P9-DUC-953

Presented to

_____

_____

_____

DATE

by

THE GIDEONS INTERNATIONAL
P.O. Box 140800
Nashville, TN 37214-0800
WWW.GIDEONS.ORG
Distributing Scriptures since 1908

Contact information for Gideons in this area:
615-564-5000 or tgi@gideons.org

Righteousness exalts a nation,
but sin is a reproach to any people.
—Proverbs 14:34

WHO ARE THE GIDEONS?

The Gideons International is an Association of Christian business and professional men, banded together in more than 190 countries for fellowship and service. The purpose of the Association is the promotion of the Gospel of Christ to all people, to the end that they might come to know the Lord Jesus Christ as their personal Saviour.

With the help of Christian friends of many different churches, Gideons have been able to place and distribute over 1.8 billion Bibles and New Testaments to hotels, motels, hospitals, penal institutions, members of armed forces, school students and those in the public nursing field.

We are pleased to present you with this copy of God's precious Word and trust that you will enjoy reading it daily.

The Bible contains the mind of God, the state of man, the way of salvation, the doom of sinners, and the happiness of believers. Its doctrines are holy, its precepts are binding, its histories are true, and its decisions are immutable. Read it to be wise, believe it to be safe, and practice it to be holy. It contains light to direct you, food to support you, and comfort to cheer you.

It is the traveler's map, the pilgrim's staff, the pilot's compass, the soldier's sword, and the Christian's charter. Here Paradise is restored, Heaven opened, and the gates of hell disclosed.

Christ is its grand subject, our good the design, and the glory of God its end.

It should fill the memory, rule the heart, and guide the feet. Read it slowly, frequently, and prayerfully. It is a mine of wealth, a paradise of glory, and a river of pleasure. It is given you in life, will be opened at the judgment, and be remembered forever. It involves the highest responsibility, will reward the greatest labor, and will condemn all who trifle with its sacred contents.

HELP IN TIME OF NEED

HELP IN TIME OF NEED

HELP WITH LIFE'S PROBLEMS

HELP WITH LIFE'S PROBLEMS

HELP WITH LIFE'S PROBLEMS

CHRISTIAN CHARACTER FOR GODLY LIVING IN TODAY'S WORLD

CHRISTIAN CHARACTER FOR GODLY LIVING IN TODAY'S WORLD

CHRISTIAN CHARACTER FOR GODLY LIVING IN TODAY'S WORLD

Patience

Romans 5:3–5	281
James 1:2–4	411
Psalm 37:7	497
Psalm 40:1	500

Peace

John 14:27	197
Romans 5:1	281
Psalm 4:8	472

Prayer

Col. 4:2	367
1 Thess. 5:17	373
James 5:16	417

Purity

1 Tim. 4:12	380
2 Tim. 2:22	385
Titus 2:6–8	389

Reading The Bible

John 5:39	173
Psalm 1:2	471
Psalm 119:97	571

Reverence

Titus 2:7	389
Hebrews 12:28	409

Righteousness

Romans 4:5	279
2 Cor. 5:21	330
Phil. 3:9	361

Self-Control

Gal. 5:23	347
2 Peter 1:6	424

Serving Others

Acts 26:16	268
Romans 15:16	297
Phil. 2:4	359
1 Peter 4:10	422

Sharing Faith

Matthew 10:19, 20	17
Prov. 11:30	606

Sincerity

1 Tim. 1:5	377
Phil. 1:10	357
1 Peter 1:22	419

Steadfastness

1 Cor. 15:58	323
Col. 1:23	364
Psalm 51:10	509
Prov. 10:4	604

Trust

Phil. 1:6	357
Psalm 37:3–5	497
Psalm 118:8	566
Prov. 3:5	595

Truth

John 14:6	196
Psalm 25:5	487
Psalm 86:15	539
Psalm 117:2	565

Victory

1 Cor. 15:57	323
1 John 5:4	434

Wisdom

Psalm 111:10	563
Prov. 1:5	593
Prov. 2:6, 7	594
Prov. 15:22	611

Worship

John 4:23	169
Psalm 29:2	490
Psalm 95:6	547

There is a verse in the Bible which has been translated into more than 1100 languages. It tells of One who loved us with an everlasting love. The verse is here recorded in 26 languages of the world which are understood by more than three-quarters of the earth's population. The verse is John 3:16.

AFRIKAANS

Want so lief het God die wêreld gehad, dat Hy sy eniggebore Seun gegee het, sodat elkeen wat in Hom glo, nie verlore mag gaan nie, maar die ewige lewe kan hê.

ARABIC

لأَنَّهُ هَكَذَا أَحَبَّ اللهُ الْعَالَمَ حَتَّى بَذَلَ
ابْنَهُ الْوَحِيدَ لِكَيْ لاَ يَهْلِكَ كُلُّ مَنْ يُؤْمِنُ
بِهِ بَلْ تَكُونُ لَهُ الْحَيَاةُ الْأَبَدِيَّةُ

ARMENIAN

Քանի որ Աստուած այնպէս
սիրեց աշխարհը որ մինչեւ
իսկ իր Միածին Որդին տուաւ,
որպէսզի ով որ հաւատայ
անոր չկորսուի, այլ ընդունի
յաւիտենական կեանքը։

CHINESE

神愛世人、甚至將他的獨
生子賜給他們叫一切信
他的、不至滅亡反得永生

DANISH

Thi således elskede Gud verden,
at han gav sin Søden enbåfor at
enhver, som tror på ham, ikke skal
fortabes, men have evigt liv.

DUTCH

Want alzo lief heeft God de
wereld gehad, dat Hij zijn enigge-
boren Zoon gegeven heeft, opdat
een ieder, die in Hem gelooft, niet
verloren ga, maar eeuwig leven
hebbe.

ENGLISH

For God so loved the world, that he gave his only Son, that whoever believes in him should not perish but have eternal life.

FINNISH

Sillä niin on Jumala maailmaa rakastanut, että hän antoi ainokaisen Poikansa, ettei yksikään, joka häneen uskoo, hukkuisi, vaan hänellä olisi iankaikkinen elämä.

FRENCH

Car Dieu a tant aimé le monde qu'il a donné son Fils unique, afin que quiconque croit en lui ne périsse point, mais qu'il ait la vie éternelle.

GERMAN

Denn also hat Gott die Welt geliebt, daß er seinen eingeborenen Sohn gab, auf daß alle, die an ihn glauben, nicht verloren werden, sondern das ewige Leben haben.

GREEK

Διότι τόσον ἠγάπησεν ὁ Θεός τὸν κόσμον, ὥστε ἔδωκε τὸν Υἱὸν αὐτοῦ τὸν μονογενῆ, διὰ νὰ μὴ ἀπολεσθῇ πᾶς ὁ πιστεύων εἰς αὐτόν, ἀλλὰ νὰ ἔχῃ ζωὴν αἰώνιον.

HEBREW

כִּי־כָכָה אָהַב הָאֱלֹהִים אֶת־הָעוֹלָם עַד־
אֲשֶׁר נָתַן אֶת־בְּנוֹ אֶת־יְחִידוֹ לְמַעַן ֹלֹא־
יֹאבַד כָּל־הַמַּאֲמִין בּוֹ כִּי אִם־יִחְיֶה חַיֵּי
עוֹלָמִים׃

HINDI

क्योंकि परमेश्वर ने संसार से ऐसा
प्रेम रखा कि अपना एकलौता पुत्र
दे दिया कि जो कोई उस पर विश्वास
करे, नष्ट न हो परन्तु शाश्वत
जीवन पाए।

ICELANDIC

Því að svo elskaði Guð heiminn,
að hann gaf son sinn eingetinn,
til þess að hver, sem á hann trúir,
glatist ekki, heldur hafi eilíft líf.

ITALIAN

Poichè Iddio ha tanto amato il mondo, che ha dato il suo unigenito Figliuolo, affinchè chiunque crede in lui non perisca, ma abbia vita eterna.

JAPANESE

神はそのひとり子を賜わったほ
どに　この世を愛して下さった。
それは御子を信じる者がひとり
も滅びないで、永遠の命を得る
ためである

KOREAN

하나님이 세상을

이처럼 사랑하사

독생자를 주셨으니

이는 저를 믿는 자

마다 멸망치 않고

영생을 얻게 하려

하심이니라

NORWEGIAN

For så har Gud elsket verden at han gav sin Sønn, den enbårne, forat hver den som tror på ham, ikke skal fortapes, men ha evig liv.

POLISH

Ponieważ Bóg tak świat kochał, że dał swego syna jedynego, aby kto wierzy w Niego nie zginął, lecz żył wiecznie.

PORTUGUESE

Porque Deus amou o mundo de tal maneira, que deu o seu Filho unigênito, para que todo aquêle que nêle crê não pereça, mas tenha a vida eterna.

RUSSIAN

Ибо так возлюбил Бог мир, что отдал Сына Своего Единородного, дабы всякий верующий в Него, не погиб, но имел жизнь вечную.

SINHALESE

මක්නිසාද දෙවියන්වහන්සේ ස්ව කීය ඒකජාතක පුතුයාණන් දෙන තරම් ලෝකයාට ප්‍රේම කළ සේක. එසේ කළේ උන්වහන්සේ කෙරෙහි අදහා ගන්නා සැමදෙනම විනාශය තොවී සදාකාල ජීවනය ලබන පිණිසය.

SPANISH

Porque de tal manera amó Dios al mundo, que ha dado á su Hijo unigénito, para que todo aquel que en él cree, no se pierda, mas tenga vida eterna.

SWEDISH

Ty så älskade Gud världen, att han utgav sin enfödde Son, på det att var och en som tror på honom skall icke förgås, utan hava evigt liv.

TAMIL

தேவன், தம்முடைய ஒரேபேறான குமாரனே விசுவாசிக்கிறவன் எவனோ அவன்கெட இறப்போகாமல் நித்தியஜீவனை அடை யும்படிக்கு, அவரைத் தந்தருளி. இப்படிஎவ்வாய் உலகத்தில் அன்புகூர்ந் தார்.

VIETNAMESE

Vì Đức Chúa Trời thươngyêu thế-gian đến nỗi đã ban Con độc sahn của Ngài, hầu cho hễ ai tin Con ấy không bị hư-mất, nhưng được sự sống đời đời.

THE
NEW TESTAMENT
OF OUR LORD AND SAVIOUR
JESUS CHRIST
WITH PSALMS AND PROVERBS

The Gideons
International

P.O. Box 140800
Nashville, TN
37214-0800

www.gideons.org

NEW TESTAMENT

ABOUT THIS BIBLE

This edition of The Holy Bible is distributed free of charge throughout the world by The Gideons International. For more information about the ministry of The Gideons, please contact: The Gideons International, Post Office Box 140800, Nashville, TN 37214-0800 USA, or visit The Gideons website at: www.gideons.org.

COPYRIGHT INFORMATION

The Holy Bible, English Standard Version® (ESV®) is copyright © Crossway, a publishing ministry of Good News Publishers, 1300 Crescent Street, Wheaton, Illinois 60187, USA. The ESV Bible text may be quoted (in written, visual, or electronic form) up to and inclusive of one thousand (1,000) verses without express written permission of the publisher, provided that the verses quoted do not amount to a complete book of the Bible nor do the verses quoted account for 50% or more of the total text of the work in which they are quoted. When quoting from the ESV in written, visual, and electronic form, the letters "ESV" must be included as part of the Scripture reference given with the quote. "ESV" and "English Standard Version" are registered trademarks of Crossway. The use of either trademark requires the permission of Crossway. The ESV Bible translation carries forward the historic stream of Bible translation in English exemplified especially by the King James Version (KJV) Bible of 1611 and subsequent essentially literal Bible translations. At the request of The Gideons—and in appreciation for their worldwide, century-plus distribution of more than 1.8 billion Bibles—Crossway is pleased to license the ESV Bible text to The Gideons, and to grant permission to The Gideons to include certain alternative readings based on the Textus Receptus, for exclusive free distribution of a Gideons edition, as follows: Bible translations of the New Testament into English and other languages are almost exclusively based on either (a) the Greek Textus Receptus manuscript tradition (which was the basis for the 1611 translation of the KJV Bible), or

(b) the Greek NA-UBS manuscript corpus (which is the basis for almost all Bible translations completed since the late 1800s). In some places in the New Testament of the ESV Gideons edition, as printed and distributed exclusively under license to The Gideons International, the Gideons edition follows the Textus Receptus manuscript tradition, which corresponds in the vast majority of instances to the corpus of New Testament Greek manuscripts known among scholars today as the Majority Text. Regarding the Old Testament, the primary textual basis for translation of the ESV Old Testament is the Masoretic text of the Hebrew Bible as found in the *Biblia Hebraica Stuttgartensia* (2nd ed. 1983); regarding the ESV New Testament, the primary textual basis for translation of the ESV New Testament is the Greek text of the 1993 editions of the *Greek New Testament* (4th corrected ed.), published by the United Bible Societies (UBS), and *Novum Testamentum Graece* (27th ed.), edited by Nestle and Aland. The ESV Bible is based on the original Greek and Hebrew sources noted above, as adapted from the English Revised Standard Version, copyright division of Christian Education of the National Council of Churches of Christ in the USA. Crossway is a not-for-profit publishing ministry of Good News Publishers, and is the sole copyright holder of the ESV (English Standard Version) Bible. Crossway exists solely for the purpose of publishing the Gospel and the Truth of God's Word, the Bible. Crossway donates a portion of the purchase of every Bible sold to help support Bible distribution and Bible teaching ministries around the world. Crossway can be found online at www.crossway.org; the online ESV Bible can be found at www.esvbible.org.

MATTHEW

CHAPTER 1

¹ The book of the genealogy of Jesus Christ, the son of David, the son of Abraham.

² Abraham was the father of Isaac, and Isaac the father of Jacob, and Jacob the father of Judah and his brothers,

³ and Judah the father of Perez and Zerah by Tamar, and Perez the father of Hezron, and Hezron the father of Ram,

⁴ and Ram the father of Amminadab, and Amminadab the father of Nahshon, and Nahshon the father of Salmon,

⁵ and Salmon the father of Boaz by Rahab, and Boaz the father of Obed by Ruth, and Obed the father of Jesse,

⁶ and Jesse the father of David the king. And David was the father of Solomon by the wife of Uriah,

⁷ and Solomon the father of Rehoboam, and Rehoboam the father of Abijah, and Abijah the father of Asa,

⁸ and Asa the father of Jehoshaphat, and Jehoshaphat the father of Joram, and Joram the father of Uzziah,

⁹ and Uzziah the father of Jotham, and Jotham the father of Ahaz, and Ahaz the father of Hezekiah,

¹⁰ and Hezekiah the father of Manasseh, and Manasseh the father of Amon, and Amon the father of Josiah,

¹¹ and Josiah the father of Jechoniah and his brothers, at the time of the deportation to Babylon.

¹² And after the deportation to Babylon: Jechoniah was the father of Shealtiel, and Shealtiel the father of Zerubbabel,

¹³ and Zerubbabel the father of Abiud, and Abiud the father of Eliakim, and Eliakim the father of Azor,

¹⁴ and Azor the father of Zadok, and Zadok the father of Achim, and Achim the father of Eliud,

¹⁵ and Eliud the father of Eleazar, and Eleazar the father of Matthan, and Matthan the father of Jacob,

¹⁶ and Jacob the father of Joseph the husband of Mary, of whom Jesus was born, who is called Christ.

¹⁷ So all the generations from Abraham to David were fourteen generations, and

from David to the deportation to Babylon fourteen generations, and from the deportation to Babylon to the Christ fourteen generations.

¹⁸ Now the birth of Jesus Christ took place in this way. When his mother Mary had been betrothed to Joseph, before they came together she was found to be with child from the Holy Spirit.

¹⁹ And her husband Joseph, being a just man and unwilling to put her to shame, resolved to divorce her quietly.

²⁰ But as he considered these things, behold, an angel of the Lord appeared to him in a dream, saying, "Joseph, son of David, do not fear to take Mary as your wife, for that which is conceived in her is from the Holy Spirit.

²¹ "She will bear a son, and you shall call his name Jesus, for he will save his people from their sins."

²² All this took place to fulfill what the Lord had spoken by the prophet:

²³ "Behold, the virgin shall conceive and bear a son, and they shall call his name Immanuel" (which means, God with us).

²⁴ When Joseph woke from sleep, he did as the angel of the Lord commanded him: he took his wife,

²⁵ but knew her not until she had given birth to her firstborn son. And he called his name Jesus.

CHAPTER 2

¹ Now after Jesus was born in Bethlehem of Judea in the days of Herod the king, behold, wise men from the east came to Jerusalem,

² saying, "Where is he who has been born king of the Jews? For we saw his star when it rose in the east and have come to worship him."

³ When Herod the king heard this, he was troubled, and all Jerusalem with him;

⁴ and assembling all the chief priests and scribes of the people, he inquired of them where the Christ was to be born.

⁵ They told him, "In Bethlehem of Judea, for so it is written by the prophet:

⁶ "'And you, O Bethlehem, in the land of Judah, are by no means least among the rulers of Judah; for from you shall come a ruler who will shepherd my people Israel.'"

⁷ Then Herod summoned the wise men secretly and ascertained from them what time the star had appeared.

⁸ And he sent them to Bethlehem, saying, "Go and search diligently for the child, and

when you have found him, bring me word, that I too may come and worship him."

⁹ After listening to the king, they went on their way. And behold, the star that they had seen when it rose in the east went before them until it came to rest over the place where the child was.

¹⁰ When they saw the star, they rejoiced exceedingly with great joy.

¹¹ And going into the house they saw the child with Mary his mother, and they fell down and worshiped him. Then, opening their treasures, they offered him gifts, gold and frankincense and myrrh.

¹² And being warned in a dream not to return to Herod, they departed to their own country by another way.

¹³ Now when they had departed, behold, an angel of the Lord appeared to Joseph in a dream and said, "Rise, take the child and his mother, and flee to Egypt, and remain there until I tell you, for Herod is about to search for the child, to destroy him."

¹⁴ And he rose and took the child and his mother by night and departed to Egypt

¹⁵ and remained there until the death of Herod. This was to fulfill what the Lord had spoken by the prophet, "Out of Egypt I called my son."

¹⁶ Then Herod, when he saw that he had been tricked by the wise men, became furious, and he sent and killed all the male children in Bethlehem and in all that region who were two years old or under, according to the time that he had ascertained from the wise men.

¹⁷ Then was fulfilled what was spoken by the prophet Jeremiah:

¹⁸ "A voice was heard in Ramah, weeping and loud lamentation, Rachel weeping for her children; she refused to be comforted, because they are no more."

¹⁹ But when Herod died, behold, an angel of the Lord appeared in a dream to Joseph in Egypt,

²⁰ saying, "Rise, take the child and his mother and go to the land of Israel, for those who sought the child's life are dead."

²¹ And he rose and took the child and his mother and went to the land of Israel.

²² But when he heard that Archelaus was reigning over Judea in place of his father Herod, he was afraid to go there, and being warned in a dream he withdrew to the district of Galilee.

²³ And he went and lived in a city called Nazareth, so that what was spoken by the prophets might be fulfilled, that he would be called a Nazarene.

CHAPTER 3

¹ In those days John the Baptist came preaching in the wilderness of Judea,

² "Repent, for the kingdom of heaven is at hand."

³ For this is he who was spoken of by the prophet Isaiah when he said, "The voice of one crying in the wilderness: 'Prepare the way of the Lord; make his paths straight.'"

⁴ Now John wore a garment of camel's hair and a leather belt around his waist, and his food was locusts and wild honey.

⁵ Then Jerusalem and all Judea and all the region about the Jordan were going out to him,

⁶ and they were baptized by him in the river Jordan, confessing their sins.

⁷ But when he saw many of the Pharisees and Sadducees coming to his baptism, he said to them, "You brood of vipers! Who warned you to flee from the wrath to come?

⁸ "Bear fruit in keeping with repentance,

⁹ "And do not presume to say to yourselves, 'We have Abraham as our father,' for I tell you, God is able from these stones to raise up children for Abraham.

¹⁰ "Even now the axe is laid to the root of the trees. Every tree therefore that does not bear good fruit is cut down and thrown into the fire.

¹¹ "I baptize you with water for repentance, but he who is coming after me is mightier than I, whose sandals I am not worthy to carry. He will baptize you with the Holy Spirit and fire.

¹² "His winnowing fork is in his hand, and he will clear his threshing floor and gather his wheat into the barn, but the chaff he will burn with unquenchable fire."

¹³ Then Jesus came from Galilee to the Jordan to John, to be baptized by him.

¹⁴ John would have prevented him, saying, "I need to be baptized by you, and do you come to me?"

¹⁵ But Jesus answered him, "Let it be so now, for thus it is fitting for us to fulfill all righteousness." Then he consented.

¹⁶ And when Jesus was baptized, immediately he went up from the water, and behold, the heavens were opened to him, and he saw

the Spirit of God descending like a dove and coming to rest on him;

17 and behold, a voice from heaven said, "This is my beloved Son, with whom I am well pleased."

CHAPTER 4

1 Then Jesus was led up by the Spirit into the wilderness to be tempted by the devil.

2 And after fasting forty days and forty nights, he was hungry.

3 And the tempter came and said to him, "If you are the Son of God, command these stones to become loaves of bread."

4 But he answered, "It is written, 'Man shall not live by bread alone, but by every word that comes from the mouth of God.'"

5 Then the devil took him to the holy city and set him on the pinnacle of the temple

6 and said to him, "If you are the Son of God, throw yourself down, for it is written, 'He will command his angels concerning you,' and 'On their hands they will bear you up, lest you strike your foot against a stone.'"

7 Jesus said to him, "Again it is written, 'You shall not put the Lord your God to the test.'"

8 Again, the devil took him to a very high mountain and showed him all the kingdoms of the world and their glory.

9 And he said to him, "All these I will give you, if you will fall down and worship me."

10 Then Jesus said to him, "Be gone, Satan! For it is written, 'You shall worship the Lord your God and him only shall you serve.'"

11 Then the devil left him, and behold, angels came and were ministering to him.

12 Now when he heard that John had been arrested, he withdrew into Galilee.

13 And leaving Nazareth he went and lived in Capernaum by the sea, in the territory of Zebulun and Naphtali,

14 so that what was spoken by the prophet Isaiah might be fulfilled:

15 "The land of Zebulun and the land of Naphtali, the way of the sea, beyond the Jordan, Galilee of the Gentiles—

16 "the people dwelling in darkness have seen a great light, and for those dwelling in the region and shadow of death, on them a light has dawned."

17 From that time Jesus began to preach, saying, "Repent, for the kingdom of heaven is at hand."

[18] While walking by the Sea of Galilee, he saw two brothers, Simon (who is called Peter) and Andrew his brother, casting a net into the sea, for they were fishermen.

[19] And he said to them, "Follow me, and I will make you fishers of men."

[20] Immediately they left their nets and followed him.

[21] And going on from there he saw two other brothers, James the son of Zebedee and John his brother, in the boat with Zebedee their father, mending their nets, and he called them.

[22] Immediately they left the boat and their father and followed him.

[23] And he went throughout all Galilee, teaching in their synagogues and proclaiming the gospel of the kingdom and healing every disease and every affliction among the people.

[24] So his fame spread throughout all Syria, and they brought him all the sick, those afflicted with various diseases and pains, those oppressed by demons, epileptics, and paralytics, and he healed them.

[25] And great crowds followed him from Galilee and the Decapolis, and from Jerusalem and Judea, and from beyond the Jordan.

CHAPTER 5

[1] Seeing the crowds, he went up on the mountain, and when he sat down, his disciples came to him.

[2] And he opened his mouth and taught them, saying:

[3] "Blessed are the poor in spirit, for theirs is the kingdom of heaven.

[4] "Blessed are those who mourn, for they shall be comforted.

[5] "Blessed are the meek, for they shall inherit the earth.

[6] "Blessed are those who hunger and thirst for righteousness, for they shall be satisfied.

[7] "Blessed are the merciful, for they shall receive mercy.

[8] "Blessed are the pure in heart, for they shall see God.

[9] "Blessed are the peacemakers, for they shall be called sons of God.

[10] "Blessed are those who are persecuted for righteousness' sake, for theirs is the kingdom of heaven.

[11] "Blessed are you when others revile you and persecute you and utter all kinds of evil against you falsely on my account.

[12] "Rejoice and be glad, for your reward is great in heaven, for so they persecuted the prophets who were before you.

¹³ "You are the salt of the earth, but if salt has lost its taste, how shall its saltiness be restored? It is no longer good for anything except to be thrown out and trampled under people's feet.

¹⁴ "You are the light of the world. A city set on a hill cannot be hidden.

¹⁵ "Nor do people light a lamp and put it under a basket, but on a stand, and it gives light to all in the house.

¹⁶ "In the same way, let your light shine before others, so that they may see your good works and give glory to your Father who is in heaven.

¹⁷ "Do not think that I have come to abolish the Law or the Prophets; I have not come to abolish them but to fulfill them.

¹⁸ "For truly, I say to you, until heaven and earth pass away, not an iota, not a dot, will pass from the Law until all is accomplished.

¹⁹ "Therefore whoever relaxes one of the least of these commandments and teaches others to do the same will be called least in the kingdom of heaven, but whoever does them and teaches them will be called great in the kingdom of heaven.

²⁰ "For I tell you, unless your righteousness exceeds that of the scribes and Pharisees, you will never enter the kingdom of heaven.

²¹ "You have heard that it was said to those of old, 'You shall not murder; and whoever murders will be liable to judgment.'

²² "But I say to you that everyone who is angry with his brother will be liable to judgment; whoever insults his brother will be liable to the council; and whoever says, 'You fool!' will be liable to the hell of fire.

²³ "So if you are offering your gift at the altar and there remember that your brother has something against you,

²⁴ "leave your gift there before the altar and go. First be reconciled to your brother, and then come and offer your gift.

²⁵ "Come to terms quickly with your accuser while you are going with him to court, lest your accuser hand you over to the judge, and the judge to the guard, and you be put in prison.

²⁶ "Truly, I say to you, you will never get out until you have paid the last penny.

²⁷ "You have heard that it was said, 'You shall not commit adultery.'

²⁸ "But I say to you that everyone who looks at a woman

with lustful intent has already committed adultery with her in his heart.

29 "If your right eye causes you to sin, tear it out and throw it away. For it is better that you lose one of your members than that your whole body be thrown into hell.

30 "And if your right hand causes you to sin, cut it off and throw it away. For it is better that you lose one of your members than that your whole body go into hell.

31 "It was also said, 'Whoever divorces his wife, let him give her a certificate of divorce.'

32 "But I say to you that everyone who divorces his wife, except on the ground of sexual immorality, makes her commit adultery, and whoever marries a divorced woman commits adultery.

33 "Again you have heard that it was said to those of old, 'You shall not swear falsely, but shall perform to the Lord what you have sworn.'

34 "But I say to you, Do not take an oath at all, either by heaven, for it is the throne of God,

35 "or by the earth, for it is his footstool, or by Jerusalem, for it is the city of the great King.

36 "And do not take an oath by your head, for you cannot make one hair white or black.

37 "Let what you say be simply 'Yes' or 'No'; anything more than this comes from evil.

38 "You have heard that it was said, 'An eye for an eye and a tooth for a tooth.'

39 "But I say to you, Do not resist the one who is evil. But if anyone slaps you on the right cheek, turn to him the other also.

40 "And if anyone would sue you and take your tunic, let him have your cloak as well.

41 "And if anyone forces you to go one mile, go with him two miles.

42 "Give to the one who begs from you, and do not refuse the one who would borrow from you.

43 "You have heard that it was said, 'You shall love your neighbor and hate your enemy.'

44 "But I say to you, Love your enemies, bless those who curse you, do good to those who hate you, and pray for those who persecute you,

45 "so that you may be sons of your Father who is in heaven. For he makes his sun rise on the evil and on the good, and sends rain on the just and on the unjust.

46 "For if you love those who

love you, what reward do you have? Do not even the tax collectors do the same?

47 "And if you greet only your brothers, what more are you doing than others? Do not even the tax collectors do the same?

48 "You therefore must be perfect, as your heavenly Father is perfect.

CHAPTER 6

1 "Beware of practicing your righteousness before other people in order to be seen by them, for then you will have no reward from your Father who is in heaven.

2 "Thus, when you give to the needy, sound no trumpet before you, as the hypocrites do in the synagogues and in the streets, that they may be praised by others. Truly, I say to you, they have received their reward.

3 "But when you give to the needy, do not let your left hand know what your right hand is doing,

4 "so that your giving may be in secret. And your Father who sees in secret will reward you.

5 "And when you pray, you must not be like the hypocrites. For they love to stand and pray in the synagogues and at the street corners, that they may be seen by others. Truly, I say to you, they have received their reward.

6 "But when you pray, go into your room and shut the door and pray to your Father who is in secret. And your Father who sees in secret will reward you.

7 "And when you pray, do not heap up empty phrases as the Gentiles do, for they think that they will be heard for their many words.

8 "Do not be like them, for your Father knows what you need before you ask him.

9 "Pray then like this: Our Father in heaven, hallowed be your name.

10 "Your kingdom come, your will be done, on earth as it is in heaven.

11 "Give us this day our daily bread,

12 "and forgive us our debts, as we also have forgiven our debtors.

13 "And lead us not into temptation, but deliver us from evil. For yours is the kingdom and the power and the glory, forever. Amen.

14 "For if you forgive others their trespasses, your heavenly Father will also forgive you,

15 "but if you do not forgive others their trespasses, neither will your Father forgive your trespasses.

16 "And when you fast, do not look gloomy like the hypocrites, for they disfigure their faces that their fasting may be seen by others. Truly, I say to you, they have received their reward.

17 "But when you fast, anoint your head and wash your face,

18 "that your fasting may not be seen by others but by your Father who is in secret. And your Father who sees in secret will reward you.

19 "Do not lay up for yourselves treasures on earth, where moth and rust destroy and where thieves break in and steal,

20 "but lay up for yourselves treasures in heaven, where neither moth nor rust destroys and where thieves do not break in and steal.

21 "For where your treasure is, there your heart will be also.

22 "The eye is the lamp of the body. So, if your eye is healthy, your whole body will be full of light,

23 "but if your eye is bad, your whole body will be full of darkness. If then the light in you is darkness, how great is the darkness!

24 "No one can serve two masters, for either he will hate the one and love the other, or he will be devoted to the one and despise the other. You cannot serve God and money.

25 "Therefore I tell you, do not be anxious about your life, what you will eat or what you will drink, nor about your body, what you will put on. Is not life more than food, and the body more than clothing?

26 "Look at the birds of the air: they neither sow nor reap nor gather into barns, and yet your heavenly Father feeds them. Are you not of more value than they?

27 "And which of you by being anxious can add a single hour to his span of life?

28 "And why are you anxious about clothing? Consider the lilies of the field, how they grow: they neither toil nor spin,

29 "yet I tell you, even Solomon in all his glory was not arrayed like one of these.

30 "But if God so clothes the grass of the field, which today is alive and tomorrow is thrown into the oven, will he not much more clothe you, O you of little faith?

31 "Therefore do not be anxious, saying, 'What shall we eat?' or 'What shall we drink?' or 'What shall we wear?'

32 "For the Gentiles seek after all these things, and your heavenly Father knows that you need them all.

33 "But seek first the kingdom of God and his righteousness, and all these things will be added to you.

34 "Therefore do not be anxious about tomorrow, for tomorrow will be anxious for itself. Sufficient for the day is its own trouble.

CHAPTER 7

1 "Judge not, that you be not judged.

2 "For with the judgment you pronounce you will be judged, and with the measure you use it will be measured to you.

3 "Why do you see the speck that is in your brother's eye, but do not notice the log that is in your own eye?

4 "Or how can you say to your brother, 'Let me take the speck out of your eye,' when there is the log in your own eye?

5 "You hypocrite, first take the log out of your own eye, and then you will see clearly to take the speck out of your brother's eye.

6 "Do not give dogs what is holy, and do not throw your pearls before pigs, lest they trample them underfoot and turn to attack you.

7 "Ask, and it will be given to you; seek, and you will find; knock, and it will be opened to you.

8 "For everyone who asks receives, and the one who seeks finds, and to the one who knocks it will be opened.

9 "Or which one of you, if his son asks him for bread, will give him a stone?

10 "Or if he asks for a fish, will give him a serpent?

11 "If you then, who are evil, know how to give good gifts to your children, how much more will your Father who is in heaven give good things to those who ask him!

12 "So whatever you wish that others would do to you, do also to them, for this is the Law and the Prophets.

13 "Enter by the narrow gate. For the gate is wide and the way is easy that leads to destruction, and those who enter by it are many.

14 "For the gate is narrow and the way is hard that leads to life, and those who find it are few.

15 "Beware of false prophets, who come to you in sheep's clothing but inwardly are ravenous wolves.

16 "You will recognize them by their fruits. Are grapes gathered from thornbushes, or figs from thistles?

17 "So, every healthy tree bears good fruit, but the diseased tree bears bad fruit.

18 "A healthy tree cannot

bear bad fruit, nor can a diseased tree bear good fruit.

¹⁹ "Every tree that does not bear good fruit is cut down and thrown into the fire.

²⁰ "Thus you will recognize them by their fruits.

²¹ "Not everyone who says to me, 'Lord, Lord,' will enter the kingdom of heaven, but the one who does the will of my Father who is in heaven.

²² "On that day many will say to me, 'Lord, Lord, did we not prophesy in your name, and cast out demons in your name, and do many mighty works in your name?'

²³ "And then will I declare to them, 'I never knew you; depart from me, you workers of lawlessness.'

²⁴ "Everyone then who hears these words of mine and does them will be like a wise man who built his house on the rock.

²⁵ "And the rain fell, and the floods came, and the winds blew and beat on that house, *but it did not fall, because* it had been founded on the rock.

²⁶ "And everyone who hears these words of mine and does not do them will be like a foolish man who built his house on the sand.

²⁷ "And the rain fell, and the floods came, and the winds blew and beat against that house, and it fell, and great was the fall of it."

²⁸ And when Jesus finished these sayings, the crowds were astonished at his teaching,

²⁹ for he was teaching them as one who had authority, and not as their scribes.

CHAPTER 8

¹ When he came down from the mountain, great crowds followed him.

² And behold, a leper came to him and knelt before him, saying, "Lord, if you will, you can make me clean."

³ And Jesus stretched out his hand and touched him, saying, "I will; be clean." And immediately his leprosy was cleansed.

⁴ And Jesus said to him, "See that you say nothing to anyone, but go; show yourself to the priest and offer the gift that Moses commanded, for a proof to them."

⁵ When he had entered Capernaum, a centurion came forward to him, appealing to him,

⁶ "Lord, my servant is lying paralyzed at home, suffering terribly."

⁷ And he said to him, "I will come and heal him."

⁸ But the centurion replied,

"Lord, I am not worthy to have you come under my roof, but only say the word, and my servant will be healed.

9 "For I too am a man under authority, with soldiers under me. And I say to one, 'Go,' and he goes, and to another, 'Come,' and he comes, and to my servant, 'Do this,' and he does it."

10 When Jesus heard this, he marveled and said to those who followed him, "Truly, I tell you, with no one in Israel have I found such faith.

11 "I tell you, many will come from east and west and recline at table with Abraham, Isaac, and Jacob in the kingdom of heaven,

12 "while the sons of the kingdom will be thrown into the outer darkness. In that place there will be weeping and gnashing of teeth."

13 And to the centurion Jesus said, "Go; let it be done for you as you have believed." And the servant was healed at that very moment.

14 And when Jesus entered Peter's house, he saw his mother-in-law lying sick with a fever.

15 He touched her hand, and the fever left her, and she rose and began to serve him.

16 That evening they brought to him many who were oppressed by demons, and he cast out the spirits with a word and healed all who were sick.

17 This was to fulfill what was spoken by the prophet Isaiah: "He took our illnesses and bore our diseases."

18 Now when Jesus saw a crowd around him, he gave orders to go over to the other side.

19 And a scribe came up and said to him, "Teacher, I will follow you wherever you go."

20 And Jesus said to him, "Foxes have holes, and birds of the air have nests, but the Son of Man has nowhere to lay his head."

21 Another of the disciples said to him, "Lord, let me first go and bury my father."

22 And Jesus said to him, "Follow me, and leave the dead to bury their own dead."

23 And when he got into the boat, his disciples followed him.

24 And behold, there arose a great storm on the sea, so that the boat was being swamped by the waves; but he was asleep.

25 And they went and woke him, saying, "Save us, Lord; we are perishing."

26 And he said to them, "Why are you afraid, O you of little faith?" Then he rose

and rebuked the winds and the sea, and there was a great calm.

²⁷ And the men marveled, saying, "What sort of man is this, that even winds and sea obey him?"

²⁸ And when he came to the other side, to the country of the Gadarenes, two demon-possessed men met him, coming out of the tombs, so fierce that no one could pass that way.

²⁹ And behold, they cried out, "What have you to do with us, O Son of God? Have you come here to torment us before the time?"

³⁰ Now a herd of many pigs was feeding at some distance from them.

³¹ And the demons begged him, saying, "If you cast us out, send us away into the herd of pigs."

³² And he said to them, "Go." So they came out and went into the pigs, and behold, the whole herd rushed down the steep bank into the sea and drowned in the waters.

³³ The herdsmen fled, and going into the city they told everything, especially what had happened to the demon-possessed men.

³⁴ And behold, all the city came out to meet Jesus, and when they saw him, they begged him to leave their region.

CHAPTER 9

¹ And getting into a boat he crossed over and came to his own city.

² And behold, some people brought to him a paralytic, lying on a bed. And when Jesus saw their faith, he said to the paralytic, "Take heart, my son; your sins are forgiven."

³ And behold, some of the scribes said to themselves, "This man is blaspheming."

⁴ But Jesus, knowing their thoughts, said, "Why do you think evil in your hearts?

⁵ "For which is easier, to say, 'Your sins are forgiven,' or to say, 'Rise and walk'?

⁶ "But that you may know that the Son of Man has authority on earth to forgive sins"—he then said to the paralytic—"Rise, pick up your bed and go home."

⁷ And he rose and went home.

⁸ When the crowds saw it, they were afraid, and they glorified God, who had given such authority to men.

⁹ As Jesus passed on from there, he saw a man called Matthew sitting at the tax booth, and he said to him, "Follow me." And he rose and followed him.

¹⁰ And as Jesus reclined at table in the house, behold, many tax collectors and sinners came and were reclining with Jesus and his disciples. ¹¹ And when the Pharisees saw this, they said to his disciples, "Why does your teacher eat with tax collectors and sinners?" ¹² But when he heard it, he said, "Those who are well have no need of a physician, but those who are sick. ¹³ Go and learn what this means, 'I desire mercy, and not sacrifice.' For I came not to call the righteous, but sinners."

¹⁴ Then the disciples of John came to him, saying, "Why do we and the Pharisees fast, but your disciples do not fast?" ¹⁵ And Jesus said to them, "Can the wedding guests mourn as long as the bridegroom is with them? The days will come when the bridegroom is taken away from them, and then they will fast. ¹⁶ No one puts a piece of unshrunk cloth on an old garment, for the patch tears away from the garment, and a worse tear is made. ¹⁷ Neither is new wine put into old wineskins. If it is, the skins burst and the wine is spilled and the skins are destroyed. But new wine is put into fresh wineskins, and so both are preserved."

¹⁸ While he was saying these things to them, behold, a ruler came in and knelt before him, saying, "My daughter has just died, but come and lay your hand on her, and she will live." ¹⁹ And Jesus rose and followed him, with his disciples.

²⁰ And behold, a woman who had suffered from a discharge of blood for twelve years came up behind him and touched the fringe of his garment, ²¹ for she said to herself, "If I only touch his garment, I will be made well." ²² Jesus turned, and seeing her he said, "Take heart, daughter; your faith has made you well." And instantly the woman was made well.

²³ And when Jesus came to the ruler's house and saw the flute players and the crowd making a commotion, ²⁴ he said, "Go away, for the girl is not dead but sleeping." And they laughed at him. ²⁵ But when the crowd had been put outside, he went in and took her by the hand, and the girl arose. ²⁶ And the report of this went through all that district.

²⁷ And as Jesus passed on from there, two blind men

followed him, crying aloud, "Have mercy on us, Son of David."

²⁸ When he entered the house, the blind men came to him, and Jesus said to them, "Do you believe that I am able to do this?" They said to him, "Yes, Lord."

²⁹ Then he touched their eyes, saying, "According to your faith be it done to you."

³⁰ And their eyes were opened. And Jesus sternly warned them, "See that no one knows about it."

³¹ But they went away and spread his fame through all that district.

³² As they were going away, behold, a demon-oppressed man who was mute was brought to him.

³³ And when the demon had been cast out, the mute man spoke. And the crowds marveled, saying, "Never was anything like this seen in Israel."

³⁴ But the Pharisees said, "He casts out demons by the prince of demons."

³⁵ And Jesus went throughout all the cities and villages, teaching in their synagogues and proclaiming the gospel of the kingdom and healing every disease and every affliction.

³⁶ When he saw the crowds, he had compassion for them, because they were harassed and helpless, like sheep without a shepherd.

³⁷ Then he said to his disciples, "The harvest is plentiful, but the laborers are few;

³⁸ "therefore pray earnestly to the Lord of the harvest to send out laborers into his harvest."

CHAPTER 10

¹ And he called to him his twelve disciples and gave them authority over unclean spirits, to cast them out, and to heal every disease and every affliction.

² The names of the twelve apostles are these: first, Simon, who is called Peter, and Andrew his brother; James the son of Zebedee, and John his brother;

³ Philip and Bartholomew; Thomas and Matthew the tax collector; James the son of Alphaeus, and Thaddaeus;

⁴ Simon the Zealot, and Judas Iscariot, who betrayed him.

⁵ These twelve Jesus sent out, instructing them, "Go nowhere among the Gentiles and enter no town of the Samaritans,

⁶ "but go rather to the lost sheep of the house of Israel.

⁷ "And proclaim as you go, saying, 'The kingdom of heaven is at hand.'

⁸ "Heal the sick, raise the dead, cleanse lepers, cast out demons. You received without paying; give without pay.

⁹ "Acquire no gold or silver or copper for your belts,

¹⁰ "no bag for your journey, or two tunics or sandals or a staff, for the laborer deserves his food.

¹¹ "And whatever town or village you enter, find out who is worthy in it and stay there until you depart.

¹² "As you enter the house, greet it.

¹³ "And if the house is worthy, let your peace come upon it, but if it is not worthy, let your peace return to you.

¹⁴ "And if anyone will not receive you or listen to your words, shake off the dust from your feet when you leave that house or town.

¹⁵ "Truly, I say to you, it will be more bearable on the day of judgment for the land of Sodom and Gomorrah than for that town.

¹⁶ "Behold, I am sending you out as sheep in the midst of wolves, so be wise as serpents and innocent as doves.

¹⁷ "Beware of men, for they will deliver you over to courts and flog you in their synagogues,

¹⁸ "and you will be dragged before governors and kings for my sake, to bear witness before them and the Gentiles.

¹⁹ "When they deliver you over, do not be anxious how you are to speak or what you are to say, for what you are to say will be given to you in that hour.

²⁰ "For it is not you who speak, but the Spirit of your Father speaking through you.

²¹ "Brother will deliver brother over to death, and the father his child, and children will rise against parents and have them put to death,

²² "and you will be hated by all for my name's sake. But the one who endures to the end will be saved.

²³ "When they persecute you in one town, flee to the next, for truly, I say to you, you will not have gone through all the towns of Israel before the Son of Man comes.

²⁴ "A disciple is not above his teacher, nor a servant above his master.

²⁵ "It is enough for the disciple to be like his teacher, and the servant like his master. If they have called the master of the house Beelzebul, how much more will they malign those of his household.

²⁶ "So have no fear of them, for nothing is covered that will not be revealed, or hidden that will not be known.

27 "What I tell you in the dark, say in the light, and what you hear whispered, proclaim on the housetops. 28 "And do not fear those who kill the body but cannot kill the soul. Rather fear him who can destroy both soul and body in hell. 29 "Are not two sparrows sold for a penny? And not one of them will fall to the ground apart from your Father. 30 "But even the hairs of your head are all numbered. 31 "Fear not, therefore; you are of more value than many sparrows. 32 "So everyone who acknowledges me before men, I also will acknowledge before my Father who is in heaven, 33 "but whoever denies me before men, I also will deny before my Father who is in heaven. 34 "Do not think that I have come to bring peace to the earth. I have not come to bring peace, but a sword. 35 "For I have come to set a man against his father, and a daughter against her mother, and a daughter-in-law against her mother-in-law. 36 "And a person's enemies will be those of his own household. 37 "Whoever loves father or mother more than me is not worthy of me, and whoever loves son or daughter more than me is not worthy of me. 38 "And whoever does not take his cross and follow me is not worthy of me. 39 "Whoever finds his life will lose it, and whoever loses his life for my sake will find it. 40 "Whoever receives you receives me, and whoever receives me receives him who sent me. 41 "The one who receives a prophet because he is a prophet will receive a prophet's reward, and the one who receives a righteous person because he is a righteous person will receive a righteous person's reward. 42 "And whoever gives one of these little ones even a cup of cold water because he is a disciple, truly, I say to you, he will by no means lose his reward."

CHAPTER 11

1 When Jesus had finished instructing his twelve disciples, he went on from there to teach and preach in their cities.

2 Now when John heard in prison about the deeds of the Christ, he sent word by his disciples 3 and said to him, "Are you the one who is to come, or shall we look for another?"

4 And Jesus answered them, "Go and tell John what you hear and see:

5 "the blind receive their sight and the lame walk, lepers are cleansed and the deaf hear, and the dead are raised up, and the poor have good news preached to them.

6 "And blessed is the one who is not offended by me."

7 As they went away, Jesus began to speak to the crowds concerning John: "What did you go out into the wilderness to see? A reed shaken by the wind?

8 "What then did you go out to see? A man dressed in soft clothing? Behold, those who wear soft clothing are in kings' houses.

9 "What then did you go out to see? A prophet? Yes, I tell you, and more than a prophet.

10 "This is he of whom it is written, 'Behold, I send my messenger before your face, who will prepare your way before you.'

11 "Truly, I say to you, among those born of women there has arisen no one greater than John the Baptist. Yet the one who is least in the kingdom of heaven is greater than he.

12 "From the days of John the Baptist until now the kingdom of heaven has suffered violence, and the violent take it by force.

13 "For all the Prophets and the Law prophesied until John,

14 "and if you are willing to accept it, he is Elijah who is to come.

15 "He who has ears to hear, let him hear.

16 "But to what shall I compare this generation? It is like children sitting in the marketplaces and calling to their playmates,

17 "'We played the flute for you, and you did not dance; we sang a dirge, and you did not mourn.'

18 "For John came neither eating nor drinking, and they say, 'He has a demon.'

19 "The Son of Man came eating and drinking, and they say, 'Look at him! A glutton and a drunkard, a friend of tax collectors and sinners!' Yet wisdom is justified by her deeds."

20 Then he began to denounce the cities where most of his mighty works had been done, because they did not repent.

21 "Woe to you, Chorazin! Woe to you, Bethsaida! For if the mighty works done in you had been done in Tyre and Sidon, they would have repented long ago in sackcloth and ashes.

22 "But I tell you, it will be more bearable on the day of judgment for Tyre and Sidon than for you.

23 "And you, Capernaum, will you be exalted to heaven? You will be brought down to Hades. For if the mighty works done in you had been done in Sodom, it would have remained until this day.

24 "But I tell you that it will be more tolerable on the day of judgment for the land of Sodom than for you."

25 At that time Jesus declared, "I thank you, Father, Lord of heaven and earth, that you have hidden these things from the wise and understanding and revealed them to little children;

26 "yes, Father, for such was your gracious will.

27 "All things have been handed over to me by my Father, and no one knows the Son except the Father, and no one knows the Father except the Son and anyone to whom the Son chooses to reveal him.

28 "Come to me, all who labor and are heavy laden, and I will give you rest.

29 "Take my yoke upon you, and learn from me, for I am gentle and lowly in heart, and you will find rest for your souls.

30 "For my yoke is easy, and my burden is light."

CHAPTER 12

1 At that time Jesus went through the grainfields on the Sabbath. His disciples were hungry, and they began to pluck heads of grain and to eat.

2 But when the Pharisees saw it, they said to him, "Look, your disciples are doing what is not lawful to do on the Sabbath."

3 He said to them, "Have you not read what David did when he was hungry, and those who were with him:

4 "how he entered the house of God and ate the bread of the Presence, which it was not lawful for him to eat nor for those who were with him, but only for the priests?

5 "Or have you not read in the Law how on the Sabbath the priests in the temple profane the Sabbath and are guiltless?

6 "I tell you, something greater than the temple is here.

7 "And if you had known what this means, 'I desire mercy, and not sacrifice,' you would not have condemned the guiltless.

8 "For the Son of Man is lord of the Sabbath."

9 He went on from there and entered their synagogue.

¹⁰ And a man was there with a withered hand. And they asked him, "Is it lawful to heal on the Sabbath?"—so that they might accuse him.

¹¹ He said to them, "Which one of you who has a sheep, if it falls into a pit on the Sabbath, will not take hold of it and lift it out?

¹² Of how much more value is a man than a sheep! So it is lawful to do good on the Sabbath."

¹³ Then he said to the man, "Stretch out your hand." And the man stretched it out, and it was restored, healthy like the other.

¹⁴ But the Pharisees went out and conspired against him, how to destroy him.

¹⁵ Jesus, aware of this, withdrew from there. And many followed him, and he healed them all

¹⁶ and ordered them not to make him known.

¹⁷ This was to fulfill what was spoken by the prophet Isaiah:

¹⁸ "Behold, my servant whom I have chosen, my beloved with whom my soul is well pleased. I will put my Spirit upon him, and he will proclaim justice to the Gentiles.

¹⁹ "He will not quarrel or cry aloud, nor will anyone hear his voice in the streets;

²⁰ "a bruised reed he will not break, and a smoldering wick he will not quench, until he brings justice to victory;

²¹ "and in his name the Gentiles will hope."

²² Then a demon-oppressed man who was blind and mute was brought to him, and he healed him, so that the man spoke and saw.

²³ And all the people were amazed, and said, "Can this be the Son of David?"

²⁴ But when the Pharisees heard it, they said, "It is only by Beelzebul, the prince of demons, that this man casts out demons."

²⁵ Knowing their thoughts, he said to them, "Every kingdom divided against itself is laid waste, and no city or house divided against itself will stand.

²⁶ "And if Satan casts out Satan, he is divided against himself. How then will his kingdom stand?

²⁷ "And if I cast out demons by Beelzebul, by whom do your sons cast them out? Therefore they will be your judges.

²⁸ "But if it is by the Spirit of God that I cast out demons, then the kingdom of God has come upon you.

²⁹ "Or how can someone enter a strong man's house and

plunder his goods, unless he first binds the strong man? Then indeed he may plunder his house.

30 "Whoever is not with me is against me, and whoever does not gather with me scatters.

31 "Therefore I tell you, every sin and blasphemy will be forgiven people, but the blasphemy against the Spirit will not be forgiven.

32 "And whoever speaks a word against the Son of Man will be forgiven, but whoever speaks against the Holy Spirit will not be forgiven, either in this age or in the age to come.

33 "Either make the tree good and its fruit good, or make the tree bad and its fruit bad, for the tree is known by its fruit.

34 "You brood of vipers! How can you speak good, when you are evil? For out of the abundance of the heart the mouth speaks.

35 "The good person out of his good treasure brings forth good, and the evil person out of his evil treasure brings forth evil.

36 "I tell you, on the day of judgment people will give account for every careless word they speak,

37 "for by your words you will be justified, and by your words you will be condemned."

38 Then some of the scribes and Pharisees answered him, saying, "Teacher, we wish to see a sign from you."

39 But he answered them, "An evil and adulterous generation seeks for a sign, but no sign will be given to it except the sign of the prophet Jonah.

40 "For just as Jonah was three days and three nights in the belly of the great fish, so will the Son of Man be three days and three nights in the heart of the earth.

41 "The men of Nineveh will rise up at the judgment with this generation and condemn it, for they repented at the preaching of Jonah, and behold, something greater than Jonah is here.

42 "The queen of the South will rise up at the judgment with this generation and condemn it, for she came from the ends of the earth to hear the wisdom of Solomon, and behold, something greater than Solomon is here.

43 "When the unclean spirit has gone out of a person, it passes through waterless places seeking rest, but finds none.

44 "Then it says, 'I will return to my house from which I came.' And when it comes, it finds the house empty, swept, and put in order.

45 "Then it goes and brings with it seven other spirits more evil than itself, and they enter and dwell there, and the last state of that person is worse than the first. So also will it be with this evil generation."

46 While he was still speaking to the people, behold, his mother and his brothers stood outside, asking to speak to him.

47 Someone told him, "Your mother and your brothers are standing outside, asking to speak to you."

48 But he replied to the man who told him, "Who is my mother, and who are my brothers?"

49 And stretching out his hand toward his disciples, he said, "Here are my mother and my brothers!

50 "For whoever does the will of my Father in heaven is my brother and sister and mother."

CHAPTER 13

1 That same day Jesus went out of the house and sat beside the sea.

2 And great crowds gathered about him, so that he got into a boat and sat down. And the whole crowd stood on the beach.

3 And he told them many things in parables, saying: "A sower went out to sow.

4 "And as he sowed, some seeds fell along the path, and the birds came and devoured them.

5 "Other seeds fell on rocky ground, where they did not have much soil, and immediately they sprang up, since they had no depth of soil,

6 "but when the sun rose they were scorched. And since they had no root, they withered away.

7 "Other seeds fell among thorns, and the thorns grew up and choked them.

8 "Other seeds fell on good soil and produced grain, some a hundredfold, some sixty, some thirty.

9 "He who has ears, let him hear."

10 Then the disciples came and said to him, "Why do you speak to them in parables?"

11 And he answered them, "To you it has been given to know the secrets of the kingdom of heaven, but to them it has not been given.

12 "For to the one who has, more will be given, and he will have an abundance, but from the one who has not, even what he has will be taken away.

13 "This is why I speak to them in parables, because

seeing they do not see, and hearing they do not hear, nor do they understand.

14 "Indeed, in their case the prophecy of Isaiah is fulfilled that says: ' 'You will indeed hear but never understand, and you will indeed see but never perceive.'.

15 4 "For this people's heart has grown dull, and with their ears they can barely hear, and their eyes they have closed, lest they should see with their eyes and hear with their ears and understand with their heart and turn, and I would heal them.'

16 "But blessed are your eyes, for they see, and your ears, for they hear.

17 "For truly, I say to you, many prophets and righteous people longed to see what you see, and did not see it, and to hear what you hear, and did not hear it.

18 "Hear then the parable of the sower:

19 "When anyone hears the word of the kingdom and does not understand it, the evil one comes and snatches away what has been sown in his heart. This is what was sown along the path.

20 "As for what was sown on rocky ground, this is the one who hears the word and immediately receives it with joy,

21 "yet he has no root in himself, but endures for a while, and when tribulation or persecution arises on account of the word, immediately he falls away.

22 "As for what was sown among thorns, this is the one who hears the word, but the cares of the world and the deceitfulness of riches choke the word, and it proves unfruitful.

23 "As for what was sown on good soil, this is the one who hears the word and understands it. He indeed bears fruit and yields, in one case a hundredfold, in another sixty, and in another thirty."

24 He put another parable before them, saying, "The kingdom of heaven may be compared to a man who sowed good seed in his field,

25 "but while his men were sleeping, his enemy came and sowed weeds among the wheat and went away.

26 "So when the plants came up and bore grain, then the weeds appeared also.

27 "And the servants of the master of the house came and said to him, 'Master, did you not sow good seed in your field? How then does it have weeds?'

28 "He said to them, 'An enemy has done this.' So the ser-

vants said to him, 'Then do you want us to go and gather them?'

29 "But he said, 'No, lest in gathering the weeds you root up the wheat along with them.

30 "'Let both grow together until the harvest, and at harvest time I will tell the reapers, Gather the weeds first and bind them in bundles to be burned, but gather the wheat into my barn.'"

31 He put another parable before them, saying, "The kingdom of heaven is like a grain of mustard seed that a man took and sowed in his field.

32 "It is the smallest of all seeds, but when it has grown it is larger than all the garden plants and becomes a tree, so that the birds of the air come and make nests in its branches."

33 He told them another parable. "The kingdom of heaven is like leaven that a woman took and hid in three measures of flour, till it was all leavened."

34 All these things Jesus said to the crowds in parables; indeed, he said nothing to them without a parable.

35 This was to fulfill what was spoken by the prophet: "I will open my mouth in parables; I will utter what has been hidden since the foundation of the world."

36 Then he left the crowds and went into the house. And his disciples came to him, saying, "Explain to us the parable of the weeds of the field."

37 He answered, "The one who sows the good seed is the Son of Man.

38 "The field is the world, and the good seed is the sons of the kingdom. The weeds are the sons of the evil one,

39 "and the enemy who sowed them is the devil. The harvest is the end of the age, and the reapers are angels.

40 "Just as the weeds are gathered and burned with fire, so will it be at the end of the age.

41 "The Son of Man will send his angels, and they will gather out of his kingdom all causes of sin and all law-breakers,

42 "and throw them into the fiery furnace. In that place there will be weeping and gnashing of teeth.

43 "Then the righteous will shine like the sun in the kingdom of their Father. He who has ears, let him hear.

44 "The kingdom of heaven is like treasure hidden in a field, which a man found and covered up. Then in his

joy he goes and sells all that he has and buys that field.

⁴⁵ "Again, the kingdom of heaven is like a merchant in search of fine pearls,

⁴⁶ "who, on finding one pearl of great value, went and sold all that he had and bought it.

⁴⁷ "Again, the kingdom of heaven is like a net that was thrown into the sea and gathered fish of every kind.

⁴⁸ "When it was full, men drew it ashore and sat down and sorted the good into containers but threw away the bad.

⁴⁹ "So it will be at the end of the age. The angels will come out and separate the evil from the righteous

⁵⁰ "and throw them into the fiery furnace. In that place there will be weeping and gnashing of teeth.

⁵¹ "Have you understood all these things?" They said to him, "Yes."

⁵² And he said to them, "Therefore every scribe who has been trained for the kingdom of heaven is like a master of a house, who brings out of his treasure what is new and what is old."

⁵³ And when Jesus had finished these parables, he went away from there,

⁵⁴ and coming to his hometown he taught them in their synagogue, so that they were astonished, and said, "Where did this man get this wisdom and these mighty works?

⁵⁵ "Is not this the carpenter's son? Is not his mother called Mary? And are not his brothers James and Joseph and Simon and Judas?

⁵⁶ "And are not all his sisters with us? Where then did this man get all these things?"

⁵⁷ And they took offense at him. But Jesus said to them, "A prophet is not without honor except in his hometown and in his own household."

⁵⁸ And he did not do any mighty works there, because of their unbelief.

CHAPTER 14

¹ At that time Herod the tetrarch heard about the fame of Jesus,

² and he said to his servants, "This is John the Baptist. He has been raised from the dead; that is why these miraculous powers are at work in him."

³ For Herod had seized John and bound him and put him in prison for the sake of Herodias, his brother Philip's wife,

⁴ because John had been saying to him, "It is not lawful for you to have her."

⁵ And though he wanted to put him to death, he feared

the people, because they held him to be a prophet.

6 But when Herod's birthday came, the daughter of Herodias danced before the company and pleased Herod,

7 so that he promised with an oath to give her whatever she might ask.

8 Prompted by her mother, she said, "Give me the head of John the Baptist here on a platter."

9 And the king was sorry, but because of his oaths and his guests he commanded it to be given.

10 He sent and had John beheaded in the prison,

11 and his head was brought on a platter and given to the girl, and she brought it to her mother.

12 And his disciples came and took the body and buried it, and they went and told Jesus.

13 Now when Jesus heard this, he withdrew from there in a boat to a desolate place by himself. But when the crowds heard it, they followed him on foot from the towns.

14 When he went ashore he saw a great crowd, and he had compassion on them and healed their sick.

15 Now when it was evening, the disciples came to him and said, "This is a desolate place, and the day is now over; send the crowds away to go into the villages and buy food for themselves."

16 But Jesus said, "They need not go away; you give them something to eat."

17 They said to him, "We have only five loaves here and two fish."

18 And he said, "Bring them here to me."

19 Then he ordered the crowds to sit down on the grass, and taking the five loaves and the two fish, he looked up to heaven and said a blessing. Then he broke the loaves and gave them to the disciples, and the disciples gave them to the crowds.

20 And they all ate and were satisfied. And they took up twelve baskets full of the broken pieces left over.

21 And those who ate were about five thousand men, besides women and children.

22 Immediately he made the disciples get into the boat and go before him to the other side, while he dismissed the crowds.

23 And after he had dismissed the crowds, he went up on the mountain by himself to pray. When evening came, he was there alone,

24 but the boat by this time was a long way from the land,

beaten by the waves, for the wind was against them.

²⁵ And in the fourth watch of the night he came to them, walking on the sea.

²⁶ But when the disciples saw him walking on the sea, they were terrified, and said, "It is a ghost!" and they cried out in fear.

²⁷ But immediately Jesus spoke to them, saying, "Take heart; it is I. Do not be afraid."

²⁸ And Peter answered him, "Lord, if it is you, command me to come to you on the water."

²⁹ He said, "Come." So Peter got out of the boat and walked on the water and came to Jesus.

³⁰ But when he saw the wind, he was afraid, and beginning to sink he cried out, "Lord, save me."

³¹ Jesus immediately reached out his hand and took hold of him, saying to him, "O you of little faith, why did you doubt?"

³² And when they got into the boat, the wind ceased.

³³ And those in the boat worshiped him, saying, "Truly you are the Son of God."

³⁴ And when they had crossed over, they came to land at Gennesaret.

³⁵ And when the men of that place recognized him, they sent around to all that region and brought to him all who were sick

³⁶ and implored him that they might only touch the fringe of his garment. And as many as touched it were made well.

CHAPTER 15

¹ Then Pharisees and scribes came to Jesus from Jerusalem and said,

² "Why do your disciples break the tradition of the elders? For they do not wash their hands when they eat."

³ He answered them, "And why do you break the commandment of God for the sake of your tradition?

⁴ "For God commanded, 'Honor your father and your mother,' and, 'Whoever reviles father or mother must surely die.'

⁵ "But you say, 'If anyone tells his father or his mother, "What you would have gained from me is given to God,"

⁶ " 'he need not honor his father.' So for the sake of your tradition you have made void the word of God.

⁷ "You hypocrites! Well did Isaiah prophesy of you, when he said:

⁸ " 'This people honors me with their lips, but their heart is far from me;

⁹ "'in vain do they worship me, teaching as doctrines the commandments of men.'"

¹⁰ And he called the people to him and said to them, "Hear and understand:

¹¹ "it is not what goes into the mouth that defiles a person, but what comes out of the mouth; this defiles a person."

¹² Then the disciples came and said to him, "Do you know that the Pharisees were offended when they heard this saying?"

¹³ He answered, "Every plant that my heavenly Father has not planted will be rooted up.

¹⁴ "Let them alone; they are blind guides. And if the blind lead the blind, both will fall into a pit."

¹⁵ But Peter said to him, "Explain the parable to us."

¹⁶ And he said, "Are you also still without understanding?

¹⁷ "Do you not see that whatever goes into the mouth passes into the stomach and is expelled?

¹⁸ "But what comes out of the mouth proceeds from the heart, and this defiles a person.

¹⁹ "For out of the heart come evil thoughts, murder, adultery, sexual immorality, theft, false witness, slander.

²⁰ "These are what defile a person. But to eat with unwashed hands does not defile anyone."

²¹ And Jesus went away from there and withdrew to the district of Tyre and Sidon.

²² And behold, a Canaanite woman from that region came out and was crying, "Have mercy on me, O Lord, Son of David; my daughter is severely oppressed by a demon."

²³ But he did not answer her a word. And his disciples came and begged him, saying, "Send her away, for she is crying out after us."

²⁴ He answered, "I was sent only to the lost sheep of the house of Israel."

²⁵ But she came and knelt before him, saying, "Lord, help me."

²⁶ And he answered, "It is not right to take the children's bread and throw it to the dogs."

²⁷ She said, "Yes, Lord, yet even the dogs eat the crumbs that fall from their masters' table."

²⁸ Then Jesus answered her, "O woman, great is your faith! Be it done for you as you desire." And her daughter was healed instantly.

²⁹ Jesus went on from there and walked beside the Sea of Galilee. And he went up on the mountain and sat down there.

30 And great crowds came to him, bringing with them the lame, the blind, the crippled, the mute, and many others, and they put them at his feet, and he healed them,

31 so that the crowd wondered, when they saw the mute speaking, the crippled healthy, the lame walking, and the blind seeing. And they glorified the God of Israel.

32 Then Jesus called his disciples to him and said, "I have compassion on the crowd because they have been with me now three days and have nothing to eat. And I am unwilling to send them away hungry, lest they faint on the way."

33 And the disciples said to him, "Where are we to get enough bread in such a desolate place to feed so great a crowd?"

34 And Jesus said to them, "How many loaves do you have?" They said, "Seven, and a few small fish."

35 And directing the crowd to sit down on the ground,

36 he took the seven loaves and the fish, and having given thanks he broke them and gave them to the disciples, and the disciples gave them to the crowds.

37 And they all ate and were satisfied. And they took up seven baskets full of the broken pieces left over.

38 Those who ate were four thousand men, besides women and children.

39 And after sending away the crowds, he got into the boat and went to the region of Magadan.

CHAPTER 16

1 And the Pharisees and Sadducees came, and to test him they asked him to show them a sign from heaven.

2 He answered them, "When it is evening, you say, 'It will be fair weather, for the sky is red.'

3 "And in the morning, 'It will be stormy today, for the sky is red and threatening.' You know how to interpret the appearance of the sky, but you cannot interpret the signs of the times.

4 "An evil and adulterous generation seeks for a sign, but no sign will be given to it except the sign of Jonah." So he left them and departed.

5 When the disciples reached the other side, they had forgotten to bring any bread.

6 Jesus said to them, "Watch and beware of the leaven of the Pharisees and Sadducees."

7 And they began discussing it among themselves, saying, "We brought no bread."

20 "For where two or three are gathered in my name, there am I among them."

21 Then Peter came up and said to him, "Lord, how often will my brother sin against me, and I forgive him? As many as seven times?"

22 Jesus said to him, "I do not say to you seven times, but seventy-seven times.

23 "Therefore the kingdom of heaven may be compared to a king who wished to settle accounts with his servants.

24 "When he began to settle, one was brought to him who owed him ten thousand talents.

25 "And since he could not pay, his master ordered him to be sold, with his wife and children and all that he had, and payment to be made.

26 "So the servant fell on his knees, imploring him, 'Have patience with me, and I will pay you everything.'

27 "And out of pity for him, the master of that servant released him and forgave him the debt.

28 "But when that same servant went out, he found one of his fellow servants who owed him a hundred denarii, and seizing him, he began to choke him, saying, 'Pay what you owe.'

29 "So his fellow servant fell down and pleaded with him, 'Have patience with me, and I will pay you.'

30 "He refused and went and put him in prison until he should pay the debt.

31 "When his fellow servants saw what had taken place, they were greatly distressed, and they went and reported to their master all that had taken place.

32 "Then his master summoned him and said to him, 'You wicked servant! I forgave you all that debt because you pleaded with me.

33 "'And should not you have had mercy on your fellow servant, as I had mercy on you?'

34 "And in anger his master delivered him to the jailers, until he should pay all his debt.

35 "So also my heavenly Father will do to every one of you, if you do not forgive your brother from your heart."

CHAPTER 19

1 Now when Jesus had finished these sayings, he went away from Galilee and entered the region of Judea beyond the Jordan.

2 And large crowds followed him, and he healed them there.

3 And Pharisees came up to

him and tested him by asking, "Is it lawful to divorce one's wife for any cause?"

4 He answered, "Have you not read that he who created them from the beginning made them male and female,

5 "and said, 'Therefore a man shall leave his father and his mother and hold fast to his wife, and the two shall become one flesh'?

6 "So they are no longer two but one flesh. What therefore God has joined together, let not man separate."

7 They said to him, "Why then did Moses command one to give a certificate of divorce and to send her away?"

8 He said to them, "Because of your hardness of heart Moses allowed you to divorce your wives, but from the beginning it was not so.

9 "And I say to you: whoever divorces his wife, except for sexual immorality, and marries another, commits adultery, and whoever marries a divorced woman commits adultery."

10 The disciples said to him, "If such is the case of a man with his wife, it is better not to marry."

11 But he said to them, "Not everyone can receive this saying, but only those to whom it is given.

12 "For there are eunuchs who have been so from birth, and there are eunuchs who have been made eunuchs by men, and there are eunuchs who have made themselves eunuchs for the sake of the kingdom of heaven. Let the one who is able to receive this receive it."

13 Then children were brought to him that he might lay his hands on them and pray. The disciples rebuked the people,

14 but Jesus said, "Let the little children come to me and do not hinder them, for to such belongs the kingdom of heaven."

15 And he laid his hands on them and went away.

16 And behold, a man came up to him, saying, "Teacher, what good deed must I do to have eternal life?"

17 And he said to him, "Why do you ask me about what is good? There is only one who is good. If you would enter life, keep the commandments."

18 He said to him, "Which ones?" And Jesus said, "You shall not murder, You shall not commit adultery, You shall not steal, You shall not bear false witness,

19 "Honor your father and mother, and, You shall love your neighbor as yourself."

20 The young man said to him, "All these I have kept. What do I still lack?"

21 Jesus said to him, "If you would be perfect, go, sell what you possess and give to the poor, and you will have treasure in heaven; and come, follow me."

22 When the young man heard this he went away sorrowful, for he had great possessions.

23 And Jesus said to his disciples, "Truly, I say to you, only with difficulty will a rich person enter the kingdom of heaven.

24 "Again I tell you, it is easier for a camel to go through the eye of a needle than for a rich person to enter the kingdom of God."

25 When the disciples heard this, they were greatly astonished, saying, "Who then can be saved?"

26 But Jesus looked at them and said, "With man this is impossible, but with God all things are possible."

27 Then Peter said in reply, "See, we have left everything and followed you. What then will we have?"

28 Jesus said to them, "Truly, I say to you, in the new world, when the Son of Man will sit on his glorious throne, you who have followed me will also sit on twelve thrones, judging the twelve tribes of Israel.

29 "And everyone who has left houses or brothers or sisters or father or mother or children or lands, for my name's sake, will receive a hundredfold and will inherit eternal life.

30 "But many who are first will be last, and the last first.

CHAPTER 20

1 "For the kingdom of heaven is like a master of a house who went out early in the morning to hire laborers for his vineyard.

2 "After agreeing with the laborers for a denarius a day, he sent them into his vineyard.

3 "And going out about the third hour he saw others standing idle in the marketplace,

4 "and to them he said, 'You go into the vineyard too, and whatever is right I will give you.'

5 "So they went. Going out again about the sixth hour and the ninth hour, he did the same.

6 "And about the eleventh hour he went out and found others standing. And he said to them, 'Why do you stand here idle all day?'

7 "They said to him, 'Because

no one has hired us.' He said to them, 'You go into the vineyard too.'

⁸ "And when evening came, the owner of the vineyard said to his foreman, 'Call the laborers and pay them their wages, beginning with the last, up to the first.'

⁹ "And when those hired about the eleventh hour came, each of them received a denarius.

¹⁰ "Now when those hired first came, they thought they would receive more, but each of them also received a denarius.

¹¹ "And on receiving it they grumbled at the master of the house,

¹² "saying, 'These last worked only one hour, and you have made them equal to us who have borne the burden of the day and the scorching heat.'

¹³ "But he replied to one of them, 'Friend, I am doing you no wrong. Did you not agree with me for a denarius?

¹⁴ " 'Take what belongs to you and go. I choose to give to this last worker as I give to you.

¹⁵ " 'Am I not allowed to do what I choose with what belongs to me? Or do you begrudge my generosity?'

¹⁶ "So the last will be first, and the first last."

¹⁷ And as Jesus was going up to Jerusalem, he took the twelve disciples aside, and on the way he said to them,

¹⁸ "See, we are going up to Jerusalem. And the Son of Man will be delivered over to the chief priests and scribes, and they will condemn him to death

¹⁹ "and deliver him over to the Gentiles to be mocked and flogged and crucified, and he will be raised on the third day."

²⁰ Then the mother of the sons of Zebedee came up to him with her sons, and kneeling before him she asked him for something.

²¹ And he said to her, "What do you want?" She said to him, "Say that these two sons of mine are to sit, one at your right hand and one at your left, in your kingdom."

²² Jesus answered, "You do not know what you are asking. Are you able to drink the cup that I am to drink?" They said to him, "We are able."

²³ He said to them, "You will drink my cup, but to sit at my right hand and at my left is not mine to grant, but it is for those for whom it has been prepared by my Father."

²⁴ And when the ten heard it, they were indignant at the two brothers.

²⁵ But Jesus called them to him and said, "You know that the rulers of the Gentiles lord it over them, and their great ones exercise authority over them.

²⁶ "It shall not be so among you. But whoever would be great among you must be your servant,

²⁷ "and whoever would be first among you must be your slave,

²⁸ "even as the Son of Man came not to be served but to serve, and to give his life as a ransom for many."

²⁹ And as they went out of Jericho, a great crowd followed him.

³⁰ And behold, there were two blind men sitting by the roadside, and when they heard that Jesus was passing by, they cried out, "Lord, have mercy on us, Son of David!"

³¹ The crowd rebuked them, telling them to be silent, but they cried out all the more, "Lord, have mercy on us, Son of David!"

³² And stopping, Jesus called them and said, "What do you want me to do for you?"

³³ They said to him, "Lord, let our eyes be opened."

³⁴ And Jesus in pity touched their eyes, and immediately they recovered their sight and followed him.

CHAPTER 21

¹ Now when they drew near to Jerusalem and came to Bethphage, to the Mount of Olives, then Jesus sent two disciples,

² saying to them, "Go into the village in front of you, and immediately you will find a donkey tied, and a colt with her. Untie them and bring them to me.

³ "If anyone says anything to you, you shall say, 'The Lord needs them,' and he will send them at once."

⁴ This took place to fulfill what was spoken by the prophet, saying,

⁵ "Say to the daughter of Zion, 'Behold, your king is coming to you, humble, and mounted on a donkey, on a colt, the foal of a beast of burden.'"

⁶ The disciples went and did as Jesus had directed them.

⁷ They brought the donkey and the colt and put on them their cloaks, and he sat on them.

⁸ Most of the crowd spread their cloaks on the road, and others cut branches from the trees and spread them on the road.

⁹ And the crowds that went before him and that followed him were shouting, "Hosanna to the Son of David! Blessed is he who comes in the name

of the Lord! Hosanna in the highest!"

10 And when he entered Jerusalem, the whole city was stirred up, saying, "Who is this?"

11 And the crowds said, "This is the prophet Jesus, from Nazareth of Galilee."

12 And Jesus entered the temple and drove out all who sold and bought in the temple, and he overturned the tables of the money-changers and the seats of those who sold pigeons.

13 He said to them, "It is written, 'My house shall be called a house of prayer,' but you make it a den of robbers."

14 And the blind and the lame came to him in the temple, and he healed them.

15 But when the chief priests and the scribes saw the wonderful things that he did, and the children crying out in the temple, "Hosanna to the Son of David!" they were indignant,

16 and they said to him, "Do you hear what these are saying?" And Jesus said to them, "Yes; have you never read, 'Out of the mouth of infants and nursing babies you have prepared praise'?"

17 And leaving them, he went out of the city to Bethany and lodged there.

18 In the morning, as he was returning to the city, he became hungry.

19 And seeing a fig tree by the wayside, he went to it and found nothing on it but only leaves. And he said to it, "May no fruit ever come from you again!" And the fig tree withered at once.

20 When the disciples saw it, they marveled, saying, "How did the fig tree wither at once?"

21 And Jesus answered them, "Truly, I say to you, if you have faith and do not doubt, you will not only do what has been done to the fig tree, but even if you say to this mountain, 'Be taken up and thrown into the sea,' it will happen.

22 "And whatever you ask in prayer, you will receive, if you have faith."

23 And when he entered the temple, the chief priests and the elders of the people came up to him as he was teaching, and said, "By what authority are you doing these things, and who gave you this authority?"

24 Jesus answered them, "I also will ask you one question, and if you tell me the answer, then I also will tell you by what authority I do these things.

25 "The baptism of John,

from where did it come? From heaven or from man?" And they discussed it among themselves, saying, "If we say, 'From heaven,' he will say to us, 'Why then did you not believe him?'

26 "But if we say, 'From man,' we are afraid of the crowd, for they all hold that John was a prophet."

27 So they answered Jesus, "We do not know." And he said to them, "Neither will I tell you by what authority I do these things.

28 "What do you think? A man had two sons. And he went to the first and said, 'Son, go and work in the vineyard today.'

29 "And he answered, 'I will not,' but afterward he changed his mind and went.

30 "And he went to the other son and said the same. And he answered, 'I go, sir,' but did not go.

31 "Which of the two did the will of his father?" They said, "The first." Jesus said to them, "Truly, I say to you, the tax collectors and the prostitutes go into the kingdom of God before you.

32 "For John came to you in the way of righteousness, and you did not believe him, but the tax collectors and the prostitutes believed him. And even when you saw it, you did not afterward change your minds and believe him.

33 "Hear another parable. There was a master of a house who planted a vineyard and put a fence around it and dug a winepress in it and built a tower and leased it to tenants, and went into another country.

34 "When the season for fruit drew near, he sent his servants to the tenants to get his fruit.

35 "And the tenants took his servants and beat one, killed another, and stoned another.

36 "Again he sent other servants, more than the first. And they did the same to them.

37 "Finally he sent his son to them, saying, 'They will respect my son.'

38 "But when the tenants saw the son, they said to themselves, 'This is the heir. Come, let us kill him and have his inheritance.'

39 "And they took him and threw him out of the vineyard and killed him.

40 "When therefore the owner of the vineyard comes, what will he do to those tenants?"

41 They said to him, "He will put those wretches to a miserable death and let out the vineyard to other tenants

who will give him the fruits in their seasons."

⁴² Jesus said to them, "Have you never read in the Scriptures: 'The stone that the builders rejected has become the cornerstone; this was the Lord's doing, and it is marvelous in our eyes'?

⁴³ "Therefore I tell you, the kingdom of God will be taken away from you and given to a people producing its fruits.

⁴⁴ "And the one who falls on this stone will be broken to pieces; and when it falls on anyone, it will crush him."

⁴⁵ When the chief priests and the Pharisees heard his parables, they perceived that he was speaking about them.

⁴⁶ And although they were seeking to arrest him, they feared the crowds, because they held him to be a prophet.

CHAPTER 22

¹ And again Jesus spoke to them in parables, saying,

² "The kingdom of heaven *may be compared to* a king who gave a wedding feast for his son,

³ "and sent his servants to call those who were invited to the wedding feast, but they would not come.

⁴ "Again he sent other servants, saying, 'Tell those who are invited, "See, I have pre-pared my dinner, my oxen and my fat calves have been slaughtered, and everything is ready. Come to the wedding feast."'

⁵ "But they paid no attention and went off, one to his farm, another to his business,

⁶ "while the rest seized his servants, treated them shamefully, and killed them.

⁷ "The king was angry, and he sent his troops and destroyed those murderers and burned their city.

⁸ "Then he said to his servants, 'The wedding feast is ready, but those invited were not worthy.

⁹ "'Go therefore to the main roads and invite to the wedding feast as many as you find.'

¹⁰ "And those servants went out into the roads and gathered all whom they found, both bad and good. So the wedding hall was filled with guests.

¹¹ "But when the king came in to look at the guests, he saw there a man who had no wedding garment.

¹² "And he said to him, 'Friend, how did you get in here without a wedding garment?' And he was speechless.

¹³ "Then the king said to the attendants, 'Bind him hand and foot and cast him into the outer darkness. In that

place there will be weeping and gnashing of teeth.'

14 "For many are called, but few are chosen."

15 Then the Pharisees went and plotted how to entangle him in his words.

16 And they sent their disciples to him, along with the Herodians, saying, "Teacher, we know that you are true and teach the way of God truthfully, and you do not care about anyone's opinion, for you are not swayed by appearances.

17 "Tell us, then, what you think: Is it lawful to pay taxes to Caesar, or not?"

18 But Jesus, aware of their malice, said, "Why put me to the test, you hypocrites?

19 "Show me the coin for the tax." And they brought him a denarius.

20 And Jesus said to them, "Whose likeness and inscription is this?"

21 They said, "Caesar's." Then he said to them, "Therefore render to Caesar the things that are Caesar's, and to God the things that are God's."

22 When they heard it, they marveled. And they left him and went away.

23 The same day Sadducees came to him, who say that there is no resurrection, and they asked him a question,

24 saying, "Teacher, Moses said, 'If a man dies having no children, his brother must marry the widow and raise up offspring for his brother.'

25 "Now there were seven brothers among us. The first married and died, and having no offspring left his wife to his brother.

26 "So too the second and third, down to the seventh.

27 "After them all, the woman died.

28 "In the resurrection, therefore, of the seven, whose wife will she be? For they all had her."

29 But Jesus answered them, "You are wrong, because you know neither the Scriptures nor the power of God.

30 "For in the resurrection they neither marry nor are given in marriage, but are like angels in heaven.

31 "And as for the resurrection of the dead, have you not read what was said to you by God:

32 "'I am the God of Abraham, and the God of Isaac, and the God of Jacob'? He is not God of the dead, but of the living."

33 And when the crowd heard it, they were astonished at his teaching.

34 But when the Pharisees heard that he had silenced the Sadducees, they gathered together.

³⁵ And one of them, a lawyer, asked him a question to test him.

³⁶ "Teacher, which is the great commandment in the Law?"

³⁷ And he said to him, "You shall love the Lord your God with all your heart and with all your soul and with all your mind.

³⁸ "This is the great and first commandment.

³⁹ "And a second is like it: You shall love your neighbor as yourself.

⁴⁰ "On these two commandments depend all the Law and the Prophets."

⁴¹ Now while the Pharisees were gathered together, Jesus asked them a question,

⁴² saying, "What do you think about the Christ? Whose son is he?" They said to him, "The son of David."

⁴³ He said to them, "How is it then that David, in the Spirit, calls him Lord, saying,

⁴⁴ "'The Lord said to my Lord, "Sit at my right hand, until I put your enemies under your feet"'?

⁴⁵ "If then David calls him Lord, how is he his son?"

⁴⁶ And no one was able to answer him a word, nor from that day did anyone dare to ask him any more questions.

CHAPTER 23

¹ Then Jesus said to the crowds and to his disciples,

² "The scribes and the Pharisees sit on Moses' seat,

³ "so do and observe whatever they tell you, but not the works they do. For they preach, but do not practice.

⁴ "They tie up heavy burdens, hard to bear, and lay them on people's shoulders, but they themselves are not willing to move them with their finger.

⁵ "They do all their deeds to be seen by others. For they make their phylacteries broad and their fringes long,

⁶ "and they love the place of honor at feasts and the best seats in the synagogues

⁷ "and greetings in the marketplaces and being called rabbi by others.

⁸ "But you are not to be called rabbi, for you have one teacher, and you are all brothers.

⁹ "And call no man your father on earth, for you have one Father, who is in heaven.

¹⁰ "Neither be called instructors, for you have one instructor, the Christ.

¹¹ "The greatest among you shall be your servant.

¹² "Whoever exalts himself will be humbled, and whoever humbles himself will be exalted.

13 "But woe to you, scribes and Pharisees, hypocrites! For you shut the kingdom of heaven in people's faces. For you neither enter yourselves nor allow those who would enter to go in.

14 "Woe to you, scribes and Pharisees, hypocrites! For you devour widows' houses and for a pretense you make long prayers; therefore you will receive the greater condemnation.

15 "Woe to you, scribes and Pharisees, hypocrites! For you travel across sea and land to make a single proselyte, and when he becomes a proselyte, you make him twice as much a child of hell as yourselves.

16 "Woe to you, blind guides, who say, 'If anyone swears by the temple, it is nothing, but if anyone swears by the gold of the temple, he is bound by his oath.'

17 "You blind fools! For which is greater, the gold or the temple that has made the gold sacred?

18 "And you say, 'If anyone swears by the altar, it is nothing, but if anyone swears by the gift that is on the altar, he is bound by his oath.'

19 "You blind men! For which is greater, the gift or the altar that makes the gift sacred?

20 "So whoever swears by the altar swears by it and by everything on it.

21 "And whoever swears by the temple swears by it and by him who dwells in it.

22 "And whoever swears by heaven swears by the throne of God and by him who sits upon it.

23 "Woe to you, scribes and Pharisees, hypocrites! For you tithe mint and dill and cumin, and have neglected the weightier matters of the law: justice and mercy and faithfulness. These you ought to have done, without neglecting the others.

24 "You blind guides, straining out a gnat and swallowing a camel!

25 "Woe to you, scribes and Pharisees, hypocrites! For you clean the outside of the cup and the plate, but inside they are full of greed and self-indulgence.

26 "You blind Pharisee! First clean the inside of the cup and the plate, that the outside also may be clean.

27 "Woe to you, scribes and Pharisees, hypocrites! For you are like whitewashed tombs, which outwardly appear beautiful, but within are full of dead people's bones and all uncleanness.

28 "So you also outwardly appear righteous to others,

but within you are full of hypocrisy and lawlessness.

29 "Woe to you, scribes and Pharisees, hypocrites! For you build the tombs of the prophets and decorate the monuments of the righteous,

30 "saying, 'If we had lived in the days of our fathers, we would not have taken part with them in shedding the blood of the prophets.'

31 "Thus you witness against yourselves that you are sons of those who murdered the prophets.

32 "Fill up, then, the measure of your fathers.

33 "You serpents, you brood of vipers, how are you to escape being sentenced to hell?

34 "Therefore I send you prophets and wise men and scribes, some of whom you will kill and crucify, and some you will flog in your synagogues and persecute from town to town,

35 "so that on you may come all the righteous blood shed on earth, from the blood of righteous Abel to the blood of Zechariah the son of Barachiah, whom you murdered between the sanctuary and the altar.

36 "Truly, I say to you, all these things will come upon this generation.

37 "O Jerusalem, Jerusalem, the city that kills the prophets and stones those who are sent to it! How often would I have gathered your children together as a hen gathers her brood under her wings, and you were not willing!

38 "See, your house is left to you desolate.

39 "For I tell you, you will not see me again, until you say, 'Blessed is he who comes in the name of the Lord.'"

CHAPTER 24

1 Jesus left the temple and was going away, when his disciples came to point out to him the buildings of the temple.

2 But he answered them, "You see all these, do you not? Truly, I say to you, there will not be left here one stone upon another that will not be thrown down."

3 As he sat on the Mount of Olives, the disciples came to him privately, saying, "Tell us, when will these things be, and what will be the sign of your coming and of the end of the age?"

4 And Jesus answered them, "See that no one leads you astray.

5 "For many will come in my name, saying, 'I am the Christ,' and they will lead many astray.

6 "And you will hear of wars and rumors of wars. See that

you are not alarmed, for this must take place, but the end is not yet.

7 "For nation will rise against nation, and kingdom against kingdom, and there will be famines and earthquakes in various places.

8 "All these are but the beginning of the birth pains.

9 "Then they will deliver you up to tribulation and put you to death, and you will be hated by all nations for my name's sake.

10 "And then many will fall away and betray one another and hate one another.

11 "And many false prophets will arise and lead many astray.

12 "And because lawlessness will be increased, the love of many will grow cold.

13 "But the one who endures to the end will be saved.

14 "And this gospel of the kingdom will be proclaimed throughout the whole world as a testimony to all nations, and then the end will come.

15 "So when you see the abomination of desolation spoken of by the prophet Daniel, standing in the holy place (let the reader understand),

16 "then let those who are in Judea flee to the mountains.

17 "Let the one who is on the housetop not go down to take what is in his house,

18 "and let the one who is in the field not turn back to take his cloak.

19 "And alas for women who are pregnant and for those who are nursing infants in those days!

20 "Pray that your flight may not be in winter or on a Sabbath.

21 "For then there will be great tribulation, such as has not been from the beginning of the world until now, no, and never will be.

22 "And if those days had not been cut short, no human being would be saved. But for the sake of the elect those days will be cut short.

23 "Then if anyone says to you, 'Look, here is the Christ!' or 'There he is!' do not believe it.

24 "For false christs and false prophets will arise and perform great signs and wonders, so as to lead astray, if possible, even the elect.

25 "See, I have told you beforehand.

26 "So, if they say to you, 'Look, he is in the wilderness,' do not go out. If they say, 'Look, he is in the inner rooms,' do not believe it.

27 "For as the lightning comes from the east and shines as far as the west, so will be the coming of the Son of Man.

²⁸ "Wherever the corpse is, there the vultures will gather.

²⁹ "Immediately after the tribulation of those days the sun will be darkened, and the moon will not give its light, and the stars will fall from heaven, and the powers of the heavens will be shaken.

³⁰ "Then will appear in heaven the sign of the Son of Man, and then all the tribes of the earth will mourn, and they will see the Son of Man coming on the clouds of heaven with power and great glory.

³¹ "And he will send out his angels with a loud trumpet call, and they will gather his elect from the four winds, from one end of heaven to the other.

³² "From the fig tree learn its lesson: as soon as its branch becomes tender and puts out its leaves, you know that summer is near.

³³ "So also, when you see all these things, you know that he is near, at the very gates.

³⁴ "Truly, I say to you, this generation will not pass away until all these things take place.

³⁵ "Heaven and earth will pass away, but my words will not pass away.

³⁶ "But concerning that day and hour no one knows, not even the angels of heaven, nor the Son, but the Father only.

³⁷ "For as were the days of Noah, so will be the coming of the Son of Man.

³⁸ "For as in those days before the flood they were eating and drinking, marrying and giving in marriage, until the day when Noah entered the ark,

³⁹ "and they were unaware until the flood came and swept them all away, so will be the coming of the Son of Man.

⁴⁰ "Then two men will be in the field; one will be taken and one left.

⁴¹ "Two women will be grinding at the mill; one will be taken and one left.

⁴² "Therefore, stay awake, for you do not know on what day your Lord is coming.

⁴³ "But know this, that if the master of the house had known in what part of the night the thief was coming, he would have stayed awake and would not have let his house be broken into.

⁴⁴ "Therefore you also must be ready, for the Son of Man is coming at an hour you do not expect.

⁴⁵ "Who then is the faithful and wise servant, whom his master has set over his household, to give them their food at the proper time?

46 "Blessed is that servant whom his master will find so doing when he comes.

47 "Truly, I say to you, he will set him over all his possessions.

48 "But if that wicked servant says to himself, 'My master is delayed,'

49 "and begins to beat his fellow servants and eats and drinks with drunkards,

50 "the master of that servant will come on a day when he does not expect him and at an hour he does not know

51 "and will cut him in pieces and put him with the hypocrites. In that place there will be weeping and gnashing of teeth.

CHAPTER 25

1 "Then the kingdom of heaven will be like ten virgins who took their lamps and went to meet the bridegroom.

2 "Five of them were foolish, and five were wise.

3 "For when the foolish took their lamps, they took no oil with them,

4 "but the wise took flasks of oil with their lamps.

5 "As the bridegroom was delayed, they all became drowsy and slept.

6 "But at midnight there was a cry, 'Here is the bridegroom! Come out to meet him.'

7 "Then all those virgins rose and trimmed their lamps.

8 "And the foolish said to the wise, 'Give us some of your oil, for our lamps are going out.'

9 "But the wise answered, saying, 'Since there will not be enough for us and for you, go rather to the dealers and buy for yourselves.'

10 "And while they were going to buy, the bridegroom came, and those who were ready went in with him to the marriage feast, and the door was shut.

11 "Afterward the other virgins came also, saying, 'Lord, lord, open to us.'

12 "But he answered, 'Truly, I say to you, I do not know you.'

13 "Watch therefore, for you know neither the day nor the hour.

14 "For it will be like a man going on a journey, who called his servants and entrusted to them his property.

15 "To one he gave five talents, to another two, to another one, to each according to his ability. Then he went away.

16 "He who had received the five talents went at once and traded with them, and he made five talents more.

17 "So also he who had the two talents made two talents more.

¹⁸ "But he who had received the one talent went and dug in the ground and hid his master's money.

¹⁹ "Now after a long time the master of those servants came and settled accounts with them.

²⁰ "And he who had received the five talents came forward, bringing five talents more, saying, 'Master, you delivered to me five talents; here I have made five talents more.'

²¹ "His master said to him, 'Well done, good and faithful servant. You have been faithful over a little; I will set you over much. Enter into the joy of your master.'

²² "And he also who had the two talents came forward, saying, 'Master, you delivered to me two talents; here I have made two talents more.'

²³ "His master said to him, 'Well done, good and faithful servant. You have been faithful over a little; I will set you over much. Enter into the joy of your master.'

²⁴ "He also who had received the one talent came forward, saying, 'Master, I knew you to be a hard man, reaping where you did not sow, and gathering where you scattered no seed,

²⁵ "so I was afraid, and I went and hid your talent in the ground. Here you have what is yours.'

²⁶ "But his master answered him, 'You wicked and slothful servant! You knew that I reap where I have not sown and gather where I scattered no seed?

²⁷ "'Then you ought to have invested my money with the bankers, and at my coming I should have received what was my own with interest.

²⁸ "'So take the talent from him and give it to him who has the ten talents.

²⁹ "'For to everyone who has will more be given, and he will have an abundance. But from the one who has not, even what he has will be taken away.

³⁰ "'And cast the worthless servant into the outer darkness. In that place there will be weeping and gnashing of teeth.'

³¹ "When the Son of Man comes in his glory, and all the angels with him, then he will sit on his glorious throne.

³² "Before him will be gathered all the nations, and he will separate people one from another as a shepherd separates the sheep from the goats.

³³ "And he will place the sheep on his right, but the goats on the left.

34 "Then the King will say to those on his right, 'Come, you who are blessed by my Father, inherit the kingdom prepared for you from the foundation of the world.

35 "'For I was hungry and you gave me food, I was thirsty and you gave me drink, I was a stranger and you welcomed me,

36 "'I was naked and you clothed me, I was sick and you visited me, I was in prison and you came to me.'

37 "Then the righteous will answer him, saying, 'Lord, when did we see you hungry and feed you, or thirsty and give you drink?

38 "'And when did we see you a stranger and welcome you, or naked and clothe you?

39 "'And when did we see you sick or in prison and visit you?'

40 "And the King will answer them, 'Truly, I say to you, as you did it to one of the least of these my brothers, you did it to me.'

41 "Then he will say to those on his left, 'Depart from me, you cursed, into the eternal fire prepared for the devil and his angels.

42 "'For I was hungry and you gave me no food, I was thirsty and you gave me no drink,

43 "'I was a stranger and you did not welcome me, naked and you did not clothe me, sick and in prison and you did not visit me.'

44 "Then they also will answer, saying, 'Lord, when did we see you hungry or thirsty or a stranger or naked or sick or in prison, and did not minister to you?'

45 "Then he will answer them, saying, 'Truly, I say to you, as you did not do it to one of the least of these, you did not do it to me.'

46 "And these will go away into eternal punishment, but the righteous into eternal life."

CHAPTER 26

1 When Jesus had finished all these sayings, he said to his disciples,

2 "You know that after two days the Passover is coming, and the Son of Man will be delivered up to be crucified."

3 Then the chief priests and the elders of the people gathered in the palace of the high priest, whose name was Caiaphas,

4 and plotted together in order to arrest Jesus by stealth and kill him.

5 But they said, "Not during the feast, lest there be an uproar among the people."

6 Now when Jesus was at

Bethany in the house of Simon the leper,

⁷ a woman came up to him with an alabaster flask of very expensive ointment, and she poured it on his head as he reclined at table.

⁸ And when the disciples saw it, they were indignant, saying, "Why this waste?

⁹ "For this could have been sold for a large sum and given to the poor."

¹⁰ But Jesus, aware of this, said to them, "Why do you trouble the woman? For she has done a beautiful thing to me.

¹¹ "For you always have the poor with you, but you will not always have me.

¹² "In pouring this ointment on my body, she has done it to prepare me for burial.

¹³ "Truly, I say to you, wherever this gospel is proclaimed in the whole world, what she has done will also be told in memory of her."

¹⁴ Then one of the twelve, whose name was Judas Iscariot, went to the chief priests

¹⁵ and said, "What will you give me if I deliver him over to you?" And they paid him thirty pieces of silver.

¹⁶ And from that moment he sought an opportunity to betray him.

¹⁷ Now on the first day of Unleavened Bread the disciples came to Jesus, saying, "Where will you have us prepare for you to eat the Passover?"

¹⁸ He said, "Go into the city to a certain man and say to him, 'The Teacher says, My time is at hand. I will keep the Passover at your house with my disciples.'"

¹⁹ And the disciples did as Jesus had directed them, and they prepared the Passover.

²⁰ When it was evening, he reclined at table with the twelve.

²¹ And as they were eating, he said, "Truly, I say to you, one of you will betray me."

²² And they were very sorrowful and began to say to him one after another, "Is it I, Lord?"

²³ He answered, "He who has dipped his hand in the dish with me will betray me.

²⁴ "The Son of Man goes as it is written of him, but woe to that man by whom the Son of Man is betrayed! It would have been better for that man if he had not been born."

²⁵ Judas, who would betray him, answered, "Is it I, Rabbi?" He said to him, "You have said so."

²⁶ Now as they were eating, Jesus took bread, and after blessing it he broke it and gave

it to the disciples, and said, "Take, eat; this is my body."

27 And he took a cup, and when he had given thanks he gave it to them, saying, "Drink of it, all of you,

28 "for this is my blood of the covenant, which is poured out for many for the forgiveness of sins.

29 "I tell you I will not drink again of this fruit of the vine until that day when I drink it new with you in my Father's kingdom."

30 And when they had sung a hymn, they went out to the Mount of Olives.

31 Then Jesus said to them, "You will all fall away because of me this night. For it is written, 'I will strike the shepherd, and the sheep of the flock will be scattered.'

32 "But after I am raised up, I will go before you to Galilee."

33 Peter answered him, "Though they all fall away because of me, I will never fall away."

34 Jesus said to him, "Truly, I tell you, this very night, before the rooster crows, you will deny me three times."

35 Peter said to him, "Even if I must die with you, I will not deny you!" And all the disciples said the same.

36 Then Jesus went with them to a place called Gethsemane, and he said to his disciples, "Sit here, while I go over there and pray."

37 And taking with him Peter and the two sons of Zebedee, he began to be sorrowful and troubled.

38 Then he said to them, "My soul is very sorrowful, even to death; remain here, and watch with me."

39 And going a little farther he fell on his face and prayed, saying, "My Father, if it be possible, let this cup pass from me; nevertheless, not as I will, but as you will."

40 And he came to the disciples and found them sleeping. And he said to Peter, "So, could you not watch with me one hour?

41 "Watch and pray that you may not enter into temptation. The spirit indeed is willing, but the flesh is weak."

42 Again, for the second time, he went away and prayed, "My Father, if this cannot pass unless I drink it, your will be done."

43 And again he came and found them sleeping, for their eyes were heavy.

44 So, leaving them again, he went away and prayed for the third time, saying the same words again.

45 Then he came to the disciples and said to them, "Are

you still sleeping and taking your rest? See, the hour is at hand, and the Son of Man is betrayed into the hands of sinners.

46 "Rise, let us be going; see, my betrayer is at hand."

47 While he was still speaking, Judas came, one of the twelve, and with him a great crowd with swords and clubs, from the chief priests and the elders of the people.

48 Now the betrayer had given them a sign, saying, "The one I will kiss is the man; seize him."

49 And he came up to Jesus at once and said, "Greetings, Rabbi!" And he kissed him.

50 Jesus said to him, "Friend, do what you came to do." Then they came up and laid hands on Jesus and seized him.

51 And behold, one of those who were with Jesus stretched out his hand and drew his sword and struck the servant of the high priest and cut off his ear.

52 Then Jesus said to him, "Put your sword back into its place. For all who take the sword will perish by the sword.

53 "Do you think that I cannot appeal to my Father, and he will at once send me more than twelve legions of angels?

54 "But how then should the Scriptures be fulfilled, that it must be so?"

55 At that hour Jesus said to the crowds, "Have you come out as against a robber, with swords and clubs to capture me? Day after day I sat in the temple teaching, and you did not seize me.

56 "But all this has taken place that the Scriptures of the prophets might be fulfilled." Then all the disciples left him and fled.

57 Then those who had seized Jesus led him to Caiaphas the high priest, where the scribes and the elders had gathered.

58 And Peter was following him at a distance, as far as the courtyard of the high priest, and going inside he sat with the guards to see the end.

59 Now the chief priests and the whole council were seeking false testimony against Jesus that they might put him to death,

60 but they found none, though many false witnesses came forward. At last two came forward

61 and said, "This man said, 'I am able to destroy the temple of God, and to rebuild it in three days.'"

62 And the high priest stood up and said, "Have you no

answer to make? What is it that these men testify against you?"

63 But Jesus remained silent. And the high priest said to him, "I adjure you by the living God, tell us if you are the Christ, the Son of God."

64 Jesus said to him, "You have said so. But I tell you, from now on you will see the Son of Man seated at the right hand of Power and coming on the clouds of heaven."

65 Then the high priest tore his robes and said, "He has uttered blasphemy. What further witnesses do we need? You have now heard his blasphemy.

66 "What is your judgment?" They answered, "He deserves death."

67 Then they spit in his face and struck him. And some slapped him,

68 saying, "Prophesy to us, you Christ! Who is it that struck you?"

69 Now Peter was sitting outside in the courtyard. And a servant girl came up to him and said, "You also were with Jesus the Galilean."

70 But he denied it before them all, saying, "I do not know what you mean."

71 And when he went out to the entrance, another servant girl saw him, and

she said to the bystanders, "This man was with Jesus of Nazareth."

72 And again he denied it with an oath: "I do not know the man."

73 After a little while the bystanders came up and said to Peter, "Certainly you too are one of them, for your accent betrays you."

74 Then he began to invoke a curse on himself and to swear, "I do not know the man." And immediately the rooster crowed.

75 And Peter remembered the saying of Jesus, "Before the rooster crows, you will deny me three times." And he went out and wept bitterly.

CHAPTER 27

1 When morning came, all the chief priests and the elders of the people took counsel against Jesus to put him to death.

2 And they bound him and led him away and delivered him over to Pilate the governor.

3 Then when Judas, his betrayer, saw that Jesus was condemned, he changed his mind and brought back the thirty pieces of silver to the chief priests and the elders,

4 saying, "I have sinned by betraying innocent blood."

They said, "What is that to us? See to it yourself."

5 And throwing down the pieces of silver into the temple, he departed, and he went and hanged himself.

6 But the chief priests, taking the pieces of silver, said, "It is not lawful to put them into the treasury, since it is blood money."

7 So they took counsel and bought with them the potter's field as a burial place for strangers.

8 Therefore that field has been called the Field of Blood to this day.

9 Then was fulfilled what had been spoken by the prophet Jeremiah, saying, "And they took the thirty pieces of silver, the price of him on whom a price had been set by some of the sons of Israel,

10 "and they gave them for the potter's field, as the Lord directed me."

11 Now Jesus stood before the governor, and the governor asked him, "Are you the King of the Jews?" Jesus said, "You have said so."

12 But when he was accused by the chief priests and elders, he gave no answer.

13 Then Pilate said to him, "Do you not hear how many things they testify against you?"

14 But he gave him no answer, not even to a single charge, so that the governor was greatly amazed.

15 Now at the feast the governor was accustomed to release for the crowd any one prisoner whom they wanted.

16 And they had then a notorious prisoner called Barabbas.

17 So when they had gathered, Pilate said to them, "Whom do you want me to release for you: Barabbas, or Jesus who is called Christ?"

18 For he knew that it was out of envy that they had delivered him up.

19 Besides, while he was sitting on the judgment seat, his wife sent word to him, "Have nothing to do with that righteous man, for I have suffered much because of him today in a dream."

20 Now the chief priests and the elders persuaded the crowd to ask for Barabbas and destroy Jesus.

21 The governor again said to them, "Which of the two do you want me to release for you?" And they said, "Barabbas."

22 Pilate said to them, "Then what shall I do with Jesus who is called Christ?" They all said, "Let him be crucified!"

23 And he said, "Why, what

evil has he done?" But they shouted all the more, "Let him be crucified!"

24 So when Pilate saw that he was gaining nothing, but rather that a riot was beginning, he took water and washed his hands before the crowd, saying, "I am innocent of this man's blood; see to it yourselves."

25 And all the people answered, "His blood be on us and on our children!"

26 Then he released for them Barabbas, and having scourged Jesus, delivered him to be crucified.

27 Then the soldiers of the governor took Jesus into the governor's headquarters, and they gathered the whole battalion before him.

28 And they stripped him and put a scarlet robe on him,

29 and twisting together a crown of thorns, they put it on his head and put a reed in his right hand. And kneeling before him, they mocked him, saying, "Hail, King of the Jews!"

30 And they spit on him and took the reed and struck him on the head.

31 And when they had mocked him, they stripped him of the robe and put his own clothes on him and led him away to crucify him.

32 As they went out, they found a man of Cyrene, Simon by name. They compelled this man to carry his cross.

33 And when they came to a place called Golgotha (which means Place of a Skull),

34 they offered him wine to drink, mixed with gall, but when he tasted it, he would not drink it.

35 And when they had crucified him, they divided his garments among them by casting lots.

36 Then they sat down and kept watch over him there.

37 And over his head they put the charge against him, which read, "This is Jesus, the King of the Jews."

38 Then two robbers were crucified with him, one on the right and one on the left.

39 And those who passed by derided him, wagging their heads

40 and saying, "You who would destroy the temple and rebuild it in three days, save yourself! If you are the Son of God, come down from the cross."

41 So also the chief priests, with the scribes and elders, mocked him, saying,

42 "He saved others; he cannot save himself. He is the King of Israel; let him

come down now from the cross, and we will believe in him.

43 "He trusts in God; let God deliver him now, if he desires him. For he said, 'I am the Son of God.'"

44 And the robbers who were crucified with him also reviled him in the same way.

45 Now from the sixth hour there was darkness over all the land until the ninth hour.

46 And about the ninth hour Jesus cried out with a loud voice, saying, "Eli, Eli, lema sabachthani?" that is, "My God, my God, why have you forsaken me?".

47 And some of the bystanders, hearing it, said, "This man is calling Elijah."

48 And one of them at once ran and took a sponge, filled it with sour wine, and put it on a reed and gave it to him to drink.

49 But the others said, "Wait, let us see whether Elijah will come to save him."

50 And Jesus cried out again with a loud voice and yielded up his spirit.

51 And behold, the curtain of the temple was torn in two, from top to bottom. And the earth shook, and the rocks were split.

52 The tombs also were opened. And many bodies of the saints who had fallen asleep were raised,

53 and coming out of the tombs after his resurrection they went into the holy city and appeared to many.

54 When the centurion and those who were with him, keeping watch over Jesus, saw the earthquake and what took place, they were filled with awe and said, "Truly this was the Son of God!"

55 There were also many women there, looking on from a distance, who had followed Jesus from Galilee, ministering to him,

56 among whom were Mary Magdalene and Mary the mother of James and Joseph and the mother of the sons of Zebedee.

57 When it was evening, there came a rich man from Arimathea, named Joseph, who also was a disciple of Jesus.

58 He went to Pilate and asked for the body of Jesus. Then Pilate ordered it to be given to him.

59 And Joseph took the body and wrapped it in a clean linen shroud

60 and laid it in his own new tomb, which he had cut in the rock. And he rolled a great stone to the entrance of the tomb and went away.

⁶¹ Mary Magdalene and the other Mary were there, sitting opposite the tomb.

⁶² The next day, that is, after the day of Preparation, the chief priests and the Pharisees gathered before Pilate

⁶³ and said, "Sir, we remember how that impostor said, while he was still alive, 'After three days I will rise.'

⁶⁴ "Therefore order the tomb to be made secure until the third day, lest his disciples go and steal him away and tell the people, 'He has risen from the dead,' and the last fraud will be worse than the first."

⁶⁵ Pilate said to them, "You have a guard of soldiers. Go, make it as secure as you can."

⁶⁶ So they went and made the tomb secure by sealing the stone and setting a guard.

CHAPTER 28

¹ Now after the Sabbath, toward the dawn of the first day of the week, Mary Magdalene and the other Mary went to see the tomb.

² And behold, there was a great earthquake, for an angel of the Lord descended from heaven and came and rolled back the stone and sat on it.

³ His appearance was like lightning, and his clothing white as snow.

⁴ And for fear of him the guards trembled and became like dead men.

⁵ But the angel said to the women, "Do not be afraid, for I know that you seek Jesus who was crucified.

⁶ "He is not here, for he has risen, as he said. Come, see the place where he lay.

⁷ "Then go quickly and tell his disciples that he has risen from the dead, and behold, he is going before you to Galilee; there you will see him. See, I have told you."

⁸ So they departed quickly from the tomb with fear and great joy, and ran to tell his disciples.

⁹ And behold, Jesus met them and said, "Greetings!" And they came up and took hold of his feet and worshiped him.

¹⁰ Then Jesus said to them, "Do not be afraid; go and tell my brothers to go to Galilee, and there they will see me."

¹¹ While they were going, behold, some of the guard went into the city and told the chief priests all that had taken place.

¹² And when they had assembled with the elders and taken counsel, they gave a sufficient sum of money to the soldiers

¹³ and said, "Tell people, 'His disciples came by night and

stole him away while we were asleep.'

14 "And if this comes to the governor's ears, we will satisfy him and keep you out of trouble."

15 So they took the money and did as they were directed. And this story has been spread among the Jews to this day.

16 Now the eleven disciples went to Galilee, to the mountain to which Jesus had directed them.

17 And when they saw him they worshiped him, but some doubted.

18 And Jesus came and said to them, "All authority in heaven and on earth has been given to me.

19 "Go therefore and make disciples of all nations, baptizing them in the name of the Father and of the Son and of the Holy Spirit,

20 "teaching them to observe all that I have commanded you. And behold, I am with you always, to the end of the age."

THE GOSPEL ACCORDING TO

MARK

CHAPTER 1

1 The beginning of the gospel of Jesus Christ, the Son of God.

2 As it is written in Isaiah the prophet, "Behold, I send my messenger before your face, who will prepare your way,

3 "the voice of one crying in the wilderness: 'Prepare the way of the Lord, make his paths straight,'"

4 John appeared, baptizing in the wilderness and proclaiming a baptism of repentance for the forgiveness of sins.

5 And all the country of Judea and all Jerusalem were going out to him and were being baptized by him in the river Jordan, confessing their sins.

6 Now John was clothed with camel's hair and wore a leather belt around his waist and ate locusts and wild honey.

7 And he preached, saying, "After me comes he who is mightier than I, the strap of whose sandals I am not worthy to stoop down and untie.

8 "I have baptized you with

water, but he will baptize you with the Holy Spirit."

⁹ In those days Jesus came from Nazareth of Galilee and was baptized by John in the Jordan.

¹⁰ And when he came up out of the water, immediately he saw the heavens being torn open and the Spirit descending on him like a dove.

¹¹ And a voice came from heaven, "You are my beloved Son; with you I am well pleased."

¹² The Spirit immediately drove him out into the wilderness.

¹³ And he was in the wilderness forty days, being tempted by Satan. And he was with the wild animals, and the angels were ministering to him.

¹⁴ Now after John was arrested, Jesus came into Galilee, proclaiming the gospel of God,

¹⁵ and saying, "The time is fulfilled, and the kingdom of God is at hand; repent and believe in the gospel."

¹⁶ Passing alongside the Sea of Galilee, he saw Simon and Andrew the brother of Simon casting a net into the sea, for they were fishermen.

¹⁷ And Jesus said to them, "Follow me, and I will make you become fishers of men."

¹⁸ And immediately they left their nets and followed him.

¹⁹ And going on a little farther, he saw James the son of Zebedee and John his brother, who were in their boat mending the nets.

²⁰ And immediately he called them, and they left their father Zebedee in the boat with the hired servants and followed him.

²¹ And they went into Capernaum, and immediately on the Sabbath he entered the synagogue and was teaching.

²² And they were astonished at his teaching, for he taught them as one who had authority, and not as the scribes.

²³ And immediately there was in their synagogue a man with an unclean spirit. And he cried out,

²⁴ "What have you to do with us, Jesus of Nazareth? Have you come to destroy us? I know who you are—the Holy One of God."

²⁵ But Jesus rebuked him, saying, "Be silent, and come out of him!"

²⁶ And the unclean spirit, convulsing him and crying out with a loud voice, came out of him.

²⁷ And they were all amazed, so that they questioned among themselves, saying, "What is this? A new

teaching with authority! He commands even the unclean spirits, and they obey him."

²⁸ And at once his fame spread everywhere throughout all the surrounding region of Galilee.

²⁹ And immediately he left the synagogue and entered the house of Simon and Andrew, with James and John.

³⁰ Now Simon's mother-in-law lay ill with a fever, and immediately they told him about her.

³¹ And he came and took her by the hand and lifted her up, and the fever left her, and she began to serve them.

³² That evening at sundown they brought to him all who were sick or oppressed by demons.

³³ And the whole city was gathered together at the door.

³⁴ And he healed many who were sick with various diseases, and cast out many demons. And he would not permit the demons to speak, because they knew him.

³⁵ And rising very early in the morning, while it was still dark, he departed and went out to a desolate place, and there he prayed.

³⁶ And Simon and those who were with him searched for him,

³⁷ and they found him and said to him, "Everyone is looking for you."

³⁸ And he said to them, "Let us go on to the next towns, that I may preach there also, for that is why I came out."

³⁹ And he went throughout all Galilee, preaching in their synagogues and casting out demons.

⁴⁰ And a leper came to him, imploring him, and kneeling said to him, "If you will, you can make me clean."

⁴¹ Moved with pity, he stretched out his hand and touched him and said to him, "I will; be clean."

⁴² And immediately the leprosy left him, and he was made clean.

⁴³ And Jesus sternly charged him and sent him away at once,

⁴⁴ and said to him, "See that you say nothing to anyone, but go, show yourself to the priest and offer for your cleansing what Moses commanded, for a proof to them."

⁴⁵ But he went out and began to talk freely about it, and to spread the news, so that Jesus could no longer openly enter a town, but was out in desolate places, and people were coming to him from every quarter.

CHAPTER 2

¹ And when he returned to Capernaum after some days, it was reported that he was at home.

² And many were gathered together, so that there was no more room, not even at the door. And he was preaching the word to them.

³ And they came, bringing to him a paralytic carried by four men.

⁴ And when they could not get near him because of the crowd, they removed the roof above him, and when they had made an opening, they let down the bed on which the paralytic lay.

⁵ And when Jesus saw their faith, he said to the paralytic, "Son, your sins are forgiven."

⁶ Now some of the scribes were sitting there, questioning in their hearts,

⁷ "Why does this man speak like that? He is blaspheming! Who can forgive sins but God alone?"

⁸ And immediately Jesus, perceiving in his spirit that they thus questioned within themselves, said to them, "Why do you question these things in your hearts?

⁹ "Which is easier, to say to the paralytic, 'Your sins are forgiven,' or to say, 'Rise, take up your bed and walk'?

¹⁰ "But that you may know that the Son of Man has authority on earth to forgive sins"— he said to the paralytic—

¹¹ "I say to you, rise, pick up your bed, and go home."

¹² And he rose and immediately picked up his bed and went out before them all, so that they were all amazed and glorified God, saying, "We never saw anything like this!"

¹³ He went out again beside the sea, and all the crowd was coming to him, and he was teaching them.

¹⁴ And as he passed by, he saw Levi the son of Alphaeus sitting at the tax booth, and he said to him, "Follow me." And he rose and followed him.

¹⁵ And as he reclined at table in his house, many tax collectors and sinners were reclining with Jesus and his disciples, for there were many who followed him.

¹⁶ And the scribes of the Pharisees, when they saw that he was eating with sinners and tax collectors, said to his disciples, "Why does he eat with tax collectors and sinners?"

¹⁷ And when Jesus heard it, he said to them, "Those who are well have no need of a

physician, but those who are sick. I came not to call the righteous, but sinners."

[18] Now John's disciples and the Pharisees were fasting. And people came and said to him, "Why do John's disciples and the disciples of the Pharisees fast, but your disciples do not fast?"

[19] And Jesus said to them, "Can the wedding guests fast while the bridegroom is with them? As long as they have the bridegroom with them, they cannot fast.

[20] "The days will come when the bridegroom is taken away from them, and then they will fast in that day.

[21] "No one sews a piece of unshrunk cloth on an old garment. If he does, the patch tears away from it, the new from the old, and a worse tear is made.

[22] "And no one puts new wine into old wineskins. If he does, the wine will burst the skins—and the wine is destroyed, and so are the skins. But new wine is for fresh wineskins."

[23] One Sabbath he was going through the grainfields, and as they made their way, his disciples began to pluck heads of grain.

[24] And the Pharisees were saying to him, "Look, why are they doing what is not lawful on the Sabbath?"

[25] And he said to them, "Have you never read what David did, when he was in need and was hungry, he and those who were with him:

[26] "how he entered the house of God, in the time of Abiathar the high priest, and ate the bread of the Presence, which it is not lawful for any but the priests to eat, and also gave it to those who were with him?"

[27] And he said to them, "The Sabbath was made for man, not man for the Sabbath.

[28] "So the Son of Man is lord even of the Sabbath."

CHAPTER 3

[1] Again he entered the synagogue, and a man was there with a withered hand.

[2] And they watched Jesus, to see whether he would heal him on the Sabbath, so that they might accuse him.

[3] And he said to the man with the withered hand, "Come here."

[4] And he said to them, "Is it lawful on the Sabbath to do good or to do harm, to save life or to kill?" But they were silent.

[5] And he looked around at them with anger, grieved at their hardness of heart, and

said to the man, "Stretch out your hand." He stretched it out, and his hand was restored.

⁶ The Pharisees went out and immediately held counsel with the Herodians against him, how to destroy him.

⁷ Jesus withdrew with his disciples to the sea, and a great crowd followed, from Galilee and Judea

⁸ and Jerusalem and Idumea and from beyond the Jordan and from around Tyre and Sidon. When the great crowd heard all that he was doing, they came to him.

⁹ And he told his disciples to have a boat ready for him because of the crowd, lest they crush him,

¹⁰ for he had healed many, so that all who had diseases pressed around him to touch him.

¹¹ And whenever the unclean spirits saw him, they fell down before him and cried out, "You are the Son of God."

¹² And he strictly ordered them not to make him known.

¹³ And he went up on the mountain and called to him those whom he desired, and they came to him.

¹⁴ And he appointed twelve (whom he also named apostles) so that they might be with him and he might send them out to preach

¹⁵ and have authority to cast out demons.

¹⁶ He appointed the twelve: Simon (to whom he gave the name Peter);

¹⁷ James the son of Zebedee and John the brother of James (to whom he gave the name Boanerges, that is, Sons of Thunder);

¹⁸ Andrew, and Philip, and Bartholomew, and Matthew, and Thomas, and James the son of Alphaeus, and Thaddaeus, and Simon the Zealot,

¹⁹ and Judas Iscariot, who betrayed him.

²⁰ Then he went home, and the crowd gathered again, so that they could not even eat.

²¹ And when his family heard it, they went out to seize him, for they were saying, "He is out of his mind."

²² And the scribes who came down from Jerusalem were saying, "He is possessed by Beelzebul," and "by the prince of demons he casts out the demons."

²³ And he called them to him and said to them in parables, "How can Satan cast out Satan?

²⁴ "If a kingdom is divided against itself, that kingdom cannot stand.

²⁵ "And if a house is divided

against itself, that house will not be able to stand.

26 "And if Satan has risen up against himself and is divided, he cannot stand, but is coming to an end.

27 "But no one can enter a strong man's house and plunder his goods, unless he first binds the strong man. Then indeed he may plunder his house.

28 "Truly, I say to you, all sins will be forgiven the children of man, and whatever blasphemies they utter,

29 "but whoever blasphemes against the Holy Spirit never has forgiveness, but is guilty of an eternal sin"—

30 for they were saying, "He has an unclean spirit."

31 And his mother and his brothers came, and standing outside they sent to him and called him.

32 And a crowd was sitting around him, and they said to him, "Your mother and your brothers are outside, seeking you."

33 And he answered them, "Who are my mother and my brothers?"

34 And looking about at those who sat around him, he said, "Here are my mother and my brothers!

35 "For whoever does the will of God, he is my brother and sister and mother."

CHAPTER 4

1 Again he began to teach beside the sea. And a very large crowd gathered about him, so that he got into a boat and sat in it on the sea, and the whole crowd was beside the sea on the land.

2 And he was teaching them many things in parables, and in his teaching he said to them:

3 "Listen! Behold, a sower went out to sow.

4 "And as he sowed, some seed fell along the path, and the birds came and devoured it.

5 "Other seed fell on rocky ground, where it did not have much soil, and immediately it sprang up, since it had no depth of soil.

6 "And when the sun rose, it was scorched, and since it had no root, it withered away.

7 "Other seed fell among thorns, and the thorns grew up and choked it, and it yielded no grain.

8 "And other seeds fell into good soil and produced grain, growing up and increasing and yielding thirtyfold and sixtyfold and a hundredfold."

9 And he said, "He who has ears to hear, let him hear."

10 And when he was alone, those around him with the

twelve asked him about the parables.

¹¹ And he said to them, "To you has been given the secret of the kingdom of God, but for those outside everything is in parables,

¹² "so that 'they may indeed see but not perceive, and may indeed hear but not understand, lest they should turn and be forgiven.'"

¹³ And he said to them, "Do you not understand this parable? How then will you understand all the parables?

¹⁴ "The sower sows the word.

¹⁵ "And these are the ones along the path, where the word is sown: when they hear, Satan immediately comes and takes away the word that is sown in them.

¹⁶ "And these are the ones sown on rocky ground: the ones who, when they hear the word, immediately receive it with joy.

¹⁷ "And they have no root in themselves, but endure for a while; then, when tribulation or persecution arises on account of the word, immediately they fall away.

¹⁸ "And others are the ones sown among thorns. They are those who hear the word,

¹⁹ "but the cares of the world and the deceitfulness of riches and the desires for other things enter in and choke the word, and it proves unfruitful.

²⁰ "But those that were sown on the good soil are the ones who hear the word and accept it and bear fruit, thirtyfold and sixtyfold and a hundredfold."

²¹ And he said to them, "Is a lamp brought in to be put under a basket, or under a bed, and not on a stand?

²² "For nothing is hidden except to be made manifest; nor is anything secret except to come to light.

²³ "If anyone has ears to hear, let him hear."

²⁴ And he said to them, "Pay attention to what you hear: with the measure you use, it will be measured to you, and still more will be added to you.

²⁵ "For to the one who has, more will be given, and from the one who has not, even what he has will be taken away."

²⁶ And he said, "The kingdom of God is as if a man should scatter seed on the ground.

²⁷ "He sleeps and rises night and day, and the seed sprouts and grows; he knows not how.

²⁸ "The earth produces by itself, first the blade, then

the ear, then the full grain in the ear.

²⁹ "But when the grain is ripe, at once he puts in the sickle, because the harvest has come."

³⁰ And he said, "With what can we compare the kingdom of God, or what parable shall we use for it?

³¹ "It is like a grain of mustard seed, which, when sown on the ground, is the smallest of all the seeds on earth,

³² "yet when it is sown it grows up and becomes larger than all the garden plants and puts out large branches, so that the birds of the air can make nests in its shade."

³³ With many such parables he spoke the word to them, as they were able to hear it.

³⁴ He did not speak to them without a parable, but privately to his own disciples he explained everything.

³⁵ On that day, when evening had come, he said to them, "Let us go across to the other side."

³⁶ And leaving the crowd, they took him with them in the boat, just as he was. And other boats were with him.

³⁷ And a great windstorm arose, and the waves were breaking into the boat, so that the boat was already filling.

³⁸ But he was in the stern, asleep on the cushion. And they woke him and said to him, "Teacher, do you not care that we are perishing?"

³⁹ And he awoke and rebuked the wind and said to the sea, "Peace! Be still!" And the wind ceased, and there was a great calm.

⁴⁰ He said to them, "Why are you so afraid? Have you still no faith?"

⁴¹ And they were filled with great fear and said to one another, "Who then is this, that even the wind and the sea obey him?"

CHAPTER 5

¹ They came to the other side of the sea, to the country of the Gerasenes.

² And when Jesus had stepped out of the boat, immediately there met him out of the tombs a man with an unclean spirit.

³ He lived among the tombs. And no one could bind him anymore, not even with a chain,

⁴ for he had often been bound with shackles and chains, but he wrenched the chains apart, and he broke the shackles in pieces. No one had the strength to subdue him.

⁵ Night and day among the tombs and on the mountains

he was always crying out and cutting himself with stones.

⁶ And when he saw Jesus from afar, he ran and fell down before him.

⁷ And crying out with a loud voice, he said, "What have you to do with me, Jesus, Son of the Most High God? I adjure you by God, do not torment me."

⁸ For he was saying to him, "Come out of the man, you unclean spirit!"

⁹ And Jesus asked him, "What is your name?" He replied, "My name is Legion, for we are many."

¹⁰ And he begged him earnestly not to send them out of the country.

¹¹ Now a great herd of pigs was feeding there on the hillside,

¹² and they begged him, saying, "Send us to the pigs; let us enter them."

¹³ So he gave them permission. And the unclean spirits came out and entered the pigs; and the herd, numbering about two thousand, rushed down the steep bank into the sea and drowned in the sea.

¹⁴ The herdsmen fled and told it in the city and in the country. And people came to see what it was that had happened.

¹⁵ And they came to Jesus and saw the demon-possessed man, the one who had had the legion, sitting there, clothed and in his right mind, and they were afraid.

¹⁶ And those who had seen it described to them what had happened to the demon-possessed man and to the pigs.

¹⁷ And they began to beg Jesus to depart from their region.

¹⁸ As he was getting into the boat, the man who had been possessed with demons begged him that he might be with him.

¹⁹ And he did not permit him but said to him, "Go home to your friends and tell them how much the Lord has done for you, and how he has had mercy on you."

²⁰ And he went away and began to proclaim in the Decapolis how much Jesus had done for him, and everyone marveled.

²¹ And when Jesus had crossed again in the boat to the other side, a great crowd gathered about him, and he was beside the sea.

²² Then came one of the rulers of the synagogue, Jairus by name, and seeing him, he fell at his feet

²³ and implored him earnestly, saying, "My little daughter is at the point of

death. Come and lay your hands on her, so that she may be made well and live."

²⁴ And he went with her. And a great crowd followed him and thronged about him.

²⁵ And there was a woman who had had a discharge of blood for twelve years,

²⁶ and who had suffered much under many physicians, and had spent all that she had, and was no better but rather grew worse.

²⁷ She had heard the reports about Jesus and came up behind him in the crowd and touched his garment.

²⁸ For she said, "If I touch even his garments, I will be made well."

²⁹ And immediately the flow of blood dried up, and she felt in her body that she was healed of her disease.

³⁰ And Jesus, perceiving in himself that power had gone out from him, immediately turned about in the crowd and said, "Who touched my garments?"

³¹ And his disciples said to him, "You see the crowd pressing around you, and yet you say, 'Who touched me?'"

³² And he looked around to see who had done it.

³³ But the woman, knowing what had happened to her, came in fear and trembling and fell down before him and told him the whole truth.

³⁴ And he said to her, "Daughter, your faith has made you well; go in peace, and be healed of your disease."

³⁵ While he was still speaking, there came from the ruler's house some who said, "Your daughter is dead. Why trouble the Teacher any further?"

³⁶ But overhearing what they said, Jesus said to the ruler of the synagogue, "Do not fear, only believe."

³⁷ And he allowed no one to follow him except Peter and James and John the brother of James.

³⁸ They came to the house of the ruler of the synagogue, and Jesus saw a commotion, people weeping and wailing loudly.

³⁹ And when he had entered, he said to them, "Why are you making a commotion and weeping? The child is not dead but sleeping."

⁴⁰ And they laughed at him. But he put them all outside and took the child's father and mother and those who were with him and went in where the child was.

⁴¹ Taking her by the hand he said to her, "Talitha cumi," which means, "Little girl, I say to you, arise."

42 And immediately the girl got up and came to his hometown, and they were immediately overcome with amazement.

43 And he strictly charged them that no one should know this, and told them to give her something to eat.

CHAPTER 6

1 He went away from there and came to his hometown, and his disciples followed him.

2 And on the Sabbath he began to teach in the synagogue, and many who heard him were astonished, saying, "Where did this man get these things? What is the wisdom given to him? How are such mighty works done by his hands?

3 "Is not this the carpenter, the son of Mary and brother of James and Joses and Judas and Simon? And are not his sisters here with us?" And they took offense at him.

4 And Jesus said to them, "A prophet is not without honor, except in his hometown and among his relatives and in his own household."

5 And he could do no mighty work there, except that he laid his hands on a few sick people and healed them.

6 And he marveled because of their unbelief. And he went about among the villages teaching.

7 And he called the twelve and began to send them out two by two, and gave them authority over the unclean spirits.

8 He charged them to take nothing for their journey except a staff— no bread, no bag, no money in their belts—

9 but to wear sandals and not put on two tunics.

10 And he said to them, "Whenever you enter a house, stay there until you depart from there.

11 "And if any place will not receive you and they will not listen to you, when you leave, shake off the dust that is on your feet as a testimony against them."

12 So they went out and proclaimed that people should repent.

13 And they cast out many demons and anointed with oil many who were sick and healed them.

14 King Herod heard of it, for Jesus' name had become known. Some said, "John the Baptist has been raised from the dead. That is why these miraculous powers are at work in him."

15 But others said, "He is Elijah!" And others said, "He

is a prophet, like one of the prophets of old."

¹⁶ But when Herod heard of it, he said, "John, whom I beheaded, has been raised."

¹⁷ For it was Herod who had sent and seized John and bound him in prison for the sake of Herodias, his brother Philip's wife, because he had married her.

¹⁸ For John had been saying to Herod, "It is not lawful for you to have your brother's wife."

¹⁹ And Herodias had a grudge against him and wanted to put him to death. But she could not,

²⁰ for Herod feared John, knowing that he was a righteous and holy man, and he kept him safe. When he heard him, he was greatly perplexed, and yet he heard him gladly.

²¹ But an opportunity came when Herod on his birthday gave a banquet for his nobles and military commanders and the leading men of Galilee.

²² For when Herodias's daughter came in and danced, she pleased Herod and his guests. And the king said to the girl, "Ask me for whatever you wish, and I will give it to you."

²³ And he vowed to her, "Whatever you ask me, I will give you, up to half of my kingdom."

²⁴ And she went out and said to her mother, "For what should I ask?" And she said, "The head of John the Baptist."

²⁵ And she came in immediately with haste to the king and asked, saying, "I want you to give me at once the head of John the Baptist on a platter."

²⁶ And the king was exceedingly sorry, but because of his oaths and his guests he did not want to break his word to her.

²⁷ And immediately the king sent an executioner with orders to bring John's head. He went and beheaded him in the prison

²⁸ and brought his head on a platter and gave it to the girl, and the girl gave it to her mother.

²⁹ When his disciples heard of it, they came and took his body and laid it in a tomb.

³⁰ The apostles returned to Jesus and told him all that they had done and taught.

³¹ And he said to them, "Come away by yourselves to a desolate place and rest a while." For many were coming and going, and they had no leisure even to eat.

³² And they went away in the boat to a desolate place by themselves.

33 Now many saw them going and recognized them, and they ran there on foot from all the towns and got there ahead of them.

34 When he went ashore he saw a great crowd, and he had compassion on them, because they were like sheep without a shepherd. And he began to teach them many things.

35 And when it grew late, his disciples came to him and said, "This is a desolate place, and the hour is now late.

36 "Send them away to go into the surrounding countryside and villages and buy themselves something to eat."

37 But he answered them, "You give them something to eat." And they said to him, "Shall we go and buy two hundred denarii worth of bread and give it to them to eat?"

38 And he said to them, "How many loaves do you have? Go and see." And when they had found out, they said, "Five, and two fish."

39 Then he commanded them all to sit down in groups on the green grass.

40 So they sat down in groups, by hundreds and by fifties.

41 And taking the five loaves and the two fish he looked up to heaven and said a blessing and broke the loaves and gave them to the disciples to set before the people. And he divided the two fish among them all.

42 And they all ate and were satisfied.

43 And they took up twelve baskets full of broken pieces and of the fish.

44 And those who ate the loaves were five thousand men.

45 Immediately he made his disciples get into the boat and go before him to the other side, to Bethsaida, while he dismissed the crowd.

46 And after he had taken leave of them, he went up on the mountain to pray.

47 And when evening came, the boat was out on the sea, and he was alone on the land.

48 And he saw that they were making headway painfully, for the wind was against them. And about the fourth watch of the night he came to them, walking on the sea. He meant to pass by them,

49 but when they saw him walking on the sea they thought it was a ghost, and cried out,

50 for they all saw him and were terrified. But immediately he spoke to them and said, "Take heart; it is I. Do not be afraid."

⁵¹ And he got into the boat with them, and the wind ceased. And they were utterly astounded,

⁵² for they did not understand about the loaves, but their hearts were hardened.

⁵³ When they had crossed over, they came to land at Gennesaret and moored to the shore.

⁵⁴ And when they got out of the boat, the people immediately recognized him

⁵⁵ and ran about the whole region and began to bring the sick people on their beds to wherever they heard he was.

⁵⁶ And wherever he came, in villages, cities, or countryside, they laid the sick in the marketplaces and implored him that they might touch even the fringe of his garment. And as many as touched it were made well.

CHAPTER 7

¹ Now when the Pharisees gathered to him, with some of the scribes who had come from Jerusalem,

² they saw that some of his disciples ate with hands that were defiled, that is, unwashed.

³ (For the Pharisees and all the Jews do not eat unless they wash their hands prop-erly, holding to the tradition of the elders,

⁴ and when they come from the marketplace, they do not eat unless they wash. And there are many other traditions that they observe, such as the washing of cups and pots and copper vessels and dining couches.)

⁵ And the Pharisees and the scribes asked him, "Why do your disciples not walk according to the tradition of the elders, but eat with defiled hands?"

⁶ And he said to them, "Well did Isaiah prophesy of you hypocrites, as it is written, 'This people honors me with their lips, but their heart is far from me;

⁷ 'in vain do they worship me, teaching as doctrines the commandments of men.'

⁸ "You leave the commandment of God and hold to the tradition of men."

⁹ And he said to them, "You have a fine way of rejecting the commandment of God in order to establish your tradition!

¹⁰ "For Moses said, 'Honor your father and your mother'; and, 'Whoever reviles father or mother must surely die.'

¹¹ "But you say, 'If a man tells his father or his mother, "Whatever you would have

gained from me is Corban"
(that is, given to God)—

12 "then you no longer permit him to do anything for his father or mother,

13 "thus making void the word of God by your tradition that you have handed down. And many such things you do."

14 And he called the people to him again and said to them, "Hear me, all of you, and understand:

15 "There is nothing outside a person that by going into him can defile him, but the things that come out of a person are what defile him.

16 "If anyone has ears to hear, let him hear."

17 And when he had entered the house and left the people, his disciples asked him about the parable.

18 And he said to them, "Then are you also without understanding? Do you not see that whatever goes into a person from outside cannot defile him,

19 "since it enters not his heart but his stomach, and is expelled?" (Thus he declared all foods clean.)

20 And he said, "What comes out of a person is what defiles him.

21 "For from within, out of the heart of man, come evil thoughts, sexual immorality, theft, murder, adultery,

22 "coveting, wickedness, deceit, sensuality, envy, slander, pride, foolishness.

23 "All these evil things come from within, and they defile a person."

24 And from there he arose and went away to the region of Tyre and Sidon. And he entered a house and did not want anyone to know, yet he could not be hidden.

25 But immediately a woman whose little daughter had an unclean spirit heard of him and came and fell down at his feet.

26 Now the woman was a Gentile, a Syrophoenician by birth. And she begged him to cast the demon out of her daughter.

27 And he said to her, "Let the children be fed first, for it is not right to take the children's bread and throw it to the dogs."

28 But she answered him, "Yes, Lord; yet even the dogs under the table eat the children's crumbs."

29 And he said to her, "For this statement you may go your way; the demon has left your daughter."

30 And she went home and found the child lying in bed and the demon gone.

31 Then he returned from the region of Tyre and went through Sidon to the Sea of Galilee, in the region of the Decapolis.

32 And they brought to him a man who was deaf and had a speech impediment, and they begged him to lay his hand on him.

33 And taking him aside from the crowd privately, he put his fingers into his ears, and after spitting touched his tongue.

34 And looking up to heaven, he sighed and said to him, "Ephphatha," that is, "Be opened."

35 And his ears were opened, his tongue was released, and he spoke plainly.

36 And Jesus charged them to tell no one. But the more he charged them, the more zealously they proclaimed it.

37 And they were astonished beyond measure, saying, "He has done all things well. He even makes the deaf hear and the mute speak."

CHAPTER 8

1 In those days, when again a great crowd had gathered, and they had nothing to eat, he called his disciples to him and said to them,

2 "I have compassion on the crowd, because they have been with me now three days and have nothing to eat.

3 "And if I send them away hungry to their homes, they will faint on the way. And some of them have come from far away."

4 And his disciples answered him, "How can one feed these people with bread here in this desolate place?"

5 And he asked them, "How many loaves do you have?" They said, "Seven."

6 And he directed the crowd to sit down on the ground. And he took the seven loaves, and having given thanks, he broke them and gave them to his disciples to set before the people; and they set them before the crowd.

7 And they had a few small fish. And having blessed them, he said that these also should be set before them.

8 And they ate and were satisfied. And they took up the broken pieces left over, seven baskets full.

9 And there were about four thousand people. And he sent them away.

10 And immediately he got into the boat with his disciples and went to the district of Dalmanutha.

11 The Pharisees came and began to argue with him,

seeking from him a sign from heaven to test him.

¹² And he sighed deeply in his spirit and said, "Why does this generation seek a sign? Truly, I say to you, no sign will be given to this generation."

¹³ And he left them, got into the boat again, and went to the other side.

¹⁴ Now they had forgotten to bring bread, and they had only one loaf with them in the boat.

¹⁵ And he cautioned them, saying, "Watch out; beware of the leaven of the Pharisees and the leaven of Herod."

¹⁶ And they began discussing with one another the fact that they had no bread.

¹⁷ And Jesus, aware of this, said to them, "Why are you discussing the fact that you have no bread? Do you not yet perceive or understand? Are your hearts hardened?

¹⁸ "Having eyes do you not see, and having ears do you not hear? And do you not remember?

¹⁹ "When I broke the five loaves for the five thousand, how many baskets full of broken pieces did you take up?" They said to him, "Twelve."

²⁰ "And the seven for the four thousand, how many baskets full of broken pieces

did you take up?" And they said to him, "Seven."

²¹ And he said to them, "Do you not yet understand?"

²² And they came to Bethsaida. And some people brought to him a blind man and begged him to touch him.

²³ And he took the blind man by the hand and led him out of the village, and when he had spit on his eyes and laid his hands on him, he asked him, "Do you see anything?"

²⁴ And he looked up and said, "I see people, but they look like trees, walking."

²⁵ Then Jesus laid his hands on his eyes again; and he opened his eyes, his sight was restored, and he saw everything clearly.

²⁶ And he sent him to his home, saying, "Do not even enter the village."

²⁷ And Jesus went on with his disciples to the villages of Caesarea Philippi. And on the way he asked his disciples, "Who do people say that I am?"

²⁸ And they told him, "John the Baptist; and others say, Elijah; and others, one of the prophets."

²⁹ And he asked them, "But who do you say that I am?" Peter answered him, "You are the Christ."

30 And he strictly charged them to tell no one about him.

31 And he began to teach them that the Son of Man must suffer many things and be rejected by the elders and the chief priests and the scribes and be killed, and after three days rise again.

32 And he said this plainly. And Peter took him aside and began to rebuke him.

33 But turning and seeing his disciples, he rebuked Peter and said, "Get behind me, Satan! For you are not setting your mind on the things of God, but on the things of man."

34 And calling the crowd to him with his disciples, he said to them, "If anyone would come after me, let him deny himself and take up his cross and follow me.

35 "For whoever would save his life will lose it, but whoever loses his life for my sake and the gospel's will save it.

36 "For what does it profit a man to gain the whole world and forfeit his soul?

37 "For what can a man give in return for his soul?

38 "For whoever is ashamed of me and of my words in this adulterous and sinful generation, of him will the Son of Man also be ashamed when he comes in the glory of his Father with the holy angels."

CHAPTER 9

1 And he said to them, "Truly, I say to you, there are some standing here who will not taste death until they see the kingdom of God after it has come with power."

2 And after six days Jesus took with him Peter and James and John, and led them up a high mountain by themselves. And he was transfigured before them,

3 and his clothes became radiant, intensely white, as no one on earth could bleach them.

4 And there appeared to them Elijah with Moses, and they were talking with Jesus.

5 And Peter said to Jesus, "Rabbi, it is good that we are here. Let us make three tents, one for you and one for Moses and one for Elijah."

6 For he did not know what to say, for they were terrified.

7 And a cloud overshadowed them, and a voice came out of the cloud, "This is my beloved Son; listen to him."

8 And suddenly, looking around, they no longer saw anyone with them but Jesus only.

9 And as they were coming down the mountain, he

charged them to tell no one what they had seen, until the Son of Man had risen from the dead.

¹⁰ So they kept the matter to themselves, questioning what this rising from the dead might mean.

¹¹ And they asked him, "Why do the scribes say that first Elijah must come?"

¹² And he said to them, "Elijah does come first to restore all things. And how is it written of the Son of Man that he should suffer many things and be treated with contempt?

¹³ "But I tell you that Elijah has come, and they did to him whatever they pleased, as it is written of him."

¹⁴ And when they came to the disciples, they saw a great crowd around them, and scribes arguing with them.

¹⁵ And immediately all the crowd, when they saw him, were greatly amazed and ran up to him and greeted him.

¹⁶ And he asked them, "What are you arguing about with them?"

¹⁷ And someone from the crowd answered him, "Teacher, I brought my son to you, for he has a spirit that makes him mute.

¹⁸ "And whenever it seizes him, it throws him down, and he foams and grinds his teeth and becomes rigid. So I asked your disciples to cast it out, and they were not able."

¹⁹ And he answered them, "O faithless generation, how long am I to be with you? How long am I to bear with you? Bring him to me."

²⁰ And they brought the boy to him. And when the spirit saw him, immediately it convulsed the boy, and he fell on the ground and rolled about, foaming at the mouth.

²¹ And Jesus asked his father, "How long has this been happening to him?" And he said, "From childhood.

²² "And it has often cast him into fire and into water, to destroy him. But if you can do anything, have compassion on us and help us."

²³ And Jesus said to him, "If you can'! All things are possible for one who believes."

²⁴ Immediately the father of the child cried out and said, "I believe; help my unbelief!"

²⁵ And when Jesus saw that a crowd was running together, he rebuked the unclean spirit, saying to it, "You mute and deaf spirit, I command you, come out of him and never enter him again."

²⁶ And after crying out and convulsing him terribly, it

came out, and the boy was like a corpse, so that most of them said, "He is dead."

27 But Jesus took him by the hand and lifted him up, and he arose.

28 And when he had entered the house, his disciples asked him privately, "Why could we not cast it out?"

29 And he said to them, "This kind cannot be driven out by anything but prayer and fasting."

30 They went on from there and passed through Galilee. And he did not want anyone to know,

31 for he was teaching his disciples, saying to them, "The Son of Man is going to be delivered into the hands of men, and they will kill him. And when he is killed, after three days he will rise."

32 But they did not understand the saying, and were afraid to ask him.

33 And they came to Capernaum. And when he was in the house he asked them, "What were you discussing on the way?"

34 But they kept silent, for on the way they had argued with one another about who was the greatest.

35 And he sat down and called the twelve. And he said to them, "If anyone would be first, he must be last of all and servant of all."

36 And he took a child and put him in the midst of them, and taking him in his arms, he said to them,

37 "Whoever receives one such child in my name receives me, and whoever receives me, receives not me but him who sent me."

38 John said to him, "Teacher, we saw someone casting out demons in your name, and we tried to stop him, because he was not following us."

39 But Jesus said, "Do not stop him, for no one who does a mighty work in my name will be able soon afterward to speak evil of me.

40 "For the one who is not against us is for us.

41 "For truly, I say to you, whoever gives you a cup of water to drink because you belong to Christ will by no means lose his reward.

42 "Whoever causes one of these little ones who believe in me to sin, it would be better for him if a great millstone were hung around his neck and he were thrown into the sea.

43 "And if your hand causes you to sin, cut it off. It is better for you to enter life crippled than with two hands to go to hell, to the unquenchable fire,

44 "'where their worm does not die and the fire is not quenched.'

45 "And if your foot causes you to sin, cut it off. It is better for you to enter life lame than with two feet to be thrown into hell,

46 "'where their worm does not die and the fire is not quenched.'

47 "And if your eye causes you to sin, tear it out. It is better for you to enter the kingdom of God with one eye than with two eyes to be thrown into hell,

48 "'where their worm does not die and the fire is not quenched.'

49 "For everyone will be salted with fire, and every sacrifice will be salted with salt.

50 "Salt is good, but if the salt has lost its saltiness, how will you make it salty again? Have salt in yourselves, and be at peace with one another."

CHAPTER 10

1 And he left there and went to the region of Judea and beyond the Jordan, and crowds gathered to him again. And again, as was his custom, he taught them.

2 And Pharisees came up and in order to test him asked, "Is it lawful for a man to divorce his wife?"

3 He answered them, "What did Moses command you?"

4 They said, "Moses allowed a man to write a certificate of divorce and to send her away."

5 And Jesus said to them, "Because of your hardness of heart he wrote you this commandment.

6 "But from the beginning of creation, 'God made them male and female.'

7 "'Therefore a man shall leave his father and mother and hold fast to his wife,

8 "'and the two shall become one flesh.' So they are no longer two but one flesh.

9 "What therefore God has joined together, let not man separate."

10 And in the house the disciples asked him again about this matter.

11 And he said to them, "Whoever divorces his wife and marries another commits adultery against her,

12 "and if she divorces her husband and marries another, she commits adultery."

13 And they were bringing children to him that he might touch them, and the disciples rebuked them.

14 But when Jesus saw it, he was indignant and said to them, "Let the children come to me; do not hinder them,

for to such belongs the kingdom of God.

¹⁵ "Truly, I say to you, whoever does not receive the kingdom of God like a child shall not enter it."

¹⁶ And he took them in his arms and blessed them, laying his hands on them.

¹⁷ And as he was setting out on his journey, a man ran up and knelt before him and asked him, "Good Teacher, what must I do to inherit eternal life?"

¹⁸ And Jesus said to him, "Why do you call me good? No one is good except God alone.

¹⁹ "You know the commandments: 'Do not murder, Do not commit adultery, Do not steal, Do not bear false witness, Do not defraud, Honor your father and mother.'"

²⁰ And he said to him, "Teacher, all these I have kept from my youth."

²¹ And Jesus, looking at him, loved him, and said to him, "You lack one thing: go, sell all that you have and give to the poor, and you will have treasure in heaven; and come, follow me."

²² Disheartened by the saying, he went away sorrowful, for he had great possessions.

²³ And Jesus looked around and said to his disciples, "How difficult it will be for those who have wealth to enter the kingdom of God!"

²⁴ And the disciples were amazed at his words. But Jesus said to them again, "Children, how difficult it is for those who trust in riches to enter the kingdom of God!

²⁵ "It is easier for a camel to go through the eye of a needle than for a rich person to enter the kingdom of God."

²⁶ And they were exceedingly astonished, and said to him, "Then who can be saved?"

²⁷ Jesus looked at them and said, "With man it is impossible, but not with God. For all things are possible with God."

²⁸ Peter began to say to him, "See, we have left everything and followed you."

²⁹ Jesus said, "Truly, I say to you, there is no one who has left house or brothers or sisters or mother or father or children or lands, for my sake and for the gospel,

³⁰ "who will not receive a hundredfold now in this time, houses and brothers and sisters and mothers and children and lands, with persecutions, and in the age to come eternal life.

³¹ "But many who are first will be last, and the last first."

³² And they were on the road, going up to Jerusalem, and Jesus was walking ahead of

them. And they were amazed, and those who followed were afraid. And taking the twelve again, he began to tell them what was to happen to him,

33 saying, "See, we are going up to Jerusalem, and the Son of Man will be delivered over to the chief priests and the scribes, and they will condemn him to death and deliver him over to the Gentiles.

34 "And they will mock him and spit on him, and flog him and kill him. And after three days he will rise."

35 And James and John, the sons of Zebedee, came up to him and said to him, "Teacher, we want you to do for us whatever we ask of you."

36 And he said to them, "What do you want me to do for you?"

37 And they said to him, "Grant us to sit, one at your right hand and one at your left, in your glory."

38 Jesus said to them, "You do not know what you are asking. Are you able to drink the cup that I drink, or to be baptized with the baptism with which I am baptized?"

39 And they said to him, "We are able." And Jesus said to them, "The cup that I drink you will drink, and with the baptism with which I am baptized, you will be baptized,

40 "but to sit at my right hand or at my left is not mine to grant, but it is for those for whom it has been prepared."

41 And when the ten heard it, they began to be indignant at James and John.

42 And Jesus called them to him and said to them, "You know that those who are considered rulers of the Gentiles lord it over them, and their great ones exercise authority over them.

43 "But it shall not be so among you. But whoever would be great among you must be your servant,

44 "and whoever would be first among you must be slave of all.

45 "For even the Son of Man came not to be served but to serve, and to give his life as a ransom for many."

46 And they came to Jericho. And as he was leaving Jericho with his disciples and a great crowd, Bartimaeus, a blind beggar, the son of Timaeus, was sitting by the roadside.

47 And when he heard that it was Jesus of Nazareth, he began to cry out and say, "Jesus, Son of David, have mercy on me!"

48 And many rebuked him, telling him to be silent. But he cried out all the more, "Son of David, have mercy on me!"

49 And Jesus stopped and said, "Call him." And they called the blind man, saying to him, "Take heart. Get up; he is calling you."

50 And throwing off his cloak, he sprang up and came to Jesus.

51 And Jesus said to him, "What do you want me to do for you?" And the blind man said to him, "Rabbi, let me recover my sight."

52 And Jesus said to him, "Go your way; your faith has made you well." And immediately he recovered his sight and followed him on the way.

CHAPTER 11

1 Now when they drew near to Jerusalem, to Bethphage and Bethany, at the Mount of Olives, Jesus sent two of his disciples

2 and said to them, "Go into the village in front of you, and immediately as you enter it you will find a colt tied, on which no one has ever sat. Untie it and bring it.

3 "If anyone says to you, 'Why are you doing this?' say, 'The Lord has need of it and will send it back here immediately.'"

4 And they went away and found a colt tied at a door outside in the street, and they untied it.

5 And some of those standing there said to them, "What are you doing, untying the colt?"

6 And they told them what Jesus had said, and they let them go.

7 And they brought the colt to Jesus and threw their cloaks on it, and he sat on it.

8 And many spread their cloaks on the road, and others spread leafy branches that they had cut from the fields.

9 And those who went before and those who followed were shouting, "Hosanna! Blessed is he who comes in the name of the Lord!

10 "Blessed is the coming kingdom of our father David! Hosanna in the highest!"

11 And he entered Jerusalem and went into the temple. And when he had looked around at everything, as it was already late, he went out to Bethany with the twelve.

12 On the following day, when they came from Bethany, he was hungry.

13 And seeing in the distance a fig tree in leaf, he went to see if he could find anything on it. When he came to it, he found nothing but leaves, for it was not the season for figs.

14 And he said to it, "May no one ever eat fruit from you

again." And his disciples heard it.

¹⁵ And they came to Jerusalem. And he entered the temple and began to drive out those who sold and those who bought in the temple, and he overturned the tables of the money-changers and the seats of those who sold pigeons.

¹⁶ And he would not allow anyone to carry anything through the temple.

¹⁷ And he was teaching them and saying to them, "Is it not written, 'My house shall be called a house of prayer for all the nations'? But you have made it a den of robbers."

¹⁸ And the chief priests and the scribes heard it and were seeking a way to destroy him, for they feared him, because all the crowd was astonished at his teaching.

¹⁹ And when evening came they went out of the city.

²⁰ As they passed by in the morning, they saw the fig tree withered away to its roots.

²¹ And Peter remembered and said to him, "Rabbi, look! The fig tree that you cursed has withered."

²² And Jesus answered them, "Have faith in God.

²³ Truly, I say to you, whoever says to this mountain, 'Be taken up and thrown into

the sea,' and does not doubt in his heart, but believes that what he says will come to pass, it will be done for him.

²⁴ "Therefore I tell you, whatever you ask in prayer, believe that you have received it, and it will be yours.

²⁵ "And whenever you stand praying, forgive, if you have anything against anyone, so that your Father also who is in heaven may forgive you your trespasses."

²⁶ "But if you do not forgive, neither will your Father who is in heaven forgive your trespasses."

²⁷ And they came again to Jerusalem. And as he was walking in the temple, the chief priests and the scribes and the elders came to him,

²⁸ and they said to him, "By what authority are you doing these things, or who gave you this authority to do them?"

²⁹ Jesus said to them, "I will ask you one question; answer me, and I will tell you by what authority I do these things.

³⁰ "Was the baptism of John from heaven or from man? Answer me."

³¹ And they discussed it with one another, saying, "If we say, 'From heaven,' he will say, 'Why then did you not believe him?'

³² "But shall we say, 'From

man'?"—they were afraid of the people, for they all held that John really was a prophet.

³³ So they answered Jesus, "We do not know." And Jesus said to them, "Neither will I tell you by what authority I do these things."

¹ And he began to speak to them in parables. "A man planted a vineyard and put a fence around it and dug a pit for the winepress and built a tower, and leased it to tenants and went into another country.

² "When the season came, he sent a servant to the tenants to get from them some of the fruit of the vineyard.

³ "And they took him and beat him and sent him away empty-handed.

⁴ "Again he sent to them another servant, and they struck him on the head and treated him shamefully.

⁵ "And he sent another, and him they killed. And so with many others: some they beat, and some they killed.

⁶ "He had still one other, a beloved son. Finally he sent him to them, saying, 'They will respect my son.'

⁷ "But those tenants said to one another, 'This is the heir. Come, let us kill him, and the inheritance will be ours.'

⁸ "And they took him and killed him and threw him out of the vineyard.

⁹ "What will the owner of the vineyard do? He will come and destroy the tenants and give the vineyard to others.

¹⁰ "Have you not read this Scripture: 'The stone that the builders rejected has become the cornerstone;

¹¹ "'this was the Lord's doing, and it is marvelous in our eyes'?"

¹² And they were seeking to arrest him but feared the people, for they perceived that he had told the parable against them. So they left him and went away.

¹³ And they sent to him some of the Pharisees and some of the Herodians, to trap him in his talk.

¹⁴ And they came and said to him, "Teacher, we know that you are true and do not care about anyone's opinion. For you are not swayed by appearances, but truly teach the way of God. Is it lawful to pay taxes to Caesar, or not? Should we pay them, or should we not?"

¹⁵ But, knowing their hypocrisy, he said to them, "Why put me to the test? Bring me a denarius and let me look at it."

¹⁶ And they brought one. And he said to them, "Whose likeness and inscription is this?" They said to him, "Caesar's."

¹⁷ Jesus said to them, "Render to Caesar the things that are Caesar's, and to God the things that are God's." And they marveled at him.

¹⁸ And Sadducees came to him, who say that there is no resurrection. And they asked him a question, saying,

¹⁹ "Teacher, Moses wrote for us that if a man's brother dies and leaves a wife, but leaves no child, the man must take the widow and raise up offspring for his brother.

²⁰ "There were seven brothers; the first took a wife, and when he died left no offspring.

²¹ "And the second took her, and died, leaving no offspring. And the third likewise.

²² "And the seven left no offspring. Last of all the woman also died.

²³ "In the resurrection, when they rise again, whose wife will she be? For the seven had her as wife."

²⁴ Jesus said to them, "Is this not the reason you are wrong, because you know neither the Scriptures nor the power of God?

²⁵ "For when they rise from the dead, they neither marry nor are given in marriage, but are like angels in heaven.

²⁶ "And as for the dead being raised, have you not read in the book of Moses, in the passage about the bush, how God spoke to him, saying, 'I am the God of Abraham, and the God of Isaac, and the God of Jacob'?

²⁷ "He is not God of the dead, but of the living. You are quite wrong."

²⁸ And one of the scribes came up and heard them disputing with one another, and seeing that he answered them well, asked him, "Which commandment is the most important of all?"

²⁹ Jesus answered, "The most important is, 'Hear, O Israel: The Lord our God, the Lord is one.

³⁰ "'And you shall love the Lord your God with all your heart and with all your soul and with all your mind and with all your strength.'

³¹ "The second is this: 'You shall love your neighbor as yourself.' There is no other commandment greater than these."

³² And the scribe said to him, "You are right, Teacher. You have truly said that he is one, and there is no other besides him.

33 "And to love him with all the heart and with all the understanding and with all the strength, and to love one's neighbor as oneself, is much more than all whole burnt-offerings and sacrifices."

34 And when Jesus saw that he answered wisely, he said to him, "You are not far from the kingdom of God." And after that no one dared to ask him any more questions.

35 And as Jesus taught in the temple, he said, "How can the scribes say that the Christ is the son of David?

36 "David himself, in the Holy Spirit, declared, 'The Lord said to my Lord, "Sit at my right hand, until I put your enemies under your feet."'

37 "David himself calls him Lord. So how is he his son?" And the great throng heard him gladly.

38 And in his teaching he said, "Beware of the scribes, who like to walk around in long robes and like greetings in the marketplaces

39 "and have the best seats in the synagogues and the places of honor at feasts,

40 "who devour widows' houses and for a pretense make long prayers. They will receive the greater condemnation."

41 And he sat down opposite the treasury and watched the people putting money into the offering box. Many rich people put in large sums.

42 And a poor widow came and put in two small copper coins, which make a penny.

43 And he called his disciples to him and said to them, "Truly, I say to you, this poor widow has put in more than all those who are contributing to the offering box.

44 "For they all contributed out of their abundance, but she out of her poverty has put in everything she had, all she had to live on."

CHAPTER 13

1 And as he came out of the temple, one of his disciples said to him, "Look, Teacher, what wonderful stones and what wonderful buildings!"

2 And Jesus said to him, "Do you see these great buildings? There will not be left here one stone upon another that will not be thrown down."

3 And as he sat on the Mount of Olives opposite the temple, Peter and James and John and Andrew asked him privately,

4 "Tell us, when will these things be, and what will be the sign when all these things are about to be accomplished?"

5 And Jesus began to say to

them, "See that no one leads you astray.

6 "Many will come in my name, saying, 'I am he!' and they will lead many astray.

7 "And when you hear of wars and rumors of wars, do not be alarmed. This must take place, but the end is not yet.

8 "For nation will rise against nation, and kingdom against kingdom. There will be earthquakes in various places; there will be famines. These are but the beginning of the birth pains.

9 "But be on your guard. For they will deliver you over to councils, and you will be beaten in synagogues, and you will stand before governors and kings for my sake, to bear witness before them.

10 "And the gospel must first be proclaimed to all nations.

11 "And when they bring you to trial and deliver you over, do not be anxious beforehand what you are to say, but say whatever is given you in that hour, for it is not you who speak, but the Holy Spirit.

12 "And brother will deliver brother over to death, and the father his child, and children will rise against parents and have them put to death.

13 "And you will be hated by all for my name's sake. But the one who endures to the end will be saved.

14 "But when you see the abomination of desolation standing where he ought not to be (let the reader understand), then let those who are in Judea flee to the mountains.

15 "Let the one who is on the housetop not go down, nor enter his house, to take anything out,

16 "and let the one who is in the field not turn back to take his cloak.

17 "And alas for women who are pregnant and for those who are nursing infants in those days!

18 "Pray that it may not happen in winter.

19 "For in those days there will be such tribulation as has not been from the beginning of the creation that God created until now, and never will be.

20 "And if the Lord had not cut short the days, no human being would be saved. But for the sake of the elect, whom he chose, he shortened the days.

21 "And then if anyone says to you, 'Look, here is the Christ!' or 'Look, there he is!' do not believe it.

22 "For false christs and false prophets will arise and perform signs and wonders, to

lead astray, if possible, the elect.

23 "But be on guard; I have told you all things beforehand.

24 "But in those days, after that tribulation, the sun will be darkened, and the moon will not give its light,

25 "and the stars will be falling from heaven, and the powers in the heavens will be shaken.

26 "And then they will see the Son of Man coming in clouds with great power and glory.

27 "And then he will send out the angels and gather his elect from the four winds, from the ends of the earth to the ends of heaven.

28 "From the fig tree learn its lesson: as soon as its branch becomes tender and puts out its leaves, you know that summer is near.

29 "So also, when you see these things taking place, you know that he is near, at the very gates.

30 "Truly, I say to you, this generation will not pass away until all these things take place.

31 "Heaven and earth will pass away, but my words will not pass away.

32 "But concerning that day or that hour, no one knows, not even the angels in heaven, nor the Son, but only the Father.

33 "Be on guard, keep awake and pray. For you do not know when the time will come.

34 "It is like a man going on a journey, when he leaves home and puts his servants in charge, each with his work, and commands the doorkeeper to stay awake.

35 "Therefore stay awake—for you do not know when the master of the house will come, in the evening, or at midnight, or when the rooster crows, or in the morning—

36 "lest he come suddenly and find you asleep.

37 "And what I say to you I say to all: Stay awake."

CHAPTER 14

1 It was now two days before the Passover and the Feast of Unleavened Bread. And the chief priests and the scribes were seeking how to arrest him by stealth and kill him,

2 for they said, "Not during the feast, lest there be an uproar from the people."

3 And while he was at Bethany in the house of Simon the leper, as he was reclining at table, a woman came with an alabaster flask of ointment of pure nard, very costly, and she broke the flask and poured it over his head.

⁴ There were some who said to themselves indignantly, "Why was the ointment wasted like that?

⁵ "For this ointment could have been sold for more than three hundred denarii and given to the poor." And they scolded her.

⁶ But Jesus said, "Leave her alone. Why do you trouble her? She has done a beautiful thing to me.

⁷ "For you always have the poor with you, and whenever you want, you can do good for them. But you will not always have me.

⁸ "She has done what she could; she has anointed my body beforehand for burial.

⁹ "And truly, I say to you, wherever the gospel is proclaimed in the whole world, what she has done will be told in memory of her."

¹⁰ Then Judas Iscariot, who was one of the twelve, went to the chief priests in order to betray him to them.

¹¹ And when they heard it, they were glad and promised to give him money. And he sought an opportunity to betray him.

¹² And on the first day of Unleavened Bread, when they sacrificed the Passover lamb, his disciples said to him, "Where will you have us go and prepare for you to eat the Passover?"

¹³ And he sent two of his disciples and said to them, "Go into the city, and a man carrying a jar of water will meet you. Follow him,

¹⁴ "and wherever he enters, say to the master of the house, 'The Teacher says, Where is my guest room, where I may eat the Passover with my disciples?'

¹⁵ "And he will show you a large upper room furnished and ready; there prepare for us."

¹⁶ And the disciples set out and went to the city and found it just as he had told them, and they prepared the Passover.

¹⁷ And when it was evening, he came with the twelve.

¹⁸ And as they were reclining at table and eating, Jesus said, "Truly, I say to you, one of you will betray me, one who is eating with me."

¹⁹ They began to be sorrowful and to say to him one after another, "Is it I?"

²⁰ He said to them, "It is one of the twelve, one who is dipping bread into the dish with me.

²¹ "For the Son of Man goes as it is written of him, but woe to that man by whom the Son of Man is betrayed! It would

have been better for that man if he had not been born."

²² And as they were eating, he took bread, and after blessing it broke it and gave it to them, and said, "Take; this is my body."

²³ And he took a cup, and when he had given thanks he gave it to them, and they all drank of it.

²⁴ And he said to them, "This is my blood of the covenant, which is poured out for many.

²⁵ "Truly, I say to you, I will not drink again of the fruit of the vine until that day when I drink it new in the kingdom of God."

²⁶ And when they had sung a hymn, they went out to the Mount of Olives.

²⁷ And Jesus said to them, "You will all fall away, for it is written, 'I will strike the shepherd, and the sheep will be scattered.'

²⁸ "But after I am raised up, I will go before you to Galilee."

²⁹ Peter said to him, "Even though they all fall away, I will not."

³⁰ And Jesus said to him, "Truly, I tell you, this very night, before the rooster crows twice, you will deny me three times."

³¹ But he said emphatically, "If I must die with you, I will not deny you." And they all said the same.

³² And they went to a place called Gethsemane. And he said to his disciples, "Sit here while I pray."

³³ And he took with him Peter and James and John, and began to be greatly distressed and troubled.

³⁴ And he said to them, "My soul is very sorrowful, even to death. Remain here and watch."

³⁵ And going a little farther, he fell on the ground and prayed that, if it were possible, the hour might pass from him.

³⁶ And he said, "Abba, Father, all things are possible for you. Remove this cup from me. Yet not what I will, but what you will."

³⁷ And he came and found them sleeping, and he said to Peter, "Simon, are you asleep? Could you not watch one hour?

³⁸ "Watch and pray that you may not enter into temptation. The spirit indeed is willing, but the flesh is weak."

³⁹ And again he went away and prayed, saying the same words.

⁴⁰ And again he came and found them sleeping, for their eyes were very heavy, and they did not know what to answer him.

41 And he came the third time and said to them, "Are you still sleeping and taking your rest? It is enough; the hour has come. The Son of Man is betrayed into the hands of sinners.

42 "Rise, let us be going; see, my betrayer is at hand."

43 And immediately, while he was still speaking, Judas came, one of the twelve, and with him a crowd with swords and clubs, from the chief priests and the scribes and the elders.

44 Now the betrayer had given them a sign, saying, "The one I will kiss is the man. Seize him and lead him away under guard."

45 And when he came, he went up to him at once and said, "Rabbi!" And he kissed him.

46 And they laid hands on him and seized him.

47 But one of those who stood by drew his sword and struck the servant of the high priest and cut off his ear.

48 And Jesus said to them, "Have you come out as against a robber, with swords and clubs to capture me?

49 "Day after day I was with you in the temple teaching, and you did not seize me. But let the Scriptures be fulfilled."

50 And they all left him and fled.

51 And a young man followed him, with nothing but a linen cloth about his body. And they seized him,

52 but he left the linen cloth and ran away naked.

53 And they led Jesus to the high priest. And all the chief priests and the elders and the scribes came together.

54 And Peter had followed him at a distance, right into the courtyard of the high priest. And he was sitting with the guards and warming himself at the fire.

55 Now the chief priests and the whole council were seeking testimony against Jesus to put him to death, but they found none.

56 For many bore false witness against him, but their testimony did not agree.

57 And some stood up and bore false witness against him, saying,

58 "We heard him say, 'I will destroy this temple that is made with hands, and in three days I will build another, not made with hands.'"

59 Yet even about this their testimony did not agree.

60 And the high priest stood up in the midst and asked Jesus, "Have you no answer to make? What is

it that these men testify against you?"

⁶¹ But he remained silent and made no answer. Again the high priest asked him, "Are you the Christ, the Son of the Blessed?"

⁶² And Jesus said, "I am, and you will see the Son of Man seated at the right hand of Power, and coming with the clouds of heaven."

⁶³ And the high priest tore his garments and said, "What further witnesses do we need?

⁶⁴ "You have heard his blasphemy. What is your decision?" And they all condemned him as deserving death.

⁶⁵ And some began to spit on him and to cover his face and to strike him, saying to him, "Prophesy!" And the guards received him with blows.

⁶⁶ And as Peter was below in the courtyard, one of the servant girls of the high priest came,

⁶⁷ and seeing Peter warming himself, she looked at him and said, "You also were with the Nazarene, Jesus."

⁶⁸ But he denied it, saying, "I neither know nor understand what you mean." And he went out into the gateway and the rooster crowed.

⁶⁹ And the servant girl saw him and began again to say to the bystanders, "This man is one of them."

⁷⁰ But again he denied it. And after a little while the bystanders again said to Peter, "Certainly you are one of them, for you are a Galilean."

⁷¹ But he began to invoke a curse on himself and to swear, "I do not know this man of whom you speak."

⁷² And immediately the rooster crowed a second time. And Peter remembered how Jesus had said to him, "Before the rooster crows twice, you will deny me three times." And he broke down and wept.

CHAPTER 15

¹ And as soon as it was morning, the chief priests held a consultation with the elders and scribes and the whole council. And they bound Jesus and led him away and delivered him over to Pilate.

² And Pilate asked him, "Are you the King of the Jews?" And he answered him, "You have said so."

³ And the chief priests accused him of many things.

⁴ And Pilate again asked him, "Have you no answer to make? See how many charges they bring against you."

⁵ But Jesus made no further answer, so that Pilate was amazed.

⁶ Now at the feast he used to release for them one prisoner for whom they asked.

⁷ And among the rebels in prison, who had committed murder in the insurrection, there was a man called Barabbas.

⁸ And the crowd came up and began to ask Pilate to do as he usually did for them.

⁹ And he answered them, saying, "Do you want me to release for you the King of the Jews?"

¹⁰ For he perceived that it was out of envy that the chief priests had delivered him up.

¹¹ But the chief priests stirred up the crowd to have him release for them Barabbas instead.

¹² And Pilate again said to them, "Then what shall I do with the man you call the King of the Jews?"

¹³ And they cried out again, "Crucify him."

¹⁴ And Pilate said to them, "Why, what evil has he done?" But they shouted all the more, "Crucify him."

¹⁵ So Pilate, wishing to satisfy the crowd, released for them Barabbas, and having scourged Jesus, he delivered him to be crucified.

¹⁶ And the soldiers led him away inside the palace (that is, the governor's headquarters), and they called together the whole battalion.

¹⁷ And they clothed him in a purple cloak, and twisting together a crown of thorns, they put it on him.

¹⁸ And they began to salute him, "Hail, King of the Jews!"

¹⁹ And they were striking his head with a reed and spitting on him and kneeling down in homage to him.

²⁰ And when they had mocked him, they stripped him of the purple cloak and put his own clothes on him. And they led him out to crucify him.

²¹ And they compelled a passerby, Simon of Cyrene, who was coming in from the country, the father of Alexander and Rufus, to carry his cross.

²² And they brought him to the place called Golgotha (which means Place of a Skull).

²³ And they offered him wine mixed with myrrh, but he did not take it.

²⁴ And they crucified him and divided his garments among them, casting lots for them, to decide what each should take.

²⁵ And it was the third hour when they crucified him.

²⁶ And the inscription of the charge against him read, "The King of the Jews."

27 And with him they crucified two *robbers, one on his right and one on his left.*

28 And the Scripture was fulfilled that says, "He was numbered with the transgressors."

29 And those who passed by derided him, wagging their heads and saying, "Aha! You who would destroy the temple and rebuild it in three days,

30 "save yourself, and come down from the cross!"

31 So also the chief priests with the scribes mocked him to one another, saying, "He saved others; he cannot save himself.

32 "Let the Christ, the King of Israel, come down now from the cross that we may see and believe." Those who were crucified with him also reviled him.

33 And when the sixth hour had come, there was darkness over the whole land until the ninth hour.

34 And at the ninth hour Jesus cried with a loud voice, "Eloi, Eloi, lema sabachthani?" which means, "My God, my God, why have you forsaken me?"

35 And some of the bystanders hearing it said, "Behold, he is calling Elijah."

36 And someone ran and filled a sponge with sour wine, put it on a reed and gave it to him to drink, saying, "Wait, let us see whether Elijah will come to take him down."

37 And Jesus uttered a loud cry and breathed his last.

38 And the curtain of the temple was torn in two, from top to bottom.

39 And when the centurion, who stood facing him, saw that in this way he breathed his last, he said, "Truly this man was the Son of God!"

40 There were also women looking on from a distance, among whom were Mary Magdalene, and Mary the mother of James the younger and of Joses, and Salome.

41 When he was in Galilee, they followed him and ministered to him, and there were also many other women who came up with him to Jerusalem.

42 And when evening had come, since it was the day of Preparation, that is, the day before the Sabbath,

43 Joseph of Arimathea, a respected member of the council, who was also himself looking for the kingdom of God, took courage and went to Pilate and asked for the body of Jesus.

44 Pilate was surprised to hear that he should have already died. And summoning

the centurion, he asked him whether he was already dead.

45 And when he learned from the centurion that he was dead, he granted the corpse to Joseph.

46 And Joseph bought a linen shroud, and taking him down, wrapped him in the linen shroud and laid him in a tomb that had been cut out of the rock. And he rolled a stone against the entrance of the tomb.

47 Mary Magdalene and Mary the mother of Joses saw where he was laid.

CHAPTER 16

1 When the Sabbath was past, Mary Magdalene, Mary the mother of James, and Salome bought spices, so that they might go and anoint him.

2 And very early on the first day of the week, when the sun had risen, they went to the tomb.

3 And they were saying to one another, "Who will roll away the stone for us from the entrance of the tomb?"

4 And looking up, they saw that the stone had been rolled back—it was very large.

5 And entering the tomb, they saw a young man sitting on the right side, dressed in a white robe, and they were alarmed.

6 And he said to them, "Do not be alarmed. You seek Jesus of Nazareth, who was crucified. He has risen; he is not here. See the place where they laid him.

7 "But go, tell his disciples and Peter that he is going before you to Galilee. There you will see him, just as he told you."

8 And they went out and fled from the tomb, for trembling and astonishment had seized them, and they said nothing to anyone, for they were afraid.

9 Now when he rose early on the first day of the week, he appeared first to Mary Magdalene, from whom he had cast out seven demons.

10 She went and told those who had been with him, as they mourned and wept.

11 But when they heard that he was alive and had been seen by her, they would not believe it.

12 After these things he appeared in another form to two of them, as they were walking into the country.

13 And they went back and told the rest, but they did not believe them.

14 Afterward he appeared to the eleven themselves as they were reclining at table, and he rebuked them for

their unbelief and hardness of heart, because they had not believed those who saw him after he had risen.

¹⁵ And he said to them, "Go into all the world and proclaim the gospel to the whole creation.

¹⁶ "Whoever believes and is baptized will be saved, but whoever does not believe will be condemned.

¹⁷ "And these signs will accompany those who believe: in my name they will cast out demons; they will speak in new tongues;

¹⁸ "they will pick up serpents with their hands; and if they drink any deadly poison, it will not hurt them; they will lay their hands on the sick, and they will recover."

¹⁹ So then the Lord Jesus, after he had spoken to them, was taken up into heaven and sat down at the right hand of God.

²⁰ And they went out and preached everywhere, while the Lord worked with them and confirmed the message by accompanying signs.

THE GOSPEL ACCORDING TO

LUKE

CHAPTER 1

¹ Inasmuch as many have undertaken to compile a narrative of the things that have been accomplished among us,

² just as those who from the beginning were eyewitnesses and ministers of the word have delivered them to us,

³ it seemed good to me also, having followed all things closely for some time past, to write an orderly account for you, most excellent Theophilus,

⁴ that you may have certainty concerning the things you have been taught.

⁵ In the days of Herod, king of Judea, there was a priest named Zechariah, of the division of Abijah. And he had a wife from the daughters of Aaron, and her name was Elizabeth.

⁶ And they were both righteous before God, walking blamelessly in all the commandments and statutes of the Lord.

⁷ But they had no child, because Elizabeth was barren,

and both were advanced in years.

⁸ Now while he was serving as priest before God when his division was on duty,

⁹ according to the custom of the priesthood, he was chosen by lot to enter the temple of the Lord and burn incense.

¹⁰ And the whole multitude of the people were praying outside at the hour of incense.

¹¹ And there appeared to him an angel of the Lord standing on the right side of the altar of incense.

¹² And Zechariah was troubled when he saw him, and fear fell upon him.

¹³ But the angel said to him, "Do not be afraid, Zechariah, for your prayer has been heard, and your wife Elizabeth will bear you a son, and you shall call his name John.

¹⁴ "And you will have joy and gladness, and many will rejoice at his birth,

¹⁵ "for he will be great before the Lord. And he must not drink wine or strong drink, and he will be filled with the Holy Spirit, even from his mother's womb.

¹⁶ "And he will turn many of the children of Israel to the Lord their God,

¹⁷ "and he will go before him in the spirit and power of Eli-jah, to turn the hearts of the fathers to the children, and the disobedient to the wisdom of the just, to make ready for the Lord a people prepared."

¹⁸ And Zechariah said to the angel, "How shall I know this? For I am an old man, and my wife is advanced in years."

¹⁹ And the angel answered him, "I am Gabriel. I stand in the presence of God, and I was sent to speak to you and to bring you this good news.

²⁰ "And behold, you will be silent and unable to speak until the day that these things take place, because you did not believe my words, which will be fulfilled in their time."

²¹ And the people were waiting for Zechariah, and they were wondering at his delay in the temple.

²² And when he came out, he was unable to speak to them, and they realized that he had seen a vision in the temple. And he kept making signs to them and remained mute.

²³ And when his time of service was ended, he went to his home.

²⁴ After these days his wife Elizabeth conceived, and for five months she kept herself hidden, saying,

²⁵ "Thus the Lord has done

for me in the days when he looked on me, to take away my reproach among people."

26 In the sixth month the angel Gabriel was sent from God to a city of Galilee named Nazareth,

27 to a virgin betrothed to a man whose name was Joseph, of the house of David. And the virgin's name was Mary.

28 And he came to her and said, "Greetings, O favored one, the Lord is with you!"

29 But she was greatly troubled at the saying, and tried to discern what sort of greeting this might be.

30 And the angel said to her, "Do not be afraid, Mary, for you have found favor with God.

31 "And behold, you will conceive in your womb and bear a son, and you shall call his name Jesus.

32 "He will be great and will be called the Son of the Most High. And the Lord God will give to him the throne of his father David,

33 "and he will reign over the house of Jacob forever, and of his kingdom there will be no end."

34 And Mary said to the angel, "How will this be, since I am a virgin?"

35 And the angel answered her, "The Holy Spirit will come upon you, and the power of the Most High will overshadow you; therefore the child to be born will be called holy-- the Son of God.

36 "And behold, your relative Elizabeth in her old age has also conceived a son, and this is the sixth month with her who was called barren.

37 "For nothing will be impossible with God."

38 And Mary said, "Behold, I am the servant of the Lord; let it be to me according to your word." And the angel departed from her.

39 In those days Mary arose and went with haste into the hill country, to a town in Judah,

40 and she entered the house of Zechariah and greeted Elizabeth.

41 And when Elizabeth heard the greeting of Mary, the baby leaped in her womb. And Elizabeth was filled with the Holy Spirit,

42 and she exclaimed with a loud cry, "Blessed are you among women, and blessed is the fruit of your womb!

43 "And why is this granted to me that the mother of my Lord should come to me?

44 "For behold, when the sound of your greeting came to my ears, the baby in my womb leaped for joy.

45 "And blessed is she who believed that there would be a fulfillment of what was spoken to her from the Lord."

46 And Mary said, "My soul magnifies the Lord,

47 "and my spirit rejoices in God my Savior,

48 "for he has looked on the humble estate of his servant. For behold, from now on all generations will call me blessed;

49 "for he who is mighty has done great things for me, and holy is his name.

50 "And his mercy is for those who fear him from generation to generation.

51 "He has shown strength with his arm; he has scattered the proud in the thoughts of their hearts;

52 "he has brought down the mighty from their thrones and exalted those of humble estate;

53 "he has filled the hungry with good things, and the rich he has sent away empty.

54 "He has helped his servant Israel, in remembrance of his mercy,

55 "as he spoke to our fathers, to Abraham and to his offspring forever."

56 And Mary remained with her about three months and returned to her home.

57 Now the time came for Elizabeth to give birth, and she bore a son.

58 And her neighbors and relatives heard that the Lord had shown great mercy to her, and they rejoiced with her.

59 And on the eighth day they came to circumcise the child. And they would have called him Zechariah after his father,

60 but his mother answered, "No; he shall be called John."

61 And they said to her, "None of your relatives is called by this name."

62 And they made signs to his father, inquiring what he wanted him to be called.

63 And he asked for a writing tablet and wrote, "His name is John." And they all wondered.

64 And immediately his mouth was opened and his tongue loosed, and he spoke, blessing God.

65 And fear came on all their neighbors. And all these things were talked about through all the hill country of Judea,

66 and all who heard them laid them up in their hearts, saying, "What then will this child be?" For the hand of the Lord was with him.

67 And his father Zechariah was filled with the Holy Spirit and prophesied, saying,

68 "Blessed be the Lord God

of Israel, for he has visited and redeemed his people

69 "and has raised up a horn of salvation for us in the house of his servant David,

70 "as he spoke by the mouth of his holy prophets from of old,

71 "that we should be saved from our enemies and from the hand of all who hate us;

72 "to show the mercy promised to our fathers and to remember his holy covenant,

73 "the oath that he swore to our father Abraham, to grant us

74 "that we, being delivered from the hand of our enemies, might serve him without fear,

75 "in holiness and righteousness before him all our days.

76 "And you, child, will be called the prophet of the Most High; for you will go before the Lord to prepare his ways,

77 "to give knowledge of salvation to his people in the forgiveness of their sins,

78 "because of the tender mercy of our God, whereby the sunrise shall visit us from on high

79 "to give light to those who sit in darkness and in the shadow of death, to guide our feet into the way of peace."

80 And the child grew and became strong in spirit, and he was in the wilderness until the day of his public appearance to Israel.

CHAPTER 2

1 In those days a decree went out from Caesar Augustus that all the world should be registered.

2 This was the first registration when Quirinius was governor of Syria.

3 And all went to be registered, each to his own town.

4 And Joseph also went up from Galilee, from the town of Nazareth, to Judea, to the city of David, which is called Bethlehem, because he was of the house and lineage of David,

5 to be registered with Mary, his betrothed, who was with child.

6 And while they were there, the time came for her to give birth.

7 And she gave birth to her firstborn son and wrapped him in swaddling cloths and laid him in a manger, because *there was no place for them* in the inn.

8 And in the same region there were shepherds out in the field, keeping watch over their flock by night.

9 And an angel of the Lord appeared to them, and the glory of the Lord shone

around them, and they were filled with great fear.

10 And the angel said to them, "Fear not, for behold, I bring you good news of great joy that will be for all the people.

11 "For unto you is born this day in the city of David a Savior, who is Christ the Lord.

12 "And this will be a sign for you: you will find a baby wrapped in swaddling cloths and lying in a manger."

13 And suddenly there was with the angel a multitude of the heavenly host praising God and saying,

14 "Glory to God in the highest, and on earth peace among those with whom he is pleased!"

15 When the angels went away from them into heaven, the shepherds said to one another, "Let us go over to Bethlehem and see this thing that has happened, which the Lord has made known to us."

16 And they went with haste and found Mary and Joseph, and the baby lying in a manger.

17 And when they saw it, they made known the saying that had been told them concerning this child.

18 And all who heard it wondered at what the shepherds told them.

19 But Mary treasured up all these things, pondering them in her heart.

20 And the shepherds returned, glorifying and praising God for all they had heard and seen, as it had been told them.

21 And at the end of eight days, when he was circumcised, he was called Jesus, the name given by the angel before he was conceived in the womb.

22 And when the time came for their purification according to the Law of Moses, they brought him up to Jerusalem to present him to the Lord

23 (as it is written in the Law of the Lord, "Every male who first opens the womb shall be called holy to the Lord")

24 and to offer a sacrifice according to what is said in the Law of the Lord, "a pair of turtledoves, or two young pigeons."

25 Now there was a man in Jerusalem, whose name was Simeon, and this man was righteous and devout, waiting for the consolation of Israel, and the Holy Spirit was upon him.

26 And it had been revealed to him by the Holy Spirit that he would not see death before he had seen the Lord's Christ.

27 And he came in the Spirit

into the temple, and when the parents brought in the child Jesus, to do for him according to the custom of the Law, ²⁸ he took him up in his arms and blessed God and said,

²⁹ "Lord, now you are letting your servant depart in peace, according to your word;

³⁰ "for my eyes have seen your salvation

³¹ "that you have prepared in the presence of all peoples,

³² "a light for revelation to the Gentiles, and for glory to your people Israel."

³³ And his father and his mother marveled at what was said about him.

³⁴ And Simeon blessed them and said to Mary his mother, "Behold, this child is appointed for the fall and rising of many in Israel, and for a sign that is opposed

³⁵ "(and a sword will pierce through your own soul also), so that thoughts from many hearts may be revealed."

³⁶ And there was a prophetess, Anna, the daughter of Phanuel, of the tribe of Asher. She was advanced in years, having lived with her husband seven years from when she was a virgin,

³⁷ and then as a widow until she was eighty-four. She did not depart from the temple,

worshiping with fasting and prayer night and day.

³⁸ And coming up at that very hour she began to give thanks to God and to speak of him to all who were waiting for the redemption of Jerusalem.

³⁹ And when they had performed everything according to the Law of the Lord, they returned into Galilee, to their own town of Nazareth.

⁴⁰ And the child grew and became strong, filled with wisdom. And the favor of God was upon him.

⁴¹ Now his parents went to Jerusalem every year at the Feast of the Passover.

⁴² And when he was twelve years old, they went up according to custom.

⁴³ And when the feast had ended, as they were returning, the boy Jesus stayed behind in Jerusalem. Joseph and his mother did not know it,

⁴⁴ but supposing him to be in the group they went a day's journey, but then they began to search for him among their relatives and acquaintances,

⁴⁵ and when they did not find him, they returned to Jerusalem, searching for him.

⁴⁶ After three days they found him in the temple, sitting among the teachers, listening to them and asking them questions.

⁴⁷ And all who heard him were amazed at his understanding and his answers.

⁴⁸ And when his parents saw him, they were astonished. And his mother said to him, "Son, why have you treated us so? Behold, your father and I have been searching for you in great distress."

⁴⁹ And he said to them, "Why were you looking for me? Did you not know that I must be in my Father's house?"

⁵⁰ And they did not understand the saying that he spoke to them.

⁵¹ And he went down with them and came to Nazareth and was submissive to them. And his mother treasured up all these things in her heart.

⁵² And Jesus increased in wisdom and in stature and in favor with God and man.

CHAPTER 3

¹ In the fifteenth year of the reign of Tiberius Caesar, Pontius Pilate being governor of Judea, and Herod being tetrarch of Galilee, and his brother Philip tetrarch of the region of Ituraea and Trachonitis, and Lysanias tetrarch of Abilene,

² during the high priesthood of Annas and Caiaphas, the word of God came to John the son of Zechariah in the wilderness.

³ And he went into all the region around the Jordan, proclaiming a baptism of repentance for the forgiveness of sins.

⁴ As it is written in the book of the words of Isaiah the prophet, "The voice of one crying in the wilderness: 'Prepare the way of the Lord, make his paths straight.

⁵ " 'Every valley shall be filled, and every mountain and hill shall be made low, and the crooked shall become straight, and the rough places shall be level ways,

⁶ " 'and all flesh shall see the salvation of God.' "

⁷ He said therefore to the crowds that came out to be baptized by him, "You brood of vipers! Who warned you to flee from the wrath to come?

⁸ "Bear fruits in keeping with repentance. And do not begin to say to yourselves, 'We have Abraham as our father.' For I tell you, God is able from these stones to raise up children for Abraham.

⁹ "Even now the axe is laid to the root of the trees. Every tree therefore that does not bear good fruit is cut down and thrown into the fire."

¹⁰ And the crowds asked him, "What then shall we do?"

¹¹ And he answered them, "Whoever has two tunics is

to share with him who has none, and whoever has food is to do likewise."

¹² Tax collectors also came to be baptized and said to him, "Teacher, what shall we do?"

¹³ And he said to them, "Collect no more than you are authorized to do."

¹⁴ Soldiers also asked him, "And we, what shall we do?" And he said to them, "Do not extort money from anyone by threats or by false accusation, and be content with your wages."

¹⁵ As the people were in expectation, and all were questioning in their hearts concerning John, whether he might be the Christ,

¹⁶ John answered them all, saying, "I baptize you with water, but he who is mightier than I is coming, the strap of whose sandals I am not worthy to untie. He will baptize you with the Holy Spirit and fire.

¹⁷ "His winnowing fork is in his hand, to clear his threshing floor and to gather the wheat into his barn, but the chaff he will burn with unquenchable fire."

¹⁸ So with many other exhortations he preached good news to the people.

¹⁹ But Herod the tetrarch, who had been reproved by him for Herodias, his brother's wife, and for all the evil things that Herod had done,

²⁰ added this to them all, that he locked up John in prison.

²¹ Now when all the people were baptized, and when Jesus also had been baptized and was praying, the heavens were opened,

²² and the Holy Spirit descended on him in bodily form, like a dove; and a voice came from heaven, "You are my beloved Son; with you I am well pleased."

²³ Jesus, when he began his ministry, was about thirty years of age, being the son (as was supposed) of Joseph, the son of Heli,

²⁴ the son of Matthat, the son of Levi, the son of Melchi, the son of Jannai, the son of Joseph,

²⁵ the son of Mattathias, the son of Amos, the son of Nahum, the son of Esli, the son of Naggai,

²⁶ the son of Maath, the son of Mattathias, the son of Semein, the son of Josech, the son of Joda,

²⁷ the son of Joanan, the son of Rhesa, the son of Zerubbabel, the son of Shealtiel, the son of Neri,

²⁸ the son of Melchi, the son of Addi, the son of Cosam, the son of Elmadam, the son of Er,

29 the son of Joshua, the son of Eliezer, the son of Jorim, the son of Matthat, the son of Levi,

30 the son of Simeon, the son of Judah, the son of Joseph, the son of Jonam, the son of Eliakim,

31 the son of Melea, the son of Menna, the son of Mattatha, the son of Nathan, the son of David,

32 the son of Jesse, the son of Obed, the son of Boaz, the son of Sala, the son of Nahshon,

33 the son of Amminadab, the son of Ram, the son of Hezron, the son of Perez, the son of Judah,

34 the son of Jacob, the son of Isaac, the son of Abraham, the son of Terah, the son of Nahor,

35 the son of Serug, the son of Reu, the son of Peleg, the son of Eber, the son of Shelah,

36 the son of Cainan, the son of Arphaxad, the son of Shem, the son of Noah, the son of Lamech,

37 the son of Methuselah, the son of Enoch, the son of Jared, the son of Mahalaleel, the son of Cainan,

38 the son of Enos, the son of Seth, the son of Adam, the son of God.

CHAPTER 4

1 And Jesus, full of the Holy Spirit, returned from the Jordan and was led by the Spirit in the wilderness

2 for forty days, being tempted by the devil. And he ate nothing during those days. And when they were ended, he was hungry.

3 The devil said to him, "If you are the Son of God, command this stone to become bread."

4 And Jesus answered him, "It is written, 'Man shall not live by bread alone, but by every word of God.'"

5 And the devil took him up and showed him all the kingdoms of the world in a moment of time,

6 and said to him, "To you I will give all this authority and their glory, for it has been delivered to me, and I give it to whom I will.

7 If you, then, will worship me, it will all be yours."

8 And Jesus answered him, "Get behind me, Satan! For it is written, 'You shall worship the Lord your God, and him only shall you serve.'"

9 And he took him to Jerusalem and set him on the pinnacle of the temple and said to him, "If you are the Son of God, throw yourself down from here,

10 "for it is written, 'He will command his angels concerning you, to guard you,'

¹¹"and 'On their hands they will bear you up, lest you strike your foot against a stone.'"

¹²And Jesus answered him, "It is said, 'You shall not put the Lord your God to the test.'"

¹³And when the devil had ended every temptation, he departed from him until an opportune time.

¹⁴And Jesus returned in the power of the Spirit to Galilee, and a report about him went out through all the surrounding country.

¹⁵And he taught in their synagogues, being glorified by all.

¹⁶And he came to Nazareth, where he had been brought up. And as was his custom, he went to the synagogue on the Sabbath day, and he stood up to read.

¹⁷And the scroll of the prophet Isaiah was given to him. He unrolled the scroll and found the place where it was written,

¹⁸"The Spirit of the Lord is upon me, because he has anointed me to proclaim good news to the poor. He has sent me to proclaim liberty to the captives and recovering of sight to the blind, to set at liberty those who are oppressed,

¹⁹"to proclaim the year of the Lord's favor."

²⁰And he rolled up the scroll and gave it back to the attendant and sat down. And the eyes of all in the synagogue were fixed on him.

²¹And he began to say to them, "Today this Scripture has been fulfilled in your hearing."

²²And all spoke well of him and marveled at the gracious words that were coming from his mouth. And they said, "Is not this Joseph's son?"

²³And he said to them, "Doubtless you will quote to me this proverb, 'Physician, heal yourself.' What we have heard you did at Capernaum, do here in your hometown as well."

²⁴And he said, "Truly, I say to you, no prophet is acceptable in his hometown.

²⁵"But in truth, I tell you, there were many widows in Israel in the days of Elijah, when the heavens were shut up three years and six months, and a great famine came over all the land,

²⁶"and Elijah was sent to none of them but only to Zarephath, in the land of Sidon, to a woman who was a widow.

²⁷"And there were many lepers in Israel in the time of the prophet Elisha, and none of them was cleansed, but only Naaman the Syrian."

²⁸When they heard these

things, all in the synagogue were filled with wrath.

29 And they rose up and drove him out of the town and brought him to the brow of the hill on which their town was built, so that they could throw him down the cliff.

30 But passing through their midst, he went away.

31 And he went down to Capernaum, a city of Galilee. And he was teaching them on the Sabbath,

32 and they were astonished at his teaching, for his word possessed authority.

33 And in the synagogue there was a man who had the spirit of an unclean demon, and he cried out with a loud voice,

34 "Ha! What have you to do with us, Jesus of Nazareth? Have you come to destroy us? I know who you are—the Holy One of God."

35 But Jesus rebuked him, saying, "Be silent and come out of him!" And when the demon had thrown him down in their midst, he came out of him, having done him no harm.

36 And they were all amazed and said to one another, "What is this word? For with authority and power he commands the unclean spirits, and they come out!"

37 And reports about him went out into every place in the surrounding region.

38 And he arose and left the synagogue and entered Simon's house. Now Simon's mother-in-law was ill with a high fever, and they appealed to him on her behalf.

39 And he stood over her and rebuked the fever, and it left her, and immediately she rose and began to serve them.

40 Now when the sun was setting, all those who had any who were sick with various diseases brought them to him, and he laid his hands on every one of them and healed them.

41 And demons also came out of many, crying, "You are the Son of God!" But he rebuked them and would not allow them to speak, because they knew that he was the Christ.

42 And when it was day, he departed and went into a desolate place. And the people sought him and came to him, and would have kept him from leaving them,

43 but he said to them, "I must preach the good news of the kingdom of God to the other towns as well; for I was sent for this purpose."

44 And he was preaching in the synagogues of Galilee.

CHAPTER 5

¹ On one occasion, while the crowd was pressing in on him to hear the word of God, he was standing by the lake of Gennesaret,

² and he saw two boats by the lake, but the fishermen had gone out of them and were washing their nets.

³ Getting into one of the boats, which was Simon's, he asked him to put out a little from the land. And he sat down and taught the people from the boat.

⁴ And when he had finished speaking, he said to Simon, "Put out into the deep and let down your nets for a catch."

⁵ And Simon answered, "Master, we toiled all night and took nothing! But at your word I will let down the nets."

⁶ And when they had done this, they enclosed a large number of fish, and their nets were breaking.

⁷ They signaled to their partners in the other boat to come and help them. And they came and filled both the boats, so that they began to sink.

⁸ But when Simon Peter saw it, he fell down at Jesus' knees, saying, "Depart from me, for I am a sinful man, O Lord."

⁹ For he and all who were with him were astonished at the catch of fish that they had taken,

¹⁰ and so also were James and John, sons of Zebedee, who were partners with Simon. And Jesus said to Simon, "Do not be afraid; from now on you will be catching men."

¹¹ And when they had brought their boats to land, they left everything and followed him.

¹² While he was in one of the cities, there came a man full of leprosy. And when he saw Jesus, he fell on his face and begged him, "Lord, if you will, you can make me clean."

¹³ And Jesus stretched out his hand and touched him, saying, "I will; be clean." And immediately the leprosy left him.

¹⁴ And he charged him to tell no one, but "go and show yourself to the priest, and make an offering for your cleansing, as Moses commanded, for a proof to them."

¹⁵ But now even more the report about him went abroad, and great crowds gathered to hear him and to be healed of their infirmities.

¹⁶ But he would withdraw to desolate places and pray.

¹⁷ On one of those days, as he was teaching, Pharisees and teachers of the law were sitting there, who had come

from every village of Galilee and Judea and from Jerusalem. And the power of the Lord was with him to heal.

¹⁸ And behold, some men were bringing on a bed a man who was paralyzed, and they were seeking to bring him in and lay him before Jesus, ¹⁹ but finding no way to bring him in, because of the crowd, they went up on the roof and let him down with his bed through the tiles into the midst before Jesus. ²⁰ And when he saw their faith, he said, "Man, your sins are forgiven you." ²¹ And the scribes and the Pharisees began to question, saying, "Who is this who speaks blasphemies? Who can forgive sins but God alone?" ²² When Jesus perceived their thoughts, he answered them, "Why do you question in your hearts? ²³ Which is easier, to say, 'Your sins are forgiven you,' or to say, 'Rise and walk'? ²⁴ "But that you may know that the Son of Man has authority on earth to forgive sins"—he said to the man who was paralyzed—"I say to you, rise, pick up your bed and go home." ²⁵ And immediately he rose up before them and picked up what he had been lying on and went home, glorifying God.

²⁶ And amazement seized them all, and they glorified God and were filled with awe, saying, "We have seen extraordinary things today."

²⁷ After this he went out and saw a tax collector named Levi, sitting at the tax booth. And he said to him, "Follow me." ²⁸ And leaving everything, he rose and followed him.

²⁹ And Levi made him a great feast in his house, and there was a large company of tax collectors and others reclining at table with them. ³⁰ And the Pharisees and their scribes grumbled at his disciples, saying, "Why do you eat and drink with tax collectors and sinners?" ³¹ And Jesus answered them, "Those who are well have no need of a physician, but those who are sick. ³² I have not come to call the righteous but sinners to repentance."

³³ And they said to him, "The disciples of John fast often and offer prayers, and so do the disciples of the Pharisees, but yours eat and drink." ³⁴ And Jesus said to them, "Can you make wedding guests fast while the bridegroom is with them?

[35] "The days will come when the bridegroom is taken away from them, and then they will fast in those days."

[36] He also told them a parable: "No one tears a piece from a new garment and puts it on an old garment. If he does, he will tear the new, and the piece from the new will not match the old.

[37] "And no one puts new wine into old wineskins. If he does, the new wine will burst the skins and it will be spilled, and the skins will be destroyed.

[38] "But new wine must be put into fresh wineskins.

[39] "And no one after drinking old wine desires new, for he says, 'The old is good.'"

CHAPTER 6

[1] On a Sabbath, while he was going through the grainfields, his disciples plucked and ate some heads of grain, rubbing them in their hands.

[2] But some of the Pharisees said, "Why are you doing what is not lawful to do on the Sabbath?"

[3] And Jesus answered them, "Have you not read what David did when he was hungry, he and those who were with him:

[4] "how he entered the house of God and took and ate the bread of the Presence, which is not lawful for any but the priests to eat, and also gave it to those with him?"

[5] And he said to them, "The Son of Man is lord of the Sabbath."

[6] On another Sabbath, he entered the synagogue and was teaching, and a man was there whose right hand was withered.

[7] And the scribes and the Pharisees watched him, to see whether he would heal on the Sabbath, so that they might find a reason to accuse him.

[8] But he knew their thoughts, and he said to the man with the withered hand, "Come and stand here." And he rose and stood there.

[9] And Jesus said to them, "I ask you, is it lawful on the Sabbath to do good or to do harm, to save life or to destroy it?"

[10] And after looking around at them all he said to him, "Stretch out your hand." And he did so, and his hand was restored.

[11] But they were filled with fury and discussed with one another what they might do to Jesus.

[12] In these days he went out to the mountain to pray, and all night he continued in prayer to God.

[13] And when day came, he called his disciples and chose

from them twelve, whom he when named apostles:

14 Simon, whom he named Peter, and Andrew his brother, and James and John, and Philip, and Bartholomew,

15 and Matthew, and Thomas, and James the son of Alphaeus, and Simon who was called the Zealot,

16 and Judas the son of James, and Judas Iscariot, who became a traitor.

17 And he came down with them and stood on a level place, with a great crowd of his disciples and a great multitude of people from all Judea and Jerusalem and the seacoast of Tyre and Sidon,

18 who came to hear him and to be healed of their diseases. And those who were troubled with unclean spirits were cured.

19 And all the crowd sought to touch him, for power came out from him and healed them all.

20 And he lifted up his eyes on his disciples, and said: "Blessed are you who are poor, for yours is the kingdom of God.

21 "Blessed are you who are hungry now, for you shall be satisfied. Blessed are you who weep now, for you shall laugh.

22 "Blessed are you when people hate you and when they exclude you and revile you and spurn your name as evil, on account of the Son of Man!

23 "Rejoice in that day, and leap for joy, for behold, your reward is great in heaven; for so their fathers did to the prophets.

24 "But woe to you who are rich, for you have received your consolation.

25 "Woe to you who are full now, for you shall be hungry. Woe to you who laugh now, for you shall mourn and weep.

26 "Woe to you, when all people speak well of you, for so their fathers did to the false prophets.

27 "But I say to you who hear, Love your enemies, do good to those who hate you,

28 "bless those who curse you, pray for those who abuse you.

29 "To one who strikes you on the cheek, offer the other also, and from one who takes away your cloak do not withhold your tunic either.

30 "Give to everyone who begs from you, and from one who takes away your goods do not demand them back.

31 "And as you wish that others would do to you, do so to them.

32 "If you love those who

love you, what benefit is that to you? For even sinners love those who love them.

33 "And if you do good to those who do good to you, what benefit is that to you? For even sinners do the same.

34 "And if you lend to those from whom you expect to receive, what credit is that to you? Even sinners lend to sinners, to get back the same amount.

35 "But love your enemies, and do good, and lend, expecting nothing in return, and your reward will be great, and you will be sons of the Most High, for he is kind to the ungrateful and the evil.

36 "Be merciful, even as your Father is merciful.

37 "Judge not, and you will not be judged; condemn not, and you will not be condemned; forgive, and you will be forgiven;

38 "give, and it will be given to you. Good measure, pressed down, shaken together, running over, will be put into your lap. For with the measure you use it will be measured back to you."

39 He also told them a parable: "Can a blind man lead a blind man? Will they not both fall into a pit?

40 "A disciple is not above his teacher, but everyone when he is fully trained will be like his teacher.

41 "Why do you see the speck that is in your brother's eye, but do not notice the log that is in your own eye?

42 "How can you say to your brother, 'Brother, let me take out the speck that is in your eye,' when you yourself do not see the log that is in your own eye? You hypocrite, first take the log out of your own eye, and then you will see clearly to take out the speck that is in your brother's eye.

43 "For no good tree bears bad fruit, nor again does a bad tree bear good fruit,

44 "for each tree is known by its own fruit. For figs are not gathered from thornbushes, nor are grapes picked from a bramble bush.

45 "The good person out of the good treasure of his heart produces good, and the evil person out of his evil treasure produces evil, for out of the abundance of the heart his mouth speaks.

46 "Why do you call me 'Lord, Lord,' and not do what I tell you?

47 "Everyone who comes to me and hears my words and does them, I will show you what he is like:

48 "he is like a man building a house, who dug deep and

laid the foundation on the rock. And when a flood arose, the stream broke against that house and could not shake it, because it had been well built.

49 "But the one who hears and does not do them is like a man who built a house on the ground without a foundation. When the stream broke against it, immediately it fell, and the ruin of that house was great."

CHAPTER 7

1 After he had finished all his sayings in the hearing of the people, he entered Capernaum.

2 Now a centurion had a servant who was sick and at the point of death, who was highly valued by him.

3 When the centurion heard about Jesus, he sent to him elders of the Jews, asking him to come and heal his servant.

4 And when they came to Jesus, they pleaded with him earnestly, saying, "He is worthy to have you do this for him,

5 "for he loves our nation, and he is the one who built us our synagogue."

6 And Jesus went with them. When he was not far from the house, the centurion sent friends, saying to him, "Lord, do not trouble yourself, for I am not worthy to have you come under my roof.

7 "Therefore I did not presume to come to you. But say the word, and let my servant be healed.

8 "For I too am a man set under authority, with soldiers under me: and I say to one, 'Go,' and he goes; and to another, 'Come,' and he comes; and to my servant, 'Do this,' and he does it."

9 When Jesus heard these things, he marveled at him, and turning to the crowd that followed him, said, "I tell you, not even in Israel have I found such faith."

10 And when those who had been sent returned to the house, they found the servant well.

11 Soon afterward he went to a town called Nain, and his disciples and a great crowd went with him.

12 As he drew near to the gate of the town, behold, a man who had died was being carried out, the only son of his mother, and she was a widow, and a considerable crowd from the town was with her.

13 And when the Lord saw her, he had compassion on her and said to her, "Do not weep."

14 Then he came up and touched the bier, and the

bearers stood still. And he said, "Young man, I say to you, arise."

15 And the dead man sat up and began to speak, and Jesus gave him to his mother.

16 Fear seized them all, and they glorified God, saying, "A great prophet has arisen among us!" and "God has visited his people!"

17 And this report about him spread through the whole of Judea and all the surrounding country.

18 The disciples of John reported all these things to him. And John,

19 calling two of his disciples to him, sent them to the Lord, saying, "Are you the one who is to come, or shall we look for another?"

20 And when the men had come to him, they said, "John the Baptist has sent us to you, saying, 'Are you the one who is to come, or shall we look for another?'"

21 In that hour he healed many people of diseases and plagues and evil spirits, and on many who were blind he bestowed sight.

22 And he answered them, "Go and tell John what you have seen and heard: the blind receive their sight, the lame walk, lepers are cleansed, and the deaf hear, the dead are raised up, the poor have good news preached to them.

23 "And blessed is the one who is not offended by me."

24 When John's messengers had gone, Jesus began to speak to the crowds concerning John: "What did you go out into the wilderness to see? A reed shaken by the wind?

25 "What then did you go out to see? A man dressed in soft clothing? Behold, those who are dressed in splendid clothing and live in luxury are in kings' courts.

26 "What then did you go out to see? A prophet? Yes, I tell you, and more than a prophet.

27 "This is he of whom it is written, 'Behold, I send my messenger before your face, who will prepare your way before you.'

28 "I tell you, among those born of women none is greater than John. Yet the one who is least in the kingdom of God is greater than he."

29 (When all the people heard this, and the tax collectors too, they declared God just, having been baptized with the baptism of John,

30 but the Pharisees and the lawyers rejected the purpose of God for themselves, not having been baptized by him.)

31 "To what then shall I com-

pare the people of this generation, and what are they like?

³² "They are like children sitting in the marketplace and calling to one another, 'We played the flute for you, and you did not dance; we sang a dirge, and you did not weep.'

³³ "For John the Baptist has come eating no bread and drinking no wine, and you say, 'He has a demon.'

³⁴ "The Son of Man has come eating and drinking, and you say, 'Look at him! A glutton and a drunkard, a friend of tax collectors and sinners!'

³⁵ "Yet wisdom is justified by all her children."

³⁶ One of the Pharisees asked him to eat with him, and he went into the Pharisee's house and reclined at the table.

³⁷ And behold, a woman of the city, who was a sinner, when she learned that he was reclining at table in the Pharisee's house, brought an alabaster flask of ointment,

³⁸ and standing behind him at his feet, weeping, began to wet his feet with her tears and wiped them with the hair of her head and kissed his feet and anointed them with the ointment.

³⁹ Now when the Pharisee who had invited him saw this, he said to himself, "If this man were a prophet, he would have known who and what sort of woman this is who is touching him, for she is a sinner."

⁴⁰ And Jesus answering said to him, "Simon, I have something to say to you." And he answered, "Say it, Teacher."

⁴¹ "A certain moneylender had two debtors. One owed five hundred denarii, and the other fifty.

⁴² "When they could not pay, he cancelled the debt of both. Now which of them will love him more?"

⁴³ Simon answered, "The one, I suppose, for whom he cancelled the larger debt." And he said to him, "You have judged rightly."

⁴⁴ Then turning toward the woman he said to Simon, "Do you see this woman? I entered your house; you gave me no water for my feet, but she has wet my feet with her tears and wiped them with her hair.

⁴⁵ "You gave me no kiss, but from the time I came in she has not ceased to kiss my feet.

⁴⁶ "You did not anoint my head with oil, but she has anointed my feet with ointment.

⁴⁷ "Therefore I tell you, her sins, which are many, are forgiven—for she loved much. But he who is forgiven little, loves little."

⁴⁸ And he said to her, "Your sins are forgiven."

⁴⁹ Then those who were at table with him began to say among themselves, "Who is this, who even forgives sins?"

⁵⁰ And he said to the woman, "Your faith has saved you; go in peace."

CHAPTER 8

¹ Soon afterward he went on through cities and villages, proclaiming and bringing the good news of the kingdom of God. And the twelve were with him,

² and also some women who had been healed of evil spirits and infirmities: Mary, called Magdalene, from whom seven demons had gone out,

³ and Joanna, the wife of Chuza, Herod's household manager, and Susanna, and many others, who provided for them out of their means.

⁴ And when a great crowd was gathering and people from town after town came to him, he said in a parable,

⁵ "A sower went out to sow his seed. And as he sowed, some fell along the path and was trampled underfoot, and the birds of the air devoured it.

⁶ "And some fell on the rock, and as it grew up, it withered away, because it had no moisture.

⁷ "And some fell among thorns, and the thorns grew up with it and choked it.

⁸ "And some fell into good soil and grew and yielded a hundredfold." As he said these things, he called out, "He who has ears to hear, let him hear."

⁹ And when his disciples asked him what this parable meant,

¹⁰ he said, "To you it has been given to know the secrets of the kingdom of God, but for others they are in parables, so that 'seeing they may not see, and hearing they may not understand.'

¹¹ "Now the parable is this: The seed is the word of God.

¹² "The ones along the path are those who have heard; then the devil comes and takes away the word from their hearts, so that they may not believe and be saved.

¹³ "And the ones on the rock are those who, when they hear the word, receive it with joy. But these have no root; they believe for a while, and in time of testing fall away.

¹⁴ "And as for what fell among the thorns, they are those who hear, but as they go on their way they are choked by the cares and riches and pleasures of life, and their fruit does not mature.

15 *"As for that in the good soil, they are those who, hearing the word, hold it fast in an honest and good heart, and bear fruit with patience.*

16 *"No one after lighting a lamp covers it with a jar or puts it under a bed, but puts it on a stand, so that those who enter may see the light.*

17 *"For nothing is hidden that will not be made manifest, nor is anything secret that will not be known and come to light.*

18 *"Take care then how you hear, for to the one who has, more will be given, and from the one who has not, even what he thinks that he has will be taken away."*

19 Then his mother and his brothers came to him, but they could not reach him because of the crowd.

20 And he was told, "Your mother and your brothers are standing outside, desiring to see you."

21 But he answered them, "My mother and my brothers are those who hear the word of God and do it."

22 One day he got into a boat with his disciples, and he said to them, "Let us go across to the other side of the lake." So they set out,

23 and as they sailed he fell asleep. And a windstorm came down on the lake, and they were filling with water and were in danger.

24 And they went and woke him, saying, "Master, Master, we are perishing!" And he awoke and rebuked the wind and the raging waves, and they ceased, and there was a calm.

25 He said to them, "Where is your faith?" And they were afraid, and they marveled, saying to one another, "Who then is this, that he commands even winds and water, and they obey him?"

26 Then they sailed to the country of the Gerasenes, which is opposite Galilee.

27 When Jesus had stepped out on land, there met him a man from the city who had demons. For a long time he had worn no clothes, and he had not lived in a house but among the tombs.

28 When he saw Jesus, he cried out and fell down before him and said with a loud voice, "What have you to do with me, Jesus, Son of the Most High God? I beg you, do not torment me."

29 For he had commanded the unclean spirit to come out of the man. (For many a time it had seized him. He was kept under guard and bound with chains and shackles, but he

would break the bonds and be driven by the demon into the desert.)

³⁰ Jesus then asked him, "What is your name?" And he said, "Legion," for many demons had entered him.

³¹ And they begged him not to command them to depart into the abyss.

³² Now a large herd of pigs was feeding there on the hillside, and they begged him to let them enter these. So he gave them permission.

³³ Then the demons came out of the man and entered the pigs, and the herd rushed down the steep bank into the lake and drowned.

³⁴ When the herdsmen saw what had happened, they fled and told it in the city and in the country.

³⁵ Then people went out to see what had happened, and they came to Jesus and found the man from whom the demons had gone, sitting at the feet of Jesus, clothed and in his right mind, and they were afraid.

³⁶ And those who had seen it told them how the demon-possessed man had been healed.

³⁷ Then all the people of the surrounding country of the Gerasenes asked him to depart from them, for they were

seized with great fear. So he got into the boat and returned.

³⁸ The man from whom the demons had gone begged that he might be with him, but Jesus sent him away, saying,

³⁹ "Return to your home, and declare how much God has done for you." And he went away, proclaiming throughout the whole city how much Jesus had done for him.

⁴⁰ Now when Jesus returned, the crowd welcomed him, for they were all waiting for him.

⁴¹ And there came a man named Jairus, who was a ruler of the synagogue. And falling at Jesus' feet, he implored him to come to his house,

⁴² for he had an only daughter, about twelve years of age, and she was dying. As Jesus went, the people pressed around him.

⁴³ And there was a woman who had had a discharge of blood for twelve years, and though she had spent all her living on physicians, she could not be healed by anyone.

⁴⁴ She came up behind him and touched the fringe of his garment, and immediately her discharge of blood ceased.

⁴⁵ And Jesus said, "Who was it that touched me?" When all denied it, Peter said, "Master,

the crowds surround you and are pressing in on you!"

⁴⁶ But Jesus said, "Someone touched me, for I perceive that power has gone out from me."

⁴⁷ And when the woman saw that she was not hidden, she came trembling, and falling down before him declared in the presence of all the people why she had touched him, and how she had been immediately healed.

⁴⁸ And he said to her, "Daughter, your faith has made you well; go in peace."

⁴⁹ While he was still speaking, someone from the ruler's house came and said, "Your daughter is dead; do not trouble the Teacher any more."

⁵⁰ But Jesus on hearing this answered him, "Do not fear; only believe, and she will be well."

⁵¹ And when he came to the house, he allowed no one to enter with him, except Peter and John and James, and the father and mother of the child.

⁵² And all were weeping and mourning for her, but he said, "Do not weep, for she is not dead but sleeping."

⁵³ And they laughed at him, knowing that she was dead.

⁵⁴ But taking her by the hand he called, saying, "Child, arise."

⁵⁵ And her spirit returned, and she got up at once. And he directed that something should be given her to eat.

⁵⁶ And her parents were amazed, but he charged them to tell no one what had happened.

CHAPTER 9

¹ And he called the twelve together and gave them power and authority over all demons and to cure diseases,

² and he sent them out to proclaim the kingdom of God and to heal.

³ And he said to them, "Take nothing for your journey, no staff, nor bag, nor bread, nor money; and do not have two tunics.

⁴ "And whatever house you enter, stay there, and from there depart.

⁵ "And wherever they do not receive you, when you leave that town shake off the dust from your feet as a testimony against them."

⁶ And they departed and went through the villages, preaching the gospel and healing everywhere.

⁷ Now Herod the tetrarch heard about all that was happening, and he was perplexed, because it was said by some that John had been raised from the dead,

8 by some that Elijah had appeared, and by others that one of the prophets of old had risen.

9 Herod said, "John I beheaded, but who is this about whom I hear such things?" And he sought to see him.

10 On their return the apostles told him all that they had done. And he took them and withdrew apart to a town called Bethsaida.

11 When the crowds learned it, they followed him, and he welcomed them and spoke to them of the kingdom of God and cured those who had need of healing.

12 Now the day began to wear away, and the twelve came and said to him, "Send the crowd away to go into the surrounding villages and countryside to find lodging and get provisions, for we are here in a desolate place."

13 But he said to them, "You give them something to eat." They said, "We have no more than five loaves and two fish—unless we are to go and buy food for all these people."

14 For there were about five thousand men. And he said to his disciples, "Have them sit down in groups of about fifty each."

15 And they did so, and had them all sit down.

16 And taking the five loaves and the two fish, he looked up to heaven and said a blessing over them. Then he broke the loaves and gave them to the disciples to set before the crowd.

17 And they all ate and were satisfied. And what was left over was picked up, twelve baskets of broken pieces.

18 Now it happened that as he was praying alone, the disciples were with him. And he asked them, "Who do the crowds say that I am?"

19 And they answered, "John the Baptist. But others say, Elijah, and others, that one of the prophets of old has risen."

20 Then he said to them, "But who do you say that I am?" And Peter answered, "The Christ of God."

21 And he strictly charged and commanded them to tell this to no one,

22 saying, "The Son of Man must suffer many things and be rejected by the elders and chief priests and scribes, and be killed, and on the third day be raised."

23 And he said to all, "If anyone would come after me, let him deny himself and take up his cross daily and follow me.

24 "For whoever would save his life will lose it, but who-

ever loses his life for my sake will save it.

²⁵ "For what does it profit a man if he gains the whole world and loses or forfeits himself?

²⁶ "For whoever is ashamed of me and of my words, of him will the Son of Man be ashamed when he comes in his glory and the glory of the Father and of the holy angels.

²⁷ "But I tell you truly, there are some standing here who will not taste death until they see the kingdom of God."

²⁸ Now about eight days after these sayings he took with him Peter and John and James and went up on the mountain to pray.

²⁹ And as he was praying, the appearance of his face was altered, and his clothing became dazzling white.

³⁰ And behold, two men were talking with him, Moses and Elijah,

³¹ who appeared in glory and spoke of his departure, which he was about to accomplish at Jerusalem.

³² Now Peter and those who were with him were heavy with sleep, but when they became fully awake they saw his glory and the two men who stood with him.

³³ And as the men were parting from him, Peter said to Jesus, "Master, it is good that we are here. Let us make three tents, one for you and one for Moses and one for Elijah"— not knowing what he said.

³⁴ As he was saying these things, a cloud came and overshadowed them, and they were afraid as they entered the cloud.

³⁵ And a voice came out of the cloud, saying, "This is my Son, my Chosen One; listen to him!"

³⁶ And when the voice had spoken, Jesus was found alone. And they kept silent and told no one in those days anything of what they had seen.

³⁷ On the next day, when they had come down from the mountain, a great crowd met him.

³⁸ And behold, a man from the crowd cried out, "Teacher, I beg you to look at my son, for he is my only child.

³⁹ "And behold, a spirit seizes him, and he suddenly cries out. It convulses him so that he foams at the mouth, and shatters him, and will hardly leave him.

⁴⁰ "And I begged your disciples to cast it out, but they could not."

⁴¹ Jesus answered, "O faithless and twisted generation, how long am I to be with you

and bear with you? Bring your son here."

⁴² While he was coming, the demon threw him to the ground and convulsed him. But Jesus rebuked the unclean spirit and healed the boy, and gave him back to his father.

⁴³ And all were astonished at the majesty of God. But while they were all marveling at everything he was doing, Jesus said to his disciples,

⁴⁴ "Let these words sink into your ears: The Son of Man is about to be delivered into the hands of men."

⁴⁵ But they did not understand this saying, and it was concealed from them, so that they might not perceive it. And they were afraid to ask him about this saying.

⁴⁶ An argument arose among them as to which of them was the greatest.

⁴⁷ But Jesus, knowing the reasoning of their hearts, took a child and put him by his side

⁴⁸ and said to them, "Whoever receives this child in my name receives me, and whoever receives me receives him who sent me. For he who is least among you all is the one who is great."

⁴⁹ John answered, "Master, we saw someone casting out demons in your name, and we tried to stop him, because he does not follow with us."

⁵⁰ But Jesus said to him, "Do not stop him, for the one who is not against you is for you."

⁵¹ When the days drew near for him to be taken up, he set his face to go to Jerusalem.

⁵² And he sent messengers ahead of him, who went and entered a village of the Samaritans, to make preparations for him.

⁵³ But the people did not receive him, because his face was set toward Jerusalem.

⁵⁴ And when his disciples James and John saw it, they said, "Lord, do you want us to tell fire to come down from heaven and consume them?"

⁵⁵ But he turned and rebuked them saying, "You do not know what manner of spirit you are of; for the Son of Man came not to destroy people's lives but to save them."

⁵⁶ And they went on to another village.

⁵⁷ As they were going along the road, someone said to him, "I will follow you wherever you go."

⁵⁸ And Jesus said to him, "Foxes have holes, and birds of the air have nests, but the Son of Man has nowhere to lay his head."

⁵⁹ To another he said, "Follow me." But he said, "Lord,

let me first go and bury my father."

⁶⁰And Jesus said to him, "Leave the dead to bury their own dead. But as for you, go and proclaim the kingdom of God."

⁶¹Yet another said, "I will follow you, Lord, but let me first say farewell to those at my home."

⁶²Jesus said to him, "No one who puts his hand to the plow and looks back is fit for the kingdom of God."

CHAPTER 10

¹After this the Lord appointed seventy-two others and sent them on ahead of him, two by two, into every town and place where he himself was about to go.

²And he said to them, "The harvest is plentiful, but the laborers are few. Therefore pray earnestly to the Lord of the harvest to send out laborers into his harvest.

³"Go your way; behold, I am sending you out as lambs in the midst of wolves.

⁴"Carry no moneybag, no knapsack, no sandals, and greet no one on the road.

⁵"Whatever house you enter, first say, 'Peace be to this house!'

⁶"And if a son of peace is there, your peace will rest upon him. But if not, it will return to you.

⁷"And remain in the same house, eating and drinking what they provide, for the laborer deserves his wages. Do not go from house to house.

⁸"Whenever you enter a town and they receive you, eat what is set before you.

⁹"Heal the sick in it and say to them, 'The kingdom of God has come near to you.'

¹⁰"But whenever you enter a town and they do not receive you, go into its streets and say,

¹¹"'Even the dust of your town that clings to our feet we wipe off against this. Nevertheless know this, that the kingdom of God has come near.'

¹²"I tell you, it will be more bearable on that day for Sodom than for that town.

¹³"Woe to you, Chorazin! Woe to you, Bethsaida! For if the mighty works done in you had been done in Tyre and Sidon, they would have repented long ago, sitting in sackcloth and ashes.

¹⁴"But it will be more bearable in the judgment for Tyre and Sidon than for you.

¹⁵"And you, Capernaum, will you be exalted to heaven? You shall be brought down to Hades.

16 "The one who hears you hears me, and the one who rejects you rejects me, and the one who rejects me rejects him who sent me."

17 The seventy-two returned with joy, saying, "Lord, even the demons are subject to us in your name!"

18 And he said to them, "I saw Satan fall like lightning from heaven.

19 "Behold, I have given you authority to tread on serpents and scorpions, and over all the power of the enemy, and nothing shall hurt you.

20 "Nevertheless, do not rejoice in this, that the spirits are subject to you, but rejoice that your names are written in heaven."

21 In that same hour he rejoiced in the Holy Spirit and said, "I thank you, Father, Lord of heaven and earth, that you have hidden these things from the wise and understanding and revealed them to little children; yes, Father, for such was your gracious will.

22 "All things have been handed over to me by my Father, and no one knows who the Son is except the Father, or who the Father is except the Son and anyone to whom the Son chooses to reveal him."

23 Then turning to the disciples he said privately, "Blessed are the eyes that see what you see!

24 "For I tell you that many prophets and kings desired to see what you see, and did not see it, and to hear what you hear, and did not hear it."

25 And behold, a lawyer stood up to put him to the test, saying, "Teacher, what shall I do to inherit eternal life?"

26 He said to him, "What is written in the Law? How do you read it?"

27 And he answered, "You shall love the Lord your God with all your heart and with all your soul and with all your strength and with all your mind, and your neighbor as yourself."

28 And he said to him, "You have answered correctly; do this, and you will live."

29 But he, desiring to justify himself, said to Jesus, "And who is my neighbor?"

30 Jesus replied, "A man was going down from Jerusalem to Jericho, and he fell among robbers, who stripped him and beat him and departed, leaving him half dead.

31 "Now by chance a priest was going down that road, and when he saw him he passed by on the other side.

32 "So likewise a Levite,

when he came to the place and saw him, passed by on the other side.

33 "But a Samaritan, as he journeyed, came to where he was, and when he saw him, he had compassion.

34 "He went to him and bound up his wounds, pouring on oil and wine. Then he set him on his own animal and brought him to an inn and took care of him.

35 "And the next day he took out two denarii and gave them to the innkeeper, saying, 'Take care of him, and whatever more you spend, I will repay you when I come back.'

36 "Which of these three, do you think, proved to be a neighbor to the man who fell among the robbers?"

37 He said, "The one who showed him mercy." And Jesus said to him, "You go, and do likewise."

38 Now as they went on their way, Jesus entered a village. And a woman named Martha welcomed him into her house.

39 And she had a sister called Mary, who sat at the Lord's feet and listened to his teaching.

40 But Martha was distracted with much serving. And she went up to him and said, "Lord, do you not care that my sister has left me to serve alone? Tell her then to help me."

41 But the Lord answered her, "Martha, Martha, you are anxious and troubled about many things,

42 "but one thing is necessary. Mary has chosen the good portion, which will not be taken away from her."

CHAPTER 11

1 Now Jesus was praying in a certain place, and when he finished, one of his disciples said to him, "Lord, teach us to pray, as John taught his disciples."

2 And he said to them, "When you pray, say: Father, hallowed be your name. Your kingdom come.

3 "Give us each day our daily bread,

4 "and forgive us our sins, for we ourselves forgive everyone who is indebted to us. And lead us not into temptation, but deliver us from evil."

5 And he said to them, "Which of you who has a friend will go to him at midnight and say to him, 'Friend, lend me three loaves,

6 "'for a friend of mine has arrived on a journey, and I have nothing to set before him';

7 "and he will answer from

within, 'Do not bother me; the door is now shut, and my children are with me in bed. I cannot get up and give you anything'?

8 "I tell you, though he will not get up and give him anything because he is his friend, yet because of his impudence he will rise and give him whatever he needs.

9 "And I tell you, ask, and it will be given to you; seek, and you will find; knock, and it will be opened to you.

10 "For everyone who asks receives, and the one who seeks finds, and to the one who knocks it will be opened.

11 "What father among you, if his son asks for bread, will give him a stone; or if he asks for a fish, will instead of a fish give him a serpent;

12 "or if he asks for an egg, will give him a scorpion?

13 "If you then, who are evil, know how to give good gifts to your children, how much more will the heavenly Father give the Holy Spirit to those who ask him!"

14 Now he was casting out a demon that was mute. When the demon had gone out, the mute man spoke, and the people marveled.

15 But some of them said, "He casts out demons by Beelzebul, the prince of demons,"

16 while others, to test him, kept seeking from him a sign from heaven.

17 But he, knowing their thoughts, said to them, "Every kingdom divided against itself is laid waste, and a divided household falls.

18 "And if Satan also is divided against himself, how will his kingdom stand? For you say that I cast out demons by Beelzebul.

19 "And if I cast out demons by Beelzebul, by whom do your sons cast them out? Therefore they will be your judges.

20 "But if it is by the finger of God that I cast out demons, then the kingdom of God has come upon you.

21 "When a strong man, fully armed, guards his own palace, his goods are safe;

22 "but when one stronger than he attacks him and overcomes him, he takes away his armor in which he trusted and divides his spoil.

23 "Whoever is not with me is against me, and whoever does not gather with me scatters.

24 "When the unclean spirit has gone out of a person, it passes through waterless places seeking rest, and finding none it says, 'I will return to my house from which I came.'

²⁵ "And when it comes, it finds the house swept and put in order.

²⁶ "Then it goes and brings seven other spirits more evil than itself, and they enter and dwell there. And the last state of that person is worse than the first."

²⁷ As he said these things, a woman in the crowd raised her voice and said to him, "Blessed is the womb that bore you, and the breasts at which you nursed!"

²⁸ But he said, "Blessed rather are those who hear the word of God and keep it!"

²⁹ When the crowds were increasing, he began to say, "This generation is an evil generation. It seeks for a sign, but no sign will be given to it except the sign of Jonah.

³⁰ "For as Jonah became a sign to the people of Nineveh, so will the Son of Man be to this generation.

³¹ "The queen of the South will rise up at the judgment with the men of this generation and condemn them, for she came from the ends of the earth to hear the wisdom of Solomon, and behold, something greater than Solomon is here.

³² "The men of Nineveh will rise up at the judgment with this generation and condemn it, for they repented at the preaching of Jonah, and behold, something greater than Jonah is here.

³³ "No one after lighting a lamp puts it in a cellar or under a basket, but on a stand, so that those who enter may see the light.

³⁴ "Your eye is the lamp of your body. When your eye is healthy, your whole body is full of light, but when it is bad, your body is full of darkness.

³⁵ "Therefore be careful lest the light in you be darkness.

³⁶ "If then your whole body is full of light, having no part dark, it will be wholly bright, as when a lamp with its rays gives you light."

³⁷ While Jesus was speaking, a Pharisee asked him to dine with him, so he went in and reclined at table.

³⁸ The Pharisee was astonished to see that he did not first wash before dinner.

³⁹ And the Lord said to him, "Now you Pharisees cleanse the outside of the cup and of the dish, but inside you are full of greed and wickedness.

⁴⁰ "You fools! Did not he who made the outside make the inside also?

⁴¹ "But give as alms those things that are within, and behold, everything is clean for you.

42 "But woe to you Pharisees! For you tithe mint and rue and every herb, and neglect justice and the love of God. These you ought to have done, without neglecting the others.

43 "Woe to you Pharisees! For you love the best seat in the synagogues and greetings in the marketplaces.

44 "Woe to you! For you are like unmarked graves, and people walk over them without knowing it."

45 One of the lawyers answered him, "Teacher, in saying these things you insult us also."

46 And he said, "Woe to you lawyers also! For you load people with burdens hard to bear, and you yourselves do not touch the burdens with one of your fingers.

47 "Woe to you! For you build the tombs of the prophets whom your fathers killed.

48 "So you are witnesses and you consent to the deeds of your fathers, for they killed them, and you build their tombs.

49 "Therefore also the Wisdom of God said, 'I will send them prophets and apostles, some of whom they will kill and persecute,'

50 "so that the blood of all the prophets, shed from the foundation of the world, may be charged against this generation,

51 "from the blood of Abel to the blood of Zechariah, who perished between the altar and the sanctuary. Yes, I tell you, it will be required of this generation.

52 "Woe to you lawyers! For you have taken away the key of knowledge. You did not enter yourselves, and you hindered those who were entering."

53 As he went away from there, the scribes and the Pharisees began to press him hard and to provoke him to speak about many things,

54 lying in wait for him, to catch him in something he might say.

CHAPTER 12

1 In the meantime, when so many thousands of the people had gathered together that they were trampling one another, he began to say to his disciples first, "Beware of the leaven of the Pharisees, which is hypocrisy.

2 "Nothing is covered up that will not be revealed, or hidden that will not be known.

3 "Therefore whatever you have said in the dark shall be heard in the light, and what you have whispered in private rooms shall be proclaimed on the housetops.

⁴ "I tell you, my friends, do not fear those who kill the body, and after that have nothing more that they can do.

⁵ "But I will warn you whom to fear: fear him who, after he has killed, has authority to cast into hell. Yes, I tell you, fear him!

⁶ "Are not five sparrows sold for two pennies? And not one of them is forgotten before God.

⁷ "Why, even the hairs of your head are all numbered. Fear not; you are of more value than many sparrows.

⁸ "And I tell you, everyone who acknowledges me before men, the Son of Man also will acknowledge before the angels of God,

⁹ "but the one who denies me before men will be denied before the angels of God.

¹⁰ "And everyone who speaks a word against the Son of Man will be forgiven, but the one who blasphemes against the Holy Spirit will not be forgiven.

¹¹ "And when they bring you before the synagogues and the rulers and the authorities, do not be anxious about how you should defend yourself or what you should say,

¹² "for the Holy Spirit will teach you in that very hour what you ought to say."

¹³ Someone in the crowd said to him, "Teacher, tell my brother to divide the inheritance with me."

¹⁴ But he said to him, "Man, who made me a judge or arbitrator over you?"

¹⁵ And he said to them, "Take care, and be on your guard against all covetousness, for one's life does not consist in the abundance of his possessions."

¹⁶ And he told them a parable, saying, "The land of a rich man produced plentifully,

¹⁷ "and he thought to himself, 'What shall I do, for I have nowhere to store my crops?'

¹⁸ "And he said, 'I will do this: I will tear down my barns and build larger ones, and there I will store all my grain and my goods.

¹⁹ " 'And I will say to my soul, "Soul, you have ample goods laid up for many years; relax, eat, drink, be merry." '

²⁰ "But God said to him, 'Fool! This night your soul is required of you, and the things you have prepared, whose will they be?'

²¹ "So is the one who lays up treasure for himself and is not rich toward God."

²² And he said to his disciples, "Therefore I tell you, do not be anxious about your life, what you will eat, nor

about your body, what you will put on.

²³ "For life is more than food, and the body more than clothing.

²⁴ "Consider the ravens: they neither sow nor reap, they have neither storehouse nor barn, and yet God feeds them. Of how much more value are you than the birds!

²⁵ "And which of you by being anxious can add a single hour to his span of life?

²⁶ "If then you are not able to do as small a thing as that, why are you anxious about the rest?

²⁷ "Consider the lilies, how they grow: they neither toil nor spin, yet I tell you, even Solomon in all his glory was not arrayed like one of these.

²⁸ "But if God so clothes the grass, which is alive in the field today, and tomorrow is thrown into the oven, how much more will he clothe you, O you of little faith!

²⁹ "And do not seek what you are to eat and what you are to drink, nor be worried.

³⁰ "For all the nations of the world seek after these things, and your Father knows that you need them.

³¹ "Instead, seek his kingdom, and these things will be added to you.

³² "Fear not, little flock, for it is your Father's good pleasure to give you the kingdom.

³³ "Sell your possessions, and give to the needy. Provide yourselves with moneybags that do not grow old, with a treasure in the heavens that does not fail, where no thief approaches and no moth destroys.

³⁴ "For where your treasure is, there will your heart be also.

³⁵ "Stay dressed for action and keep your lamps burning,

³⁶ "and be like men who are waiting for their master to come home from the wedding feast, so that they may open the door to him at once when he comes and knocks.

³⁷ "Blessed are those servants whom the master finds awake when he comes. Truly, I say to you, he will dress himself for service and have them recline at table, and he will come and serve them.

³⁸ "If he comes in the second watch, or in the third, and finds them awake, blessed are those servants!

³⁹ "But know this, that if the master of the house had known at what hour the thief was coming, he would not have left his house to be broken into.

⁴⁰ "You also must be ready, for the Son of Man is coming at an hour you do not expect."

⁴¹ Peter said, "Lord, are you telling this parable for us or for all?"

⁴² And the Lord said, "Who then is the faithful and wise manager, whom his master will set over his household, to give them their portion of food at the proper time?

⁴³ "Blessed is that servant whom his master will find so doing when he comes.

⁴⁴ "Truly, I say to you, he will set him over all his possessions.

⁴⁵ "But if that servant says to himself, 'My master is delayed in coming,' and begins to beat the male and female servants, and to eat and drink and get drunk,

⁴⁶ "the master of that servant will come on a day when he does not expect him and at an hour he does not know, and will cut him in pieces and put him with the unfaithful.

⁴⁷ "And that servant who knew his master's will but did not get ready or act according to his will, will receive a severe beating.

⁴⁸ "But the one who did not know, and did what deserved a beating, will receive a light beating. Everyone to whom much was given, of him much will be required, and from him to whom they entrust-ed much, they will demand the more.

⁴⁹ "I came to cast fire on the earth, and would that it were already kindled!

⁵⁰ "I have a baptism to be baptized with, and how great is my distress until it is accomplished!

⁵¹ "Do you think that I have come to give peace on earth? No, I tell you, but rather division.

⁵² "For from now on in one house there will be five divided, three against two and two against three.

⁵³ "They will be divided, father against son and son against father, mother against daughter and daughter against mother, mother-in-law against her daughter-in-law and daughter-in-law against mother-in-law."

⁵⁴ He also said to the crowds, "When you see a cloud rising in the west, you say at once, 'A shower is coming.' And so it happens.

⁵⁵ "And when you see the south wind blowing, you say, 'There will be scorching heat,' and it happens.

⁵⁶ "You hypocrites! You know how to interpret the appearance of earth and sky, but why do you not know how to interpret the present time?

⁵⁷ "And why do you not

judge for yourselves what is right?

58 "As you go with your accuser before the magistrate, make an effort to settle with him on the way, lest he drag you to the judge, and the judge hand you over to the officer, and the officer put you in prison.

59 "I tell you, you will never get out until you have paid the very last penny."

CHAPTER 13

1 There were some present at that very time who told him about the Galileans whose blood Pilate had mingled with their sacrifices.

2 And he answered them, "Do you think that these Galileans were worse sinners than all the other Galileans, because they suffered in this way?

3 "No, I tell you; but unless you repent, you will all likewise perish.

4 "Or those eighteen on whom the tower in Siloam fell and killed them: do you think that they were worse offenders than all the others who lived in Jerusalem?

5 "No, I tell you; but unless you repent, you will all likewise perish."

6 And he told this parable: "A man had a fig tree plant-ed in his vineyard, and he came seeking fruit on it and found none.

7 "And he said to the vine-dresser, 'Look, for three years now I have come seeking fruit on this fig tree, and I find none. Cut it down. Why should it use up the ground?'

8 "And he answered him, 'Sir, let it alone this year also, until I dig around it and put on manure.

9 "'Then if it should bear fruit next year, well and good; but if not, you can cut it down.'"

10 Now he was teaching in one of the synagogues on the Sabbath.

11 And behold, there was a woman who had had a disabling spirit for eighteen years. She was bent over and could not fully straighten herself.

12 When Jesus saw her, he called her over and said to her, "Woman, you are freed from your disability."

13 And he laid his hands on her, and immediately she was made straight, and she glorified God.

14 But the ruler of the synagogue, indignant because Jesus had healed on the Sabbath, said to the people, "There are six days in which work ought to be done. Come on those days and be healed, and not on the Sabbath day."

¹⁵ Then the Lord answered him, "You hypocrites! Does not each of you on the Sabbath untie his ox or his donkey from the manger and lead it away to water it?

¹⁶ "And ought not this woman, a daughter of Abraham whom Satan bound for eighteen years, be loosed from this bond on the Sabbath day?"

¹⁷ As he said these things, all his adversaries were put to shame, and all the people rejoiced at all the glorious things that were done by him.

¹⁸ He said therefore, "What is the kingdom of God like? And to what shall I compare it?

¹⁹ "It is like a grain of mustard seed that a man took and sowed in his garden, and it grew and became a tree, and the birds of the air made nests in its branches."

²⁰ And again he said, "To what shall I compare the kingdom of God?

²¹ "It is like leaven that a woman took and hid in three measures of flour, until it was all leavened."

²² He went on his way through towns and villages, teaching and journeying toward Jerusalem.

²³ And someone said to him, "Lord, will those who are saved be few?" And he said to them,

²⁴ "Strive to enter through the narrow door. For many, I tell you, will seek to enter and will not be able.

²⁵ "When once the master of the house has risen and shut the door, and you begin to stand outside and to knock at the door, saying, 'Lord, open to us,' then he will answer you, 'I do not know where you come from.'

²⁶ "Then you will begin to say, 'We ate and drank in your presence, and you taught in our streets.'

²⁷ "But he will say, 'I tell you, I do not know where you come from. Depart from me, all you workers of evil!'

²⁸ "In that place there will be weeping and gnashing of teeth, when you see Abraham and Isaac and Jacob and all the prophets in the kingdom of God but you yourselves cast out.

²⁹ "And people will come from east and west, and from north and south, and recline at table in the kingdom of God.

³⁰ "And behold, some are last who will be first, and some are first who will be last."

³¹ At that very hour some Pharisees came and said to him, "Get away from here, for Herod wants to kill you."

³² And he said to them, "Go

and tell that fox, 'Behold, I cast out demons and perform cures today and tomorrow, and the third day I finish my course.

33 "'Nevertheless, I must go on my way today and tomorrow and the day following, for it cannot be that a prophet should perish away from Jerusalem.'

34 "O Jerusalem, Jerusalem, the city that kills the prophets and stones those who are sent to it! How often would I have gathered your children together as a hen gathers her brood under her wings, and you were not willing!

35 "Behold, your house is forsaken. And I tell you, you will not see me until you say, 'Blessed is he who comes in the name of the Lord!'"

CHAPTER 14

1 One Sabbath, when he went to dine at the house of a ruler of the Pharisees, they were watching him carefully.

2 And behold, there was a man before him who had dropsy.

3 And Jesus responded to the lawyers and Pharisees, saying, "Is it lawful to heal on the Sabbath, or not?"

4 But they remained silent. Then he took him and healed him and sent him away.

5 And he said to them, "Which of you, having a son or an ox that has fallen into a well on a Sabbath day, will not immediately pull him out?"

6 And they could not reply to these things.

7 Now he told a parable to those who were invited, when he noticed how they chose the places of honor, saying to them,

8 "When you are invited by someone to a wedding feast, do not sit down in a place of honor, lest someone more distinguished than you be invited by him,

9 "and he who invited you both will come and say to you, 'Give your place to this person,' and then you will begin with shame to take the lowest place.

10 "But when you are invited, go and sit in the lowest place, so that when your host comes he may say to you, 'Friend, move up higher.' Then you will be honored in the presence of all who sit at table with you.

11 "For everyone who exalts himself will be humbled, and he who humbles himself will be exalted."

12 He said also to the man who had invited him, "When you give a dinner or a banquet, do not invite your

friends or your brothers or your relatives or rich neighbors, lest they also invite you in return and you be repaid.

13 "But when you give a feast, invite the poor, the crippled, the lame, the blind,

14 "and you will be blessed, because they cannot repay you. For you will be repaid at the resurrection of the just."

15 When one of those who reclined at table with him heard these things, he said to him, "Blessed is everyone who will eat bread in the kingdom of God!"

16 But he said to him, "A man once gave a great banquet and invited many.

17 "And at the time for the banquet he sent his servant to say to those who had been invited, 'Come, for everything is now ready.'

18 "But they all alike began to make excuses. The first said to him, 'I have bought a field, and I must go out and see it. Please have me excused.'

19 "And another said, 'I have bought five yoke of oxen, and I go to examine them. Please have me excused.'

20 "And another said, 'I have married a wife, and therefore I cannot come.'

21 "So the servant came and reported these things to his master. Then the master of the house became angry and said to his servant, 'Go out quickly to the streets and lanes of the city, and bring in the poor and crippled and blind and lame.'

22 "And the servant said, 'Sir, what you commanded has been done, and still there is room.'

23 "And the master said to the servant, 'Go out to the highways and hedges and compel people to come in, that my house may be filled.

24 " 'For I tell you, none of those men who were invited shall taste my banquet.' "

25 Now great crowds accompanied him, and he turned and said to them,

26 "If anyone comes to me and does not hate his own father and mother and wife and children and brothers and sisters, yes, and even his own life, he cannot be my disciple.

27 "Whoever does not bear his own cross and come after me cannot be my disciple.

28 "For which of you, desiring to build a tower, does not first sit down and count the cost, whether he has enough to complete it?

29 "Otherwise, when he has laid a foundation and is not able to finish, all who see it begin to mock him,

30 "saying, 'This man began

to build and was not able to finish.'

³¹ "Or what king, going out to encounter another king in war, will not sit down first and deliberate whether he is able with ten thousand to meet him who comes against him with twenty thousand?

³² "And if not, while the other is yet a great way off, he sends a delegation and asks for terms of peace.

³³ "So therefore, any one of you who does not renounce all that he has cannot be my disciple.

³⁴ "Salt is good, but if salt has lost its taste, how shall its saltiness be restored?

³⁵ "It is of no use either for the soil or for the manure pile. It is thrown away. He who has ears to hear, let him hear."

CHAPTER 15

¹ Now the tax collectors and sinners were all drawing near to hear him.

² And the Pharisees and the scribes grumbled, saying, "This man receives sinners and eats with them."

³ So he told them this parable:

⁴ "What man of you, having a hundred sheep, if he has lost one of them, does not leave the ninety-nine in the open country, and go after the one that is lost, until he finds it?

⁵ "And when he has found it, he lays it on his shoulders, rejoicing.

⁶ "And when he comes home, he calls together his friends and his neighbors, saying to them, 'Rejoice with me, for I have found my sheep that was lost.'

⁷ "Just so, I tell you, there will be more joy in heaven over one sinner who repents than over ninety-nine righteous persons who need no repentance.

⁸ "Or what woman, having ten silver coins, if she loses one coin, does not light a lamp and sweep the house and seek diligently until she finds it?

⁹ "And when she has found it, she calls together her friends and neighbors, saying, 'Rejoice with me, for I have found the coin that I had lost.'

¹⁰ "Just so, I tell you, there is joy before the angels of God over one sinner who repents."

¹¹ And he said, "There was a man who had two sons.

¹² "And the younger of them said to his father, 'Father, give me the share of property that is coming to me.' And he divided his property between them.

¹³ "Not many days later, the younger son gathered all he

had and took a journey into a far country, and there he squandered his property in reckless living.

¹⁴ "And when he had spent everything, a severe famine arose in that country, and he began to be in need.

¹⁵ "So he went and hired himself out to one of the citizens of that country, who sent him into his fields to feed pigs.

¹⁶ "And he was longing to be fed with the pods that the pigs ate, and no one gave him anything.

¹⁷ "But when he came to himself, he said, 'How many of my father's hired servants have more than enough bread, but I perish here with hunger!

¹⁸ "'I will arise and go to my father, and I will say to him, "Father, I have sinned against heaven and before you.

¹⁹ "'I am no longer worthy to be called your son. Treat me as one of your hired servants."'

²⁰ "And he arose and came to his father. But while he was still a long way off, his father saw him and felt compassion, and ran and embraced him and kissed him.

²¹ "And the son said to him, 'Father, I have sinned against heaven and before you. I am no longer worthy to be called your son.'

²² "But the father said to his servants, 'Bring quickly the best robe, and put it on him, and put a ring on his hand, and shoes on his feet.

²³ "'And bring the fattened calf and kill it, and let us eat and celebrate.

²⁴ "'For this my son was dead, and is alive again; he was lost, and is found.' And they began to celebrate.

²⁵ "Now his older son was in the field, and as he came and drew near to the house, he heard music and dancing.

²⁶ "And he called one of the servants and asked what these things meant.

²⁷ "And he said to him, 'Your brother has come, and your father has killed the fattened calf, because he has received him back safe and sound.'

²⁸ "But he was angry and refused to go in. His father came out and entreated him,

²⁹ "but he answered his father, 'Look, these many years I have served you, and I never disobeyed your command, yet you never gave me a young goat, that I might celebrate with my friends.

³⁰ "'But when this son of yours came, who has devoured your property with prostitutes, you killed the fattened calf for him!'

³¹ "And he said to him, 'Son,

you are always with me, and all that is mine is yours.

32 "It was fitting to celebrate and be glad, for this your brother was dead, and is alive; he was lost, and is found.'"

CHAPTER 16

1 He also said to the disciples, "There was a rich man who had a manager, and charges were brought to him that this man was wasting his possessions.

2 "And he called him and said to him, 'What is this that I hear about you? Turn in the account of your management, for you can no longer be manager.'

3 "And the manager said to himself, 'What shall I do, since my master is taking the management away from me? I am not strong enough to dig, and I am ashamed to beg.

4 "'I have decided what to do, so that when I am removed from management, people may receive me into their houses.'

5 "So, summoning his master's debtors one by one, he said to the first, 'How much do you owe my master?'

6 "He said, 'A hundred measures of oil.' He said to him, 'Take your bill, and sit down quickly and write fifty.'

7 "Then he said to another, 'And how much do you owe?' He said, 'A hundred measures of wheat.' He said to him, 'Take your bill, and write eighty.'

8 "The master commended the dishonest manager for his shrewdness. For the sons of this world are more shrewd in dealing with their own generation than the sons of light.

9 "And I tell you, make friends for yourselves by means of unrighteous wealth, so that when it fails they may receive you into the eternal dwellings.

10 "One who is faithful in a very little is also faithful in much, and one who is dishonest in a very little is also dishonest in much.

11 "If then you have not been faithful in the unrighteous wealth, who will entrust to you the true riches?

12 "And if you have not been faithful in that which is another's, who will give you that which is your own?

13 "No servant can serve two masters, for either he will hate the one and love the other, or he will be devoted to the one and despise the other. You cannot serve God and money."

14 The Pharisees, who were lovers of money, heard all these things, and they ridiculed him.

15 And he said to them,

"You are those who justify yourselves before men, but God knows your hearts. For what is exalted among men is an abomination in the sight of God.

16 "The Law and the Prophets were until John; since then the good news of the kingdom of God is preached, and everyone forces his way into it.

17 "But it is easier for heaven and earth to pass away than for one dot of the Law to become void.

18 "Everyone who divorces his wife and marries another commits adultery, and he who marries a woman divorced from her husband commits adultery.

19 "There was a rich man who was clothed in purple and fine linen and who feasted sumptuously every day.

20 "And at his gate was laid a poor man named Lazarus, covered with sores,

21 "who desired to be fed with what fell from the rich man's table. Moreover, even the dogs came and licked his sores.

22 "The poor man died and was carried by the angels to Abraham's side. The rich man also died and was buried,

23 "and in Hades, being in torment, he lifted up his eyes and saw Abraham far off and Lazarus at his side.

24 "And he called out, 'Father Abraham, have mercy on me, and send Lazarus to dip the end of his finger in water and cool my tongue, for I am in anguish in this flame.'

25 "But Abraham said, 'Child, remember that you in your lifetime received your good things, and Lazarus in like manner bad things; but now he is comforted here, and you are in anguish.

26 "'And besides all this, between us and you a great chasm has been fixed, in order that those who would pass from here to you may not be able, and none may cross from there to us.'

27 "And he said, 'Then I beg you, father, to send him to my father's house—

28 "'for I have five brothers—so that he may warn them, lest they also come into this place of torment.'

29 "But Abraham said, 'They have Moses and the Prophets; let them hear them.'

30 "And he said, 'No, father Abraham, but if someone goes to them from the dead, they will repent.'

31 "He said to him, 'If they do not hear Moses and the Prophets, neither will they be convinced if someone should rise from the dead.'"

CHAPTER 17

¹ And he said to his disciples, "Temptations to sin are sure to come, but woe to the one through whom they come!

² "It would be better for him if a millstone were hung around his neck and he were cast into the sea than that he should cause one of these little ones to sin.

³ "Pay attention to yourselves! If your brother sins, rebuke him, and if he repents, forgive him,

⁴ "and if he sins against you seven times in the day, and turns to you seven times, saying, 'I repent,' you must forgive him."

⁵ The apostles said to the Lord, "Increase our faith!"

⁶ And the Lord said, "If you had faith like a grain of mustard seed, you could say to this mulberry tree, 'Be uprooted and planted in the sea,' and it would obey you.

⁷ "Will any one of you who has a servant plowing or keeping sheep say to him when he has come in from the field, 'Come at once and recline at table'?

⁸ "Will he not rather say to him, 'Prepare supper for me, and dress properly, and serve me while I eat and drink, and afterward you will eat and drink'?

⁹ "Does he thank the servant because he did what was commanded?

¹⁰ "So you also, when you have done all that you were commanded, say, 'We are unworthy servants; we have only done what was our duty.'"

¹¹ On the way to Jerusalem he was passing along between Samaria and Galilee.

¹² And as he entered a village, he was met by ten lepers, who stood at a distance

¹³ and lifted up their voices, saying, "Jesus, Master, have mercy on us."

¹⁴ When he saw them he said to them, "Go and show yourselves to the priests." And as they went they were cleansed.

¹⁵ Then one of them, when he saw that he was healed, turned back, praising God with a loud voice;

¹⁶ and he fell on his face at Jesus' feet, giving him thanks. Now he was a Samaritan.

¹⁷ Then Jesus answered, "Were not ten cleansed? Where are the nine?

¹⁸ "Was no one found to return and give praise to God except this foreigner?"

¹⁹ And he said to him, "Rise and go your way; your faith has made you well."

²⁰ Being asked by the Pharisees when the kingdom of

God would come, he answered them, "The kingdom of God is not coming in ways that can be observed,

²¹ "nor will they say, 'Look, here it is!' or 'There!' for behold, the kingdom of God is in the midst of you."

²² And he said to the disciples, "The days are coming when you will desire to see one of the days of the Son of Man, and you will not see it.

²³ "And they will say to you, 'Look, there!' or 'Look, here!' Do not go out or follow them.

²⁴ "For as the lightning flashes and lights up the sky from one side to the other, so will the Son of Man be in his day.

²⁵ "But first he must suffer many things and be rejected by this generation.

²⁶ "Just as it was in the days of Noah, so will it be in the days of the Son of Man.

²⁷ "They were eating and drinking and marrying and being given in marriage, until the day when Noah entered the ark, and the flood came and destroyed them all.

²⁸ "Likewise, just as it was in the days of Lot—they were eating and drinking, buying and selling, planting and building,

²⁹ "but on the day when Lot went out from Sodom, fire and sulfur rained from heaven and destroyed them all—

³⁰ "so will it be on the day when the Son of Man is revealed.

³¹ "On that day, let the one who is on the housetop, with his goods in the house, not come down to take them away, and likewise let the one who is in the field not turn back.

³² "Remember Lot's wife.

³³ "Whoever seeks to preserve his life will lose it, but whoever loses his life will keep it.

³⁴ "I tell you, in that night there will be two in one bed. One will be taken and the other left.

³⁵ "There will be two women grinding together. One will be taken and the other left.

³⁶ "Two men will be in the field; one will be taken and the other left."

³⁷ And they said to him, "Where, Lord?" He said to them, "Where the corpse is, there the vultures will gather."

CHAPTER 18

¹ And he told them a parable to the effect that they ought always to pray and not lose heart.

² He said, "In a certain city there was a judge who

neither feared God nor respected man.

³ "And there was a widow in that city who kept coming to him and saying, 'Give me justice against my adversary.'

⁴ "For a while he refused, but afterward he said to himself, 'Though I neither fear God nor respect man,

⁵ " 'yet because this widow keeps bothering me, I will give her justice, so that she will not beat me down by her continual coming.' "

⁶ And the Lord said, "Hear what the unrighteous judge says.

⁷ "And will not God give justice to his elect, who cry to him day and night? Will he delay long over them?

⁸ "I tell you, he will give justice to them speedily. Nevertheless, when the Son of Man comes, will he find faith on earth?"

⁹ He also told this parable to some who trusted in themselves that they were righteous, and treated others with contempt:

¹⁰ "Two men went up into the temple to pray, one a Pharisee and the other a tax collector.

¹¹ "The Pharisee, standing by himself, prayed thus: 'God, I thank you that I am not like other men, extortioners, unjust, adulterers, or even like this tax collector.

¹² " 'I fast twice a week; I give tithes of all that I get.'

¹³ "But the tax collector, standing far off, would not even lift up his eyes to heaven, but beat his breast, saying, 'God, be merciful to me, a sinner!'

¹⁴ "I tell you, this man went down to his house justified, rather than the other. For everyone who exalts himself will be humbled, but the one who humbles himself will be exalted."

¹⁵ Now they were bringing even infants to him that he might touch them. And when the disciples saw it, they rebuked them.

¹⁶ But Jesus called them to him, saying, "Let the children come to me, and do not hinder them, for to such belongs the kingdom of God.

¹⁷ "Truly, I say to you, whoever does not receive the kingdom of God like a child shall not enter it."

¹⁸ And a ruler asked him, "Good Teacher, what must I do to inherit eternal life?"

¹⁹ And Jesus said to him, "Why do you call me good? No one is good except God alone.

²⁰ "You know the commandments: 'Do not commit adultery, Do not murder, Do

not steal, Do not bear false witness, Honor your father and mother.'"

21 And he said, "All these I have kept from my youth."

22 When Jesus heard this, he said to him, "One thing you still lack. Sell all that you have and distribute to the poor, and you will have treasure in heaven; and come, follow me."

23 But when he heard these things, he became very sad, for he was extremely rich.

24 Jesus, seeing that he had become sad, said, "How difficult it is for those who have wealth to enter the kingdom of God!

25 "For it is easier for a camel to go through the eye of a needle than for a rich person to enter the kingdom of God."

26 Those who heard it said, "Then who can be saved?"

27 But he said, "What is impossible with man is possible with God."

28 And Peter said, "See, we have left our homes and followed you."

29 And he said to them, "Truly, I say to you, there is no one who has left house or wife or brothers or parents or children, for the sake of the kingdom of God,

30 "who will not receive many times more in this time, and in the age to come eternal life."

31 And taking the twelve, he said to them, "See, we are going up to Jerusalem, and everything that is written about the Son of Man by the prophets will be accomplished.

32 "For he will be delivered over to the Gentiles and will be mocked and shamefully treated and spit upon.

33 "And after flogging him, they will kill him, and on the third day he will rise."

34 But they understood none of these things. This saying was hidden from them, and they did not grasp what was said.

35 As he drew near to Jericho, a blind man was sitting by the roadside begging.

36 And hearing a crowd going by, he inquired what this meant.

37 They told him, "Jesus of Nazareth is passing by."

38 And he cried out, "Jesus, Son of David, have mercy on me!"

39 And those who were in front rebuked him, telling him to be silent. But he cried out all the more, "Son of David, have mercy on me!"

40 And Jesus stopped and commanded him to be brought to him. And when he came near, he asked him,

⁴¹ "What do you want me to do for you?" He said, "Lord, let me recover my sight."

⁴² And Jesus said to him, "Recover your sight; your faith has made you well."

⁴³ And immediately he recovered his sight and followed him, glorifying God. And all the people, when they saw it, gave praise to God.

CHAPTER 19

¹ He entered Jericho and was passing through.

² And behold, there was a man named Zacchaeus. He was a chief tax collector and was rich.

³ And he was seeking to see who Jesus was, but on account of the crowd he could not, because he was small in stature.

⁴ So he ran on ahead and climbed up into a sycamore tree to see him, for he was about to pass that way.

⁵ And when Jesus came to the place, he looked up and said to him, "Zacchaeus, hurry and come down, for I must stay at your house today."

⁶ So he hurried and came down and received him joyfully.

⁷ And when they saw it, they all grumbled, "He has gone in to be the guest of a man who is a sinner."

⁸ And Zacchaeus stood and said to the Lord, "Behold, Lord, the half of my goods I give to the poor. And if I have defrauded anyone of anything, I restore it fourfold."

⁹ And Jesus said to him, "Today salvation has come to this house, since he also is a son of Abraham.

¹⁰ "For the Son of Man came to seek and to save the lost."

¹¹ As they heard these things, he proceeded to tell a parable, because he was near to Jerusalem, and because they supposed that the kingdom of God was to appear immediately.

¹² He said therefore, "A nobleman went into a far country to receive for himself a kingdom and then return.

¹³ "Calling ten of his servants, he gave them ten minas, and said to them, 'Engage in business until I come.'

¹⁴ "But his citizens hated him and sent a delegation after him, saying, 'We do not want this man to reign over us.'

¹⁵ "When he returned, having received the kingdom, he ordered these servants to whom he had given the money to be called to him, that he might know what they had gained by doing business.

¹⁶ "The first came before

him, saying, 'Lord, your mina has made ten minas more.'

17 "And he said to him, 'Well done, good servant! Because you have been faithful in a very little, you shall have authority over ten cities.'

18 "And the second came, saying, 'Lord, your mina has made five minas.'

19 "And he said to him, 'And you are to be over five cities.'

20 "Then another came, saying, 'Lord, here is your mina, which I kept laid away in a handkerchief;

21 "'for I was afraid of you, because you are a severe man. You take what you did not deposit, and reap what you did not sow.'

22 "He said to him, 'I will condemn you with your own words, you wicked servant! You knew that I was a severe man, taking what I did not deposit and reaping what I did not sow?

23 "'Why then did you not put my money in the bank, and at my coming I might have collected it with interest?'

24 "And he said to those who stood by, 'Take the mina from him, and give it to the one who has the ten minas.'

25 "And they said to him, 'Lord, he has ten minas!'

26 "'I tell you that to everyone who has, more will be given, but from the one who has not, even what he has will be taken away.

27 "'But as for these enemies of mine, who did not want me to reign over them, bring them here and slaughter them before me.'"

28 And when he had said these things, he went on ahead, going up to Jerusalem.

29 When he drew near to Bethphage and Bethany, at the mount that is called Olivet, he sent two of the disciples,

30 saying, "Go into the village in front of you, where on entering you will find a colt tied, on which no one has ever yet sat. Untie it and bring it here.

31 "If anyone asks you, 'Why are you untying it?' you shall say this: 'The Lord has need of it.'"

32 So those who were sent went away and found it just as he had told them.

33 And as they were untying the colt, its owners said to them, "Why are you untying the colt?"

34 And they said, "The Lord has need of it."

35 And they brought it to Jesus, and throwing their cloaks on the colt, they set Jesus on it.

36 And as he rode along,

they spread their cloaks on the road.

³⁷ As he was drawing near—already on the way down the Mount of Olives—the whole multitude of his disciples began to rejoice and praise God with a loud voice for all the mighty works that they had seen,

³⁸ saying, "Blessed is the King who comes in the name of the Lord! Peace in heaven and glory in the highest!"

³⁹ And some of the Pharisees in the crowd said to him, "Teacher, rebuke your disciples."

⁴⁰ He answered, "I tell you, if these were silent, the very stones would cry out."

⁴¹ And when he drew near and saw the city, he wept over it,

⁴² saying, "Would that you, even you, had known on this day the things that make for peace! But now they are hidden from your eyes.

⁴³ "For the days will come upon you, when your enemies will set up a barricade around you and surround you and hem you in on every side

⁴⁴ "and tear you down to the ground, you and your children within you. And they will not leave one stone upon another in you, because you did not know the time of your visitation."

⁴⁵ And he entered the temple and began to drive out those who sold,

⁴⁶ saying to them, "It is written, 'My house shall be a house of prayer,' but you have made it a den of robbers."

⁴⁷ And he was teaching daily in the temple. The chief priests and the scribes and the principal men of the people were seeking to destroy him,

⁴⁸ but they did not find anything they could do, for all the people were hanging on his words.

CHAPTER 20

¹ One day, as Jesus was teaching the people in the temple and preaching the gospel, the chief priests and the elders with the scribes came up

² and said to him, "Tell us by what authority you do these things, or who it is that gave you this authority."

³ He answered them, "I also will ask you a question. Now tell me,

⁴ "was the baptism of John from heaven or from man?"

⁵ And they discussed it with one another, saying, "If we say, 'From heaven,' he will say, 'Why did you not believe him?'

6 "But if we say, 'From man,' all the people will stone us to death, for they are convinced that John was a prophet."

7 So they answered that they did not know where it came from.

8 And Jesus said to them, "Neither will I tell you by what authority I do these things."

9 And he began to tell the people this parable: "A man planted a vineyard and let it out to tenants and went into another country for a long while.

10 "When the time came, he sent a servant to the tenants, so that they would give him some of the fruit of the vineyard. But the tenants beat him and sent him away empty-handed.

11 "And he sent another servant. But they also beat and treated him shamefully, and sent him away empty-handed.

12 "And he sent yet a third. This one also they wounded and cast out.

13 "Then the owner of the vineyard said, 'What shall I do? I will send my beloved son; perhaps they will respect him.'

14 "But when the tenants saw him, they said to themselves, 'This is the heir. Let us kill him, so that the inheritance may be ours.'

15 "And they threw him out of the vineyard and killed him. What then will the owner of the vineyard do to them?

16 "He will come and destroy those tenants and give the vineyard to others." When they heard this, they said, "Surely not!"

17 But he looked directly at them and said, "What then is this that is written: 'The stone that the builders rejected has become the cornerstone'?

18 "Everyone who falls on that stone will be broken to pieces, and when it falls on anyone, it will crush him."

19 The scribes and the chief priests sought to lay hands on him at that very hour, for they perceived that he had told this parable against them, but they feared the people.

20 So they watched him and sent spies, who pretended to be sincere, that they might catch him in something he said, so as to deliver him up to the authority and jurisdiction of the governor.

21 So they asked him, "Teacher, we know that you speak and teach rightly, and show no partiality, but truly teach the way of God.

²² "Is it lawful for us to give tribute to Caesar, or not?"

²³ But he perceived their craftiness, and said to them,

²⁴ "Show me a denarius. Whose likeness and inscription does it have?" They said, "Caesar's."

²⁵ He said to them, "Then render to Caesar the things that are Caesar's, and to God the things that are God's."

²⁶ And they were not able in the presence of the people to catch him in what he said, but marveling at his answer they became silent.

²⁷ There came to him some Sadducees, those who deny that there is a resurrection,

²⁸ and they asked him a question, saying, "Teacher, Moses wrote for us that if a man's brother dies, having a wife but no children, the man must take the widow and raise up offspring for his brother.

²⁹ "Now there were seven brothers. The first took a wife, and died without children.

³⁰ "And the second

³¹ "and the third took her, and likewise all seven left no children and died.

³² "Afterward the woman also died.

³³ "In the resurrection, therefore, whose wife will the woman be? For the seven had her as wife."

³⁴ And Jesus said to them, "The sons of this age marry and are given in marriage,

³⁵ "but those who are considered worthy to attain to that age and to the resurrection from the dead neither marry nor are given in marriage,

³⁶ "for they cannot die anymore, because they are equal to angels and are sons of God, being sons of the resurrection.

³⁷ "But that the dead are raised, even Moses showed, in the passage about the bush, where he calls the Lord the God of Abraham and the God of Isaac and the God of Jacob.

³⁸ "Now he is not God of the dead, but of the living, for all live to him."

³⁹ Then some of the scribes answered, "Teacher, you have spoken well."

⁴⁰ For they no longer dared to ask him any question.

⁴¹ But he said to them, "How can they say that the Christ is David's son?

⁴² "For David himself says in the Book of Psalms, 'The Lord said to my Lord, "Sit at my right hand,

⁴³ "'"until I make your enemies your footstool."'

⁴⁴ "David thus calls him Lord, so how is he his son?"

⁴⁵ And in the hearing of all the people he said to his disciples,

⁴⁶ "Beware of the scribes, who like to walk around in long robes, and love greetings in the marketplaces and the best seats in the synagogues and the places of honor at feasts,

⁴⁷ "who devour widows' houses and for a pretense make long prayers. They will receive the greater condemnation."

CHAPTER 21

¹ Jesus looked up and saw the rich putting their gifts into the offering box,

² and he saw a poor widow put in two small copper coins.

³ And he said, "Truly, I tell you, this poor widow has put in more than all of them.

⁴ "For they all contributed out of their abundance, but she out of her poverty put in all she had to live on."

⁵ And while some were speaking of the temple, how it was adorned with noble stones and offerings, he said,

⁶ "As for these things that you see, the days will come when there will not be left here one stone upon another that will not be thrown down."

⁷ And they asked him, "Teacher, when will these things be, and what will be the sign when these things are about to take place?"

⁸ And he said, "See that you are not led astray. For many will come in my name, saying, 'I am he!' and, 'The time is at hand!' Do not go after them.

⁹ "And when you hear of wars and tumults, do not be terrified, for these things must first take place, but the end will not be at once."

¹⁰ Then he said to them, "Nation will rise against nation, and kingdom against kingdom.

¹¹ "There will be great earthquakes, and in various places famines and pestilences. And there will be terrors and great signs from heaven.

¹² "But before all this they will lay their hands on you and persecute you, delivering you up to the synagogues and prisons, and you will be brought before kings and governors for my name's sake.

¹³ "This will be your opportunity to bear witness.

¹⁴ "Settle it therefore in your minds not to meditate beforehand how to answer,

¹⁵ "for I will give you a mouth and wisdom, which none of your adversaries will be able to withstand or contradict.

16 "You will be delivered up even by parents and brothers and relatives and friends, and some of you they will put to death.

17 "You will be hated by all for my name's sake.

18 "But not a hair of your head will perish.

19 "By your endurance you will gain your lives.

20 "But when you see Jerusalem surrounded by armies, then know that its desolation has come near.

21 "Then let those who are in Judea flee to the mountains, and let those who are inside the city depart, and let not those who are out in the country enter it,

22 "for these are days of vengeance, to fulfill all that is written.

23 "Alas for women who are pregnant and for those who are nursing infants in those days! For there will be great distress upon the earth and wrath against this people.

24 "They will fall by the edge of the sword and be led captive among all nations, and Jerusalem will be trampled underfoot by the Gentiles, until the times of the Gentiles are fulfilled.

25 "And there will be signs in sun and moon and stars, and on the earth distress of nations in perplexity because of the roaring of the sea and the waves,

26 "people fainting with fear and with foreboding of what is coming on the world. For the powers of the heavens will be shaken.

27 "And then they will see the Son of Man coming in a cloud with power and great glory.

28 "Now when these things begin to take place, straighten up and raise your heads, because your redemption is drawing near."

29 And he told them a parable: "Look at the fig tree, and all the trees.

30 "As soon as they come out in leaf, you see for yourselves and know that the summer is already near.

31 "So also, when you see these things taking place, you know that the kingdom of God is near.

32 "Truly, I say to you, this generation will not pass away until all has taken place.

33 "Heaven and earth will pass away, but my words will not pass away.

34 "But watch yourselves lest your hearts be weighed down with dissipation and drunkenness and cares of this life, and that day come upon you suddenly like a trap.

35 "For it will come upon all who dwell on the face of the *whole earth*.

36 "But stay awake at all times, praying that *you may have strength to escape all these things that are going to take place*, and to stand before the Son of Man."

37 And every day he was teaching in the temple, but at night he went out and lodged on the mount called Olivet.

38 And early in the morning all the people came to him in the temple to hear him.

CHAPTER 22

1 Now the Feast of Unleavened Bread drew near, which is called the Passover.

2 And the chief priests and the scribes were seeking how to put him to death, for they feared the people.

3 Then Satan entered into Judas called Iscariot, who was of the number of the twelve.

4 He went away and conferred with the chief priests and officers how he might betray him to them.

5 And they were glad, and agreed to give him money.

6 So he consented and sought an opportunity to betray him to them in the absence of a crowd.

7 Then came the day of Unleavened Bread, on which the Passover lamb had to be sacrificed.

8 *So Jesus sent* Peter and John, saying, "Go and prepare the Passover for us, that we may eat it."

9 They said to him, "Where will you have us prepare it?"

10 He said to them, "Behold, when you have entered the city, a man carrying a jar of water will meet you. Follow him into the house that he enters

11 "and tell the master of the house, 'The Teacher says to you, Where is the guest room, where I may eat the Passover with my disciples?'

12 "And he will show you a large upper room furnished; prepare it there."

13 And they went and found it just as he had told them, and they prepared the Passover.

14 And when the hour came, he reclined at table, and the apostles with him.

15 And he said to them, "I have earnestly desired to eat this Passover with you before I suffer.

16 "For I tell you I will not eat it until it is fulfilled in the kingdom of God."

17 And he took a cup, and when he had given thanks he said, "Take this, and divide it among yourselves.

18 "For I tell you that from now on I will not drink of the fruit of the vine until the kingdom of God comes."

19 And he took bread, and when he had given thanks, he broke it and gave it to them, saying, "This is my body, which is given for you. Do this in remembrance of me."

20 And likewise the cup after they had eaten, saying, "This cup that is poured out for you is the new covenant in my blood.

21 "But behold, the hand of him who betrays me is with me on the table.

22 "For the Son of Man goes as it has been determined, but woe to that man by whom he is betrayed!"

23 And they began to question one another, which of them it could be who was going to do this.

24 A dispute also arose among them, as to which of them was to be regarded as the greatest.

25 And he said to them, "The kings of the Gentiles exercise lordship over them, and those in authority over them are called benefactors.

26 "But not so with you. Rather, let the greatest among you become as the youngest, and the leader as one who serves.

27 "For who is the greater, one who reclines at table or one who serves? Is it not the one who reclines at table? But I am among you as the one who serves.

28 "You are those who have stayed with me in my trials,

29 "and I assign to you, as my Father assigned to me, a kingdom,

30 "that you may eat and drink at my table in my kingdom and sit on thrones judging the twelve tribes of Israel.

31 "Simon, Simon, behold, Satan demanded to have you, that he might sift you like wheat,

32 "but I have prayed for you that your faith may not fail. And when you have turned again, strengthen your brothers."

33 Peter said to him, "Lord, I am ready to go with you both to prison and to death."

34 Jesus said, "I tell you, Peter, the rooster will not crow this day, until you deny three times that you know me."

35 And he said to them, "When I sent you out with no moneybag or knapsack or sandals, did you lack anything?" They said, "Nothing."

36 He said to them, "But now let the one who has a moneybag take it, and likewise a knapsack. And let the one

who has no sword sell his cloak and buy one.

37 "For I tell you that this Scripture must be fulfilled in me: 'And he was numbered with the transgressors.' For what is written about me has its fulfillment."

38 And they said, "Look, Lord, here are two swords." And he said to them, "It is enough."

39 And he came out and went, as was his custom, to the Mount of Olives, and the disciples followed him.

40 And when he came to the place, he said to them, "Pray that you may not enter into temptation."

41 And he withdrew from them about a stone's throw, and knelt down and prayed,

42 saying, "Father, if you are willing, remove this cup from me. Nevertheless, not my will, but yours, be done."

43 And there appeared to him an angel from heaven, strengthening him.

44 And being in an agony he prayed more earnestly; and his sweat became like great drops of blood falling down to the ground.

45 And when he rose from prayer, he came to the disciples and found them sleeping for sorrow,

46 and he said to them, "Why are you sleeping? Rise and pray that you may not enter into temptation."

47 While he was still speaking, there came a crowd, and the man called Judas, one of the twelve, was leading them. He drew near to Jesus to kiss him,

48 but Jesus said to him, "Judas, would you betray the Son of Man with a kiss?"

49 And when those who were around him saw what would follow, they said, "Lord, shall we strike with the sword?"

50 And one of them struck the servant of the high priest and cut off his right ear.

51 But Jesus said, "No more of this!" And he touched his ear and healed him.

52 Then Jesus said to the chief priests and officers of the temple and elders, who had come out against him, "Have you come out as against a robber, with swords and clubs?

53 "When I was with you day after day in the temple, you did not lay hands on me. But this is your hour, and the power of darkness."

54 Then they seized him and led him away, bringing him into the high priest's house, and Peter was following at a distance.

⁵⁵ And when they had kindled a fire in the middle of the courtyard and sat down together, Peter sat down among them.

⁵⁶ Then a servant girl, seeing him as he sat in the light and looking closely at him, said, "This man also was with him."

⁵⁷ But he denied it, saying, "Woman, I do not know him."

⁵⁸ And a little later someone else saw him and said, "You also are one of them." But Peter said, "Man, I am not."

⁵⁹ And after an interval of about an hour still another insisted, saying, "Certainly this man also was with him, for he too is a Galilean."

⁶⁰ But Peter said, "Man, I do not know what you are talking about." And immediately, while he was still speaking, the rooster crowed.

⁶¹ And the Lord turned and looked at Peter. And Peter remembered the saying of the Lord, how he had said to him, "Before the rooster crows today, you will deny me three times."

⁶² And he went out and wept bitterly.

⁶³ Now the men who were holding Jesus in custody were mocking him as they beat him.

⁶⁴ They also blindfolded him and kept asking him, "Prophesy! Who is it that struck you?"

⁶⁵ And they said many other things against him, blaspheming him.

⁶⁶ When day came, the assembly of the elders of the people gathered together, both chief priests and scribes. And they led him away to their council, and they said,

⁶⁷ "If you are the Christ, tell us." But he said to them, "If I tell you, you will not believe,

⁶⁸ "and if I ask you, you will not answer.

⁶⁹ "But from now on the Son of Man shall be seated at the right hand of the power of God."

⁷⁰ So they all said, "Are you the Son of God, then?" And he said to them, "You say that I am."

⁷¹ Then they said, "What further testimony do we need? We have heard it ourselves from his own lips."

CHAPTER 23

¹ Then the whole company of them arose and brought him before Pilate.

² And they began to accuse him, saying, "We found this man misleading our nation and forbidding us to give tribute to Caesar, and saying that he himself is Christ, a king."

3 And Pilate asked him, "Are you the King of the Jews?" And he answered him, "You have said so."

4 Then Pilate said to the chief priests and the crowds, "I find no guilt in this man."

5 But they were urgent, saying, "He stirs up the people, teaching throughout all Judea, from Galilee even to this place."

6 When Pilate heard this, he asked whether the man was a Galilean.

7 And when he learned that he belonged to Herod's jurisdiction, he sent him over to Herod, who was himself in Jerusalem at that time.

8 When Herod saw Jesus, he was very glad, for he had long desired to see him, because he had heard about him, and he was hoping to see some sign done by him.

9 So he questioned him at some length, but he made no answer.

10 The chief priests and the scribes stood by, vehemently accusing him.

11 And Herod with his soldiers treated him with contempt and mocked him. Then, arraying him in splendid clothing, he sent him back to Pilate.

12 And Herod and Pilate became friends with each other that very day, for before this they had been at enmity with each other.

13 Pilate then called together the chief priests and the rulers and the people,

14 and said to them, "You brought me this man as one who was misleading the people. And after examining him before you, behold, I did not find this man guilty of any of your charges against him.

15 "Neither did Herod, for he sent him back to us. Look, nothing deserving death has been done by him.

16 "I will therefore punish and release him."

17 Now he was obliged to release one man to them at the festival.

18 But they all cried out together, "Away with this man, and release to us Barabbas"—

19 a man who had been thrown into prison for an insurrection started in the city and for murder.

20 Pilate addressed them once more, desiring to release Jesus,

21 but they kept shouting, "Crucify, crucify him!"

22 A third time he said to them, "Why, what evil has he done? I have found in him no guilt deserving death. I will therefore punish and release him."

23 But they were urgent, demanding with loud cries that he should be crucified. And their voices prevailed.

24 So Pilate decided that their demand should be granted.

25 He released the man who had been thrown into prison for insurrection and murder, for whom they asked, but he delivered Jesus over to their will.

26 And as they led him away, they seized one Simon of Cyrene, who was coming in from the country, and laid on him the cross, to carry it behind Jesus.

27 And there followed him a great multitude of the people and of women who were mourning and lamenting for him.

28 But turning to them Jesus said, "Daughters of Jerusalem, do not weep for me, but weep for yourselves and for your children.

29 "For behold, the days are coming when they will say, 'Blessed are the barren and the wombs that never bore and the breasts that never nursed!'

30 "Then they will begin to say to the mountains, 'Fall on us,' and to the hills, 'Cover us.'

31 "For if they do these things when the wood is green, what will happen when it is dry?"

32 Two others, who were criminals, were led away to be put to death with him.

33 And when they came to the place that is called The Skull, there they crucified him, and the criminals, one on his right and one on his left.

34 And Jesus said, "Father, forgive them, for they know not what they do." And they cast lots to divide his garments.

35 And the people stood by, watching, but the rulers scoffed at him, saying, "He saved others; let him save himself, if he is the Christ of God, his Chosen One!"

36 The soldiers also mocked him, coming up and offering him sour wine

37 and saying, "If you are the King of the Jews, save yourself!"

38 There was also an inscription over him, "This is the King of the Jews."

39 One of the criminals who were hanged railed at him, saying, "Are you not the Christ? Save yourself and us!"

40 But the other rebuked him, saying, "Do you not fear God, since you are under the same sentence of condemnation?

41 "And we indeed justly, for we are receiving the due reward of our deeds; but this man has done nothing wrong."

42 And he said, "Jesus, remember me when you come into your kingdom."

43 And he said to him, "Truly, I say to you, today you will be with me in Paradise."

44 It was now about the sixth hour, and there was darkness over the whole land until the ninth hour,

45 while the sun's light failed. And the curtain of the temple was torn in two.

46 Then Jesus, calling out with a loud voice, said, "Father, into your hands I commit my spirit!" And having said this he breathed his last.

47 Now when the centurion saw what had taken place, he praised God, saying, "Certainly this man was innocent!"

48 And all the crowds that had assembled for this spectacle, when they saw what had taken place, returned home beating their breasts.

49 And all his acquaintances and the women who had followed him from Galilee stood at a distance watching these things.

50 Now there was a man named Joseph, from the Jewish town of Arimathea. He was a member of the council, a good and righteous man,

51 who had not consented to their decision and action; and he was looking for the kingdom of God.

52 This man went to Pilate and asked for the body of Jesus.

53 Then he took it down and wrapped it in a linen shroud and laid him in a tomb cut in stone, where no one had ever yet been laid.

54 It was the day of Preparation, and the Sabbath was beginning.

55 The women who had come with him from Galilee followed and saw the tomb and how his body was laid.

56 Then they returned and prepared spices and ointments. On the Sabbath they rested according to the commandment.

CHAPTER 24

1 But on the first day of the week, at early dawn, they went to the tomb, taking the spices they had prepared.

2 And they found the stone rolled away from the tomb,

3 but when they went in they did not find the body of the Lord Jesus.

4 While they were perplexed about this, behold, two men

stood by them in dazzling apparel.

5 And as they were frightened and bowed their faces to the ground, the men said to them, "Why do you seek the living among the dead?

6 "He is not here, but has risen. Remember how he told you, while he was still in Galilee,

7 "that the Son of Man must be delivered into the hands of sinful men and be crucified and on the third day rise."

8 And they remembered his words,

9 and returning from the tomb they told all these things to the eleven and to all the rest.

10 Now it was Mary Magdalene and Joanna and Mary the mother of James and the other women with them who told these things to the apostles,

11 but these words seemed to them an idle tale, and they did not believe them.

12 But Peter rose and ran to the tomb; stooping and looking in, he saw the linen cloths by themselves; and he went home marveling at what had happened.

13 That very day two of them were going to a village named Emmaus, about seven miles from Jerusalem,

14 and they were talking with each other about all these things that had happened.

15 While they were talking and discussing together, Jesus himself drew near and went with them.

16 But their eyes were kept from recognizing him.

17 And he said to them, "What is this conversation that you are holding with each other as you walk?" And they stood still, looking sad.

18 Then one of them, named Cleopas, answered him, "Are you the only visitor to Jerusalem who does not know the things that have happened there in these days?"

19 And he said to them, "What things?" And they said to him, "Concerning Jesus of Nazareth, a man who was a prophet mighty in deed and word before God and all the people,

20 "and how our chief priests and rulers delivered him up to be condemned to death, and crucified him.

21 "But we had hoped that he was the one to redeem Israel. Yes, and besides all this, it is now the third day since these things happened.

22 "Moreover, some women of our company amazed us.

They were at the tomb early in the morning,

23 "and when they did not find his body, they came back saying that they had even seen a vision of angels, who said that he was alive.

24 "Some of those who were with us went to the tomb and found it just as the women had said, but him they did not see."

25 And he said to them, "O foolish ones, and slow of heart to believe all that the prophets have spoken!

26 "Was it not necessary that the Christ should suffer these things and enter into his glory?"

27 And beginning with Moses and all the Prophets, he interpreted to them in all the Scriptures the things concerning himself.

28 So they drew near to the village to which they were going. He acted as if he were going farther,

29 but they urged him strongly, saying, "Stay with us, for it is toward evening and the day is now far spent." So he went in to stay with them.

30 When he was at table with them, he took the bread and blessed and broke it and gave it to them.

31 And their eyes were opened, and they recognized him. And he vanished from their sight.

32 They said to each other, "Did not our hearts burn within us while he talked to us on the road, while he opened to us the Scriptures?"

33 And they rose that same hour and returned to Jerusalem. And they found the eleven and those who were with them gathered together,

34 saying, "The Lord has risen indeed, and has appeared to Simon!"

35 Then they told what had happened on the road, and how he was known to them in the breaking of the bread.

36 As they were talking about these things, Jesus himself stood among them, and said to them, "Peace to you!"

37 But they were startled and frightened and thought they saw a spirit.

38 And he said to them, "Why are you troubled, and why do doubts arise in your hearts?

39 "See my hands and my feet, that it is I myself. Touch me, and see. For a spirit does not have flesh and bones as you see that I have."

40 And when he had said this, he showed them his hands and his feet.

41 And while they still

disbelieved for joy and were marveling, he said to them, "Have you anything here to eat?"

⁴² They gave him a piece of broiled fish,

⁴³ and he took it and ate before them.

⁴⁴ Then he said to them, "These are my words that I spoke to you while I was still with you, that everything written about me in the Law of Moses and the Prophets and the Psalms must be fulfilled."

⁴⁵ Then he opened their minds to understand the Scriptures,

⁴⁶ and said to them, "Thus it is written, that the Christ should suffer and on the third day rise from the dead,

⁴⁷ "and that repentance and forgiveness of sins should be proclaimed in his name to all nations, beginning from Jerusalem.

⁴⁸ "You are witnesses of these things.

⁴⁹ "And behold, I am sending the promise of my Father upon you. But stay in the city until you are clothed with power from on high."

⁵⁰ Then he led them out as far as Bethany, and lifting up his hands he blessed them.

⁵¹ While he blessed them, he parted from them and was carried up into heaven.

⁵² And they worshiped him and returned to Jerusalem with great joy,

⁵³ and were continually in the temple blessing God.

THE GOSPEL ACCORDING TO

JOHN

CHAPTER 1

¹ In the beginning was the Word, and the Word was with God, and the Word was God.

² He was in the beginning with God.

³ All things were made through him, and without him was not any thing made that was made.

⁴ In him was life, and the life was the light of men.

⁵ The light shines in the darkness, and the darkness has not overcome it.

⁶ There was a man sent from God, whose name was John.

⁷ He came as a witness, to bear witness about the light,

that all might believe through him.

⁸ He was not the light, but came to bear witness about the light.

⁹ The true light, which gives light to everyone, was coming into the world.

¹⁰ He was in the world, and the world was made through him, yet the world did not know him.

¹¹ He came to his own, and his own people did not receive him.

¹² But to all who did receive him, who believed in his name, he gave the right to become children of God,

¹³ who were born, not of blood nor of the will of the flesh nor of the will of man, but of God.

¹⁴ And the Word became flesh and dwelt among us, and we have seen his glory, glory as of the only Son from the Father, full of grace and truth.

¹⁵ (John bore witness about him, and cried out, "This was he of whom I said, 'He who comes after me ranks before me, because he was before me.'")

¹⁶ For from his fullness we have all received, grace upon grace.

¹⁷ For the law was given through Moses; grace and truth came through Jesus Christ.

¹⁸ No one has ever seen God; the only God, who is at the Father's side, he has made him known.

¹⁹ And this is the testimony of John, when the Jews sent priests and Levites from Jerusalem to ask him, "Who are you?"

²⁰ He confessed, and did not deny, but confessed, "I am not the Christ."

²¹ And they asked him, "What then? Are you Elijah?" He said, "I am not." "Are you the Prophet?" And he answered, "No."

²² So they said to him, "Who are you? We need to give an answer to those who sent us. What do you say about yourself?"

²³ He said, "I am the voice of one crying out in the wilderness, 'Make straight the way of the Lord,' as the prophet Isaiah said."

²⁴ (Now they had been sent from the Pharisees.)

²⁵ They asked him, "Then why are you baptizing, if you are neither the Christ, nor Elijah, nor the Prophet?"

²⁶ John answered them, "I baptize with water, but among you stands one you do not know,

²⁷ "even he who comes after

me, the strap of whose sandal I am not worthy to untie."

28 These things took place in Bethany across the Jordan, where John was baptizing.

29 The next day he saw Jesus coming toward him, and said, "Behold, the Lamb of God, who takes away the sin of the world!

30 "This is he of whom I said, 'After me comes a man who ranks before me, because he was before me.'

31 I myself did not know him, but for this purpose I came baptizing with water, that he might be revealed to Israel."

32 And John bore witness: "I saw the Spirit descend from heaven like a dove, and it remained on him.

33 "I myself did not know him, but he who sent me to baptize with water said to me, 'He on whom you see the Spirit descend and remain, this is he who baptizes with the Holy Spirit.'

34 "And I have seen and have borne witness that this is the Son of God."

35 The next day again John was standing with two of his disciples,

36 and he looked at Jesus as he walked by and said, "Behold, the Lamb of God!"

37 The two disciples heard him say this, and they followed Jesus.

38 Jesus turned and saw them following and said to them, "What are you seeking?" And they said to him, "Rabbi" (which means Teacher), "where are you staying?"

39 He said to them, "Come and you will see." So they came and saw where he was staying, and they stayed with him that day, for it was about the tenth hour.

40 One of the two who heard John speak and followed Jesus was Andrew, Simon Peter's brother.

41 He first found his own brother Simon and said to him, "We have found the Messiah" (which means Christ).

42 He brought him to Jesus. Jesus looked at him and said, "You are Simon the son of John. You shall be called Cephas" (which means Peter).

43 The next day Jesus decided to go to Galilee. He found Philip and said to him, "Follow me."

44 Now Philip was from Bethsaida, the city of Andrew and Peter.

45 Philip found Nathanael and said to him, "We have found him of whom Moses in the Law and also the prophets wrote, Jesus of Nazareth, the son of Joseph."

⁴⁶ Nathanael said to him, "Can anything good come out of Nazareth?" Philip said to him, "Come and see."

⁴⁷ Jesus saw Nathanael coming toward him and said of him, "Behold, an Israelite indeed, in whom there is no deceit!"

⁴⁸ Nathanael said to him, "How do you know me?" Jesus answered him, "Before Philip called you, when you were under the fig tree, I saw you."

⁴⁹ Nathanael answered him, "Rabbi, you are the Son of God! You are the King of Israel!"

⁵⁰ Jesus answered him, "Because I said to you, 'I saw you under the fig tree,' do you believe? You will see greater things than these."

⁵¹ And he said to him, "Truly, truly, I say to you, you will see heaven opened, and the angels of God ascending and descending on the Son of Man."

CHAPTER 2

¹ On the third day there was a wedding at Cana in Galilee, and the mother of Jesus was there.

² Jesus also was invited to the wedding with his disciples.

³ When the wine ran out, the mother of Jesus said to him, "They have no wine."

⁴ And Jesus said to her, "Woman, what does this have to do with me? My hour has not yet come."

⁵ His mother said to the servants, "Do whatever he tells you."

⁶ Now there were six stone water jars there for the Jewish rites of purification, each holding twenty or thirty gallons.

⁷ Jesus said to the servants, "Fill the jars with water." And they filled them up to the brim.

⁸ And he said to them, "Now draw some out and take it to the master of the feast." So they took it.

⁹ When the master of the feast tasted the water now become wine, and did not know where it came from (though the servants who had drawn the water knew), the master of the feast called the bridegroom

¹⁰ and said to him, "Everyone serves the good wine first, and when people have drunk freely, then the poor wine. But you have kept the good wine until now."

¹¹ This, the first of his signs, Jesus did at Cana in Galilee, and manifested his glory. And his disciples believed in him.

¹² After this he went down to Capernaum, with his mother and his brothers and his disciples, and they stayed there for a few days.

¹³ The Passover of the Jews was at hand, and Jesus went up to Jerusalem.

¹⁴ In the temple he found those who were selling oxen and sheep and pigeons, and the money-changers sitting there.

¹⁵ And making a whip of cords, he drove them all out of the temple, with the sheep and oxen. And he poured out the coins of the money-changers and overturned their tables.

¹⁶ And he told those who sold the pigeons, "Take these things away; do not make my Father's house a house of trade."

¹⁷ His disciples remembered that it was written, "Zeal for your house will consume me."

¹⁸ So the Jews said to him, "What sign do you show us for doing these things?"

¹⁹ Jesus answered them, "Destroy this temple, and in three days I will raise it up."

²⁰ The Jews then said, "It has taken forty-six years to build this temple, and will you raise it up in three days?"

²¹ But he was speaking about the temple of his body.

²² When therefore he was raised from the dead, his disciples remembered that he had said this, and they believed the Scripture and the word that Jesus had spoken.

²³ Now when he was in Jerusalem at the Passover Feast, many believed in his name when they saw the signs that he was doing.

²⁴ But Jesus on his part did not entrust himself to them, because he knew all people

²⁵ and needed no one to bear witness about man, for he himself knew what was in man.

CHAPTER 3

¹ Now there was a man of the Pharisees named Nicodemus, a ruler of the Jews.

² This man came to Jesus by night and said to him, "Rabbi, we know that you are a teacher come from God, for no one can do these signs that you do unless God is with him."

³ Jesus answered him, "Truly, truly, I say to you, unless one is born again he cannot see the kingdom of God."

⁴ Nicodemus said to him, "How can a man be born when he is old? Can he enter a second time into his mother's womb and be born?"

⁵ Jesus answered, "Truly, truly, I say to you, unless one is born of water and the Spirit, he cannot enter the kingdom of God.

⁶ "That which is born of the flesh is flesh, and that which is born of the Spirit is spirit.

⁷ "Do not marvel that I said to you, 'You must be born again.'

⁸ "The wind blows where it wishes, and you hear its sound, but you do not know where it comes from or where it goes. So it is with everyone who is born of the Spirit."

⁹ Nicodemus said to him, "How can these things be?"

¹⁰ Jesus answered him, "Are you the teacher of Israel and yet you do not understand these things?

¹¹ "Truly, truly, I say to you, we speak of what we know, and bear witness to what we have seen, but you do not receive our testimony.

¹² "If I have told you earthly things and you do not believe, how can you believe if I tell you heavenly things?

¹³ "No one has ascended into heaven except he who descended from heaven, the Son of Man.

¹⁴ "And as Moses lifted up the serpent in the wilderness, so must the Son of Man be lifted up,

¹⁵ "that whoever believes in him may have eternal life.

¹⁶ "For God so loved the world, that he gave his only Son, that whoever believes in him should not perish but have eternal life.

¹⁷ "For God did not send his Son into the world to condemn the world, but in order that the world might be saved through him.

¹⁸ "Whoever believes in him is not condemned, but whoever does not believe is condemned already, because he has not believed in the name of the only Son of God.

¹⁹ "And this is the judgment: the light has come into the world, and people loved the darkness rather than the light because their works were evil.

²⁰ "For everyone who does wicked things hates the light and does not come to the light, lest his works should be exposed.

²¹ "But whoever does what is true comes to the light, so that it may be clearly seen that his works have been carried out in God."

²² After this Jesus and his disciples went into the Judean countryside, and he remained there with them and was baptizing.

²³ John also was baptizing at Aenon near Salim, because

water was plentiful there, and people were coming and being baptized

²⁴ (for John had not yet been put in prison).

²⁵ Now a discussion arose between some of John's disciples and a Jew over purification.

²⁶ And they came to John and said to him, "Rabbi, he who was with you across the Jordan, to whom you bore witness—look, he is baptizing, and all are going to him."

²⁷ John answered, "A person cannot receive even one thing unless it is given him from heaven.

²⁸ "You yourselves bear me witness, that I said, 'I am not the Christ, but I have been sent before him.'

²⁹ "The one who has the bride is the bridegroom. The friend of the bridegroom, who stands and hears him, rejoices greatly at the bridegroom's voice. Therefore this joy of mine is now complete.

³⁰ "He must increase, but I must decrease."

³¹ He who comes from above is above all. He who is of the earth belongs to the earth and speaks in an earthly way. He who comes from heaven is above all.

³² He bears witness to what he has seen and heard, yet no one receives his testimony.

³³ Whoever receives his testimony sets his seal to this, that God is true.

³⁴ For he whom God has sent utters the words of God, for he gives the Spirit without measure.

³⁵ The Father loves the Son and has given all things into his hand.

³⁶ Whoever believes in the Son has eternal life; whoever does not obey the Son shall not see life, but the wrath of God remains on him.

CHAPTER 4

¹ Now when Jesus learned that the Pharisees had heard that Jesus was making and baptizing more disciples than John

² (although Jesus himself did not baptize, but only his disciples),

³ he left Judea and departed again for Galilee.

⁴ And he had to pass through Samaria.

⁵ So he came to a town of Samaria called Sychar, near the field that Jacob had given to his son Joseph.

⁶ Jacob's well was there; so Jesus, wearied as he was from his journey, was sitting beside the well. It was about the sixth hour.

⁷ A woman from Samaria

came to draw water. Jesus said to her, "Give me a drink."

8 (For his disciples had gone away into the city to buy food.)

9 The Samaritan woman said to him, "How is it that you, a Jew, ask for a drink from me, a woman of Samaria?" (For Jews have no dealings with Samaritans.)

10 Jesus answered her, "If you knew the gift of God, and who it is that is saying to you, 'Give me a drink,' you would have asked him, and he would have given you living water."

11 The woman said to him, "Sir, you have nothing to draw water with, and the well is deep. Where do you get that living water?

12 "Are you greater than our father Jacob? He gave us the well and drank from it himself, as did his sons and his livestock."

13 Jesus said to her, "Everyone who drinks of this water will be thirsty again,

14 "but whoever drinks of the water that I will give him will never be thirsty again. The water that I will give him will become in him a spring of water welling up to eternal life."

15 The woman said to him, "Sir, give me this water, so that I will not be thirsty or have to come here to draw water."

16 Jesus said to her, "Go, call your husband, and come here."

17 The woman answered him, "I have no husband." Jesus said to her, "You are right in saying, 'I have no husband';

18 "for you have had five husbands, and the one you now have is not your husband. What you have said is true."

19 The woman said to him, "Sir, I perceive that you are a prophet.

20 "Our fathers worshiped on this mountain, but you say that in Jerusalem is the place where people ought to worship."

21 Jesus said to her, "Woman, believe me, the hour is coming when neither on this mountain nor in Jerusalem will you worship the Father.

22 "You worship what you do not know; we worship what we know, for salvation is from the Jews.

23 "But the hour is coming, and is now here, when the true worshipers will worship the Father in spirit and truth, for the Father is seeking such people to worship him.

24 "God is spirit, and those who worship him must worship in spirit and truth."

25 The woman said to him,

"I know that Messiah is coming (he who is called Christ). When he comes, he will tell us all things."

²⁶ Jesus said to her, "I who speak to you am he."

²⁷ Just then his disciples came back. They marveled that he was talking with a woman, but no one said, "What do you seek?" or, "Why are you talking with her?"

²⁸ So the woman left her water jar and went away into town and said to the people, ²⁹ "Come, see a man who told me all that I ever did. Can this be the Christ?" ³⁰ They went out of the town and were coming to him.

³¹ Meanwhile the disciples were urging him, saying, "Rabbi, eat." ³² But he said to them, "I have food to eat that you do not know about." ³³ So the disciples said to one another, "Has anyone brought him something to eat?" ³⁴ Jesus said to them, "My food is to do the will of him who sent me and to accomplish his work. ³⁵ "Do you not say, 'There are yet four months, then comes the harvest'? Look, I tell you, lift up your eyes, and see that the fields are white for harvest.

³⁶ "Already the one who reaps is receiving wages and gathering fruit for eternal life, so that sower and reaper may rejoice together. ³⁷ "For here the saying holds true, 'One sows and another reaps.' ³⁸ "I sent you to reap that for which you did not labor. Others have labored, and you have entered into their labor."

³⁹ Many Samaritans from that town believed in him because of the woman's testimony, "He told me all that I ever did." ⁴⁰ So when the Samaritans came to him, they asked him to stay with him, and he stayed there two days. ⁴¹ And many more believed because of his word. ⁴² They said to the woman, "It is no longer because of what you said that we believe, for we have heard for ourselves, and we know that this is indeed the Savior of the world."

⁴³ After the two days he departed for Galilee. ⁴⁴ (For Jesus himself had testified that a prophet has no honor in his own hometown.) ⁴⁵ So when he came to Galilee, the Galileans welcomed him, having seen all that he had done in Jerusalem at the

feast. For they too had gone to the feast.

⁴⁶ So he came again to Cana in Galilee, where he had made the water wine. And at Capernaum there was an official whose son was ill.

⁴⁷ When this man heard that Jesus had come from Judea to Galilee, he went to him and asked him to come down and heal his son, for he was at the point of death.

⁴⁸ So Jesus said to him, "Unless you see signs and wonders you will not believe."

⁴⁹ The official said to him, "Sir, come down before my child dies."

⁵⁰ Jesus said to him, "Go; your son will live." The man believed the word that Jesus spoke to him and went on his way.

⁵¹ As he was going down, his servants met him and told him that his son was recovering.

⁵² So he asked them the hour when he began to get better, and they said to him, "Yesterday at the seventh hour the fever left him."

⁵³ The father knew that was the hour when Jesus had said to him, "Your son will live." And he himself believed, and all his household.

⁵⁴ This was now the second sign that Jesus did when he had come from Judea to Galilee.

CHAPTER 5

¹ After this there was a feast of the Jews, and Jesus went up to Jerusalem.

² Now there is in Jerusalem by the Sheep Gate a pool, in Aramaic called Bethesda, which has five roofed colonnades.

³ In these lay a multitude of invalids—blind, lame, and paralyzed—waiting for the moving of the water;

⁴ for an angel of the Lord went down at certain seasons into the pool, and stirred the water: whoever stepped in first after the stirring of the water was healed of whatever disease he had.

⁵ One man was there who had been an invalid for thirty-eight years.

⁶ When Jesus saw him lying there and knew that he had already been there a long time, he said to him, "Do you want to be healed?"

⁷ The sick man answered him, "Sir, I have no one to put me into the pool when the water is stirred up, and while I am going another steps down before me."

⁸ Jesus said to him, "Get up, take up your bed, and walk."

⁹ And at once the man was

healed, and he took up his bed and walked. Now that day was the Sabbath.

¹⁰ So the Jews said to the man who had been healed, "It is the Sabbath, and it is not lawful for you to take up your bed."

¹¹ But he answered them, "The man who healed me, that man said to me, 'Take up your bed, and walk.'"

¹² They asked him, "Who is the man who said to you, 'Take up your bed and walk?'"

¹³ Now the man who had been healed did not know who it was, for Jesus had withdrawn, as there was a crowd in the place.

¹⁴ Afterward Jesus found him in the temple and said to him, "See, you are well! Sin no more, that nothing worse may happen to you."

¹⁵ The man went away and told the Jews that it was Jesus who had healed him.

¹⁶ And this was why the Jews were persecuting Jesus, because he was *doing these things* on the Sabbath.

¹⁷ But Jesus answered them, "My Father is working until now, and I am working."

¹⁸ This was why the Jews were seeking all the more to kill him, because not only was he breaking the Sabbath, but he was even calling God his own Father, making himself equal with God.

¹⁹ So Jesus said to them, "Truly, truly, I say to you, the Son can do nothing of his own accord, but only what he sees the Father doing. For whatever the Father does, that the Son does likewise.

²⁰ "For the Father loves the Son and shows him all that he himself is doing. And greater works than these will he show him, so that you may marvel.

²¹ "For as the Father raises the dead and gives them life, so also the Son gives life to whom he will.

²² "The Father judges no one, but has given all judgment to the Son,

²³ "that all may honor the Son, just as they honor the Father. Whoever does not honor the Son does not honor the Father who sent him.

²⁴ "Truly, truly, I say to you, whoever hears my word and believes him who sent me *has eternal life.* He does not come into judgment, but has passed from death to life.

²⁵ "Truly, truly, I say to you, an hour is coming, and is now here, when the dead will hear the voice of the Son of God, and those who hear will live.

²⁶ "For as the Father has life

in himself, so he has granted the Son also to have life in himself.

27 "And he has given him authority to execute judgment, because he is the Son of Man.

28 "Do not marvel at this, for an hour is coming when all who are in the tombs will hear his voice

29 "and come out, those who have done good to the resurrection of life, and those who have done evil to the resurrection of judgment.

30 "I can do nothing on my own. As I hear, I judge, and my judgment is just, because I seek not my own will but the will of him who sent me.

31 "If I alone bear witness about myself, my testimony is not true.

32 "There is another who bears witness about me, and I know that the testimony that he bears about me is true.

33 "You sent to John, and he has borne witness to the truth.

34 "Not that the testimony that I receive is from man, but I say these things so that you may be saved.

35 "He was a burning and shining lamp, and you were willing to rejoice for a while in his light.

36 "But the testimony that I have is greater than that of John. For the works that the Father has given me to accomplish, the very works that I am doing, bear witness about me that the Father has sent me.

37 "And the Father who sent me has himself borne witness about me. His voice you have never heard, his form you have never seen,

38 "and you do not have his word abiding in you, for you do not believe the one whom he has sent.

39 "You search the Scriptures because you think that in them you have eternal life; and it is they that bear witness about me,

40 "yet you refuse to come to me that you may have life.

41 "I do not receive glory from people.

42 "But I know that you do not have the love of God within you.

43 "I have come in my Father's name, and you do not receive me. If another comes in his own name, you will receive him.

44 "How can you believe, when you receive glory from one another and do not seek the glory that comes from the only God?

45 "Do not think that I will accuse you to the Father. There is one who accuses you:

Moses, on whom you have set your hope.

46 "For if you believed Moses, you would believe me; for he wrote of me.

47 "But if you do not believe his writings, how will you believe my words?"

CHAPTER 6

1 After this Jesus went away to the other side of the Sea of Galilee, which is the Sea of Tiberias.

2 And a large crowd was following him, because they saw the signs that he was doing on the sick.

3 Jesus went up on the mountain, and there he sat down with his disciples.

4 Now the Passover, the feast of the Jews, was at hand.

5 Lifting up his eyes, then, and seeing that a large crowd was coming toward him, Jesus said to Philip, "Where are we to buy bread, so that these people may eat?"

6 He said this to test him, for he himself knew what he would do.

7 Philip answered him, "Two hundred denarii worth of bread would not be enough for each of them to get a little."

8 One of his disciples, Andrew, Simon Peter's brother, said to him,

9 "There is a boy here who has five barley loaves and two fish, but what are they for so many?"

10 Jesus said, "Have the people sit down." Now there was much grass in the place. So the men sat down, about five thousand in number.

11 Jesus then took the loaves, and when he had given thanks, he distributed them to those who were seated. So also the fish, as much as they wanted.

12 And when they had eaten their fill, he told his disciples, "Gather up the leftover fragments, that nothing may be lost."

13 So they gathered them up and filled twelve baskets with fragments from the five barley loaves left by those who had eaten.

14 When the people saw the sign that he had done, they said, "This is indeed the Prophet who is to come into the world!"

15 Perceiving then that they were about to come and take him by force to make him king, Jesus withdrew again to the mountain by himself.

16 When evening came, his disciples went down to the sea,

17 got into a boat, and started across the sea to Capernaum.

It was now dark, and Jesus had not yet come to them.

18 The sea became rough because a strong wind was blowing.

19 When they had rowed about three or four miles, they saw Jesus walking on the sea and coming near the boat, and they were frightened.

20 But he said to them, "It is I; do not be afraid."

21 Then they were glad to take him into the boat, and immediately the boat was at the land to which they were going.

22 On the next day the crowd that remained on the other side of the sea saw that there had been only one boat there, and that Jesus had not entered the boat with his disciples, but that his disciples had gone away alone.

23 Other boats from Tiberias came near the place where they had eaten the bread after the Lord had given thanks.

24 So when the crowd saw that Jesus was not there, nor his disciples, they themselves got into the boats and went to Capernaum, seeking Jesus.

25 When they found him on the other side of the sea, they said to him, "Rabbi, when did you come here?"

26 Jesus answered them, "Truly, truly, I say to you, you are seeking me, not because you saw signs, but because you ate your fill of the loaves.

27 "Do not work for the food that perishes, but for the food that endures to eternal life, which the Son of Man will give to you. For on him God the Father has set his seal."

28 Then they said to him, "What must we do, to be doing the works of God?"

29 Jesus answered them, "This is the work of God, that you believe in him whom he has sent."

30 So they said to him, "Then what sign do you do, that we may see and believe you? What work do you perform?

31 "Our fathers ate the manna in the wilderness; as it is written, 'He gave them bread from heaven to eat.'"

32 Jesus then said to them, "Truly, truly, I say to you, it was not Moses who gave you the bread from heaven, but my Father gives you the true bread from heaven.

33 "For the bread of God is he who comes down from heaven and gives life to the world."

34 They said to him, "Sir, give us this bread always."

35 Jesus said to them, "I am the bread of life; whoever comes to me shall not hunger,

and whoever believes in me shall never thirst.

³⁶ "But I said to you that you have seen me and yet do not believe.

³⁷ "All that the Father gives me will come to me, and whoever comes to me I will never cast out.

³⁸ "For I have come down from heaven, not to do my own will but the will of him who sent me.

³⁹ "And this is the will of him who sent me, that I should lose nothing of all that he has given me, but raise it up on the last day.

⁴⁰ "For this is the will of my Father, that everyone who looks on the Son and believes in him should have eternal life, and I will raise him up on the last day."

⁴¹ So the Jews grumbled about him, because he said, "I am the bread that came down from heaven."

⁴² They said, "Is not this Jesus, the son of Joseph, whose father and mother we know? How does he now say, 'I have come down from heaven'?"

⁴³ Jesus answered them, "Do not grumble among yourselves.

⁴⁴ "No one can come to me unless the Father who sent me draws him. And I will raise him up on the last day.

⁴⁵ "It is written in the Prophets, 'And they will all be taught by God.' Everyone who has heard and learned from the Father comes to me—

⁴⁶ "not that anyone has seen the Father except he who is from God; he has seen the Father.

⁴⁷ "Truly, truly, I say to you, whoever believes has eternal life.

⁴⁸ "I am the bread of life.

⁴⁹ "Your fathers ate the manna in the wilderness, and they died.

⁵⁰ "This is the bread that comes down from heaven, so that one may eat of it and not die.

⁵¹ "I am the living bread that came down from heaven. If anyone eats of this bread, he will live forever. And the bread that I will give for the life of the world is my flesh."

⁵² The Jews then disputed among themselves, saying, "How can this man give us his flesh to eat?"

⁵³ So Jesus said to them, "Truly, truly, I say to you, unless you eat the flesh of the Son of Man and drink his blood, you have no life in you.

⁵⁴ "Whoever feeds on my flesh and drinks my blood has eternal life, and I will raise him up on the last day.

⁵⁵ "For my flesh is true food, and my blood is true drink.

⁵⁶ "Whoever feeds on my flesh and drinks my blood abides in me, and I in him.

⁵⁷ "As the living Father sent me, and I live because of the Father, so whoever feeds on me, he also will live because of me.

⁵⁸ "This is the bread that came down from heaven, not like the bread the fathers ate, and died. Whoever feeds on this bread will live forever."

⁵⁹ Jesus said these things in the synagogue, as he taught at Capernaum.

⁶⁰ When many of his disciples heard it; they said, "This is a hard saying; who can listen to it?"

⁶¹ But Jesus, knowing in himself that his disciples were grumbling about this, said to them, "Do you take offense at this?

⁶² "Then what if you were to see the Son of Man ascending to where he was before?

⁶³ "It is the Spirit who gives life; the flesh is no help at all. The words that I have spoken to you are spirit and life.

⁶⁴ "But there are some of you who do not believe." (For Jesus knew from the beginning who those were who did not believe, and who it was who would betray him.)

⁶⁵ And he said, "This is why I told you that no one can come to me unless it is granted him by the Father."

⁶⁶ After this many of his disciples turned back and no longer walked with him.

⁶⁷ So Jesus said to the Twelve, "Do you want to go away as well?"

⁶⁸ Simon Peter answered him, "Lord, to whom shall we go? You have the words of eternal life,

⁶⁹ "and we have believed, and have come to know, that you are the Holy One of God."

⁷⁰ Jesus answered them; "Did I not choose you, the Twelve? And yet one of you is a devil."

⁷¹ He spoke of Judas the son of Simon Iscariot, for he, one of the Twelve, was going to betray him.

CHAPTER 7

¹ After this Jesus went about in Galilee. He would not go about in Judea, because the Jews were seeking to kill him.

² Now the Jews' Feast of Booths was at hand.

³ So his brothers said to him, "Leave here and go to Judea, that your disciples also may see the works you are doing.

⁴ "For no one works in secret if he seeks to be known

openly. If you do these things, show yourself to the world."

5 For not even his brothers believed in him.

6 Jesus said to them, "My time has not yet come, but your time is always here.

7 "The world cannot hate you, but it hates me because I testify about it that its works are evil.

8 "You go up to the feast. I am not yet going up to this feast, for my time has not yet fully come."

9 After saying this, he remained in Galilee.

10 But after his brothers had gone up to the feast, then he also went up, not publicly but in private.

11 The Jews were looking for him at the feast, and saying, "Where is he?"

12 And there was much muttering about him among the people. While some said, "He is a good man," others said, "No, he is leading the people astray."

13 Yet for fear of the Jews no one spoke openly of him.

14 About the middle of the feast Jesus went up into the temple and began teaching.

15 The Jews therefore marveled, saying, "How is it that this man has learning, when he has never studied?"

16 So Jesus answered them, "My teaching is not mine, but his who sent me.

17 "If anyone's will is to do God's will, he will know whether the teaching is from God or whether I am speaking on my own authority.

18 "The one who speaks on his own authority seeks his own glory; but the one who seeks the glory of him who sent him is true, and in him there is no falsehood.

19 "Has not Moses given you the law? Yet none of you keeps the law. Why do you seek to kill me?"

20 The crowd answered, "You have a demon! Who is seeking to kill you?"

21 Jesus answered them, "I did one work, and you all marvel at it.

22 "Moses gave you circumcision (not that it is from Moses, but from the fathers), and you circumcise a man on the Sabbath.

23 "If on the Sabbath a man receives circumcision, so that the law of Moses may not be broken, are you angry with me because on the Sabbath I made a man's whole body well?

24 "Do not judge by appearances, but judge with right judgment."

25 Some of the people of Je-

rusalem therefore said, "Is not this the man whom they seek to kill?

26 "And here he is, speaking openly, and they say nothing to him! Can it be that the authorities really know that this is the Christ?

27 "But we know where this man comes from, and when the Christ appears, no one will know where he comes from."

28 So Jesus proclaimed, as he taught in the temple, "You know me, and you know where I come from. But I have not come of my own accord. He who sent me is true, and him you do not know.

29 "I know him, for I come from him, and he sent me."

30 So they were seeking to arrest him, but no one laid a hand on him, because his hour had not yet come.

31 Yet many of the people believed in him. They said, "When the Christ appears, will he do more signs than this man has done?"

32 The Pharisees heard the crowd muttering these things about him, and the chief priests and Pharisees sent officers to arrest him.

33 Jesus then said, "I will be with you a little longer, and then I am going to him who sent me.

34 "You will seek me and you will not find me. Where I am you cannot come."

35 The Jews said to one another, "Where does this man intend to go that we will not find him? Does he intend to go to the Dispersion among the Greeks and teach the Greeks?

36 "What does he mean by saying, 'You will seek me and you will not find me,' and, 'Where I am you cannot come'?"

37 On the last day of the feast, the great day, Jesus stood up and cried out, "If anyone thirsts, let him come to me and drink.

38 "Whoever believes in me, as the Scripture has said, 'Out of his heart will flow rivers of living water.'"

39 Now this he said about the Spirit, whom those who believed in him were to receive, for as yet the Spirit had not been given, because Jesus was not yet glorified.

40 When they heard these words, some of the people said, "This really is the Prophet."

41 Others said, "This is the Christ." But some said, "Is the Christ to come from Galilee?

42 "Has not the Scripture said that the Christ comes from the offspring of David,

and comes from Bethlehem, the village where David was?"

43 So there was a division among the people over him.

44 Some of them wanted to arrest him, but no one laid hands on him.

45 The officers then came to the chief priests and Pharisees, who said to them, "Why did you not bring him?"

46 The officers answered, "No one ever spoke like this man!"

47 The Pharisees answered them, "Have you also been deceived?

48 "Have any of the authorities or the Pharisees believed in him?

49 "But this crowd that does not know the law is accursed."

50 Nicodemus, who had gone to him before, and who was one of them, said to them,

51 "Does our law judge a man without first giving him a hearing and learning what he does?"

52 They replied, "Are you from Galilee too? Search and see that no prophet arises from Galilee."

53 They went each to his own house,

CHAPTER 8

1 but Jesus went to the Mount of Olives.

2 Early in the morning he came again to the temple. All the people came to him, and he sat down and taught them.

3 The scribes and the Pharisees brought a woman who had been caught in adultery, and placing her in the midst

4 they said to him, "Teacher, this woman has been caught in the act of adultery.

5 "Now in the Law Moses commanded us to stone such women. So what do you say?"

6 This they said to test him, that they might have some charge to bring against him. Jesus bent down and wrote with his finger on the ground.

7 And as they continued to ask him, he stood up and said to them, "Let him who is without sin among you be the first to throw a stone at her."

8 And once more he bent down and wrote on the ground.

9 But when they heard it, they went away one by one, beginning with the older ones, and Jesus was left alone with the woman standing before him.

10 Jesus stood up and said to her, "Woman, where are they? Has no one condemned you?"

11 She said, "No one, Lord." And Jesus said, "Neither do I condemn you; go, and from now on sin no more."

¹² Again Jesus spoke to them, saying, "I am the light of the world. Whoever follows me will not walk in darkness, but will have the light of life."

¹³ So the Pharisees said to him, "You are bearing witness about yourself; your testimony is not true."

¹⁴ Jesus answered, "Even if I do bear witness about myself, my testimony is true, for I know where I came from and where I am going, but you do not know where I come from or where I am going.

¹⁵ "You judge according to the flesh; I judge no one.

¹⁶ "Yet even if I do judge, my judgment is true, for it is not I alone who judge, but I and the Father who sent me.

¹⁷ "In your Law it is written that the testimony of two people is true.

¹⁸ "I am the one who bears witness about myself, and the Father who sent me bears witness about me."

¹⁹ They said to him therefore, "Where is your Father?" Jesus answered, "You know neither me nor my Father. If you knew me, you would know my Father also."

²⁰ These words he spoke in the treasury, as he taught in the temple; but no one arrested him, because his hour had not yet come.

²¹ So he said to them again, "I am going away, and you will seek me, and you will die in your sin. Where I am going, you cannot come."

²² So the Jews said, "Will he kill himself, since he says, 'Where I am going, you cannot come'?"

²³ He said to them, "You are from below; I am from above. You are of this world; I am not of this world.

²⁴ "I told you that you would die in your sins, for unless you believe that I am he you will die in your sins."

²⁵ So they said to him, "Who are you?" Jesus said to them, "Just what I have been telling you from the beginning.

²⁶ "I have much to say about you and much to judge, but he who sent me is true, and I declare to the world what I have heard from him."

²⁷ They did not understand that he had been speaking to them about the Father.

²⁸ So Jesus said to them, "When you have lifted up the Son of Man, then you will know that I am he, and that I do nothing on my own authority, but speak just as the Father taught me.

²⁹ "And he who sent me is with me. He has not left me

alone, for I always do the things that are pleasing to him."

30 As he was saying these things, many believed in him.

31 So Jesus said to the Jews who had believed him, "If you abide in my word, you are truly my disciples,

32 "and you will know the truth, and the truth will set you free."

33 They answered him, "We are offspring of Abraham and have never been enslaved to anyone. How is it that you say, 'You will become free'?"

34 Jesus answered them, "Truly, truly, I say to you, everyone who practices sin is a slave to sin.

35 "The slave does not remain in the house forever; the son remains forever.

36 "So if the Son sets you free, you will be free indeed.

37 "I know that you are offspring of Abraham; yet you seek to kill me because my word finds no place in you.

38 "I speak of what I have seen with my Father, and you do what you have heard from your father."

39 They answered him, "Abraham is our father." Jesus said to them, "If you were Abraham's children, you would be doing the works Abraham did,

40 "but now you seek to kill me, a man who has told you the truth that I heard from God. This is not what Abraham did.

41 "You are doing the works your father did." They said to him, "We were not born of sexual immorality. We have one Father—even God."

42 Jesus said to them, "If God were your Father, you would love me, for I came from God and I am here. I came not of my own accord, but he sent me.

43 "Why do you not understand what I say? It is because you cannot bear to hear my word.

44 "You are of your father the devil, and your will is to do your father's desires. He was a murderer from the beginning, and does not stand in the truth, because there is no truth in him. When he lies, he speaks out of his own character, for he is a liar and the father of lies.

45 "But because I tell the truth, you do not believe me.

46 "Which one of you convicts me of sin? If I tell the truth, why do you not believe me?

47 "Whoever is of God hears the words of God. The reason why you do not hear them is that you are not of God."

⁴⁸ The Jews answered him, "Are we not right in saying that you are a Samaritan and have a demon?"

⁴⁹ Jesus answered, "I do not have a demon, but I honor my Father, and you dishonor me.

⁵⁰ "Yet I do not seek my own glory; there is One who seeks it, and he is the judge.

⁵¹ "Truly, truly, I say to you, if anyone keeps my word, he will never see death."

⁵² The Jews said to him, "Now we know that you have a demon! Abraham died, as did the prophets, yet you say, 'If anyone keeps my word, he will never taste death.'

⁵³ "Are you greater than our father Abraham, who died? And the prophets died! Who do you make yourself out to be?"

⁵⁴ Jesus answered, "If I glorify myself, my glory is nothing. It is my Father who glorifies me, of whom you say, 'He is our God.'

⁵⁵ "But you have not known him. I know him. If I were to say that I do not know him, I would be a liar like you, but I do know him and I keep his word.

⁵⁶ "Your father Abraham rejoiced that he would see my day. He saw it and was glad."

⁵⁷ So the Jews said to him, "You are not yet fifty years old, and have you seen Abraham?"

⁵⁸ Jesus said to them, "Truly, truly, I say to you, before Abraham was, I am."

⁵⁹ So they picked up stones to throw at him, but Jesus hid himself and went out of the temple.

CHAPTER 9

¹ As he passed by, he saw a man blind from birth.

² And his disciples asked him, "Rabbi, who sinned, this man or his parents, that he was born blind?"

³ Jesus answered, "It was not that this man sinned, or his parents, but that the works of God might be displayed in him.

⁴ "We must work the works of him who sent me while it is day; night is coming, when no one can work.

⁵ "As long as I am in the world, I am the light of the world."

⁶ Having said these things, he spit on the ground and made mud with the saliva. Then he anointed the man's eyes with the mud

⁷ and said to him, "Go, wash in the pool of Siloam" (which means Sent). So he went and washed and came back seeing.

⁸ The neighbors and those

who had seen him before as a beggar were saying, "Is this not the man who used to sit and beg?"

⁹ Some said, "It is he." Others said, "No, but he is like him." He kept saying, "I am the man."

¹⁰ So they said to him, "Then how were your eyes opened?"

¹¹ He answered, "The man called Jesus made mud and anointed my eyes and said to me, 'Go to Siloam and wash.' So I went and washed and received my sight."

¹² They said to him, "Where is he?" He said, "I do not know."

¹³ They brought to the Pharisees the man who had formerly been blind.

¹⁴ Now it was a Sabbath day when Jesus made the mud and opened his eyes.

¹⁵ So the Pharisees again asked him how he had received his sight. And he said to them, "He put mud on my eyes, and I washed, and I see."

¹⁶ Some of the Pharisees said, "This man is not from God, for he does not keep the Sabbath." But others said, "How can a man who is a sinner do such signs?" And there was a division among them.

¹⁷ So they said again to the blind man, "What do you say about him, since he has opened your eyes?" He said, "He is a prophet."

¹⁸ The Jews did not believe that he had been blind and had received his sight, until they called the parents of the man who had received his sight

¹⁹ and asked them, "Is this your son, who you say was born blind? How then does he now see?"

²⁰ His parents answered, "We know that this is our son and that he was born blind.

²¹ "But how he now sees we do not know, nor do we know who opened his eyes. Ask him; he is of age. He will speak for himself."

²² (His parents said these things because they feared the Jews, for the Jews had already agreed that if anyone should confess Jesus to be Christ, he was to be put out of the synagogue.)

²³ Therefore his parents said, "He is of age; ask him."

²⁴ So for the second time they called the man who had been blind and said to him, "Give glory to God. We know that this man is a sinner."

²⁵ He answered, "Whether he is a sinner I do not know. One thing I do know, that though I was blind, now I see."

²⁶ They said to him, "What

did he do to you? How did he open your eyes?"

²⁷ He answered them, "I have told you already, and you would not listen. Why do you want to hear it again? Do you also want to become his disciples?"

²⁸ And they reviled him, saying, "You are his disciple, but we are disciples of Moses. ²⁹ "We know that God has spoken to Moses, but as for this man, we do not know where he comes from."

³⁰ The man answered, "Why, this is an amazing thing! You do not know where he comes from, and yet he opened my eyes. ³¹ "We know that God does not listen to sinners, but if anyone is a worshiper of God and does his will, God listens to him. ³² "Never since the world began has it been heard that anyone opened the eyes of a man born blind. ³³ "If this man were not from God, he could do nothing."

³⁴ They answered him, "You were born in utter sin, and would you teach us?" And they cast him out.

³⁵ Jesus heard that they had cast him out, and having found him he said, "Do you believe in the Son of Man?"

³⁶ He answered, "And who

is he, sir, that I may believe in him?"

³⁷ Jesus said to him, "You have seen him, and it is he who is speaking to you."

³⁸ He said, "Lord, I believe," and he worshiped him.

³⁹ Jesus said, "For judgment I came into this world, that those who do not see may see, and those who see may become blind."

⁴⁰ Some of the Pharisees near him heard these things, and said to him, "Are we also blind?"

⁴¹ Jesus said to them, "If you were blind, you would have no guilt; but now that you say, 'We see,' your guilt remains.

CHAPTER 10

¹ "Truly, truly, I say to you, he who does not enter the sheepfold by the door but climbs in by another way, that man is a thief and a robber.

² "But he who enters by the door is the shepherd of the sheep.

³ "To him the gatekeeper opens. The sheep hear his voice, and he calls his own sheep by name and leads them out.

⁴ "When he has brought out all his own, he goes before them, and the sheep follow him, for they know his voice.

⁵ "A stranger they will not

follow, but they will flee from him, for they do not know the voice of strangers."

⁶ This figure of speech Jesus used with them, but they did not understand what he was saying to them.

⁷ So Jesus again said to them, "Truly, truly, I say to you, I am the door of the sheep.

⁸ "All who came before me are thieves and robbers, but the sheep did not listen to them.

⁹ "I am the door. If anyone enters by me, he will be saved and will go in and out and find pasture.

¹⁰ "The thief comes only to steal and kill and destroy. I came that they may have life and have it abundantly.

¹¹ "I am the good shepherd. The good shepherd lays down his life for the sheep.

¹² "He who is a hired hand and not a shepherd, who does not own the sheep, sees the wolf coming and leaves the sheep and flees, and the wolf snatches them and scatters them.

¹³ "He flees because he is a hired hand and cares nothing for the sheep.

¹⁴ "I am the good shepherd. I know my own and my own know me,

¹⁵ "just as the Father knows me and I know the Father; and I lay down my life for the sheep.

¹⁶ "And I have other sheep that are not of this fold. I must bring them also, and they will listen to my voice. So there will be one flock, one shepherd.

¹⁷ "For this reason the Father loves me, because I lay down my life that I may take it up again.

¹⁸ "No one takes it from me, but I lay it down of my own accord. I have authority to lay it down, and I have authority to take it up again. This charge I have received from my Father."

¹⁹ There was again a division among the Jews because of these words.

²⁰ Many of them said, "He has a demon, and is insane; why listen to him?"

²¹ Others said, "These are not the words of one who is oppressed by a demon. Can a demon open the eyes of the blind?"

²² At that time the Feast of Dedication took place at Jerusalem. It was winter,

²³ and Jesus was walking in the temple, in the colonnade of Solomon.

²⁴ So the Jews gathered around him and said to him, "How long will you keep us

in suspense? If you are the Christ, tell us plainly."

²⁵ Jesus answered them, "I told you, and you do not believe. The works that I do in my Father's name bear witness about me,

²⁶ "but you do not believe because you are not among my sheep.

²⁷ "My sheep hear my voice, and I know them, and they follow me.

²⁸ "I give them eternal life, and they will never perish, and no one will snatch them out of my hand.

²⁹ "My Father, who has given them to me, is greater than all, and no one is able to snatch them out of the Father's hand.

³⁰ "I and the Father are one."

³¹ The Jews picked up stones again to stone him.

³² Jesus answered them, "I have shown you many good works from the Father; for which of them are you going to stone me?"

³³ The Jews answered him, "It is not for a good work that we are going to stone you but for blasphemy, because you, being a man, make yourself God."

³⁴ Jesus answered them, "Is it not written in your Law, 'I said, you are gods'?

³⁵ "If he called them gods to whom the word of God came—and Scripture cannot be broken—

³⁶ "do you say of him whom the Father consecrated and sent into the world, 'You are blaspheming,' because I said, 'I am the Son of God'?

³⁷ "If I am not doing the works of my Father, then do not believe me;

³⁸ "but if I do them, even though you do not believe me, believe the works, that you may know and understand that the Father is in me and I am in the Father."

³⁹ Again they sought to arrest him, but he escaped from their hands.

⁴⁰ He went away again across the Jordan to the place where John had been baptizing at first, and there he remained.

⁴¹ And many came to him. And they said, "John did no sign, but everything that John said about this man was true."

⁴² And many believed in him there.

CHAPTER 11

¹ Now a certain man was ill, Lazarus of Bethany, the village of Mary and her sister Martha.

² It was Mary who anointed the Lord with ointment and wiped his feet with her

hair, whose brother Lazarus was ill.

³ So the sisters sent to him, saying, "Lord, he whom you love is ill."

⁴ But when Jesus heard it he said, "This illness does not lead to death. It is for the glory of God, so that the Son of God may be glorified through it."

⁵ Now Jesus loved Martha and her sister and Lazarus.

⁶ So, when he heard that Lazarus was ill, he stayed two days longer in the place where he was.

⁷ Then after this he said to the disciples, "Let us go to Judea again."

⁸ The disciples said to him, "Rabbi, the Jews were just now seeking to stone you, and are you going there again?"

⁹ Jesus answered, "Are there not twelve hours in the day? If anyone walks in the day, he does not stumble, because he sees the light of this world.

¹⁰ "But if anyone walks in the night, he stumbles, because the light is not in him."

¹¹ After saying these things, he said to them, "Our friend Lazarus has fallen asleep, but I go to awaken him."

¹² The disciples said to him, "Lord, if he has fallen asleep, he will recover."

¹³ Now Jesus had spoken of his death, but they thought that he meant taking rest in sleep.

¹⁴ Then Jesus told them plainly, "Lazarus has died,

¹⁵ "and for your sake I am glad that I was not there, so that you may believe. But let us go to him."

¹⁶ So Thomas, called the Twin, said to his fellow disciples, "Let us also go, that we may die with him."

¹⁷ Now when Jesus came, he found that Lazarus had already been in the tomb four days.

¹⁸ Bethany was near Jerusalem, about two miles off,

¹⁹ and many of the Jews had come to Martha and Mary to console them concerning their brother.

²⁰ So when Martha heard that Jesus was coming, she went and met him, but Mary remained seated in the house.

²¹ Martha said to Jesus, "Lord, if you had been here, my brother would not have died.

²² "But even now I know that whatever you ask from God, God will give you."

²³ Jesus said to her, "Your brother will rise again."

²⁴ Martha said to him, "I know that he will rise again

in the resurrection on the last day."

25 Jesus said to her, "I am the resurrection and the life. Whoever believes in me, though he die, yet shall he live,

26 "and everyone who lives and believes in me shall never die. Do you believe this?"

27 She said to him, "Yes, Lord; I believe that you are the Christ, the Son of God, who is coming into the world."

28 When she had said this, she went and called her sister Mary, saying in private, "The Teacher is here and is calling for you."

29 And when she heard it, she rose quickly and went to him.

30 Now Jesus had not yet come into the village, but was still in the place where Martha had met him.

31 When the Jews who were with her in the house, consoling her, saw Mary rise quickly and go out, they followed her, supposing that she was going to the tomb to weep there.

32 Now when Mary came to where Jesus was and saw him, she fell at his feet, saying to him, "Lord, if you had been here, my brother would not have died."

33 When Jesus saw her weeping, and the Jews who had come with her also weeping, he was deeply moved in his spirit and greatly troubled.

34 And he said, "Where have you laid him?" They said to him, "Lord, come and see."

35 Jesus wept.

36 So the Jews said, "See how he loved him!"

37 But some of them said, "Could not he who opened the eyes of the blind man also have kept this man from dying?"

38 Then Jesus, deeply moved again, came to the tomb. It was a cave, and a stone lay against it.

39 Jesus said, "Take away the stone." Martha, the sister of the dead man, said to him, "Lord, by this time there will be an odor, for he has been dead four days."

40 Jesus said to her, "Did I not tell you that if you believed you would see the glory of God?"

41 So they took away the stone. And Jesus lifted up his eyes and said, "Father, I thank you that you have heard me.

42 "I knew that you always hear me, but I said this on account of the people standing around, that they may believe that you sent me."

43 When he had said these

things, he cried out with a loud voice, "Lazarus, come out."

44 The man who had died came out, his hands and feet bound with linen strips, and his face wrapped with a cloth. Jesus said to them, "Unbind him, and let him go."

45 Many of the Jews therefore, who had come with Mary and had seen what he did, believed in him,

46 but some of them went to the Pharisees and told them what Jesus had done.

47 So the chief priests and the Pharisees gathered the council and said, "What are we to do? For this man performs many signs.

48 "If we let him go on like this, everyone will believe in him, and the Romans will come and take away both our place and our nation."

49 But one of them, Caiaphas, who was high priest that year, said to them, "You know nothing at all.

50 "Nor do you understand that it is better for you that one man should die for the people, not that the whole nation should perish."

51 He did not say this of his own accord, but being high priest that year he prophesied that Jesus would die for the nation,

52 and not for the nation only, but also to gather into one the children of God who are scattered abroad.

53 So from that day on they made plans to put him to death.

54 Jesus therefore no longer walked openly among the Jews, but went from there to the region near the wilderness, to a town called Ephraim, and there he stayed with the disciples.

55 Now the Passover of the Jews was at hand, and many went up from the country to Jerusalem before the Passover to purify themselves.

56 They were looking for Jesus and saying to one another as they stood in the temple, "What do you think? That he will not come to the feast at all?"

57 Now the chief priests and the Pharisees had given orders that if anyone knew where he was, he should let them know, so that they might arrest him.

CHAPTER 12

1 Six days before the Passover, Jesus therefore came to Bethany, where Lazarus was, whom Jesus had raised from the dead.

2 So they gave a dinner for him there. Martha served, and

Lazarus was one of those reclining with him at table.

3 Mary therefore took a pound of expensive ointment made from pure nard, and anointed the feet of Jesus and wiped his feet with her hair. The house was filled with the fragrance of the perfume.

4 But Judas Iscariot, one of his disciples (he who was about to betray him), said,

5 "Why was this ointment not sold for three hundred denarii and given to the poor?"

6 He said this, not because he cared about the poor, but because he was a thief, and having charge of the moneybag he used to help himself to what was put into it.

7 Jesus said, "Leave her alone, so that she may keep it for the day of my burial.

8 "For the poor you always have with you, but you do not always have me."

9 When the large crowd of the Jews learned that Jesus was there, they came, not only on account of him but also to see Lazarus, whom he had raised from the dead.

10 So the chief priests made plans to put Lazarus to death as well,

11 because on account of him many of the Jews were going away and believing in Jesus.

12 The next day the large crowd that had come to the feast heard that Jesus was coming to Jerusalem.

13 So they took branches of palm trees and went out to meet him, crying out, "Hosanna! Blessed is he who comes in the name of the Lord, even the King of Israel!"

14 And Jesus found a young donkey and sat on it, just as it is written,

15 "Fear not, daughter of Zion; behold, your king is coming, sitting on a donkey's colt!"

16 His disciples did not understand these things at first, but when Jesus was glorified, then they remembered that these things had been written about him and had been done to him.

17 The crowd that had been with him when he called Lazarus out of the tomb and raised him from the dead continued to bear witness.

18 The reason why the crowd went to meet him was that they heard he had done this sign.

19 So the Pharisees said to one another, "You see that you are gaining nothing. Look, the world has gone after him."

20 Now among those who

went up to worship at the feast were some Greeks.

²¹ So these came to Philip, who was from Bethsaida in Galilee, and asked him, "Sir, we wish to see Jesus."

²² Philip went and told Andrew; Andrew and Philip went and told Jesus.

²³ And Jesus answered them, "The hour has come for the Son of Man to be glorified.

²⁴ "Truly, truly, I say to you, unless a grain of wheat falls into the earth and dies, it remains alone; but if it dies, it bears much fruit.

²⁵ "Whoever loves his life loses it, and whoever hates his life in this world will keep it for eternal life.

²⁶ "If anyone serves me, he must follow me; and where I am, there will my servant be also. If anyone serves me, the Father will honor him.

²⁷ "Now is my soul troubled. And what shall I say? 'Father, save me from this hour'? But for this purpose I have come to this hour.

²⁸ "Father, glorify your name." Then a voice came from heaven: "I have glorified it, and I will glorify it again."

²⁹ The crowd that stood there and heard it said that it had thundered. Others said, "An angel has spoken to him."

³⁰ Jesus answered, "This voice has come for your sake, not mine.

³¹ "Now is the judgment of this world; now will the ruler of this world be cast out.

³² "And I, when I am lifted up from the earth, will draw all people to myself."

³³ He said this to show by what kind of death he was going to die.

³⁴ So the crowd answered him, "We have heard from the Law that the Christ remains forever. How can you say that the Son of Man must be lifted up? Who is this Son of Man?"

³⁵ So Jesus said to them, "The light is among you for a little while longer. Walk while you have the light, lest darkness overtake you. The one who walks in the darkness does not know where he is going.

³⁶ "While you have the light, believe in the light, that you may become sons of light." When Jesus had said these things, he departed and hid himself from them.

³⁷ Though he had done so many signs before them, they still did not believe in him,

³⁸ so that the word spoken by the prophet Isaiah might be fulfilled: "Lord, who has believed what he heard from

us, and to whom has the arm of the Lord been revealed?"

³⁹ Therefore they could not believe. For again Isaiah said,

⁴⁰ "He has blinded their eyes and hardened their heart, lest they see with their eyes, and understand with their heart, and turn, and I would heal them."

⁴¹ Isaiah said these things because he saw his glory and spoke of him.

⁴² Nevertheless, many even of the authorities believed in him, but for fear of the Pharisees they did not confess it, so that they would not be put out of the synagogue;

⁴³ for they loved the glory that comes from man more than the glory that comes from God.

⁴⁴ And Jesus cried out and said, "Whoever believes in me, believes not in me but in him who sent me.

⁴⁵ And whoever sees me sees him who sent me.

⁴⁶ "I have come into the world as light, so that whoever believes in me may not remain in darkness.

⁴⁷ "If anyone hears my words and does not keep them, I do not judge him; for I did not come to judge the world but to save the world.

⁴⁸ "The one who rejects me and does not receive my words has a judge; the word that I have spoken will judge him on the last day.

⁴⁹ "For I have not spoken on my own authority, but the Father who sent me has himself given me a commandment—what to say and what to speak.

⁵⁰ "And I know that his commandment is eternal life. What I say, therefore, I say as the Father has told me."

CHAPTER 13

¹ Now before the Feast of the Passover, when Jesus knew that his hour had come to depart out of this world to the Father, having loved his own who were in the world, he loved them to the end.

² During supper, when the devil had already put it into the heart of Judas Iscariot, Simon's son, to betray him,

³ Jesus, knowing that the Father had given all things into his hands, and that he had come from God and was going back to God,

⁴ rose from supper. He laid aside his outer garments, and taking a towel, tied it around his waist.

⁵ Then he poured water into a basin and began to wash the disciples' feet and to wipe them with the towel that was wrapped around him.

⁶ He came to Simon Peter, who said to him, "Lord, do you wash my feet?"

⁷ Jesus answered him, "What I am doing you do not understand now, but afterward you will understand."

⁸ Peter said to him, "You shall never wash my feet." Jesus answered him, "If I do not wash you, you have no share with me."

⁹ Simon Peter said to him, "Lord, not my feet only but also my hands and my head!"

¹⁰ Jesus said to him, "The one who has bathed does not need to wash, except for his feet, but is completely clean. And you are clean, but not every one of you."

¹¹ For he knew who was to betray him; that was why he said, "Not all of you are clean."

¹² When he had washed their feet and put on his outer garments and resumed his place, he said to them, "Do you understand what I have done to you?

¹³ You call me Teacher and Lord, and you are right, for so I am.

¹⁴ If I then, your Lord and Teacher, have washed your feet, you also ought to wash one another's feet.

¹⁵ For I have given you an example, that you also should do just as I have done to you.

¹⁶ "Truly, truly, I say to you, a servant is not greater than his master, nor is a messenger greater than the one who sent him.

¹⁷ "If you know these things, blessed are you if you do them.

¹⁸ "I am not speaking of all of you; I know whom I have chosen. But the Scripture will be fulfilled, 'He who ate my bread has lifted his heel against me.'

¹⁹ "I am telling you this now, before it takes place, that when it does take place you may believe that I am he.

²⁰ "Truly, truly, I say to you, whoever receives the one I send receives me, and whoever receives me receives the one who sent me."

²¹ After saying these things, Jesus was troubled in his spirit, and testified, "Truly, truly, I say to you, one of you will betray me."

²² The disciples looked at one another, uncertain of whom he spoke.

²³ One of his disciples, whom Jesus loved, was reclining at table at Jesus' side,

²⁴ so Simon Peter motioned to him to ask Jesus of whom he was speaking.

²⁵ So that disciple, leaning back against Jesus, said to him, "Lord, who is it?"

²⁶ Jesus answered, "It is he to whom I will give this morsel of bread when I have dipped it." So when he had dipped the morsel, he gave it to Judas, the son of Simon Iscariot.

²⁷ Then after he had taken the morsel, Satan entered into him. Jesus said to him, "What you are going to do, do quickly."

²⁸ Now no one at the table knew why he said this to him.

²⁹ Some thought that, because Judas had the money-bag, Jesus was telling him, "Buy what we need for the feast," or that he should give something to the poor.

³⁰ So, after receiving the morsel of bread, he immediately went out. And it was night.

³¹ When he had gone out, Jesus said, "Now is the Son of Man glorified, and God is glorified in him.

³² "If God is glorified in him, God will also glorify him in himself, and glorify him at once.

³³ "Little children, yet a little while I am with you. You will seek me, and just as I said to the Jews, so now I also say to you, 'Where I am going you cannot come.'

³⁴ "A new commandment I give to you, that you love one

another: just as I have loved you, you also are to love one another.

³⁵ "By this all people will know that you are my disciples, if you have love for one another."

³⁶ Simon Peter said to him, "Lord, where are you going?" Jesus answered him, "Where I am going you cannot follow me now, but you will follow afterward."

³⁷ Peter said to him, "Lord, why can I not follow you now? I will lay down my life for you."

³⁸ Jesus answered, "Will you lay down your life for me? Truly, truly, I say to you, the rooster will not crow till you have denied me three times.

CHAPTER 14

¹ "Let not your hearts be troubled. Believe in God; believe also in me.

² "In my Father's house are many rooms; if it were not so, I would have told you; for I go to prepare a place for you.

³ "And if I go and prepare a place for you, I will come again and will take you to myself, that where I am you may be also.

⁴ "And you know the way to where I am going."

⁵ Thomas said to him, "Lord, we do not know where you

are going. How can we know the way?"

6 Jesus said to him, "I am the way, and the truth, and the life. No one comes to the Father except through me.

7 "If you had known me, you would have known my Father also. From now on you do know him and have seen him."

8 Philip said to him, "Lord, show us the Father, and it is enough for us."

9 Jesus said to him, "Have I been with you so long, and you still do not know me, Philip? Whoever has seen me has seen the Father. How can you say, 'Show us the Father'?

10 "Do you not believe that I am in the Father and the Father is in me? The words that I say to you I do not speak on my own authority, but the Father who dwells in me does his works.

11 "Believe me that I am in the Father and the Father is in me, or else believe on account of the works themselves.

12 "Truly, truly, I say to you, whoever believes in me will also do the works that I do; and greater works than these will he do, because I am going to the Father.

13 "Whatever you ask in my name, this I will do, that the Father may be glorified in the Son.

14 "If you ask me anything in my name, I will do it.

15 "If you love me, you will keep my commandments.

16 "And I will ask the Father, and he will give you another Helper, to be with you forever,

17 "even the Spirit of truth, whom the world cannot receive, because it neither sees him nor knows him. You know him, for he dwells with you and will be in you.

18 "I will not leave you as orphans; I will come to you.

19 "Yet a little while and the world will see me no more, but you will see me. Because I live, you also will live.

20 "In that day you will know that I am in my Father, and you in me, and I in you.

21 "Whoever has my commandments and keeps them, he it is who loves me. And he who loves me will be loved by my Father, and I will love him and manifest myself to him."

22 Judas (not Iscariot) said to him, "Lord, how is it that you will manifest yourself to us, and not to the world?"

23 Jesus answered him, "If anyone loves me, he will keep my word, and my Father will love him, and we will come to him and make our home with him.

CHAPTER 15

24 "Whoever does not love me does not keep my words. And the word that you hear is not mine but the Father's who sent me.

25 "These things I have spoken to you while I am still with you.

26 "But the Helper, the Holy Spirit, whom the Father will send in my name, he will teach you all things and bring to your remembrance all that I have said to you.

27 "Peace I leave with you; my peace I give to you. Not as the world gives do I give to you. Let not your hearts be troubled, neither let them be afraid.

28 "You heard me say to you, 'I am going away, and I will come to you.' If you loved me, you would have rejoiced, because I am going to the Father, for the Father is greater than I.

29 "And now I have told you before it takes place, so that when it does take place you may believe.

30 "I will no longer talk much with you, for the ruler of this world is coming. He has no claim on me,

31 "but I do as the Father has commanded me, so that the world may know that I love the Father. Rise, let us go from here.

1 "I am the true vine, and my Father is the vinedresser.

2 "Every branch in me that does not bear fruit he takes away, and every branch that does bear fruit he prunes, that it may bear more fruit.

3 "Already you are clean because of the word that I have spoken to you.

4 "Abide in me, and I in you. As the branch cannot bear fruit by itself, unless it abides in the vine, neither can you, unless you abide in me.

5 "I am the vine; you are the branches. Whoever abides in me and I in him, he it is that bears much fruit, for apart from me you can do nothing.

6 "If anyone does not abide in me he is thrown away like a branch and withers; and the branches are gathered, thrown into the fire, and burned.

7 "If you abide in me, and my words abide in you, ask whatever you wish, and it will be done for you.

8 "By this my Father is glorified, that you bear much fruit and so prove to be my disciples.

9 "As the Father has loved me, so have I loved you. Abide in my love.

10 "If you keep my commandments, you will abide

in my love, just as I have kept my Father's commandments and abide in his love.

¹¹ "These things I have spoken to you, that my joy may be in you, and that your joy may be full.

¹² "This is my commandment, that you love one another as I have loved you.

¹³ "Greater love has no one than this, that someone lay down his life for his friends.

¹⁴ "You are my friends if you do what I command you.

¹⁵ "No longer do I call you servants, for the servant does not know what his master is doing; but I have called you friends, for all that I have heard from my Father I have made known to you.

¹⁶ "You did not choose me, but I chose you and appointed you that you should go and bear fruit and that your fruit should abide, so that whatever you ask the Father in my name, he may give it to you.

¹⁷ "These things I command you, so that you will love one another.

¹⁸ "If the world hates you, know that it has hated me before it hated you.

¹⁹ "If you were of the world, the world would love you as its own; but because you are not of the world, but I chose you out of the world, therefore the world hates you.

²⁰ "Remember the word that I said to you: 'A servant is not greater than his master.' If they persecuted me, they will also persecute you. If they kept my word, they will also keep yours.

²¹ "But all these things they will do to you on account of my name, because they do not know him who sent me.

²² "If I had not come and spoken to them, they would not have been guilty of sin, but now they have no excuse for their sin.

²³ "Whoever hates me hates my Father also.

²⁴ "If I had not done among them the works that no one else did, they would not be guilty of sin, but now they have seen and hated both me and my Father.

²⁵ "But the word that is written in their Law must be fulfilled: 'They hated me without a cause.'

²⁶ "But when the Helper comes, whom I will send to you from the Father, the Spirit of truth, who proceeds from the Father, he will bear witness about me.

²⁷ "And you also will bear witness, because you have been with me from the beginning.

CHAPTER 16

1 "I have said all these things to you to keep you from falling away.

2 "They will put you out of the synagogues. Indeed, the hour is coming when whoever kills you will think he is offering service to God.

3 "And they will do these things because they have not known the Father, nor me.

4 "But I have said these things to you, that when their hour comes you may remember that I told them to you. I did not say these things to you from the beginning, because I was with you.

5 "But now I am going to him who sent me, and none of you asks me, 'Where are you going?'

6 "But because I have said these things to you, sorrow has filled your heart.

7 "Nevertheless, I tell you the truth: it is to your advantage that I go away, for if I do not go away, the Helper will not come to you. But if I go, I will send him to you.

8 "And when he comes, he will convict the world concerning sin and righteousness and judgment;

9 "concerning sin, because they do not believe in me;

10 "concerning righteousness, because I go to the Father, and you will see me no longer;

11 "concerning judgment, because the ruler of this world is judged.

12 "I still have many things to say to you, but you cannot bear them now.

13 "When the Spirit of truth comes, he will guide you into all the truth, for he will not speak on his own authority, but whatever he hears he will speak, and he will declare to you the things that are to come.

14 "He will glorify me, for he will take what is mine and declare it to you.

15 "All that the Father has is mine; therefore I said that he will take what is mine and declare it to you.

16 "A little while, and you will see me no longer; and again a little while, and you will see me."

17 So some of his disciples said to one another, "What is this that he says to us, 'A little while, and you will not see me, and again a little while, and you will see me'; and, 'because I am going to the Father'?"

18 So they were saying, "What does he mean by 'a little while'? We do not know what he is talking about."

19 Jesus knew that they

wanted to ask him, so he said to them, "Is this what you are asking yourselves, what I meant by saying, 'A little while and you will not see me, and again a little while and you will see me'?

20 "Truly, truly, I say to you, you will weep and lament, but the world will rejoice. You will be sorrowful, but your sorrow will turn into joy.

21 "When a woman is giving birth, she has sorrow because her hour has come, but when she has delivered the baby, she no longer remembers the anguish, for joy that a human being has been born into the world.

22 "So also you have sorrow now, but I will see you again, and your hearts will rejoice, and no one will take your joy from you.

23 "In that day you will ask nothing of me. Truly, truly, I say to you, whatever you ask of the Father in my name, he will give it to you.

24 "Until now you have asked nothing in my name. Ask, and you will receive, that your joy may be full.

25 "I have said these things to you in figures of speech. The hour is coming when I will no longer speak to you in figures of speech but will tell you plainly about the Father.

26 "In that day you will ask in my name, and I do not say to you that I will ask the Father on your behalf;

27 "for the Father himself loves you, because you have loved me and have believed that I came from God.

28 "I came from the Father and have come into the world, and now I am leaving the world and going to the Father."

29 His disciples said, "Ah, now you are speaking plainly and not using figurative speech!

30 "Now we know that you know all things and do not need anyone to question you; this is why we believe that you came from God."

31 Jesus answered them, "Do you now believe?

32 "Behold, the hour is coming, indeed it has come, when you will be scattered, each to his own home, and will leave me alone. Yet I am not alone, for the Father is with me.

33 "I have said these things to you, that in me you may have peace. In the world you will have tribulation. But take heart; I have overcome the world."

CHAPTER 17

1 When Jesus had spoken these words, he lifted up his

eyes to heaven, and said, "Father, the hour has come; glorify your Son that the Son may glorify you,

² "since you have given him authority over all flesh, to give eternal life to all whom you have given him.

³ "And this is eternal life, that they know you the only true God, and Jesus Christ whom you have sent.

⁴ "I glorified you on earth, having accomplished the work that you gave me to do.

⁵ "And now, Father, glorify me in your own presence with the glory that I had with you before the world existed.

⁶ "I have manifested your name to the people whom you gave me out of the world. Yours they were, and you gave them to me, and they have kept your word.

⁷ "Now they know that everything that you have given me is from you.

⁸ "For I have given them the words that you gave me, and they have received them and have come to know in truth that I came from you; and they have believed that you sent me.

⁹ "I am praying for them. I am not praying for the world but for those whom you have given me, for they are yours.

¹⁰ "All mine are yours, and yours are mine, and I am glorified in them.

¹¹ "And I am no longer in the world, but they are in the world, and I am coming to you. Holy Father, keep them in your name, which you have given me, that they may be one, even as we are one.

¹² "While I was with them, I kept them in your name, which you have given me. I have guarded them, and not one of them has been lost except the son of destruction, that the Scripture might be fulfilled.

¹³ "But now I am coming to you, and these things I speak in the world, that they may have my joy fulfilled in themselves.

¹⁴ "I have given them your word, and the world has hated them because they are not of the world, just as I am not of the world.

¹⁵ "I do not ask that you take them out of the world, but that you keep them from the evil one.

¹⁶ "They are not of the world, just as I am not of the world.

¹⁷ "Sanctify them in the truth; your word is truth.

¹⁸ "As you sent me into the world, so I have sent them into the world.

¹⁹ "And for their sake I consecrate myself, that they

also may be sanctified in truth.

20 "I do not ask for these only, but also for those who will believe in me through their word,

21 "that they may all be one, just as you, Father, are in me, and I in you, that they also may be in us, so that the world may believe that you have sent me.

22 "The glory that you have given me I have given to them, that they may be one even as we are one,

23 "I in them and you in me, that they may become perfectly one, so that the world may know that you sent me and loved them even as you loved me.

24 "Father, I desire that they also, whom you have given me, may be with me where I am, to see my glory that you have given me because you loved me before the foundation of the world.

25 "O righteous Father, even though the world *does not know* you, I know you, and these know that you have sent me.

26 "I made known to them your name, and I will continue to make it known, that the love with which you have loved me may be in them, and I in them."

CHAPTER 18

1 When Jesus had spoken these words, he went out with his disciples across the brook Kidron, where there was a garden, which he and his disciples entered.

2 Now Judas, who betrayed him, also knew the place, for Jesus often met there with his disciples.

3 So Judas, having procured a band of soldiers and some officers from the chief priests and the Pharisees, went there with lanterns and torches and weapons.

4 Then Jesus, knowing all that would happen to him, came forward and said to them, "Whom do you seek?"

5 They answered him, "Jesus of Nazareth." Jesus said to them, "I am he." Judas, who betrayed him, was standing with them.

6 When Jesus said to them, "I am he," they drew back and fell to the ground.

7 So he asked them again, "Whom do you seek?" And they said, "Jesus of Nazareth."

8 Jesus answered, "I told you that I am he. So, if you seek me, let these men go."

9 This was to fulfil the word that he had spoken: "Of those whom you gave me I have lost not one."

10 Then Simon Peter, having

a sword, drew it and struck the high priest's servant and cut off his right ear. (The servant's name was Malchus.)

¹¹ So Jesus said to Peter, "Put your sword into its sheath; shall I not drink the cup that the Father has given me?"

¹² So the band of soldiers and their captain and the officers of the Jews arrested Jesus and bound him.

¹³ First they led him to Annas, for he was the father-in-law of Caiaphas, who was high priest that year.

¹⁴ It was Caiaphas who had advised the Jews that it would be expedient that one man should die for the people.

¹⁵ Simon Peter followed Jesus, and so did another disciple. Since that disciple was known to the high priest, he entered with Jesus into the courtyard of the high priest,

¹⁶ but Peter stood outside at the door. So the other disciple, who was known to the high priest, went out and spoke to the servant girl who kept watch at the door, and brought Peter in.

¹⁷ The servant girl at the door said to Peter, "You also are not one of this man's disciples, are you?" He said, "I am not."

¹⁸ Now the servants and officers had made a charcoal fire, because it was cold, and they were standing and warming themselves. Peter also was with them, standing and warming himself.

¹⁹ The high priest then questioned Jesus about his disciples and his teaching.

²⁰ Jesus answered him, "I have spoken openly to the world. I have always taught in synagogues and in the temple, where all Jews come together. I have said nothing in secret.

²¹ "Why do you ask me? Ask those who have heard me what I said to them; they know what I said."

²² When he had said these things, one of the officers standing by struck Jesus with his hand, saying, "Is that how you answer the high priest?"

²³ Jesus answered him, "If what I said is wrong, bear witness about the wrong; but if what I said is right, why do you strike me?"

²⁴ Annas then sent him bound to Caiaphas the high priest.

²⁵ Now Simon Peter was standing and warming himself. So they said to him, "You also are not one of his disciples, are you?" He denied it and said, "I am not."

²⁶ One of the servants of the high priest, a relative of the

man whose ear Peter had cut off, asked, "Did I not see you in the garden with him?"

27 Peter again denied it, and at once a rooster crowed.

28 Then they led Jesus from the house of Caiaphas to the governor's headquarters. It was early morning. They themselves did not enter the governor's headquarters, so that they would not be defiled, but could eat the Passover.

29 So Pilate went outside to them and said, "What accusation do you bring against this man?"

30 They answered him, "If this man were not doing evil, we would not have delivered him over to you."

31 Pilate said to them, "Take him yourselves and judge him by your own law." The Jews said to him, "It is not lawful for us to put anyone to death."

32 This was to fulfill the word that Jesus had spoken to show by what kind of death he was going to die.

33 So Pilate entered his headquarters again and called Jesus and said to him, "Are you the King of the Jews?"

34 Jesus answered, "Do you say this of your own accord, or did others say it to you about me?"

35 Pilate answered, "Am I a Jew? Your own nation and the chief priests have delivered you over to me. What have you done?"

36 Jesus answered, "My kingdom is not of this world. If my kingdom were of this world, my servants would have been fighting, that I might not be delivered over to the Jews. But my kingdom is not from the world."

37 Then Pilate said to him, "So you are a king?" Jesus answered, "You say that I am a king. For this purpose I was born and for this purpose I have come into the world— to bear witness to the truth. Everyone who is of the truth listens to my voice."

38 Pilate said to him, "What is truth?" After he had said this, he went back outside to the Jews and told them, "I find no guilt in him.

39 "But you have a custom that I should release one man for you at the Passover. So do you want me to release to you the King of the Jews?"

40 They cried out again, "Not this man, but Barabbas!" Now Barabbas was a robber.

CHAPTER 19

1 Then Pilate took Jesus and flogged him.

2 And the soldiers twisted

together a crown of thorns and put it on his head and arrayed him in a purple robe.

3 They came up to him, saying, "Hail, King of the Jews!" and struck him with their hands.

4 Pilate went out again and said to them, "See, I am bringing him out to you that you may know that I find no guilt in him."

5 So Jesus came out, wearing the crown of thorns and the purple robe. Pilate said to them, "Behold the man!"

6 When the chief priests and the officers saw him, they cried out, "Crucify him, crucify him!" Pilate said to them, "Take him yourselves and crucify him, for I find no guilt in him."

7 The Jews answered him, "We have a law, and according to that law he ought to die because he has made himself the Son of God."

8 When Pilate heard this statement, he was even more afraid.

9 He entered his headquarters again and said to Jesus, "Where are you from?" But Jesus gave him no answer.

10 So Pilate said to him, "You will not speak to me? Do you not know that I have authority to release you and authority to crucify you?"

11 Jesus answered him, "You would have no authority over me at all unless it had been given you from above. Therefore he who delivered me over to you has the greater sin."

12 From then on Pilate sought to release him, but the Jews cried out, "If you release this man, you are not Caesar's friend. Everyone who makes himself a king opposes Caesar."

13 So when Pilate heard these words, he brought Jesus out and sat down on the judgment seat at a place called The Stone Pavement, and in Aramaic Gabbatha.

14 Now it was the day of Preparation of the Passover. It was about the sixth hour. He said to the Jews, "Behold your King!"

15 They cried out, "Away with him, away with him, crucify him!" Pilate said to them, "Shall I crucify your King?" The chief priests answered, "We have no king but Caesar."

16 So he delivered him over to them to be crucified. So they took Jesus,

17 and he went out, bearing his own cross, to the place called The Place of a Skull, which in Aramaic is called Golgotha.

18 There they crucified him,

and with him two others, one on either side, and Jesus between them.

19 Pilate also wrote an inscription and put it on the cross. It read, "Jesus of Nazareth, the King of the Jews." 20 Many of the Jews read this inscription, for the place where Jesus was crucified was near the city, and it was written in Aramaic, in Latin, and in Greek. 21 So the chief priests of the Jews said to Pilate, "Do not write, 'The King of the Jews,' but rather, 'This man said, I am King of the Jews.'" 22 Pilate answered, "What I have written I have written."

23 When the soldiers had crucified Jesus, they took his garments and divided them into four parts, one part for each soldier; also his tunic. But the tunic was seamless, woven in one piece from top to bottom, 24 so they said to one another, "Let us not tear it, but cast lots for it to see whose it shall be." This was to fulfill the Scripture which says, "They divided my garments among them, and for my clothing they cast lots." So the soldiers did these things, 25 but standing by the cross of Jesus were his mother and his mother's sister, Mary the wife of Clopas, and Mary Magdalene. 26 When Jesus saw his mother and the disciple whom he loved standing nearby, he said to his mother, "Woman, behold, your son!" 27 Then he said to the disciple, "Behold, your mother!" And from that hour the disciple took her to his own home.

28 After this, Jesus, knowing that all was now finished, said (to fulfill the Scripture), "I thirst." 29 A jar full of sour wine stood there, so they put a sponge full of the sour wine on a hyssop branch and held it to his mouth. 30 When Jesus had received the sour wine, he said, "It is finished," and he bowed his head and gave up his spirit.

31 Since it was the day of Preparation, and so that the bodies would not remain on the cross on the Sabbath (for that Sabbath was a high day), the Jews asked Pilate that their legs might be broken and that they might be taken away. 32 So the soldiers came and broke the legs of the first, and of the other who had been crucified with him. 33 But when they came to Jesus and saw that he was

already dead, they did not break his legs.

34 But one of the soldiers pierced his side with a spear, and at once there came out blood and water.

35 He who saw it has borne witness—his testimony is true, and he knows that he is telling the truth—that you also may believe.

36 For these things took place that the Scripture might be fulfilled: "Not one of his bones will be broken."

37 And again another Scripture says, "They will look on him whom they have pierced."

38 After these things Joseph of Arimathea, who was a disciple of Jesus, but secretly for fear of the Jews, asked Pilate that he might take away the body of Jesus, and Pilate gave him permission. So he came and took away his body.

39 Nicodemus also, who earlier had come to Jesus by night, came bringing a mixture of myrrh and aloes, about seventy-five pounds in weight.

40 So they took the body of Jesus and bound it in linen cloths with the spices, as is the burial custom of the Jews.

41 Now in the place where he was crucified there was a garden, and in the garden a new tomb in which no one had yet been laid.

42 So because of the Jewish day of Preparation, since the tomb was close at hand, they laid Jesus there.

CHAPTER 20

1 Now on the first day of the week Mary Magdalene came to the tomb early, while it was still dark, and saw that the stone had been taken away from the tomb.

2 So she ran and went to Simon Peter and the other disciple, the one whom Jesus loved, and said to them, "They have taken the Lord out of the tomb, and we do not know where they have laid him."

3 So Peter went out with the other disciple, and they were going toward the tomb.

4 Both of them were running together, but the other disciple outran Peter and reached the tomb first.

5 And stooping to look in, he saw the linen cloths lying there, but he did not go in.

6 Then Simon Peter came, following him, and went into the tomb. He saw the linen cloths lying there,

7 and the face cloth, which had been on Jesus' head, not lying with the linen cloths

but folded up in a place by itself.

8 Then the other disciple, who had reached the tomb first, also went in, and he saw and believed;

9 for as yet they did not understand the Scripture, that he must rise from the dead.

10 Then the disciples went back to their homes.

11 But Mary stood weeping outside the tomb, and as she wept she stooped to look into the tomb.

12 And she saw two angels in white, sitting where the body of Jesus had lain, one at the head and one at the feet.

13 They said to her, "Woman, why are you weeping?" She said to them, "They have taken away my Lord, and I do not know where they have laid him."

14 Having said this, she turned around and saw Jesus standing, but she did not know that it was Jesus.

15 Jesus said to her, "Woman, why are you weeping? Whom are you seeking?" Supposing him to be the gardener, she said to him, "Sir, if you have carried him away, tell me where you have laid him, and I will take him away."

16 Jesus said to her, "Mary." She turned and said to him in Aramaic, "Rabboni!" (which means Teacher).

17 Jesus said to her, "Do not cling to me, for I have not yet ascended to the Father; but go to my brothers and say to them, 'I am ascending to my Father and your Father, to my God and your God.'"

18 Mary Magdalene went and announced to the disciples, "I have seen the Lord"—and that he had said these things to her.

19 On the evening of that day, the first day of the week, the doors being locked where the disciples were for fear of the Jews, Jesus came and stood among them and said to them, "Peace be with you."

20 When he had said this, he showed them his hands and his side. Then the disciples were glad when they saw the Lord.

21 Jesus said to them again, "Peace be with you. As the Father has sent me, even so I am sending you."

22 And when he had said this, he breathed on them and said to them, "Receive the Holy Spirit.

23 "If you forgive the sins of any, they are forgiven them; if you withhold forgiveness from any, it is withheld."

24 Now Thomas, one of the Twelve, called the Twin, was

not with them when Jesus came.

25 So the other disciples told him, "We have seen the Lord." But he said to them, "Unless I see in his hands the mark of the nails, and place my finger into the mark of the nails, and place my hand into his side, I will never believe."

26 Eight days later, his disciples were inside again, and Thomas was with them. Although the doors were locked, Jesus came and stood among them and said, "Peace be with you."

27 Then he said to Thomas, "Put your finger here, and see my hands; and put out your hand, and place it in my side. Do not disbelieve, but believe."

28 Thomas answered him, "My Lord and my God!"

29 Jesus said to him, "Have you believed because you have seen me? Blessed are those who have not seen and yet have believed."

30 Now Jesus did many other signs in the presence of the disciples, which are not written in this book;

31 but these are written so that you may believe that Jesus is the Christ, the Son of God, and that by believing you may have life in his name.

CHAPTER 21

1 After this Jesus revealed himself again to the disciples by the Sea of Tiberias, and he revealed himself in this way.

2 Simon Peter, Thomas (called the Twin), Nathanael of Cana in Galilee, the sons of Zebedee, and two others of his disciples were together.

3 Simon Peter said to them, "I am going fishing." They said to him, "We will go with you." They went out and got into the boat, but that night they caught nothing.

4 Just as day was breaking, Jesus stood on the shore; yet the disciples did not know that it was Jesus.

5 Jesus said to them, "Children, do you have any fish?" They answered him, "No."

6 He said to them, "Cast the net on the right side of the boat, and you will find some." So they cast it, and now they were not able to haul it in, because of the quantity of fish.

7 That disciple whom Jesus loved therefore said to Peter, "It is the Lord!" When Simon Peter heard that it was the Lord, he put on his outer garment, for he was stripped for work, and threw himself into the sea.

8 The other disciples came in the boat, dragging the net

full of fish, for they were not far from the land, but about a hundred yards off.

⁹ When they got out on land, they saw a charcoal fire in place, with fish laid out on it, and bread.

¹⁰ Jesus said to them, "Bring some of the fish that you have just caught."

¹¹ So Simon Peter went aboard and hauled the net ashore, full of large fish, 153 of them. And although there were so many, the net was not torn.

¹² Jesus said to them, "Come and have breakfast." Now none of the disciples dared ask him, "Who are you?" They knew it was the Lord.

¹³ Jesus came and took the bread and gave it to them, and so with the fish.

¹⁴ This was now the third time that Jesus was revealed to the disciples after he was raised from the dead.

¹⁵ When they had finished breakfast, Jesus said to Simon Peter, "Simon, son of John, do you love me more than these?" He said to him, "Yes, Lord; you know that I love you." He said to him, "Feed my lambs."

¹⁶ He said to him a second time, "Simon, son of John, do you love me?" He said to him, "Yes, Lord; you know that I love you." He said to him, "Tend my sheep."

¹⁷ He said to him the third time, "Simon, son of John, do you love me?" Peter was grieved because he said to him the third time, "Do you love me?" and he said to him, "Lord, you know everything; you know that I love you." Jesus said to him, "Feed my sheep.

¹⁸ "Truly, truly, I say to you, when you were young, you used to dress yourself and walk wherever you wanted, but when you are old, you will stretch out your hands, and another will dress you and carry you where you do not want to go."

¹⁹ (This he said to show by what kind of death he was to glorify God.) And after saying this he said to him, "Follow me."

²⁰ Peter turned and saw the disciple whom Jesus loved following them, the one who also had leaned back against him during the supper and had said, "Lord, who is it that is going to betray you?"

²¹ When Peter saw him, he said to Jesus, "Lord, what about this man?"

²² Jesus said to him, "If it is my will that he remain until I come, what is that to you? You follow me!"

23 So the saying spread abroad among the brothers that this disciple was not to die; yet Jesus did not say to him that he was not to die, but, "If it is my will that he remain until I come, what is that to you?"

24 This is the disciple who is bearing witness about these things, and who has written these things, and we know that his testimony is true.

25 Now there are also many other things that Jesus did. Were every one of them to be written, I suppose that the world itself could not contain the books that would be written.

THE ACTS

OF THE APOSTLES

CHAPTER 1

1 In the first book, O Theophilus, I have dealt with all that Jesus began to do and teach,

2 until the day when he was taken up, after he had given commands through the Holy Spirit to the apostles whom he had chosen.

3 He presented himself alive to them after his suffering by many proofs, appearing to them during forty days and speaking about the kingdom of God.

4 And while staying with them he ordered them not to depart from Jerusalem, but to wait for the promise of the Father, which, he said, "you heard from me;

5 "for John baptized with water, but you will be baptized with the Holy Spirit not many days from now."

6 So when they had come together, they asked him, "Lord, will you at this time restore the kingdom to Israel?"

7 He said to them, "It is not for you to know times or seasons that the Father has fixed by his own authority.

8 "But you will receive power when the Holy Spirit has come upon you, and you will be my witnesses in Jerusalem and in all Judea and Samaria, and to the end of the earth."

9 And when he had said these things, as they were looking on, he was lifted up, and a cloud took him out of their sight.

10 And while they were gazing into heaven as he went,

behold, two men stood by them in white robes,

[11] and said, "Men of Galilee, why do you stand looking into heaven? This Jesus, who was taken up from you into heaven, will come in the same way as you saw him go into heaven."

[12] Then they returned to Jerusalem from the mount called Olivet, which is near Jerusalem, a Sabbath day's journey away.

[13] And when they had entered, they went up to the upper room, where they were staying, Peter and John and James and Andrew, Philip and Thomas, Bartholomew and Matthew, James the son of Alphaeus and Simon the Zealot and Judas the son of James.

[14] All these with one accord were devoting themselves to prayer, together with the women and Mary the mother of Jesus, and his brothers.

[15] In those days Peter stood up among the brothers (the company of persons was in all about 120) and said,

[16] "Brothers, the Scripture had to be fulfilled, which the Holy Spirit spoke beforehand by the mouth of David concerning Judas, who became a guide to those who arrested Jesus.

[17] "For he was numbered among us and was allotted his share in this ministry."

[18] (Now this man acquired a field with the reward of his wickedness, and falling headlong he burst open in the middle and all his bowels gushed out.

[19] And it became known to all the inhabitants of Jerusalem, so that the field was called in their own language Akeldama, that is, Field of Blood.)

[20] "For it is written in the Book of Psalms, 'May his camp become desolate, and let there be no one to dwell in it'; and, 'Let another take his office.'

[21] "So one of the men who have accompanied us during all the time that the Lord Jesus went in and out among us,

[22] "beginning from the baptism of John until the day when he was taken up from us—one of these men must become with us a witness to his resurrection."

[23] And they put forward two, Joseph called Barsabbas, who was also called Justus, and Matthias.

[24] And they prayed and said, "You, Lord, who know the hearts of all, show which one of these two you have chosen

25 "to take the place in this ministry and apostleship from which Judas turned aside to go to his own place."

26 And they cast lots for them, and the lot fell on Matthias, and he was numbered with the eleven apostles.

CHAPTER 2

1 When the day of Pentecost arrived, they were all together in one place.

2 And suddenly there came from heaven a sound like a mighty rushing wind, and it filled the entire house where they were sitting.

3 And divided tongues as of fire appeared to them and rested on each one of them.

4 And they were all filled with the Holy Spirit and began to speak in other tongues as the Spirit gave them utterance.

5 Now there were dwelling in Jerusalem Jews, devout men from every nation under heaven.

6 And at this sound the multitude came together, and they were bewildered, because each one was hearing them speak in his own language.

7 And they were amazed and astonished, saying, "Are not all these who are speaking Galileans?

8 "And how is it that we hear, each of us in his own native language?

9 "Parthians and Medes and Elamites and residents of Mesopotamia, Judea and Cappadocia, Pontus and Asia,

10 "Phrygia and Pamphylia, Egypt and the parts of Libya belonging to Cyrene, and visitors from Rome,

11 "both Jews and proselytes, Cretans and Arabians—we hear them telling in our own tongues the mighty works of God."

12 And all were amazed and perplexed, saying to one another, "What does this mean?"

13 But others mocking said, "They are filled with new wine."

14 But Peter, standing with the eleven, lifted up his voice and addressed them: "Men of Judea and all who dwell in Jerusalem, let this be known to you, and give ear to my words.

15 "For these people are not drunk, as you suppose, since it is only the third hour of the day.

16 "But this is what was uttered through the prophet Joel:

17 "'And in the last days it shall be, God declares, that I will pour out my Spirit on all flesh, and your sons and your

daughters shall prophesy, and your young men shall see visions, and your old men shall dream dreams;

18 "'even on my male servants and female servants in those days I will pour out my Spirit, and they shall prophesy.

19 "'And I will show wonders in the heavens above and signs on the earth below, blood, and fire, and vapor of smoke;

20 "'the sun shall be turned to darkness and the moon to blood, before the day of the Lord comes, the great and magnificent day.

21 "'And it shall come to pass that everyone who calls upon the name of the Lord shall be saved.'

22 "Men of Israel, hear these words: Jesus of Nazareth, a man attested to you by God with mighty works and wonders and signs that God did through him in your midst, as you yourselves know—

23 "this Jesus, delivered up according to the definite plan and foreknowledge of God, you crucified and killed by the hands of lawless men.

24 "God raised him up, loosing the pangs of death, because it was not possible for him to be held by it.

25 "For David says concerning him, 'I saw the Lord always before me, for he is at my right hand that I may not be shaken;

26 "'therefore my heart was glad, and my tongue rejoiced; my flesh also will dwell in hope.

27 "'For you will not abandon my soul to Hades, or let your Holy One see corruption.

28 "'You have made known to me the paths of life; you will make me full of gladness with your presence.'

29 "Brothers, I may say to you with confidence about the patriarch David that he both died and was buried, and his tomb is with us to this day.

30 "Being therefore a prophet, and knowing that God had sworn with an oath to him that he would set one of his descendants on his throne,

31 "he foresaw and spoke about the resurrection of the Christ, that he was not abandoned to Hades, nor did his flesh see corruption.

32 "This Jesus God raised up, and of that we all are witnesses.

33 "Being therefore exalted at the right hand of God, and having received from the Father the promise of the Holy Spirit, he has poured out this that you yourselves are seeing and hearing.

34 "For David did not as-

cend into the heavens, but he himself says, 'The Lord said to my Lord, "Sit at my right hand,

35 " ' "until I make your enemies your footstool." '

36 "Let all the house of Israel therefore know for certain that God has made him both Lord and Christ, this Jesus whom you crucified."

37 Now when they heard this they were cut to the heart, and said to Peter and the rest of the apostles, "Brothers, what shall we do?"

38 And Peter said to them, "Repent and be baptized every one of you in the name of Jesus Christ for the forgiveness of your sins, and you will receive the gift of the Holy Spirit.

39 "For the promise is for you and for your children and for all who are far off, everyone whom the Lord our God calls to himself."

40 And with many other words he bore witness and continued to exhort them, saying, "Save yourselves from this crooked generation."

41 So those who received his word were baptized, and there were added that day about three thousand souls.

42 And they devoted themselves to the apostles' teaching and the fellowship, to the breaking of bread and the prayers.

43 And awe came upon every soul, and many wonders and signs were being done through the apostles.

44 And all who believed were together and had all things in common.

45 And they were selling their possessions and belongings and distributing the proceeds to all, as any had need.

46 And day by day, attending the temple together and breaking bread in their homes, they received their food with glad and generous hearts,

47 praising God and having favor with all the people. And the Lord added to their number day by day those who were being saved.

CHAPTER 3

1 Now Peter and John were going up to the temple at the hour of prayer, the ninth hour.

2 And a man lame from birth was being carried, whom they laid daily at the gate of the temple that is called the Beautiful Gate to ask alms of those entering the temple.

3 Seeing Peter and John about to go into the temple, he asked to receive alms.

4 And Peter directed his gaze

at him, as did John, and said, "Look at us."

⁵ And he fixed his attention on them, expecting to receive something from them.

⁶ But Peter said, "I have no silver and gold, but what I do have I give to you. In the name of Jesus Christ of Nazareth, rise up and walk!"

⁷ And he took him by the right hand and raised him up, and immediately his feet and ankles were made strong.

⁸ And leaping up he stood and began to walk, and entered the temple with them, walking and leaping and praising God.

⁹ And all the people saw him walking and praising God,

¹⁰ and recognized him as the one who sat at the Beautiful Gate of the temple, asking for alms. And they were filled with wonder and amazement at what had happened to him.

¹¹ While they clung to Peter and John, all the people, utterly astounded, ran together to them in the portico called Solomon's.

¹² And when Peter saw it he addressed the people: "Men of Israel, why do you wonder at this, or why do you stare at us, as though by our own power or piety we have made him walk?

¹³ "The God of Abraham, the God of Isaac, and the God of Jacob, the God of our fathers, glorified his servant Jesus, whom you delivered over and denied in the presence of Pilate, when he had decided to release him.

¹⁴ "But you denied the Holy and Righteous One, and asked for a murderer to be granted to you,

¹⁵ "and you killed the Author of life, whom God raised from the dead. To this we are witnesses.

¹⁶ "And his name—by faith in his name—has made this man strong whom you see and know, and the faith that is through Jesus has given the man this perfect health in the presence of you all.

¹⁷ "And now, brothers, I know that you acted in ignorance, as did also your rulers.

¹⁸ "But what God foretold by the mouth of all the prophets, that his Christ would suffer, he thus fulfilled.

¹⁹ "Repent therefore, and turn back, that your sins may be blotted out,

²⁰ "that times of refreshing may come from the presence of the Lord, and that he may send the Christ appointed for you, Jesus,

²¹ "whom heaven must receive until the time for restoring all the things about which

God spoke by the mouth of his holy prophets long ago.

²² "Moses said, 'The Lord God will raise up for you a prophet like me from your brothers. You shall listen to him in whatever he tells you.

²³ "And it shall be that every soul who does not listen to that prophet shall be destroyed from the people.'

²⁴ "And all the prophets who have spoken, from Samuel and those who came after him, also proclaimed these days.

²⁵ "You are the sons of the prophets and of the covenant that God made with your fathers, saying to Abraham, 'And in your offspring shall all the families of the earth be blessed.'

²⁶ "God, having raised up his servant, sent him to you first, to bless you by turning every one of you from your wickedness."

CHAPTER 4

¹ And as they were speaking to the people, the priests and the captain of the temple and the Sadducees came upon them,

² greatly annoyed because they were teaching the people and proclaiming in Jesus the resurrection from the dead.

³ And they arrested them and put them in custody un-

til the next day, for it was already evening.

⁴ But many of those who had heard the word believed, and the number of the men came to about five thousand.

⁵ On the next day their rulers and elders and scribes gathered together in Jerusalem,

⁶ with Annas the high priest and Caiaphas and John and Alexander, and all who were of the high-priestly family.

⁷ And when they had set them in the midst, they inquired, "By what power or by what name did you do this?"

⁸ Then Peter, filled with the Holy Spirit, said to them, "Rulers of the people and elders,

⁹ "if we are being examined today concerning a good deed done to a crippled man, by what means this man has been healed,

¹⁰ "let it be known to all of you and to all the people of Israel that by the name of Jesus Christ of Nazareth, whom you crucified, whom God raised from the dead—by him this man is standing before you well.

¹¹ "This Jesus is the stone that was rejected by you, the builders, which has become the cornerstone.

¹² "And there is salvation in

no one else, for there is no other name under heaven given among men by which we must be saved."

13 Now when they saw the boldness of Peter and John, and perceived that they were uneducated, common men, they were astonished. And they recognized that they had been with Jesus.

14 But seeing the man who was healed standing beside them, they had nothing to say in opposition.

15 But when they had commanded them to leave the council, they conferred with one another,

16 saying, "What shall we do with these men? For that a notable sign has been performed through them is evident to all the inhabitants of Jerusalem, and we cannot deny it.

17 "But in order that it may spread no further among the people, let us warn them to speak no more to anyone in this name."

18 So they called them and charged them not to speak or teach at all in the name of Jesus.

19 But Peter and John answered them, "Whether it is right in the sight of God to listen to you rather than to God, you must judge,

20 "for we cannot but speak of what we have seen and heard."

21 And when they had further threatened them, they let them go, finding no way to punish them, because of the people, for all were praising God for what had happened.

22 For the man on whom this sign of healing was performed was more than forty years old.

23 When they were released, they went to their friends and reported what the chief priests and the elders had said to them.

24 And when they heard it, they lifted their voices together to God and said, "Sovereign Lord, who made the heaven and the earth and the sea and everything in them,

25 "who through the mouth of our father David, your servant, said by the Holy Spirit, 'Why did the Gentiles rage, and the peoples plot in vain?

26 " 'The kings of the earth set themselves, and the rulers were gathered together, against the Lord and against his Anointed'—

27 "for truly in this city there were gathered together against your holy servant Jesus, whom you anointed, both Herod and Pontius

Pilate, along with the Gentiles and the peoples of Israel,

28 "to do whatever your hand and your plan had predestined to take place.

29 "And now, Lord, look upon their threats and grant to your servants to continue to speak your word with all boldness,

30 "while you stretch out your hand to heal, and signs and wonders are performed through the name of your holy servant Jesus."

31 And when they had prayed, the place in which they were gathered together was shaken, and they were all filled with the Holy Spirit and continued to speak the word of God with boldness.

32 Now the full number of those who believed were of one heart and soul, and no one said that any of the things that belonged to him was his own, but they had everything in common.

33 And with great power the apostles were giving their testimony to the resurrection of the Lord Jesus, and great grace was upon them all.

34 There was not a needy person among them, for as many as were owners of lands or houses sold them and brought the proceeds of what was sold

35 and laid it at the apostles' feet, and it was distributed to each as any had need.

36 Thus Joseph, who was also called by the apostles Barnabas (which means son of encouragement), a Levite, a native of Cyprus,

37 sold a field that belonged to him and brought the money and laid it at the apostles' feet.

CHAPTER 5

1 But a man named Ananias, with his wife Sapphira, sold a piece of property,

2 and with his wife's knowledge he kept back for himself some of the proceeds and brought only a part of it and laid it at the apostles' feet.

3 But Peter said, "Ananias, why has Satan filled your heart to lie to the Holy Spirit and to keep back for yourself part of the proceeds of the land?

4 "While it remained unsold, did it not remain your own? And after it was sold, was it not at your disposal? Why is it that you have contrived this deed in your heart? You have not lied to man but to God."

5 When Ananias heard these words, he fell down and breathed his last. And great fear came upon all who heard of it.

6 The young men rose and

wrapped him up and carried him out and buried him.

⁷ After an interval of about three hours his wife came in, not knowing what had happened.

⁸ And Peter said to her, "Tell me whether you sold the land for so much." And she said, "Yes, for so much."

⁹ But Peter said to her, "How is it that you have agreed together to test the Spirit of the Lord? Behold, the feet of those who have buried your husband are at the door, and they will carry you out."

¹⁰ Immediately she fell down at his feet and breathed her last. When the young men came in they found her dead, and they carried her out and buried her beside her husband.

¹¹ And great fear came upon the whole church and upon all who heard of these things.

¹² Now many signs and wonders were regularly done among the people by the hands of the apostles. And they were all together in Solomon's Portico.

¹³ None of the rest dared join them, but the people held them in high esteem.

¹⁴ And more than ever believers were added to the Lord, multitudes of both men and women,

¹⁵ so that they even carried out the sick into the streets and laid them on cots and mats, that as Peter came by at least his shadow might fall on some of them.

¹⁶ The people also gathered from the towns around Jerusalem, bringing the sick and those afflicted with unclean spirits, and they were all healed.

¹⁷ But the high priest rose up, and all who were with him (that is, the party of the Sadducees), and filled with jealousy

¹⁸ they arrested the apostles and put them in the public prison.

¹⁹ But during the night an angel of the Lord opened the prison doors and brought them out, and said,

²⁰ "Go and stand in the temple and speak to the people all the words of this Life."

²¹ And when they heard this, they entered the temple at daybreak and began to teach. Now when the high priest came, and those who were with him, they called together the council, all the senate of the people of Israel, and sent to the prison to have them brought.

²² But when the officers came, they did not find them in the prison, so they returned and reported,

23 "We found the prison securely locked and the guards standing at the doors, but when we opened them we found no one inside."

24 Now when the captain of the temple and the chief priests heard these words, they were greatly perplexed about them, wondering what this would come to.

25 And someone came and told them, "Look! The men whom you put in prison are standing in the temple and teaching the people."

26 Then the captain with the officers went and brought them, but not by force, for they were afraid of being stoned by the people.

27 And when they had brought them, they set them before the council. And the high priest questioned them,

28 saying, "We strictly charged you not to teach in this name, yet here you have filled Jerusalem with your teaching, and you intend to bring this man's blood upon us."

29 But Peter and the apostles answered, "We must obey God rather than men.

30 "The God of our fathers raised Jesus, whom you killed by hanging him on a tree.

31 "God exalted him at his right hand as Leader and Savior, to give repentance to Israel and forgiveness of sins.

32 "And we are witnesses to these things, and so is the Holy Spirit, whom God has given to those who obey him."

33 When they heard this, they were enraged and wanted to kill them.

34 But a Pharisee in the council named Gamaliel, a teacher of the law held in honor by all the people, stood up and gave orders to put the men outside for a little while.

35 And he said to them, "Men of Israel, take care what you are about to do with these men.

36 "For before these days Theudas rose up, claiming to be somebody, and a number of men, about four hundred, joined him. He was killed, and all who followed him were dispersed and came to nothing.

37 "After him Judas the Galilean rose up in the days of the census and drew away some of the people after him. He too perished, and all who followed him were scattered.

38 "So in the present case I tell you, keep away from these men and let them alone, for if this plan or this undertaking is of man, it will fail;

39 "but if it is of God, you will not be able to overthrow them. You might even be found opposing God!" So they took his advice,

40 and when they had called in the apostles, they beat them and charged them not to speak in the name of Jesus, and let them go.

41 Then they left the presence of the council, rejoicing that they were counted worthy to suffer dishonor for the name.

42 And every day, in the temple and from house to house, they did not cease teaching and preaching that the Christ is Jesus.

CHAPTER 6

1 Now in these days when the disciples were increasing in number, a complaint by the Hellenists arose against the Hebrews because their widows were being neglected in the daily distribution.

2 And the twelve summoned the full number of the disciples and said, "It is not right that we should give up preaching the word of God to serve tables.

3 "Therefore, brothers, pick out from among you seven men of good repute, full of the Spirit and of wisdom, whom we will appoint to this duty.

4 "But we will devote ourselves to prayer and to the ministry of the word."

5 And what they said pleased the whole gathering, and they chose Stephen, a man full of faith and of the Holy Spirit, and Philip, and Prochorus, and Nicanor, and Timon, and Parmenas, and Nicolaus, a proselyte of Antioch.

6 These they set before the apostles, and they prayed and laid their hands on them.

7 And the word of God continued to increase, and the number of the disciples multiplied greatly in Jerusalem, and a great many of the priests became obedient to the faith.

8 And Stephen, full of grace and power, was doing great wonders and signs among the people.

9 Then some of those who belonged to the synagogue of the Freedmen (as it was called), and of the Cyrenians, and of the Alexandrians, and of those from Cilicia and Asia, rose up and disputed with Stephen.

10 But they could not withstand the wisdom and the Spirit with which he was speaking.

11 Then they secretly instigated men who said, "We

have heard him speak blasphemous words against Moses and God."

12 And they stirred up the people and the elders and the scribes, and they came upon him and seized him and brought him before the council,

13 and they set up false witnesses who said, "This man never ceases to speak words against this holy place and the law,

14 "for we have heard him say that this Jesus of Nazareth will destroy this place and will change the customs that Moses delivered to us."

15 And gazing at him, all who sat in the council saw that his face was like the face of an angel.

CHAPTER 7

1 And the high priest said, "Are these things so?"

2 And Stephen said: "Brothers and fathers, hear me. The God of glory appeared to our father Abraham when he was in Mesopotamia, before he lived in Haran,

3 "and said to him, 'Go out from your land and from your kindred and go into the land that I will show you.'

4 "Then he went out from the land of the Chaldeans and lived in Haran. And after his father died, God removed him from there into this land in which you are now living.

5 "Yet he gave him no inheritance in it, not even a foot's length, but promised to give it to him as a possession and to his offspring after him, though he had no child.

6 "And God spoke to this effect—that his offspring would be sojourners in a land belonging to others, who would enslave them and afflict them four hundred years.

7 "'But I will judge the nation that they serve,' said God, 'and after that they shall come out and worship me in this place.'

8 "And he gave him the covenant of circumcision. And so Abraham became the father of Isaac, and circumcised him on the eighth day, and Isaac became the father of Jacob, and Jacob of the twelve patriarchs.

9 "And the patriarchs, jealous of Joseph, sold him into Egypt; but God was with him

10 "and rescued him out of all his afflictions and gave him favor and wisdom before Pharaoh, king of Egypt, who made him ruler over Egypt and over all his household.

11 "Now there came a famine throughout all Egypt and Canaan, and great affliction,

and our fathers could find no food.

12 "But when Jacob heard that there was grain in Egypt, he sent out our fathers on their first visit.

13 And on the second visit Joseph made himself known to his brothers, and Joseph's family became known to Pharaoh.

14 "And Joseph sent and summoned Jacob his father and all his kindred, seventy-five persons in all.

15 "And Jacob went down into Egypt, and he died, he and our fathers,

16 "and they were carried back to Shechem and laid in the tomb that Abraham had bought for a sum of silver from the sons of Hamor in Shechem.

17 "But as the time of the promise drew near, which God had granted to Abraham, the people increased and multiplied in Egypt

18 "until there arose over Egypt another king who did not know Joseph.

19 "He dealt shrewdly with our race and forced our fathers to expose their infants, so that they would not be kept alive.

20 "At this time Moses was born; and he was beautiful in God's sight. And he was

brought up for three months in his father's house,

21 "and when he was exposed, Pharaoh's daughter adopted him and brought him up as her own son.

22 "And Moses was instructed in all the wisdom of the Egyptians, and he was mighty in his words and deeds.

23 "When he was forty years old, it came into his heart to visit his brothers, the children of Israel.

24 "And seeing one of them being wronged, he defended the oppressed man and avenged him by striking down the Egyptian.

25 "He supposed that his brothers would understand that God was giving them salvation by his hand, but they did not understand.

26 "And on the following day he appeared to them as they were quarreling and tried to reconcile them, saying, 'Men, you are brothers. Why do you wrong each other?'

27 "But the man who was wronging his neighbor thrust him aside, saying, 'Who made you a ruler and a judge over us?

28 " 'Do you want to kill me as you killed the Egyptian yesterday?'

29 "At this retort Moses fled and became an exile in the

land of Midian, where he became the father of two sons.

30 "Now when forty years had passed, an angel appeared to him in the wilderness of Mount Sinai, in a flame of fire in a bush.

31 "When Moses saw it, he was amazed at the sight, and as he drew near to look, there came the voice of the Lord:

32 "'I am the God of your fathers, the God of Abraham and of Isaac and of Jacob.' And Moses trembled and did not dare to look.

33 "Then the Lord said to him, 'Take off the sandals from your feet, for the place where you are standing is holy ground.

34 "'I have surely seen the affliction of my people who are in Egypt, and have heard their groaning, and I have come down to deliver them. And now come, I will send you to Egypt.'

35 "This Moses, whom they rejected, saying, 'Who made you a ruler and a judge?'—this man God sent as both ruler and redeemer by the hand of the angel who appeared to him in the bush.

36 "This man led them out, performing wonders and signs in Egypt and at the Red Sea and in the wilderness for forty years.

37 "This is the Moses who said to the Israelites, 'God will raise up for you a prophet like me from your brothers.'

38 "This is the one who was in the congregation in the wilderness with the angel who spoke to him at Mount Sinai, and with our fathers. He received living oracles to give to us.

39 "Our fathers refused to obey him, but thrust him aside, and in their hearts they turned to Egypt,

40 "saying to Aaron, 'Make for us gods who will go before us. As for this Moses who led us out from the land of Egypt, we do not know what has become of him.'

41 "And they made a calf in those days, and offered a sacrifice to the idol and were rejoicing in the works of their hands.

42 "But God turned away and gave them over to worship the host of heaven, as it is written in the book of the prophets: 'Did you bring to me slain beasts and sacrifices, during the forty years in the wilderness, O house of Israel?

43 "'You took up the tent of Moloch and the star of your god Rephan, the images that you made to worship; and I will send you into exile beyond Babylon.'

44 "Our fathers had the tent of witness in the wilderness, just as he who spoke to Moses directed him to make it, according to the pattern that he had seen.

45 "Our fathers in turn brought it in with Joshua when they dispossessed the nations that God drove out before our fathers. So it was until the days of David,

46 "who found favor in the sight of God and asked to find a dwelling place for the God of Jacob.

47 "But it was Solomon who built a house for him.

48 "Yet the Most High does not dwell in houses made by hands, as the prophet says,

49 "'Heaven is my throne, and the earth is my footstool. What kind of house will you build for me, says the Lord, or what is the place of my rest?

50 "'Did not my hand make all these things?'

51 "You stiff-necked people, uncircumcised in heart and ears, you always resist the Holy Spirit. As your fathers did, so do you.

52 "Which of the prophets did your fathers not persecute? And they killed those who announced beforehand the coming of the Righteous One, whom you have now betrayed and murdered,

53 "you who received the law as delivered by angels and did not keep it."

54 Now when they heard these things they were enraged, and they ground their teeth at him.

55 But he, full of the Holy Spirit, gazed into heaven and saw the glory of God, and Jesus standing at the right hand of God.

56 And he said, "Behold, I see the heavens opened, and the Son of Man standing at the right hand of God."

57 But they cried out with a loud voice and stopped their ears and rushed together at him.

58 Then they cast him out of the city and stoned him. And the witnesses laid down their garments at the feet of a young man named Saul.

59 And as they were stoning Stephen, he called out, "Lord Jesus, receive my spirit."

60 And falling to his knees he cried out with a loud voice, "Lord, do not hold this sin against them." And when he had said this, he fell asleep.

CHAPTER 8

1 And Saul approved of his execution. And there arose on that day a great persecution against the church in Jerusa-

lem, and they were all scattered throughout the regions of Judea and Samaria, except the apostles.

² Devout men buried Stephen and made great lamentation over him.

³ But Saul was ravaging the church, and entering house after house, he dragged off men and women and committed them to prison.

⁴ Now those who were scattered went about preaching the word.

⁵ Philip went down to the city of Samaria and proclaimed to them the Christ.

⁶ And the crowds with one accord paid attention to what was being said by Philip when they heard him and saw the signs that he did.

⁷ For unclean spirits, crying out with a loud voice, came out of many who had them, and many who were paralyzed or lame were healed.

⁸ So there was much joy in that city.

⁹ But there was a man named Simon, who had previously practiced magic in the city and amazed the people of Samaria, saying that he himself was somebody great.

¹⁰ They all paid attention to him, from the least to the greatest, saying, "This man is the power of God that is called Great."

¹¹ And they paid attention to him because for a long time he had amazed them with his magic.

¹² But when they believed Philip as he preached good news about the kingdom of God and the name of Jesus Christ, they were baptized, both men and women.

¹³ Even Simon himself believed, and after being baptized he continued with Philip. And seeing signs and great miracles performed, he was amazed.

¹⁴ Now when the apostles at Jerusalem heard that Samaria had received the word of God, they sent to them Peter and John,

¹⁵ who came down and prayed for them that they might receive the Holy Spirit,

¹⁶ for he had not yet fallen on any of them, but they had only been baptized in the name of the Lord Jesus.

¹⁷ Then they laid their hands on them and they received the Holy Spirit.

¹⁸ Now when Simon saw that the Spirit was given through the laying on of the apostles' hands, he offered them money,

¹⁹ saying, "Give me this power also, so that anyone on

whom I lay my hands may receive the Holy Spirit."

20 But Peter said to him, "May your silver perish with you, because you thought you could obtain the gift of God with money!

21 "You have neither part nor lot in this matter, for your heart is not right before God.

22 "Repent, therefore, of this wickedness of yours, and pray to the Lord that, if possible, the intent of your heart may be forgiven you.

23 "For I see that you are in the gall of bitterness and in the bond of iniquity."

24 And Simon answered, "Pray for me to the Lord, that nothing of what you have said may come upon me."

25 Now when they had testified and spoken the word of the Lord, they returned to Jerusalem, preaching the gospel to many villages of the Samaritans.

26 Now an angel of the Lord said to Philip, "Rise and go toward the south to the road that goes down from Jerusalem to Gaza." This is a desert place.

27 And he rose and went. And there was an Ethiopian, a eunuch, a court official of Candace, queen of the Ethiopians, who was in charge of all her treasure. He had come to Jerusalem to worship

28 and was returning, seated in his chariot, and he was reading the prophet Isaiah.

29 And the Spirit said to Philip, "Go over and join this chariot."

30 So Philip ran to him and heard him reading Isaiah the prophet and asked, "Do you understand what you are reading?"

31 And he said, "How can I, unless someone guides me?" And he invited Philip to come up and sit with him.

32 Now the passage of the Scripture that he was reading was this: "Like a sheep he was led to the slaughter and like a lamb before its shearer is silent, so he opens not his mouth.

33 "In his humiliation justice was denied him. Who can describe his generation? For his life is taken away from the earth."

34 And the eunuch said to Philip, "About whom, I ask you, does the prophet say this, about himself or about someone else?"

35 Then Philip opened his mouth, and beginning with this Scripture he told him the good news about Jesus.

36 And as they were going along the road they came to some water, and the eunuch said, "See, here is water! What

prevents me from being baptized?"

37 And Philip said, "If you believe with all your heart, you may." And he replied, "I believe that Jesus Christ is the Son of God."

38 And he commanded the chariot to stop, and they both went down into the water, Philip and the eunuch, and he baptized him.

39 And when they came up out of the water, the Spirit of the Lord carried Philip away, and the eunuch saw him no more, and went on his way rejoicing.

40 But Philip found himself at Azotus, and as he passed through he preached the gospel to all the towns until he came to Caesarea.

CHAPTER 9

1 But Saul, still breathing threats and murder against the disciples of the Lord, went to the high priest

2 and asked him for letters to the synagogues at Damascus, so that if he found any belonging to the Way, men or women, he might bring them bound to Jerusalem.

3 Now as he went on his way, he approached Damascus, and suddenly a light from heaven shone around him.

4 And falling to the ground he heard a voice saying to him, "Saul, Saul, why are you persecuting me?"

5 And he said, "Who are you, Lord?" And he said, "I am Jesus, whom you are persecuting.

6 "But rise and enter the city, and you will be told what you are to do."

7 The men who were traveling with him stood speechless, hearing the voice but seeing no one.

8 Saul rose from the ground, and although his eyes were opened, he saw nothing. So they led him by the hand and brought him into Damascus.

9 And for three days he was without sight, and neither ate nor drank.

10 Now there was a disciple at Damascus named Ananias. The Lord said to him in a vision, "Ananias." And he said, "Here I am, Lord."

11 And the Lord said to him, "Rise and go to the street called Straight, and at the house of Judas look for a man of Tarsus named Saul, for behold, he is praying,

12 "and he has seen in a vision a man named Ananias come in and lay his hands on him so that he might regain his sight."

13 And Ananias answered, "Lord, I have heard from

many about this man, how much evil he has done to your saints at Jerusalem.

14 "And here he has authority from the chief priests to bind all who call on your name."

15 But the Lord said to him, "Go, for he is a chosen instrument of mine to carry my name before the Gentiles and kings and the children of Israel.

16 "For I will show him how much he must suffer for the sake of my name."

17 So Ananias departed and entered the house. And laying his hands on him he said, "Brother Saul, the Lord Jesus who appeared to you on the road by which you came has sent me so that you may regain your sight and be filled with the Holy Spirit."

18 And immediately something like scales fell from his eyes, and he regained his sight. Then he rose and was baptized;

19 and taking food, he was strengthened. For some days he was with the disciples at Damascus.

20 And immediately he proclaimed Jesus in the synagogues, saying, "He is the Son of God."

21 And all who heard him were amazed and said, "Is not this the man who made having in Jerusalem of those who called upon this name? And has he not come here for this purpose, to bring them bound before the chief priests?"

22 But Saul increased all the more in strength, and confounded the Jews who lived in Damascus by proving that Jesus was the Christ.

23 When many days had passed, the Jews plotted to kill him,

24 but their plot became known to Saul. They were watching the gates day and night in order to kill him,

25 but his disciples took him by night and let him down through an opening in the wall, lowering him in a basket.

26 And when he had come to Jerusalem, he attempted to join the disciples. And they were all afraid of him, for they did not believe that he was a disciple.

27 But Barnabas took him and brought him to the apostles and declared to them how on the road he had seen the Lord, who spoke to him, and how at Damascus he had preached boldly in the name of Jesus.

28 So he went in and out among them at Jerusalem, preaching boldly in the name of the Lord.

29 And he spoke and disputed against the Hellenists. But they were seeking to kill him.

30 And when the brothers learned this, they brought him down to Caesarea and sent him off to Tarsus.

31 So the church throughout all Judea and Galilee and Samaria had peace and was being built up. And walking in the fear of the Lord and in the comfort of the Holy Spirit, it multiplied.

32 Now as Peter went here and there among them all, he came down also to the saints who lived at Lydda.

33 There he found a man named Aeneas, bedridden for eight years, who was paralyzed.

34 And Peter said to him, "Aeneas, Jesus Christ heals you; rise and make your bed." And immediately he rose.

35 And all the residents of Lydda and Sharon saw him, and they turned to the Lord.

36 Now there was in Joppa a disciple named Tabitha, which, translated, means Dorcas. She was full of good works and acts of charity.

37 In those days she became ill and died, and when they had washed her, they laid her in an upper room.

38 Since Lydda was near Joppa, the disciples, hearing that Peter was there, sent two men to him, urging him, "Please come to us without delay."

39 So Peter rose and went with them. And when he arrived, they took him to the upper room. All the widows stood beside him weeping and showing tunics and other garments that Dorcas made while she was with them.

40 But Peter put them all outside, and knelt down and prayed; and turning to the body he said, "Tabitha, arise." And she opened her eyes, and when she saw Peter she sat up.

41 And he gave her his hand and raised her up. Then calling the saints and widows, he presented her alive.

42 And it became known throughout all Joppa, and many believed in the Lord.

43 And he stayed in Joppa for many days with one Simon, a tanner.

CHAPTER 10

1 At Caesarea there was a man named Cornelius, a centurion of what was known as the Italian Cohort,

2 a devout man who feared God with all his household, gave alms generously to the people, and prayed continually to God.

3 About the ninth hour of

the day he saw clearly in a vision an angel of God come in and say to him, "Cornelius."

4 And he stared at him in terror and said, "What is it, Lord?" And he said to him, "Your prayers and your alms have ascended as a memorial before God.

5 "And now send men to Joppa and bring one Simon who is called Peter.

6 "He is lodging with one Simon, a tanner, whose house is by the sea."

7 When the angel who spoke to him had departed, he called two of his servants and a devout soldier from among those who attended him,

8 and having related everything to them, he sent them to Joppa.

9 The next day, as they were on their journey and approaching the city, Peter went up on the housetop about the sixth hour to pray.

10 And he became hungry and wanted something to eat, but while they were preparing it, he fell into a trance

11 and saw the heavens opened and something like a great sheet descending, being let down by its four corners upon the earth.

12 In it were all kinds of animals and reptiles and birds of the air.

13 And there came a voice to him: "Rise, Peter; kill and eat."

14 But Peter said, "By no means, Lord; for I have never eaten anything that is common or unclean."

15 And the voice came to him again a second time, "What God has made clean, do not call common."

16 This happened three times, and the thing was taken up at once to heaven.

17 Now while Peter was inwardly perplexed as to what the vision that he had seen might mean, behold, the men who were sent by Cornelius, having made inquiry for Simon's house, stood at the gate

18 and called out to ask whether Simon who was called Peter was lodging there.

19 And while Peter was pondering the vision, the Spirit said to him, "Behold, three men are looking for you.

20 "Rise and go down and accompany them without hesitation, for I have sent them."

21 And Peter went down to the men and said, "I am the one you are looking for. What is the reason for your coming?"

22 And they said, "Cornelius, a centurion, an upright and God-fearing man, who is well spoken of by the whole Jewish

nation, was directed by a holy angel to send for you to come to his house and to hear what you have to say."

²³ So he invited them in to be his guests. The next day he rose and went away with them, and some of the brothers from Joppa accompanied him.

²⁴ And on the following day they entered Caesarea. Cornelius was expecting them and had called together his relatives and close friends.

²⁵ When Peter entered, Cornelius met him and fell down at his feet and worshiped him.

²⁶ But Peter lifted him up, saying, "Stand up; I too am a man."

²⁷ And as he talked with him, he went in and found many persons gathered.

²⁸ And he said to them, "You yourselves know how unlawful it is for a Jew to associate with or to visit anyone of another nation, but God has shown me that I should not call any person common or unclean.

²⁹ "So when I was sent for, I came without objection. I ask then why you sent for me."

³⁰ And Cornelius said, "Four days ago, about this hour, I was praying in my house at the ninth hour, and behold, a man stood before me in bright clothing

³¹ "and said, 'Cornelius, your prayer has been heard and your alms have been remembered before God.

³² "'Send therefore to Joppa and ask for Simon who is called Peter. He is lodging in the house of Simon, a tanner, by the sea.'

³³ "So I sent for you at once, and you have been kind enough to come. Now therefore we are all here in the presence of God to hear all that you have been commanded by the Lord."

³⁴ So Peter opened his mouth and said: "Truly I understand that God shows no partiality,

³⁵ "but in every nation anyone who fears him and does what is right is acceptable to him.

³⁶ "As for the word that he sent to Israel, preaching good news of peace through Jesus Christ (he is Lord of all),

³⁷ "you yourselves know what happened throughout all Judea, beginning from Galilee after the baptism that John proclaimed:

³⁸ "how God anointed Jesus of Nazareth with the Holy Spirit and with power. He went about doing good and healing all who were

oppressed by the devil, for God was with him.

39 "And we are witnesses of all that he did both in the country of the Jews and in Jerusalem. They put him to death by hanging him on a tree,

40 "but God raised him on the third day and made him to appear,

41 "not to all the people but to us who had been chosen by God as witnesses, who ate and drank with him after he rose from the dead.

42 "And he commanded us to preach to the people and to testify that he is the one appointed by God to be judge of the living and the dead.

43 "To him all the prophets bear witness that everyone who believes in him receives forgiveness of sins through his name."

44 While Peter was still saying these things, the Holy Spirit fell on all who heard the word.

45 And the believers from among the circumcised who had come with Peter were amazed, because the gift of the Holy Spirit was poured out even on the Gentiles.

46 For they were hearing them speaking in tongues and extolling God. Then Peter declared,

47 "Can anyone withhold water for baptizing these people, who have received the Holy Spirit just as we have?"

48 And he commanded them to be baptized in the name of Jesus Christ. Then they asked him to remain for some days.

CHAPTER 11

1 Now the apostles and the brothers who were throughout Judea heard that the Gentiles also had received the word of God.

2 So when Peter went up to Jerusalem, the circumcision party criticized him, saying,

3 "You went to uncircumcised men and ate with them."

4 But Peter began and explained it to them in order:

5 "I was in the city of Joppa praying, and in a trance I saw a vision, something like a great sheet descending, being let down from heaven by its four corners, and it came down to me.

6 "Looking at it closely, I observed animals and beasts of prey and reptiles and birds of the air.

7 "And I heard a voice saying to me, 'Rise, Peter; kill and eat.'

8 "But I said, 'By no means, Lord; for nothing common

or unclean has ever entered my mouth.'

9 "But the voice answered a second time from heaven, 'What God has made clean, do not call common.'

10 "This happened three times, and all was drawn up again into heaven.

11 "And behold, at that very moment three men arrived at the house in which we were, sent to me from Caesarea.

12 "And the Spirit told me to go with them, making no distinction. These six brothers also accompanied me, and we entered the man's house.

13 "And he told us how he had seen the angel stand in his house and say, 'Send to Joppa and bring Simon who is called Peter;

14 " 'he will declare to you a message by which you will be saved, you and all your household.'

15 "As I began to speak, the Holy Spirit fell on them just as on us at the beginning.

16 "And I remembered the word of the Lord, how he said, 'John baptized with water, but you will be baptized with the Holy Spirit.'

17 "If then God gave the same gift to them as he gave to us when we believed in the Lord Jesus Christ, who was I that I could stand in God's way?"

18 When they heard these things they fell silent. And they glorified God, saying, "Then to the Gentiles also God has granted repentance that leads to life."

19 Now those who were scattered because of the persecution that arose over Stephen traveled as far as Phoenicia and Cyprus and Antioch, speaking the word to no one except Jews.

20 But there were some of them, men of Cyprus and Cyrene, who on coming to Antioch spoke to the Hellenists also, preaching the Lord Jesus.

21 And the hand of the Lord was with them, and a great number who believed turned to the Lord.

22 The report of this came to the ears of the church in Jerusalem, and they sent Barnabas to Antioch.

23 When he came and saw the grace of God, he was glad, and he exhorted them all to remain faithful to the Lord with steadfast purpose,

24 for he was a good man, full of the Holy Spirit and of faith. And a great many people were added to the Lord.

25 So Barnabas went to Tarsus to look for Saul,

26 and when he had found him, he brought him to

Antioch. For a whole year they met with the church and taught a great many people. And in Antioch the disciples were first called Christians.

27 Now in these days prophets came down from Jerusalem to Antioch.

28 And one of them named Agabus stood up and foretold by the Spirit that there would be a great famine over all the world (this took place in the days of Claudius).

29 So the disciples determined, every one according to his ability, to send relief to the brothers living in Judea.

30 And they did so, sending it to the elders by the hand of Barnabas and Saul.

CHAPTER 12

1 About that time Herod the king laid violent hands on some who belonged to the church.

2 He killed James the brother of John with the sword,

3 and when he saw that it pleased the Jews, he proceeded to arrest Peter also. This was during the days of Unleavened Bread.

4 And when he had seized him, he put him in prison, delivering him over to four squads of soldiers to guard him, intending after the Passover to bring him out to the people.

5 So Peter was kept in prison, but earnest prayer for him was made to God by the church.

6 Now when Herod was about to bring him out, on that very night, Peter was sleeping between two soldiers, bound with two chains, and sentries before the door were guarding the prison.

7 And behold, an angel of the Lord stood next to him, and a light shone in the cell. He struck Peter on the side and woke him, saying, "Get up quickly." And the chains fell off his hands.

8 And the angel said to him, "Dress yourself and put on your sandals." And he did so. And he said to him, "Wrap your cloak around you and follow me."

9 And he went out and followed him. He did not know that what was being done by the angel was real, but thought he was seeing a vision.

10 When they had passed the first and the second guard, they came to the iron gate leading into the city. It opened for them of its own accord, and they went out and went along one street,

and immediately the angel left him.

¹¹ When Peter came to himself, he said, "Now I am sure that the Lord has sent his angel and rescued me from the hand of Herod and from all that the Jewish people were expecting."

¹² When he realized this, he went to the house of Mary, the mother of John whose other name was Mark, where many were gathered together and were praying.

¹³ And when he knocked at the door of the gateway, a servant girl named Rhoda came to answer.

¹⁴ Recognizing Peter's voice, in her joy she did not open the gate but ran in and reported that Peter was standing at the gate.

¹⁵ They said to her, "You are out of your mind." But she kept insisting that it was so, and they kept saying, "It is his angel!"

¹⁶ But Peter continued knocking, and when they opened, they saw him and were amazed.

¹⁷ But motioning to them with his hand to be silent, he described to them how the Lord had brought him out of the prison. And he said, "Tell these things to James and to the brothers."

Then he departed and went to another place.

¹⁸ Now when day came, there was no little disturbance among the soldiers over what had become of Peter.

¹⁹ And after Herod searched for him and did not find him, he examined the sentries and ordered that they should be put to death. Then he went down from Judea to Caesarea and spent time there.

²⁰ Now Herod was angry with the people of Tyre and Sidon, and they came to him with one accord, and having persuaded Blastus, the king's chamberlain, they asked for peace, because their country depended on the king's country for food.

²¹ On an appointed day Herod put on his royal robes, took his seat upon the throne, and delivered an oration to them.

²² And the people were shouting, "The voice of a god, and not of a man!"

²³ Immediately an angel of the Lord struck him down, because he did not give God the glory, and he was eaten by worms and breathed his last.

²⁴ But the word of God increased and multiplied.

²⁵ And Barnabas and Saul returned from Jerusalem when they had completed their

service, bringing with them John, whose other name was Mark.

CHAPTER 13

1 Now there were in the church at Antioch prophets and teachers, Barnabas, Simeon who was called Niger, Lucius of Cyrene, Manaen a lifelong friend of Herod the tetrarch, and Saul.

2 While they were worshiping the Lord and fasting, the Holy Spirit said, "Set apart for me Barnabas and Saul for the work to which I have called them."

3 Then after fasting and praying they laid their hands on them and sent them off.

4 So, being sent out by the Holy Spirit, they went down to Seleucia, and from there they sailed to Cyprus.

5 When they arrived at Salamis, they proclaimed the word of God in the synagogues of the Jews. And they had John to assist them.

6 When they had gone *through* the whole island as far as Paphos, they came upon a certain magician, a Jewish false prophet named Bar-Jesus.

7 He was with the proconsul, Sergius Paulus, a man of intelligence, who summoned Barnabas and Saul and sought to hear the word of God.

8 But Elymas the magician (for that is the meaning of his name) opposed them, seeking to turn the proconsul away from the faith.

9 But Saul, who was also called Paul, filled with the Holy Spirit, looked intently at him

10 and said, "You son of the devil, you enemy of all righteousness, full of all deceit and villainy, will you not stop making crooked the straight paths of the Lord?

11 "And now, behold, the hand of the Lord is upon you, and you will be blind and unable to see the sun for a time." Immediately mist and darkness fell upon him, and he went about seeking people to lead him by the hand.

12 Then the proconsul believed, when he saw what had occurred, for he was astonished at the teaching of the Lord.

13 Now Paul and his companions set sail from Paphos and came to Perga in Pamphylia. And John left them and returned to Jerusalem,

14 but they went on from Perga and came to Antioch in Pisidia. And on the Sabbath day they went into the synagogue and sat down.

¹⁵ After the reading from the Law and the Prophets, the rulers of the synagogue sent a message to them, saying, "Brothers, if you have any word of encouragement for the people, say it."

¹⁶ So Paul stood up, and motioning with his hand said: "Men of Israel and you who fear God, listen.

¹⁷ "The God of this people Israel chose our fathers and made the people great during their stay in the land of Egypt, and with uplifted arm he led them out of it.

¹⁸ "And for about forty years he put up with them in the wilderness.

¹⁹ "And after destroying seven nations in the land of Canaan, he gave them their land as an inheritance.

²⁰ "All this took about 450 years. And after that he gave them judges until Samuel the prophet.

²¹ "Then they asked for a king, and God gave them Saul the son of Kish, a man of the tribe of Benjamin, for forty years.

²² "And when he had removed him, he raised up David to be their king, of whom he testified and said, 'I have found in David the son of Jesse a man after my heart, who will do all my will.'

²³ "Of this man's offspring God has brought to Israel a Savior, Jesus, as he promised.

²⁴ "Before his coming, John had proclaimed a baptism of repentance to all the people of Israel.

²⁵ "And as John was finishing his course, he said, 'What do you suppose that I am? I am not he. No, but behold, after me one is coming, the sandals of whose feet I am not worthy to untie.'

²⁶ "Brothers, sons of the family of Abraham, and those among you who fear God, to us has been sent the message of this salvation.

²⁷ "For those who live in Jerusalem and their rulers, because they did not recognize him nor understand the utterances of the prophets, which are read every Sabbath, fulfilled them by condemning him.

²⁸ "And though they found in him no guilt worthy of death, they asked Pilate to have him executed.

²⁹ "And when they had carried out all that was written of him, they took him down from the tree and laid him in a tomb.

³⁰ "But God raised him from the dead,

³¹ "and for many days he appeared to those who had

come up with him from Galilee to Jerusalem, who are now his witnesses to the people.

32 "And we bring you the good news that what God promised to the fathers,

33 "this he has fulfilled to us their children by raising Jesus, as also it is written in the second Psalm, 'You are my Son, today I have begotten you.'

34 "And as for the fact that he raised him from the dead, no more to return to corruption, he has spoken in this way, 'I will give you the holy and sure blessings of David.'

35 "Therefore he says also in another psalm, 'You will not let your Holy One see corruption.'

36 "For David, after he had served the purpose of God in his own generation, fell asleep and was laid with his fathers and saw corruption.

37 "but he whom God raised up did not see corruption.

38 "Let it be known to you therefore, brothers, that through this man forgiveness of sins is proclaimed to you,

39 "and by him everyone who believes is freed from everything from which you could not be freed by the law of Moses.

40 "Beware, therefore, lest what is said in the Prophets should come about:

41 "'Look, you scoffers, be astounded and perish; for I am doing a work in your days, a work that you will not believe, even if one tells it to you.'"

42 As they went out, the people begged that these things might be told them the next Sabbath.

43 And after the meeting of the synagogue broke up, many Jews and devout converts to Judaism followed Paul and Barnabas, who, as they spoke with them, urged them to continue in the grace of God.

44 The next Sabbath almost the whole city gathered to hear the word of the Lord.

45 But when the Jews saw the crowds, they were filled with jealousy and began to contradict what was spoken by Paul, reviling him.

46 And Paul and Barnabas spoke out boldly, saying, "It was necessary that the word of God be spoken first to you. Since you thrust it aside and judge yourselves unworthy of eternal life, behold, we are turning to the Gentiles.

47 "For so the Lord has commanded us, saying, 'I have made you a light for the Gentiles, that you may

bring salvation to the ends of the earth.'"

⁴⁸ And when the Gentiles heard this, they began rejoicing and glorifying the word of the Lord, and as many as were appointed to eternal life believed.

⁴⁹ And the word of the Lord was spreading throughout the whole region.

⁵⁰ But the Jews incited the devout women of high standing and the leading men of the city, stirred up persecution against Paul and Barnabas, and drove them out of their district.

⁵¹ But they shook off the dust from their feet against them and went to Iconium.

⁵² And the disciples were filled with joy and with the Holy Spirit.

CHAPTER 14

¹ Now at Iconium they entered together into the Jewish synagogue and spoke in such a way that a great number of both Jews and Greeks believed.

² But the unbelieving Jews stirred up the Gentiles and poisoned their minds against the brothers.

³ So they remained for a long time, speaking boldly for the Lord, who bore witness to the word of his grace, grant-

ing signs and wonders to be done by their hands.

⁴ But the people of the city were divided; some sided with the Jews and some with the apostles.

⁵ When an attempt was made by both Gentiles and Jews, with their rulers, to mistreat them and to stone them,

⁶ they learned of it and fled to Lystra and Derbe, cities of Lycaonia, and to the surrounding country,

⁷ and there they continued to preach the gospel.

⁸ Now at Lystra there was a man sitting who could not use his feet. He was crippled from birth and had never walked.

⁹ He listened to Paul speaking. And Paul, looking intently at him and seeing that he had faith to be made well,

¹⁰ said in a loud voice, "Stand upright on your feet." And he sprang up and began walking.

¹¹ And when the crowds saw what Paul had done, they lifted up their voices, saying in Lycaonian, "The gods have come down to us in the likeness of men!"

¹² Barnabas they called Zeus, and Paul, Hermes, because he was the chief speaker.

¹³ And the priest of Zeus,

whose temple was at the entrance to the city, brought oxen and garlands to the gates and wanted to offer sacrifice with the crowds.

14 But when the apostles Barnabas and Paul heard of it, they tore their garments and rushed out into the crowd, crying out,

15 "Men, why are you doing these things? We also are men, of like nature with you, and we bring you good news, that you should turn from these vain things to a living God, who made the heaven and the earth and the sea and all that is in them.

16 "In past generations he allowed all the nations to walk in their own ways.

17 "Yet he did not leave himself without witness, for he did good by giving you rains from heaven and fruitful seasons, satisfying your hearts with food and gladness."

18 Even with these words they scarcely restrained the *people from offering* sacrifice to them.

19 But Jews came from Antioch and Iconium, and having persuaded the crowds, they stoned Paul and dragged him out of the city, supposing that he was dead.

20 But when the disciples gathered about him, he rose up and entered the city, and on the next day he went on with Barnabas to Derbe.

21 When they had preached the gospel to that city and had made many disciples, they returned to Lystra and to Iconium and to Antioch,

22 strengthening the souls of the disciples, encouraging them to continue in the faith, *and* saying that through many tribulations we must enter the kingdom of God.

23 And when they had appointed elders for them in every church, with prayer and fasting they committed them to the Lord in whom they had believed.

24 Then they passed through Pisidia and came to Pamphylia.

25 And when they had spoken the word in Perga, they went down to Attalia,

26 and from there they sailed to Antioch, where they had been commended to the grace of *God for the work that* they had fulfilled.

27 And when they arrived and gathered the church together, they declared all that God had done with them, and how he had opened a door of faith to the Gentiles.

28 And they remained no little time with the disciples.

¹ But some men came down from Judea and were teaching the brothers, "Unless you are circumcised according to the custom of Moses, you cannot be saved."

² And after Paul and Barnabas had no small dissension and debate with them, Paul and Barnabas and some of the others were appointed to go up to Jerusalem to the apostles and the elders about this question.

³ So, being sent on their way by the church, they passed through both Phoenicia and Samaria, describing in detail the conversion of the Gentiles, and brought great joy to all the brothers.

⁴ When they came to Jerusalem, they were welcomed by the church and the apostles and the elders, and they declared all that God had done with them.

⁵ But some believers who belonged to the party of the Pharisees rose up and said, "It is necessary to circumcise them and to order them to keep the law of Moses."

⁶ The apostles and the elders were gathered together to consider this matter.

⁷ And after there had been much debate, Peter stood up and said to them, "Brothers, you know that in the early days God made a choice among you, that by my mouth the Gentiles should hear the word of the gospel and believe.

⁸ "And God, who knows the heart, bore witness to them, by giving them the Holy Spirit just as he did to us,

⁹ "and he made no distinction between us and them, having cleansed their hearts by faith.

¹⁰ "Now, therefore, why are you putting God to the test by placing a yoke on the neck of the disciples that neither our fathers nor we have been able to bear?

¹¹ "But we believe that we will be saved through the grace of the Lord Jesus, just as they will."

¹² And all the assembly fell silent, and they listened to Barnabas and Paul as they related what signs and wonders God had done through them among the Gentiles.

¹³ After they finished speaking, James replied, "Brothers, listen to me.

¹⁴ "Simeon has related how God first visited the Gentiles, to take from them a people for his name.

¹⁵ "And with this the words of the prophets agree, just as it is written,

16 " 'After this I will return, and I will rebuild the tent of David that has fallen; I will rebuild its ruins, and I will restore it,

17 " 'that the remnant of mankind may seek the Lord, and all the Gentiles who are called by my name, says the Lord, who makes these things

18 " known from of old.'

19 "Therefore my judgment is that we should not trouble those of the Gentiles who turn to God,

20 "but should write to them to abstain from the things polluted by idols, and from sexual immorality, and from what has been strangled, and from blood.

21 "For from ancient generations Moses has had in every city those who proclaim him, for he is read every Sabbath in the synagogues."

22 "Then it seemed good to the apostles and the elders, with the whole church, to choose men from among *them* and send them to Antioch with Paul and Barnabas. They sent Judas called Barsabbas, and Silas, leading men among the brothers,

23 with the following letter: "The brothers, both the apostles and the elders, to the brothers who are of the Gentiles in Antioch and Syria and Cilicia, greetings.

24 "Since we have heard that some persons have gone out from us and troubled you with words, unsettling your minds, although we gave them no instructions,

25 "it has seemed good to us, having come to one accord, to choose men and send them to you with our beloved Barnabas and Paul,

26 "men who have risked their lives for the name of our Lord Jesus Christ.

27 "We have therefore sent Judas and Silas, who themselves will tell you the same things by word of mouth.

28 "For it has seemed good to the Holy Spirit and to us to lay on you no greater burden than these requirements:

29 "that you abstain from what has been sacrificed to idols, and from blood, and from what has been strangled, and from sexual immorality. If you keep yourselves *from these, you will do well.* Farewell."

30 So when they were sent off, they went down to Antioch, and having gathered the congregation together, they delivered the letter.

31 And when they had read it, they rejoiced because of its encouragement.

32 And Judas and Silas, who were themselves prophets, encouraged and strengthened the brothers with many words.

33 And after they had spent some time, they were sent off in peace by the brothers to those who had sent them.

34 But it seemed good to Silas to remain there.

35 But Paul and Barnabas remained in Antioch, teaching and preaching the word of the Lord, with many others also.

36 And after some days Paul said to Barnabas, "Let us return and visit the brothers in every city where we proclaimed the word of the Lord, and see how they are."

37 Now Barnabas wanted to take with them John called Mark.

38 But Paul thought best not to take with them one who had withdrawn from them in Pamphylia and had not gone with them to the work.

39 And there arose a sharp disagreement, so that they separated from each other. Barnabas took Mark with him and sailed away to Cyprus,

40 but Paul chose Silas and departed, having been commended by the brothers to the grace of the Lord.

41 And he went through Syria and Cilicia, strengthening the churches.

1 Paul came also to Derbe and to Lystra. A disciple was there, named Timothy, the son of a Jewish woman who was a believer, but his father was a Greek.

2 He was well spoken of by the brothers at Lystra and Iconium.

3 Paul wanted Timothy to accompany him, and he took him and circumcised him because of the Jews who were in those places, for they all knew that his father was a Greek.

4 As they went on their way through the cities, they delivered to them for observance the decisions that had been reached by the apostles and elders who were in Jerusalem.

5 So the churches were strengthened in the faith, and they increased in numbers daily.

6 And they went through the region of Phrygia and Galatia, having been forbidden by the Holy Spirit to speak the word in Asia.

7 And when they had come up to Mysia, they attempted to go into Bithynia, but the Spirit of Jesus did not allow them.

8 So, passing by Mysia, they went down to Troas.

9 And a vision appeared to Paul in the night: a man

of Macedonia was standing there, urging him and saying, "Come over to Macedonia and help us."

10 And when Paul had seen the vision, immediately we sought to go on into Macedonia, concluding that God had called us to preach the gospel to them.

11 So, setting sail from Troas, we made a direct voyage to Samothrace, and the following day to Neapolis,

12 and from there to Philippi, which is a leading city of the district of Macedonia and a Roman colony. We remained in this city some days.

13 And on the Sabbath day we went out the gate to the riverside, where we supposed there was a place of prayer, and we sat down and spoke to the women who had come together.

14 One who heard us was a woman named Lydia, from the city of Thyatira, a seller of purple goods, who was a worshiper of God. The Lord opened her heart to pay attention to what was said by Paul.

15 And after she was baptized, and her household as well, she urged us, saying, "If you have judged me to be faithful to the Lord, come to my house and stay." And she prevailed upon us.

16 As we were going to the place of prayer, we were met by a slave girl who had a spirit of divination and brought her owners much gain by fortune-telling.

17 She followed Paul and us, crying out, "These men are servants of the Most High God, who proclaim to you the way of salvation."

18 And this she kept doing for many days. Paul, having become greatly annoyed, turned and said to the spirit, "I command you in the name of Jesus Christ to come out of her." And it came out that very hour.

19 But when her owners saw that their hope of gain was gone, they seized Paul and Silas and dragged them into the marketplace before the rulers.

20 And when they had brought them to the magistrates, they said, "These men are Jews, and they are disturbing our city.

21 "They advocate customs that are not lawful for us as Romans to accept or practice."

22 The crowd joined in attacking them, and the magistrates tore the garments off them and gave orders to beat them with rods.

23 And when they had inflicted many blows upon them, they threw them into prison, ordering the jailer to keep them safely.

24 Having received this order, he put them into the inner prison and fastened their feet in the stocks.

25 About midnight Paul and Silas were praying and singing hymns to God, and the prisoners were listening to them,

26 and suddenly there was a great earthquake, so that the foundations of the prison were shaken. And immediately all the doors were opened, and everyone's bonds were unfastened.

27 When the jailer woke and saw that the prison doors were open, he drew his sword and was about to kill himself, supposing that the prisoners had escaped.

28 But Paul cried with a loud voice, "Do not harm yourself, for we are all here."

29 And the jailer called for lights and rushed in, and trembling with fear he fell down before Paul and Silas.

30 Then he brought them out and said, "Sirs, what must I do to be saved?"

31 And they said, "Believe in the Lord Jesus, and you will be saved, you and your household."

32 And they spoke the word of the Lord to him and to all who were in his house.

33 And he took them the same hour of the night and washed their wounds; and he was baptized at once, he and all his family.

34 Then he brought them up into his house and set food before them. And he rejoiced along with his entire household that he had believed in God.

35 But when it was day, the magistrates sent the police, saying, "Let those men go."

36 And the jailer reported these words to Paul, saying, "The magistrates have sent to let you go. Therefore come out now and go in peace."

37 But Paul said to them, "They have beaten us publicly, uncondemned, men who are Roman citizens, and have thrown us into prison; and do they now throw us out secretly? No! Let them come themselves and take us out."

38 The police reported these words to the magistrates, and they were afraid when they heard that they were Roman citizens.

39 So they came and apologized to them. And they took them out and asked them to leave the city.

⁴⁰ So they went out of the prison and visited Lydia. And when they had seen the brothers, they encouraged them and departed.

CHAPTER 17

¹ Now when they had passed through Amphipolis and Apollonia, they came to Thessalonica, where there was a synagogue of the Jews.

² And Paul went in, as was his custom, and on three Sabbath days he reasoned with them from the Scriptures,

³ explaining and proving that it was necessary for the Christ to suffer and to rise from the dead, and saying, "This Jesus, whom I proclaim to you, is the Christ."

⁴ And some of them were persuaded and joined Paul and Silas, as did a great many of the devout Greeks and not a few of the leading women.

⁵ But the Jews were jealous, and taking some wicked men of the rabble, they formed a mob, set the city in an uproar, and attacked the house of Jason, seeking to bring them out to the crowd.

⁶ And when they could not find them, they dragged Jason and some of the brothers before the city authorities, shouting, "These men who have turned the world upside down have come here also,

⁷ "and Jason has received them, and they are all acting against the decrees of Caesar, saying that there is another king, Jesus."

⁸ And the people and the city authorities were disturbed when they heard these things.

⁹ And when they had taken money as security from Jason and the rest, they let them go.

¹⁰ The brothers immediately sent Paul and Silas away by night to Berea, and when they arrived they went into the Jewish synagogue.

¹¹ Now these Jews were more noble than those in Thessalonica; they received the word with all eagerness, examining the Scriptures daily to see if these things were so.

¹² Many of them therefore believed, with not a few Greek women of high standing as well as men.

¹³ But when the Jews from Thessalonica learned that the word of God was proclaimed by Paul at Berea also, they came there too, agitating and stirring up the crowds.

¹⁴ Then the brothers immediately sent Paul off on his way to the sea, but Silas and Timothy remained there.

¹⁵ Those who conducted

Paul brought him as far as Athens, and after receiving a command for Silas and Timothy to come to him as soon as possible, they departed.

¹⁶ Now while Paul was waiting for them at Athens, his spirit was provoked within him as he saw that the city was full of idols.

¹⁷ So he reasoned in the synagogue with the Jews and the devout persons, and in the marketplace every day with those who happened to be there.

¹⁸ Some of the Epicurean and Stoic philosophers also conversed with him. And some said, "What does this babbler wish to say?" Others said, "He seems to be a preacher of foreign divinities"—because he was preaching Jesus and the resurrection.

¹⁹ And they took him and brought him to the Areopagus, saying, "May we know what this new teaching is that you are presenting?

²⁰ "For you bring some strange things to our ears. We wish to know therefore what these things mean."

²¹ Now all the Athenians and the foreigners who lived there would spend their time in nothing except telling or hearing something new.

²² So Paul, standing in the midst of the Areopagus, said: "Men of Athens, I perceive that in every way you are very religious.

²³ "For as I passed along and observed the objects of your worship, I found also an altar with this inscription, 'To the unknown god.' What therefore you worship as unknown, this I proclaim to you.

²⁴ "The God who made the world and everything in it, being Lord of heaven and earth, does not live in temples made by man,

²⁵ "nor is he served by human hands, as though he needed anything, since he himself gives to all mankind life and breath and everything.

²⁶ "And he made from one man every nation of mankind to live on all the face of the earth, having determined allotted periods and the boundaries of their dwelling place,

²⁷ "that they should seek God, and perhaps feel their way toward him and find him. Yet he is actually not far from each one of us,

²⁸ "for 'In him we live and move and have our being'; as even some of your own poets have said, 'For we are indeed his offspring.'

²⁹ "Being then God's offspring, we ought not to think

that the divine being is like gold or silver or stone, an image formed by the art and imagination of man.

30 "The times of ignorance God overlooked, but now he commands all people everywhere to repent,

31 "because he has fixed a day on which he will judge the world in righteousness by a man whom he has appointed; and of this he has given assurance to all by raising him from the dead."

32 Now when they heard of the resurrection of the dead, some mocked. But others said, "We will hear you again about this."

33 So Paul went out from their midst.

34 But some men joined him and believed, among whom also were Dionysius the Areopagite and a woman named Damaris and others with them.

CHAPTER 18

1 After this Paul left Athens and went to Corinth.

2 And he found a Jew named Aquila, a native of Pontus, recently come from Italy with his wife Priscilla, because Claudius had commanded all the Jews to leave Rome. And he went to see them,

3 and because he was of the same trade he stayed with them and worked, for they were tentmakers by trade.

4 And he reasoned in the synagogue every Sabbath, and tried to persuade Jews and Greeks.

5 When Silas and Timothy arrived from Macedonia, Paul was occupied with the word, testifying to the Jews that the Christ was Jesus.

6 And when they opposed and reviled him, he shook out his garments and said to them, "Your blood be on your own heads! I am innocent. From now on I will go to the Gentiles."

7 And he left there and went to the house of a man named Titius Justus, a worshiper of God. His house was next door to the synagogue.

8 Crispus, the ruler of the synagogue, believed in the Lord, together with his entire household. And many of the Corinthians hearing Paul believed and were baptized.

9 And the Lord said to Paul one night in a vision, "Do not be afraid, but go on speaking and do not be silent,

10 "for I am with you, and no one will attack you to harm you, for I have many in this city who are my people."

11 And he stayed a year and

six months, teaching the word of God among them.

[12] But when Gallio was pro-consul of Achaia, the Jews made a united attack on Paul and brought him before the tribunal,

[13] saying, "This man is persuading people to worship God contrary to the law."

[14] But when Paul was about to open his mouth, Gallio said to the Jews, "If it were a matter of wrongdoing or vicious crime, O Jews, I would have reason to accept your complaint.

[15] "But since it is a matter of questions about words and names and your own law, see to it yourselves. I refuse to be a judge of these things."

[16] And he drove them from the tribunal.

[17] And they all seized Sosthenes, the ruler of the synagogue, and beat him in front of the tribunal. But Gallio paid no attention to any of this.

[18] After this, Paul stayed many days longer and then took leave of the brothers and set sail for Syria, and with him Priscilla and Aquila. At Cenchreae he had cut his hair, for he was under a vow.

[19] And they came to Ephesus, and he left them there, but he himself went into the synagogue and rea... the Jews.

[20] When they asked him to stay for a longer period, he declined.

[21] But on taking leave of them he said, "I will return to you if God wills," and he set sail from Ephesus.

[22] When he had landed at Caesarea, he went up and greeted the church, and then went down to Antioch.

[23] After spending some time there, he departed and went from one place to the next through the region of Galatia and Phrygia, strengthening all the disciples.

[24] Now a Jew named Apollos, a native of Alexandria, came to Ephesus. He was an eloquent man, competent in the Scriptures.

[25] He had been instructed in the way of the Lord. And being fervent in spirit, he spoke and taught accurately the things concerning Jesus, though he knew only the baptism of John.

[26] He began to speak boldly in the synagogue, but when Priscilla and Aquila heard him, they took him aside and explained to him the way of God more accurately.

[27] And when he wished to cross to Achaia, the brothers encouraged him and wrote to

the disciples to welcome him. When he arrived, he greatly *helped those who through grace had believed,*

28 for he powerfully refuted the Jews in public, showing by the Scriptures that the Christ was Jesus.

CHAPTER 19

1 And it happened that while Apollos was at Corinth, Paul passed through the inland country and came to Ephesus. There he found some disciples.

2 And he said to them, "Did you receive the Holy Spirit when you believed?" And they said, "No, we have not even heard that there is a Holy Spirit."

3 And he said, "Into what then were you baptized?" They said, "Into John's baptism."

4 And Paul said, "John baptized with the baptism of repentance, telling the people to believe in the one who was to come after him, that is, Jesus."

5 On hearing this, they were baptized in the name of the Lord Jesus.

6 And when Paul had laid his hands on them, the Holy Spirit came on them, and they began speaking in tongues and prophesying.

7 There were about twelve men in all.

8 And he entered the synagogue and for three months spoke boldly, reasoning and persuading them about the kingdom of God.

9 But when some became stubborn and continued in unbelief, speaking evil of the Way before the congregation, he withdrew from them and took the disciples with him, reasoning daily in the hall of Tyrannus.

10 This continued for two years, so that all the residents of Asia heard the word of the Lord, both Jews and Greeks.

11 And God was doing extraordinary miracles by the hands of Paul,

12 so that even handkerchiefs or aprons that had touched his skin were carried away to the sick, and their diseases left them and the evil spirits came out of them.

13 Then some of the itinerant Jewish exorcists undertook to invoke the name of the Lord Jesus over those who had evil spirits, saying, "I adjure you by the Jesus whom Paul proclaims."

14 Seven sons of a Jewish high priest named Sceva were doing this.

15 But the evil spirit answered them, "Jesus I know,

and Paul I recognize, but who are you?"

16 And the man in whom was the evil spirit leaped on them, mastered all of them and overpowered them, so that they fled out of that house naked and wounded.

17 And this became known to all the residents of Ephesus, both Jews and Greeks. And fear fell upon them all, and the name of the Lord Jesus was extolled.

18 Also many of those who were now believers came, confessing and divulging their practices.

19 And a number of those who had practiced magic arts brought their books together and burned them in the sight of all. And they counted the value of them and found it came to fifty thousand pieces of silver.

20 So the word of the Lord continued to increase and prevail mightily.

21 Now after these events Paul resolved in the Spirit to pass through Macedonia and Achaia and go to Jerusalem, saying, "After I have been there, I must also see Rome."

22 And having sent into Macedonia two of his helpers, Timothy and Erastus, he himself stayed in Asia for a while.

23 About that time there arose no little disturbance concerning the Way.

24 For a man named Demetrius, a silversmith, who made silver shrines of Artemis, brought to no little business to the craftsmen.

25 These he gathered together, with the workmen in similar trades, and said, "Men, you know that from this business we have our wealth.

26 "And you see and hear that not only in Ephesus but in almost all of Asia this Paul has persuaded and turned away a great many people, saying that gods made with hands are not gods.

27 "And there is danger not only that this trade of ours may come into disrepute but also that the temple of the great goddess Artemis may be counted as nothing, and that she may even be deposed from her magnificence, she whom all Asia and the world worship."

28 When they heard this they were enraged and were crying out, "Great is Artemis of the Ephesians!"

29 So the city was filled with the confusion, and they rushed together into the theater, dragging with them Gaius and Aristarchus,

Macedonians who were Paul's companions in travel.

30 But when Paul wished to go in among the crowd, the disciples would not let him.

31 And even some of the Asiarchs, who were friends of his, sent to him and were urging him not to venture into the theater.

32 Now some cried out one thing, some another, for the assembly was in confusion, and most of them did not know why they had come together.

33 Some of the crowd prompted Alexander, whom the Jews had put forward. And Alexander, motioning with his hand, wanted to make a defense to the crowd.

34 But when they recognized that he was a Jew, for about two hours they all cried out with one voice, "Great is Artemis of the Ephesians!"

35 And when the town clerk had quieted the crowd, he said, "Men of Ephesus, who is there who does not know that the city of the Ephesians is temple keeper of the great Artemis, and of the sacred stone that fell from the sky?

36 "Seeing then that these things cannot be denied, you ought to be quiet and do nothing rash.

37 "For you have brought these men here who are neither sacrilegious nor blasphemers of our goddess.

38 "If therefore Demetrius and the craftsmen with him have a complaint against anyone, the courts are open, and there are proconsuls. Let them bring charges against one another.

39 "But if you seek anything further, it shall be settled in the regular assembly.

40 "For we really are in danger of being charged with rioting today, since there is no cause that we can give to justify this commotion."

41 And when he had said these things, he dismissed the assembly.

CHAPTER 20

1 After the uproar ceased, Paul sent for the disciples, and after encouraging them, he said farewell and departed for Macedônia.

2 When he had gone through those regions and had given them much encouragement, he came to Greece.

3 There he spent three months, and when a plot was made against him by the Jews as he was about to set sail for Syria, he decided to return through Macedonia.

4 Sopater the Berean, son of Pyrrhus, accompanied him;

and of the Thessalonians, Aristarchus and Secundus; and Gaius of Derbe, and Timothy; and the Asians, Tychicus and Trophimus.

5 These went on ahead and were waiting for us at Troas,

6 but we sailed away from Philippi after the days of Unleavened Bread, and in five days we came to them at Troas, where we stayed for seven days.

7 On the first day of the week, when we were gathered together to break bread, Paul talked with them, intending to depart on the next day, and he prolonged his speech until midnight.

8 There were many lamps in the upper room where we were gathered.

9 And a young man named Eutychus, sitting at the window, sank into a deep sleep as Paul talked still longer. And being overcome by sleep, he fell down from the third story and was taken up dead.

10 But Paul went down and bent over him, and taking him in his arms, said, "Do not be alarmed, for his life is in him."

11 And when Paul had gone up and had broken bread and eaten, he conversed with them a long while, until daybreak, and so departed.

12 And they took the youth away alive, and were not a little comforted.

13 But going ahead to the ship, we set sail for Assos, intending to take Paul aboard there, for so he had arranged, intending himself to go by land.

14 And when he met us at Assos, we took him on board and went to Mitylene.

15 And sailing from there we came the following day opposite Chios; the next day we touched at Samos; and the day after that we went to Miletus.

16 For Paul had decided to sail past Ephesus, so that he might not have to spend time in Asia, for he was hastening to be at Jerusalem, if possible, on the day of Pentecost.

17 Now from Miletus he sent to Ephesus and called the elders of the church to come to him.

18 And when they came to him, he said to them: "You yourselves know how I lived among you the whole time from the first day that I set foot in Asia,

19 "serving the Lord with all humility and with tears and with trials that happened to me through the plots of the Jews;

20 "how I did not shrink

from declaring to you anything that was profitable, and teaching you in public and from house to house,

21 "testifying both to Jews and to Greeks of repentance toward God and of faith in our Lord Jesus Christ.

22 "And now, behold, I am going to Jerusalem, constrained by the Spirit, not knowing what will happen to me there,

23 "except that the Holy Spirit testifies to me in every city that imprisonment and afflictions await me.

24 "But I do not account my life of any value nor as precious to myself, if only I may finish my course and the ministry that I received from the Lord Jesus, to testify to the gospel of the grace of God.

25 "And now, behold, I know that none of you among whom I have gone about proclaiming the kingdom will see my face again.

26 "Therefore I testify to you this day that I am innocent of the blood of all,

27 "for I did not shrink from declaring to you the whole counsel of God.

28 "Pay careful attention to yourselves and to all the flock, in which the Holy Spirit has made you overseers, to care for the church of God, which he purchased with his own blood.

29 "I know that after my departure fierce wolves will come in among you, not sparing the flock;

30 "and from among your own selves will arise men speaking twisted things, to draw away the disciples after them.

31 "Therefore be alert, remembering that for three years I did not cease night or day to admonish every one with tears.

32 "And now I commend you to God and to the word of his grace, which is able to build you up and to give you the inheritance among all those who are sanctified.

33 "I coveted no one's silver or gold or apparel.

34 "You yourselves know that these hands ministered to my necessities and to those who were with me.

35 "In all things I have shown you that by working hard in this way we must help the weak and remember the words of the Lord Jesus, how he himself said, 'It is more blessed to give than to receive.'"

36 And when he had said these things, he knelt down and prayed with them all.

37 And there was much weep-

ing on the part of all; they embraced Paul and kissed him,

³⁸ being sorrowful most of all because of the word he had spoken, that they would not see his face again. And they accompanied him to the ship.

CHAPTER 21

¹ And when we had parted from them and set sail, we came by a straight course to Cos, and the next day to Rhodes, and from there to Patara.

² And having found a ship crossing to Phoenicia, we went aboard and set sail.

³ When we had come in sight of Cyprus, leaving it on the left we sailed to Syria and landed at Tyre, for there the ship was to unload its cargo.

⁴ And having sought out the disciples, we stayed there for seven days. And through the Spirit they were telling Paul not to go on to Jerusalem.

⁵ When our days there were ended, we departed and went on our journey, and they all, with wives and children, accompanied us until we were outside the city. And kneeling down on the beach, we prayed

⁶ and said farewell to one another. Then we went on board the ship, and they returned home.

⁷ When we had finished the voyage from Tyre, we arrived at Ptolemais, and we greeted the brothers and stayed with them for one day.

⁸ On the next day we departed and came to Caesarea, and we entered the house of Philip the evangelist, who was one of the seven, and stayed with him.

⁹ He had four unmarried daughters, who prophesied.

¹⁰ While we were staying for many days, a prophet named Agabus came down from Judea.

¹¹ And coming to us, he took Paul's belt and bound his own feet and hands and said, "Thus says the Holy Spirit, 'This is how the Jews at Jerusalem will bind the man who owns this belt and deliver him into the hands of the Gentiles.'"

¹² When we heard this, we and the people there urged him not to go up to Jerusalem.

¹³ Then Paul answered, "What are you doing, weeping and breaking my heart? For I am ready not only to be imprisoned but even to die in Jerusalem for the name of the Lord Jesus."

¹⁴ And since he would not be persuaded, we ceased and said, "Let the will of the Lord be done."

¹⁵ After these days we got

ready and went up to Jerusalem.

16 And some of the disciples from Caesarea went with us, bringing us to the house of Mnason of Cyprus, an early disciple, with whom we should lodge.

17 When we had come to Jerusalem, the brothers received us gladly.

18 On the following day Paul went in with us to James, and all the elders were present.

19 After greeting them, he related one by one the things that God had done among the Gentiles through his ministry.

20 And when they heard it, they glorified God. And they said to him, "You see, brother, how many thousands there are among the Jews of those who have believed. They are all zealous for the law,

21 "and they have been told about you that you teach all the Jews who are among the Gentiles to forsake Moses, telling them not to circumcise their children or walk according to our customs.

22 "What then is to be done? They will certainly hear that you have come.

23 "Do therefore what we tell you. We have four men who are under a vow;

24 "take these men and purify yourself along with them and pay their expenses, so that they may shave their heads. Thus all will know that there is nothing in what they have been told about you, but that you yourself also live in observance of the law.

25 "But as for the Gentiles who have believed, we have sent a letter with our judgment that they should abstain from what has been sacrificed to idols, and from blood, and from what has been strangled, and from sexual immorality."

26 Then Paul took the men, and the next day he purified himself along with them and went into the temple, giving notice when the days of purification would be fulfilled and the offering presented for each one of them.

27 When the seven days were almost completed, the Jews from Asia, seeing him in the temple, stirred up the whole crowd and laid hands on him,

28 crying out, "Men of Israel, help! This is the man who is teaching everyone everywhere against the people and the law and this place. Moreover, he even brought Greeks into the temple and has defiled this holy place."

29 For they had previously

seen Trophimus the Ephesian with him in the city, and they supposed that Paul had brought him into the temple.

30 Then all the city was stirred up, and the people ran together. They seized Paul and dragged him out of the temple, and at once the gates were shut.

31 And as they were seeking to kill him, word came to the tribune of the cohort that all Jerusalem was in confusion.

32 He at once took soldiers and centurions and ran down to them. And when they saw the tribune and the soldiers, they stopped beating Paul.

33 Then the tribune came up and arrested him and ordered him to be bound with two chains. He inquired who he was and what he had done.

34 Some in the crowd were shouting one thing, some another. And as he could not learn the facts because of the uproar, he ordered him to be brought into the barracks.

35 And when he came to the steps, he was actually carried by the soldiers because of the violence of the crowd,

36 for the mob of the people followed, crying out, "Away with him!"

37 As Paul was about to be brought into the barracks, he said to the tribune, "May I say something to you?" And he said, "Do you know Greek?

38 "Are you not the Egyptian, then, who recently stirred up a revolt and led the four thousand men of the Assassins out into the wilderness?"

39 Paul replied, "I am a Jew, from Tarsus in Cilicia, a citizen of no obscure city. I beg you, permit me to speak to the people."

40 And when he had given him permission, Paul, standing on the steps, motioned with his hand to the people. And when there was a great hush, he addressed them in the Hebrew language, saying:

CHAPTER 22

1 "Brothers and fathers, hear the defense that I now make before you."

2 And when they heard that he was addressing them in the Hebrew language, they became even more quiet. And he said:

3 "I am a Jew, born in Tarsus in Cilicia, but brought up in this city, educated at the feet of Gamaliel according to the strict manner of the law of our fathers, being zealous for God as all of you are this day.

4 "I persecuted this Way to the death, binding and delivering to prison both men and women,

5 "as the high priest and the whole council of elders can bear me witness. From them I received letters to the brothers, and I journeyed toward Damascus to take those also who were there and bring them in bonds to Jerusalem to be punished.

6 "As I was on my way and drew near to Damascus, about noon a great light from heaven suddenly shone around me.

7 "And I fell to the ground and heard a voice saying to me, 'Saul, Saul, why are you persecuting me?'

8 "And I answered, 'Who are you, Lord?' And he said to me, 'I am Jesus of Nazareth, whom you are persecuting.'

9 "Now those who were with me saw the light but did not understand the voice of the one who was speaking to me.

10 "And I said, 'What shall I do, Lord?' And the Lord said to me, 'Rise, and go into Damascus, and there you will be told all that is appointed for you to do.'

11 "And since I could not see because of the brightness of that light, I was led by the hand by those who were with me, and came into Damascus.

12 "And one Ananias, a devout man according to the law, well spoken of by all the Jews who lived there,

13 "came to me, and standing by me said to me, 'Brother Saul, receive your sight.' And at that very hour I received my sight and saw him.

14 "And he said, 'The God of our fathers appointed you to know his will, to see the Righteous One and to hear a voice from his mouth;

15 " 'for you will be a witness for him to everyone of what you have seen and heard.

16 " 'And now why do you wait? Rise and be baptized and wash away your sins, calling on his name.'

17 "When I had returned to Jerusalem and was praying in the temple, I fell into a trance

18 "and saw him saying to me, 'Make haste and get out of Jerusalem quickly, because they will not accept your testimony about me.'

19 "And I said, 'Lord, they themselves know that in one synagogue after another I imprisoned and beat those who believed in you.

20 "And when the blood of Stephen your witness was being shed, I myself was standing by and approving and watching over the garments of those who killed him.'

21 "And he said to me, 'Go,

for I will send you far away to the Gentiles.'"

²² Up to this word they listened to him. Then they raised their voices and said, "Away with such a fellow from the earth! For he should not be allowed to live."

²³ And as they were shouting and throwing off their cloaks and flinging dust into the air,

²⁴ the tribune ordered him to be brought into the barracks, saying that he should be examined by flogging, to find out why they were shouting against him like this.

²⁵ But when they had stretched him out for the whips, Paul said to the centurion who was standing by, "Is it lawful for you to flog a man who is a Roman citizen and uncondemned?"

²⁶ When the centurion heard this, he went to the tribune and said to him, "What are you about to do? For this man is a Roman citizen."

²⁷ So the tribune came and said to him, "Tell me, are you a Roman citizen?" And he said, "Yes."

²⁸ The tribune answered, "I bought this citizenship for a large sum." Paul said, "But I am a citizen by birth."

²⁹ So those who were about to examine him withdrew from him immediately, and the tribune also was afraid, for he realized that Paul was a Roman citizen and that he had bound him.

³⁰ But on the next day, desiring to know the real reason why he was being accused by the Jews, he unbound him and commanded the chief priests and all the council to meet, and he brought Paul down and set him before them.

CHAPTER 23

¹ And looking intently at the council, Paul said, "Brothers, I have lived my life before God in all good conscience up to this day."

² And the high priest Ananias commanded those who stood by him to strike him on the mouth.

³ Then Paul said to him, "God is going to strike you, you whitewashed wall! Are you sitting to judge me according to the law, and yet contrary to the law you order me to be struck?"

⁴ Those who stood by said, "Would you revile God's high priest?"

⁵ And Paul said, "I did not know, brothers, that he was the high priest, for it is

written, 'You shall not speak evil of a ruler of your people.' "

6 Now when Paul perceived that one part were Sadducees and the other Pharisees, he cried out in the council, "Brothers, I am a Pharisee, a son of Pharisees. It is with respect to the hope and the resurrection of the dead that I am on trial."

7 And when he had said this, a dissension arose between the Pharisees and the Sadducees, and the assembly was divided.

8 For the Sadducees say that there is no resurrection, nor angel, nor spirit, but the Pharisees acknowledge them all.

9 Then a great clamor arose, and some of the scribes of the Pharisees' party stood up and contended sharply, "We find nothing wrong in this man. What if a spirit or an angel spoke to him?"

10 And when the dissension became violent, the tribune, afraid that Paul *would* be torn to pieces by them, commanded the soldiers to go down and take him away from among them by force and bring him into the barracks.

11 The following night the Lord stood by him and said, "Take courage, for as you have testified to the facts about me in Jerusalem, so you must testify also in Rome."

12 When it was day, the Jews made a plot and bound themselves by an oath neither to eat nor drink till they had killed Paul.

13 There were more than forty who made this conspiracy.

14 They went to the chief priests and elders and said, "We have strictly bound ourselves by an oath to taste no food till we have killed Paul.

15 Now therefore you, along with the council, give notice to the tribune to bring him down to you, as though you were going to determine his case more exactly. And we are ready to kill him before he comes near."

16 Now the son of Paul's sister heard of their ambush, so he went and entered the barracks and told Paul.

17 Paul called one of the centurions and said, "Take this young man to the tribune, for he has something to tell him."

18 So he took him and brought him to the tribune and said, "Paul the prisoner called me and asked me to bring this young man to you, as he has something to say to you."

19 The tribune took him by the hand, and going aside

asked him privately, "What is it that you have to tell me?"

20 And he said, "The Jews have agreed to ask you to bring Paul down to the council tomorrow, as though they were going to inquire somewhat more closely about him.

21 "But do not be persuaded by them, for more than forty of their men are lying in ambush for him, who have bound themselves by an oath neither to eat nor drink till they have killed him. And now they are ready, waiting for your consent."

22 So the tribune dismissed the young man, charging him, "Tell no one that you have informed me of these things."

23 Then he called two of the centurions and said, "Get ready two hundred soldiers, with seventy horsemen and two hundred spearmen to go as far as Caesarea at the third hour of the night.

24 "Also provide mounts for Paul to ride and bring him safely to Felix the governor."

25 And he wrote a letter to this effect:

26 "Claudius Lysias, to his Excellency the governor Felix, greetings.

27 "This man was seized by the Jews and was about to be killed by them when I came upon them with the soldiers and rescued him, having learned that he was a Roman citizen.

28 "And desiring to know the charge for which they were accusing him, I brought him down to their council.

29 "I found that he was being accused about questions of their law, but charged with nothing deserving death or imprisonment.

30 "And when it was disclosed to me that there would be a plot against the man, I sent him to you at once, ordering his accusers also to state before you what they have against him."

31 So the soldiers, according to their instructions, took Paul and brought him by night to Antipatris.

32 And on the next day they returned to the barracks, letting the horsemen go on with him.

33 When they had come to Caesarea and delivered the letter to the governor, they presented Paul also before him.

34 On reading the letter, he asked what province he was from. And when he learned that he was from Cilicia,

35 he said, "I will give you a hearing when your accusers arrive." And he commanded

him to be guarded in Herod's praetorium.

CHAPTER 24

1 And after five days the high priest Ananias came down with some elders and a spokesman, one Tertullus. They laid before the governor their case against Paul.

2 And when he had been summoned, Tertullus began to accuse him, saying: "Since through you we enjoy much peace, and since by your foresight, most excellent Felix, reforms are being made for this nation,

3 "in every way and everywhere we accept this with all gratitude.

4 "But, to detain you no further, I beg you in your kindness to hear us briefly.

5 "For we have found this man a plague, one who stirs up riots among all the Jews throughout the world and is a ringleader of the sect of the Nazarenes.

6 "He even tried *to profane the temple, but* we seized him and we would have judged him *according to our law.

7 "But the chief captain Lysias came and with great violence took him out of our hands,

8 "commanding his accusers to come before you. By examining him yourself you will* be able to find out from him about everything of which we accuse him."

9 The Jews also joined in the charge, affirming that all these things were so.

10 And when the governor had nodded to him to speak, Paul replied: "Knowing that for many years you have been a judge over this nation, I cheerfully make my defense.

11 "You can verify that it is not more than twelve days since I went up to worship in Jerusalem,

12 "and they did not find me disputing with anyone or stirring up a crowd, either in the temple or in the synagogues or in the city.

13 "Neither can they prove to you what they now bring up against me.

14 "But this I confess to you, that according to the Way, which they call a sect, I worship the *God of* our fathers, *believing* everything laid down by the Law and written in the Prophets,

15 "having a hope in God, which these men themselves accept, that there will be a resurrection of both the just and the unjust.

16 "So I always take pains to have a clear conscience toward both God and man.

¹⁷ "Now after several years I came to bring alms to my nation and to present offerings.

¹⁸ "While I was doing this, they found me purified in the temple, without any crowd or tumult. But some Jews from Asia—

¹⁹ "they ought to be here before you and to make an accusation, should they have anything against me.

²⁰ "Or else let these men themselves say what wrongdoing they found when I stood before the council,

²¹ "other than this one thing that I cried out while standing among them: 'It is with respect to the resurrection of the dead that I am on trial before you this day.'"

²² But Felix, having a rather accurate knowledge of the Way, put them off, saying, "When Lysias the tribune comes down, I will decide your case."

²³ Then he gave orders to the centurion that he should be kept in custody but have some liberty, and that none of his friends should be prevented from attending to his needs.

²⁴ After some days Felix came with his wife Drusilla, who was Jewish, and he sent for Paul and heard him speak about faith in Christ Jesus.

²⁵ And as he reasoned about righteousness and self-control and the coming judgment, Felix was alarmed and said, "Go away for the present. When I get an opportunity I will summon you."

²⁶ At the same time he hoped that money would be given him by Paul. So he sent for him often and conversed with him.

²⁷ When two years had elapsed, Felix was succeeded by Porcius Festus. And desiring to do the Jews a favor, Felix left Paul in prison.

CHAPTER 25

¹ Now three days after Festus had arrived in the province, he went up to Jerusalem from Caesarea.

² And the chief priests and the principal men of the Jews laid out their case against Paul, and they urged him,

³ asking as a favor against Paul that he summon him to Jerusalem—because they were planning an ambush to kill him on the way.

⁴ Festus replied that Paul was being kept at Caesarea and that he himself intended to go there shortly.

⁵ "So," said he, "let the men of authority among you go down with me, and if there is anything wrong about the

man, let them bring charges against him."

⁶ After he stayed among them not more than eight or ten days, he went down to Caesarea. And the next day he took his seat on the tribunal and ordered Paul to be brought.

⁷ When he had arrived, the Jews who had come down from Jerusalem stood around him, bringing many and serious charges against him that they could not prove.

⁸ Paul argued in his defense, "Neither against the law of the Jews, nor against the temple, nor against Caesar have I committed any offense."

⁹ But Festus, wishing to do the Jews a favor, said to Paul, "Do you wish to go up to Jerusalem and there be tried on these charges before me?"

¹⁰ But Paul said, "I am standing before Caesar's tribunal, where I ought to be tried. To the Jews I have done no wrong, as you yourself know very well.

¹¹ "If then I am a wrongdoer and have committed anything for which I deserve to die, I do not seek to escape death. But if there is nothing to their charges against me, no one can give me up to them. I appeal to Caesar."

¹² Then Paul, when he had conferred with his council, answered, "To Caesar you have appealed; to Caesar you shall go."

¹³ Now when some days had passed, Agrippa the king and Bernice arrived at Caesarea and greeted Festus.

¹⁴ And as they stayed there many days, Festus laid Paul's case before the king, saying, "There is a man left prisoner by Felix,

¹⁵ "and when I was at Jerusalem, the chief priests and the elders of the Jews laid out their case against him, asking for a sentence of condemnation against him.

¹⁶ "I answered them that it was not the custom of the Romans to give up anyone before the accused met the accusers face to face and had opportunity to make his defense concerning the charge laid against him.

¹⁷ "So when they came together here, I made no delay, but on the next day took my seat on the tribunal and ordered the man to be brought.

¹⁸ "When the accusers stood up, they brought no charge in his case of such evils as I supposed.

¹⁹ "Rather they had certain points of dispute with him about their own religion and about a certain Jesus, who

was dead, but whom Paul asserted to be alive.

20 "Being at a loss how to investigate these questions, I asked whether he wanted to go to Jerusalem and be tried there regarding them.

21 "But when Paul had appealed to be kept in custody for the decision of the emperor, I ordered him to be held until I could send him to Caesar."

22 Then Agrippa said to Festus, "I would like to hear the man myself." "Tomorrow," said he, "you will hear him."

23 So on the next day Agrippa and Bernice came with great pomp, and they entered the audience hall with the military tribunes and the prominent men of the city. Then, at the command of Festus, Paul was brought in.

24 And Festus said, "King Agrippa and all who are present with us, you see this man about whom the whole Jewish people petitioned me, both in Jerusalem and here, shouting that he ought not to live any longer.

25 "But I found that he had done nothing deserving death. And as he himself appealed to the emperor, I decided to go ahead and send him.

26 "But I have nothing definite to write to my lord about him. Therefore I have brought him before you all, and especially before you, King Agrippa, so that, after we have examined him, I may have something to write.

27 "For it seems to me unreasonable, in sending a prisoner, not to indicate the charges against him."

CHAPTER 26

1 So Agrippa said to Paul, "You have permission to speak for yourself." Then Paul stretched out his hand and made his defense:

2 "I consider myself fortunate that it is before you, King Agrippa, I am going to make my defense today against all the accusations of the Jews.

3 "especially because you are familiar with all the customs and controversies of the Jews. Therefore I beg you to listen to me patiently.

4 "My manner of life from my youth, spent from the beginning among my own nation and in Jerusalem, is known by all the Jews.

5 "They have known for a long time, if they are willing to testify, that according to the strictest party of our religion I have lived as a Pharisee.

6 "And now I stand here on trial because of my hope in

the promise made by God to our fathers,

7 "to which our twelve tribes hope to attain, as they earnestly worship night and day. And for this hope I am accused by Jews, O king!

8 "Why is it thought incredible by any of you that God raises the dead?

9 "I myself was convinced that I ought to do many things in opposing the name of Jesus of Nazareth.

10 "And I did so in Jerusalem. I not only locked up many of the saints in prison after receiving authority from the chief priests, but when they were put to death I cast my vote against them.

11 "And I punished them often in all the synagogues and tried to make them blaspheme, and in raging fury against them I persecuted them even to foreign cities.

12 "In this connection I journeyed to Damascus with the authority and commission of the chief priests.

13 "At midday, O king, I saw on the way a light from heaven, brighter than the sun, that shone around me and those who journeyed with me.

14 "And when we had all fallen to the ground, I heard a voice saying to me in the Hebrew language, 'Saul, Saul, why are you persecuting me? It is hard for you to kick against the goads.'

15 "And I said, 'Who are you, Lord?' And the Lord said, 'I am Jesus whom you are persecuting.

16 "'But rise and stand upon your feet, for I have appeared to you for this purpose, to appoint you as a servant and witness to the things in which you have seen me and to those in which I will appear to you,

17 "'delivering you from your people and from the Gentiles—to whom I am sending you

18 "'to open their eyes, so that they may turn from darkness to light and from the power of Satan to God, that they may receive forgiveness of sins and a place among those who are sanctified by faith in me.'

19 "Therefore, O King Agrippa, I was not disobedient to the heavenly vision,

20 "but declared first to those in Damascus, then in Jerusalem and throughout all the region of Judea, and also to the Gentiles, that they should repent and turn to God, performing deeds in keeping with their repentance.

21 "For this reason the Jews seized me in the temple and tried to kill me.

²² "To this day I have had the help that comes from God, and so I stand here testifying both to small and great, saying nothing but what the prophets and Moses said would come to pass:

²³ "that the Christ must suffer and that, by being the first to rise from the dead, he would proclaim light both to our people and to the Gentiles."

²⁴ And as he was saying these things in his defense, Festus said with a loud voice, "Paul, you are out of your mind; your great learning is driving you out of your mind."

²⁵ But Paul said, "I am not out of my mind, most excellent Festus, but I am speaking true and rational words.

²⁶ "For the king knows about these things, and to him I speak boldly. For I am persuaded that none of these things has escaped his notice, for this has not been done in a corner.

²⁷ "King Agrippa, do you believe the prophets? I know that you believe."

²⁸ And Agrippa said to Paul, "In a short time would you persuade me to be a Christian?"

²⁹ And Paul said, "Whether short or long, I would to God that not only you but also all who hear me this day might become such as I am—except for these chains."

³⁰ Then the king rose, and the governor and Bernice and those who were sitting with them.

³¹ And when they had withdrawn, they said to one another, "This man is doing nothing to deserve death or imprisonment."

³² And Agrippa said to Festus, "This man could have been set free if he had not appealed to Caesar."

CHAPTER 27

¹ And when it was decided that we should sail for Italy, they delivered Paul and some other prisoners to a centurion of the Augustan Cohort named Julius.

² And embarking in a ship of Adramyttium, which was about to sail to the ports along the coast of Asia, we put to sea, accompanied by Aristarchus, a Macedonian from Thessalonica.

³ The next day we put in at Sidon. And Julius treated Paul kindly and gave him leave to go to his friends and be cared for.

⁴ And putting out to sea from there we sailed under the lee of Cyprus, because the winds were against us.

5 And when we had sailed across the open sea along the coast of Cilicia and Pamphylia, we came to Myra in Lycia.

6 There the centurion found a ship of Alexandria sailing for Italy and put us on board.

7 We sailed slowly for a number of days and arrived with difficulty off Cnidus, and as the wind did not allow us to go farther, we sailed under the lee of Crete off Salmone.

8 Coasting along it with difficulty, we came to a place called Fair Havens, near which was the city of Lasea.

9 Since much time had passed, and the voyage was now dangerous because even the Fast was already over, Paul advised them,

10 saying, "Sirs, I perceive that the voyage will be with injury and much loss, not only of the cargo and the ship, but also of our lives."

11 But the centurion paid more attention to the pilot and to the owner of the ship than to what Paul said.

12 And because the harbor was not suitable to spend the winter in, the majority decided to put out to sea from there, on the chance that somehow they could reach Phoenix, a harbor of Crete, facing both southwest and northwest, and spend the winter there.

13 Now when the south wind blew gently, supposing that they had obtained their purpose, they weighed anchor and sailed along Crete, close to the shore.

14 But soon a tempestuous wind, called the northeaster, struck down from the land.

15 And when the ship was caught and could not face the wind, we gave way to it and were driven along.

16 Running under the lee of a small island called Cauda, we managed with difficulty to secure the ship's boat.

17 After hoisting it up, they used supports to undergird the ship. Then, fearing that they would run aground on the Syrtis, they lowered the gear, and thus they were driven along.

18 Since we were violently storm-tossed, they began the next day to jettison the cargo.

19 And on the third day they threw the ship's tackle overboard with their own hands.

20 When neither sun nor stars appeared for many days, and no small tempest lay on us, all hope of our being saved was at last abandoned.

21 Since they had been without food for a long time, Paul

stood up among them and said, "Men, you should have listened to me and not have set sail from Crete and incurred this injury and loss.

22 "Yet now I urge you to take heart, for there will be no loss of life among you, but only of the ship.

23 "For this very night there stood before me an angel of the God to whom I belong and whom I worship,

24 "and he said, 'Do not be afraid, Paul; you must stand before Caesar. And behold, God has granted you all those who sail with you.'

25 "So take heart, men, for I have faith in God that it will be exactly as I have been told.

26 "But we must run aground on some island."

27 When the fourteenth night had come, as we were being driven across the Adriatic Sea, about midnight the sailors suspected that they were nearing land.

28 So they took a sounding and found twenty fathoms. A little farther on they took a sounding again and found fifteen fathoms.

29 And fearing that we might run on the rocks, they let down four anchors from the stern and prayed for day to come.

30 And as the sailors were seeking to escape from the ship, and had lowered the ship's boat into the sea under pretense of laying out anchors from the bow,

31 Paul said to the centurion and the soldiers, "Unless these men stay in the ship, you cannot be saved."

32 Then the soldiers cut away the ropes of the ship's boat and let it go.

33 As day was about to dawn, Paul urged them all to take some food, saying, "Today is the fourteenth day that you have continued in suspense and without food, having taken nothing.

34 "Therefore I urge you to take some food. For it will give you strength, for not a hair is to perish from the head of any of you."

35 And when he had said these things, he took bread, and giving thanks to God in the presence of all he broke it and began to eat.

36 Then they all were encouraged and ate some food themselves.

37 (We were in all 276 persons in the ship.)

38 And when they had eaten enough, they lightened the ship, throwing out the wheat into the sea.

39 Now when it was day, they did not recognize the

land, but they noticed a bay with a beach, on which they planned if possible to run the ship ashore.

40 So they cast off the anchors and left them in the sea, at the same time loosening the ropes that tied the rudders. Then hoisting the foresail to the wind they made for the beach.

41 But striking a reef, they ran the vessel aground. The bow stuck and remained immovable, and the stern was being broken up by the surf.

42 The soldiers' plan was to kill the prisoners, lest any should swim away and escape.

43 But the centurion, wishing to save Paul, kept them from carrying out their plan. He ordered those who could swim to jump overboard first and make for the land,

44 and the rest on planks or on pieces of the ship. And so it was that all were brought safely to land.

CHAPTER 28

1 After we were brought safely through, we then learned that the island was called Malta.

2 The native people showed us unusual kindness, for they kindled a fire and welcomed us all, because it had begun to rain and was cold.

3 When Paul had gathered a bundle of sticks and put them on the fire, a viper came out because of the heat and fastened on his hand.

4 When the native people saw the creature hanging from his hand, they said to one another, "No doubt this man is a murderer. Though he has escaped from the sea, Justice has not allowed him to live."

5 He, however, shook off the creature into the fire and suffered no harm.

6 They were waiting for him to swell up or suddenly fall down dead. But when they had waited a long time and saw no misfortune come to him, they changed their minds and said that he was a god.

7 Now in the neighborhood of that place were lands belonging to the chief man of the island, named Publius, who received us and entertained us hospitably for three days.

8 It happened that the father of Publius lay sick with fever and dysentery. And Paul visited him and prayed, and putting his hands on him healed him.

9 And when this had taken place, the rest of the people on the island who had dis-

eases also came and were cured.

¹⁰ They also honored us greatly, and when we were about to sail, they put on board whatever we needed.

¹¹ After three months we set sail in a ship that had wintered in the island, a ship of Alexandria, with the twin gods as a figurehead.

¹² Putting in at Syracuse, we stayed there for three days.

¹³ And from there we made a circuit and arrived at Rhegium. And after one day a south wind sprang up, and on the second day we came to Puteoli.

¹⁴ There we found brothers and were invited to stay with them for seven days. And so we came to Rome.

¹⁵ And the brothers there, when they heard about us, came as far as the Forum of Appius and Three Taverns to meet us. On seeing them, Paul thanked God and took courage.

¹⁶ And when we came into Rome, Paul was allowed to stay by himself, with the soldier who guarded him.

¹⁷ After three days he called together the local leaders of the Jews, and when they had gathered, he said to them, "Brothers, though I had done nothing against our people or the customs of our fathers, yet I was delivered as a prisoner from Jerusalem into the hands of the Romans.

¹⁸ "When they had examined me, they wished to set me at liberty, because there was no reason for the death penalty in my case.

¹⁹ "But because the Jews objected, I was compelled to appeal to Caesar—though I had no charge to bring against my nation.

²⁰ "For this reason, therefore, I have asked to see you and speak with you, since it is because of the hope of Israel that I am wearing this chain."

²¹ And they said to him, "We have received no letters from Judea about you, and none of the brothers coming here has reported or spoken any evil about you.

²² "But we desire to hear from you what your views are, for with regard to this sect we know that everywhere it is spoken against."

²³ When they had appointed a day for him, they came to him at his lodging in greater numbers. From morning till evening he expounded to them, testifying to the kingdom of God and trying to convince them about Jesus both from the Law of Moses and from the Prophets.

24 And some were convinced by what he said, but others disbelieved.

25 And disagreeing among themselves, they departed after Paul had made one statement: "The Holy Spirit was right in saying to your fathers through Isaiah the prophet:

26 " 'Go to this people, and say, "You will indeed hear but never understand, and you will indeed see but never perceive."

27 " 'For this people's heart has grown dull, and with their ears they can barely hear, and their eyes they have closed; lest they should see with their eyes and hear with their ears and understand with their heart and turn, and I would heal them.'

28 "Therefore let it be known to you that this salvation of God has been sent to the Gentiles; they will listen."

29 And when he had said these words, the Jews departed, having much dispute among themselves.

30 He lived there two whole years at his own expense, and welcomed all who came to him,

31 proclaiming the kingdom of God and teaching about the Lord Jesus Christ with all boldness and without hindrance.

THE LETTER OF PAUL TO THE

ROMANS

CHAPTER 1

1 Paul, a servant of Christ Jesus, called to be an apostle, set apart for the *gospel of God*,

2 which he promised beforehand through his prophets in the holy Scriptures,

3 concerning his Son, who was descended from David according to the flesh

4 and was declared to be the Son of God in power according to the Spirit of holiness by his resurrection from the dead, Jesus Christ our Lord,

5 through whom we have received grace and apostleship to bring about the obedience of faith for the sake of his name among all the nations,

6 including you who are called to belong to Jesus Christ,

7 To all those in Rome who are loved by God and called to be saints: Grace to you

and peace from God our Father and the Lord Jesus Christ.

⁸ First, I thank my God through Jesus Christ for all of you, because your faith is proclaimed in all the world.

⁹ For God is my witness, whom I serve with my spirit in the gospel of his Son, that without ceasing I mention you

¹⁰ always in my prayers, asking that somehow by God's will I may now at last succeed in coming to you.

¹¹ For I long to see you, that I may impart to you some spiritual gift to strengthen you—

¹² that is, that we may be mutually encouraged by each other's faith, both yours and mine.

¹³ I do not want you to be unaware, brothers, that I have often intended to come to you (but thus far have been prevented), in order that I may reap some harvest among you as well as among the rest of the Gentiles.

¹⁴ I am under obligation both to Greeks and to barbarians, both to the wise and to the foolish.

¹⁵ So I am eager to preach the gospel to you also who are in Rome.

¹⁶ For I am not ashamed of the gospel, for it is the power of God for salvation to every-one who believes, to the Jew first and also to the Greek.

¹⁷ For in it the righteousness of God is revealed from faith for faith, as it is written, "The righteous shall live by faith."

¹⁸ For the wrath of God is revealed from heaven against all ungodliness and unrighteousness of men, who by their unrighteousness suppress the truth.

¹⁹ For what can be known about God is plain to them, because God has shown it to them.

²⁰ For his invisible attributes, namely, his eternal power and divine nature, have been clearly perceived, ever since the creation of the world, in the things that have been made. So they are without excuse.

²¹ For although they knew God, they did not honor him as God or give thanks to him, but they became futile in their thinking, and their foolish hearts were darkened.

²² Claiming to be wise, they became fools,

²³ and exchanged the glory of the immortal God for images resembling mortal man and birds and animals and creeping things.

²⁴ Therefore God gave them up in the lusts of their hearts

to impurity, to the dishonoring of their bodies among themselves,

25 because they exchanged the truth about God for a lie and worshiped and served the creature rather than the Creator, who is blessed forever! Amen.

26 For this reason God gave them up to dishonorable passions. For their women exchanged natural relations for those that are contrary to nature;

27 and the men likewise gave up natural relations with women and were consumed with passion for one another, men committing shameless acts with men and receiving in themselves the due penalty for their error.

28 And since they did not see fit to acknowledge God, God gave them up to a debased mind to do what ought not to be done.

29 They were filled with all manner of unrighteousness, evil, covetousness, malice. They are full of envy, murder, strife, deceit, maliciousness. They are gossips,

30 slanderers, haters of God, insolent, haughty, boastful, inventors of evil, disobedient to parents,

31 foolish, faithless, heartless, ruthless.

32 Though they know God's righteous decree that those who practice such things deserve to die, they not only do them but give approval to those who practice them.

CHAPTER 2

1 Therefore you have no excuse, O man, every one of you who judges. For in passing judgment on another you condemn yourself, because you, the judge, practice the very same things.

2 We know that the judgment of God rightly falls on those who practice such things.

3 Do you suppose, O man—you who judge those who practice such things and yet do them yourself—that you will escape the judgment of God?

4 Or do you presume on the riches of his kindness and forbearance and patience, not knowing that God's kindness is meant to lead you to repentance?

5 But because of your hard and impenitent heart you are storing up wrath for yourself on the day of wrath when God's righteous judgment will be revealed.

6 He will render to each one according to his works:

7 to those who by patience

in well-doing seek for glory and honor and immortality, he will give eternal life;

⁸ but for those who are self-seeking and do not obey the truth, but obey unrighteousness, there will be wrath and fury.

⁹ There will be tribulation and distress for every human being who does evil, the Jew first and also the Greek,

¹⁰ but glory and honor and peace for everyone who does good, the Jew first and also the Greek.

¹¹ For God shows no partiality.

¹² For all who have sinned without the law will also perish without the law, and all who have sinned under the law will be judged by the law.

¹³ For it is not the hearers of the law who are righteous before God, but the doers of the law who will be justified.

¹⁴ For when Gentiles, who do not have the law, by nature do what the law requires, they are a law to themselves, even though they do not have the law.

¹⁵ They show that the work of the law is written on their hearts, while their conscience also bears witness, and their conflicting thoughts accuse or even excuse them

¹⁶ on that day when, according to my gospel, God judges the secrets of men by Christ Jesus.

¹⁷ But if you call yourself a Jew and rely on the law and boast in God

¹⁸ and know his will and approve what is excellent, because you are instructed from the law;

¹⁹ and if you are sure that you yourself are a guide to the blind, a light to those who are in darkness,

²⁰ an instructor of the foolish, a teacher of children, having in the law the embodiment of knowledge and truth—

²¹ you then who teach others, do you not teach yourself? While you preach against stealing, do you steal?

²² You who say that one must not commit adultery, do you commit adultery? You who abhor idols, do you rob temples?

²³ You who boast in the law dishonor God by breaking the law.

²⁴ For, as it is written, "The name of God is blasphemed among the Gentiles because of you."

²⁵ For circumcision indeed is of value if you obey the law, but if you break the law, your circumcision becomes uncircumcision.

²⁶ So, if a man who is uncircumcised keeps the precepts of the law, will not his uncircumcision be regarded as circumcision?

²⁷ Then he who is physically uncircumcised but keeps the law will condemn you who have the written code and circumcision but break the law.

²⁸ For no one is a Jew who is merely one outwardly, nor is circumcision outward and physical.

²⁹ For a Jew is one inwardly, and circumcision is a matter of the heart, by the Spirit, not by the letter. His praise is not from man but from God.

CHAPTER 3

¹ Then what advantage has the Jew? Or what is the value of circumcision?

² Much in every way. To begin with, the Jews were entrusted with the oracles of God.

³ What if some were unfaithful? Does their faithlessness nullify the faithfulness of God?

⁴ By no means! Let God be true though every one were a liar, as it is written, "That you may be justified in your words, and prevail when you are judged."

⁵ But if our unrighteousness serves to show the righteousness of God, what shall we say? That God is unrighteous to inflict wrath on us? (I speak in a human way.)

⁶ By no means! For then how could God judge the world?

⁷ But if through my lie God's truth abounds to his glory, why am I still being condemned as a sinner?

⁸ And why not do evil that good may come?—as some people slanderously charge us with saying. Their condemnation is just.

⁹ What then? Are we Jews any better off? No, not at all. For we have already charged that all, both Jews and Greeks, are under sin,

¹⁰ as it is written: "None is righteous, no, not one;

¹¹ "no one understands; no one seeks for God.

¹² "All have turned aside; together they have become worthless; no one does good, not even one."

¹³ "Their throat is an open grave; they use their tongues to deceive." "The venom of asps is under their lips."

¹⁴ "Their mouth is full of curses and bitterness."

¹⁵ "Their feet are swift to shed blood;

¹⁶ "in their paths are ruin and misery,

¹⁷ "and the way of peace they have not known."

18 "There is no fear of God before their eyes."

19 Now we know that whatever the law says it speaks to those who are under the law, so that every mouth may be stopped, and the whole world may be held accountable to God.

20 For by works of the law no human being will be justified in his sight, since through the law comes knowledge of sin.

21 But now the righteousness of God has been manifested apart from the law, although the Law and the Prophets bear witness to it—

22 the righteousness of God through faith in Jesus Christ for all who believe. For there is no distinction:

23 for all have sinned and fall short of the glory of God,

24 and are justified by his grace as a gift, through the redemption that is in Christ Jesus,

25 whom God put forward as a propitiation by his blood, to be received by faith. This was to show God's righteousness, because in his divine forbearance he had passed over former sins.

26 It was to show his righteousness at the present time, so that he might be just and the justifier of the one who has faith in Jesus.

27 Then what becomes of our boasting? It is excluded. By what kind of law? By a law of works? No, but by the law of faith.

28 For we hold that one is justified by faith apart from works of the law.

29 Or is God the God of Jews only? Is he not the God of Gentiles also? Yes, of Gentiles also,

30 since God is one—who will justify the circumcised by faith and the uncircumcised through faith.

31 Do we then overthrow the law by this faith? By no means! On the contrary, we uphold the law.

CHAPTER 4

1 What then shall we say was gained by Abraham, our forefather according to the flesh?

2 For if Abraham was justified by works, he has something to boast about, but not before God.

3 For what does the Scripture say? "Abraham believed God, and it was counted to him as righteousness."

4 Now to the one who works, his wages are not counted as a gift but as his due.

5 And to the one who does not work but believes in him who justifies the ungodly, his

faith is counted as righteousness,

⁶ just as David also speaks of the blessing of the one to whom God counts righteousness apart from works:

⁷ "Blessed are those whose lawless deeds are forgiven, and whose sins are covered;

⁸ "blessed is the man against whom the Lord will not count his sin."

⁹ Is this blessing then only for the circumcised, or also for the uncircumcised? For we say that faith was counted to Abraham as righteousness.

¹⁰ How then was it counted to him? Was it before or after he had been circumcised? It was not after, but before he was circumcised.

¹¹ He received the sign of circumcision as a seal of the righteousness that he had by faith while he was still uncircumcised. The purpose was to make him the father of all who believe without being circumcised, so that righteousness would be counted to them as well,

¹² and to make him the father of the circumcised who are not merely circumcised but who also walk in the footsteps of the faith that our father Abraham had before he was circumcised.

¹³ For the promise to Abraham and his offspring that he would be heir of the world did not come through the law but through the righteousness of faith.

¹⁴ For if it is the adherents of the law who are to be the heirs, faith is null and the promise is void.

¹⁵ For the law brings wrath, but where there is no law there is no transgression.

¹⁶ That is why it depends on faith, in order that the promise may rest on grace and be guaranteed to all his offspring—not only to the adherent of the law but also to the one who shares the faith of Abraham, who is the father of us all,

¹⁷ as it is written, "I have made you the father of many nations"—in the presence of the God in whom he believed, who gives life to the dead and calls into existence the things that do not exist.

¹⁸ In hope he believed against hope, that he should become the father of many nations, as he had been told, "So shall your offspring be."

¹⁹ He did not weaken in faith when he considered his own body, which was as good as dead (since he was about a hundred years old), or when he considered the barrenness of Sarah's womb.

20 No unbelief made him waver concerning the promise of God, but he grew strong in his faith as he gave glory to God,

21 fully convinced that God was able to do what he had promised.

22 That is why his faith was "counted to him as righteousness."

23 But the words "it was counted to him" were not written for his sake alone,

24 but for ours also. It will be counted to us who believe in him who raised from the dead Jesus our Lord,

25 who was delivered up for our trespasses and raised for our justification.

CHAPTER 5

1 Therefore, since we have been justified by faith, we have peace with God through our Lord Jesus Christ.

2 Through him we have also obtained access by faith into this grace in which we stand, and we rejoice in hope of the glory of God.

3 Not only that, but we rejoice in our sufferings, knowing that suffering produces endurance,

4 and endurance produces character, and character produces hope,

5 and hope does not put us to shame, because God's love has been poured into our hearts through the Holy Spirit who has been given to us.

6 For while we were still weak, at the right time Christ died for the ungodly.

7 For one will scarcely die for a righteous person—though perhaps for a good person one would dare even to die—

8 but God shows his love for us in that while we were still sinners, Christ died for us.

9 Since, therefore, we have now been justified by his blood, much more shall we be saved by him from the wrath of God.

10 For if while we were enemies we were reconciled to God by the death of his Son, much more, now that we are reconciled, shall we be saved by his life.

11 More than that, we also rejoice in God through our Lord Jesus Christ, through whom we have now received reconciliation.

12 Therefore, just as sin came into the world through one man, and death through sin, and so death spread to all men because all sinned—

13 for sin indeed was in the world before the law was given, but sin is not counted where there is no law.

14 Yet death reigned from Adam to Moses, even over those whose sinning was not like the transgression of Adam, who was a type of the one who was to come.

15 But the free gift is not like the trespass. For if many died through one man's trespass, much more have the grace of God and the free gift by the grace of that one man Jesus Christ abounded for many.

16 And the free gift is not like the result of that one man's sin. For the judgment following one trespass brought condemnation, but the free gift following many trespasses brought justification.

17 For if, because of one man's trespass, death reigned through that one man, much more will those who receive the abundance of grace and the free gift of righteousness reign in life through the one man Jesus Christ.

18 Therefore, as one trespass led to condemnation for all men, so one act of righteousness leads to justification and life for all men.

19 For as by the one man's disobedience the many were made sinners, so by the one man's obedience the many will be made righteous.

20 Now the law came in to increase the trespass, but where sin increased, grace abounded all the more,

21 so that, as sin reigned in death, grace also might reign through righteousness leading to eternal life through Jesus Christ our Lord.

CHAPTER 6

1 What shall we say then? Are we to continue in sin that grace may abound?

2 By no means! How can we who died to sin still live in it?

3 Do you not know that all of us who have been baptized into Christ Jesus were baptized into his death?

4 We were buried therefore with him by baptism into death, in order that, just as Christ was raised from the dead by the glory of the Father, we too might walk in newness of life.

5 For if we have been united with him in a death like his, we shall certainly be united with him in a resurrection like his.

6 We know that our old self was crucified with him in order that the body of sin might be brought to nothing, so that we would no longer be enslaved to sin.

7 For one who has died has been set free from sin.

8 Now if we have died with Christ, we believe that we will also live with him.

9 We know that Christ, being raised from the dead, will never die again; death no longer has dominion over him.

10 For the death he died he died to sin, once for all, but the life he lives he lives to God.

11 So you also must consider yourselves dead to sin and alive to God in Christ Jesus.

12 Let not sin therefore reign in your mortal body, to make you obey its passions.

13 Do not present your members to sin as instruments for unrighteousness, but present yourselves to God as those who have been brought from death to life, and your members to God as instruments for righteousness.

14 For sin will have no dominion over you, since you are not under law but under grace.

15 What then? Are we to sin because we are not under law but under grace? By no means!

16 Do you not know that if you present yourselves to anyone as obedient slaves, you are slaves of the one whom you obey, either of

sin, which leads to death, or of obedience, which leads to righteousness?

17 But thanks be to God, that you who were once slaves of sin have become obedient from the heart to the standard of teaching to which you were committed,

18 and, having been set free from sin, have become slaves of righteousness.

19 I am speaking in human terms, because of your natural limitations. For just as you once presented your members as slaves to impurity and to lawlessness leading to more lawlessness, so now present your members as slaves to righteousness leading to sanctification.

20 For when you were slaves of sin, you were free in regard to righteousness.

21 But what fruit were you getting at that time from the things of which you are now ashamed? For the end of those things is death.

22 But now that you have been set free from sin and have become slaves of God, the fruit you get leads to sanctification and its end, eternal life.

23 For the wages of sin is death, but the free gift of God is eternal life in Christ Jesus our Lord.

CHAPTER 7

¹ Or do you not know, brothers—for I am speaking to those who know the law—that the law is binding on a person only as long as he lives?

² For a married woman is bound by law to her husband while he lives, but if her husband dies she is released from the law of marriage.

³ Accordingly, she will be called an adulteress if she lives with another man while her husband is alive. But if her husband dies, she is free from that law, and if she marries another man she is not an adulteress.

⁴ Likewise, my brothers, you also have died to the law through the body of Christ, so that you may belong to another, to him who has been raised from the dead, in order that we may bear fruit for God.

⁵ For while we were living in the flesh, our sinful passions, aroused by the law, were at work in our members to bear fruit for death.

⁶ But now we are released from the law, having died to that which held us captive, so that we serve in the new way of the Spirit and not in the old way of the written code.

⁷ What then shall we say? That the law is sin? By no means! Yet if it had not been for the law, I would not have known sin. For I would not have known what it is to covet if the law had not said, "You shall not covet."

⁸ But sin, seizing an opportunity through the commandment, produced in me all kinds of covetousness. For apart from the law, sin lies dead.

⁹ I was once alive apart from the law, but when the commandment came, sin came alive and I died.

¹⁰ The very commandment that promised life proved to be death to me.

¹¹ For sin, seizing an opportunity through the commandment, deceived me and through it killed me.

¹² So the law is holy, and the commandment is holy and righteous and good.

¹³ Did that which is good, then, bring death to me? By no means! It was sin, producing death in me through what is good, in order that sin might be shown to be sin, and through the commandment might become sinful beyond measure.

¹⁴ For we know that the law is spiritual, but I am of the flesh, sold under sin.

¹⁵ For I do not understand

my own actions. For I do not do what I want, but I do the very thing I hate.

¹⁶ Now if I do what I do not want, I agree with the law, that it is good.

¹⁷ So now it is no longer I who do it, but sin that dwells within me.

¹⁸ For I know that nothing good dwells in me, that is, in my flesh. For I have the desire to do what is right, but not the ability to carry it out.

¹⁹ For I do not do the good I want, but the evil I do not want is what I keep on doing.

²⁰ Now if I do what I do not want, it is no longer I who do it, but sin that dwells within me.

²¹ So I find it to be a law that when I want to do right, evil lies close at hand.

²² For I delight in the law of God, in my inner being,

²³ but I see in my members another law waging war against the law of my mind and making me captive to the law of sin that dwells in my members.

²⁴ Wretched man that I am! Who will deliver me from this body of death?

²⁵ Thanks be to God through Jesus Christ our Lord! So then, I myself serve the law of God with my mind, but with my flesh I serve the law of sin.

CHAPTER 8

¹ There is therefore now no condemnation for those who are in Christ Jesus, who walk not according to the flesh (but according to the Spirit).

² For the law of the Spirit of life has set you free in Christ Jesus from the law of sin and death.

³ For God has done what the law, weakened by the flesh, could not do. By sending his own Son in the likeness of sinful flesh and for sin, he condemned sin in the flesh,

⁴ in order that the righteous requirement of the law might be fulfilled in us, who walk not according to the flesh but according to the Spirit.

⁵ For those who live according to the flesh set their minds on the things of the flesh, but those who live according to the Spirit set their minds on the things of the Spirit.

⁶ For to set the mind on the flesh is death, but to set the mind on the Spirit is life and peace.

⁷ For the mind that is set on the flesh is hostile to God, for it does not submit to God's law; indeed, it cannot.

⁸ Those who are in the flesh cannot please God.

⁹ You, however, are not in the flesh but in the Spirit, if

in fact the Spirit of God dwells in you. Anyone who does not have the Spirit of Christ does not belong to him.

10 But if Christ is in you, although the body is dead because of sin, the Spirit is life because of righteousness.

11 If the Spirit of him who raised Jesus from the dead dwells in you, he who raised Christ Jesus from the dead will also give life to your mortal bodies through his Spirit who dwells in you.

12 So then, brothers, we are debtors, not to the flesh, to live according to the flesh.

13 For if you live according to the flesh you will die, but if by the Spirit you put to death the deeds of the body, you will live.

14 For all who are led by the Spirit of God are sons of God.

15 For you did not receive the spirit of slavery to fall back into fear, but you have received the Spirit of adoption as sons, by whom we cry, "Abba! Father!"

16 The Spirit himself bears witness with our spirit that we are children of God,

17 and if children, then heirs—heirs of God and fellow heirs with Christ, provided we suffer with him in order that we may also be glorified with him.

18 For I consider that the sufferings of this present time are not worth comparing with the glory that is to be revealed to us.

19 For the creation waits with eager longing for the revealing of the sons of God.

20 For the creation was subjected to futility, not willingly, but because of him who subjected it, in hope

21 that the creation itself will be set free from its bondage to corruption and obtain the freedom of the glory of the children of God.

22 For we know that the whole creation has been groaning together in the pains of childbirth until now.

23 And not only the creation, but we ourselves, who have the firstfruits of the Spirit, groan inwardly as we wait eagerly for adoption as sons, the redemption of our bodies.

24 For in this hope we were saved. Now hope that is seen is not hope. For who hopes for what he sees?

25 But if we hope for what we do not see, we wait for it with patience.

26 Likewise the Spirit helps us in our weakness. For we do not know what to pray for as we ought, but the Spirit himself intercedes for us

with groanings too deep for words.

²⁷ And he who searches hearts knows what is the mind of the Spirit, because the Spirit intercedes for the saints according to the will of God.

²⁸ And we know that for those who love God all things work together for good, for those who are called according to his purpose.

²⁹ For those whom he foreknew he also predestined to be conformed to the image of his Son, in order that he might be the firstborn among many brothers.

³⁰ And those whom he predestined he also called, and those whom he called he also justified, and those whom he justified he also glorified.

³¹ What then shall we say to these things? If God is for us, who can be against us?

³² He who did not spare his own Son but gave him up for us all, how will he not also with him graciously give us all things?

³³ Who shall bring any charge against God's elect? It is God who justifies.

³⁴ Who is to condemn? Christ Jesus is the one who died—more than that, who was raised—who is at the right hand of God, who indeed is interceding for us.

³⁵ Who shall separate us from the love of Christ? Shall tribulation, or distress, or persecution, or famine, or nakedness, or danger, or sword?

³⁶ As it is written, "For your sake we are being killed all the day long; we are regarded as sheep to be slaughtered."

³⁷ No, in all these things we are more than conquerors through him who loved us.

³⁸ For I am sure that neither death nor life, nor angels nor rulers, nor things present nor things to come, nor powers,

³⁹ nor height nor depth, nor anything else in all creation, will be able to separate us from the love of God in Christ Jesus our Lord.

CHAPTER 9

¹ I am speaking the truth in Christ—I am not lying; my conscience bears me witness in the Holy Spirit—

² that I have great sorrow and unceasing anguish in my heart.

³ For I could wish that I myself were accursed and cut off from Christ for the sake of my brothers, my kinsmen according to the flesh.

⁴ They are Israelites, and to them belong the adoption, the glory, the covenants, the

giving of the law, the worship, and the promises.

⁵ To them belong the patriarchs, and from their race, according to the flesh, is the Christ, who is God over all, blessed forever. Amen.

⁶ But it is not as though the word of God has failed. For not all who are descended from Israel belong to Israel,

⁷ and not all are children of Abraham because they are his offspring, but "Through Isaac shall your offspring be named."

⁸ This means that it is not the children of the flesh who are the children of God, but the children of the promise are counted as offspring.

⁹ For this is what the promise said: "About this time next year I will return, and Sarah shall have a son."

¹⁰ And not only so, but also when Rebekah had conceived children by one man, our forefather Isaac,

¹¹ though they were not yet born and had done nothing either good or bad—in order that God's purpose of election might continue, not because of works but because of him who calls—

¹² she was told, "The older will serve the younger."

¹³ As it is written, "Jacob I loved, but Esau I hated."

¹⁴ What shall we say then? Is there injustice on God's part? By no means!

¹⁵ For he says to Moses, "I will have mercy on whom I have mercy, and I will have compassion on whom I have compassion."

¹⁶ So then it depends not on human will or exertion, but on God, who has mercy.

¹⁷ For the Scripture says to Pharaoh, "For this very purpose I have raised you up, that I might show my power in you, and that my name might be proclaimed in all the earth."

¹⁸ So then he has mercy on whomever he wills, and he hardens whomever he wills.

¹⁹ You will say to me then, "Why does he still find fault? For who can resist his will?"

²⁰ But who are you, O man, to answer back to God? Will what is molded say to its molder, "Why have you made me like this?"

²¹ Has the potter no right over the clay, to make out of the same lump one vessel for honorable use and another for dishonorable use?

²² What if God, desiring to show his wrath and to make known his power, has endured with much patience vessels of wrath prepared for destruction,

23 in order to make known the riches of his glory for vessels of mercy, which he has prepared beforehand for glory—

24 even us whom he has called, not from the Jews only but also from the Gentiles?

25 As indeed he says in Hosea, "Those who were not my people I will call 'my people,' and her who was not beloved I will call 'beloved.'"

26 "And in the very place where it was said to them, 'You are not my people,' there they will be called 'sons of the living God.'"

27 And Isaiah cries out concerning Israel: "Though the number of the sons of Israel be as the sand of the sea, only a remnant of them will be saved,

28 "for the Lord will carry out his sentence upon the earth fully and without delay."

29 And as Isaiah predicted, "If the Lord of hosts had not left us offspring, we would have been like Sodom and become like Gomorrah."

30 What shall we say, then? That Gentiles who did not pursue righteousness have attained it, that is, a righteousness that is by faith;

31 but that Israel who pursued a law that would lead to righteousness did not succeed in reaching that law.

32 Why? Because they did not pursue it by faith, but as if it were based on works. They have stumbled over the stumbling stone,

33 as it is written, "Behold, I am laying in Zion a stone of stumbling, and a rock of offense; and whoever believes in him will not be put to shame."

CHAPTER 10

1 Brothers, my heart's desire and prayer to God for them is that they may be saved.

2 For I bear them witness that they have a zeal for God, but not according to knowledge.

3 For, being ignorant of the righteousness of God, and seeking to establish their own, they did not submit to God's righteousness.

4 For Christ is the end of the law for righteousness to everyone who believes.

5 For Moses writes about the righteousness that is based on the law, that the person who does the commandments shall live by them.

6 But the righteousness based on faith says, "Do not say in your heart, 'Who will ascend into heaven?'" (that is, to bring Christ down)

7 "or 'Who will descend into the abyss?'" (that is, to bring Christ up from the dead).

8 But what does it say? "The word is near you, in your mouth and in your heart" (that is, the word of faith that we proclaim);

9 because, if you confess with your mouth that Jesus is Lord and believe in your heart that God raised him from the dead, you will be saved.

10 For with the heart one believes and is justified, and with the mouth one confesses and is saved.

11 For the Scripture says, "Everyone who believes in him will not be put to shame."

12 For there is no distinction between Jew and Greek; for the same Lord is Lord of all, bestowing his riches on all who call on him.

13 For "everyone who calls on the name of the Lord will be saved."

14 How then will they call on him in whom they have not believed? And how are they to believe in him of whom they have never heard? And how are they to hear without someone preaching?

15 And how are they to preach unless they are sent? As it is written, "How beautiful are the feet of those who preach the good news!"

16 But they have not all obeyed the gospel. For Isaiah says, "Lord, who has believed what he has heard from us?"

17 So faith comes from hearing, and hearing through the word of Christ.

18 But I ask, have they not heard? Indeed they have, for "Their voice has gone out to all the earth, and their words to the ends of the world."

19 But I ask, did Israel not understand? First Moses says, "I will make you jealous of those who are not a nation; with a foolish nation I will make you angry."

20 Then Isaiah is so bold as to say, "I have been found by those who did not seek me; I have shown myself to those who did not ask for me."

21 But of Israel he says, "All day long I have held out my hands to a disobedient and contrary people."

CHAPTER 11

1 I ask, then, has God rejected his people? By no means! For I myself am an Israelite, a descendant of Abraham, a member of the tribe of Benjamin.

2 God has not rejected his people whom he foreknew. Do you not know what the Scripture says of Elijah, how he appeals to God against Israel?

3 "Lord, they have killed your prophets, they have demolished your altars, and I alone am left, and they seek my life."

4 But what is God's reply to him? "I have kept for myself seven thousand men who have not bowed the knee to Baal."

5 So too at the present time there is a remnant, chosen by grace.

6 But if it is by grace, it is no longer on the basis of works; otherwise grace would no longer be grace.

7 What then? Israel failed to obtain what it was seeking. The elect obtained it, but the rest were hardened,

8 as it is written, "God gave them a spirit of stupor, eyes that would not see and ears that would not hear, down to this very day."

9 And David says, "Let their table become a snare and a trap, a stumbling block and a retribution for them;

10 "let their eyes be darkened so that they cannot see, and bend their backs forever."

11 So I ask, did they stumble in order that they might fall? By no means! Rather through their trespass salvation has come to the Gentiles, so as to make Israel jealous.

12 Now if their trespass means riches for the world, and if their failure means riches for the Gentiles, how much more will their full inclusion mean!

13 Now I am speaking to you Gentiles. Inasmuch then as I am an apostle to the Gentiles, I magnify my ministry

14 in order somehow to make my fellow Jews jealous, and thus save some of them.

15 For if their rejection means the reconciliation of the world, what will their acceptance mean but life from the dead?

16 If the dough offered as firstfruits is holy, so is the whole lump, and if the root is holy, so are the branches.

17 But if some of the branches were broken off, and you, although a wild olive shoot, were grafted in among the others and now share in the nourishing root of the olive tree,

18 do not be arrogant toward the branches. If you are, remember it is not you who support the root, but the root that supports you.

19 Then you will say, "Branches were broken off so that I might be grafted in."

20 That is true. They were broken off because of their unbelief, but you stand fast through faith. So do not become proud, but fear.

21 For if God did not spare the natural branches, neither will he spare you.

22 Note then the kindness and the severity of God: severity toward those who have fallen, but God's kindness to you, provided you continue in his kindness. Otherwise you too will be cut off.

23 And even they, if they do not continue in their unbelief, will be grafted in, for God has the power to graft them in again.

24 For if you were cut from what is by nature a wild olive tree, and grafted, contrary to nature, into a cultivated olive tree, how much more will these, the natural branches, be grafted back into their own olive tree.

25 Lest you be wise in your own sight, I do not want you to be unaware of this mystery, brothers: a partial hardening has come upon Israel, until the fullness of the Gentiles has come in.

26 And in this way all Israel will be saved, as it is written, "The Deliverer will come from Zion, he will banish ungodliness from Jacob";

27 "and this will be my covenant with them when I take away their sins."

28 As regards the gospel, they are enemies for your sake. But as regards election, they are beloved for the sake of their forefathers.

29 For the gifts and the calling of God are irrevocable.

30 For just as you were at one time disobedient to God but now have received mercy because of their disobedience,

31 so they too have now been disobedient in order that by the mercy shown to you they also may now receive mercy.

32 For God has consigned all to disobedience, that he may have mercy on all.

33 Oh, the depth of the riches and wisdom and knowledge of God! How unsearchable are his judgments and how inscrutable his ways!

34 "For who has known the mind of the Lord, or who has been his counselor?"

35 "Or who has given a gift to him that he might be repaid?"

36 For from him and through him and to him are all things. To him be glory forever. Amen.

CHAPTER 12

1 I appeal to you therefore, brothers, by the mercies of God, to present your bodies as a living sacrifice, holy and acceptable to God, which is your spiritual worship.

² Do not be conformed to this world, but be transformed by the renewal of your mind, that by testing you may discern what is the will of God, what is good and acceptable and perfect.

³ For by the grace given to me I say to everyone among you not to think of himself more highly than he ought to think, but to think with sober judgment, each according to the measure of faith that God has assigned.

⁴ For as in one body we have many members, and the members do not all have the same function,

⁵ so we, though many, are one body in Christ, and individually members one of another.

⁶ Having gifts that differ according to the grace given to us, let us use them: if prophecy, in proportion to our faith;

⁷ if service, in our serving; the one who teaches, in his teaching;

⁸ the one who exhorts, in his exhortation; the one who contributes, in generosity; the one who leads, with zeal; the one who does acts of mercy, with cheerfulness.

⁹ Let love be genuine. Abhor what is evil; hold fast to what is good.

¹⁰ Love one another with brotherly affection. Outdo one another in showing honor.

¹¹ Do not be slothful in zeal, be fervent in spirit, serve the Lord.

¹² Rejoice in hope, be patient in tribulation, be constant in prayer.

¹³ Contribute to the needs of the saints and seek to show hospitality.

¹⁴ Bless those who persecute you; bless and do not curse them.

¹⁵ Rejoice with those who rejoice, weep with those who weep.

¹⁶ Live in harmony with one another. Do not be haughty, but associate with the lowly. Never be wise in your own sight.

¹⁷ Repay no one evil for evil, but give thought to do what is honorable in the sight of all.

¹⁸ If possible, so far as it depends on you, live peaceably with all.

¹⁹ Beloved, never avenge yourselves, but leave it to the wrath of God, for it is written, "Vengeance is mine, I will repay, says the Lord."

²⁰ To the contrary, "if your enemy is hungry, feed him; if he is thirsty, give him something to drink; for by so doing you will heap burning coals on his head."

²¹ Do not be overcome by evil, but overcome evil with good.

CHAPTER 13

¹ Let every person be subject to the governing authorities. For there is no authority except from God, and those that exist have been instituted by God.

² Therefore whoever resists the authorities resists what God has appointed, and those who resist will incur judgment.

³ For rulers are not a terror to good conduct, but to bad. Would you have no fear of the one who is in authority? Then do what is good, and you will receive his approval,

⁴ for he is God's servant for your good. But if you do wrong, be afraid, for he does not bear the sword in vain. For he is the servant of God, an avenger who carries out God's wrath on the wrongdoer.

⁵ Therefore one must be in subjection, not only to avoid God's wrath but also for the sake of conscience.

⁶ For because of this you also pay taxes, for the authorities are ministers of God, attending to this very thing.

⁷ Pay to all what is owed to them: taxes to whom taxes are owed, revenue to whom revenue is owed, respect to whom respect is owed, honor to whom honor is owed.

⁸ Owe no one anything, except to love each other, for the one who loves another has fulfilled the law.

⁹ For the commandments, "You shall not commit adultery, You shall not murder, You shall not steal, You shall not covet," and any other commandment, are summed up in this word: "You shall love your neighbor as yourself."

¹⁰ Love does no wrong to a neighbor; therefore love is the fulfilling of the law.

¹¹ Besides this you know the time, that the hour has come for you to wake from sleep. For salvation is nearer to us now than when we first believed.

¹² The night is far gone; the day is at hand. So then let us cast off the works of darkness and put on the armor of light.

¹³ Let us walk properly as in the daytime, not in orgies and drunkenness, not in sexual immorality and sensuality, not in quarreling and jealousy.

¹⁴ But put on the Lord Jesus Christ, and make no provision for the flesh, to gratify its desires.

¹ As for the one who is weak in faith, welcome him, but not to quarrel over opinions.

² One person believes he may eat anything, while the weak person eats only vegetables.

³ Let not the one who eats despise the one who abstains, and let not the one who abstains pass judgment on the one who eats, for God has welcomed him.

⁴ Who are you to pass judgment on the servant of another? It is before his own master that he stands or falls. And he will be upheld, for the Lord is able to make him stand.

⁵ One person esteems one day as better than another, while another esteems all days alike. Each one should be fully convinced in his own mind.

⁶ The one who observes the day, observes it in honor of the Lord. The one who eats, eats in honor of the Lord, since he gives thanks to God, while the one who abstains, abstains in honor of the Lord and gives thanks to God.

⁷ For none of us lives to himself, and none of us dies to himself.

⁸ For if we live, we live to the Lord, and if we die, we die to the Lord. So then, whether we live or whether we die, we are the Lord's.

⁹ For to this end Christ died and lived again, that he might be Lord both of the dead and of the living.

¹⁰ Why do you pass judgment on your brother? Or you, why do you despise your brother? For we will all stand before the judgment seat of God;

¹¹ for it is written, "As I live, says the Lord, every knee shall bow to me, and every tongue shall confess to God."

¹² So then each of us will give an account of himself to God.

¹³ Therefore let us not pass judgment on one another any longer, but rather decide never to put a stumbling block or hindrance in the way of a brother.

¹⁴ I know and am persuaded in the Lord Jesus that nothing is unclean in itself, but it is unclean for anyone who thinks it unclean.

¹⁵ For if your brother is grieved by what you eat, you are no longer walking in love. By what you eat, do not destroy the one for whom Christ died.

¹⁶ So do not let what you regard as good be spoken of as evil.

¹⁷ For the kingdom of God

is not a matter of eating and drinking but of righteousness and peace and joy in the Holy Spirit.

¹⁸ Whoever thus serves Christ is acceptable to God and approved by men.

¹⁹ So then let us pursue what makes for peace and for mutual upbuilding.

²⁰ Do not, for the sake of food, destroy the work of God. Everything is indeed clean, but it is wrong for anyone to make another stumble by what he eats.

²¹ It is good not to eat meat or drink wine or do anything that causes your brother to stumble.

²² The faith that you have, keep between yourself and God. Blessed is the one who has no reason to pass judgment on himself for what he approves.

²³ But whoever has doubts is condemned if he eats, because the eating is not from faith. For whatever does not proceed from faith is sin.

CHAPTER 15

¹ We who are strong have an obligation to bear with the failings of the weak, and not to please ourselves.

² Let each of us please his neighbor for his good, to build him up.

³ For Christ did not please himself, but as it is written, "The reproaches of those who reproached you fell on me."

⁴ For whatever was written in former days was written for our instruction, that through endurance and through the encouragement of the Scriptures we might have hope.

⁵ May the God of endurance and encouragement grant you to live in such harmony with one another, in accord with Christ Jesus,

⁶ that together you may with one voice glorify the God and Father of our Lord Jesus Christ.

⁷ Therefore welcome one another as Christ has welcomed you, for the glory of God.

⁸ For I tell you that Christ became a servant to the circumcised to show God's truthfulness, in order to confirm the promises given to the patriarchs,

⁹ and in order that the Gentiles might glorify God for his mercy. As it is written, "Therefore I will praise you among the Gentiles, and sing to your name."

¹⁰ And again it is said, "Rejoice, O Gentiles, with his people."

¹¹ And again, "Praise the

Lord, all you Gentiles, and let all the peoples extol him."

¹² And again Isaiah says, "The root of Jesse will come, even he who arises to rule the Gentiles; in him will the Gentiles hope."

¹³ May the God of hope fill you with all joy and peace in believing, so that by the power of the Holy Spirit you may abound in hope.

¹⁴ I myself am satisfied about you, my brothers, that you yourselves are full of goodness, filled with all knowledge and able to instruct one another.

¹⁵ But on some points I have written to you very boldly by way of reminder, because of the grace given me by God

¹⁶ to be a minister of Christ Jesus to the Gentiles in the priestly service of the gospel of God, so that the offering of the Gentiles may be acceptable, sanctified by the Holy Spirit.

¹⁷ In Christ Jesus, then, I have reason to be proud of my work for God.

¹⁸ For I will not venture to speak of anything except what Christ has accomplished through me to bring the Gentiles to obedience—by word and deed,

¹⁹ by the power of signs and wonders, by the power of the Spirit of God—so that from Jerusalem and all the way around to Illyricum I have fulfilled the ministry of the gospel of Christ;

²⁰ and thus I make it my ambition to preach the gospel, not where Christ has already been named, lest I build on someone else's foundation,

²¹ but as it is written, "Those who have never been told of him will see, and those who have never heard will understand."

²² This is the reason why I have so often been hindered from coming to you.

²³ But now, since I no longer have any room for work in these regions, and since I have longed for many years to come to you,

²⁴ I hope to see you in passing as I go to Spain, and to be helped on my journey there by you, once I have enjoyed your company for a while.

²⁵ At present, however, I am going to Jerusalem bringing aid to the saints.

²⁶ For Macedonia and Achaia have been pleased to make some contribution for the poor among the saints at Jerusalem.

²⁷ For they were pleased to do it, and indeed they owe it to them. For if the Gentiles have come to share in their

spiritual blessings, they ought also to be of service to them in material blessings.

²⁸ When therefore I have completed this and have delivered to them what has been collected, I will leave for Spain by way of you.

²⁹ I know that when I come to you I will come in the fullness of the blessing of Christ.

³⁰ I appeal to you, brothers, by our Lord Jesus Christ and by the love of the Spirit, to strive together with me in your prayers to God on my behalf,

³¹ that I may be delivered from the unbelievers in Judea, and that my service for Jerusalem may be acceptable to the saints,

³² so that by God's will I may come to you with joy and be refreshed in your company.

³³ May the God of peace be with you all. Amen.

CHAPTER 16

¹ I commend to you our sister Phoebe, a servant of the church at Cenchreae,

² that you may welcome her in the Lord in a way worthy of the saints, and help her in whatever she may need from you, for she has been a patron of many and of myself as well.

³ Greet Prisca and Aquila, my fellow workers in Christ Jesus,

⁴ who risked their necks for my life, to whom not only I give thanks but all the churches of the Gentiles give thanks as well.

⁵ Greet also the church in their house. Greet my beloved Epaenetus, who was the first convert to Christ in Asia.

⁶ Greet Mary, who has worked hard for you.

⁷ Greet Andronicus and Junia, my kinsmen and my fellow prisoners. They are well known to the apostles, and they were in Christ before me.

⁸ Greet Ampliatus, my beloved in the Lord.

⁹ Greet Urbanus, our fellow worker in Christ, and my beloved Stachys.

¹⁰ Greet Apelles, who is approved in Christ. Greet those who belong to the family of Aristobulus.

¹¹ Greet my kinsman Herodion. Greet those in the Lord who belong to the family of Narcissus.

¹² Greet those workers in the Lord, Tryphaena and Tryphosa. Greet the beloved Persis, who has worked hard in the Lord.

¹³ Greet Rufus, chosen in the Lord; also his mother, who has been a mother to me as well.

¹⁴ Greet Asyncritus, Phlegon, Hermes, Patrobas, Hermas, and the brothers who are with them.

¹⁵ Greet Philologus, Julia, Nereus and his sister, and Olympas, and all the saints who are with them.

¹⁶ Greet one another with a holy kiss. All the churches of Christ greet you.

¹⁷ I appeal to you, brothers, to watch out for those who cause divisions and create obstacles contrary to the doctrine that you have been taught; avoid them.

¹⁸ For such persons do not serve our Lord Christ, but their own appetites, and by smooth talk and flattery they deceive the hearts of the naive.

¹⁹ For your obedience is known to all, so that I rejoice over you, but I want you to be wise as to what is good and innocent as to what is evil.

²⁰ The God of peace will soon crush Satan under your feet. The grace of our Lord Jesus Christ be with you.

²¹ Timothy, my fellow worker, greets you; so do Lucius and Jason and Sosipater, my kinsmen.

²² I Tertius, who wrote this letter, greet you in the Lord.

²³ Gaius, who is host to me and to the whole church, greets you. Erastus, the city treasurer, and our brother Quartus, greet you.

²⁴ The grace of our Lord Jesus Christ be with you all. Amen.

²⁵ Now to him who is able to strengthen you according to my gospel and the preaching of Jesus Christ, according to the revelation of the mystery that was kept secret for long ages

²⁶ but has now been disclosed and through the prophetic writings has been made known to all nations, according to the command of the eternal God, to bring about the obedience of faith—

²⁷ to the only wise God be glory forevermore through Jesus Christ! Amen.

THE FIRST LETTER OF PAUL TO THE CORINTHIANS

1 CORINTHIANS

CHAPTER 1

1 Paul, called by the will of God to be an apostle of Christ Jesus, and our brother Sosthenes,

2 To the church of God that is in Corinth, to those sanctified in Christ Jesus, called to be saints together with all those who in every place call upon the name of our Lord Jesus Christ, both their Lord and ours:

3 Grace to you and peace from God our Father and the Lord Jesus Christ.

4 I give thanks to my God always for you because of the grace of God that was given you in Christ Jesus,

5 that in every way you were enriched in him in all speech and all knowledge—

6 even as the testimony about Christ was confirmed among you—

7 so that you are not lacking in any gift, as you wait for the revealing of our Lord Jesus Christ,

8 who will sustain you to the end, guiltless in the day of our Lord Jesus Christ.

9 God is faithful, by whom you were called into the fellowship of his Son, Jesus Christ our Lord.

10 I appeal to you, brothers, by the name of our Lord Jesus Christ, that all of you agree, and that there be no divisions among you, but that you be united in the same mind and the same judgment.

11 For it has been reported to me by Chloe's people that there is quarreling among you, my brothers.

12 What I mean is that each one of you says, "I follow Paul," or "I follow Apollos," or "I follow Cephas," or "I follow Christ."

13 Is Christ divided? Was Paul crucified for you? Or were you baptized in the name of Paul?

14 I thank God that I baptized none of you except Crispus and Gaius,

15 so that no one may say that you were baptized in my name.

16 (I did baptize also the household of Stephanas. Beyond that, I do not know

whether I baptized anyone else.)

¹⁷ For Christ did not send me to baptize but to preach the gospel, and not with words of eloquent wisdom, lest the cross of Christ be emptied of its power.

¹⁸ For the word of the cross is folly to those who are perishing, but to us who are being saved it is the power of God.

¹⁹ For it is written, "I will destroy the wisdom of the wise, and the discernment of the discerning I will thwart."

²⁰ Where is the one who is wise? Where is the scribe? Where is the debater of this age? Has not God made foolish the wisdom of the world?

²¹ For since, in the wisdom of God, the world did not know God through wisdom, it pleased God through the folly of what we preach to save those who believe.

²² For Jews demand signs and Greeks seek wisdom,

²³ but we preach Christ crucified, a stumbling block to Jews and folly to Gentiles,

²⁴ but to those who are called, both Jews and Greeks, Christ the power of God and the wisdom of God.

²⁵ For the foolishness of God is wiser than men, and the weakness of God is stronger than men.

²⁶ For consider your calling, brothers: not many of you were wise according to worldly standards, not many were powerful, not many were of noble birth.

²⁷ But God chose what is foolish in the world to shame the wise; God chose what is weak in the world to shame the strong;

²⁸ God chose what is low and despised in the world, even things that are not, to bring to nothing things that are,

²⁹ so that no human being might boast in the presence of God.

³⁰ And because of him you are in Christ Jesus, who became to us wisdom from God, righteousness and sanctification and redemption,

³¹ so that, as it is written, "Let the one who boasts, boast in the Lord."

CHAPTER 2

¹ And I, when I came to you, brothers, did not come proclaiming to you the testimony of God with lofty speech or wisdom.

² For I decided to know nothing among you except Jesus Christ and him crucified.

³ And I was with you in

weakness and in fear and much trembling,

4 and my speech and my message were not in plausible words of wisdom, but in demonstration of the Spirit and of power,

5 so that your faith might not rest in the wisdom of men but in the power of God.

6 Yet among the mature we do impart wisdom, although it is not a wisdom of this age or of the rulers of this age, who are doomed to pass away.

7 But we impart a secret and hidden wisdom of God, which God decreed before the ages for our glory.

8 None of the rulers of this age understood this, for if they had, they would not have crucified the Lord of glory.

9 But, as it is written, "What no eye has seen, nor ear heard, nor the heart of man has imagined, what God has prepared for those who love him"—

10 these things God has revealed to us through the Spirit. For the Spirit searches everything, even the depths of God.

11 For who knows a person's thoughts except the spirit of that person, which is in him? So also no one comprehends the thoughts of God except the Spirit of God.

12 Now we have received not the spirit of the world, but the Spirit who is from God, that we might understand the things freely given us by God.

13 And we impart this in words not taught by human wisdom but taught by the Spirit, interpreting spiritual truths to those who are spiritual.

14 The natural person does not accept the things of the Spirit of God, for they are folly to him, and he is not able to understand them because they are spiritually discerned.

15 The spiritual person judges all things, but is himself to be judged by no one.

16 "For who has understood the mind of the Lord so as to instruct him?" But we have the mind of Christ.

CHAPTER 3

1 But I, brothers, could not address you as spiritual people, but as people of the flesh, as infants in Christ.

2 I fed you with milk, not solid food, for you were not ready for it. And even now you are not yet ready,

3 for you are still of the flesh. For while there is jealousy and strife among you, are you not of the flesh and behaving only in a human way?

4 For when one says, "I fol-

low Paul," and another, "I follow Apollos," are you not being merely human?

⁵ What then is Apollos? What is Paul? Servants through whom you believed, as the Lord assigned to each.

⁶ I planted, Apollos watered, but God gave the growth.

⁷ So neither he who plants nor he who waters is anything, but only God who gives the growth.

⁸ He who plants and he who waters are one, and each will receive his wages according to his labor.

⁹ For we are God's fellow workers. You are God's field, God's building.

¹⁰ According to the grace of God given to me, like a skilled master builder I laid a foundation, and someone else is building upon it. Let each one take care how he builds upon it.

¹¹ For no one can lay a foundation other than that which is laid, which is Jesus Christ.

¹² Now if anyone builds on the foundation with gold, silver, precious stones, wood, hay, straw—

¹³ each one's work will become manifest, for the Day will disclose it, because it will be revealed by fire, and the fire will test what sort of work each one has done.

¹⁴ If the work that anyone has built on the foundation survives, he will receive a reward.

¹⁵ If anyone's work is burned up, he will suffer loss, though he himself will be saved, but only as through fire.

¹⁶ Do you not know that you are God's temple and that God's Spirit dwells in you?

¹⁷ If anyone destroys God's temple, God will destroy him. For God's temple is holy, and you are that temple.

¹⁸ Let no one deceive himself. If anyone among you thinks that he is wise in this age, let him become a fool that he may become wise.

¹⁹ For the wisdom of this world is folly with God. For it is written, "He catches the wise in their craftiness,"

²⁰ and again, "The Lord knows the thoughts of the wise, that they are futile."

²¹ So let no one boast in men. For all things are yours,

²² whether Paul or Apollos or Cephas or the world or life or death or the present or the future—all are yours,

²³ and you are Christ's, and Christ is God's.

CHAPTER 4

¹ This is how one should regard us, as servants of Christ

and stewards of the mysteries of God.

² Moreover, it is required of stewards that they be found faithful.

³ But with me it is a very small thing that I should be judged by you or by any human court. In fact, I do not even judge myself.

⁴ For I am not aware of anything against myself, but I am not thereby acquitted. It is the Lord who judges me.

⁵ Therefore do not pronounce judgment before the time, before the Lord comes, who will bring to light the things now hidden in darkness and will disclose the purposes of the heart. Then each one will receive his commendation from God.

⁶ I have applied all these things to myself and Apollos for your benefit, brothers, that you may learn by us not to go beyond what is written, that none of you may be puffed up in favor of one against another.

⁷ For who sees anything different in you? What do you have that you did not receive? If then you received it, why do you boast as if you did not receive it?

⁸ Already you have all you want! Already you have become rich! Without us you have become kings! And would that you did reign, so that we might share the rule with you!

⁹ For I think that God has exhibited us apostles as last of all, like men sentenced to death, because we have become a spectacle to the world, to angels, and to men.

¹⁰ We are fools for Christ's sake, but you are wise in Christ. We are weak, but you are strong. You are held in honor, but we in disrepute.

¹¹ To the present hour we hunger and thirst, we are poorly dressed and buffeted and homeless,

¹² and we labor, working with our own hands. When reviled, we bless; when persecuted, we endure;

¹³ when slandered, we entreat. We have become, and are still, like the scum of the world, the refuse of all things.

¹⁴ I do not write these things to make you ashamed, but to admonish you as my beloved children.

¹⁵ For though you have countless guides in Christ, you do not have many fathers. For I became your father in Christ Jesus through the gospel.

¹⁶ I urge you, then, be imitators of me.

¹⁷ That is why I sent you

Timothy, my beloved and faithful child in the Lord, to remind you of my ways in Christ, as I teach them everywhere in every church. ¹⁸ Some are arrogant, as though I were not coming to you. ¹⁹ But I will come to you soon, if the Lord wills, and I will find out not the talk of these arrogant people but their power. ²⁰ For the kingdom of God does not consist in talk but in power. ²¹ What do you wish? Shall I come to you with a rod, or with love in a spirit of gentleness?

CHAPTER 5

¹ It is actually reported that there is sexual immorality among you, and of a kind that is not tolerated even among pagans, for a man has his father's wife. ² And you are arrogant! Ought you not rather to mourn? Let him who has done this be removed from among you.

³ For though absent in body, I am present in spirit; and as if present, I have already pronounced judgment on the one who did such a thing. ⁴ When you are assembled in the name of the Lord Jesus and my spirit is present, with the power of our Lord Jesus, ⁵ you are to deliver this man to Satan for the destruction of the flesh, so that his spirit may be saved in the day of the Lord.

⁶ Your boasting is not good. Do you not know that a little leaven leavens the whole lump? ⁷ Cleanse out the old leaven that you may be a new lump, as you really are unleavened. For Christ, our Passover lamb, has been sacrificed. ⁸ Let us therefore celebrate the festival, not with the old leaven, the leaven of malice and evil, but with the unleavened bread of sincerity and truth.

⁹ I wrote to you in my letter not to associate with sexually immoral people— ¹⁰ not at all meaning the sexually immoral of this world, or the greedy and swindlers, or idolaters, since then you would need to go out of the world. ¹¹ But now I am writing to you not to associate with anyone who bears the name of brother if he is guilty of sexual immorality or greed, or is an idolater, reviler, drunkard, or swindler—not even to eat with such a one. ¹² For what have I to do

with judging outsiders? Is it not those inside the church whom you are to judge?

13 God judges those outside. "Purge the evil person from among you."

1 When one of you has a grievance against another, does he dare go to law before the unrighteous instead of the saints?

2 Or do you not know that the saints will judge the world? And if the world is to be judged by you, are you incompetent to try trivial cases?

3 Do you not know that we are to judge angels? How much more, then, matters pertaining to this life!

4 So if you have such cases, why do you lay them before those who have no standing in the church?

5 I say this to your shame. Can it be that there is no one among you wise enough to settle a dispute between the brothers,

6 but brother goes to law against brother, and that before unbelievers?

7 To have lawsuits at all with one another is already a defeat for you. Why not rather suffer wrong? Why not rather be defrauded?

8 But you yourselves wrong and defraud—even your own brothers!

9 Or do you not know that the unrighteous will not inherit the kingdom of God? Do not be deceived: neither the sexually immoral, nor idolaters, nor adulterers, nor men who practice homosexuality,

10 nor thieves, nor the greedy, nor drunkards, nor revilers, nor swindlers will inherit the kingdom of God.

11 And such were some of you. But you were washed, you were sanctified, you were justified in the name of the Lord Jesus Christ and by the Spirit of our God.

12 "All things are lawful for me," but not all things are helpful. "All things are lawful for me," but I will not be dominated by anything.

13 "Food is meant for the stomach and the stomach for food"—and God will destroy both one and the other. The body is not meant for sexual immorality, but for the Lord, and the Lord for the body.

14 And God raised the Lord and will also raise us up by his power.

15 Do you not know that your bodies are members of Christ? Shall I then take the members of Christ and make them members of a prostitute? Never!

¹⁶ Or do you not know that he who is joined to a prostitute becomes one body with her? For, as it is written, "The two will become one flesh."

¹⁷ But he who is joined to the Lord becomes one spirit with him.

¹⁸ Flee from sexual immorality. Every other sin a person commits is outside the body, but the sexually immoral person sins against his own body.

¹⁹ Or do you not know that your body is a temple of the Holy Spirit within you, whom you have from God? You are not your own,

²⁰ for you were bought with a price. So glorify God in your body.

CHAPTER 7

¹ Now concerning the matters about which you wrote: "It is good for a man not to have sexual relations with a woman."

² But because of the temptation to sexual immorality, each man should have his own wife and each woman her own husband.

³ The husband should give to his wife her conjugal rights, and likewise the wife to her husband.

⁴ For the wife does not have authority over her own body, but the husband does. Likewise the husband does not have authority over his own body, but the wife does.

⁵ Do not deprive one another, except perhaps by agreement for a limited time, that you may devote yourselves to prayer; but then come together again, so that Satan may not tempt you because of your lack of self-control.

⁶ Now as a concession, not a command, I say this.

⁷ I wish that all were as I myself am. But each has his own gift from God, one of one kind and one of another.

⁸ To the unmarried and the widows I say that it is good for them to remain single as I am.

⁹ But if they cannot exercise self-control, they should marry. For it is better to marry than to burn with passion.

¹⁰ To the married I give this charge (not I, but the Lord): the wife should not separate from her husband

¹¹ (but if she does, she should remain unmarried or else be reconciled to her husband), and the husband should not divorce his wife.

¹² To the rest I say (I, not the Lord) that if any brother has a wife who is an unbeliever, and she consents to live with him, he should not divorce her.

¹³ If any woman has a husband who is an unbeliever, and he consents to live with her, she should not divorce him.

¹⁴ For the unbelieving husband is made holy because of his wife, and the unbelieving wife is made holy because of her husband. Otherwise your children would be unclean, but as it is, they are holy.

¹⁵ But if the unbelieving partner separates, let it be so. In such cases the brother or sister is not enslaved. God has called you to peace.

¹⁶ For how do you know, wife, whether you will save your husband? Or how do you know, husband, whether you will save your wife?

¹⁷ Only let each person lead the life that the Lord has assigned to him, and to which God has called him. This is my rule in all the churches.

¹⁸ Was anyone at the time of his call already circumcised? Let him not seek to remove the marks of circumcision. Was anyone at the time of his call uncircumcised? Let him not seek circumcision.

¹⁹ For neither circumcision counts for anything nor uncircumcision, but keeping the commandments of God.

²⁰ Each one should remain in the condition in which he was called.

²¹ Were you a bondservant when called? Do not be concerned about it. (But if you can gain your freedom, avail yourself of the opportunity.)

²² For he who was called in the Lord as a bondservant is a freedman of the Lord. Likewise he who was free when called is a bondservant of Christ.

²³ You were bought with a price; do not become bondservants of men.

²⁴ So, brothers, in whatever condition each was called, there let him remain with God.

²⁵ Now concerning the betrothed, I have no command from the Lord, but I give my judgment as one who by the Lord's mercy is trustworthy.

²⁶ I think that in view of the present distress it is good for a person to remain as he is.

²⁷ Are you bound to a wife? Do not seek to be free. Are you free from a wife? Do not seek a wife.

²⁸ But if you do marry, you have not sinned, and if a betrothed woman marries, she has not sinned. Yet those who marry will have worldly troubles, and I would spare you that.

²⁹ This is what I mean,

brothers: the appointed time has grown very short. From now on, let those who have wives live as though they had none,

³⁰ and those who mourn as though they were not mourning, and those who rejoice as though they were not rejoicing, and those who buy as though they had no goods,

³¹ and those who deal with the world as though they had no dealings with it. For the present form of this world is passing away.

³² I want you to be free from anxieties. The unmarried man is anxious about the things of the Lord, how to please the Lord.

³³ But the married man is anxious about worldly things, how to please his wife,

³⁴ and his interests are divided. And the unmarried or betrothed woman is anxious about the things of the Lord, how to be holy in body and spirit. But the married woman is anxious about worldly things, how to please her husband.

³⁵ I say this for your own benefit, not to lay any restraint upon you, but to promote good order and to secure your undivided devotion to the Lord.

³⁶ If anyone thinks that he is not behaving properly toward his betrothed, if his passions are strong, and it has to be, let him do as he wishes: let them marry—it is no sin.

³⁷ But whoever is firmly established in his heart, being under no necessity but having his desire under control, and has determined this in his heart, to keep her as his betrothed, he will do well.

³⁸ So then he who marries his betrothed does well, and he who refrains from marriage will do even better.

³⁹ A wife is bound to her husband as long as he lives. But if her husband dies, she is free to be married to whom she wishes, only in the Lord.

⁴⁰ Yet in my judgment she is happier if she remains as she is. And I think that I too have the Spirit of God.

CHAPTER 8

¹ Now concerning food offered to idols: we know that "all of us possess knowledge." This "knowledge" puffs up, but love builds up.

² If anyone imagines that he knows something, he does not yet know as he ought to know.

³ But if anyone loves God, he is known by God.

⁴ Therefore, as to the eating of food offered to idols,

we know that "an idol has no real existence," and that "there is no God but one."

⁵ For although there may be so-called gods in heaven or on earth—as indeed there are many "gods" and many "lords"—

⁶ yet for us there is one God, the Father, from whom are all things and for whom we exist, and one Lord, Jesus Christ, through whom are all things and through whom we exist.

⁷ However, not all possess this knowledge. But some, through former association with idols, eat food as really offered to an idol, and their conscience, being weak, is defiled.

⁸ Food will not commend us to God. We are no worse off if we do not eat, and no better off if we do.

⁹ But take care that this right of yours does not somehow become a stumbling block to the weak.

¹⁰ For if anyone sees you who have knowledge eating in an idol's temple, will he not be encouraged, if his conscience is weak, to eat food offered to idols?

¹¹ And so by your knowledge this weak person is destroyed, the brother for whom Christ died.

¹² Thus, sinning against your brothers and wounding their conscience when it is weak, you sin against Christ.

¹³ Therefore, if food makes my brother stumble, I will never eat meat, lest I make my brother stumble.

CHAPTER 9

¹ Am I not free? Am I not an apostle? Have I not seen Jesus our Lord? Are not you my workmanship in the Lord?

² If to others I am not an apostle, at least I am to you, for you are the seal of my apostleship in the Lord.

³ This is my defense to those who would examine me.

⁴ Do we not have the right to eat and drink?

⁵ Do we not have the right to take along a believing wife, as do the other apostles and the brothers of the Lord and Cephas?

⁶ Or is it only Barnabas and I who have no right to refrain from working for a living?

⁷ Who serves as a soldier at his own expense? Who plants a vineyard without eating any of its fruit? Or who tends a flock without getting some of the milk?

⁸ Do I say these things on human authority? Does not the Law say the same?

⁹ For it is written in the Law

of Moses, "You shall not muzzle an ox when it treads out the grain." Is it for oxen that God is concerned?

¹⁰ Does he not certainly speak for our sake? It was written for our sake, because the plowman should plow in hope and the thresher thresh in hope of sharing in the crop.

¹¹ If we have sown spiritual things among you, is it too much if we reap material things from you?

¹² If others share this rightful claim on you, do not we even more? Nevertheless, we have not made use of this right, but we endure anything rather than put an obstacle in the way of the gospel of Christ.

¹³ Do you not know that those who are employed in the temple service get their food from the temple, and those who serve at the altar share in the sacrificial offerings?

¹⁴ In the same way, the Lord commanded that those who proclaim the gospel should get their living by the gospel.

¹⁵ But I have made no use of any of these rights, nor am I writing these things to secure any such provision. For I would rather die than have anyone deprive me of my ground for boasting.

¹⁶ For if I preach the gospel, that gives me no ground for boasting. For necessity is laid upon me. Woe to me if I do not preach the gospel!

¹⁷ For if I do this of my own will, I have a reward, but if not of my own will, I am still entrusted with a stewardship.

¹⁸ What then is my reward? That in my preaching I may present the gospel free of charge, so as not to make full use of my right in the gospel.

¹⁹ For though I am free from all, I have made myself a servant to all, that I might win more of them.

²⁰ To the Jews I became as a Jew, in order to win Jews. To those under the law I became as one under the law (though not being myself under the law) that I might win those under the law.

²¹ To those outside the law I became as one outside the law (not being outside the law of God but under the law of Christ) that I might win those outside the law.

²² To the weak I became weak, that I might win the weak. I have become all things to all people, that by all means I might save some.

²³ I do it all for the sake of the gospel, that I may share with them in its blessings.

²⁴ Do you not know that in a race all the runners run, but only one receives the prize? So run that you may obtain it.

²⁵ Every athlete exercises self-control in all things. They do it to receive a perishable wreath, but we an imperishable.

²⁶ So I do not run aimlessly; I do not box as one beating the air.

²⁷ But I discipline my body and keep it under control, lest after preaching to others I myself should be disqualified.

CHAPTER 10

¹ For I do not want you to be unaware, brothers, that our fathers were all under the cloud, and all passed through the sea,

² and all were baptized into Moses in the cloud and in the sea,

³ and all ate the same spiritual food,

⁴ and all drank the same spiritual drink. For they drank from the spiritual Rock that followed them, and the Rock was Christ.

⁵ Nevertheless, with most of them God was not pleased, for they were overthrown in the wilderness.

⁶ Now these things took place as examples for us, that we might not desire evil as they did.

⁷ Do not be idolaters as some of them were; as it is written, "The people sat down to eat and drink and rose up to play."

⁸ We must not indulge in sexual immorality as some of them did, and twenty-three thousand fell in a single day.

⁹ We must not put Christ to the test, as some of them did and were destroyed by serpents,

¹⁰ nor grumble, as some of them did and were destroyed by the Destroyer.

¹¹ Now these things happened to them as an example, but they were written down for our instruction, on whom the end of the ages has come.

¹² Therefore let anyone who thinks that he stands take heed lest he fall.

¹³ No temptation has overtaken you that is not common to man. God is faithful, and he will not let you be tempted beyond your ability, but with the temptation he will also provide the way of escape, that you may be able to endure it.

¹⁴ Therefore, my beloved, flee from idolatry.

¹⁵ I speak as to sensible people; judge for yourselves what I say.

16 The cup of blessing that we bless, is it not a participation in the blood of Christ? The bread that we break, is it not a participation in the body of Christ?

17 Because there is one bread, we who are many are one body, for we all partake of the one bread.

18 Consider the people of Israel: are not those who eat the sacrifices participants in the altar?

19 What do I imply then? That food offered to idols is anything, or that an idol is anything?

20 No, I imply that what pagans sacrifice they offer to demons and not to God. I do not want you to be participants with demons.

21 You cannot drink the cup of the Lord and the cup of demons. You cannot partake of the table of the Lord and the table of demons.

22 Shall we provoke the Lord to jealousy? Are we stronger than he?

23 "All things are lawful," but not all things are helpful. "All things are lawful," but not all things build up.

24 Let no one seek his own good, but the good of his neighbor.

25 Eat whatever is sold in the meat market without raising any question on the ground of conscience.

26 For "the earth is the Lord's, and the fullness thereof."

27 If one of the unbelievers invites you to dinner and you are disposed to go, eat whatever is set before you without raising any question on the ground of conscience.

28 But if someone says to you, "This has been offered in sacrifice," then do not eat it, for the sake of the one who informed you, and for the sake of conscience—

29 I do not mean your conscience, but his. For why should my liberty be determined by someone else's conscience?

30 If I partake with thankfulness, why am I denounced because of that for which I give thanks?

31 So, whether you eat or drink, or whatever you do, do all to the glory of God.

32 Give no offense to Jews or to Greeks or to the church of God,

33 just as I try to please everyone in everything I do, not seeking my own advantage, but that of many, that they may be saved.

CHAPTER 11

1 Be imitators of me, as I am of Christ.

2 Now I commend you because you remember me in everything and maintain the traditions even as I delivered them to you.

3 But I want you to understand that the head of every man is Christ, the head of a wife is her husband, and the head of Christ is God.

4 Every man who prays or prophesies with his head covered dishonors his head,

5 but every wife who prays or prophesies with her head uncovered dishonors her head, since it is the same as if her head were shaven.

6 For if a wife will not cover her head, then she should cut her hair short. But since it is disgraceful for a wife to cut off her hair or shave her head, let her cover her head.

7 For a man ought not to cover his head, since he is the image and glory of God, but woman is the glory of man.

8 For man was not made from woman, but woman from man.

9 Neither was man created for woman, but woman for man.

10 That is why a wife ought to have a symbol of authority on her head, because of the angels.

11 Nevertheless, in the Lord woman is not independent of man nor man of woman;

12 for as woman was made from man, so man is now born of woman. And all things are from God.

13 Judge for yourselves: is it proper for a wife to pray to God with her head uncovered?

14 Does not nature itself teach you that if a man wears long hair it is a disgrace for him,

15 but if a woman has long hair, it is her glory? For her hair is given to her for a covering.

16 If anyone is inclined to be contentious, we have no such practice, nor do the churches of God.

17 But in the following instructions I do not commend you, because when you come together it is not for the better but for the worse.

18 For, in the first place, when you come together as a church, I hear that there are divisions among you. And I believe it in part,

19 for there must be factions among you in order that those who are genuine among you may be recognized.

20 When you come together, it is not the Lord's supper that you eat.

21 For in eating, each one

goes ahead with his own meal. One goes hungry, another gets drunk.

²² What! Do you not have houses to eat and drink in? Or do you despise the church of God and humiliate those who have nothing? What shall I say to you? Shall I commend you in this? No, I will not.

²³ For I received from the Lord what I also delivered to you, that the Lord Jesus on the night when he was betrayed took bread,

²⁴ and when he had given thanks, he broke it, and said, "Take, eat; this is my body which is broken for you. Do this in remembrance of me."

²⁵ In the same way also he took the cup, after supper, saying, "This cup is the new covenant in my blood. Do this, as often as you drink it, in remembrance of me."

²⁶ For as often as you eat this bread and drink the cup, you proclaim the Lord's death until he comes.

²⁷ Whoever, therefore, eats the bread or drinks the cup of the Lord in an unworthy manner will be guilty concerning the body and blood of the Lord.

²⁸ Let a person examine himself, then, and so eat of the bread and drink of the cup.

²⁹ For anyone who eats and drinks without discerning the body eats and drinks judgment on himself.

³⁰ That is why many of you are weak and ill, and some have died.

³¹ But if we judged ourselves truly, we would not be judged.

³² But when we are judged by the Lord, we are disciplined so that we may not be condemned along with the world.

³³ So then, my brothers, when you come together to eat, wait for one another—

³⁴ if anyone is hungry, let him eat at home—so that when you come together it will not be for judgment. About the other things I will give directions when I come.

CHAPTER 12

¹ Now concerning spiritual gifts, brothers, I do not want you to be uninformed.

² You know that when you were pagans you were led astray to mute idols, however you were led.

³ Therefore I want you to understand that no one speaking in the Spirit of God ever says "Jesus is accursed!" and no one can say "Jesus is Lord" except in the Holy Spirit.

⁴ Now there are varieties of gifts, but the same Spirit;

⁵ and there are varieties of service, but the same Lord;

⁶ and there are varieties of activities, but it is the same God who empowers them all in everyone.

⁷ To each is given the manifestation of the Spirit for the common good.

⁸ For to one is given through the Spirit the utterance of wisdom, and to another the utterance of knowledge according to the same Spirit,

⁹ to another faith by the same Spirit, to another gifts of healing by the one Spirit,

¹⁰ to another the working of miracles, to another prophecy, to another the ability to distinguish between spirits, to another various kinds of tongues, to another the interpretation of tongues.

¹¹ All these are empowered by one and the same Spirit, who apportions to each one individually as he wills.

¹² For just as the body is one and has many members, and all the members of the body, though many, are one body, so it is with Christ.

¹³ For in one Spirit we were all baptized into one body—Jews or Greeks, slaves or free—and all were made to drink of one Spirit.

¹⁴ For the body does not consist of one member but of many.

¹⁵ If the foot should say, "Because I am not a hand, I do not belong to the body," that would not make it any less a part of the body.

¹⁶ And if the ear should say, "Because I am not an eye, I do not belong to the body," that would not make it any less a part of the body.

¹⁷ If the whole body were an eye, where would be the sense of hearing? If the whole body were an ear, where would be the sense of smell?

¹⁸ But as it is, God arranged the members in the body, each one of them, as he chose.

¹⁹ If all were a single member, where would the body be?

²⁰ As it is, there are many parts, yet one body.

²¹ The eye cannot say to the hand, "I have no need of you," nor again the head to the feet, "I have no need of you."

²² On the contrary, the parts of the body that seem to be weaker are indispensable,

²³ and on those parts of the body that we think less honorable we bestow the greater honor, and our unpresentable parts are treated with greater modesty,

²⁴ which our more presentable parts do not require. But

God has so composed the body, giving greater honor to the part that lacked it,

25 that there may be no division in the body, but that the members may have the same care for one another.

26 If one member suffers, all suffer together; if one member is honored, all rejoice together.

27 Now you are the body of Christ and individually members of it.

28 And God has appointed in the church first apostles, second prophets, third teachers, then miracles, then gifts of healing, helping, administrating, and various kinds of tongues.

29 Are all apostles? Are all prophets? Are all teachers? Do all work miracles?

30 Do all possess gifts of healing? Do all speak with tongues? Do all interpret?

31 But earnestly desire the higher gifts. And I will show you a still more excellent way.

CHAPTER 13

1 If I speak in the tongues of men and of angels, but have not love, I am a noisy gong or a clanging cymbal.

2 And if I have prophetic powers, and understand all mysteries and all knowledge, and if I have all faith, so as to remove mountains, but have not love, I am nothing.

3 If I give away all I have, and if I deliver up my body to be burned, but have not love, I gain nothing.

4 Love is patient and kind; love does not envy or boast; it is not arrogant

5 or rude. It does not insist on its own way; it is not irritable or resentful;

6 it does not rejoice at wrongdoing, but rejoices with the truth.

7 Love bears all things, believes all things, hopes all things, endures all things.

8 Love never ends. As for prophecies, they will pass away; as for tongues, they will cease; as for knowledge, it will pass away.

9 For we know in part and we prophesy in part,

10 but when the perfect comes, the partial will pass away.

11 When I was a child, I spoke like a child, I thought like a child, I reasoned like a child. When I became a man, I gave up childish ways.

12 For now we see in a mirror dimly, but then face to face. Now I know in part; then I shall know fully, even as I have been fully known.

¹³ So now faith, hope, and love abide, these three; but the greatest of these is love.

CHAPTER 14

¹ Pursue love, and earnestly desire the spiritual gifts, especially that you may prophesy.

² For one who speaks in a tongue speaks not to men but to God; for no one understands him, but he utters mysteries in the Spirit.

³ On the other hand, the one who prophesies speaks to people for their upbuilding and encouragement and consolation.

⁴ The one who speaks in a tongue builds up himself, but the one who prophesies builds up the church.

⁵ Now I want you all to speak in tongues, but even more to prophesy. The one who prophesies is greater than the one who speaks in tongues, unless someone interprets, so that the church may be built up.

⁶ Now, brothers, if I come to you speaking in tongues, how will I benefit you unless I bring you some revelation or knowledge or prophecy or teaching?

⁷ If even lifeless instruments, such as the flute or the harp, do not give distinct notes, how will anyone know what is played?

⁸ And if the bugle gives an indistinct sound, who will get ready for battle?

⁹ So with yourselves, if with your tongue you utter speech that is not intelligible, how will anyone know what is said? For you will be speaking into the air.

¹⁰ There are doubtless many different languages in the world, and none is without meaning,

¹¹ but if I do not know the meaning of the language, I will be a foreigner to the speaker and the speaker a foreigner to me.

¹² So with yourselves, since you are eager for manifestations of the Spirit, strive to excel in building up the church.

¹³ Therefore, one who speaks in a tongue should pray that he may interpret.

¹⁴ For if I pray in a tongue, my spirit prays but my mind is unfruitful.

¹⁵ What am I to do? I will pray with my spirit, but I will pray with my mind also; I will sing praise with my spirit, but I will sing with my mind also.

¹⁶ Otherwise, if you give thanks with your spirit, how can anyone in the position of an outsider say "Amen"

to your thanksgiving when he does not know what you are saying?

¹⁷ For you may be giving thanks well enough, but the other person is not being built up.

¹⁸ I thank God that I speak in tongues more than all of you.

¹⁹ Nevertheless, in church I would rather speak five words with my mind in order to instruct others, than ten thousand words in a tongue.

²⁰ Brothers, do not be children in your thinking. Be infants in evil, but in your thinking be mature.

²¹ In the Law it is written, "By people of strange tongues and by the lips of foreigners will I speak to this people, and even then they will not listen to me, says the Lord."

²² Thus tongues are a sign not for believers but for unbelievers, while prophecy is a sign not for unbelievers but for believers.

²³ If, therefore, the whole church comes together and all speak in tongues, and outsiders or unbelievers enter, will they not say that you are out of your minds?

²⁴ But if all prophesy, and an unbeliever or outsider enters, he is convicted by all, he is called to account by all,

²⁵ the secrets of his heart are disclosed, and so, falling on his face, he will worship God and declare that God is really among you.

²⁶ What then, brothers? When you come together, each one has a hymn, a lesson, a revelation, a tongue, or an interpretation. Let all things be done for building up.

²⁷ If any speak in a tongue, let there be only two or at most three, and each in turn, and let someone interpret.

²⁸ But if there is no one to interpret, let each of them keep silent in church and speak to himself and to God.

²⁹ Let two or three prophets speak, and let the others weigh what is said.

³⁰ If a revelation is made to another sitting there, let the first be silent.

³¹ For you can all prophesy one by one, so that all may learn and all be encouraged,

³² and the spirits of prophets are subject to prophets.

³³ For God is not a God of confusion but of peace. As in all the churches of the saints,

³⁴ the women should keep silent in the churches. For they are not permitted to speak, but should be in submission, as the Law also says.

³⁵ If there is anything they

desire to learn, let them ask their husbands at home. For it is shameful for a woman to speak in church.

36 Or was it from you that the word of God came? Or are you the only ones it has reached?

37 If anyone thinks that he is a prophet, or spiritual, he should acknowledge that the things I am writing to you are a command of the Lord.

38 If anyone does not recognize this, he is not recognized.

39 So, my brothers, earnestly desire to prophesy, and do not forbid speaking in tongues.

40 But all things should be done decently and in order.

CHAPTER 15

1 Now I would remind you, brothers, of the gospel I preached to you, which you received, in which you stand,

2 and by which you are being saved, if you hold fast to the word I preached to you—unless you believed in vain.

3 For I delivered to you as of first importance what I also received: that Christ died for our sins in accordance with the Scriptures,

4 that he was buried, that he was raised on the third day in accordance with the Scriptures,

5 and that he appeared to Cephas, then to the twelve.

6 Then he appeared to more than five hundred brothers at one time, most of whom are still alive, though some have fallen asleep.

7 Then he appeared to James, then to all the apostles.

8 Last of all, as to one untimely born, he appeared also to me.

9 For I am the least of the apostles, unworthy to be called an apostle, because I persecuted the church of God.

10 But by the grace of God I am what I am, and his grace toward me was not in vain. On the contrary, I worked harder than any of them, though it was not I, but the grace of God that is with me.

11 Whether then it was I or they, so we preach and so you believed.

12 Now if Christ is proclaimed as raised from the dead, how can some of you say that there is no resurrection of the dead?

13 But if there is no resurrection of the dead, then not even Christ has been raised.

14 And if Christ has not been raised, then our preaching is in vain and your faith is in vain.

¹⁵ We are even found to be misrepresenting God, because we testified about God that he raised Christ, whom he did not raise if it is true that the dead are not raised.

¹⁶ For if the dead are not raised, not even Christ has been raised.

¹⁷ And if Christ has not been raised, your faith is futile and you are still in your sins.

¹⁸ Then those also who have fallen asleep in Christ have perished.

¹⁹ If in Christ we have hope in this life only, we are of all people most to be pitied.

²⁰ But in fact Christ has been raised from the dead, the firstfruits of those who have fallen asleep.

²¹ For as by a man came death, by a man has come also the resurrection of the dead.

²² For as in Adam all die, so also in Christ shall all be made alive.

²³ But each in his own order: Christ the firstfruits, then at his coming those who belong to Christ.

²⁴ Then comes the end, when he delivers the kingdom to God the Father after destroying every rule and every authority and power.

²⁵ For he must reign until he has put all his enemies under his feet.

²⁶ The last enemy to be destroyed is death.

²⁷ For "God has put all things in subjection under his feet." But when it says, "all things are put in subjection," it is plain that he is excepted who put all things in subjection under him.

²⁸ When all things are subjected to him, then the Son himself will also be subjected to him who put all things in subjection under him, that God may be all in all.

²⁹ Otherwise, what do people mean by being baptized on behalf of the dead? If the dead are not raised at all, why are people baptized on their behalf?

³⁰ Why are we in danger every hour?

³¹ I protest, brothers, by my pride in you, which I have in Christ Jesus our Lord, I die every day!

³² What do I gain if, humanly speaking, I fought with beasts at Ephesus? If the dead are not raised, "Let us eat and drink, for tomorrow we die."

³³ Do not be deceived: "Bad company ruins good morals."

³⁴ Wake up from your drunken stupor, as is right, and do not go on sinning. For some have no knowledge of God. I say this to your shame.

³⁵ But someone will ask,

"How are the dead raised? With what kind of body do they come?"

³⁶ You foolish person! What you sow does not come to life unless it dies.

³⁷ And what you sow is not the body that is to be, but a bare kernel, perhaps of wheat or of some other grain.

³⁸ But God gives it a body as he has chosen, and to each kind of seed its own body.

³⁹ For not all flesh is the same, but there is one kind for humans, another for animals, another for birds, and another for fish.

⁴⁰ There are heavenly bodies and earthly bodies, but the glory of the heavenly is of one kind, and the glory of the earthly is of another.

⁴¹ There is one glory of the sun, and another glory of the moon, and another glory of the stars; for star differs from star in glory.

⁴² So is it with the resurrection of the dead. What is sown is perishable; what is raised is imperishable.

⁴³ It is sown in dishonor; it is raised in glory. It is sown in weakness; it is raised in power.

⁴⁴ It is sown a natural body; it is raised a spiritual body. If there is a natural body, there is also a spiritual body.

⁴⁵ Thus it is written, "The first man Adam became a living being"; the last Adam became a life-giving spirit.

⁴⁶ But it is not the spiritual that is first but the natural, and then the spiritual.

⁴⁷ The first man was from the earth, a man of dust; the second man is from heaven.

⁴⁸ As was the man of dust, so also are those who are of the dust, and as is the man of heaven, so also are those who are of heaven.

⁴⁹ Just as we have borne the image of the man of dust, we shall also bear the image of the man of heaven.

⁵⁰ I tell you this, brothers: flesh and blood cannot inherit the kingdom of God, nor does the perishable inherit the imperishable.

⁵¹ Behold! I tell you a mystery. We shall not all sleep, but we shall all be changed,

⁵² in a moment, in the twinkling of an eye, at the last trumpet. For the trumpet will sound, and the dead will be raised imperishable, and we shall be changed.

⁵³ For this perishable body must put on the imperishable, and this mortal body must put on immortality.

⁵⁴ When the perishable puts on the imperishable, and the mortal puts on immortality,

then shall come to pass the saying that is written: "Death is swallowed up in victory.

⁵⁵ "O death, where is your victory? O death, where is your sting?"

⁵⁶ The sting of death is sin, and the power of sin is the law.

⁵⁷ But thanks be to God, who gives us the victory through our Lord Jesus Christ.

⁵⁸ Therefore, my beloved brothers, be steadfast, immovable, always abounding in the work of the Lord, knowing that in the Lord your labor is not in vain.

CHAPTER 16

¹ Now concerning the collection for the saints: as I directed the churches of Galatia, so you also are to do.

² On the first day of every week, each of you is to put something aside and store it up, as he may prosper, so that there will be no collecting when I come.

³ And when I arrive, I will send those whom you accredit by letter to carry your gift to Jerusalem.

⁴ If it seems advisable that I should go also, they will accompany me.

⁵ I will visit you after passing through Macedonia, for I intend to pass through Macedonia,

⁶ and perhaps I will stay with you or even spend the winter, so that you may help me on my journey, wherever I go.

⁷ For I do not want to see you now just in passing. I hope to spend some time with you, if the Lord permits.

⁸ But I will stay in Ephesus until Pentecost,

⁹ for a wide door for effective work has opened to me, and there are many adversaries.

¹⁰ When Timothy comes, see that you put him at ease among you, for he is doing the work of the Lord, as I am.

¹¹ So let no one despise him. Help him on his way in peace, that he may return to me, for I am expecting him with the brothers.

¹² Now concerning our brother Apollos, I strongly urged him to visit you with the other brothers, but it was not at all his will to come now. He will come when he has opportunity.

¹³ Be watchful, stand firm in the faith, act like men, be strong.

¹⁴ Let all that you do be done in love.

¹⁵ Now I urge you, brothers—you know that the household of Stephanas were the first converts in Achaia,

and that they have devoted themselves to the service of the saints—

¹⁶ be subject to such as these, and to every fellow worker and laborer.

¹⁷ I rejoice at the coming of Stephanas and Fortunatus and Achaicus, because they have made up for your absence,

¹⁸ for they refreshed my spirit as well as yours. Give recognition to such people.

¹⁹ The churches of Asia send you greetings. Aquila and Prisca, together with the church in their house, send you hearty greetings in the Lord.

²⁰ All the brothers send you greetings. Greet one another with a holy kiss.

²¹ I, Paul, write this greeting with my own hand.

²² If anyone has no love for the Lord, let him be accursed. Our Lord, come!

²³ The grace of the Lord Jesus be with you.

²⁴ My love be with you all in Christ Jesus. Amen.

THE SECOND LETTER OF PAUL TO THE CORINTHIANS

2 CORINTHIANS

CHAPTER 1

¹ Paul, an apostle of Christ Jesus by the will of God, and Timothy our brother, To the church of God that is at Corinth, with all the saints who are in the whole of Achaia:

² Grace to you and peace from God our Father and the Lord Jesus Christ.

³ Blessed be the God and Father of our Lord Jesus Christ, the Father of mercies and God of all comfort,

⁴ who comforts us in all our affliction, so that we may be able to comfort those who are in any affliction, with the comfort with which we ourselves are comforted by God.

⁵ For as we share abundantly in Christ's sufferings, so through Christ we share abundantly in comfort too.

⁶ If we are afflicted, it is for your comfort and salvation; and if we are comforted, it is for your comfort, which you experience when you patient-

ly endure the same sufferings that we suffer.

⁷ Our hope for you is unshaken, for we know that as you share in our sufferings, you will also share in our comfort.

⁸ For we do not want you to be unaware, brothers, of the affliction we experienced in Asia. For we were so utterly burdened beyond our strength that we despaired of life itself.

⁹ Indeed, we felt that we had received the sentence of death. But that was to make us rely not on ourselves but on God who raises the dead.

¹⁰ He delivered us from such a deadly peril, and he will deliver us. On him we have set our hope that he will deliver us again.

¹¹ You also must help us by prayer, so that many will give thanks on our behalf for the blessing granted us through the prayers of many.

¹² For our boast is this, the testimony of our conscience, that we behaved in the world with simplicity and godly sincerity, not by earthly wisdom but by the grace of God, and supremely so toward you.

¹³ For we are not writing to you anything other than what you read and understand and

I hope you will fully understand—

¹⁴ just as you did partially understand us— that on the day of our Lord Jesus you will boast of us as we will boast of you.

¹⁵ Because I was sure of this, I wanted to come to you first, so that you might have a second experience of grace.

¹⁶ I wanted to visit you on my way to Macedonia, and to come back to you from Macedonia and have you send me on my way to Judea.

¹⁷ Was I vacillating when I wanted to do this? Do I make my plans according to the flesh, ready to say "Yes, yes" and "No, no" at the same time?

¹⁸ As surely as God is faithful, our word to you has not been Yes and No.

¹⁹ For the Son of God, Jesus Christ, whom we proclaimed among you, Silvanus and Timothy and I, was not Yes and No, but in him it is always Yes.

²⁰ For all the promises of God find their Yes in him. That is why it is through him that we utter our Amen to God for his glory.

²¹ And it is God who establishes us with you in Christ, and has anointed us,

²² and who has also put

his seal on us and given us his Spirit in our hearts as a guarantee.

23 But I call God to witness against me—it was to spare you that I refrained from coming again to Corinth.

24 Not that we lord it over your faith, but we work with you for your joy, for you stand firm in your faith.

CHAPTER 2

1 For I made up my mind not to make another painful visit to you.

2 For if I cause you pain, who is there to make me glad but the one whom I have pained?

3 And I wrote as I did, so that when I came I might not suffer pain from those who should have made me rejoice, for I felt sure of all of you, that my joy would be the joy of you all.

4 For I wrote to you out of much affliction and anguish of heart and with many tears, not to cause you pain but to let you know the abundant love that I have for you.

5 Now if anyone has caused pain, he has caused it not to me, but in some measure—not to put it too severely—to all of you.

6 For such a one, this punishment by the majority is enough,

7 so you should rather turn to forgive and comfort him, or he may be overwhelmed by excessive sorrow.

8 So I beg you to reaffirm your love for him.

9 For this is why I wrote, that I might test you and know whether you are obedient in everything.

10 Anyone whom you forgive, I also forgive. Indeed, what I have forgiven, if I have forgiven anything, has been for your sake in the presence of Christ,

11 so that we would not be outwitted by Satan; for we are not ignorant of his designs.

12 When I came to Troas to preach the gospel of Christ, even though a door was opened for me in the Lord,

13 my spirit was not at rest because I did not find my brother Titus there. So I took leave of them and went on to Macedonia.

14 But thanks be to God, who in Christ always leads us in triumphal procession, and through us spreads the fragrance of the knowledge of him everywhere.

15 For we are the aroma of Christ to God among those who are being saved and among those who are perishing,

16 to one a fragrance from

death to death, to the other a fragrance from life to life. Who is sufficient for these things?

17 For we are not, like so many, peddlers of God's word, but as men of sincerity, as commissioned by God, in the sight of God we speak in Christ.

CHAPTER 3

1 Are we beginning to commend ourselves again? Or do we need, as some do, letters of recommendation to you, or from you?

2 You yourselves are our letter of recommendation, written on our hearts, to be known and read by all.

3 And you show that you are a letter from Christ delivered by us, written not with ink but with the Spirit of the living God, not on tablets of stone but on tablets of human hearts.

4 Such is the confidence that we have through Christ toward God.

5 Not that we are sufficient in ourselves to claim anything as coming from us, but our sufficiency is from God,

6 who has made us sufficient to be ministers of a new covenant, not of the letter but of the Spirit. For the letter kills, but the Spirit gives life.

7 Now if the ministry of death, carved in letters on stone, came with such glory that the Israelites could not gaze at Moses' face because of its glory, which was being brought to an end,

8 will not the ministry of the Spirit have even more glory?

9 For if there was glory in the ministry of condemnation, the ministry of righteousness must far exceed it in glory.

10 Indeed, in this case, what once had glory has come to have no glory at all, because of the glory that surpasses it.

11 For if what was being brought to an end came with glory, much more will what is permanent have glory.

12 Since we have such a hope, we are very bold,

13 not like Moses, who would put a veil over his face so that the Israelites might not gaze at the outcome of what was being brought to an end.

14 But their minds were hardened. For to this day, when they read the old covenant, that same veil remains unlifted, because only through Christ is it taken away.

15 Yes, to this day whenever Moses is read a veil lies over their hearts.

16 But when one turns to the Lord, the veil is removed.

17 Now the Lord is the Spirit, and where the Spirit of the Lord is, there is freedom.

18 And we all, with unveiled face, beholding the glory of the Lord, are being transformed into the same image from one degree of glory to another. For this comes from the Lord who is the Spirit.

CHAPTER 4

1 Therefore, having this ministry by the mercy of God, we do not lose heart.

2 But we have renounced disgraceful, underhanded ways. We refuse to practice cunning or to tamper with God's word, but by the open statement of the truth we would commend ourselves to everyone's conscience in the sight of God.

3 And even if our gospel is veiled, it is veiled to those who are perishing.

4 In their case the god of this world has blinded the minds of the unbelievers, to keep them from seeing the light of the gospel of the glory of Christ, who is the image of God.

5 For what we proclaim is not ourselves, but Jesus Christ as Lord, with ourselves as your servants for Jesus' sake.

6 For God, who said, "Let light shine out of darkness," has shone in our hearts to give the light of the knowledge of the glory of God in the face of Jesus Christ.

7 But we have this treasure in jars of clay, to show that the surpassing power belongs to God and not to us.

8 We are afflicted in every way, but not crushed; perplexed, but not driven to despair;

9 persecuted, but not forsaken; struck down, but not destroyed;

10 always carrying in the body the death of Jesus, so that the life of Jesus may also be manifested in our bodies.

11 For we who live are always being given over to death for Jesus' sake, so that the life of Jesus also may be manifested in our mortal flesh.

12 So death is at work in us, but life in you.

13 Since we have the same spirit of faith according to what has been written, "I believed, and so I spoke," we also believe, and so we also speak,

14 knowing that he who raised the Lord Jesus will raise us also with Jesus and bring us with you into his presence.

¹⁵ For it is all for your sake, so that as grace extends to more and more people it may increase thanksgiving, to the glory of God.

¹⁶ So we do not lose heart. Though our outer self is wasting away, our inner self is being renewed day by day.

¹⁷ For this light momentary affliction is preparing for us an eternal weight of glory beyond all comparison,

¹⁸ as we look not to the things that are seen but to the things that are unseen. For the things that are seen are transient, but the things that are unseen are eternal.

CHAPTER 5

¹ For we know that if the tent that is our earthly home is destroyed, we have a building from God, a house not made with hands, eternal in the heavens.

² For in this tent we groan, longing to put on our heavenly dwelling,

³ if indeed by putting it on we may not be found naked.

⁴ For while we are still in this tent, we groan, being burdened—not that we would be unclothed, but that we would be further clothed, so that what is mortal may be swallowed up by life.

⁵ He who has prepared us for this very thing is God, who has given us the Spirit as a guarantee.

⁶ So we are always of good courage. We know that while we are at home in the body we are away from the Lord,

⁷ for we walk by faith, not by sight.

⁸ Yes, we are of good courage, and we would rather be away from the body and at home with the Lord.

⁹ So whether we are at home or away, we make it our aim to please him:

¹⁰ For we must all appear before the judgment seat of Christ, so that each one may receive what is due for what he has done in the body, whether good or evil.

¹¹ Therefore, knowing the fear of the Lord, we persuade others. But what we are is known to God, and I hope it is known also to your conscience.

¹² We are not commending ourselves to you again but giving you cause to boast about us, so that you may be able to answer those who boast about outward appearance and not about what is in the heart.

¹³ For if we are beside ourselves, it is for God; if we are in our right mind, it is for you.

14 For the love of Christ controls us, because we have concluded this: that one has died for all, therefore all have died;

15 and he died for all, that those who live might no longer live for themselves but for him who for their sake died and was raised.

16 From now on, therefore, we regard no one according to the flesh. Even though we once regarded Christ according to the flesh, we regard him thus no longer.

17 Therefore, if anyone is in Christ, he is a new creation. The old has passed away; behold, the new has come.

18 All this is from God, who through Christ reconciled us to himself and gave us the ministry of reconciliation;

19 that is, in Christ God was reconciling the world to himself, not counting their trespasses against them, and entrusting to us the message of reconciliation.

20 Therefore, we are ambassadors for Christ, God making his appeal through us. We implore you on behalf of Christ, be reconciled to God.

21 For our sake he made him to be sin who knew no sin, so that in him we might become the righteousness of God.

CHAPTER 6

1 Working together with him, then, we appeal to you not to receive the grace of God in vain.

2 For he says, "In a favorable time I listened to you, and in a day of salvation I have helped you." Behold, now is the favorable time; behold, now is the day of salvation.

3 We put no obstacle in anyone's way, so that no fault may be found with our ministry,

4 but as servants of God we commend ourselves in every way: by great endurance, in afflictions, hardships, calamities,

5 beatings, imprisonments, riots, labors, sleepless nights, hunger;

6 by purity, knowledge, patience, kindness, the Holy Spirit, genuine love;

7 by truthful speech, and the power of God; with the weapons of righteousness for the right hand and for the left;

8 through honor and dishonor, through slander and praise. We are treated as impostors, and yet are true;

9 as unknown, and yet well known; as dying, and behold, we live; as punished, and yet not killed;

10 as sorrowful, yet always

rejoicing; as poor, yet making many rich; as having nothing, yet possessing everything.

¹¹ We have spoken freely to you, Corinthians; our heart is wide open.

¹² You are not restricted by us, but you are restricted in your own affections.

¹³ In return (I speak as to children) widen your hearts also.

¹⁴ Do not be unequally yoked with unbelievers. For what partnership has righteousness with lawlessness? Or what fellowship has light with darkness?

¹⁵ What accord has Christ with Belial? Or what portion does a believer share with an unbeliever?

¹⁶ What agreement has the temple of God with idols? For we are the temple of the living God; as God said, "I will make my dwelling among them and walk among them, and I will be their God, and they shall be my people.

¹⁷ "Therefore go out from their midst, and be separate from them, says the Lord, and touch no unclean thing; then I will welcome you,

¹⁸ "and I will be a father to you, and you shall be sons and daughters to me, says the Lord Almighty."

CHAPTER 7

¹ Since we have these promises, beloved, let us cleanse ourselves from every defilement of body and spirit, bringing holiness to completion in the fear of God.

² Make room in your hearts for us. We have wronged no one, we have corrupted no one, we have taken advantage of no one.

³ I do not say this to condemn you, for I said before that you are in our hearts, to die together and to live together.

⁴ I am acting with great boldness toward you; I have great pride in you; I am filled with comfort. In all our affliction, I am overflowing with joy.

⁵ For even when we came into Macedonia, our bodies had no rest, but we were afflicted at every turn—fighting without and fear within.

⁶ But God, who comforts the downcast, comforted us by the coming of Titus,

⁷ and not only by his coming but also by the comfort with which he was comforted by you, as he told us of your longing, your mourning, your zeal for me, so that I rejoiced still more.

⁸ For even if I made you grieve with my letter, I do

not regret it—though I did regret it, for I see that that letter grieved you, though only for a while.

9 As it is, I rejoice, not because you were grieved, but because you were grieved into repenting. For you felt a godly grief, so that you suffered no loss through us.

10 For godly grief produces a repentance that leads to salvation without regret, whereas worldly grief produces death.

11 For see what earnestness this godly grief has produced in you, but also what eagerness to clear yourselves, what indignation, what fear, what longing, what zeal, what punishment! At every point you have proved yourselves innocent in the matter.

12 So although I wrote to you, it was not for the sake of the one who did the wrong, nor for the sake of the one who suffered the wrong, but in order that your earnestness for us might be revealed to you in the sight of God.

13 Therefore we are comforted. And besides our own comfort, we rejoiced still more at the joy of Titus, because his spirit has been refreshed by you all.

14 For whatever boasts I made to him about you, I was not put to shame. But just as everything we said to you was true, so also our boasting before Titus has proved true.

15 And his affection for you is even greater, as he remembers the obedience of you all, how you received him with fear and trembling.

16 I rejoice, because I have complete confidence in you.

CHAPTER 8

1 We want you to know, brothers, about the grace of God that is given among the churches of Macedonia,

2 for in a severe test of affliction, their abundance of joy and their extreme poverty have overflowed in a wealth of generosity on their part.

3 For they gave according to their means, as I can testify, and beyond their means, of their own accord,

4 begging us earnestly for the favor of taking part in the relief of the saints—

5 and this, not as we expected, but they gave themselves first to the Lord and then by the will of God to us.

6 Accordingly, we urged Titus that as he had started, so he should complete among you this act of grace.

7 But as you excel in everything—in faith, in speech,

in knowledge, in all earnestness, and in our love for you—see that you excel in this act of grace also.

8 I say this not as a command, but to prove by the earnestness of others that your love also is genuine.

9 For you know the grace of our Lord Jesus Christ, that though he was rich, yet for your sake he became poor, so that you by his poverty might become rich.

10 And in this matter I give my judgment: this benefits you, who a year ago started not only to do this work but also to desire to do it.

11 So now finish doing it as well, so that your readiness in desiring it may be matched by your completing it out of what you have.

12 For if the readiness is there, it is acceptable according to what a person has, not according to what he does not have.

13 For I do not mean that others should be eased and you burdened, but that as a matter of fairness

14 your abundance at the present time should supply their need, so that their abundance may supply your need, that there may be fairness.

15 As it is written, "Whoever gathered much had nothing left over, and whoever gathered little had no lack."

16 But thanks be to God, who put into the heart of Titus the same earnest care I have for you.

17 For he not only accepted our appeal, but being himself very earnest he is going to you of his own accord.

18 With him we are sending the brother who is famous among all the churches for his preaching of the gospel.

19 And not only that, but he has been appointed by the churches to travel with us as we carry out this act of grace that is being ministered by us, for the glory of the Lord himself and to show our good will.

20 We take this course so that no one should blame us about this generous gift that is being administered by us,

21 for we aim at what is honorable not only in the Lord's sight but also in the sight of man.

22 And with them we are sending our brother whom we have often tested and found earnest in many matters, but who is now more earnest than ever because of his great confidence in you.

23 As for Titus, he is my partner and fellow worker for your benefit. And as for

our brothers, they are messengers of the churches, the glory of Christ.

24 So give proof before the churches of your love and of our boasting about you to these men.

CHAPTER 9

1 Now it is superfluous for me to write to you about the ministry for the saints,

2 for I know your readiness, of which I boast about you to the people of Macedonia, saying that Achaia has been ready since last year. And your zeal has stirred up most of them.

3 But I am sending the brothers so that our boasting about you may not prove empty in this matter, so that you may be ready, as I said you would be.

4 Otherwise, if some Macedonians come with me and find that you are not ready, we would be humiliated—to say nothing of you—for being so confident.

5 So I thought it necessary to urge the brothers to go on ahead to you and arrange in advance for the gift you have promised, so that it may be ready as a willing gift, not as an exaction.

6 The point is this: whoever sows sparingly will also reap sparingly, and whoever sows bountifully will also reap bountifully.

7 Each one must give as he has decided in his heart, not reluctantly or under compulsion, for God loves a cheerful giver.

8 And God is able to make all grace abound to you, so that having all sufficiency in all things at all times, you may abound in every good work.

9 As it is written, "He has distributed freely, he has given to the poor; his righteousness endures forever."

10 He who supplies seed to the sower and bread for food will supply and multiply your seed for sowing and increase the harvest of your righteousness.

11 You will be enriched in every way to be generous in every way, which through us will produce thanksgiving to God.

12 For the ministry of this service is not only supplying the needs of the saints but is also overflowing in many thanksgivings to God.

13 By their approval of this service, they will glorify God because of your submission that comes from your confession of the gospel of Christ, and the generosity of your

contribution for them and for all others, ¹⁴ while they long for you and pray for you, because of the surpassing grace of God upon you.

¹⁵ Thanks be to God for his inexpressible gift!

CHAPTER 10

¹ I, Paul, myself entreat you, by the meekness and gentleness of Christ—I who am humble when face to face with you, but bold toward you when I am away!—

² I beg of you that when I am present I may not have to show boldness with such confidence as I count on showing against some who suspect us of walking according to the flesh.

³ For though we walk in the flesh, we are not waging war according to the flesh.

⁴ For the weapons of our warfare are not of the flesh but have divine power to destroy strongholds.

⁵ We destroy arguments and every lofty opinion raised against the knowledge of God, and take every thought captive to obey Christ,

⁶ being ready to punish every disobedience, when your obedience is complete.

⁷ Look at what is before your eyes. If anyone is confident that he is Christ's, let him remind himself that just as he is Christ's, so also are we.

⁸ For even if I boast a little too much of our authority, which the Lord gave for building you up and not for destroying you, I will not be ashamed.

⁹ I do not want to appear to be frightening you with my letters.

¹⁰ For they say, "His letters are weighty and strong, but his bodily presence is weak, and his speech of no account."

¹¹ Let such a person understand that what we say by letter when absent, we do when present.

¹² Not that we dare to classify or compare ourselves with some of those who are commending themselves. But when they measure themselves by one another and compare themselves with one another, they are without understanding.

¹³ But we will not boast beyond limits, but will boast only with regard to the area of influence God assigned to us, to reach even to you.

¹⁴ For we are not overextending ourselves, as though we did not reach you. For we were the first to come all the

way to you with the gospel of Christ.

¹⁵ We do not boast beyond limit in the labors of others. But our hope is that as your faith increases, our area of influence among you may be greatly enlarged,

¹⁶ so that we may preach the gospel in lands beyond you, without boasting of work already done in another's area of influence.

¹⁷ "Let the one who boasts, boast in the Lord."

¹⁸ For it is not the one who commends himself who is approved, but the one whom the Lord commends.

CHAPTER 11

¹ I wish you would bear with me in a little foolishness. Do bear with me!

² For I feel a divine jealousy for you, since I betrothed you to one husband, to present you as a pure virgin to Christ.

³ But I am afraid that as the serpent deceived Eve by his cunning, your thoughts will be led astray from a sincere and pure devotion to Christ.

⁴ For if someone comes and proclaims another Jesus than the one we proclaimed, or if you receive a different spirit from the one you received, or if you accept a different gospel from the one you accepted, you put up with it readily enough.

⁵ Indeed, I consider that I am not in the least inferior to these super-apostles.

⁶ Even if I am unskilled in speaking, I am not so in knowledge; indeed, in every way we have made this plain to you in all things.

⁷ Or did I commit a sin in humbling myself so that you might be exalted, because I preached God's gospel to you free of charge?

⁸ I robbed other churches by accepting support from them in order to serve you.

⁹ And when I was with you and was in need, I did not burden anyone, for the brothers who came from Macedonia supplied my need. So I refrained and will refrain from burdening you in any way.

¹⁰ As the truth of Christ is in me, this boasting of mine will not be silenced in the regions of Achaia.

¹¹ And why? Because I do not love you? God knows I do!

¹² And what I am doing I will continue to do, in order to undermine the claim of those who would like to claim that in their boasted mission they work on the same terms as we do.

¹³ For such men are false apostles, deceitful workmen, disguising themselves as apostles of Christ.

¹⁴ And no wonder, for even Satan disguises himself as an angel of light.

¹⁵ So it is no surprise if his servants, also, disguise themselves as servants of righteousness. Their end will correspond to their deeds.

¹⁶ I repeat, let no one think me foolish. But even if you do, accept me as a fool, so that I too may boast a little.

¹⁷ What I am saying with this boastful confidence, I say not as the Lord would but as a fool.

¹⁸ Since many boast according to the flesh, I too will boast.

¹⁹ For you gladly bear with fools, being wise yourselves!

²⁰ For you bear it if someone makes slaves of you, or devours you, or takes advantage of you, or puts on airs, or strikes you in the face.

²¹ To my shame, I must say, we were too weak for that! But whatever anyone else dares to boast of—I am speaking as a fool—I also dare to boast of that.

²² Are they Hebrews? So am I. Are they Israelites? So am I. Are they offspring of Abraham? So am I.

²³ Are they servants of Christ? I am a better one—I am talking like a madman—with far greater labors, far more imprisonments, with countless beatings, and often near death.

²⁴ Five times I received at the hands of the Jews the forty lashes less one.

²⁵ Three times I was beaten with rods. Once I was stoned. Three times I was shipwrecked; a night and a day I was adrift at sea;

²⁶ on frequent journeys, in danger from rivers, danger from robbers, danger from my own people, danger from Gentiles, danger in the city, danger in the wilderness, danger at sea, danger from false brothers;

²⁷ in toil and hardship, through many a sleepless night, in hunger and thirst, often without food, in cold and exposure.

²⁸ And, apart from other things, there is the daily pressure on me of my anxiety for all the churches.

²⁹ Who is weak, and I am not weak? Who is made to fall, and I am not indignant?

³⁰ If I must boast, I will boast of the things that show my weakness.

³¹ The God and Father of the Lord Jesus, he who is blessed

forever, knows that I am not lying.

³² At Damascus, the governor under King Aretas was guarding the city of Damascus in order to seize me,

³³ but I was let down in a basket through a window in the wall and escaped his hands.

CHAPTER 12

¹ I must go on boasting. Though there is nothing to be gained by it, I will go on to visions and revelations of the Lord.

² I know a man in Christ who fourteen years ago was caught up to the third heaven—whether in the body or out of the body I do not know, God knows.

³ And I know that this man was caught up into paradise—whether in the body or out of the body I do not know, God knows—

⁴ and he heard things that cannot be told, which man may not utter.

⁵ On behalf of this man I will boast, but on my own behalf I will not boast, except of my weaknesses—

⁶ though if I should wish to boast, I would not be a fool, for I would be speaking the truth; but I refrain from it, so that no one may think more of me than he sees in me or hears from me.

⁷ So to keep me from becoming conceited because of the surpassing greatness of the revelations, a thorn was given me in the flesh, a messenger of Satan to harass me, to keep me from becoming conceited.

⁸ Three times I pleaded with the Lord about this, that it should leave me.

⁹ But he said to me, "My grace is sufficient for you, for my power is made perfect in weakness." Therefore I will boast all the more gladly of my weaknesses, so that the power of Christ may rest upon me.

¹⁰ For the sake of Christ, then, I am content with weaknesses, insults, hardships, persecutions, and calamities. For when I am weak, then I am strong.

¹¹ I have been a fool! You forced me to it, for I ought to have been commended by you. For I was not at all inferior to these super-apostles, even though I am nothing.

¹² The signs of a true apostle were performed among you with utmost patience, with signs and wonders and mighty works.

¹³ For in what were you less favored than the rest of the churches, except that I myself

did not burden you? Forgive me this wrong!

¹⁴ Here for the third time I am ready to come to you. And I will not be a burden, for I seek not what is yours but you. For children are not obligated to save up for their parents, but parents for their children.

¹⁵ I will most gladly spend and be spent for your souls. If I love you more, am I to be loved less?

¹⁶ But granting that I myself did not burden you, I was crafty, you say, and got the better of you by deceit.

¹⁷ Did I take advantage of you through any of those whom I sent to you?

¹⁸ I urged Titus to go, and sent the brother with him. Did Titus take advantage of you? Did we not act in the same spirit? Did we not take the same steps?

¹⁹ Have you been thinking all along that we have been defending ourselves to you? It is in the sight of God that we have been speaking in Christ, and all for your upbuilding, beloved.

²⁰ For I fear that perhaps when I come I may find you not as I wish, and that you may find me not as you wish—that perhaps there may be quarreling, jealousy, anger, hostility, slander, gossip, conceit, and disorder.

²¹ I fear that when I come again my God may humble me before you, and I may have to mourn over many of those who sinned earlier and have not repented of the impurity, sexual immorality, and sensuality that they have practiced.

CHAPTER 13

¹ This is the third time I am coming to you. Every charge must be established by the evidence of two or three witnesses.

² I warned those who sinned before and all the others, and I warn them now while absent, as I did when present on my second visit, that if I come again I will not spare them—

³ since you seek proof that Christ is speaking in me. He is not weak in dealing with you, but is powerful among you.

⁴ For he was crucified in weakness, but lives by the power of God. For we also are weak in him, but in dealing with you we will live with him by the power of God.

⁵ Examine yourselves, to see whether you are in the faith. Test yourselves. Or do you not realize this about yourselves, that Jesus Christ is in you?—

unless indeed you fail to meet the test!

6 I hope you will find out that we have not failed the test.

7 But we pray to God that you may not do wrong—not that we may appear to have met the test, but that you may do what is right, though we may seem to have failed.

8 For we cannot do anything against the truth, but only for the truth.

9 For we are glad when we are weak and you are strong. Your restoration is what we pray for.

10 For this reason I write these things while I am away from you, that when I come I may not have to be severe in my use of the authority that the Lord has given me for building up and not for tearing down.

11 Finally, brothers, rejoice. Aim for restoration, comfort one another, agree with one another, live in peace; and the God of love and peace will be with you.

12 Greet one another with a holy kiss.

13 All the saints greet you.

14 The grace of the Lord Jesus Christ and the love of God and the fellowship of the Holy Spirit be with you all.

THE LETTER OF PAUL TO THE

GALATIANS

CHAPTER 1

1 Paul, an apostle—not from men nor through man, but through Jesus Christ and God the Father, who raised him from the dead—

2 and all the brothers who are with me, To the churches of Galatia:

3 Grace to you and peace from God our Father and the Lord Jesus Christ,

4 who gave himself for our sins to deliver us from the present evil age, according to the will of our God and Father,

5 to whom be the glory forever and ever. Amen.

6 I am astonished that you are so quickly deserting him who called you in the grace of Christ and are turning to a different gospel—

7 not that there is another one, but there are some who trouble you and want to distort the gospel of Christ.

8 But even if we or an angel

from heaven should preach to you a gospel contrary to the one we preached to you, let him be accursed.

9 As we have said before, so now I say again: If anyone is preaching to you a gospel contrary to the one you received, let him be accursed.

10 For am I now seeking the approval of man, or of God? Or am I trying to please man? If I were still trying to please man, I would not be a servant of Christ.

11 For I would have you know, brothers, that the gospel that was preached by me is not man's gospel.

12 For I did not receive it from any man, nor was I taught it, but I received it through a revelation of Jesus Christ.

13 For you have heard of my former life in Judaism, how I persecuted the church of God violently and tried to destroy it.

14 And I was advancing in Judaism beyond many of my own age among my people, so extremely zealous was I for the traditions of my fathers.

15 But when he who had set me apart before I was born, and who called me by his grace,

16 was pleased to reveal his Son to me, in order that I might preach him among the Gentiles, I did not immediately consult with anyone;

17 nor did I go up to Jerusalem to those who were apostles before me, but I went away into Arabia, and returned again to Damascus.

18 Then after three years I went up to Jerusalem to visit Cephas and remained with him fifteen days.

19 But I saw none of the other apostles except James the Lord's brother.

20 (In what I am writing to you, before God, I do not lie!)

21 Then I went into the regions of Syria and Cilicia.

22 And I was still unknown in person to the churches of Judea that are in Christ.

23 They only were hearing it said, "He who used to persecute us is now preaching the faith he once tried to destroy."

24 And they glorified God because of me.

CHAPTER 2

1 Then after fourteen years I went up again to Jerusalem with Barnabas, taking Titus along with me.

2 I went up because of a revelation and set before them (though privately before those who seemed influential) the gospel that I proclaim among the Gentiles, in order

to make sure I was not running or had not run in vain.

³ But even Titus, who was with me, was not forced to be circumcised, though he was a Greek.

⁴ Yet because of false brothers secretly brought in—who slipped in to spy out our freedom that we have in Christ Jesus, so that they might bring us into slavery—

⁵ to them we did not yield in submission even for a moment, so that the truth of the gospel might be preserved for you.

⁶ And from those who seemed to be influential (what they were makes no difference to me; God shows no partiality)—those, I say, who seemed influential added nothing to me.

⁷ On the contrary, when they saw that I had been entrusted with the gospel to the uncircumcised, just as Peter had been entrusted with the gospel to the circumcised

⁸ (for he who worked through Peter for his apostolic ministry to the circumcised worked also through me for mine to the Gentiles),

⁹ and when James and Cephas and John, who seemed to be pillars, perceived the grace that was given to me, they gave the right hand of fellowship to Barnabas and me, that we should go to the Gentiles and they to the circumcised.

¹⁰ Only, they asked us to remember the poor, the very thing I was eager to do.

¹¹ But when Cephas came to Antioch, I opposed him to his face, because he stood condemned.

¹² For before certain men came from James, he was eating with the Gentiles; but when they came he drew back and separated himself, fearing the circumcision party.

¹³ And the rest of the Jews acted hypocritically along with him, so that even Barnabas was led astray by their hypocrisy.

¹⁴ But when I saw that their conduct was not in step with the truth of the gospel, I said to Cephas before them all, "If you, though a Jew, live like a Gentile and not like a Jew, how can you force the Gentiles to live like Jews?"

¹⁵ We ourselves are Jews by birth and not Gentile sinners;

¹⁶ yet we know that a person is not justified by works of the law but through faith in Jesus Christ, so we also have believed in Christ Jesus, in order to be justified by faith in Christ and not by

works of the law, because by works of the law no one will be justified.

¹⁷ But if, in our endeavor to be justified in Christ, we too were found to be sinners, is Christ then a servant of sin? Certainly not!

¹⁸ For if I rebuild what I tore down, I prove myself to be a transgressor.

¹⁹ For through the law I died to the law, so that I might live to God.

²⁰ I have been crucified with Christ. It is no longer I who live, but Christ who lives in me. And the life I now live in the flesh I live by faith in the Son of God, who loved me and gave himself for me.

²¹ I do not nullify the grace of God, for if righteousness were through the law, then Christ died for no purpose.

CHAPTER 3

¹ O foolish Galatians! Who has bewitched you? It was before your eyes that Jesus Christ was publicly portrayed as crucified.

² Let me ask you only this: Did you receive the Spirit by works of the law or by hearing with faith?

³ Are you so foolish? Having begun by the Spirit, are you now being perfected by the flesh?

⁴ Did you suffer so many things in vain—if indeed it was in vain?

⁵ Does he who supplies the Spirit to you and works miracles among you do so by works of the law, or by hearing with faith—

⁶ just as Abraham "believed God, and it was counted to him as righteousness"?

⁷ Know then that it is those of faith who are the sons of Abraham.

⁸ And the Scripture, foreseeing that God would justify the Gentiles by faith, preached the gospel beforehand to Abraham, saying, "In you shall all the nations be blessed."

⁹ So then, those who are of faith are blessed along with Abraham, the man of faith.

¹⁰ For all who rely on works of the law are under a curse; for it is written, "Cursed be everyone who does not abide by all things written in the Book of the Law, and do them."

¹¹ Now it is evident that no one is justified before God by the law, for "The righteous shall live by faith."

¹² But the law is not of faith, rather "The one who does them shall live by them."

¹³ Christ redeemed us from the curse of the law by

becoming a curse for us— for it is written, "Cursed is everyone who is hanged on a tree"—

14 so that in Christ Jesus the blessing of Abraham might come to the Gentiles, so that we might receive the promised Spirit through faith.

15 To give a human example, brothers: even with a man-made covenant, no one annuls it or adds to it once it has been ratified.

16 Now the promises were made to Abraham and to his offspring. It does not say, "And to offsprings," referring to many, but referring to one, "And to your offspring," who is Christ.

17 This is what I mean: the law, which came 430 years afterward, does not annul a covenant previously ratified by God, so as to make the promise void.

18 For if the inheritance comes by the law, it no longer comes by promise; but God gave it to Abraham by a promise.

19 Why then the law? It was added because of transgressions, until the offspring should come to whom the promise had been made, and it was put in place through angels by an intermediary.

20 Now an intermediary implies more than one, but God is one.

21 Is the law then contrary to the promises of God? Certainly not! For if a law had been given that could give life, then righteousness would indeed be by the law.

22 But the Scripture imprisoned everything under sin, so that the promise by faith in Jesus Christ might be given to those who believe.

23 Now before faith came, we were held captive under the law, imprisoned until the coming faith would be revealed.

24 So then, the law was our guardian until Christ came, in order that we might be justified by faith.

25 But now that faith has come, we are no longer under a guardian,

26 for in Christ Jesus you are all sons of God, through faith.

27 For as many of you as were baptized into Christ have put on Christ.

28 There is neither Jew nor Greek, there is neither slave nor free, there is no male and female, for you are all one in Christ Jesus.

29 And if you are Christ's, then you are Abraham's offspring, heirs according to promise.

CHAPTER 4

¹ I mean that the heir, as long as he is a child, is no different from a slave, though he is the owner of everything,

² but he is under guardians and managers until the date set by his father.

³ In the same way we also, when we were children, were enslaved to the elementary principles of the world.

⁴ But when the fullness of time had come, God sent forth his Son, born of woman, born under the law,

⁵ to redeem those who were under the law, so that we might receive adoption as sons.

⁶ And because you are sons, God has sent the Spirit of his Son into our hearts, crying, "Abba! Father!"

⁷ So you are no longer a slave, but a son, and if a son, then an heir through God.

⁸ Formerly, when you did not know God, you were enslaved to those that by nature are not gods.

⁹ But now that you have come to know God, or rather to be known by God, how can you turn back again to the weak and worthless elementary principles of the world, whose slaves you want to be once more?

¹⁰ You observe days and months and seasons and years!

¹¹ I am afraid I may have labored over you in vain.

¹² Brothers, I entreat you, become as I am, for I also have become as you are. You did me no wrong.

¹³ You know it was because of a bodily ailment that I preached the gospel to you at first,

¹⁴ and though my condition was a trial to you, you did not scorn or despise me, but received me as an angel of God, as Christ Jesus.

¹⁵ What then has become of your blessedness? For I testify to you that, if possible, you would have gouged out your eyes and given them to me.

¹⁶ Have I then become your enemy by telling you the truth?

¹⁷ They make much of you, but for no good purpose. They want to shut you out, that you may make much of them.

¹⁸ It is always good to be made much of for a good purpose, and not only when I am present with you,

¹⁹ my little children, for whom I am again in the anguish of childbirth until Christ is formed in you!

²⁰ I wish I could be present

with you now and change my tone, for I am perplexed about you.

²¹ Tell me, you who desire to be under the law, do you not listen to the law? ²² For it is written that Abraham had two sons, one by a slave woman and one by a free woman. ²³ But the son of the slave was born according to the flesh, while the son of the free woman was born through promise. ²⁴ Now this may be interpreted allegorically: these women are two covenants. One is from Mount Sinai, bearing children for slavery; she is Hagar. ²⁵ Now Hagar is Mount Sinai in Arabia; she corresponds to the present Jerusalem, for she is in slavery with her children. ²⁶ But the Jerusalem above is free, and she is our mother. ²⁷ For it is written, "Rejoice, O barren one who does not bear; break forth and cry aloud, you who are not in labor! For the children of the desolate one will be more than those of the one who has a husband." ²⁸ Now you, brothers, like Isaac, are children of promise. ²⁹ But just as at that time he who was born according to the flesh persecuted him who was born according to the Spirit, so also it is now. ³⁰ But what does the Scripture say? "Cast out the slave woman and her son, for the son of the slave woman shall not inherit with the son of the free woman." ³¹ So, brothers, we are not children of the slave but of the free woman.

CHAPTER 5

¹ For freedom Christ has set us free; stand firm therefore, and do not submit again to a yoke of slavery.

² Look: I, Paul, say to you that if you accept circumcision, Christ will be of no advantage to you. ³ I testify again to every man who accepts circumcision that he is obligated to keep the whole law. ⁴ You are severed from Christ, you who would be justified by the law; you have fallen away from grace. ⁵ For through the Spirit, by faith, we ourselves eagerly wait for the hope of righteousness. ⁶ For in Christ Jesus neither circumcision nor uncircumcision counts for anything, but only faith working through love.

⁷ You were running well.

Who hindered you from obeying the truth?

⁸ This persuasion is not from him who calls you.

⁹ A little leaven leavens the whole lump.

¹⁰ I have confidence in the Lord that you will take no other view, and the one who is troubling you will bear the penalty, whoever he is.

¹¹ But if I, brothers, still preach circumcision, why am I still being persecuted? In that case the offense of the cross has been removed.

¹² I wish those who unsettle you would emasculate themselves!

¹³ For you were called to freedom, brothers. Only do not use your freedom as an opportunity for the flesh, but through love serve one another.

¹⁴ For the whole law is fulfilled in one word: "You shall love your neighbor as yourself."

¹⁵ But if you bite and devour one another, watch out that you are not consumed by one another.

¹⁶ But I say, walk by the Spirit, and you will not gratify the desires of the flesh.

¹⁷ For the desires of the flesh are against the Spirit, and the desires of the Spirit are against the flesh, for these are opposed to each other, to keep you from doing the things you want to do.

¹⁸ But if you are led by the Spirit, you are not under the law.

¹⁹ Now the works of the flesh are evident: sexual immorality, impurity, sensuality,

²⁰ idolatry, sorcery, enmity, strife, jealousy, fits of anger, rivalries, dissensions, divisions,

²¹ envy, drunkenness, orgies, and things like these. I warn you, as I warned you before, that those who do such things will not inherit the kingdom of God.

²² But the fruit of the Spirit is love, joy, peace, patience, kindness, goodness, faithfulness,

²³ gentleness, self-control; against such things there is no law.

²⁴ And those who belong to Christ Jesus have crucified the flesh with its passions and desires.

²⁵ If we live by the Spirit, let us also keep in step with the Spirit.

²⁶ Let us not become conceited, provoking one another, envying one another.

CHAPTER 6

¹ Brothers, if anyone is caught in any transgression, you who

are spiritual should restore him in a spirit of gentleness. Keep watch on yourself, lest you too be tempted.

[2] Bear one another's burdens, and so fulfill the law of Christ.

[3] For if anyone thinks he is something, when he is nothing, he deceives himself.

[4] But let each one test his own work, and then his reason to boast will be in himself alone and not in his neighbor.

[5] For each will have to bear his own load.

[6] Let the one who is taught the word share all good things with the one who teaches.

[7] Do not be deceived: God is not mocked, for whatever one sows, that will he also reap.

[8] For the one who sows to his own flesh will from the flesh reap corruption, but the one who sows to the Spirit will from the Spirit reap eternal life.

[9] And let us not grow weary of doing good, for in due season we will reap, if we do not give up.

[10] So then, as we have opportunity, let us do good to everyone, and especially to those who are of the household of faith.

[11] See with what large letters I am writing to you with my own hand.

[12] It is those who want to make a good showing in the flesh who would force you to be circumcised, and only in order that they may not be persecuted for the cross of Christ.

[13] For even those who are circumcised do not themselves keep the law, but they desire to have you circumcised that they may boast in your flesh.

[14] But far be it from me to boast except in the cross of our Lord Jesus Christ, by which the world has been crucified to me, and I to the world.

[15] For neither circumcision counts for anything, nor uncircumcision, but a new creation.

[16] And as for all who walk by this rule, peace and mercy be upon them, and upon the Israel of God.

[17] From now on let no one cause me trouble, for I bear on my body the marks of Jesus.

[18] The grace of our Lord Jesus Christ be with your spirit, brothers. Amen.

THE LETTER OF PAUL TO THE

EPHESIANS

CHAPTER 1

¹ Paul, an apostle of Christ Jesus by the will of God, To the saints who are in Ephesus, and are faithful in Christ Jesus:

² Grace to you and peace from God our Father and the Lord Jesus Christ.

³ Blessed be the God and Father of our Lord Jesus Christ, who has blessed us in Christ with every spiritual blessing in the heavenly places,

⁴ even as he chose us in him before the foundation of the world, that we should be holy and blameless before him. In love

⁵ he predestined us for adoption as sons through Jesus Christ, according to the purpose of his will,

⁶ to the praise of his glorious grace, with which he has blessed us in the Beloved.

⁷ In him we have redemption through his blood, the forgiveness of our trespasses, according to the riches of his grace,

⁸ which he lavished upon us, in all wisdom and insight

⁹ making known to us the mystery of his will, according to his purpose, which he set forth in Christ

¹⁰ as a plan for the fullness of time, to unite all things in him, things in heaven and things on earth.

¹¹ In him we have obtained an inheritance, having been predestined according to the purpose of him who works all things according to the counsel of his will,

¹² so that we who were the first to hope in Christ might be to the praise of his glory.

¹³ In him you also, when you heard the word of truth, the gospel of your salvation, and believed in him, were sealed with the promised Holy Spirit,

¹⁴ who is the guarantee of our inheritance until we acquire possession of it, to the praise of his glory.

¹⁵ For this reason, because I have heard of your faith in the Lord Jesus and your love toward all the saints,

¹⁶ I do not cease to give thanks for you, remembering you in my prayers,

¹⁷ that the God of our Lord

Jesus Christ, the Father of glory, may give you the Spirit of wisdom and of revelation in the knowledge of him,

¹⁸ having the eyes of your hearts enlightened, that you may know what is the hope to which he has called you, what are the riches of his glorious inheritance in the saints,

¹⁹ and what is the immeasurable greatness of his power toward us who believe, according to the working of his great might

²⁰ that he worked in Christ when he raised him from the dead and seated him at his right hand in the heavenly places,

²¹ far above all rule and authority and power and dominion, and above every name that is named, not only in this age but also in the one to come.

²² And he put all things under his feet and gave him as head over all things to the church,

²³ which is his body, the fullness of him who fills all in all.

CHAPTER 2

¹ And you were dead in the trespasses and sins

² in which you once walked, following the course of this world, following the prince of the power of the air, the spirit that is now at work in the sons of disobedience—

³ among whom we all once lived in the passions of our flesh, carrying out the desires of the body and the mind, and were by nature children of wrath, like the rest of mankind.

⁴ But God, being rich in mercy, because of the great love with which he loved us,

⁵ even when we were dead in our trespasses, made us alive together with Christ—by grace you have been saved—

⁶ and raised us up with him and seated us with him in the heavenly places in Christ Jesus,

⁷ so that in the coming ages he might show the immeasurable riches of his grace in kindness toward us in Christ Jesus.

⁸ For by grace you have been saved through faith. And this is not your own doing; it is the gift of God,

⁹ not a result of works, so that no one may boast.

¹⁰ For we are his workmanship, created in Christ Jesus for good works, which God prepared beforehand, that we should walk in them.

¹¹ Therefore remember that at one time you Gentiles in the flesh, called "the uncircumcision" by what is called

the circumcision, which is made in the flesh by hands—

¹² remember that you were at that time separated from Christ, alienated from the commonwealth of Israel and strangers to the covenants of promise, having no hope and without God in the world.

¹³ But now in Christ Jesus you who once were far off have been brought near by the blood of Christ.

¹⁴ For he himself is our peace, who has made us both one and has broken down in his flesh the dividing wall of hostility

¹⁵ by abolishing the law of commandments expressed in ordinances, that he might create in himself one new man in place of the two, so making peace,

¹⁶ and might reconcile us both to God in one body through the cross, thereby killing the hostility.

¹⁷ And he came and preached peace to you who were far off and peace to those who were near.

¹⁸ For through him we both have access in one Spirit to the Father.

¹⁹ So then you are no longer strangers and aliens, but you are fellow citizens with the saints and members of the household of God,

²⁰ built on the foundation of the apostles and prophets, Christ Jesus himself being the cornerstone,

²¹ in whom the whole structure, being joined together, grows into a holy temple in the Lord.

²² In him you also are being built together into a dwelling place for God by the Spirit.

CHAPTER 3

¹ For this reason I, Paul, a prisoner for Christ Jesus on behalf of you Gentiles—

² assuming that you have heard of the stewardship of God's grace that was given to me for you,

³ how the mystery was made known to me by revelation, as I have written briefly.

⁴ When you read this, you can perceive my insight into the mystery of Christ,

⁵ which was not made known to the sons of men in other generations as it has now been revealed to his holy apostles and prophets by the Spirit.

⁶ This mystery is that the Gentiles are fellow heirs, members of the same body, and partakers of the promise in Christ Jesus through the gospel.

⁷ Of this gospel I was made a minister according to the

gift of God's grace, which was given me by the working of his power.

⁸ To me, though I am the very least of all the saints, this grace was given, to preach to the Gentiles the unsearchable riches of Christ,

⁹ and to bring to light for everyone what is the plan of the mystery hidden for ages in God who created all things,

¹⁰ so that through the church the manifold wisdom of God might now be made known to the rulers and authorities in the heavenly places.

¹¹ This was according to the eternal purpose that he has realized in Christ Jesus our Lord,

¹² in whom we have boldness and access with confidence through our faith in him.

¹³ So I ask you not to lose heart over what I am suffering for you, which is your glory.

¹⁴ For this reason I bow my knees before the Father,

¹⁵ from whom every family in heaven and on earth is named,

¹⁶ that according to the riches of his glory he may grant you to be strengthened with power through his Spirit in your inner being,

¹⁷ so that Christ may dwell in your hearts through faith—that you, being rooted and grounded in love,

¹⁸ may have strength to comprehend with all the saints what is the breadth and length and height and depth,

¹⁹ and to know the love of Christ that surpasses knowledge, that you may be filled with all the fullness of God.

²⁰ Now to him who is able to do far more abundantly than all that we ask or think, according to the power at work within us,

²¹ to him be glory in the church and in Christ Jesus throughout all generations, forever and ever. Amen.

CHAPTER 4

¹ I therefore, a prisoner for the Lord, urge you to walk in a manner worthy of the calling to which you have been called,

² with all humility and gentleness, with patience, bearing with one another in love,

³ eager to maintain the unity of the Spirit in the bond of peace.

⁴ There is one body and one Spirit—just as you were called to the one hope that belongs to your call—

⁵ one Lord, one faith, one baptism,

⁶ one God and Father of all,

who is over all and through all and in all.

7 But grace was given to each one of us according to the measure of Christ's gift.

8 Therefore it says, "When he ascended on high he led a host of captives, and he gave gifts to men."

9 (In saying, "He ascended," what does it mean but that he had also descended into the lower regions, the earth?

10 He who descended is the one who also ascended far above all the heavens, that he might fill all things.)

11 And he gave the apostles, the prophets, the evangelists, the shepherds and teachers,

12 to equip the saints for the work of ministry, for building up the body of Christ,

13 until we all attain to the unity of the faith and of the knowledge of the Son of God, to mature manhood, to the measure of the stature of the fullness of Christ,

14 so that we may no longer be children, tossed to and fro by the waves and carried about by every wind of doctrine, by human cunning, by craftiness in deceitful schemes.

15 Rather, speaking the truth in love, we are to grow up in every way into him who is the head, into Christ,

16 from whom the whole body, joined and held together by every joint with which it is equipped, when each part is working properly, makes the body grow so that it builds itself up in love.

17 Now this I say and testify in the Lord, that you must no longer walk as the Gentiles do, in the futility of their minds.

18 They are darkened in their understanding, alienated from the life of God because of the ignorance that is in them, due to their hardness of heart.

19 They have become callous and have given themselves up to sensuality, greedy to practice every kind of impurity.

20 But that is not the way you learned Christ!—

21 assuming that you have heard about him and were taught in him, as the truth is in Jesus,

22 to put off your old self, which belongs to your former manner of life and is corrupt through deceitful desires,

23 and to be renewed in the spirit of your minds,

24 and to put on the new self, created after the likeness of God in true righteousness and holiness.

25 Therefore, having put away falsehood, let each one

of you speak the truth with his neighbor, for we are members one of another.

26 Be angry and do not sin; do not let the sun go down on your anger,

27 and give no opportunity to the devil.

28 Let the thief no longer steal, but rather let him labor, doing honest work with his own hands, so that he may have something to share with anyone in need.

29 Let no corrupting talk come out of your mouths, but only such as is good for building up, as fits the occasion, that it may give grace to those who hear.

30 And do not grieve the Holy Spirit of God, by whom you were sealed for the day of redemption.

31 Let all bitterness and wrath and anger and clamor and slander be put away from you, along with all malice.

32 Be kind to one another, tenderhearted, forgiving one another, as God in Christ forgave you.

CHAPTER 5

1 Therefore be imitators of God, as beloved children.

2 And walk in love, as Christ loved us and gave himself up for us, a fragrant offering and sacrifice to God.

3 But sexual immorality and all impurity or covetousness must not even be named among you, as is proper among saints.

4 Let there be no filthiness nor foolish talk nor crude joking, which are out of place, but instead let there be thanksgiving.

5 For you may be sure of this, that everyone who is sexually immoral or impure, or who is covetous (that is, an idolater), has no inheritance in the kingdom of Christ and God.

6 Let no one deceive you with empty words, for because of these things the wrath of God comes upon the sons of disobedience.

7 Therefore do not become partners with them;

8 for at one time you were darkness, but now you are light in the Lord. Walk as children of light

9 (for the fruit of light is found in all that is good and right and true),

10 and try to discern what is pleasing to the Lord.

11 Take no part in the unfruitful works of darkness, but instead expose them.

12 For it is shameful even to speak of the things that they do in secret.

13 But when anything is ex-

posed by the light, it becomes visible,

¹⁴ for anything that becomes visible is light. Therefore it says, "Awake, O sleeper, and arise from the dead, and Christ will shine on you."

¹⁵ Look carefully then how you walk, not as unwise but as wise,

¹⁶ making the best use of the time, because the days are evil.

¹⁷ Therefore do not be foolish, but understand what the will of the Lord is.

¹⁸ And do not get drunk with wine, for that is debauchery, but be filled with the Spirit,

¹⁹ addressing one another in psalms and hymns and spiritual songs, singing and making melody to the Lord with your heart,

²⁰ giving thanks always and for everything to God the Father in the name of our Lord Jesus Christ,

²¹ submitting to one another out of reverence for Christ.

²² Wives, submit to your own husbands, as to the Lord.

²³ For the husband is the head of the wife even as Christ is the head of the church, his body, and is himself its Savior.

²⁴ Now as the church submits to Christ, so also wives should submit in everything to their husbands.

²⁵ Husbands, love your wives, as Christ loved the church and gave himself up for her,

²⁶ that he might sanctify her, having cleansed her by the washing of water with the word,

²⁷ so that he might present the church to himself in splendor, without spot or wrinkle or any such thing, that she might be holy and without blemish.

²⁸ In the same way husbands should love their wives as their own bodies. He who loves his wife loves himself.

²⁹ For no one ever hated his own flesh, but nourishes and cherishes it, just as Christ does the church,

³⁰ because we are members of his body.

³¹ "Therefore a man shall leave his father and mother and hold fast to his wife, and the two shall become one flesh."

³² This mystery is profound, and I am saying that it refers to Christ and the church.

³³ However, let each one of you love his wife as himself, and let the wife see that she respects her husband.

CHAPTER 6

¹ Children, obey your parents in the Lord, for this is right.

2 "Honor your father and mother" (this is the first commandment with a promise),

3 "that it may go well with you and that you may live long in the land."

4 Fathers, do not provoke your children to anger, but bring them up in the discipline and instruction of the Lord.

5 Bondservants, obey your earthly masters with fear and trembling, with a sincere heart, as you would Christ,

6 not by the way of eye-service, as people-pleasers, but as bondservants of Christ, doing the will of God from the heart,

7 rendering service with a good will as to the Lord and not to man,

8 knowing that whatever good anyone does, this he will receive back from the Lord, whether he is a bondservant or is free.

9 Masters, do the same to them, and stop your threatening, knowing that he who is both their Master and yours is in heaven, and that there is no partiality with him.

10 Finally, be strong in the Lord and in the strength of his might.

11 Put on the whole armor of God, that you may be able to stand against the schemes of the devil.

12 For we do not wrestle against flesh and blood, but against the rulers, against the authorities, against the cosmic powers over this present darkness, against the spiritual forces of evil in the heavenly places.

13 Therefore take up the whole armor of God, that you may be able to withstand in the evil day, and having done all, to stand firm.

14 Stand therefore, having fastened on the belt of truth, and having put on the breastplate of righteousness,

15 and, as shoes for your feet, having put on the readiness given by the gospel of peace.

16 In all circumstances take up the shield of faith, with which you can extinguish all the flaming darts of the evil one;

17 and take the helmet of salvation, and the sword of the Spirit, which is the word of God,

18 praying at all times in the Spirit, with all prayer and supplication. To that end keep alert with all perseverance, making supplication for all the saints,

19 and also for me, that words may be given to me in opening my mouth boldly to proclaim the mystery of the gospel,

20 for which I am an ambassador in chains, that I may declare it boldly, as I ought to speak.

21 So that you also may know how I am and what I am doing, Tychicus the beloved brother and faithful minister in the Lord will tell you everything.

22 I have sent him to you for this very purpose, that you may know how we are, and that he may encourage your hearts.

23 Peace be to the brothers, and love with faith, from God the Father and the Lord Jesus Christ.

24 Grace be with all who love our Lord Jesus Christ with love incorruptible.

THE LETTER OF PAUL TO THE

PHILIPPIANS

CHAPTER 1

1 Paul and Timothy, servants of Christ Jesus, To all the saints in Christ Jesus who are at Philippi, with the overseers and deacons:

2 Grace to you and peace from God our Father and the Lord Jesus Christ.

3 I thank my God in all my remembrance of you,

4 always in every prayer of mine for you all making my prayer with joy,

5 because of your partnership in the gospel from the first day until now.

6 And I am sure of this, that he who began a good work in you will bring it to completion at the day of Jesus Christ.

7 It is right for me to feel this way about you all, because I hold you in my heart, for you are all partakers with me of grace, both in my imprisonment and in the defense and confirmation of the gospel.

8 For God is my witness, how I yearn for you all with the affection of Christ Jesus.

9 And it is my prayer that your love may abound more and more, with knowledge and all discernment,

10 so that you may approve what is excellent, and so be pure and blameless for the day of Christ,

11 filled with the fruit of righteousness that comes through Jesus Christ, to the glory and praise of God.

12 I want you to know, brothers, that what has happened to me has really served to advance the gospel,

13 so that it has become known throughout the whole imperial guard and to all the rest that my imprisonment is for Christ.

14 And most of the brothers, having become confident in the Lord by my imprisonment, are much more bold to speak the word without fear.

15 Some indeed preach Christ from envy and rivalry, but others from good will.

16 The latter do it out of love, knowing that I am put here for the defense of the gospel.

17 The former proclaim Christ out of selfish ambition, not sincerely but thinking to afflict me in my imprisonment.

18 What then? Only that in every way, whether in pretense or in truth, Christ is proclaimed, and in that I rejoice. Yes, and I will rejoice,

19 for I know that through your prayers and the help of the Spirit of Jesus Christ this will turn out for my deliverance,

20 as it is my eager expectation and hope that I will not be at all ashamed, but that with full courage now as always Christ will be honored in my body, whether by life or by death.

21 For to me to live is Christ, and to die is gain.

22 If I am to live in the flesh, that means fruitful labor for me. Yet which I shall choose I cannot tell.

23 I am hard pressed between the two. My desire is to depart and be with Christ, for that is far better.

24 But to remain in the flesh is more necessary on your account.

25 Convinced of this, I know that I will remain and continue with you all, for your progress and joy in the faith,

26 so that in me you may have ample cause to glory in Christ Jesus, because of my coming to you again.

27 Only let your manner of life be worthy of the gospel of Christ, so that whether I come and see you or am absent, I may hear of you that you are standing firm in one spirit, with one mind striving side by side for the faith of the gospel,

28 and not frightened in anything by your opponents. This is a clear sign to them of their destruction, but of your salvation, and that from God.

29 For it has been granted to you that for the sake of Christ

you should not only believe in him but also suffer for his sake,

30 engaged in the same conflict that you saw I had and now hear that I still have.

CHAPTER 2

1 So if there is any encouragement in Christ, any comfort from love, any participation in the Spirit, any affection and sympathy,

2 complete my joy by being of the same mind, having the same love, being in full accord and of one mind.

3 Do nothing from selfish ambition or conceit, but in humility count others more significant than yourselves.

4 Let each of you look not only to his own interests, but also to the interests of others.

5 Have this mind among yourselves, which is yours in Christ Jesus,

6 who, though he was in the form of God, did not count equality with God a thing to be grasped,

7 but emptied himself, by taking the form of a servant, being born in the likeness of men.

8 And being found in human form, he humbled himself by becoming obedient to the point of death, even death on a cross.

9 Therefore God has highly exalted him and bestowed on him the name that is above every name,

10 so that at the name of Jesus every knee should bow, in heaven and on earth and under the earth,

11 and every tongue confess that Jesus Christ is Lord, to the glory of God the Father.

12 Therefore, my beloved, as you have always obeyed, so now, not only as in my presence but much more in my absence, work out your own salvation with fear and trembling,

13 for it is God who works in you, both to will and to work for his good pleasure.

14 Do all things without grumbling or disputing,

15 that you may be blameless and innocent, children of God without blemish in the midst of a crooked and twisted generation, among whom you shine as lights in the world,

16 holding fast to the word of life, so that in the day of Christ I may be proud that I did not run in vain or labor in vain.

17 Even if I am to be poured out as a drink offering upon the sacrificial offering of your faith, I am glad and rejoice with you all.

18 Likewise you also should be glad and rejoice with me.

19 I hope in the Lord Jesus to send Timothy to you soon, so that I too may be cheered by news of you.

20 For I have no one like him, who will be genuinely concerned for your welfare.

21 For they all seek their own interests, not those of Jesus Christ.

22 But you know Timothy's proven worth, how as a son with a father he has served with me in the gospel.

23 I hope therefore to send him just as soon as I see how it will go with me,

24 and I trust in the Lord that shortly I myself will come also.

25 I have thought it necessary to send to you Epaphroditus my brother and fellow worker and fellow soldier, and your messenger and minister to my need,

26 for he has been longing for you all and has been distressed because you heard that he was ill.

27 Indeed he was ill, near to death. But God had mercy on him, and not only on him but on me also, lest I should have sorrow upon sorrow.

28 I am the more eager to send him, therefore, that you may rejoice at seeing him again, and that I may be less anxious.

29 So receive him in the Lord with all joy, and honor such men,

30 for he nearly died for the work of Christ, risking his life to complete what was lacking in your service to me.

CHAPTER 3

1 Finally, my brothers, rejoice in the Lord. To write the same things to you is no trouble to me and is safe for you.

2 Look out for the dogs, look out for the evildoers, look out for those who mutilate the flesh.

3 For we are the circumcision, who worship by the Spirit of God and glory in Christ Jesus and put no confidence in the flesh—

4 though I myself have reason for confidence in the flesh also. If anyone else thinks he has reason for confidence in the flesh, I have more:

5 circumcised on the eighth day, of the people of Israel, of the tribe of Benjamin, a Hebrew of Hebrews; as to the law, a Pharisee;

6 as to zeal, a persecutor of the church; as to righteousness under the law, blameless.

7 But whatever gain I had, I

counted as loss for the sake of Christ.

[8] Indeed, I count everything as loss because of the surpassing worth of knowing Christ Jesus my Lord. For his sake I have suffered the loss of all things and count them as rubbish, in order that I may gain Christ

[9] and be found in him, not having a righteousness of my own that comes from the law, but that which comes through faith in Christ, the righteousness from God that depends on faith—

[10] that I may know him and the power of his resurrection, and may share his sufferings, becoming like him in his death,

[11] that by any means possible I may attain the resurrection from the dead.

[12] Not that I have already obtained this or am already perfect, but I press on to make it my own, because Christ Jesus has made me his own.

[13] Brothers, I do not consider that I have made it my own. But one thing I do: forgetting what lies behind and straining forward to what lies ahead,

[14] I press on toward the goal for the prize of the upward call of God in Christ Jesus.

[15] Let those of us who are mature think this way, and if in anything you think otherwise, God will reveal that also to you.

[16] Only let us hold true to what we have attained.

[17] Brothers, join in imitating me, and keep your eyes on those who walk according to the example you have in us.

[18] For many, of whom I have often told you and now tell you even with tears, walk as enemies of the cross of Christ.

[19] Their end is destruction, their god is their belly, and they glory in their shame, with minds set on earthly things.

[20] But our citizenship is in heaven, and from it we await a Savior, the Lord Jesus Christ,

[21] who will transform our lowly body to be like his glorious body, by the power that enables him even to subject all things to himself.

CHAPTER 4

[1] Therefore, my brothers, whom I love and long for, my joy and crown, stand firm thus in the Lord, my beloved.

[2] I entreat Euodia and I entreat Syntyche to agree in the Lord.

[3] Yes, I ask you also, true companion, help these women, who have labored side by side with me in the gospel

together with Clement and the rest of my fellow workers, whose names are in the book of life.

⁴ Rejoice in the Lord always; again I will say, rejoice.

⁵ Let your reasonableness be known to everyone. The Lord is at hand;

⁶ do not be anxious about anything, but in everything by prayer and supplication with thanksgiving let your requests be made known to God.

⁷ And the peace of God, which surpasses all understanding, will guard your hearts and your minds in Christ Jesus.

⁸ Finally, brothers, whatever is true, whatever is honorable, whatever is just, whatever is pure, whatever is lovely, whatever is commendable, if there is any excellence, if there is anything worthy of praise, think about these things.

⁹ What you have learned and received and heard and seen in me—practice these things, and the God of peace will be with you.

¹⁰ I rejoiced in the Lord greatly that now at length you have revived your concern for me. You were indeed concerned for me, but you had no opportunity.

¹¹ Not that I am speaking of being in need, for I have learned in whatever situation I am to be content.

¹² I know how to be brought low, and I know how to abound. In any and every circumstance, I have learned the secret of facing plenty and hunger, abundance and need.

¹³ I can do all things through him who strengthens me.

¹⁴ Yet it was kind of you to share my trouble.

¹⁵ And you Philippians yourselves know that in the beginning of the gospel, when I left Macedonia, no church entered into partnership with me in giving and receiving, except you only.

¹⁶ Even in Thessalonica you sent me help for my needs once and again.

¹⁷ Not that I seek the gift, but I seek the fruit that increases to your credit.

¹⁸ I have received full payment, and more. I am well supplied, having received from Epaphroditus the gifts you sent, a fragrant offering, a sacrifice acceptable and pleasing to God.

¹⁹ And my God will supply every need of yours according to his riches in glory in Christ Jesus.

²⁰ To our God and Father be glory forever and ever. Amen.

²¹ Greet every saint in Christ Jesus. The brothers who are with me greet you.

²² All the saints greet you, especially those of Caesar's household.

²³ The grace of the Lord Jesus Christ be with your spirit.

THE LETTER OF PAUL TO THE

COLOSSIANS

CHAPTER 1

¹ Paul, an apostle of Christ Jesus by the will of God, and Timothy our brother,

² To the saints and faithful brothers in Christ at Colossae: Grace to you and peace from God our Father.

³ We always thank God, the Father of our Lord Jesus Christ, when we pray for you,

⁴ since we heard of your faith in Christ Jesus and of the love that you have for all the saints,

⁵ because of the hope laid up for you in heaven. Of this you have heard before in the word of the truth, the gospel,

⁶ which has come to you, as indeed in the whole world it is bearing fruit and increasing—as it also does among you, since the day you heard it and understood the grace of God in truth,

⁷ just as you learned it from Epaphras our beloved fellow servant. He is a faithful minister of Christ on your behalf

⁸ and has made known to us your love in the Spirit.

⁹ And so, from the day we heard, we have not ceased to pray for you, asking that you may be filled with the knowledge of his will in all spiritual wisdom and understanding,

¹⁰ so as to walk in a manner worthy of the Lord, fully pleasing to him, bearing fruit in every good work and increasing in the knowledge of God.

¹¹ May you be strengthened with all power, according to his glorious might, for all endurance and patience with joy,

¹² giving thanks to the Father, who has qualified you to share in the inheritance of the saints in light.

¹³ He has delivered us from the domain of darkness and transferred us to the kingdom of his beloved Son,

14 in whom we have redemption through his blood, the forgiveness of sins.

15 He is the image of the invisible God, the firstborn of all creation.

16 For by him all things were created, in heaven and on earth, visible and invisible, whether thrones or dominions or rulers or authorities—all things were created through him and for him.

17 And he is before all things, and in him all things hold together.

18 And he is the head of the body, the church. He is the beginning, the firstborn from the dead, that in everything he might be preeminent.

19 For in him all the fullness of God was pleased to dwell,

20 and through him to reconcile to himself all things, whether on earth or in heaven, making peace through the blood of his cross.

21 And you, who once were alienated and hostile in mind, doing evil deeds,

22 he has now reconciled in his body of flesh by his death, in order to present you holy and blameless and above reproach before him,

23 if indeed you continue in the faith, stable and steadfast, not shifting from the hope of the gospel that you heard, which has been proclaimed in all creation under heaven, and of which I, Paul, became a minister.

24 Now I rejoice in my sufferings for your sake, and in my flesh I am filling up what is lacking in Christ's afflictions for the sake of his body, that is, the church,

25 of which I became a minister according to the stewardship from God that was given to me for you, to make the word of God fully known,

26 the mystery hidden for ages and generations but now revealed to his saints.

27 To them God chose to make known how great among the Gentiles are the riches of the glory of this mystery, which is Christ in you, the hope of glory.

28 Him we proclaim, warning everyone and teaching everyone with all wisdom, that we may present everyone mature in Christ.

29 For this I toil, struggling with all his energy that he powerfully works within me.

CHAPTER 2

1 For I want you to know how great a struggle I have for you and for those at Laodicea and for all who have not seen me face to face,

2 that their hearts may be

encouraged, being knit together in love, to reach all the riches of full assurance of understanding and the knowledge of God's mystery, which is Christ,

³ in whom are hidden all the treasures of wisdom and knowledge.

⁴ I say this in order that no one may delude you with plausible arguments.

⁵ For though I am absent in body, yet I am with you in spirit, rejoicing to see your good order and the firmness of your faith in Christ.

⁶ Therefore, as you received Christ Jesus the Lord, so walk in him,

⁷ rooted and built up in him and established in the faith, just as you were taught, abounding in thanksgiving.

⁸ See to it that no one takes you captive by philosophy and empty deceit, according to human tradition, according to the elemental spirits of the world, and not according to Christ.

⁹ For in him the whole fullness of deity dwells bodily,

¹⁰ and you have been filled in him, who is the head of all rule and authority.

¹¹ In him also you were circumcised with a circumcision made without hands, by putting off the body of the flesh, by the circumcision of Christ,

¹² having been buried with him in baptism, in which you were also raised with him through faith in the powerful working of God, who raised him from the dead.

¹³ And you, who were dead in your trespasses and the uncircumcision of your flesh, God made alive together with him, having forgiven us all our trespasses,

¹⁴ by canceling the record of debt that stood against us with its legal demands. This he set aside, nailing it to the cross.

¹⁵ He disarmed the rulers and authorities and put them to open shame, by triumphing over them in him.

¹⁶ Therefore let no one pass judgment on you in questions of food and drink, or with regard to a festival or a new moon or a Sabbath.

¹⁷ These are a shadow of the things to come, but the substance belongs to Christ.

¹⁸ Let no one disqualify you, insisting on asceticism and worship of angels, going on in detail about visions, puffed up without reason by his sensuous mind,

¹⁹ and not holding fast to the Head, from whom the whole body, nourished and knit

together through its joints and ligaments, grows with a growth that is from God.

20 If with Christ you died to the elemental spirits of the world, why, as if you were still alive in the world, do you submit to regulations—

21 "Do not handle, Do not taste, Do not touch"

22 (referring to things that all perish as they are used)—according to human precepts and teachings?

23 These have indeed an appearance of wisdom in promoting self-made religion and asceticism and severity to the body, but they are of no value in stopping the indulgence of the flesh.

CHAPTER 3

1 If then you have been raised with Christ, seek the things that are above, where Christ is, seated at the right hand of God.

2 Set your minds on things that are above, not on things that are on earth.

3 For you have died, and your life is hidden with Christ in God.

4 When Christ who is your life appears, then you also will appear with him in glory.

5 Put to death therefore what is earthly in you: sexual immorality, impurity, passion, evil desire, and covetousness, which is idolatry.

6 On account of these the wrath of God is coming.

7 In these you too once walked, when you were living in them.

8 But now you must put them all away: anger, wrath, malice, slander, and obscene talk from your mouth.

9 Do not lie to one another, seeing that you have put off the old self with its practices

10 and have put on the new self, which is being renewed in knowledge after the image of its creator.

11 Here there is not Greek and Jew, circumcised and uncircumcised, barbarian, Scythian, slave, free; but Christ is all, and in all.

12 Put on then, as God's chosen ones, holy and beloved, compassionate hearts, kindness, humility, meekness, and patience,

13 bearing with one another and, if one has a complaint against another, forgiving each other; as the Lord has forgiven you, so you also must forgive.

14 And above all these put on love, which binds everything together in perfect harmony.

15 And let the peace of Christ rule in your hearts, to which

indeed you were called in one body. And be thankful.

¹⁶ Let the word of Christ dwell in you richly, teaching and admonishing one another in all wisdom, singing psalms and hymns and spiritual songs, with thankfulness in your hearts to God.

¹⁷ And whatever you do, in word or deed, do everything in the name of the Lord Jesus, giving thanks to God the Father through him.

¹⁸ Wives, submit to your husbands, as is fitting in the Lord.

¹⁹ Husbands, love your wives, and do not be harsh with them.

²⁰ Children, obey your parents in everything, for this pleases the Lord.

²¹ Fathers, do not provoke your children, lest they become discouraged.

²² Bondservants, obey in everything those who are your earthly masters, not by way of eye-service, as people-pleasers, but with sincerity of heart, fearing the Lord.

²³ Whatever you do, work heartily, as for the Lord and not for men,

²⁴ knowing that from the Lord you will receive the inheritance as your reward. You are serving the Lord Christ.

²⁵ For the wrongdoer will be paid back for the wrong he has done, and there is no partiality.

CHAPTER 4

¹ Masters, treat your bond-servants justly and fairly, knowing that you also have a Master in heaven.

² Continue steadfastly in prayer, being watchful in it with thanksgiving.

³ At the same time, pray also for us, that God may open to us a door for the word, to declare the mystery of Christ, on account of which I am in prison—

⁴ that I may make it clear, which is how I ought to speak.

⁵ Walk in wisdom toward outsiders, making the best use of the time.

⁶ Let your speech always be gracious, seasoned with salt, so that you may know how you ought to answer each person.

⁷ Tychicus will tell you all about my activities. He is a beloved brother and faithful minister and fellow servant in the Lord.

⁸ I have sent him to you for this very purpose, that you may know how we are and that he may encourage your hearts,

⁹ and with him Onesimus, our faithful and beloved brother, who is one of you.

They will tell you of everything that has taken place here.

¹⁰ Aristarchus my fellow prisoner greets you, and Mark the cousin of Barnabas (concerning whom you have received instructions—if he comes to you, welcome him), ¹¹ and Jesus who is called Justus. These are the only men of the circumcision among my fellow workers for the kingdom of God, and they have been a comfort to me.

¹² Epaphras, who is one of you, a servant of Christ Jesus, greets you, always struggling on your behalf in his prayers, that you may stand mature and fully assured in all the will of God. ¹³ For I bear him witness that he has worked hard for you and for those in Laodicea and in Hierapolis.

¹⁴ Luke the beloved physician greets you, as does Demas.

¹⁵ Give my greetings to the brothers at Laodicea, and to Nympha and the church in her house.

¹⁶ And when this letter has been read among you, have it also read in the church of the Laodiceans; and see that you also read the letter from Laodicea.

¹⁷ And say to Archippus, "See that you fulfill the ministry that you have received in the Lord."

¹⁸ I, Paul, write this greeting with my own hand. Remember my chains. Grace be with you.

THE FIRST LETTER OF PAUL TO THE THESSALONIANS

1 THESSALONIANS

CHAPTER 1

¹ Paul, Silvanus, and Timothy,
To the church of the Thessalonians in God the Father and the Lord Jesus Christ: Grace to you and peace.

¹.² We give thanks to God always for all of you, constantly mentioning you in our prayers, ³ remembering before our God and Father your work of faith and labor of love and steadfastness of hope in our Lord Jesus Christ.

⁴ For we know, brothers

loved by God, that he has chosen you,

⁵ because our gospel came to you not only in word, but also in power and in the Holy Spirit and with full conviction. You know what kind of men we proved to be among you for your sake.

⁶ And you became imitators of us and of the Lord, for you received the word in much affliction, with the joy of the Holy Spirit,

⁷ so that you became an example to all the believers in Macedonia and in Achaia.

⁸ For not only has the word of the Lord sounded forth from you in Macedonia and Achaia, but your faith in God has gone forth everywhere, so that we need not say anything.

⁹ For they themselves report concerning us the kind of reception we had among you, and how you turned to God from idols to serve the living and true God,

¹⁰ and to wait for his Son from heaven, whom he raised from the dead, Jesus who delivers us from the wrath to come.

CHAPTER 2

¹ For you yourselves know, brothers, that our coming to you was not in vain.

² But though we had already suffered and been shamefully treated at Philippi, as you know, we had boldness in our God to declare to you the gospel of God in the midst of much conflict.

³ For our appeal does not spring from error or impurity or any attempt to deceive,

⁴ but just as we have been approved by God to be entrusted with the gospel, so we speak, not to please man, but to please God who tests our hearts.

⁵ For we never came with words of flattery, as you know, nor with a pretext for greed—God is witness.

⁶ Nor did we seek glory from people, whether from you or from others, though we could have made demands as apostles of Christ.

⁷ But we were gentle among you, like a nursing mother taking care of her own children.

⁸ So, being affectionately desirous of you, we were ready to share with you not only the gospel of God but also our own selves, because you had become very dear to us.

⁹ For you remember, brothers, our labor and toil: we worked night and day, that we might not be a burden to any of you, while we proclaimed to you the gospel of God.

¹⁰ You are witnesses, and

God also, how holy and righteous and blameless was our conduct toward you believers.

¹¹ For you know how, like a father with his children,

¹² we exhorted each one of you and encouraged you and charged you to walk in a manner worthy of God, who calls you into his own kingdom and glory.

¹³ And we also thank God constantly for this, that when you received the word of God, which you heard from us, you accepted it not as the word of men but as what it really is, the word of God, which is at work in you believers.

¹⁴ For you, brothers, became imitators of the churches of God in Christ Jesus that are in Judea. For you suffered the same things from your own countrymen as they did from the Jews,

¹⁵ who killed both the Lord Jesus and the prophets, and drove us out, and displease God and oppose all mankind

¹⁶ by hindering us from speaking to the Gentiles that they might be saved—so as always to fill up the measure of their sins. But wrath has come upon them at last!

¹⁷ But since we were torn away from you, brothers, for a short time, in person not in heart, we endeavored the more eagerly and with great desire to see you face to face,

¹⁸ because we wanted to come to you—I, Paul, again and again—but Satan hindered us.

¹⁹ For what is our hope or joy or crown of boasting before our Lord Jesus at his coming? Is it not you?

²⁰ For you are our glory and joy.

CHAPTER 3

¹ Therefore when we could bear it no longer, we were willing to be left behind at Athens alone,

² and we sent Timothy, our brother and God's coworker in the gospel of Christ, to establish and exhort you in your faith,

³ that no one be moved by these afflictions. For you yourselves know that we are destined for this.

⁴ For when we were with you, we kept telling you beforehand that we were to suffer affliction, just as it has come to pass, and just as you know.

⁵ For this reason, when I could bear it no longer, I sent to learn about your faith, for fear that somehow the tempter had tempted you and our labor would be in vain.

⁶ But now that Timothy has come to us from you, and has

brought us the good news of your faith and love and reported that you always remember us kindly and long to see us, as we long to see you—

7 for this reason, brothers, in all our distress and affliction we have been comforted about you through your faith.

8 For now we live, if you are standing fast in the Lord.

9 For what thanksgiving can we return to God for you, for all the joy that we feel for your sake before our God,

10 as we pray most earnestly night and day that we may see you face to face and supply what is lacking in your faith?

11 Now may our God and Father himself, and our Lord Jesus, direct our way to you,

12 and may the Lord make you increase and abound in love for one another and for all, as we do for you,

13 so that he may establish your hearts blameless in holiness before our God and Father, at the coming of our Lord Jesus with all his saints.

CHAPTER 4

1 Finally, then, brothers, we ask and urge you in the Lord Jesus, that as you received from us how you ought to walk and to please God, just as you are doing, that you do so more and more.

2 For you know what instructions we gave you through the Lord Jesus.

3 For this is the will of God, your sanctification: that you abstain from sexual immorality;

4 that each one of you know how to control his own body in holiness and honor,

5 not in the passion of lust like the Gentiles who do not know God;

6 that no one transgress and wrong his brother in this matter, because the Lord is an avenger in all these things, as we told you beforehand and solemnly warned you.

7 For God has not called us for impurity, but in holiness.

8 Therefore whoever disregards this, disregards not man but God, who gives his Holy Spirit to you.

9 Now concerning brotherly love you have no need for anyone to write to you, for you yourselves have been taught by God to love one another,

10 for that indeed is what you are doing to all the brothers throughout Macedonia. But we urge you, brothers, to do this more and more,

11 and to aspire to live quietly, and to mind your own affairs, and to work with your hands, as we instructed you,

12 so that you may walk

properly before outsiders and be dependent on no one.

13 But we do not want you to be uninformed, brothers, about those who are asleep, that you may not grieve as others do who have no hope.

14 For since we believe that Jesus died and rose again, even so, through Jesus, God will bring with him those who have fallen asleep.

15 For this we declare to you by a word from the Lord, that we who are alive, who are left until the coming of the Lord, will not precede those who have fallen asleep.

16 For the Lord himself will descend from heaven with a cry of command, with the voice of an archangel, and with the sound of the trumpet of God. And the dead in Christ will rise first.

17 Then we who are alive, who are left, will be caught up together with them in the clouds to meet the Lord in the air, and so we will always be with the Lord.

18 Therefore encourage one another with these words.

CHAPTER 5

1 Now concerning the times and the seasons, brothers, you have no need to have anything written to you.

2 For you yourselves are ful-ly aware that the day of the Lord will come like a thief in the night.

3 While people are saying, "There is peace and security," then sudden destruction will come upon them as labor pains come upon a pregnant woman, and they will not escape.

4 But you are not in darkness, brothers, for that day to surprise you like a thief.

5 For you are all children of light, children of the day. We are not of the night or of the darkness.

6 So then let us not sleep, as others do, but let us keep awake and be sober.

7 For those who sleep, sleep at night, and those who get drunk, are drunk at night.

8 But since we belong to the day, let us be sober, having put on the breastplate of faith and love, and for a helmet the hope of salvation.

9 For God has not destined us for wrath, but to obtain salvation through our Lord Jesus Christ,

10 who died for us so that whether we are awake or asleep we might live with him.

11 Therefore encourage one another and build one another up, just as you are doing.

12 We ask you, brothers,

to respect those who labor among you and are over you in the Lord and admonish you,

13 and to esteem them very highly in love because of their work. Be at peace among yourselves.

14 And we urge you, brothers, admonish the idle, encourage the fainthearted, help the weak, be patient with them all.

15 See that no one repays anyone evil for evil, but always seek to do good to one another and to everyone.

16 Rejoice always,

17 pray without ceasing,

18 give thanks in all circumstances; for this is the will of God in Christ Jesus for you.

19 Do not quench the Spirit.

20 Do not despise prophecies,

21 but test everything; hold fast what is good.

22 Abstain from every form of evil.

23 Now may the God of peace himself sanctify you completely, and may your whole spirit and soul and body be kept blameless at the coming of our Lord Jesus Christ.

24 He who calls you is faithful; he will surely do it.

25 Brothers, pray for us.

26 Greet all the brothers with a holy kiss.

27 I put you under oath before the Lord to have this letter read to all the brothers.

28 The grace of our Lord Jesus Christ be with you.

THE SECOND LETTER OF PAUL TO THE THESSALONIANS

2 THESSALONIANS

CHAPTER 1

1 Paul, Silvanus, and Timothy, To the church of the Thessalonians in God our Father and the Lord Jesus Christ:

2 Grace to you and peace from God our Father and the Lord Jesus Christ.

3 We ought always to give thanks to God for you, brothers, as is right, because your faith is growing abundantly, and the love of every one of you for one another is increasing.

4 Therefore we ourselves

boast about you in the churches of God for your steadfastness and faith in all your persecutions and in the afflictions that you are enduring.

⁵ This is evidence of the righteous judgment of God, that you may be considered worthy of the kingdom of God, for which you are also suffering—

⁶ since indeed God considers it just to repay with affliction those who afflict you,

⁷ and to grant relief to you who are afflicted as well as to us, when the Lord Jesus is revealed from heaven with his mighty angels

⁸ in flaming fire, inflicting vengeance on those who do not know God and on those who do not obey the gospel of our Lord Jesus.

⁹ They will suffer the punishment of eternal destruction, away from the presence of the Lord and from the glory of his might,

¹⁰ when he comes on that day to be glorified in his saints, and to be marveled at among all who have believed, because our testimony to you was believed.

¹¹ To this end we always pray for you, that our God may make you worthy of his calling and may fulfill every resolve for good and every work of faith by his power,

¹² so that the name of our Lord Jesus may be glorified in you, and you in him, according to the grace of our God and the Lord Jesus Christ.

CHAPTER 2

¹ Now concerning the coming of our Lord Jesus Christ and our being gathered together to him, we ask you, brothers,

² not to be quickly shaken in mind or alarmed, either by a spirit or a spoken word, or a letter seeming to be from us, to the effect that the day of the Lord has come.

³ Let no one deceive you in any way. For that day will not come, unless the rebellion comes first, and the man of lawlessness is revealed, the son of destruction,

⁴ who opposes and exalts himself against every so-called god or object of worship, so that he takes his seat in the temple of God, proclaiming himself to be God.

⁵ Do you not remember that when I was still with you I told you these things?

⁶ And you know what is restraining him now so that he may be revealed in his time.

⁷ For the mystery of law-

lessness is already at work. Only he who now restrains it will do so until he is out of the way.

8 And then the lawless one will be revealed, whom the Lord Jesus will kill with the breath of his mouth and bring to nothing by the appearance of his coming.

9 The coming of the lawless one is by the activity of Satan with all power and false signs and wonders,

10 and with all wicked deception for those who are perishing, because they refused to love the truth and so be saved.

11 Therefore God sends them a strong delusion, so that they may believe what is false,

12 in order that all may be condemned who did not believe the truth but had pleasure in unrighteousness.

13 But we ought always to give thanks to God for you, brothers beloved by the Lord, because God chose you from the beginning to be saved, through sanctification by the Spirit and belief in the truth.

14 To this he called you through our gospel, so that you may obtain the glory of our Lord Jesus Christ.

15 So then, brothers, stand firm and hold to the traditions that you were taught by us, either by our spoken word or by our letter.

16 Now may our Lord Jesus Christ himself, and God our Father, who loved us and gave us eternal comfort and good hope through grace,

17 comfort your hearts and establish them in every good work and word.

CHAPTER 3

1 Finally, brothers, pray for us, that the word of the Lord may speed ahead and be honored, as happened among you,

2 and that we may be delivered from wicked and evil men. For not all have faith.

3 But the Lord is faithful. He will establish you and guard you against the evil one.

4 And we have confidence in the Lord about you, that you are doing and will do the things that we command.

5 May the Lord direct your hearts to the love of God and to the steadfastness of Christ.

6 Now we command you, brothers, in the name of our Lord Jesus Christ, that you keep away from any brother who is walking in idleness and not in accord with the tradition that you received from us.

7 For you yourselves know how you ought to imitate

us, because we were not idle when we were with you,

⁸ nor did we eat anyone's bread without paying for it, but with toil and labor we worked night and day, that we might not be a burden to any of you.

⁹ It was not because we do not have that right, but to give you in ourselves an example to imitate.

¹⁰ For even when we were with you, we would give you this command: If anyone is not willing to work, let him not eat.

¹¹ For we hear that some among you walk in idleness, not busy at work, but busybodies.

¹² Now such persons we command and encourage in the Lord Jesus Christ to do their work quietly and to earn their own living.

¹³ As for you, brothers, do not grow weary in doing good.

¹⁴ If anyone does not obey what we say in this letter, take note of that person, and have nothing to do with him, that he may be ashamed.

¹⁵ Do not regard him as an enemy, but warn him as a brother.

¹⁶ Now may the Lord of peace himself give you peace at all times in every way. The Lord be with you all.

¹⁷ I, Paul, write this greeting with my own hand. This is the sign of genuineness in every letter of mine; it is the way I write.

¹⁸ The grace of our Lord Jesus Christ be with you all.

THE FIRST LETTER OF PAUL TO TIMOTHY

1 TIMOTHY

CHAPTER 1

¹ Paul, an apostle of Christ Jesus by command of God our Savior and of Christ Jesus our hope,

² To Timothy, my true child in the faith: Grace, mercy, and peace from God the Father and Christ Jesus our Lord.

³ As I urged you when I was going to Macedonia, remain at Ephesus so that you may charge certain persons not to teach any different doctrine,

⁴ nor to devote themselves to myths and endless genealogies, which promote speculations rather than the

stewardship from God that is by faith.

⁵ The aim of our charge is love that issues from a pure heart and a good conscience and a sincere faith.

⁶ Certain persons, by swerving from these, have wandered away into vain discussion,

⁷ desiring to be teachers of the law, without understanding either what they are saying or the things about which they make confident assertions.

⁸ Now we know that the law is good, if one uses it lawfully,

⁹ understanding this, that the law is not laid down for the just but for the lawless and disobedient, for the ungodly and sinners, for the unholy and profane, for those who strike their fathers and mothers, for murderers,

¹⁰ the sexually immoral, men who practice homosexuality, enslavers, liars, perjurers, and whatever else is contrary to sound doctrine,

¹¹ in accordance with the gospel of the glory of the blessed God with which I have been entrusted.

¹² I thank him who has given me strength, Christ Jesus our Lord, because he judged me faithful, appointing me to his service,

¹³ though formerly I was a blasphemer, persecutor, and insolent opponent. But I received mercy because I had acted ignorantly in unbelief,

¹⁴ and the grace of our Lord overflowed for me with the faith and love that are in Christ Jesus.

¹⁵ The saying is trustworthy and deserving of full acceptance, that Christ Jesus came into the world to save sinners, of whom I am the foremost.

¹⁶ But I received mercy for this reason, that in me, as the foremost, Jesus Christ might display his perfect patience as an example to those who were to believe in him for eternal life.

¹⁷ To the King of the ages, immortal, invisible, the only God, be honor and glory forever and ever. Amen.

¹⁸ This charge I entrust to you, Timothy, my child, in accordance with the prophecies previously made about you, that by them you may wage the good warfare,

¹⁹ holding faith and a good conscience. By rejecting this, some have made shipwreck of their faith,

²⁰ among whom are Hymenaeus and Alexander, whom I have handed over to Satan that they may learn not to blaspheme.

CHAPTER 2

¹ First of all, then, I urge that supplications, prayers, intercessions, and thanksgivings be made for all people,

² for kings and all who are in high positions, that we may lead a peaceful and quiet life, godly and dignified in every way.

³ This is good, and it is pleasing in the sight of God our Savior,

⁴ who desires all people to be saved and to come to the knowledge of the truth.

⁵ For there is one God, and there is one mediator between God and men, the man Christ Jesus,

⁶ who gave himself as a ransom for all, which is the testimony given at the proper time.

⁷ For this I was appointed a preacher and an apostle (I am telling the truth, I am not lying), a teacher of the Gentiles in faith and truth.

⁸ I desire then that in every place the men should pray, lifting holy hands without anger or quarreling;

⁹ likewise also that women should adorn themselves in respectable apparel, with modesty and self-control, not with braided hair and gold or pearls or costly attire,

¹⁰ but with what is proper for women who profess godliness—with good works.

¹¹ Let a woman learn quietly with all submissiveness.

¹² I do not permit a woman to teach or to exercise authority over a man; rather, she is to remain quiet.

¹³ For Adam was formed first, then Eve;

¹⁴ and Adam was not deceived, but the woman was deceived and became a transgressor.

¹⁵ Yet she will be saved through childbearing—if they continue in faith and love and holiness, with self-control.

CHAPTER 3

¹ The saying is trustworthy: If anyone aspires to the office of overseer, he desires a noble task.

² Therefore an overseer must be above reproach, the husband of one wife, soberminded, self-controlled, respectable, hospitable, able to teach,

³ not a drunkard, not violent but gentle, not quarrelsome, not a lover of money.

⁴ He must manage his own household well, with all dignity keeping his children submissive,

⁵ for if someone does not know how to manage his own

household, how will he care for God's church?

⁶ He must not be a recent convert, or he may become puffed up with conceit and fall into the condemnation of the devil.

⁷ Moreover, he must be well thought of by outsiders, so that he may not fall into disgrace, into a snare of the devil.

⁸ Deacons likewise must be dignified, not double-tongued, not addicted to much wine, not greedy for dishonest gain.

⁹ They must hold the mystery of the faith with a clear conscience.

¹⁰ And let them also be tested first; then let them serve as deacons if they prove themselves blameless.

¹¹ Their wives likewise must be dignified, not slanderers, but sober-minded, faithful in all things.

¹² Let deacons each be the husband of one wife, managing their children and their own households well.

¹³ For those who serve well as deacons gain a good standing for themselves and also great confidence in the faith that is in Christ Jesus.

¹⁴ I hope to come to you soon, but I am writing these things to you so that,

¹⁵ if I delay, you may know how one ought to behave in the household of God, which is the church of the living God, a pillar and buttress of the truth.

¹⁶ Great indeed, we confess, is the mystery of godliness: God was manifested in the flesh, justified in the Spirit, seen by angels, proclaimed among the nations, believed on in the world, taken up in glory.

CHAPTER 4

¹ Now the Spirit expressly says that in later times some will depart from the faith by devoting themselves to deceitful spirits and teachings of demons,

² through the insincerity of liars whose consciences are seared,

³ who forbid marriage and require abstinence from foods that God created to be received with thanksgiving by those who believe and know the truth.

⁴ For everything created by God is good, and nothing is to be rejected if it is received with thanksgiving,

⁵ for it is made holy by the word of God and prayer.

⁶ If you put these things before the brothers, you will be a good servant of Christ Jesus,

being trained in the words of the faith and of the good doctrine that you have followed.

7 Have nothing to do with irreverent, silly myths. Rather train yourself for godliness;

8 for while bodily training is of some value, godliness is of value in every way, as it holds promise for the present life and also for the life to come.

9 The saying is trustworthy and deserving of full acceptance.

10 For to this end we toil and strive, because we have our hope set on the living God, who is the Savior of all people, especially of those who believe.

11 Command and teach these things.

12 Let no one despise you for your youth, but set the believers an example in speech, in conduct, in love, in faith, in purity.

13 Until I come, devote yourself to the public reading of Scripture, to exhortation, to teaching.

14 Do not neglect the gift you have, which was given to you by prophecy when the council of elders laid their hands on you.

15 Practice these things, immerse yourself in them, so that all may see your progress.

16 Keep a close watch on yourself and on the teaching. Persist in this, for by so doing you will save both yourself and your hearers.

CHAPTER 5

1 Do not rebuke an older man but encourage him as you would a father, younger men as brothers,

2 older women as mothers, younger women as sisters, in all purity.

3 Honor widows who are truly widows.

4 But if a widow has children or grandchildren, let them first learn to show godliness to their own household and to make some return to their parents, for this is pleasing in the sight of God.

5 She who is truly a widow, left all alone, has set her hope on God and continues in supplications and prayers night and day,

6 but she who is self-indulgent is dead even while she lives.

7 Command these things as well, so that they may be without reproach.

8 But if anyone does not provide for his relatives, and especially for members of his household, he has denied the faith and is worse than an unbeliever.

9 Let a widow be enrolled if she is not less than sixty years of age, having been the wife of one husband,

10 and having a reputation for good works: if she has brought up children, has shown hospitality, has washed the feet of the saints, has cared for the afflicted, and has devoted herself to every good work.

11 But refuse to enroll younger widows, for when their passions draw them away from Christ, they desire to marry

12 and so incur condemnation for having abandoned their former faith.

13 Besides that, they learn to be idlers, going about from house to house, and not only idlers, but also gossips and busybodies, saying what they should not.

14 So I would have younger widows marry, bear children, manage their households, and give the adversary no occasion for slander.

15 For some have already strayed after Satan.

16 If any believing woman has relatives who are widows, let her care for them. Let the church not be burdened, so that it may care for those who are truly widows.

17 Let the elders who rule well be considered worthy of double honor, especially those who labor in preaching and teaching.

18 For the Scripture says, "You shall not muzzle an ox when it treads out the grain," and, "The laborer deserves his wages."

19 Do not admit a charge against an elder except on the evidence of two or three witnesses.

20 As for those who persist in sin, rebuke them in the presence of all, so that the rest may stand in fear.

21 In the presence of God and of Christ Jesus and of the elect angels I charge you to keep these rules without prejudging, doing nothing from partiality.

22 Do not be hasty in the laying on of hands, nor take part in the sins of others; keep yourself pure.

23 (No longer drink only water, but use a little wine for the sake of your stomach and your frequent ailments.)

24 The sins of some people are conspicuous, going before them to judgment, but the sins of others appear later.

25 So also good works are conspicuous, and even those that are not cannot remain hidden.

CHAPTER 6

¹ Let all who are under a yoke as bondservants regard their own masters as worthy of all honor, so that the name of God and the teaching may not be reviled.

² Those who have believing masters must not be disrespectful on the ground that they are brothers; rather they must serve all the better since those who benefit by their good service are believers and beloved. Teach and urge these things.

³ If anyone teaches a different doctrine and does not agree with the sound words of our Lord Jesus Christ and the teaching that accords with godliness,

⁴ he is puffed up with conceit and understands nothing. He has an unhealthy craving for controversy and for quarrels about words, which produce envy, dissension, slander, evil suspicions,

⁵ and constant friction among people who are depraved in mind and deprived of the truth, imagining that godliness is a means of gain.

⁶ But godliness with contentment is great gain,

⁷ for we brought nothing into the world, and we cannot take anything out of the world.

⁸ But if we have food and clothing, with these we will be content.

⁹ But those who desire to be rich fall into temptation, into a snare, into many senseless and harmful desires that plunge people into ruin and destruction.

¹⁰ For the love of money is a root of all kinds of evils. It is through this craving that some have wandered away from the faith and pierced themselves with many pangs.

¹¹ But as for you, O man of God, flee these things. Pursue righteousness, godliness, faith, love, steadfastness, gentleness.

¹² Fight the good fight of the faith. Take hold of the eternal life to which you were called and about which you made the good confession in the presence of many witnesses.

¹³ I charge you in the presence of God, who gives life to all things, and of Christ Jesus, who in his testimony before Pontius Pilate made the good confession,

¹⁴ to keep the commandment unstained and free from reproach until the appearing of our Lord Jesus Christ,

¹⁵ which he will display at the proper time—he who is

the blessed and only Sovereign, the King of kings and Lord of lords,

16 who alone has immortality, who dwells in unapproachable light, whom no one has ever seen or can see. To him be honor and eternal dominion. Amen.

17 As for the rich in this present age, charge them not to be haughty, nor to set their hopes on the uncertainty of riches, but on God, who richly provides us with everything to enjoy.

18 They are to do good, to be rich in good works, to be generous and ready to share,

19 thus storing up treasure for themselves as a good foundation for the future, so that they may take hold of that which is truly life.

20 O Timothy, guard the deposit entrusted to you. Avoid the irreverent babble and contradictions of what is falsely called "knowledge,"

21 for by professing it some have swerved from the faith. Grace be with you.

THE SECOND LETTER OF PAUL TO TIMOTHY

2 TIMOTHY

CHAPTER 1

1 Paul, an apostle of Christ Jesus by the will of God according to the promise of the life that is in Christ Jesus,

2 To Timothy, my beloved child: Grace, mercy, and peace from God the Father and Christ Jesus our Lord.

3 I thank God whom I serve, as did my ancestors, with a clear conscience, as I remember you constantly in my prayers night and day.

4 As I remember your tears, I long to see you, that I may be filled with joy.

5 I am reminded of your sincere faith, a faith that dwelt first in your grandmother Lois and your mother Eunice and now, I am sure, dwells in you as well.

6 For this reason I remind you to fan into flame the gift of God, which is in you through the laying on of my hands,

7 for God gave us a spirit not of fear but of power and love and self-control.

8 Therefore do not be ashamed of the testimony about our Lord, nor of me his

prisoner, but share in suffering for the gospel by the power of God,

9 who saved us and called us to a holy calling, not because of our works but because of his own purpose and grace, which he gave us in Christ Jesus before the ages began,

10 and which now has been manifested through the appearing of our Savior Christ Jesus, who abolished death and brought life and immortality to light through the gospel,

11 for which I was appointed a preacher and apostle and teacher,

12 which is why I suffer as I do. But I am not ashamed, for I know whom I have believed, and I am convinced that he is able to guard until that Day what has been entrusted to me.

13 Follow the pattern of the sound words that you have heard from me, in the faith and love that are in Christ Jesus.

14 By the Holy Spirit who dwells within us, guard the good deposit entrusted to you.

15 You are aware that all who are in Asia turned away from me, among whom are Phygelus and Hermogenes.

16 May the Lord grant mercy to the household of Onesiphorus, for he often refreshed me and was not ashamed of my chains,

17 but when he arrived in Rome he searched for me earnestly and found me—

18 may the Lord grant him to find mercy from the Lord on that Day!—and you well know all the service he rendered at Ephesus.

CHAPTER 2

1 You then, my child, be strengthened by the grace that is in Christ Jesus,

2 and what you have heard from me in the presence of many witnesses entrust to faithful men who will be able to teach others also.

3 Share in suffering as a good soldier of Christ Jesus.

4 No soldier gets entangled in civilian pursuits, since his aim is to please the one who enlisted him.

5 An athlete is not crowned unless he competes according to the rules.

6 It is the hard-working farmer who ought to have the first share of the crops.

7 Think over what I say, for the Lord will give you understanding in everything.

8 Remember Jesus Christ, risen from the dead, the off-

spring of David, as preached in my gospel,

9 for which I am suffering, bound with chains as a criminal. But the word of God is not bound!

10 Therefore I endure everything for the sake of the elect, that they also may obtain the salvation that is in Christ Jesus with eternal glory.

11 The saying is trustworthy, for: If we have died with him, we will also live with him;

12 if we endure, we will also reign with him; if we deny him, he also will deny us;

13 if we are faithless, he remains faithful— for he cannot deny himself.

14 Remind them of these things, and charge them before God not to quarrel about words, which does no good, but only ruins the hearers.

15 Do your best to present yourself to God as one approved, a worker who has no need to be ashamed, rightly handling the word of truth.

16 But avoid irreverent babble, for it will lead people into more and more ungodliness,

17 and their talk will spread like gangrene. Among them are Hymenaeus and Philetus,

18 who have swerved from the truth, saying that the resurrection has already happened. They are upsetting the faith of some.

19 But God's firm foundation stands, bearing this seal: "The Lord knows those who are his," and, "Let everyone who names the name of the Lord depart from iniquity."

20 Now in a great house there are not only vessels of gold and silver but also of wood and clay, some for honorable use, some for dishonorable.

21 Therefore, if anyone cleanses himself from what is dishonorable, he will be a vessel for honorable use, set apart as holy, useful to the master of the house, ready for every good work.

22 So flee youthful passions and pursue righteousness, faith, love, and peace, along with those who call on the Lord from a pure heart.

23 Have nothing to do with foolish, ignorant controversies; you know that they breed quarrels.

24 And the Lord's servant must not be quarrelsome but kind to everyone, able to teach, patiently enduring evil,

25 correcting his opponents with gentleness. God may perhaps grant them repentance leading to a knowledge of the truth,

26 and they may come to their senses and escape from the snare of the devil, after being captured by him to do his will.

CHAPTER 3

1 But understand this, that in the last days there will come times of difficulty.

2 For people will be lovers of self, lovers of money, proud, arrogant, abusive, disobedient to their parents, ungrateful, unholy,

3 heartless, unappeasable, slanderous, without self-control, brutal, not loving good,

4 treacherous, reckless, swollen with conceit, lovers of pleasure rather than lovers of God,

5 having the appearance of godliness, but denying its power. Avoid such people.

6 For among them are those who creep into households and capture weak women, burdened with sins and led astray by various passions,

7 always learning and never able to arrive at a knowledge of the truth.

8 Just as Jannes and Jambres opposed Moses, so these men also oppose the truth, men corrupted in mind and disqualified regarding the faith.

9 But they will not get very far, for their folly will be plain to all, as was that of those two men.

10 You, however, have followed my teaching, my conduct, my aim in life, my faith, my patience, my love, my steadfastness,

11 my persecutions and sufferings that happened to me at Antioch, at Iconium, and at Lystra—which persecutions I endured; yet from them all the Lord rescued me.

12 Indeed, all who desire to live a godly life in Christ Jesus will be persecuted,

13 while evil people and impostors will go on from bad to worse, deceiving and being deceived.

14 But as for you, continue in what you have learned and have firmly believed, knowing from whom you learned it

15 and how from childhood you have been acquainted with the sacred writings, which are able to make you wise for salvation through faith in Christ Jesus.

16 All Scripture is breathed out by God and profitable for teaching, for reproof, for correction, and for training in righteousness,

17 that the man of God may be complete, equipped for every good work.

CHAPTER 4

¹ I charge you in the presence of God and of Christ Jesus, who is to judge the living and the dead, and by his appearing and his kingdom:

² preach the word; be ready in season and out of season; reprove, rebuke, and exhort, with complete patience and teaching.

³ For the time is coming when people will not endure sound teaching, but having itching ears they will accumulate for themselves teachers to suit their own passions,

⁴ and will turn away from listening to the truth and wander off into myths.

⁵ As for you, always be sober-minded, endure suffering, do the work of an evangelist, fulfill your ministry.

⁶ For I am already being poured out as a drink offering, and the time of my departure has come.

⁷ I have fought the good fight, I have finished the race, I have kept the faith.

⁸ Henceforth there is laid up for me the crown of righteousness, which the Lord, the righteous judge, will award to me on that Day, and not only to me but also to all who have loved his appearing.

⁹ Do your best to come to me soon.

¹⁰ For Demas, in love with this present world, has deserted me and gone to Thessalonica. Crescens has gone to Galatia, Titus to Dalmatia.

¹¹ Luke alone is with me. Get Mark and bring him with you, for he is very useful to me for ministry.

¹² Tychicus I have sent to Ephesus.

¹³ When you come, bring the cloak that I left with Carpus at Troas, also the books, and above all the parchments.

¹⁴ Alexander the coppersmith did me great harm; the Lord will repay him according to his deeds.

¹⁵ Beware of him yourself, for he strongly opposed our message.

¹⁶ At my first defense no one came to stand by me, but all deserted me. May it not be charged against them!

¹⁷ But the Lord stood by me and strengthened me, so that through me the message might be fully proclaimed and all the Gentiles might hear it. So I was rescued from the lion's mouth.

¹⁸ The Lord will rescue me from every evil deed and bring me safely into his heavenly kingdom. To him be the glory forever and ever. Amen.

¹⁹ Greet Prisca and Aquila, and the household of Onesiphorus.

²⁰ Erastus remained at Corinth, and I left Trophimus, who was ill, at Miletus.

²¹ Do your best to come before winter. Eubulus sends greetings to you, as do Pudens and Linus and Claudia and all the brothers.

²² The Lord be with your spirit. Grace be with you.

THE LETTER OF PAUL TO

TITUS

CHAPTER 1

¹ Paul, a servant of God and an apostle of Jesus Christ, for the sake of the faith of God's elect and their knowledge of the truth, which accords with godliness,

² in hope of eternal life, which God, who never lies, promised before the ages began

³ and at the proper time manifested in his word through the preaching with which I have been entrusted by the command of God our Savior;

⁴ To Titus, my true child in a common faith: Grace and peace from God the Father and Christ Jesus our Savior.

⁵ This is why I left you in Crete, so that you might put what remained into order, and appoint elders in every town as I directed you—

⁶ if anyone is above reproach, the husband of one wife, and his children are believers and not open to the charge of debauchery or insubordination.

⁷ For an overseer, as God's steward, must be above reproach. He must not be arrogant or quick-tempered or a drunkard or violent or greedy for gain,

⁸ but hospitable, a lover of good, self-controlled, upright, holy, and disciplined.

⁹ He must hold firm to the trustworthy word as taught, so that he may be able to give instruction in sound doctrine and also to rebuke those who contradict it.

¹⁰ For there are many who are insubordinate, empty talkers and deceivers, especially those of the circumcision party.

¹¹ They must be silenced, since they are upsetting whole families by teaching for shameful gain what they ought not to teach.

¹² One of the Cretans, a prophet of their own, said, "Cretans are always liars, evil beasts, lazy gluttons."

¹³ This testimony is true. Therefore rebuke them sharply, that they may be sound in the faith,

¹⁴ not devoting themselves to Jewish myths and the commands of people who turn away from the truth.

¹⁵ To the pure, all things are pure, but to the defiled and unbelieving, nothing is pure; but both their minds and their consciences are defiled.

¹⁶ They profess to know God, but they deny him by their works. They are detestable, disobedient, unfit for any good work.

CHAPTER 2

¹ But as for you, teach what accords with sound doctrine.

² Older men are to be sober-minded, dignified, self-controlled, sound in faith, in love, and in steadfastness.

³ Older women likewise are to be reverent in behavior, not slanderers or slaves to much wine. They are to teach what is good,

⁴ and so train the young women to love their husbands and children,

⁵ to be self-controlled, pure, working at home, kind, and submissive to their own husbands, that the word of God may not be reviled.

⁶ Likewise, urge the younger men to be self-controlled.

⁷ Show yourself in all respects to be a model of good works, and in your teaching show integrity, dignity,

⁸ and sound speech that cannot be condemned, so that an opponent may be put to shame, having nothing evil to say about us.

⁹ Bondservants are to be submissive to their own masters in everything; they are to be well-pleasing, not argumentative,

¹⁰ not pilfering, but showing all good faith, so that in everything they may adorn the doctrine of God our Savior.

¹¹ For the grace of God has appeared, bringing salvation for all people,

¹² training us to renounce ungodliness and worldly passions, and to live self-controlled, upright, and godly lives in the present age,

¹³ waiting for our blessed

hope, the appearing of the glory of our great God and Savior Jesus Christ,

¹⁴ who gave himself for us to redeem us from all lawlessness and to purify for himself a people for his own possession who are zealous for good works.

¹⁵ Declare these things; exhort and rebuke with all authority. Let no one disregard you.

CHAPTER 3

¹ Remind them to be submissive to rulers and authorities, to be obedient, to be ready for every good work,

² to speak evil of no one, to avoid quarreling, to be gentle, and to show perfect courtesy toward all people.

³ For we ourselves were once foolish, disobedient, led astray, slaves to various passions and pleasures, passing our days in malice and envy, hated by others and hating one another.

⁴ But when the goodness and loving kindness of God our Savior appeared,

⁵ he saved us, not because of works done by us in righteousness, but according to his own mercy, by the washing of regeneration and renewal of the Holy Spirit,

⁶ whom he poured out on us richly through Jesus Christ our Savior,

⁷ so that being justified by his grace we might become heirs according to the hope of eternal life.

⁸ The saying is trustworthy, and I want you to insist on these things, so that those who have believed in God may be careful to devote themselves to good works. These things are excellent and profitable for people.

⁹ But avoid foolish controversies, genealogies, dissensions, and quarrels about the law, for they are unprofitable and worthless.

¹⁰ As for a person who stirs up division, after warning him once and then twice, have nothing more to do with him,

¹¹ knowing that such a person is warped and sinful; he is self-condemned.

¹² When I send Artemas or Tychicus to you, do your best to come to me at Nicopolis, for I have decided to spend the winter there.

¹³ Do your best to speed Zenas the lawyer and Apollos on their way; see that they lack nothing.

¹⁴ And let our people learn to devote themselves to good works, so as to help cases of

urgent need, and not be unfruitful.

15 All who are with me send greetings to you. Greet those who love us in the faith. Grace be with you all.

THE LETTER OF PAUL TO

PHILEMON

1 Paul, a prisoner for Christ Jesus, and Timothy our brother, To Philemon our beloved fellow worker

2 and Apphia our sister and Archippus our fellow soldier, and the church in your house:

3 Grace to you and peace from God our Father and the Lord Jesus Christ.

4 I thank my God always when I remember you in my prayers,

5 because I hear of your love and of the faith that you have toward the Lord Jesus and for all the saints,

6 and I pray that the sharing of your faith may become effective for the full knowledge of every good thing that is in us for the sake of Christ.

7 For I have derived much joy and comfort from your love, my brother, because the hearts of the saints have been refreshed through you.

8 Accordingly, though I am bold enough in Christ to command you to do what is required,

9 yet for love's sake I prefer to appeal to you—I, Paul, an old man and now a prisoner also for Christ Jesus—

10 I appeal to you for my child, Onesimus, whose father I became in my imprisonment.

11 (Formerly he was useless to you, but now he is indeed useful to you and to me.)

12 I am sending him back to you, sending my very heart.

13 I would have been glad to keep him with me, in order that he might serve me on your behalf during my imprisonment for the gospel,

14 but I preferred to do nothing without your consent in order that your goodness might not be by compulsion but of your own accord.

15 For this perhaps is why he was parted from you for a while, that you might have him back forever,

16 no longer as a bond-servant but more than a bondservant, as a beloved brother—especially to me, but how much more to you, both in the flesh and in the Lord.

17 So if you consider me your partner, receive him as you would receive me.

18 If he has wronged you at all, or owes you anything, charge that to my account.

19 I, Paul, write this with my own hand: I will repay it—to say nothing of your owing me even your own self.

20 Yes, brother, I want some benefit from you in the Lord. Refresh my heart in Christ.

21 Confident of your obedience, I write to you, knowing that you will do even more than I say.

22 At the same time, prepare a guest room for me, for I am hoping that through your prayers I will be graciously given to you.

23 Epaphras, my fellow prisoner in Christ Jesus, sends greetings to you,

24 and so do Mark, Aristarchus, Demas, and Luke, my fellow workers.

25 The grace of the Lord Jesus Christ be with your spirit.

THE LETTER TO THE

HEBREWS

CHAPTER 1

1 Long ago, at many times and in many ways, God spoke to our fathers by the prophets,

2 but in these last days he has spoken to us by his Son, whom he appointed the heir of all things, through whom also he created the world.

3 He is the radiance of the glory of God and the exact imprint of his nature, and he upholds the universe by the word of his power. After making purification for sins, he sat down at the right hand of the Majesty on high,

4 having become as much superior to angels as the name he has inherited is more excellent than theirs.

5 For to which of the angels did God ever say, "You are my Son, today I have begotten you"? Or again, "I will be to him a father, and he shall be to me a son"?

⁶ And again, when he brings the firstborn into the world, he says, "Let all God's angels worship him."

⁷ Of the angels he says, "He makes his angels winds, and his ministers a flame of fire."

⁸ But of the Son he says, "Your throne, O God, is forever and ever, the scepter of uprightness is the scepter of your kingdom.

⁹ You have loved righteousness and hated wickedness; therefore God, your God, has anointed you with the oil of gladness beyond your companions."

¹⁰ And, "You, Lord, laid the foundation of the earth in the beginning, and the heavens are the work of your hands;

¹¹ "they will perish, but you remain; they will all wear out like a garment,

¹² "like a robe you will roll them up, like a garment they will be changed. But you are the same, and your years will have no end.

¹³ And to which of the angels has he ever said, "Sit at my right hand until I make your enemies a footstool for your feet"?

¹⁴ Are they not all ministering spirits sent out to serve for the sake of those who are to inherit salvation?

CHAPTER 2

¹ Therefore we must pay much closer attention to what we have heard, lest we drift away from it.

² For since the message declared by angels proved to be reliable, and every transgression or disobedience received a just retribution,

³ how shall we escape if we neglect such a great salvation? It was declared at first by the Lord, and it was attested to us by those who heard,

⁴ while God also bore witness by signs and wonders and various miracles and by gifts of the Holy Spirit distributed according to his will.

⁵ For it was not to angels that God subjected the world to come, of which we are speaking.

⁶ It has been testified somewhere, "What is man, that you are mindful of him, or the son of man, that you care for him?

⁷ You made him for a little while lower than the angels; you have crowned him with glory and honor,

⁸ "putting everything in subjection under his feet." Now in putting everything in subjection to him, he left nothing outside his control. At present, we do not yet see everything in subjection to him.

⁹ But we see him who for a little while was made lower than the angels, namely Jesus, crowned with glory and honor because of the suffering of death, so that by the grace of God he might taste death for everyone.

¹⁰ For it was fitting that he, for whom and by whom all things exist, in bringing many sons to glory, should make the founder of their salvation perfect through suffering.

¹¹ For he who sanctifies and those who are sanctified all have one source. That is why he is not ashamed to call them brothers,

¹² saying, "I will tell of your name to my brothers; in the midst of the congregation I will sing your praise."

¹³ And again, "I will put my trust in him." And again, "Behold, I and the children God has given me."

¹⁴ Since therefore the children share in flesh and blood, he himself likewise partook of the same things, that through death he might destroy the one who has the power of death, that is, the devil,

¹⁵ and deliver all those who through fear of death were subject to lifelong slavery.

¹⁶ For surely it is not angels that he helps, but he helps the offspring of Abraham.

¹⁷ Therefore he had to be made like his brothers in every respect, so that he might become a merciful and faithful high priest in the service of God, to make propitiation for the sins of the people.

¹⁸ For because he himself has suffered when tempted, he is able to help those who are being tempted.

CHAPTER 3

¹ Therefore, holy brothers, you who share in a heavenly calling, consider Jesus, the apostle and high priest of our confession,

² who was faithful to him who appointed him, just as Moses also was faithful in all God's house.

³ For Jesus has been counted worthy of more glory than Moses—as much more glory as the builder of a house has more honor than the house itself.

⁴ (For every house is built by someone, but the builder of all things is God.)

⁵ Now Moses was faithful in all God's house as a servant, to testify to the things that were to be spoken later,

⁶ but Christ is faithful over God's house as a son. And

we are his house if indeed we hold fast our confidence and our boasting in our hope.

7 Therefore, as the Holy Spirit says, "Today, if you hear his voice,

8 "do not harden your hearts as in the rebellion, on the day of testing in the wilderness,

9 "where your fathers put me to the test and saw my works for forty years.

10 "Therefore I was provoked with that generation, and said, 'They always go astray in their heart; they have not known my ways.'

11 "As I swore in my wrath, 'They shall not enter my rest.'"

12 Take care, brothers, lest there be in any of you an evil, unbelieving heart, leading you to fall away from the living God.

13 But exhort one another every day, as long as it is called "today," that none of you may be hardened by the deceitfulness of sin.

14 For we have come to share in Christ, if indeed we hold our original confidence firm to the end.

15 As it is said, "Today, if you hear his voice, do not harden your hearts as in the rebellion."

16 For who were those who heard and yet rebelled? Was it not all those who left Egypt led by Moses?

17 And with whom was he provoked for forty years? Was it not with those who sinned, whose bodies fell in the wilderness?

18 And to whom did he swear that they would not enter his rest, but to those who were disobedient?

19 So we see that they were unable to enter because of unbelief.

CHAPTER 4

1 Therefore, while the promise of entering his rest still stands, let us fear lest any of you should seem to have failed to reach it.

2 For good news came to us just as to them, but the message they heard did not benefit them, because they were not united by faith with those who listened.

3 For we who have believed enter that rest, as he has said, "As I swore in my wrath, 'They shall not enter my rest,'" although his works were finished from the foundation of the world.

4 For he has somewhere spoken of the seventh day in this way: "And God rested on the seventh day from all his works."

5 And again in this passage

he said, "They shall not enter my rest."

⁶ Since therefore it remains for some to enter it, and those who formerly received the good news failed to enter because of disobedience,

⁷ again he appoints a certain day, "Today," saying through David so long afterward, in the words already quoted, "Today, if you hear his voice, do not harden your hearts."

⁸ For if Joshua had given them rest, God would not have spoken of another day later on.

⁹ So then, there remains a Sabbath rest for the people of God,

¹⁰ for whoever has entered God's rest has also rested from his works as God did from his.

¹¹ Let us therefore strive to enter that rest, so that no one may fall by the same sort of disobedience.

¹² For the word of God is living and active, sharper than any two-edged sword, piercing to the division of soul and of spirit, of joints and of marrow, and discerning the thoughts and intentions of the heart.

¹³ And no creature is hidden from his sight, but all are naked and exposed to the eyes of him to whom we must give account.

¹⁴ Since then we have a great high priest who has passed through the heavens, Jesus, the Son of God, let us hold fast our confession.

¹⁵ For we do not have a high priest who is unable to sympathize with our weaknesses, but one who in every respect has been tempted as we are, yet without sin.

¹⁶ Let us then with confidence draw near to the throne of grace, that we may receive mercy and find grace to help in time of need.

CHAPTER 5

¹ For every high priest chosen from among men is appointed to act on behalf of men in relation to God, to offer gifts and sacrifices for sins.

² He can deal gently with the ignorant and wayward, since he himself is beset with weakness.

³ Because of this he is obligated to offer sacrifice for his own sins just as he does for those of the people.

⁴ And no one takes this honor for himself, but only when called by God, just as Aaron was.

⁵ So also Christ did not exalt himself to be made a high priest, but was appointed by

him who said to him, "You are my Son, today I have begotten you";

⁶ as he says also in another place, "You are a priest forever, after the order of Melchizedek."

⁷ In the days of his flesh, Jesus offered up prayers and supplications, with loud cries and tears, to him who was able to save him from death, and he was heard because of his reverence.

⁸ Although he was a son, he learned obedience through what he suffered.

⁹ And being made perfect, he became the source of eternal salvation to all who obey him,

¹⁰ being designated by God a high priest after the order of Melchizedek.

¹¹ About this we have much to say, and it is hard to explain, since you have become dull of hearing.

¹² For though by this time you ought to be teachers, you need someone to teach you again the basic principles of the oracles of God. You need milk, not solid food,

¹³ for everyone who lives on milk is unskilled in the word of righteousness, since he is a child.

¹⁴ But solid food is for the mature, for those who have their powers of discernment trained by constant practice to distinguish good from evil.

CHAPTER 6

¹ Therefore let us leave the elementary doctrine of Christ and go on to maturity, not laying again a foundation of repentance from dead works and of faith toward God,

² and of instruction about washings, the laying on of hands, the resurrection of the dead, and eternal judgment.

³ And this we will do if God permits.

⁴ For it is impossible, in the case of those who have once been enlightened, who have tasted the heavenly gift, and have shared in the Holy Spirit,

⁵ and have tasted the goodness of the word of God and the powers of the age to come,

⁶ and then have fallen away, to restore them again to repentance, since they are crucifying once again the Son of God to their own harm and holding him up to contempt.

⁷ For land that has drunk the rain that often falls on it, and produces a crop useful to those for whose sake it is cultivated, receives a blessing from God.

⁸ But if it bears thorns and

thistles, it is worthless and near to being cursed, and its end is to be burned.

9 Though we speak in this way, yet in your case, beloved, we feel sure of better things—things that belong to salvation.

10 For God is not unjust so as to overlook your work and the love that you have shown for his name in serving the saints, as you still do.

11 And we desire each one of you to show the same earnestness to have the full assurance of hope until the end,

12 so that you may not be sluggish, but imitators of those who through faith and patience inherit the promises.

13 For when God made a promise to Abraham, since he had no one greater by whom to swear, he swore by himself,

14 saying, "Surely I will bless you and multiply you."

15 And thus Abraham, having patiently waited, obtained the promise.

16 For people swear by something greater than themselves, and in all their disputes an oath is final for confirmation.

17 So when God desired to show more convincingly to the heirs of the promise the unchangeable character of his purpose, he guaranteed it with an oath,

18 so that by two unchangeable things, in which it is impossible for God to lie, we who have fled for refuge might have strong encouragement to hold fast to the hope set before us.

19 We have this as a sure and steadfast anchor of the soul, a hope that enters into the inner place behind the curtain,

20 where Jesus has gone as a forerunner on our behalf, having become a high priest forever after the order of Melchizedek.

CHAPTER 7

1 For this Melchizedek, king of Salem, priest of the Most High God, met Abraham returning from the slaughter of the kings and blessed him,

2 and to him Abraham apportioned a tenth part of everything. He is first, by translation of his name, king of righteousness, and then he is also king of Salem, that is, king of peace.

3 He is without father or mother or genealogy, having neither beginning of days nor end of life, but resembling the Son of God he continues a priest forever.

4 See how great this man was to whom Abraham the

patriarch gave a tenth of the spoils!

5 And those descendants of Levi who receive the priestly office have a commandment in the law to take tithes from the people, that is, from their brothers, though these also are descended from Abraham.

6 But this man who does not have his descent from them received tithes from Abraham and blessed him who had the promises.

7 It is beyond dispute that the inferior is blessed by the superior.

8 In the one case tithes are received by mortal men, but in the other case, by one of whom it is testified that he lives.

9 One might even say that Levi himself, who receives tithes, paid tithes through Abraham,

10 for he was still in the loins of his ancestor when Melchizedek met him.

11 Now if perfection had been attainable through the Levitical priesthood (for under it the people received the law), what further need would there have been for another priest to arise after the order of Melchizedek, rather than one named after the order of Aaron?

12 For when there is a change in the priesthood, there is necessarily a change in the law as well.

13 For the one of whom these things are spoken belonged to another tribe, from which no one has ever served at the altar.

14 For it is evident that our Lord was descended from Judah, and in connection with that tribe Moses said nothing about priests.

15 This becomes even more evident when another priest arises in the likeness of Melchizedek,

16 who has become a priest, not on the basis of a legal requirement concerning bodily descent, but by the power of an indestructible life.

17 For it is witnessed of him, "You are a priest forever, after the order of Melchizedek."

18 For on the one hand, a former commandment is set aside because of its weakness and uselessness

19 (for the law made nothing perfect); but on the other hand, a better hope is introduced, through which we draw near to God.

20 And it was not without an oath. For those who formerly became priests were made such without an oath,

21 but this one was made a priest with an oath by the

one who said to him: "The Lord has sworn and will not change his mind, 'You are a priest forever.'"

²² This makes Jesus the guarantor of a better covenant.

²³ The former priests were many in number, because they were prevented by death from continuing in office,

²⁴ but he holds his priesthood permanently, because he continues forever.

²⁵ Consequently, he is able to save to the uttermost those who draw near to God through him, since he always lives to make intercession for them.

²⁶ For it was indeed fitting that we should have such a high priest, holy, innocent, unstained, separated from sinners, and exalted above the heavens.

²⁷ He has no need, like those high priests, to offer sacrifices daily, first for his own sins and then for those of the people, since he did this once for all when he offered up himself.

²⁸ For the law appoints men in their weakness as high priests, but the word of the oath, which came later than the law, appoints a Son who has been made perfect forever.

CHAPTER 8

¹ Now the point in what we are saying is this: we have such a high priest, one who is seated at the right hand of the throne of the Majesty in heaven,

² a minister in the holy places, in the true tent that the Lord set up, not man.

³ For every high priest is appointed to offer gifts and sacrifices; thus it is necessary for this priest also to have something to offer.

⁴ Now if he were on earth, he would not be a priest at all, since there are priests who offer gifts according to the law.

⁵ They serve a copy and shadow of the heavenly things. For when Moses was about to erect the tent, he was instructed by God, saying, "See that you make everything according to the pattern that was shown you on the mountain."

⁶ But as it is, Christ has obtained a ministry that is as much more excellent than the old as the covenant he mediates is better, since it is enacted on better promises.

⁷ For if that first covenant had been faultless, there would have been no occasion to look for a second.

⁸ For he finds fault with

them when he says: "Behold, the days are coming, declares the Lord, when I will establish a new covenant with the house of Israel and with the house of Judah,

9 "not like the covenant that I made with their fathers on the day when I took them by the hand to bring them out of the land of Egypt. For they did not continue in my covenant, and so I showed no concern for them, declares the Lord.

10 "For this is the covenant that I will make with the house of Israel after those days, declares the Lord: I will put my laws into their minds, and write them on their hearts, and I will be their God, and they shall be my people.

11 "And they shall not teach, each one his neighbor and each one his brother, saying, 'Know the Lord,' for they shall all know me, from the least of them to the greatest.

12 "For I will be merciful toward their iniquities, and I will remember their sins no more."

13 In speaking of a new covenant, he makes the first one obsolete. And what is becoming obsolete and growing old is ready to vanish away.

CHAPTER 9

1 Now even the first covenant had regulations for worship and an earthly place of holiness.

2 For a tent was prepared, the first section, in which were the lampstand and the table and the bread of the Presence. It is called the Holy Place.

3 Behind the second curtain was a second section called the Most Holy Place,

4 having the golden altar of incense and the ark of the covenant covered on all sides with gold, in which was a golden urn holding the manna, and Aaron's staff that budded, and the tablets of the covenant.

5 Above it were the cherubim of glory overshadowing the mercy seat. Of these things we cannot now speak in detail.

6 These preparations having thus been made, the priests go regularly into the first section, performing their ritual duties,

7 but into the second only the high priest goes, and he but once a year, and not without taking blood, which he offers for himself and for the unintentional sins of the people.

8 By this the Holy Spirit

indicates that the way into the holy places is not yet opened as long as the first section is still standing

9 (which is symbolic for the present age). According to this arrangement, gifts and sacrifices are offered that cannot perfect the conscience of the worshiper,

10 but deal only with food and drink and various washings, regulations for the body imposed until the time of reformation.

11 But when Christ appeared as a high priest of the good things that have come, then through the greater and more perfect tent (not made with hands, that is, not of this creation)

12 he entered once for all into the holy places, not by means of the blood of goats and calves but by means of his own blood, thus securing an eternal redemption.

13 For if the blood of goats and bulls, and the sprinkling of defiled persons with the ashes of a heifer, sanctify for the purification of the flesh,

14 how much more will the blood of Christ, who through the eternal Spirit offered himself without blemish to God, purify our conscience from dead works to serve the living God.

15 Therefore he is the mediator of a new covenant, so that those who are called may receive the promised eternal inheritance, since a death has occurred that redeems them from the transgressions committed under the first covenant.

16 For where a will is involved, the death of the one who made it must be established.

17 For a will takes effect only at death, since it is not in force as long as the one who made it is alive.

18 Therefore not even the first covenant was inaugurated without blood.

19 For when every commandment of the law had been declared by Moses to all the people, he took the blood of calves and goats, with water and scarlet wool and hyssop, and sprinkled both the book itself and all the people,

20 saying, "This is the blood of the covenant that God commanded for you."

21 And in the same way he sprinkled with the blood both the tent and all the vessels used in worship.

22 Indeed, under the law almost everything is purified with blood, and without the shedding of blood there is no forgiveness of sins.

23 Thus it was necessary for the copies of the heavenly things to be purified with these rites, but the heavenly things themselves with better sacrifices than these.

24 For Christ has entered, not into holy places made with hands, which are copies of the true things, but into heaven itself, now to appear in the presence of God on our behalf.

25 Nor was it to offer himself repeatedly, as the high priest enters the holy places every year with blood not his own,

26 for then he would have had to suffer repeatedly since the foundation of the world. But as it is, he has appeared once for all at the end of the ages to put away sin by the sacrifice of himself.

27 And just as it is appointed for man to die once, and after that comes judgment,

28 so Christ, having been offered once to bear the sins of many, will appear a second time, not to deal with sin but to save those who are eagerly waiting for him.

CHAPTER 10

1 For since the law has but a shadow of the good things to come instead of the true form of these realities, it can nev-er, by the same sacrifices that are continually offered every year, make perfect those who draw near.

2 Otherwise, would they not have ceased to be offered, since the worshipers, having once been cleansed, would no longer have any consciousness of sins?

3 But in these sacrifices there is a reminder of sins every year.

4 For it is impossible for the blood of bulls and goats to take away sins.

5 Consequently, when Christ came into the world, he said, "Sacrifices and offerings you have not desired, but a body have you prepared for me;

6 "in burnt offerings and sin offerings you have taken no pleasure.

7 "Then I said, 'Behold, I have come to do your will, O God, as it is written of me in the scroll of the book.'"

8 When he said above, "You have neither desired nor taken pleasure in sacrifices and offerings and burnt offerings and sin offerings" (these are offered according to the law),

9 then he added, "Behold, I have come to do your will." He does away with the first in order to establish the second.

10 And by that will we have

been sanctified through the offering of the body of Jesus Christ once for all.

11 And every priest stands daily at his service, offering repeatedly the same sacrifices, which can never take away sins.

12 But when Christ had offered for all time a single sacrifice for sins, he sat down at the right hand of God,

13 waiting from that time until his enemies should be made a footstool for his feet.

14 For by a single offering he has perfected for all time those who are being sanctified.

15 And the Holy Spirit also bears witness to us; for after saying,

16 "This is the covenant that I will make with them after those days, declares the Lord: I will put my laws on their hearts, and write them on their minds,"

17 then he adds, "I will remember their sins and their lawless deeds no more."

18 Where there is forgiveness of these, there is no longer any offering for sin.

19 Therefore, brothers, since we have confidence to enter the holy places by the blood of Jesus,

20 by the new and living way that he opened for us through the curtain, that is, through his flesh,

21 and since we have a great priest over the house of God,

22 let us draw near with a true heart in full assurance of faith, with our hearts sprinkled clean from an evil conscience and our bodies washed with pure water.

23 Let us hold fast the confession of our hope without wavering, for he who promised is faithful.

24 And let us consider how to stir up one another to love and good works,

25 not neglecting to meet together, as is the habit of some, but encouraging one another, and all the more as you see the Day drawing near.

26 For if we go on sinning deliberately after receiving the knowledge of the truth, there no longer remains a sacrifice for sins,

27 but a fearful expectation of judgment, and a fury of fire that will consume the adversaries.

28 Anyone who has set aside the law of Moses dies without mercy on the evidence of two or three witnesses.

29 How much worse punishment, do you think, will be deserved by the one who has trampled underfoot the Son of God, and has profaned the

the blood of the covenant by which he was sanctified, and has outraged the Spirit of grace?

30 For we know him who said, "Vengeance is mine; I will repay." And again, "The Lord will judge his people."

31 It is a fearful thing to fall into the hands of the living God.

32 But recall the former days when, after you were enlightened, you endured a hard struggle with sufferings,

33 sometimes being publicly exposed to reproach and affliction, and sometimes being partners with those so treated.

34 For you had compassion on those in prison, and you joyfully accepted the plundering of your property, since you knew that you yourselves had a better possession and an abiding one.

35 Therefore do not throw away your confidence, which has a great reward.

36 For you have need of endurance, so that when you have done the will of God you may receive what is promised.

37 For, "Yet a little while, and the coming one will come and will not delay;

38 "but my righteous one shall live by faith, and if he shrinks back, my soul has no pleasure in him."

39 But we are not of those who shrink back and are destroyed, but of those who have faith and preserve their souls.

CHAPTER 11

1 Now faith is the assurance of things hoped for, the conviction of things not seen.

2 For by it the people of old received their commendation.

3 By faith we understand that the universe was created by the word of God, so that what is seen was not made out of things that are visible.

4 By faith Abel offered to God a more acceptable sacrifice than Cain, through which he was commended as righteous, God commending him by accepting his gifts. And through his faith, though he died, he still speaks.

5 By faith Enoch was taken up so that he should not see death, and he was not found, because God had taken him. Now before he was taken he was commended as having pleased God.

6 And without faith it is impossible to please him, for whoever would draw near to God must believe that he

exists and that he rewards those who seek him.

⁷ By faith Noah, being warned by God concerning events as yet unseen, in reverent fear constructed an ark for the saving of his household. By this he condemned the world and became an heir of the righteousness that comes by faith.

⁸ By faith Abraham obeyed when he was called to go out to a place that he was to receive as an inheritance. And he went out, not knowing where he was going.

⁹ By faith he went to live in the land of promise, living as in a foreign land, living in tents with Isaac and Jacob, heirs with him of the same promise.

¹⁰ For he was looking forward to the city that has foundations, whose designer and builder is God.

¹¹ By faith Sarah herself received power to conceive, even when she was past the age, since she considered him faithful who had promised.

¹² Therefore from one man, and him as good as dead, were born descendants as many as the stars of heaven and as many as the innumerable grains of sand by the seashore.

¹³ These all died in faith, not having received the things promised, but having seen them and greeted them from afar, and having acknowledged that they were strangers and exiles on the earth.

¹⁴ For people who speak thus make it clear that they are seeking a homeland.

¹⁵ If they had been thinking of that land from which they had gone out, they would have had opportunity to return.

¹⁶ But as it is, they desire a better country, that is, a heavenly one. Therefore God is not ashamed to be called their God, for he has prepared for them a city.

¹⁷ By faith Abraham, when he was tested, offered up Isaac, and he who had received the promises was in the act of offering up his only son,

¹⁸ of whom it was said, "Through Isaac shall your offspring be named."

¹⁹ He considered that God was able even to raise him from the dead, from which, figuratively speaking, he did receive him back.

²⁰ By faith Isaac invoked future blessings on Jacob and Esau.

²¹ By faith Jacob, when dying, blessed each of the sons of Joseph, bowing in worship over the head of his staff.

22 By faith Joseph, at the end of his life, made mention of the exodus of the Israelites and gave directions concerning his bones.

23 By faith Moses, when he was born, was hidden for three months by his parents, because they saw that the child was beautiful, and they were not afraid of the king's edict.

24 By faith Moses, when he was grown up, refused to be called the son of Pharaoh's daughter,

25 choosing rather to be mistreated with the people of God than to enjoy the fleeting pleasures of sin.

26 He considered the reproach of Christ greater wealth than the treasures of Egypt, for he was looking to the reward.

27 By faith he left Egypt, not being afraid of the anger of the king, for he endured as seeing him who is invisible.

28 By faith he kept the Passover and sprinkled the blood, so that the Destroyer of the firstborn might not touch them.

29 By faith the people crossed the Red Sea as on dry land, but the Egyptians, when they attempted to do the same, were drowned.

30 By faith the walls of Jericho fell down after they had been encircled for seven days.

31 By faith Rahab the prostitute did not perish with those who were disobedient, because she had given a friendly welcome to the spies.

32 And what more shall I say? For time would fail me to tell of Gideon, Barak, Samson, Jephthah, of David and Samuel and the prophets—

33 who through faith conquered kingdoms, enforced justice, obtained promises, stopped the mouths of lions,

34 quenched the power of fire, escaped the edge of the sword, were made strong out of weakness, became mighty in war, put foreign armies to flight.

35 Women received back their dead by resurrection. Some were tortured, refusing to accept release, so that they might rise again to a better life.

36 Others suffered mocking and flogging, and even chains and imprisonment.

37 They were stoned, they were sawn in two, they were tempted, they were killed with the sword. They went about in skins of sheep and goats, destitute, afflicted, mistreated—

38 of whom the world was not worthy—wandering about in deserts and mountains, and in dens and caves of the earth.

39 And all these, though commended through their faith, did not receive what was promised,

40 since God had provided something better for us, that apart from us they should not be made perfect.

CHAPTER 12

1 Therefore, since we are surrounded by so great a cloud of witnesses, let us also lay aside every weight, and sin which clings so closely, and let us run with endurance the race that is set before us,

2 looking to Jesus, the founder and perfecter of our faith, who for the joy that was set before him endured the cross, despising the shame, and is seated at the right hand of the throne of God.

3 Consider him who endured from sinners such hostility against himself, so that you may not grow weary or fainthearted.

4 In your struggle against sin you have not yet resisted to the point of shedding your blood.

5 And have you forgotten the exhortation that addresses you as sons? "My son, do not regard lightly the discipline of the Lord, nor be weary when reproved by him.

6 "For the Lord disciplines the one he loves, and chastises every son whom he receives."

7 It is for discipline that you have to endure. God is treating you as sons. For what son is there whom his father does not discipline?

8 If you are left without discipline, in which all have participated, then you are illegitimate children and not sons.

9 Besides this, we have had earthly fathers who disciplined us and we respected them. Shall we not much more be subject to the Father of spirits and live?

10 For they disciplined us for a short time as it seemed best to them, but he disciplines us for our good, that we may share his holiness.

11 For the moment all discipline seems painful rather than pleasant, but later it yields the peaceful fruit of righteousness to those who have been trained by it.

12 Therefore lift your drooping hands and strengthen your weak knees,

13 and make straight paths for your feet, so that what is

lame may not be put out of joint but rather be healed.

¹⁴ Strive for peace with everyone, and for the holiness without which no one will see *the Lord.*

¹⁵ See to it that no one fails to obtain the grace of God; that no "root of bitterness" springs up and causes trouble, and by it many become defiled;

¹⁶ that no one is sexually immoral or unholy like Esau, who sold his birthright for a single meal.

¹⁷ For you know that afterward, when he desired to inherit the blessing, he was rejected, for he found no chance to repent, though he sought it with tears.

¹⁸ For you have not come to what may be touched, a blazing fire and darkness and gloom and a tempest

¹⁹ and the sound of a trumpet and a voice whose words made the hearers beg that no further messages be spoken to them.

²⁰ For they could not endure the order that was given, "If even a beast touches the mountain, it shall be stoned."

²¹ Indeed, so terrifying was the sight that Moses said, "I tremble with fear."

²² But you have come to Mount Zion and to the city of the living God, the heavenly Jerusalem, and to innumerable angels in festal gathering,

²³ and to the assembly of the firstborn who are enrolled in heaven, and to God, the judge of all, and to the spirits of the righteous made perfect,

²⁴ and to Jesus, the mediator of a new covenant, and to the sprinkled blood that speaks a better word than the blood of Abel.

²⁵ See that you do not refuse him who is speaking. For if they did not escape when they refused him who warned them on earth, much less will we escape if we reject him who warns from heaven.

²⁶ At that time his voice shook the earth, but now he has promised, "Yet once more I will shake not only the earth but also the heavens."

²⁷ This phrase, "Yet once more," indicates the removal of things that are shaken—that is, things that have been made—in order that the things that cannot be shaken may remain.

²⁸ Therefore let us be grateful for receiving a kingdom that cannot be shaken, and thus let us offer to God acceptable worship, with reverence and awe,

²⁹ for our God is a consuming fire.

CHAPTER 13

¹ Let brotherly love continue.

² Do not neglect to show hospitality to strangers, for thereby some have entertained angels unawares.

³ Remember those who are in prison, as though in prison with them, and those who are mistreated, since you also are in the body.

⁴ Let marriage be held in honor among all, and let the marriage bed be undefiled, for God will judge the sexually immoral and adulterous.

⁵ Keep your life free from love of money, and be content with what you have, for he has said, "I will never leave you nor forsake you."

⁶ So we can confidently say, "The Lord is my helper; I will not fear; what can man do to me?"

⁷ Remember your leaders, those who spoke to you the word of God. Consider the outcome of their way of life, and imitate their faith.

⁸ Jesus Christ is the same yesterday and today and forever.

⁹ Do not be led away by diverse and strange teachings, for it is good for the heart to be strengthened by grace, not by foods, which have not benefited those devoted to them.

¹⁰ We have an altar from which those who serve the tent have no right to eat.

¹¹ For the bodies of those animals whose blood is brought into the holy places by the high priest as a sacrifice for sin are burned outside the camp.

¹² So Jesus also suffered outside the gate in order to sanctify the people through his own blood.

¹³ Therefore let us go to him outside the camp and bear the reproach he endured.

¹⁴ For here we have no lasting city, but we seek the city that is to come.

¹⁵ Through him then let us continually offer up a sacrifice of praise to God, that is, the fruit of lips that acknowledge his name.

¹⁶ Do not neglect to do good and to share what you have, for such sacrifices are pleasing to God.

¹⁷ Obey your leaders and submit to them, for they are keeping watch over your souls, as those who will have to give an account. Let them do this with joy and not with groaning, for that would be of no advantage to you.

¹⁸ Pray for us, for we are sure that we have a clear conscience, desiring to act honorably in all things.

19 I urge you the more earnestly to do this in order that I may be restored to you the sooner.

20 Now may the God of peace who brought again from the dead our Lord Jesus, the great shepherd of the sheep, through the blood of the eternal covenant,

21 equip you with everything good that you may do his will, working in us that which is pleasing in his sight, through Jesus Christ, to whom be glory forever and ever. Amen.

22 I appeal to you, brothers, bear with my word of exhortation, for I have written to you briefly.

23 You should know that our brother Timothy has been released, with whom I shall see you if he comes soon.

24 Greet all your leaders and all the saints. Those who come from Italy send you greetings.

25 Grace be with all of you.

THE LETTER OF

JAMES

CHAPTER 1

1 James, a servant of God and of the Lord Jesus Christ, To the twelve tribes in the Dispersion: Greetings.

2 Count it all joy, my brothers, when you meet trials of various kinds,

3 for you know that the testing of your faith produces steadfastness.

4 And let steadfastness have its full effect, that you may be perfect and complete, lacking in nothing.

5 If any of you lacks wisdom, let him ask God, who gives generously to all without reproach, and it will be given him.

6 But let him ask in faith, with no doubting, for the one who doubts is like a wave of the sea that is driven and tossed by the wind.

7 For that person must not suppose that he will receive anything from the Lord;

8 he is a double-minded man, unstable in all his ways.

9 Let the lowly brother boast in his exaltation,

10 and the rich in his humiliation, because like a flower of the grass he will pass away.

¹¹ For the sun rises with its scorching heat and withers the grass; its flower falls, and its beauty perishes. So also will the rich man fade away in the midst of his pursuits.

¹² Blessed is the man who remains steadfast under trial, for when he has stood the test he will receive the crown of life, which God has promised to those who love him.

¹³ Let no one say when he is tempted, "I am being tempted by God," for God cannot be tempted with evil, and he himself tempts no one.

¹⁴ But each person is tempted when he is lured and enticed by his own desire.

¹⁵ Then desire when it has conceived gives birth to sin, and sin when it is fully grown brings forth death.

¹⁶ Do not be deceived, my beloved brothers.

¹⁷ Every good gift and every perfect gift is from above, coming down from the Father of lights with whom there is no variation *or shadow due* to change.

¹⁸ Of his own will he brought us forth by the word of truth, that we should be a kind of firstfruits of his creatures.

¹⁹ Know this, my beloved brothers: let every person be quick to hear, slow to speak, slow to anger;

²⁰ for the anger of man does not produce the righteousness of God.

²¹ Therefore put away all filthiness and rampant wickedness and receive with meekness the implanted word, which is able to save your souls.

²² But be doers of the word, and not hearers only, deceiving yourselves.

²³ For if anyone is a hearer of the word and not a doer, he is like a man who looks intently at his natural face in a mirror.

²⁴ For he looks at himself and goes away and at once forgets what he was like.

²⁵ But the one who looks into the perfect law, the law of liberty, and perseveres, being no hearer who forgets but a doer who acts, he will be blessed in his doing.

²⁶ If anyone thinks he is religious and does not bridle his tongue but deceives his heart, this person's religion is worthless.

²⁷ Religion that is pure and undefiled before God, the Father, is this: to visit orphans and widows in their affliction, and to keep oneself unstained from the world.

CHAPTER 2

¹ My brothers, show no partiality as you hold the faith

in our Lord Jesus Christ, the Lord of glory.

² For if a man wearing a gold ring and fine clothing comes into your assembly, and a poor man in shabby clothing also comes in,

³ and if you pay attention to the one who wears the fine clothing and say, "You sit here in a good place," while you say to the poor man, "You stand over there," or, "Sit down at my feet,"

⁴ have you not then made distinctions among yourselves and become judges with evil thoughts?

⁵ Listen, my beloved brothers, has not God chosen those who are poor in the world to be rich in faith and heirs of the kingdom, which he has promised to those who love him?

⁶ But you have dishonored the poor man. Are not the rich the ones who oppress you, and the ones who drag you into court?

⁷ Are they not the ones who blaspheme the honorable name by which you were called?

⁸ If you really fulfill the royal law according to the Scripture, "You shall love your neighbor as yourself," you are doing well.

⁹ But if you show partiality, you are committing sin and are convicted by the law as transgressors.

¹⁰ For whoever keeps the whole law but fails in one point has become accountable for all of it.

¹¹ For he who said, "Do not commit adultery," also said, "Do not murder." If you do not commit adultery but do murder, you have become a transgressor of the law.

¹² So speak and so act as those who are to be judged under the law of liberty.

¹³ For judgment is without mercy to one who has shown no mercy. Mercy triumphs over judgment.

¹⁴ What good is it, my brothers, if someone says he has faith but does not have works? Can that faith save him?

¹⁵ If a brother or sister is poorly clothed and lacking in daily food,

¹⁶ and one of you says to them, "Go in peace, be warmed and filled," without giving them the things needed for the body, what good is that?

¹⁷ So also faith by itself, if it does not have works, is dead.

¹⁸ But someone will say, "You have faith and I have works." Show me your faith apart from your works, and

I will show you my faith by my works.

¹⁹ You believe that God is one; you do well. Even the demons believe—and shudder!

²⁰ Do you want to be shown, you foolish person, that faith apart from works is useless?

²¹ Was not Abraham our father justified by works when he offered up his son Isaac on the altar?

²² You see that faith was active along with his works, and faith was completed by his works;

²³ and the Scripture was fulfilled that says, "Abraham believed God, and it was counted to him as righteousness"—and he was called a friend of God.

²⁴ You see that a person is justified by works and not by faith alone.

²⁵ And in the same way was not also Rahab the prostitute justified by works when she received the messengers and sent them out by another way?

²⁶ For as the body apart from the spirit is dead, so also faith apart from works is dead.

CHAPTER 3

¹ Not many of you should become teachers, my brothers, for you know that we who teach will be judged with greater strictness.

² For we all stumble in many ways. And if anyone does not stumble in what he says, he is a perfect man, able also to bridle his whole body.

³ If we put bits into the mouths of horses so that they obey us, we guide their whole bodies as well.

⁴ Look at the ships also: though they are so large and are driven by strong winds, they are guided by a very small rudder wherever the will of the pilot directs.

⁵ So also the tongue is a small member, yet it boasts of great things. How great a forest is set ablaze by such a small fire!

⁶ And the tongue is a fire, a world of unrighteousness. The tongue is set among our members, staining the whole body, setting on fire the entire course of life, and set on fire by hell.

⁷ For every kind of beast and bird, of reptile and sea creature, can be tamed and has been tamed by mankind,

⁸ but no human being can tame the tongue. It is a restless evil, full of deadly poison.

⁹ With it we bless our Lord and Father, and with it we curse people who are made in the likeness of God.

10 From the same mouth come blessing and cursing. My brothers, these things ought not to be so.

11 Does a spring pour forth from the same opening both fresh and salt water?

12 Can a fig tree, my brothers, bear olives, or a grapevine produce figs? Neither can a salt pond yield fresh water.

13 Who is wise and understanding among you? By his good conduct let him show his works in the meekness of wisdom.

14 But if you have bitter jealousy and selfish ambition in your hearts, do not boast and be false to the truth.

15 This is not the wisdom that comes down from above, but is earthly, unspiritual, demonic.

16 For where jealousy and selfish ambition exist, there will be disorder and every vile practice.

17 But the wisdom from above is first pure, then peaceable, gentle, open to reason, full of mercy and good fruits, impartial and sincere.

18 And a harvest of righteousness is sown in peace by those who make peace.

CHAPTER 4

1 What causes quarrels and what causes fights among you? Is it not this, that your passions are at war within you?

2 You desire and do not have, so you murder. You covet and cannot obtain, so you fight and quarrel. You do not have, because you do not ask.

3 You ask and do not receive, because you ask wrongly, to spend it on your passions.

4 You adulterous people! Do you not know that friendship with the world is enmity with God? Therefore whoever wishes to be a friend of the world makes himself an enemy of God.

5 Or do you suppose it is to no purpose that the Scripture says, "He yearns jealously over the spirit that he has made to dwell in us"?

6 But he gives more grace. Therefore it says, "God opposes the proud, but gives grace to the humble."

7 Submit yourselves therefore to God. Resist the devil, and he will flee from you.

8 Draw near to God, and he will draw near to you. Cleanse your hands, you sinners, and purify your hearts, you double-minded.

9 Be wretched and mourn and weep. Let your laughter be turned to mourning and your joy to gloom.

10 Humble yourselves before the Lord, and he will exalt you.

11 Do not speak evil against one another, brothers. The one who speaks against a brother or judges his brother, speaks evil against the law and judges the law. But if you judge the law, you are not a doer of the law but a judge.

12 There is only one lawgiver and judge, he who is able to save and to destroy. But who are you to judge your neighbor?

13 Come now, you who say, "Today or tomorrow we will go into such and such a town and spend a year there and trade and make a profit"—

14 yet you do not know what tomorrow will bring. What is your life? For you are a mist that appears for a little time and then vanishes.

15 Instead you ought to say, "If the Lord wills, we will live and do this or that."

16 As it is, you boast in your arrogance. All such boasting is evil.

17 So whoever knows the right thing to do and fails to do it, for him it is sin.

CHAPTER 5

1 Come now, you rich, weep and howl for the miseries that are coming upon you.

2 Your riches have rotted and your garments are moth-eaten.

3 Your gold and silver have corroded, and their corrosion will be evidence against you and will eat your flesh like fire. You have laid up treasure in the last days.

4 Behold, the wages of the laborers who mowed your fields, which you kept back by fraud, are crying out against you, and the cries of the harvesters have reached the ears of the Lord of hosts.

5 You have lived on the earth in luxury and in self-indulgence. You have fattened your hearts in a day of slaughter.

6 You have condemned and murdered the righteous person. He does not resist you.

7 Be patient, therefore, brothers, until the coming of the Lord. See how the farmer waits for the precious fruit of the earth, being patient about it, until it receives the early and the late rains.

8 You also, be patient. Establish your hearts, for the coming of the Lord is at hand.

9 Do not grumble against one another, brothers, so that you may not be judged; behold, the Judge is standing at the door.

¹⁰ As an example of suffering and patience, brothers, take the prophets who spoke in the name of the Lord.

¹¹ Behold, we consider those blessed who remained steadfast. You have heard of the steadfastness of Job, and you have seen the purpose of the Lord, how the Lord is compassionate and merciful.

¹² But above all, my brothers, do not swear, either by heaven or by earth or by any other oath, but let your "yes" be yes and your "no" be no, so that you may not fall under condemnation.

¹³ Is anyone among you suffering? Let him pray. Is anyone cheerful? Let him sing praise.

¹⁴ Is anyone among you sick? Let him call for the elders of the church, and let them pray over him, anointing him with oil in the name of the Lord.

¹⁵ And the prayer of faith will save the one who is sick, and the Lord will raise him up. And if he has committed sins, he will be forgiven.

¹⁶ Therefore, confess your sins to one another and pray for one another, that you may be healed. The prayer of a righteous person has great power as it is working.

¹⁷ Elijah was a man with a nature like ours, and he prayed fervently that it might not rain, and for three years and six months it did not rain on the earth.

¹⁸ Then he prayed again, and heaven gave rain, and the earth bore its fruit.

¹⁹ My brothers, if anyone among you wanders from the truth and someone brings him back,

²⁰ let him know that whoever brings back a sinner from his wandering will save his soul from death and will cover a multitude of sins.

THE FIRST LETTER OF PETER

1 PETER

CHAPTER 1

¹ Peter, an apostle of Jesus Christ, To those who are elect exiles of the Dispersion in Pontus, Galatia, Cappadocia, Asia, and Bithynia,

² according to the foreknowledge of God the Father,

in the sanctification of the Spirit, for obedience to Jesus Christ and for sprinkling with his blood: May grace and peace be multiplied to you.

³ Blessed be the God and Father of our Lord Jesus Christ! According to his great mercy, he has caused us to be born again to a living hope through the resurrection of Jesus Christ from the dead,

⁴ to an inheritance that is imperishable, undefiled, and unfading, kept in heaven for you,

⁵ who by God's power are being guarded through faith for a salvation ready to be revealed in the last time.

⁶ In this you rejoice, though now for a little while, if necessary, you have been grieved by various trials,

⁷ so that the tested genuineness of your faith—more precious than gold that perishes though it is tested by fire—may be found to result in praise and glory and honor at the revelation of Jesus Christ.

⁸ Though you have not seen him, you love him. Though you do not now see him, you believe in him and rejoice with joy that is inexpressible and filled with glory,

⁹ obtaining the outcome of your faith, the salvation of your souls.

¹⁰ Concerning this salvation, the prophets who prophesied about the grace that was to be yours searched and inquired carefully,

¹¹ inquiring what person or time the Spirit of Christ in them was indicating when he predicted the sufferings of Christ and the subsequent glories.

¹² It was revealed to them that they were serving not themselves but you, in the things that have now been announced to you through those who preached the good news to you by the Holy Spirit sent from heaven, things into which angels long to look.

¹³ Therefore, preparing your minds for action, and being sober-minded, set your hope fully on the grace that will be brought to you at the revelation of Jesus Christ.

¹⁴ As obedient children, do not be conformed to the passions of your former ignorance,

¹⁵ but as he who called you is holy, you also be holy in all your conduct,

¹⁶ since it is written, "You shall be holy, for I am holy."

¹⁷ And if you call on him as Father who judges impartially according to each one's deeds, conduct yourselves with fear

throughout the time of your exile,

¹⁸ knowing that you were redeemed from the futile ways inherited from your forefathers, not with perishable things such as silver or gold,

¹⁹ but with the precious blood of Christ, like that of a lamb without blemish or spot.

²⁰ He was foreknown before the foundation of the world but was made manifest in the last times for the sake of you

²¹ who through him are believers in God, who raised him from the dead and gave him glory, so that your faith and hope are in God.

²² Having purified your souls by your obedience to the truth for a sincere brotherly love, love one another earnestly from a pure heart,

²³ since you have been born again, not of perishable seed but of imperishable, through the living and abiding word of God;

²⁴ for "All flesh is like grass and all its glory like the flower of grass. The grass withers, and the flower falls,

²⁵ "but the word of the Lord remains forever." And this word is the good news that was preached to you.

¹ So put away all malice and all deceit and hypocrisy and envy and all slander.

² Like newborn infants, long for the pure spiritual milk, that by it you may grow up into salvation—

³ if indeed you have tasted that the Lord is good.

⁴ As you come to him, a living stone rejected by men but in the sight of God chosen and precious,

⁵ you yourselves like living stones are being built up as a spiritual house, to be a holy priesthood, to offer spiritual sacrifices acceptable to God through Jesus Christ.

⁶ For it stands in Scripture: "Behold, I am laying in Zion a stone, a cornerstone chosen and precious, and whoever believes in him will not be put to shame."

⁷ So the honor is for you who believe, but for those who do not believe, "The stone that the builders rejected has become the cornerstone,"

⁸ and "A stone of stumbling, and a rock of offense." They stumble because they disobey the word, as they were destined to do.

⁹ But you are a chosen race, a royal priesthood, a holy nation, a people for his own possession, that you may

proclaim the excellencies of him who called you out of darkness into his marvelous light.

¹⁰ Once you were not a people, but now you are God's people; once you had not received mercy, but now you have received mercy.

¹¹ Beloved, I urge you as sojourners and exiles to abstain from the passions of the flesh, which wage war against your soul.

¹² Keep your conduct among the Gentiles honorable, so that when they speak against you as evildoers, they may see your good deeds and glorify God on the day of visitation.

¹³ Be subject for the Lord's sake to every human institution, whether it be to the emperor as supreme,

¹⁴ or to governors as sent by him to punish those who do evil and to praise those who do good.

¹⁵ For this is the will of God, that by doing good you should put to silence the ignorance of foolish people.

¹⁶ Live as people who are free, not using your freedom as a cover-up for evil, but living as servants of God.

¹⁷ Honor everyone. Love the brotherhood. Fear God. Honor the emperor.

¹⁸ Servants, be subject to your masters with all respect, not only to the good and gentle but also to the unjust.

¹⁹ For this is a gracious thing, when, mindful of God, one endures sorrows while suffering unjustly.

²⁰ For what credit is it if, when you sin and are beaten for it, you endure? But if when you do good and suffer for it you endure, this is a gracious thing in the sight of God.

²¹ For to this you have been called, because Christ also suffered for you, leaving you an example, so that you might follow in his steps.

²² He committed no sin, neither was deceit found in his mouth.

²³ When he was reviled, he did not revile in return; when he suffered, he did not threaten, but continued entrusting himself to him who judges justly.

²⁴ He himself bore our sins in his body on the tree, that we might die to sin and live to righteousness. By his wounds you have been healed.

²⁵ For you were straying like sheep, but have now returned to the Shepherd and Overseer of your souls.

CHAPTER 3

¹ Likewise, wives, be subject to your own husbands, so that

even if some do not obey the word, they may be won without a word by the conduct of their wives,

² when they see your respectful and pure conduct.

³ Do not let your adorning be external—the braiding of hair and the putting on of gold jewelry, or the clothing you wear—

⁴ but let your adorning be the hidden person of the heart with the imperishable beauty of a gentle and quiet spirit, which in God's sight is very precious.

⁵ For this is how the holy women who hoped in God used to adorn themselves, by submitting to their own husbands,

⁶ as Sarah obeyed Abraham, calling him lord. And you are her children, if you do good and do not fear anything that is frightening.

⁷ Likewise, husbands, live with your wives in an understanding way, showing honor to the woman as the weaker vessel, since they are heirs with you of the grace of life, so that your prayers may not be hindered.

⁸ Finally, all of you, have unity of mind, sympathy, brotherly love, a tender heart, and a humble mind.

⁹ Do not repay evil for evil or reviling for reviling, but on the contrary, bless, for to this you were called, that you may obtain a blessing.

¹⁰ For "Whoever desires to love life and see good days, let him keep his tongue from evil and his lips from speaking deceit;

¹¹ "let him turn away from evil and do good; let him seek peace and pursue it.

¹² "For the eyes of the Lord are on the righteous, and his ears are open to their prayer. But the face of the Lord is against those who do evil."

¹³ Now who is there to harm you if you are zealous for what is good?

¹⁴ But even if you should suffer for righteousness' sake, you will be blessed. Have no fear of them, nor be troubled,

¹⁵ but in your hearts honor Christ the Lord as holy, always being prepared to make a defense to anyone who asks you for a reason for the hope that is in you; yet do it with gentleness and respect,

¹⁶ having a good conscience, so that, when you are slandered, those who revile your good behavior in Christ may be put to shame.

¹⁷ For it is better to suffer for doing good, if that should be God's will, than for doing evil.

¹⁸ For Christ also suffered

once for sins, the righteous for the unrighteous, that he might bring us to God, being put to death in the flesh but made alive in the spirit,

19 in which he went and proclaimed to the spirits in prison,

20 because they formerly did not obey, when God's patience waited in the days of Noah, while the ark was being prepared, in which a few, that is, eight persons, were brought safely through water.

21 Baptism, which corresponds to this, now saves you, not as a removal of dirt from the body but as an appeal to God for a good conscience, through the resurrection of Jesus Christ,

22 who has gone into heaven and is at the right hand of God, with angels, authorities, and powers having been subjected to him.

CHAPTER 4

1 Since therefore Christ suffered in the flesh, arm yourselves with the same way of thinking, for whoever has suffered in the flesh has ceased from sin,

2 so as to live for the rest of the time in the flesh no longer for human passions but for the will of God.

3 For the time that is past suffices for doing what the Gentiles want to do, living in sensuality, passions, drunkenness, orgies, drinking parties, and lawless idolatry.

4 With respect to this they are surprised when you do not join them in the same flood of debauchery, and they malign you;

5 but they will give account to him who is ready to judge the living and the dead.

6 For this is why the gospel was preached even to those who are dead, that though judged in the flesh the way people are, they might live in the spirit the way God does.

7 The end of all things is at hand; therefore be self-controlled and sober-minded for the sake of your prayers.

8 Above all, keep loving one another earnestly, since love covers a multitude of sins.

9 Show hospitality to one another without grumbling.

10 As each has received a gift, use it to serve one another, as good stewards of God's varied grace:

11 whoever speaks, as one who speaks oracles of God; whoever serves, as one who serves by the strength that God supplies—in order that in everything God may be glorified through Jesus Christ.

To him belong glory and dominion forever and ever. Amen.

¹² Beloved, do not be surprised at the fiery trial when it comes upon you to test you, as though something strange were happening to you.

¹³ But rejoice insofar as you share Christ's sufferings, that you may also rejoice and be glad when his glory is revealed.

¹⁴ If you are insulted for the name of Christ, you are blessed, because the Spirit of glory and of God rests upon you.

¹⁵ But let none of you suffer as a murderer or a thief or an evildoer or as a meddler.

¹⁶ Yet if anyone suffers as a Christian, let him not be ashamed, but let him glorify God in that name.

¹⁷ For it is time for judgment to begin at the household of God; and if it begins with us, what will be the outcome for those who do not obey the gospel of God?

¹⁸ And "If the righteous is scarcely saved, what will become of the ungodly and the sinner?"

¹⁹ Therefore let those who suffer according to God's will entrust their souls to a faithful Creator while doing good.

CHAPTER 5

¹ So I exhort the elders among you, as a fellow elder and a witness of the sufferings of Christ, as well as a partaker in the glory that is going to be revealed:

² shepherd the flock of God that is among you, exercising oversight, not under compulsion, but willingly, as God would have you; not for shameful gain, but eagerly;

³ not domineering over those in your charge, but being examples to the flock.

⁴ And when the chief Shepherd appears, you will receive the unfading crown of glory.

⁵ Likewise, you who are younger, be subject to the elders. Clothe yourselves, all of you, with humility toward one another, for "God opposes the proud but gives grace to the humble."

⁶ Humble yourselves, therefore, under the mighty hand of God so that at the proper time he may exalt you,

⁷ casting all your anxieties on him, because he cares for you.

⁸ Be sober-minded; be watchful. Your adversary the devil prowls around like a roaring lion, seeking someone to devour.

⁹ Resist him, firm in your

faith, knowing that the same kinds of suffering are being experienced by your brotherhood throughout the world.

¹⁰ And after you have suffered a little while, the God of all grace, who has called you to his eternal glory in Christ, will himself restore, confirm, strengthen, and establish you.

¹¹ To him be the dominion forever and ever. Amen.

¹² By Silvanus, a faithful brother as I regard him, I have written briefly to you, exhorting and declaring that this is the true grace of God. Stand firm in it.

¹³ She who is at Babylon, who is likewise chosen, sends you greetings; and so does Mark, my son.

¹⁴ Greet one another with the kiss of love. Peace to all of you who are in Christ.

THE SECOND LETTER OF PETER

2 PETER

CHAPTER 1

¹ Simeon Peter, a servant and apostle of Jesus Christ, To those who have obtained a faith of equal standing with ours by the righteousness of our God and Savior Jesus Christ:

² May grace and peace be multiplied to you in the knowledge of God and of Jesus our Lord.

³ His divine power has granted to us all things that pertain to life and godliness, through the knowledge of him who called us to his own glory and excellence,

⁴ by which he has granted to us his precious and very great promises, so that through them you may become partakers of the divine nature, having escaped from the corruption that is in the world because of sinful desire.

⁵ For this very reason, make every effort to supplement your faith with virtue, and virtue with knowledge,

⁶ and knowledge with self-control, and self-control with steadfastness, and steadfastness with godliness,

⁷ and godliness with brotherly affection, and brotherly affection with love.

⁸ For if these qualities are yours and are increasing, they keep you from being

ineffective or unfruitful in the knowledge of our Lord Jesus Christ.

⁹ For whoever lacks these qualities is so nearsighted that he is blind, having forgotten that he was cleansed from his former sins.

¹⁰ Therefore, brothers, be all the more diligent to confirm your calling and election, for if you practice these qualities you will never fall.

¹¹ For in this way there will be richly provided for you an entrance into the eternal kingdom of our Lord and Savior Jesus Christ.

¹² Therefore I intend always to remind you of these qualities, though you know them and are established in the truth that you have.

¹³ I think it right, as long as I am in this body, to stir you up by way of reminder,

¹⁴ since I know that the putting off of my body will be soon, as our Lord Jesus Christ made clear to me.

¹⁵ And I will make every effort so that after my departure you may be able at any time to recall these things.

¹⁶ For we did not follow cleverly devised myths when we made known to you the power and coming of our Lord Jesus Christ, but we were eyewitnesses of his majesty.

¹⁷ For when he received honor and glory from God the Father, and the voice was borne to him by the Majestic Glory, "This is my beloved Son, with whom I am well pleased,"

¹⁸ we ourselves heard this very voice borne from heaven, for we were with him on the holy mountain.

¹⁹ And we have the prophetic word more fully confirmed, to which you will do well to pay attention as to a lamp shining in a dark place, until the day dawns and the morning star rises in your hearts,

²⁰ knowing this first of all, that no prophecy of Scripture comes from someone's own interpretation.

²¹ For no prophecy was ever produced by the will of man, but men spoke from God as they were carried along by the Holy Spirit.

CHAPTER 2

¹ But false prophets also arose among the people, just as there will be false teachers among you, who will secretly bring in destructive heresies, even denying the Master who bought them, bringing upon themselves swift destruction.

² And many will follow their sensuality, and because of them the way of truth will be blasphemed.

³ And in their greed they will exploit you with false words. Their condemnation from long ago is not idle, and their destruction is not asleep.

⁴ For if God did not spare angels when they sinned, but cast them into hell and committed them to chains of gloomy darkness to be kept until the judgment;

⁵ if he did not spare the ancient world, but preserved Noah, a herald of righteousness, with seven others, when he brought a flood upon the world of the ungodly;

⁶ if by turning the cities of Sodom and Gomorrah to ashes he condemned them to extinction, making them an example of what is going to happen to the ungodly;

⁷ and if he rescued righteous Lot, greatly distressed by the sensual conduct of the wicked

⁸ (for as that righteous man lived among them day after day, he was tormenting his righteous soul over their lawless deeds that he saw and heard);

⁹ then the Lord knows how to rescue the godly from trials, and to keep the unrighteous under punishment until the day of judgment,

¹⁰ and especially those who indulge in the lust of defiling passion and despise authority. Bold and willful, they do not tremble as they blaspheme the glorious ones,

¹¹ whereas angels, though greater in might and power, do not pronounce a blasphemous judgment against them before the Lord.

¹² But these, like irrational animals, creatures of instinct, born to be caught and destroyed, blaspheming about matters of which they are ignorant, will also be destroyed in their destruction,

¹³ suffering wrong as the wage for their wrongdoing. They count it pleasure to revel in the daytime. They are blots and blemishes, reveling in their deceptions, while they feast with you.

¹⁴ They have eyes full of adultery, insatiable for sin. They entice unsteady souls. They have hearts trained in greed. Accursed children!

¹⁵ Forsaking the right way, they have gone astray. They have followed the way of Balaam, the son of Beor, who loved gain from wrongdoing,

¹⁶ but was rebuked for his own transgression; a speechless donkey spoke with human voice and restrained the prophet's madness.

¹⁷ These are waterless

springs and mists driven by a storm. For them the gloom of utter darkness has been reserved.

18 For, speaking loud boasts of folly, they entice by sensual passions of the flesh those who are barely escaping from those who live in error.

19 They promise them freedom, but they themselves are slaves of corruption. For whatever overcomes a person, to that he is enslaved.

20 For if, after they have escaped the defilements of the world through the knowledge of our Lord and Savior Jesus Christ, they are again entangled in them and overcome, the last state has become worse for them than the first.

21 For it would have been better for them never to have known the way of righteousness than after knowing it to turn back from the holy commandment delivered to them.

22 What the true proverb says has happened to them: "The dog returns to its own vomit, and the sow, after washing herself, returns to wallow in the mire."

CHAPTER 3

1 This is now the second letter that I am writing to you, beloved. In both of them I am stirring up your sincere mind by way of reminder,

2 that you should remember the predictions of the holy prophets and the commandment of the Lord and Savior through your apostles.

3 knowing this first of all, that scoffers will come in the last days with scoffing, following their own sinful desires.

4 They will say, "Where is the promise of his coming? For ever since the fathers fell asleep, all things are continuing as they were from the beginning of creation."

5 For they deliberately overlook this fact, that the heavens existed long ago, and the earth was formed out of water and through water by the word of God,

6 and that by means of these the world that then existed was deluged with water and perished.

7 But by the same word the heavens and earth that now exist are stored up for fire, being kept until the day of judgment and destruction of the ungodly.

8 But do not overlook this one fact, beloved, that with the Lord one day is as a thousand years, and a thousand years as one day.

9 The Lord is not slow to

fulfill his promise as some count slowness, but is patient toward you, not wishing that any should perish, but that all should reach repentance.

10 But the day of the Lord will come like a thief, and then the heavens will pass away with a roar, and the heavenly bodies will be burned up and dissolved, and the earth and the works that are done on it will be exposed.

11 Since all these things are thus to be dissolved, what sort of people ought you to be in lives of holiness and godliness,

12 waiting for and hastening the coming of the day of God, because of which the heavens will be set on fire and dissolved, and the heavenly bodies will melt as they burn!

13 But according to his promise we are waiting for new heavens and a new earth in which righteousness dwells.

14 Therefore, beloved, since you are waiting for these, be diligent to be found by him without spot or blemish, and at peace.

15 And count the patience of our Lord as salvation, just as our beloved brother Paul also wrote to you according to the wisdom given him,

16 as he does in all his letters when he speaks in them of these matters. There are some things in them that are hard to understand, which the ignorant and unstable twist to their own destruction, as they do the other Scriptures.

17 You therefore, beloved, knowing this beforehand, take care that you are not carried away with the error of lawless people and lose your own stability.

18 But grow in the grace and knowledge of our Lord and Savior Jesus Christ. To him be the glory both now and to the day of eternity. Amen.

THE FIRST LETTER OF JOHN

1 JOHN

CHAPTER 1

1 That which was from the beginning, which we have heard, which we have seen with our eyes, which we looked upon and have touched with our hands, concerning the word of life—

² the life was made manifest, and we have seen it, and testify to it and proclaim to you the eternal life, which was with the Father and was made manifest to us—

³ that which we have seen and heard we proclaim also to you, so that you too may have fellowship with us; and indeed our fellowship is with the Father and with his Son Jesus Christ.

⁴ And we are writing these things so that our joy may be complete.

⁵ This is the message we have heard from him and proclaim to you, that God is light, and in him is no darkness at all.

⁶ If we say we have fellowship with him while we walk in darkness, we lie and do not practice the truth.

⁷ But if we walk in the light, as he is in the light, we have fellowship with one another, and the blood of Jesus his Son cleanses us from all sin.

⁸ If we say we have no sin, we deceive ourselves, and the truth is not in us.

⁹ If we confess our sins, he is faithful and just to forgive us our sins and to cleanse us from all unrighteousness.

¹⁰ If we say we have not sinned, we make him a liar, and his word is not in us.

CHAPTER 2

¹ My little children, I am writing these things to you so that you may not sin. But if anyone does sin, we have an advocate with the Father, Jesus Christ the righteous.

² He is the propitiation for our sins, and not for ours only but also for the sins of the whole world.

³ And by this we know that we have come to know him, if we keep his commandments.

⁴ Whoever says "I know him" but does not keep his commandments is a liar, and the truth is not in him,

⁵ but whoever keeps his word, in him truly the love of God is perfected. By this we may know that we are in him:

⁶ whoever says he abides in him ought to walk in the same way in which he walked.

⁷ Beloved, I am writing you no new commandment, but an old commandment that you had from the beginning. The old commandment is the word that you have heard.

⁸ At the same time, it is a new commandment that I am writing to you, which is true in him and in you, because the darkness is passing away and the true light is already shining.

⁹ Whoever says he is in the

light and hates his brother is still in darkness.

¹⁰ Whoever loves his brother abides in the light, and in him there is no cause for stumbling.

¹¹ But whoever hates his brother is in the darkness and walks in the darkness, and does not know where he is going, because the darkness has blinded his eyes.

¹² I am writing to you, little children, because your sins are forgiven for his name's sake.

¹³ I am writing to you, fathers, because you know him who is from the beginning. I am writing to you, young men, because you have overcome the evil one. I write to you, children, because you know the Father.

¹⁴ I write to you, fathers, because you know him who is from the beginning. I write to you, young men, because you are strong, and the word of God abides in you, and you have overcome the evil one.

¹⁵ Do not love the world or *the things in the world*. If anyone loves the world, the love of the Father is not in him.

¹⁶ For all that is in the world—the desires of the flesh and the desires of the eyes and pride of life—

is not from the Father but is from the world.

¹⁷ And the world is passing away along with its desires, but whoever does the will of God abides forever.

¹⁸ Children, it is the last hour, and as you have heard that antichrist is coming, so now many antichrists have come. Therefore we know that it is the last hour.

¹⁹ They went out from us, but they were not of us; for if they had been of us, they would have continued with us. But they went out, that it might become plain that they all are not of us.

²⁰ But you have been anointed by the Holy One, and you all have knowledge.

²¹ I write to you, not because you do not know the truth, but because you know it, and because no lie is of the truth.

²² Who is the liar but he who denies that Jesus is the Christ? This is the antichrist, he who denies the Father and the Son.

²³ No one who denies the Son has the Father. Whoever confesses the Son has the Father also.

²⁴ Let what you heard from the beginning abide in you. If what you heard from the beginning abides in you, then

you too will abide in the Son and in the Father.

25 And this is the promise that he made to us—eternal life.

26 I write these things to you about those who are trying to deceive you.

27 But the anointing that you received from him abides in you, and you have no need that anyone should teach you. But as his anointing teaches you about everything, and is true, and is no lie—just as it has taught you, abide in him.

28 And now, little children, abide in him, so that when he appears we may have confidence and not shrink from him in shame at his coming.

29 If you know that he is righteous, you may be sure that everyone who practices righteousness has been born of him.

CHAPTER 3

1 See what kind of love the Father has given to us, that we should be called children of God; and so we are. The reason why the world does not know us is that it did not know him.

2 Beloved, we are God's children now, and what we will be has not yet appeared; but we know that when he appears we shall be like him,

because we shall see him as he is.

3 And everyone who thus hopes in him purifies himself as he is pure.

4 Everyone who makes a practice of sinning also practices lawlessness; sin is lawlessness.

5 You know that he appeared in order to take away sins, and in him there is no sin.

6 No one who abides in him keeps on sinning; no one who keeps on sinning has either seen him or known him.

7 Little children, let no one deceive you. Whoever practices righteousness is righteous, as he is righteous.

8 Whoever makes a practice of sinning is of the devil, for the devil has been sinning from the beginning. The reason the Son of God appeared was to destroy the works of the devil.

9 No one born of God makes a practice of sinning, for God's seed abides in him, and he cannot keep on sinning because he has been born of God.

10 By this it is evident who are the children of God, and who are the children of the devil: whoever does not practice righteousness is not of God, nor is the one who does not love his brother.

¹¹ For this is the message that you have heard from the beginning, that we should love one another.

¹² We should not be like Cain, who was of the evil one and murdered his brother. And why did he murder him? Because his own deeds were evil and his brother's righteous.

¹³ Do not be surprised, brothers, that the world hates you.

¹⁴ We know that we have passed out of death into life, because we love the brothers. Whoever does not love abides in death.

¹⁵ Everyone who hates his brother is a murderer, and you know that no murderer has eternal life abiding in him.

¹⁶ By this we know love, that he laid down his life for us, and we ought to lay down our lives for the brothers.

¹⁷ But if anyone has the world's goods and sees his brother in need, yet closes his heart against him, how does God's love abide in him?

¹⁸ Little children, let us not love in word or talk but in deed and in truth.

¹⁹ By this we shall know that we are of the truth and reassure our heart before him;

²⁰ for whenever our heart condemns us, God is greater than our heart, and he knows everything.

²¹ Beloved, if our heart does not condemn us, we have confidence before God;

²² and whatever we ask we receive from him, because we keep his commandments and do what pleases him.

²³ And this is his commandment, that we believe in the name of his Son Jesus Christ and love one another, just as he has commanded us.

²⁴ Whoever keeps his commandments abides in God, and God in him. And by this we know that he abides in us, by the Spirit whom he has given us.

CHAPTER 4

¹ Beloved, do not believe every spirit, but test the spirits to see whether they are from God, for many false prophets have gone out into the world.

² By this you know the Spirit of God: every spirit that confesses that Jesus Christ has come in the flesh is from God,

³ and every spirit that does not confess Jesus is not from God. This is the spirit of the antichrist, which you heard was coming and now is in the world already.

⁴ Little children, you are from God and have overcome them, for he who is in

you is greater than he who is in the world.

⁵ They are from the world; therefore they speak from the world, and the world listens to them.

⁶ We are from God. Whoever knows God listens to us; whoever is not from God does not listen to us. By this we know the Spirit of truth and the spirit of error.

⁷ Beloved, let us love one another, for love is from God, and whoever loves has been born of God and knows God.

⁸ Anyone who does not love does not know God, because God is love.

⁹ In this the love of God was made manifest among us, that God sent his only Son into the world, so that we might live through him.

¹⁰ In this is love, not that we have loved God but that he loved us and sent his Son to be the propitiation for our sins.

¹¹ Beloved, if God so loved us, we also ought to love one another.

¹² No one has ever seen God; if we love one another, God abides in us and his love is perfected in us.

¹³ By this we know that we abide in him and he in us, because he has given us of his Spirit.

¹⁴ And we have seen and testify that the Father has sent his Son to be the Savior of the world.

¹⁵ Whoever confesses that Jesus is the Son of God, God abides in him, and he in God.

¹⁶ So we have come to know and to believe the love that God has for us. God is love, and whoever abides in love abides in God, and God abides in him.

¹⁷ By this is love perfected with us, so that we may have confidence for the day of judgment, because as he is so also are we in this world.

¹⁸ There is no fear in love, but perfect love casts out fear. For fear has to do with punishment, and whoever fears has not been perfected in love.

¹⁹ We love because he first loved us.

²⁰ If anyone says, "I love God," and hates his brother, he is a liar; for he who does not love his brother whom he has seen cannot love God whom he has not seen.

²¹ And this commandment we have from him: whoever loves God must also love his brother.

CHAPTER 5

¹ Everyone who believes that Jesus is the Christ has been

born of God, and everyone who loves the Father loves whoever has been born of him.

2 By this we know that we love the children of God, when we love God and obey his commandments.

3 For this is the love of God, that we keep his commandments. And his commandments are not burdensome.

4 For everyone who has been born of God overcomes the world. And this is the victory that has overcome the world—our faith.

5 Who is it that overcomes the world except the one who believes that Jesus is the Son of God?

6 This is he who came by water and blood—Jesus Christ; not by the water only but by the water and the blood. And the Spirit is the one who testifies, because the Spirit is the truth.

7 For there are three that testify:

8 the Spirit and the water and the blood; and these three agree.

9 If we receive the testimony of men, the testimony of God is greater, for this is the testimony of God that he has borne concerning his Son.

10 Whoever believes in the Son of God has the testimony in himself. Whoever does not believe God has made him a liar, because he has not believed in the testimony that God has borne concerning his Son.

11 And this is the testimony, that God gave us eternal life, and this life is in his Son.

12 Whoever has the Son has life; whoever does not have the Son of God does not have life.

13 I write these things to you who believe in the name of the Son of God that you may know that you have eternal life.

14 And this is the confidence that we have toward him, that if we ask anything according to his will he hears us.

15 And if we know that he hears us in whatever we ask, we know that we have the requests that we have asked of him.

16 If anyone sees his brother committing a sin not leading to death, he shall ask, and God will give him life—to those who commit sins that do not lead to death. There is sin that leads to death; I do not say that one should pray for that.

17 All wrongdoing is sin, but there is sin that does not lead to death.

18 We know that everyone

who has been born of God does not keep on sinning, but he who was born of God protects him, and the evil one does not touch him.

¹⁹ We know that we are from God, and the whole world lies in the power of the evil one.

²⁰ And we know that the Son of God has come and has given us understanding, so that we may know him who is true; and we are in him who is true, in his Son Jesus Christ. He is the true God and eternal life.

²¹ Little children, keep yourselves from idols.

THE SECOND LETTER OF JOHN

2 JOHN

¹ The elder to the elect lady and her children, whom I love in truth, and not only I, but also all who know the truth,

² because of the truth that abides in us and will be with us forever:

³ Grace, mercy, and peace will be with us, from God the Father and from Jesus Christ the Father's Son, in truth and love.

⁴ I rejoiced greatly to find some of your children walking in the truth, just as we were commanded by the Father.

⁵ And now I ask you, dear lady—not as though I were writing you a new commandment, but the one we have had from the beginning—that we love one another.

⁶ And this is love, that we walk according to his commandments; this is the commandment, just as you have heard from the beginning, so that you should walk in it.

⁷ For many deceivers have gone out into the world, those who do not confess the coming of Jesus Christ in the flesh. Such a one is the deceiver and the antichrist.

⁸ Watch yourselves, so that you may not lose what we have worked for, but may win a full reward.

⁹ Everyone who goes on ahead and does not abide in the teaching of Christ, does not have God. Whoever abides in the teaching has both the Father and the Son.

¹⁰ If anyone comes to you and does not bring this

teaching, do not receive him into your house or give him any greeting. [11] for whoever greets him takes part in his wicked works.

[12] Though I have much to write to you, I would rather not use paper and ink. Instead I hope to come to you and talk face to face, so that our joy may be complete.

[13] The children of your elect sister greet you.

THE THIRD LETTER OF JOHN

3 JOHN

[1] The elder to the beloved Gaius, whom I love in truth.

[2] Beloved, I pray that all may go well with you and that you may be in good health, as it goes well with your soul.

[3] For I rejoiced greatly when the brothers came and testified to your truth, as indeed you are walking in the truth.

[4] I have no greater joy than to hear that my children are walking in the truth.

[5] Beloved, it is a faithful thing you do in all your efforts for these brothers, strangers as they are,

[6] who testified to your love before the church. You will do well to send them on their journey in a manner worthy of God.

[7] For they have gone out for the sake of the name, accepting nothing from the Gentiles.

[8] Therefore we ought to support people like these, that we may be fellow workers for the truth.

[9] I have written something to the church, but Diotrephes, who likes to put himself first, does not acknowledge our authority.

[10] So if I come, I will bring up what he is doing, talking wicked nonsense against us. And not content with that, he refuses to welcome the brothers, and also stops those who want to and puts them out of the church.

[11] Beloved, do not imitate evil but imitate good. Whoever does good is from God; whoever does evil has not seen God.

[12] Demetrius has received a good testimony from everyone, and from the truth itself. We also add our testimony,

and you know that our testimony is true.

¹³ I had much to write to you, but I would rather not write with pen and ink.

¹⁴ I hope to see you soon, and we will talk face to face.

¹⁵ Peace be to you. The friends greet you. Greet the friends, each by name.

THE LETTER OF

JUDE

¹ Jude, a servant of Jesus Christ and brother of James, To those who are called, beloved in God the Father and kept for Jesus Christ:

² May mercy, peace, and love be multiplied to you.

³ Beloved, although I was very eager to write to you about our common salvation, I found it necessary to write appealing to you to contend for the faith that was once for all delivered to the saints.

⁴ For certain people have crept in unnoticed who long ago were designated for this condemnation, ungodly people, who pervert the grace of our God into sensuality and deny our only Master and Lord, Jesus Christ.

⁵ Now I want to remind you, although you once fully knew it, that Jesus, who saved a people out of the land of Egypt, afterward destroyed those who did not believe.

⁶ And the angels who did not stay within their own position of authority, but left their proper dwelling, he has kept in eternal chains under gloomy darkness until the judgment of the great day—

⁷ just as Sodom and Gomorrah and the surrounding cities, which likewise indulged in sexual immorality and pursued unnatural desire, serve as an example by undergoing a punishment of eternal fire.

⁸ Yet in like manner these people also, relying on their dreams, defile the flesh, reject authority, and blaspheme the glorious ones.

⁹ But when the archangel Michael, contending with the devil, was disputing about the body of Moses, he did not presume to pronounce a blasphemous judgment, but said, "The Lord rebuke you."

¹⁰ But these people blaspheme all that they do not

understand, and they are destroyed by all that they, like unreasoning animals, understand instinctively.

[11] Woe to them! For they walked in the way of Cain and abandoned themselves for the sake of gain to Balaam's error and perished in Korah's rebellion.

[12] These are hidden reefs at your love feasts, as they feast with you without fear, shepherds feeding themselves; waterless clouds, swept along by winds; fruitless trees in late autumn, twice dead, uprooted;

[13] wild waves of the sea, casting up the foam of their own shame; wandering stars, for whom the gloom of utter darkness has been reserved forever.

[14] It was also about these that Enoch, the seventh from Adam, prophesied, saying, "Behold, the Lord comes with ten thousands of his holy ones,

[15] "to execute judgment on all and to convict all the ungodly of all their deeds of ungodliness that they have committed in such an ungodly way, and of all the harsh things that ungodly sinners have spoken against him."

[16] These are grumblers, malcontents, following their own sinful desires; they are loud-mouthed boasters, showing favoritism to gain advantage.

[17] But you must remember, beloved, the predictions of the apostles of our Lord Jesus Christ.

[18] They said to you, "In the last time there will be scoffers, following their own ungodly passions."

[19] It is these who cause divisions, worldly people, devoid of the Spirit.

[20] But you, beloved, building yourselves up in your most holy faith and praying in the Holy Spirit,

[21] keep yourselves in the love of God, waiting for the mercy of our Lord Jesus Christ that leads to eternal life.

[22] And have mercy on those who doubt;

[23] save others by snatching them out of the fire; to others show mercy with fear, hating even the garment stained by the flesh.

[24] Now to him who is able to keep you from stumbling and to present you blameless before the presence of his glory with great joy,

[25] to the only God, our Savior, through Jesus Christ our Lord, be glory, majesty, dominion, and authority, before all time and now and forever. Amen.

THE REVELATION

TO JOHN

CHAPTER 1

¹ The revelation of Jesus Christ, which God gave him to show to his servants the things that must soon take place. He made it known by sending his angel to his servant John,

² who bore witness to the word of God and to the testimony of Jesus Christ, even to all that he saw.

³ Blessed is the one who reads aloud the words of this prophecy, and blessed are those who hear, and who keep what is written in it, for the time is near.

⁴ John to the seven churches that are in Asia: Grace to you and peace from him who is and who was and who is to come, and from the seven spirits who are before his throne,

⁵ and from Jesus Christ the faithful witness, the firstborn from the dead, and the ruler of kings on earth. To him who loves us and has freed us from our sins through his blood

⁶ and made us a kingdom, priests to his God and Father,

to him be glory and dominion forever and ever. Amen.

⁷ Behold, he is coming with the clouds, and every eye will see him, even those who pierced him, and all tribes of the earth will wail on account of him. Even so. Amen.

⁸ "I am the Alpha and the Omega," says the Lord God, "who is and who was and who is to come, the Almighty."

⁹ I, John, your brother and partner in the tribulation and the kingdom and the patient endurance that are in Jesus, was on the island called Patmos on account of the word of God and the testimony of Jesus.

¹⁰ I was in the Spirit on the Lord's day, and I heard behind me a loud voice like a trumpet

¹¹ saying, "Write what you see in a book and send it to the seven churches, to Ephesus and to Smyrna and to Pergamum and to Thyatira and to Sardis and to Philadelphia and to Laodicea."

¹² Then I turned to see the voice that was speaking to me, and on turning I saw seven golden lampstands,

13 and in the midst of the lampstands one like a son of man, clothed with a long robe and with a golden sash around his chest.

14 The hairs of his head were white, like white wool, like snow. His eyes were like a flame of fire,

15 his feet were like burnished bronze, refined in a furnace, and his voice was like the roar of many waters.

16 In his right hand he held seven stars, from his mouth came a sharp two-edged sword, and his face was like the sun shining in full strength.

17 When I saw him, I fell at his feet as though dead. But he laid his right hand on me, saying, "Fear not, I am the first and the last,

18 "and the living one. I died, and behold I am alive forevermore, and I have the keys of Death and Hades.

19 "Write therefore the things that you have seen, those that are and those that are to take place after this.

20 "As for the mystery of the seven stars that you saw in my right hand, and the seven golden lampstands, the seven stars are the angels of the seven churches, and the seven lampstands are the seven churches.

CHAPTER 2

1 "To the angel of the church in Ephesus write: 'The words of him who holds the seven stars in his right hand, who walks among the seven golden lampstands.

2 "I know your works, your toil and your patient endurance, and how you cannot bear with those who are evil, but have tested those who call themselves apostles and are not, and found them to be false.

3 "I know you are enduring patiently and bearing up for my name's sake, and you have not grown weary.

4 "But I have this against you, that you have abandoned the love you had at first.

5 "Remember therefore from where you have fallen; repent, and do the works you did at first. If not, I will come to you and remove your lampstand from its place, unless you repent.

6 "Yet this you have: you hate the works of the Nicolaitans, which I also hate.

7 "He who has an ear, let him hear what the Spirit says to the churches. To the one who conquers I will grant to eat of the tree of life, which is in the paradise of God.'

8 "And to the angel of the church in Smyrna write:

'The words of the first and the last, who died and came to life.

9 " 'I know your tribulation and your poverty (but you are rich) and the slander of those who say that they are Jews and are not, but are a synagogue of Satan.

10 " 'Do not fear what you are about to suffer. Behold, the devil is about to throw some of you into prison, that you may be tested, and for ten days you will have tribulation. Be faithful unto death, and I will give you the crown of life.

11 " 'He who has an ear, let him hear what the Spirit says to the churches. The one who conquers will not be hurt by the second death.'

12 "And to the angel of the church in Pergamum write: 'The words of him who has the sharp two-edged sword.

13 " 'I know where you dwell, where Satan's throne is. Yet you hold fast my name, and you did not deny my faith even in the days of Antipas my faithful witness, who was killed among you, where Satan dwells.

14 " 'But I have a few things against you: you have some there who hold the teaching of Balaam, who taught Balak to put a stumbling block be-fore the sons of Israel, so that they might eat food sacrificed to idols and practice sexual immorality.

15 " 'So also you have some who hold the teaching of the Nicolaitans.

16 " 'Therefore repent. If not, I will come to you soon and war against them with the sword of my mouth.

17 " 'He who has an ear, let him hear what the Spirit says to the churches. To the one who conquers I will give some of the hidden manna, and I will give him a white stone, with a new name written on the stone that no one knows except the one who receives it.'

18 "And to the angel of the church in Thyatira write: 'The words of the Son of God, who has eyes like a flame of fire, and whose feet are like burnished bronze.

19 " 'I know your works, your love and faith and service and patient endurance, and that your latter works exceed the first.

20 " 'But I have this against you, that you tolerate that woman Jezebel, who calls herself a prophetess and is teaching and seducing my servants to practice sexual immorality and to eat food sacrificed to idols.

21 " 'I gave her time to repent, but she refuses to repent of her sexual immorality.

22 " 'Behold, I will throw her onto a sickbed, and those who commit adultery with her I will throw into great tribulation, unless they repent of her works,

23 " 'and I will strike her children dead. And all the churches will know that I am he who searches mind and heart, and I will give to each of you according to your works.

24 " 'But to the rest of you in Thyatira, who do not hold this teaching, who have not learned what some call the deep things of Satan, to you I say, I do not lay on you any other burden.

25 " 'Only hold fast what you have until I come.

26 " 'The one who conquers and who keeps my works until the end, to him I will give authority over the nations,

27 " 'and he will rule them with a rod of iron, as when *earthen pots are broken in pieces,* even as I myself have received authority from my Father.

28 " 'And I will give him the morning star.

29 " 'He who has an ear, let him hear what the Spirit says to the churches.'

1 "And to the angel of the church in Sardis write: 'The words of him who has the seven spirits of God and the seven stars. I know your works. You have the reputation of being alive, but you are dead.

2 " 'Wake up, and strengthen what remains and is about to die, for I have not found your works complete in the sight of my God.

3 " 'Remember, then, what you received and heard. Keep it, and repent. If you will not wake up, I will come like a thief, and you will not know at what hour I will come against you.

4 " 'Yet you have still a few names in Sardis, people who have not soiled their garments, and they will walk with me in white, for they are worthy.

5 " 'The one who conquers will be clothed thus in white garments, and I will never blot his name out of the book of life. *I will confess his name* before my Father and before his angels.

6 " 'He who has an ear, let him hear what the Spirit says to the churches.'

7 "And to the angel of the church in Philadelphia write: 'The words of the holy one,

the true one, who has the key of David, who opens and no one will shut, who shuts and no one opens.

8 "I know your works. Behold, I have set before you an open door, which no one is able to shut. I know that you have but little power, and yet you have kept my word and have not denied my name.

9 "Behold, I will make those of the synagogue of Satan who say that they are Jews and are not, but lie—behold, I will make them come and bow down before your feet, and they will learn that I have loved you.

10 "Because you have kept my word about patient endurance, I will keep you from the hour of trial that is coming on the whole world, to try those who dwell on the earth.

11 "I am coming soon. Hold fast what you have, so that no one may seize your crown.

12 "The one who conquers, I will make him a pillar in the temple of my God. Never shall he go out of it, and I will write on him the name of my God, and the name of the city of my God, the new Jerusalem, which comes down from my God out of heaven, and my own new name.

13 "He who has an ear, let him hear what the Spirit says to the churches.'

14 "And to the angel of the church in Laodicea write: 'The words of the Amen, the faithful and true witness, the beginning of God's creation.

15 "I know your works: you are neither cold nor hot. Would that you were either cold or hot!

16 "So, because you are lukewarm, and neither hot nor cold, I will spit you out of my mouth.

17 "For you say, I am rich, I have prospered, and I need nothing, not realizing that you are wretched, pitiable, poor, blind, and naked.

18 "I counsel you to buy from me gold refined by fire, so that you may be rich, and white garments so that you may clothe yourself and the shame of your nakedness may not be seen, and salve to anoint your eyes, so that you may see.

19 "Those whom I love, I reprove and discipline, so be zealous and repent.

20 "Behold, I stand at the door and knock. If anyone hears my voice and opens the door, I will come in to him and eat with him, and he with me.

21 "The one who conquers,

I will grant him to sit with me on my throne, as I also conquered and sat down with my Father on his throne. ²² "He who has an ear, let him hear what the Spirit says to the churches.'"

CHAPTER 4

¹ After this I looked, and behold, a door standing open in heaven! And the first voice, which I had heard speaking to me like a trumpet, said, "Come up here, and I will show you what must take place after this."

² At once I was in the Spirit, and behold, a throne stood in heaven, with one seated on the throne.

³ And he who sat there had the appearance of jasper and carnelian, and around the throne was a rainbow that had the appearance of an emerald.

⁴ Around the throne were twenty-four thrones, and seated on the thrones were twenty-four elders, clothed in white garments, with golden crowns on their heads.

⁵ From the throne came flashes of lightning, and rumblings and peals of thunder, and before the throne were burning seven torches of fire, which are the seven spirits of God,

⁶ and before the throne there was as it were a sea of glass, like crystal. And around the throne, on each side of the throne, are four living creatures, full of eyes in front and behind:

⁷ the first living creature like a lion, the second living creature like an ox, the third living creature with the face of a man, and the fourth living creature like an eagle in flight.

⁸ And the four living creatures, each of them with six wings, are full of eyes all around and within, and day and night they never cease to say, "Holy, holy, holy, is the Lord God Almighty, who was and is and is to come!"

⁹ And whenever the living creatures give glory and honor and thanks to him who is seated on the throne, who lives forever and ever,

¹⁰ the twenty-four elders fall down before him who is seated on the throne and worship him who lives forever and ever. They cast their crowns before the throne, saying,

¹¹ "Worthy are you, our Lord and God, to receive glory and honor and power, for you created all things, and by your will they existed and were created."

CHAPTER 5

¹ Then I saw in the right hand of him who was seated on the throne a scroll written within and on the back, sealed with seven seals.

² And I saw a mighty angel proclaiming with a loud voice, "Who is worthy to open the scroll and break its seals?"

³ And no one in heaven or on earth or under the earth was able to open the scroll or to look into it,

⁴ and I began to weep loudly because no one was found worthy to open the scroll or to look into it.

⁵ And one of the elders said to me, "Weep no more; behold, the Lion of the tribe of Judah, the Root of David, has conquered, so that he can open the scroll and its seven seals."

⁶ And between the throne and the four living creatures and among the elders I saw a Lamb standing, as though it had been slain, with seven horns and with seven eyes, which are the seven spirits of God sent out into all the earth.

⁷ And he went and took the scroll from the right hand of him who was seated on the throne.

⁸ And when he had taken the scroll, the four living creatures and the twenty-four elders fell down before the Lamb, each holding a harp, and golden bowls full of incense, which are the prayers of the saints.

⁹ And they sang a new song, saying, "Worthy are you to take the scroll and to open its seals, for you were slain, and by your blood you ransomed people for God from every tribe and language and people and nation,

¹⁰ "and you have made them a kingdom and priests to our God, and they shall reign on the earth."

¹¹ Then I looked, and I heard around the throne and the living creatures and the elders the voice of many angels, numbering myriads of myriads and thousands of thousands,

¹² saying with a loud voice, "Worthy is the Lamb who was slain, to receive power and wealth and wisdom and might and honor and glory and blessing!"

¹³ And I heard every creature in heaven and on earth and under the earth and in the sea, and all that is in them, saying, "To him who sits on the throne and to the Lamb be blessing and honor and glory and might forever and ever!"

14 And the four living creatures said, "Amen!" and the elders fell down and worshiped.

CHAPTER 6

1 Now I watched when the Lamb opened one of the seven seals, and I heard one of the four living creatures say with a voice like thunder, "Come!"

2 And I looked, and behold, a white horse! And its rider had a bow, and a crown was given to him, and he came out conquering, and to conquer.

3 When he opened the second seal, I heard the second living creature say, "Come!"

4 And out came another horse, bright red. Its rider was permitted to take peace from the earth, so that people should slay one another, and he was given a great sword.

5 When he opened the third seal, I heard the third living creature say, "Come!" And I looked, and behold, a black horse! And its rider had a pair of scales in his hand.

6 And I heard what seemed to be a voice in the midst of the four living creatures, saying, "A quart of wheat for a denarius, and three quarts of barley for a denarius, and do not harm the oil and wine!"

7 When he opened the fourth seal, I heard the voice of the fourth living creature say, "Come!"

8 And I looked, and behold, a pale horse! And its rider's name was Death, and Hades followed him. And they were given authority over a fourth of the earth, to kill with sword and with famine and with pestilence and by wild beasts of the earth.

9 When he opened the fifth seal, I saw under the altar the souls of those who had been slain for the word of God and for the witness they had borne.

10 They cried out with a loud voice, "O Sovereign Lord, holy and true, how long before you will judge and avenge our blood on those who dwell on the earth?"

11 Then they were each given a white robe and told to rest a little longer, until the number of their fellow servants and their brothers should be complete, who were to be killed as they themselves had been.

12 When he opened the sixth seal, I looked, and behold, there was a great earthquake, and the sun became black as sackcloth, the full moon became like blood,

13 and the stars of the sky fell to the earth as the fig tree sheds its winter fruit when shaken by a gale,

¹⁴ The sky vanished like a scroll that is being rolled up, and every mountain and island was removed from its place.

¹⁵ Then the kings of the earth and the great ones and the generals and the rich and the powerful, and everyone, slave and free, hid themselves in the caves and among the rocks of the mountains,

¹⁶ calling to the mountains and rocks, "Fall on us and hide us from the face of him who is seated on the throne, and from the wrath of the Lamb,

¹⁷ "for the great day of their wrath has come, and who can stand?"

CHAPTER 7

¹ After this I saw four angels standing at the four corners of the earth, holding back the four winds of the earth, that no wind might blow on earth or sea or against any tree.

² Then I saw another angel ascending from the rising of the sun, with the seal of the living God, and he called with a loud voice to the four angels who had been given power to harm earth and sea,

³ saying, "Do not harm the earth or the sea or the trees, until we have sealed the servants of our God on their foreheads."

⁴ And I heard the number of the sealed, 144,000, sealed from every tribe of the sons of Israel:

⁵ 12,000 from the tribe of Judah were sealed, 12,000 from the tribe of Reuben, 12,000 from the tribe of Gad,

⁶ 12,000 from the tribe of Asher, 12,000 from the tribe of Naphtali, 12,000 from the tribe of Manasseh,

⁷ 12,000 from the tribe of Simeon, 12,000 from the tribe of Levi, 12,000 from the tribe of Issachar,

⁸ 12,000 from the tribe of Zebulun, 12,000 from the tribe of Joseph, 12,000 from the tribe of Benjamin were sealed.

⁹ After this I looked, and behold, a great multitude that no one could number, from every nation, from all tribes and peoples and languages, standing before the throne and before the Lamb, clothed in white robes, with palm branches in their hands,

¹⁰ and crying out with a loud voice, "Salvation belongs to our God who sits on the throne, and to the Lamb!"

¹¹ And all the angels were standing around the throne and around the elders and the four living creatures,

and they fell on their faces before the throne and worshiped God,

12 saying, "Amen! Blessing and glory and wisdom and thanksgiving and honor and power and might be to our God forever and ever! Amen."

13 Then one of the elders addressed me, saying, "Who are these, clothed in white robes, and from where have they come?"

14 I said to him, "Sir, you know." And he said to me, "These are the ones coming out of the great tribulation. They have washed their robes and made them white in the blood of the Lamb.

15 "Therefore they are before the throne of God, and serve him day and night in his temple; and he who sits on the throne will shelter them with his presence.

16 "They shall hunger no more, neither thirst anymore; the sun shall not strike them, nor any scorching heat.

17 "For the Lamb in the midst of the throne will be their shepherd, and he will guide them to springs of living water, and God will wipe away every tear from their eyes."

CHAPTER 8

1 When the Lamb opened the seventh seal, there was silence in heaven for about half an hour.

2 Then I saw the seven angels who stand before God, and seven trumpets were given to them.

3 And another angel came and stood at the altar with a golden censer, and he was given much incense to offer with the prayers of all the saints on the golden altar before the throne,

4 and the smoke of the incense, with the prayers of the saints, rose before God from the hand of the angel.

5 Then the angel took the censer and filled it with fire from the altar and threw it on the earth, and there were peals of thunder, rumblings, flashes of lightning, and an earthquake.

6 Now the seven angels who had the seven trumpets prepared to blow them.

7 The first angel blew his trumpet, and there followed hail and fire, mixed with blood, and these were thrown upon the earth. And a third of the earth was burned up, and a third of the trees were burned up, and all green grass was burned up.

8 The second angel blew his trumpet, and something like a great mountain, burning with fire, was thrown into

the sea, and a third of the sea became blood.

9 A third of the living creatures in the sea died, and a third of the ships were destroyed.

10 The third angel blew his trumpet, and a great star fell from heaven, blazing like a torch, and it fell on a third of the rivers and on the springs of water.

11 The name of the star is Wormwood. A third of the waters became wormwood, and many people died from the water, because it had been made bitter.

12 The fourth angel blew his trumpet, and a third of the sun was struck, and a third of the moon, and a third of the stars, so that a third of their light might be darkened, and a third of the day might be kept from shining, and likewise a third of the night.

13 Then I looked, and I heard an eagle crying with a loud voice as it flew directly overhead, "Woe, woe, woe to those who dwell on the earth, at the blasts of the other trumpets that the three angels are about to blow!"

CHAPTER 9

1 And the fifth angel blew his trumpet, and I saw a star fallen from heaven to earth, and he was given the key to the shaft of the bottomless pit.

2 He opened the shaft of the bottomless pit, and from the shaft rose smoke like the smoke of a great furnace, and the sun and the air were darkened with the smoke from the shaft.

3 Then from the smoke came locusts on the earth, and they were given power like the power of scorpions of the earth.

4 They were told not to harm the grass of the earth or any green plant or any tree, but only those people who do not have the seal of God on their foreheads.

5 They were allowed to torment them for five months, but not to kill them, and their torment was like the torment of a scorpion when it stings someone.

6 And in those days people will seek death and will not find it. They will long to die, but death will flee from them.

7 In appearance the locusts were like horses prepared for battle: on their heads were what looked like crowns of gold; their faces were like human faces,

8 their hair like women's hair, and their teeth like lions' teeth;

9 they had breastplates like

breastplates of iron, and the noise of their wings was like the noise of many chariots with horses rushing into battle.

10 They have tails and stings like scorpions, and their power to hurt people for five months is in their tails.

11 They have as king over them the angel of the bottomless pit. His name in Hebrew is Abaddon, and in Greek he is called Apollyon.

12 The first woe has passed; behold, two woes are still to come.

13 Then the sixth angel blew his trumpet, and I heard a voice from the four horns of the golden altar before God,

14 saying to the sixth angel who had the trumpet, "Release the four angels who are bound at the great river Euphrates."

15 So the four angels, who had been prepared for the hour, the day, the month, and the year, were released to kill a third of mankind.

16 The number of mounted troops was twice ten thousand times ten thousand; I heard their number.

17 And this is how I saw the horses in my vision and those who rode them: they wore breastplates the color of fire and of sapphire and of sulfur,

and the heads of the horses were like lions' heads, and fire and smoke and sulfur came out of their mouths.

18 By these three plagues a third of mankind was killed, by the fire and smoke and sulfur coming out of their mouths.

19 For the power of the horses is in their mouths and in their tails, for their tails are like serpents with heads, and by means of them they wound.

20 The rest of mankind, who were not killed by these plagues, did not repent of the works of their hands nor give up worshiping demons and idols of gold and silver and bronze and stone and wood, which cannot see or hear or walk,

21 nor did they repent of their murders or their sorceries or their sexual immorality or their thefts.

CHAPTER 10

1 Then I saw another mighty angel coming down from heaven, wrapped in a cloud, with a rainbow over his head, and his face was like the sun, and his legs like pillars of fire.

2 He had a little scroll open in his hand. And he set his right foot on the sea, and his left foot on the land,

³ and called out with a loud voice, like a lion roaring. When he called out, the seven thunders sounded.

⁴ And when the seven thunders had sounded, I was about to write, but I heard a voice from heaven saying, "Seal up what the seven thunders have said, and do not write it down."

⁵ And the angel whom I saw standing on the sea and on the land raised his right hand to heaven

⁶ and swore by him who lives forever and ever, who created heaven and what is in it, the earth and what is in it, and the sea and what is in it, that there would be no more delay,

⁷ but that in the days of the trumpet call to be sounded by the seventh angel, the mystery of God would be fulfilled, just as he announced to his servants the prophets.

⁸ Then the voice that I had heard from heaven spoke to me again, saying, "Go, take the scroll that is open in the hand of the angel who is standing on the sea and on the land."

⁹ So I went to the angel and told him to give me the little scroll. And he said to me, "Take and eat it; it will make your stomach bitter, but in your mouth it will be sweet as honey."

¹⁰ And I took the little scroll from the hand of the angel and ate it. It was sweet as honey in my mouth, but when I had eaten it my stomach was made bitter.

¹¹ And I was told, "You must again prophesy about many peoples and nations and languages and kings."

CHAPTER 11

¹ Then I was given a measuring rod like a staff, and I was told, "Rise and measure the temple of God and the altar and those who worship there,

² "but do not measure the court outside the temple; leave that out, for it is given over to the nations, and they will trample the holy city for forty-two months.

³ "And I will grant authority to my two witnesses, and they will prophesy for 1,260 days, clothed in sackcloth."

⁴ These are the two olive trees and the two lampstands that stand before the Lord of the earth.

⁵ And if anyone would harm them, fire pours from their mouth and consumes their foes. If anyone would harm them, this is how he is doomed to be killed.

⁶ They have the power to shut the sky, that no rain may fall during the days of their prophesying, and they have power over the waters to turn them into blood and to strike the earth with every kind of plague, as often as they desire.

⁷ And when they have finished their testimony, the beast that rises from the bottomless pit will make war on them and conquer them and kill them,

⁸ and their dead bodies will lie in the street of the great city that symbolically is called Sodom and Egypt, where their Lord was crucified.

⁹ For three and a half days some from the peoples and tribes and languages and nations will gaze at their dead bodies and refuse to let them be placed in a tomb,

¹⁰ and those who dwell on the earth will rejoice over them and make merry and exchange presents, because these two prophets had been a torment to those who dwell on the earth.

¹¹ But after the three and a half days a breath of life from God entered them, and they stood up on their feet, and great fear fell on those who saw them.

¹² Then they heard a loud voice from heaven saying to them, "Come up here!" And they went up to heaven in a cloud, and their enemies watched them.

¹³ And at that hour there was a great earthquake, and a tenth of the city fell. Seven thousand people were killed in the earthquake, and the rest were terrified and gave glory to the God of heaven.

¹⁴ The second woe has passed; behold, the third woe is soon to come.

¹⁵ Then the seventh angel blew his trumpet, and there were loud voices in heaven, saying, "The kingdom of the world has become the kingdom of our Lord and of his Christ, and he shall reign forever and ever."

¹⁶ And the twenty-four elders who sit on their thrones before God fell on their faces and worshiped God,

¹⁷ saying, "We give thanks to you, Lord God Almighty, who is and who was, for you have taken your great power and begun to reign.

¹⁸ "The nations raged, but your wrath came, and the time for the dead to be judged, and for rewarding your servants, the prophets and saints, and those who fear your name, both small and great, and for

destroying the destroyers of the earth."

19 Then God's temple in heaven was opened, and the ark of his covenant was seen within his temple. There were flashes of lightning, rumblings, peals of thunder, an earthquake, and heavy hail.

CHAPTER 12

1 And a great sign appeared in heaven: a woman clothed with the sun, with the moon under her feet, and on her head a crown of twelve stars.

2 She was pregnant and was crying out in birth pains and the agony of giving birth.

3 And another sign appeared in heaven: behold, a great red dragon, with seven heads and ten horns, and on his heads seven diadems.

4 His tail swept down a third of the stars of heaven and cast them to the earth. And the dragon stood before the woman who was about to give birth, so that when she bore her child he might devour it.

5 She gave birth to a male child, one who is to rule all the nations with a rod of iron, but her child was caught up to God and to his throne,

6 and the woman fled into the wilderness, where she has a place prepared by God, in which she is to be nourished for 1,260 days.

7 Now war arose in heaven, Michael and his angels fighting against the dragon. And the dragon and his angels fought back,

8 but he was defeated, and there was no longer any place for them in heaven.

9 And the great dragon was thrown down, that ancient serpent, who is called the devil and Satan, the deceiver of the whole world— he was thrown down to the earth, and his angels were thrown down with him.

10 And I heard a loud voice in heaven, saying, "Now the salvation and the power and the kingdom of our God and the authority of his Christ have come, for the accuser of our brothers has been thrown down, who accuses them day and night before our God.

11 "And they have conquered him by the blood of the Lamb and by the word of their testimony, for they loved not their lives even unto death.

12 "Therefore, rejoice, O heavens and you who dwell in them! But woe to you, O earth and sea, for the devil has come down to you in great wrath, because he knows that his time is short!"

13 And when the dragon

saw that he had been thrown down to the earth, he pursued the woman who had given birth to the male child.

¹⁴ But the woman was given the two wings of the great eagle so that she might fly from the serpent into the wilderness, to the place where she is to be nourished for a time, and times, and half a time.

¹⁵ The serpent poured water like a river out of his mouth after the woman, to sweep her away with a flood.

¹⁶ But the earth came to the help of the woman, and the earth opened its mouth and swallowed the river that the dragon had poured from his mouth.

¹⁷ Then the dragon became furious with the woman and went off to make war on the rest of her offspring, on those who keep the commandments of God and hold to the testimony of Jesus. And he stood on the sand of the sea.

CHAPTER 13

¹ And I saw a beast rising out of the sea, with ten horns and seven heads, with ten diadems on its horns and blasphemous names on its heads.

² And the beast that I saw was like a leopard; its feet were like a bear's, and its mouth was like a lion's mouth. And to it the dragon gave his power and his throne and great authority.

³ One of its heads seemed to have a mortal wound, but its mortal wound was healed, and the whole earth marveled as they followed the beast.

⁴ And they worshiped the dragon, for he had given his authority to the beast, and they worshiped the beast, saying, "Who is like the beast, and who can fight against it?"

⁵ And the beast was given a mouth uttering haughty and blasphemous words, and it was allowed to exercise authority for forty-two months.

⁶ It opened its mouth to utter blasphemies against God, blaspheming his name and his dwelling, that is, those who dwell in heaven.

⁷ Also it was allowed to make war on the saints and to conquer them. And authority was given it over every tribe and people and language and nation,

⁸ and all who dwell on earth will worship it, everyone whose name has not been written before the foundation of the world in the book of life of the Lamb who was slain.

⁹ If anyone has an ear, let him hear:

¹⁰ If anyone is to be taken captive, to captivity he goes; if

anyone is to be slain with the sword, with the sword must he be slain. Here is a call for the endurance and faith of the saints.

11 Then I saw another beast rising out of the earth. It had two horns like a lamb and it spoke like a dragon.

12 It exercises all the authority of the first beast in its presence, and makes the earth and its inhabitants worship the first beast, whose mortal wound was healed.

13 It performs great signs, even making fire come down from heaven to earth in front of people,

14 and by the signs that it is allowed to work in the presence of the beast it deceives those who dwell on earth, telling them to make an image for the beast that was wounded by the sword and yet lived.

15 And it was allowed to give breath to the image of the beast, so that the image of the beast might even speak and might cause those who would not worship the image of the beast to be slain.

16 Also it causes all, both small and great, both rich and poor, both free and slave, to be marked on the right hand or the forehead,

17 so that no one can buy or sell unless he has the mark, that is, the name of the beast or the number of its name.

18 This calls for wisdom: let the one who has understanding calculate the number of the beast, for it is the number of a man, and his number is 666.

CHAPTER 14

1 Then I looked, and behold, on Mount Zion stood the Lamb, and with him 144,000 who had his name and his Father's name written on their foreheads.

2 And I heard a voice from heaven like the roar of many waters and like the sound of loud thunder. The voice I heard was like the sound of harpists playing on their harps,

3 and they were singing a new song before the throne and before the four living creatures and before the elders. No one could learn that song except the 144,000 who had been redeemed from the earth.

4 It is these who have not defiled themselves with women, for they are virgins. It is these who follow the Lamb wherever he goes. These have been redeemed from mankind as firstfruits for God and the Lamb,

⁵ and in their mouth no lie was found, for they are blameless.

⁶ Then I saw another angel flying directly overhead, with an eternal gospel to proclaim to those who dwell on earth, to every nation and tribe and language and people.

⁷ And he said with a loud voice, "Fear God and give him glory, because the hour of his judgment has come, and worship him who made heaven and earth, the sea and the springs of water."

⁸ Another angel, a second, followed, saying, "Fallen, fallen is Babylon the great, she who made all nations drink the wine of the passion of her sexual immorality."

⁹ And another angel, a third, followed them, saying with a loud voice, "If anyone worships the beast and its image and receives a mark on his forehead or on his hand,

¹⁰ "he also will drink the wine of God's wrath, poured full strength into the cup of his anger, and he will be tormented with fire and sulfur in the presence of the holy angels and in the presence of the Lamb.

¹¹ "And the smoke of their torment goes up forever and ever, and they have no rest, day or night, these worshipers of the beast and its image, and whoever receives the mark of its name."

¹² Here is a call for the endurance of the saints, those who keep the commandments of God and their faith in Jesus.

¹³ And I heard a voice from heaven saying, "Write this: Blessed are the dead who die in the Lord from now on." "Blessed indeed," says the Spirit, "that they may rest from their labors, for their deeds follow them!"

¹⁴ Then I looked, and behold, a white cloud, and seated on the cloud one like a son of man, with a golden crown on his head, and a sharp sickle in his hand.

¹⁵ And another angel came out of the temple, calling with a loud voice to him who sat on the cloud, "Put in your sickle, and reap, for the hour to reap has come, for the harvest of the earth is fully ripe."

¹⁶ So he who sat on the cloud swung his sickle across the earth, and the earth was reaped.

¹⁷ Then another angel came out of the temple in heaven, and he too had a sharp sickle.

¹⁸ And another angel came out from the altar, the angel who has authority over the fire, and he called with a

loud voice to the one who had the sharp sickle, "Put in your sickle and gather the clusters from the vine of the earth, for its grapes are ripe."

¹⁹ So the angel swung his sickle across the earth and gathered the grape harvest of the earth and threw it into the great winepress of the wrath of God.

²⁰ And the winepress was trodden outside the city, and blood flowed from the winepress, as high as a horse's bridle, for 1,600 stadia.

CHAPTER 15

¹ Then I saw another sign in heaven, great and amazing, seven angels with seven plagues, which are the last, for with them the wrath of God is finished.

² And I saw what appeared to be a sea of glass mingled with fire—and also those who had conquered the beast and its image and the number of its name, standing beside the sea of glass with harps of God in their hands.

³ And they sing the song of Moses, the servant of God, and the song of the Lamb, saying, "Great and amazing are your deeds, O Lord God the Almighty! Just and true are your ways, O King of the nations!

⁴ "Who will not fear, O Lord, and glorify your name? For you alone are holy. All nations will come and worship you, for your righteous acts have been revealed."

⁵ After this I looked, and the sanctuary of the tent of witness in heaven was opened,

⁶ and out of the sanctuary came the seven angels with the seven plagues, clothed in pure, bright linen, with golden sashes around their chests.

⁷ And one of the four living creatures gave to the seven angels seven golden bowls full of the wrath of God who lives forever and ever,

⁸ and the sanctuary was filled with smoke from the glory of God and from his power, and no one could enter the sanctuary until the seven plagues of the seven angels were finished.

CHAPTER 16

¹ Then I heard a loud voice from the temple telling the seven angels, "Go and pour out on the earth the seven bowls of the wrath of God."

² So the first angel went and poured out his bowl on the earth, and harmful and painful sores came upon the people who bore the mark of

the beast and worshiped its image.

3 The second angel poured out his bowl into the sea, and it became like the blood of a corpse, and every living thing died that was in the sea.

4 The third angel poured out his bowl into the rivers and the springs of water, and they became blood.

5 And I heard the angel in charge of the waters say, "Just are you, O Holy One, who is and who was, for you brought these judgments!

6 "For they have shed the blood of saints and prophets, and you have given them blood to drink. It is what they deserve!"

7 And I heard the altar saying, "Yes, Lord God the Almighty, true and just are your judgments!"

8 The fourth angel poured out his bowl on the sun, and it was allowed to scorch people with fire.

9 They were scorched by the fierce heat, and they cursed the name of God who had power over these plagues. They did not repent and give him glory.

10 The fifth angel poured out his bowl on the throne of the beast, and its kingdom was plunged into darkness. People gnawed their tongues in anguish

11 and cursed the God of heaven for their pain and sores. They did not repent of their deeds.

12 The sixth angel poured out his bowl on the great river Euphrates, and its water was dried up, to prepare the way for the kings from the east.

13 And I saw, coming out of the mouth of the dragon and out of the mouth of the beast and out of the mouth of the false prophet, three unclean spirits like frogs.

14 For they are demonic spirits, performing signs, who go abroad to the kings of the whole world, to assemble them for battle on the great day of God the Almighty.

15 ("Behold, I am coming like a thief! Blessed is the one who stays awake, keeping his garments on, that he may not go about naked and be seen exposed!")

16 And they assembled them at the place that in Hebrew is called Armageddon.

17 The seventh angel poured out his bowl into the air, and a loud voice came out of the temple, from the throne, saying, "It is done!"

18 And there were flashes of lightning, rumblings, peals of thunder, and a great

earthquake such as there had never been since man was on the earth, so great was that earthquake.

19 The great city was split into three parts, and the cities of the nations fell, and God remembered Babylon the great, to make her drain the cup of the wine of the fury of his wrath.

20 And every island fled away, and no mountains were to be found.

21 And great hailstones, about one hundred pounds each, fell from heaven on people; and they cursed God for the plague of the hail, because the plague was so severe.

CHAPTER 17

1 Then one of the seven angels who had the seven bowls came and said to me, "Come, I will show you the judgment of the great prostitute who is seated on many waters,

2 "with whom the kings of the earth have committed sexual immorality, and with the wine of whose sexual immorality the dwellers on earth have become drunk."

3 And he carried me away in the Spirit into a wilderness, and I saw a woman sitting on a scarlet beast that was full of blasphemous names, and it had seven heads and ten horns.

4 The woman was arrayed in purple and scarlet, and adorned with gold and jewels and pearls, holding in her hand a golden cup full of abominations and the impurities of her sexual immorality.

5 And on her forehead was written a name of mystery: "Babylon the great, mother of prostitutes and of earth's abominations."

6 And I saw the woman, drunk with the blood of the saints, the blood of the martyrs of Jesus. When I saw her, I marveled greatly.

7 But the angel said to me, "Why do you marvel? I will tell you the mystery of the woman, and of the beast with seven heads and ten horns that carries her.

8 "The beast that you saw was, and is not, and is about to rise from the bottomless pit and go to destruction. And the dwellers on earth whose names have not been written in the book of life from the foundation of the world will marvel to see the beast, because it was and is not and is to come.

9 "This calls for a mind with wisdom: the seven heads are

seven mountains on which the woman is seated;

¹⁰ "they are also seven kings, five of whom have fallen, one is, the other has not yet come, and when he does come he must remain only a little while.

¹¹ "As for the beast that was and is not, it is an eighth but it belongs to the seven, and it goes to destruction.

¹² "And the ten horns that you saw are ten kings who have not yet received royal power, but they are to receive authority as kings for one hour, together with the beast.

¹³ "These are of one mind, and they hand over their power and authority to the beast.

¹⁴ "They will make war on the Lamb, and the Lamb will conquer them, for he is Lord of lords and King of kings, and those with him are called and chosen and faithful."

¹⁵ And the angel said to me, "The waters that you saw, where the prostitute is seated, are peoples and multitudes and nations and languages.

¹⁶ "And the ten horns that you saw, they and the beast will hate the prostitute. They will make her desolate and naked, and devour her flesh and burn her up with fire,

¹⁷ "for God has put it into their hearts to carry out his purpose by being of one mind and handing over their royal power to the beast, until the words of God are fulfilled.

¹⁸ "And the woman that you saw is the great city that has dominion over the kings of the earth."

CHAPTER 18

¹ After this I saw another angel coming down from heaven, having great authority, and the earth was made bright with his glory.

² And he called out with a mighty voice, "Fallen, fallen is Babylon the great! She has become a dwelling place for demons, a haunt for every unclean spirit, a haunt for every unclean bird, a haunt for every unclean and detestable beast.

³ "For all nations have drunk the wine of the passion of her sexual immorality, and the kings of the earth have committed immorality with her, and the merchants of the earth have grown rich from the power of her luxurious living."

⁴ Then I heard another voice from heaven saying, "Come out of her, my people, lest you take part in her sins, lest you share in her plagues;

5 "for her sins are heaped high as heaven, and God has remembered her iniquities.

6 "Pay her back as she herself has paid back others, and repay her double for her deeds; mix a double portion for her in the cup she mixed.

7 "As she glorified herself and lived in luxury, so give her a like measure of torment and mourning, since in her heart she says, 'I sit as a queen, I am no widow, and mourning I shall never see.'

8 "For this reason her plagues will come in a single day, death and mourning and famine, and she will be burned up with fire; for mighty is the Lord God who has judged her."

9 And the kings of the earth, who committed sexual immorality and lived in luxury with her, will weep and wail over her when they see the smoke of her burning.

10 They will stand far off, in fear of her torment, and say, "Alas! Alas! You great city, you mighty city, Babylon! For in a single hour your judgment has come."

11 And the merchants of the earth weep and mourn for her, since no one buys their cargo anymore;

12 cargo of gold, silver, jewels, pearls, fine linen, purple cloth, silk, scarlet cloth, all kinds of scented wood, all kinds of articles of ivory, all kinds of articles of costly wood, bronze, iron and marble,

13 cinnamon, spice, incense, myrrh, frankincense, wine, oil, fine flour, wheat, cattle and sheep, horses and chariots, and slaves, that is, human souls.

14 "The fruit for which your soul longed has gone from you, and all your delicacies and your splendors are lost to you, never to be found again!"

15 The merchants of these wares, who gained wealth from her, will stand far off, in fear of her torment, weeping and mourning aloud,

16 "Alas, alas, for the great city that was clothed in fine linen, in purple and scarlet, adorned with gold, with jewels, and with pearls!

17 "For in a single hour all this wealth has been laid waste." And all shipmasters and seafaring men, sailors and all whose trade is on the sea, stood far off

18 and cried out as they saw the smoke of her burning, "What city was like the great city?"

19 And they threw dust on

their heads as they wept and mourned, crying out, "Alas, alas, for the great city where all who had ships at sea grew rich by her wealth! For in a single hour she has been laid waste.

20 "Rejoice over her, O heaven, and you saints and apostles and prophets, for God has given judgment for you against her!"

21 Then a mighty angel took up a stone like a great millstone and threw it into the sea, saying, "So will Babylon the great city be thrown down with violence, and will be found no more;

22 "and the sound of harpists and musicians, of flute players and trumpeters, will be heard in you no more, and a craftsman of any craft will be found in you no more, and the sound of the mill will be heard in you no more,

23 "and the light of a lamp will shine in you no more, and the voice of bridegroom and bride will be heard in you no more, for your merchants were the great ones of the earth, and all nations were deceived by your sorcery.

24 "And in her was found the blood of prophets and of saints, and of all who have been slain on earth."

CHAPTER 19

1 After this I heard what seemed to be the loud voice of a great multitude in heaven, crying out, "Hallelujah! Salvation and glory and power belong to our God,

2 "for his judgments are true and just; for he has judged the great prostitute who corrupted the earth with her immorality, and has avenged on her the blood of his servants."

3 Once more they cried out, "Hallelujah! The smoke from her goes up forever and ever."

4 And the twenty-four elders and the four living creatures fell down and worshiped God who was seated on the throne, saying, "Amen. Hallelujah!"

5 And from the throne came a voice saying, "Praise our God, all you his servants, you who fear him, small and great."

6 Then I heard what seemed to be the voice of a great multitude, like the roar of many waters and like the sound of mighty peals of thunder, crying out, "Hallelujah! For the Lord our God the Almighty reigns.

7 "Let us rejoice and exult and give him the glory, for the marriage of the Lamb has come, and his Bride has made herself ready;

⁸ "it was granted her to clothe herself with fine linen, bright and pure"— for the fine linen is the righteous deeds of the saints.

⁹ And the angel said to me, "Write this: Blessed are those who are invited to the marriage supper of the Lamb." And he said to me, "These are the true words of God."

¹⁰ Then I fell down at his feet to worship him, but he said to me, "You must not do that! I am a fellow servant with you and your brothers who hold to the testimony of Jesus. Worship God." For the testimony of Jesus is the spirit of prophecy.

¹¹ Then I saw heaven opened, and behold, a white horse! The one sitting on it is called Faithful and True, and in righteousness he judges and makes war.

¹² His eyes are like a flame of fire, and on his head are many diadems, and he has a name written that no one knows but himself.

¹³ He is clothed in a robe dipped in blood, and the name by which he is called is The Word of God.

¹⁴ And the armies of heaven, arrayed in fine linen, white and pure, were following him on white horses.

¹⁵ From his mouth comes a sharp sword with which to strike down the nations, and he will rule them with a rod of iron. He will tread the winepress of the fury of the wrath of God the Almighty.

¹⁶ On his robe and on his thigh he has a name written, King of kings and Lord of lords.

¹⁷ Then I saw an angel standing in the sun, and with a loud voice he called to all the birds that fly directly overhead, "Come, gather for the great supper of God,

¹⁸ "to eat the flesh of kings, the flesh of captains, the flesh of mighty men, the flesh of horses and their riders, and the flesh of all men, both free and slave, both small and great."

¹⁹ And I saw the beast and the kings of the earth with their armies gathered to make war against him who was sitting on the horse and against his army.

²⁰ And the beast was captured, and with it the false prophet who in its presence had done the signs by which he deceived those who had received the mark of the beast and those who worshiped its image. These two were thrown alive into the lake of fire that burns with sulfur.

²¹ And the rest were slain by

the sword that came from the mouth of him who was sitting on the horse, and all the birds were gorged with their flesh.

CHAPTER 20

¹ Then I saw an angel coming down from heaven, holding in his hand the key to the bottomless pit and a great chain.

² And he seized the dragon, that ancient serpent, who is the devil and Satan, and bound him for a thousand years,

³ and threw him into the pit, and shut it and sealed it over him, so that he might not deceive the nations any longer, until the thousand years were ended. After that he must be released for a little while.

⁴ Then I saw thrones, and seated on them were those to whom the authority to judge was committed. Also I saw the souls of those who had been beheaded for the testimony of Jesus and for the word of God, and those who had not worshiped the beast or its image and had not received its mark on their foreheads or their hands. They came to life and reigned with Christ for a thousand years.

⁵ The rest of the dead did not come to life until the thousand years were ended. This is the first resurrection.

⁶ Blessed and holy is the one who shares in the first resurrection! Over such the second death has no power, but they will be priests of God and of Christ, and they will reign with him for a thousand years.

⁷ And when the thousand years are ended, Satan will be released from his prison

⁸ and will come out to deceive the nations that are at the four corners of the earth, Gog and Magog, to gather them for battle; their number is like the sand of the sea.

⁹ And they marched up over the broad plain of the earth and surrounded the camp of the saints and the beloved city, but fire came down from heaven and consumed them,

¹⁰ and the devil who had deceived them was thrown into the lake of fire and sulfur where the beast and the false prophet were, and they will be tormented day and night forever and ever.

¹¹ Then I saw a great white throne and him who was seated on it. From his presence earth and sky fled away, and no place was found for them.

¹² And I saw the dead, great and small, standing before the throne, and books were opened. Then another book was opened, which is the

book of life. And the dead were judged by what was written in the books, according to what they had done.

¹³ And the sea gave up the dead who were in it, Death and Hades gave up the dead who were in them, and they were judged, each one of them, according to what they had done.

¹⁴ Then Death and Hades were thrown into the lake of fire. This is the second death, the lake of fire.

¹⁵ And if anyone's name was not found written in the book of life, he was thrown into the lake of fire.

CHAPTER 21

¹ Then I saw a new heaven and a new earth, for the first heaven and the first earth had passed away, and the sea was no more.

² And I saw the holy city, new Jerusalem, coming down out of heaven from God, prepared as a bride adorned for her husband.

³ And I heard a loud voice from the throne saying, "Behold, the dwelling place of God is with man. He will dwell with them, and they will be his people, and God himself will be with them as their God.

⁴ "He will wipe away every tear from their eyes, and death shall be no more, neither shall there be mourning, nor crying, nor pain anymore, for the former things have passed away."

⁵ And he who was seated on the throne said, "Behold, I am making all things new." Also he said, "Write this down, for these words are trustworthy and true."

⁶ And he said to me, "It is done! I am the Alpha and the Omega, the beginning and the end. To the thirsty I will give from the spring of the water of life without payment.

⁷ "The one who conquers will have this heritage, and I will be his God and he will be my son.

⁸ "But as for the cowardly, the faithless, the detestable, as for murderers, the sexually immoral, sorcerers, idolaters, and all liars, their portion will be in the lake that burns with fire and sulfur, which is the second death."

⁹ Then came one of the seven angels who had the seven bowls full of the seven last plagues and spoke to me, saying, "Come, I will show you the Bride, the wife of the Lamb."

¹⁰ And he carried me away in the Spirit to a great, high mountain, and showed me

the holy city Jerusalem coming down out of heaven from God,

¹¹ having the glory of God, its radiance like a most rare jewel, like a jasper, clear as crystal.

¹² It had a great, high wall, with twelve gates, and at the gates twelve angels, and on the gates the names of the twelve tribes of the sons of Israel were inscribed—

¹³ on the east three gates, on the north three gates, on the south three gates, and on the west three gates.

¹⁴ And the wall of the city had twelve foundations, and on them were the twelve names of the twelve apostles of the Lamb.

¹⁵ And the one who spoke with me had a measuring rod of gold to measure the city and its gates and walls.

¹⁶ The city lies foursquare, its length the same as its width. And he measured the city with his rod, 12,000 stadia. Its length and width and height are equal.

¹⁷ He also measured its wall, 144 cubits by human measurement, which is also an angel's measurement.

¹⁸ The wall was built of jasper, while the city was pure gold, like clear glass.

¹⁹ The foundations of the wall of the city were adorned with every kind of jewel. The first was jasper, the second sapphire, the third agate, the fourth emerald,

²⁰ the fifth onyx, the sixth carnelian, the seventh chrysolite, the eighth beryl, the ninth topaz, the tenth chrysoprase, the eleventh jacinth, the twelfth amethyst.

²¹ And the twelve gates were twelve pearls, each of the gates made of a single pearl, and the street of the city was pure gold, like transparent glass.

²² And I saw no temple in the city, for its temple is the Lord God the Almighty and the Lamb.

²³ And the city has no need of sun or moon to shine on it, for the glory of God gives it light, and its lamp is the Lamb.

²⁴ By its light will the nations walk, and the kings of the earth will bring their glory into it,

²⁵ and its gates will never be shut by day—and there will be no night there.

²⁶ They will bring into it the glory and the honor of the nations.

²⁷ But nothing unclean will ever enter it, nor anyone who does what is detestable or false, but only those who are

written in the Lamb's book of life.

CHAPTER 22

¹ Then the angel showed me the river of the water of life, bright as crystal, flowing from the throne of God and of the Lamb

² through the middle of the street of the city; also, on either side of the river, the tree of life with its twelve kinds of fruit, yielding its fruit each month. The leaves of the tree were for the healing of the nations.

³ No longer will there be anything accursed, but the throne of God and of the Lamb will be in it, and his servants will worship him.

⁴ They will see his face, and his name will be on their foreheads.

⁵ And night will be no more. They will need no light of lamp or sun, for the Lord God will be their light, and they will reign forever and ever.

⁶ And he said to me, "These words are trustworthy and true. And the Lord, the God of the spirits of the prophets, has sent his angel to show his servants what must soon take place."

⁷ "And behold, I am coming soon. Blessed is the one who keeps the words of the prophecy of this book."

⁸ I, John, am the one who heard and saw these things. And when I heard and saw them, I fell down to worship at the feet of the angel who showed them to me,

⁹ but he said to me, "You must not do that! I am a fellow servant with you and your brothers the prophets, and with those who keep the words of this book. Worship God."

¹⁰ And he said to me, "Do not seal up the words of the prophecy of this book, for the time is near.

¹¹ "Let the evildoer still do evil, and the filthy still be filthy, and the righteous still do right, and the holy still be holy."

¹² "Behold, I am coming soon, bringing my recompense with me, to repay each one for what he has done.

¹³ "I am the Alpha and the Omega, the first and the last, the beginning and the end."

¹⁴ Blessed are those who wash their robes, so that they may have the right to the tree of life and that they may enter the city by the gates.

¹⁵ Outside are the dogs and sorcerers and the sexually immoral and murderers and idolaters, and everyone

who loves and practices falsehood.

¹⁶ "I, Jesus, have sent my angel to testify to you about these things for the churches. I am the root and the descendant of David, the bright morning star."

¹⁷ The Spirit and the Bride say, "Come." And let the one who hears say, "Come." And let the one who is thirsty come; let the one who desires take the water of life without price.

¹⁸ I warn everyone who hears the words of the prophecy of this book: if anyone adds to them, God will add to him the plagues described in this book,

¹⁹ and if anyone takes away from the words of the book of this prophecy, God will take away his share in the tree of life and in the holy city, which are described in this book.

²⁰ He who testifies to these things says, "Surely I am coming soon." Amen. Come, Lord Jesus!

²¹ The grace of the Lord Jesus be with all. Amen.

THE
PSALMS

THE PSALMS

PSALM 1

¹ Blessed is the man who walks not in the counsel of the wicked, nor stands in the way of sinners, nor sits in the seat of scoffers;

² but his delight is in the law of the LORD, and on his law he meditates day and night.

³ He is like a tree planted by streams of water that yields its fruit in its season, and its leaf does not wither. In all that he does, he prospers.

⁴ The wicked are not so, but are like chaff that the wind drives away.

⁵ Therefore the wicked will not stand in the judgment, nor sinners in the congregation of the righteous;

⁶ for the LORD knows the way of the righteous, but the way of the wicked will perish.

PSALM 2

¹ Why do the nations rage and the peoples plot in vain?

² The kings of the earth set themselves, and the rulers take counsel together, against the LORD and against his Anointed, saying,

³ "Let us burst their bonds apart and cast away their cords from us."

⁴ He who sits in the heavens laughs; the Lord holds them in derision.

⁵ Then he will speak to them in his wrath, and terrify them in his fury, saying,

⁶ "As for me, I have set my King on Zion, my holy hill."

⁷ I will tell of the decree: The LORD said to me, "You are my Son; today I have begotten you.

⁸ Ask of me, and I will make the nations your heritage, and the ends of the earth your possession.

⁹ You shall break them with a rod of iron and dash them in pieces like a potter's vessel."

¹⁰ Now therefore, O kings, be wise; be warned, O rulers of the earth.

¹¹ Serve the LORD with fear, and rejoice with trembling.

¹² Kiss the Son, lest he be angry, and you perish in the way, for his wrath is quickly kindled. Blessed are all who take refuge in him.

PSALM 3

A Psalm of David, when he fled from Absalom his son.

¹ O LORD, how many are my foes! Many are rising against me;

² many are saying of my soul, there is no salvation for him in God. Selah.

³ But you, O LORD, are a shield about me, my glory, and the lifter of my head.

⁴ I cried aloud to the LORD, and he answered me from his holy hill. Selah.

⁵ I lay down and slept; I woke again, for the LORD sustained me.

⁶ I will not be afraid of many thousands of people who have set themselves against me all around.

⁷ Arise, O LORD! Save me, O my God! For you strike all my enemies on the cheek; you break the teeth of the wicked.

⁸ Salvation belongs to the LORD; your blessing be on your people! Selah.

PSALM 4

To the choirmaster: with stringed instruments. A Psalm of David.

¹ Answer me when I call, O God of my righteousness! You have given me relief when I was in distress. Be gracious to me and hear my prayer!

² O men, how long shall my honor be turned into shame? How long will you love vain words and seek after lies? Selah.

³ But know that the LORD has set apart the godly for himself; the LORD hears when I call to him.

⁴ Be angry, and do not sin; ponder in your own hearts on your beds, and be silent. Selah.

⁵ Offer right sacrifices, and put your trust in the LORD.

⁶ There are many who say, "Who will show us some good? Lift up the light of your face upon us, O LORD!"

⁷ You have put more joy in my heart than they have when their grain and wine abound.

⁸ In peace I will both lie down and sleep; for you alone, O LORD, make me dwell in safety.

PSALM 5

To the choirmaster: for the flutes. A Psalm of David.

¹ Give ear to my words, O LORD; consider my groaning.

² Give attention to the sound of my cry, my King and my God, for to you do I pray.

³ O LORD, in the morning you hear my voice; in the morning I prepare a sacrifice for you and watch.

⁴ For you are not a God

who delights in wickedness; evil may not dwell with you.

5 The boastful shall not stand before your eyes; you hate all evildoers.

6 You destroy those who speak lies; the LORD abhors the bloodthirsty and deceitful man.

7 But I, through the abundance of your steadfast love, will enter your house. I will bow down toward your holy temple in the fear of you.

8 Lead me, O LORD, in your righteousness because of my enemies; make your way straight before me.

9 For there is no truth in their mouth; their inmost self is destruction; their throat is an open grave; they flatter with their tongue.

10 Make them bear their guilt, O God; let them fall by their own counsels; because of the abundance of their transgressions cast them out, for they have rebelled against you.

11 But let all who take refuge in you rejoice; let them ever sing for joy, and spread your protection over them, that those who love your name may exult in you.

12 For you bless the righteous, O LORD; you cover him with favor as with a shield.

PSALM 6

To the choirmaster: with stringed instruments; according to The Sheminith.
A Psalm of David.

1 O LORD, rebuke me not in your anger, nor discipline me in your wrath.

2 Be gracious to me, O LORD, for I am languishing; heal me, O LORD, for my bones are troubled.

3 My soul also is greatly troubled. But you, O LORD— how long?

4 Turn, O LORD, deliver my life; save me for the sake of your steadfast love.

5 For in death there is no remembrance of you; in Sheol who will give you praise?

6 I am weary with my moaning; every night I flood my bed with tears; I drench my couch with my weeping.

7 My eye wastes away because of grief; it grows weak because of all my foes.

8 Depart from me, all you workers of evil, for the LORD has heard the sound of my weeping.

9 The LORD has heard my plea; the LORD accepts my prayer.

10 All my enemies shall be ashamed and greatly troubled; they shall turn back and be put to shame in a moment.

PSALM 7

A Shiggaion of David, which he sang to the LORD concerning the words of Cush, a Benjaminite.

¹ O LORD my God, in you do I take refuge; save me from all my pursuers and deliver me,

² lest like a lion they tear my soul apart, rending it in pieces, with none to deliver.

³ O LORD my God, if I have done this, if there is wrong in my hands,

⁴ if I have repaid my friend with evil or plundered my enemy without cause,

⁵ let the enemy pursue my soul and overtake it, and let him trample my life to the ground and lay my glory in the dust. Selah.

⁶ Arise, O LORD, in your anger; lift yourself up against the fury of my enemies; awake for me; you have appointed a judgment.

⁷ Let the assembly of the peoples be gathered about you; over it return on high.

⁸ The LORD judges the peoples; judge me, O LORD, according to my righteousness and according to the integrity that is in me.

⁹ Oh, let the evil of the wicked come to an end, and may you establish the righteous— you who test the minds and hearts, O righteous God!

¹⁰ My shield is with God, who saves the upright in heart.

¹¹ God is a righteous judge, and a God who feels indignation every day.

¹² If a man does not repent, God will whet his sword; he has bent and readied his bow;

¹³ he has prepared for him his deadly weapons, making his arrows fiery shafts.

¹⁴ Behold, the wicked man conceives evil and is pregnant with mischief and gives birth to lies.

¹⁵ He makes a pit, digging it out, and falls into the hole that he has made.

¹⁶ His mischief returns upon his own head, and on his own skull his violence descends.

¹⁷ I will give to the LORD the thanks due to his righteousness, and I will sing praise to the name of the LORD, the Most High.

PSALM 8

To the choirmaster: according to The Gittith. A Psalm of David.

¹ O LORD, our Lord, how majestic is your name in all the earth! You have set your glory above the heavens.

² Out of the mouth of babies and infants, you have established strength because of your foes, to still the enemy and the avenger.

3 When I look at your heavens, the work of your fingers, the moon and the stars, which you have set in place,

4 what is man that you are mindful of him, and the son of man that you care for him?

5 Yet you have made him a little lower than the heavenly beings and crowned him with glory and honor.

6 You have given him dominion over the works of your hands; you have put all things under his feet,

7 all sheep and oxen, and also the beasts of the field,

8 the birds of the heavens, and the fish of the sea, whatever passes along the paths of the seas.

9 O LORD, our Lord, how majestic is your name in all the earth!

PSALM 9

To the choirmaster: according to Muth-labben. A Psalm of David.

1 I will give thanks to the LORD with my whole heart; I will recount all of your wonderful deeds.

2 I will be glad and exult in you; I will sing praise to your name, O Most High.

3 When my enemies turn back, they stumble and perish before your presence.

4 For you have maintained my just cause; you have sat on the throne, giving righteous judgment.

5 You have rebuked the nations; you have made the wicked perish; you have blotted out their name forever and ever.

6 The enemy came to an end in everlasting ruins; their cities you rooted out; the very memory of them has perished.

7 But the LORD sits enthroned forever; he has established his throne for justice,

8 and he judges the world with righteousness; he judges the peoples with uprightness.

9 The LORD is a stronghold for the oppressed, a stronghold in times of trouble.

10 And those who know your name put their trust in you, for you, O LORD, have not forsaken those who seek you.

11 Sing praises to the LORD, who sits enthroned in Zion! Tell among the peoples his deeds!

12 For he who avenges blood is mindful of them; he does not forget the cry of the afflicted.

13 Be gracious to me, O LORD! See my affliction from those who hate me, O you who lift me up from the gates of death,

14 that I may recount all

your praises, that in the gates of the daughter of Zion I may rejoice in your salvation.

¹⁵ The nations have sunk in the pit that they made; in the net that they hid, their own foot has been caught.

¹⁶ The LORD has made himself known; he has executed judgment; the wicked is snared in the work of their own hands. Higgaion. Selah.

¹⁷ The wicked shall return to Sheol, all the nations that forget God.

¹⁸ For the needy shall not always be forgotten, and the hope of the poor shall not perish forever.

¹⁹ Arise, O LORD! Let not man prevail; let the nations be judged before you!

²⁰ Put them in fear, O LORD! Let the nations know that they are but men! Selah.

PSALM 10

¹ Why, O LORD, do you stand far away? Why do you hide yourself in times of trouble?

² In arrogance the wicked hotly pursue the poor; let them be caught in the schemes that they have devised.

³ For the wicked boasts of the desires of his soul, and the one greedy for gain curses and renounces the LORD.

⁴ In the pride of his face the wicked does not seek him; all his thoughts are, "There is no God."

⁵ His ways prosper at all times; your judgments are on high, out of his sight; as for all his foes, he puffs at them.

⁶ He says in his heart, "I shall not be moved; throughout all generations I shall not meet adversity."

⁷ His mouth is filled with cursing and deceit and oppression; under his tongue are mischief and iniquity.

⁸ He sits in ambush in the villages; in hiding places he murders the innocent. His eyes stealthily watch for the helpless;

⁹ he lurks in ambush like a lion in his thicket; he lurks that he may seize the poor; he seizes the poor when he draws him into his net.

¹⁰ The helpless are crushed, sink down, and fall by his might.

¹¹ He says in his heart, "God has forgotten, he has hidden his face, he will never see it."

¹² Arise, O LORD; O God, lift up your hand; forget not the afflicted.

¹³ Why does the wicked renounce God and say in his heart, "You will not call to account"?

14 But you do see, for you note mischief and vexation, that you may take it into your hands; to you the helpless commits himself; you have been the helper of the fatherless.

15 Break the arm of the wicked and evildoer; call his wickedness to account till you find none.

16 The LORD is king forever and ever; the nations perish from his land.

17 O LORD, you hear the desire of the afflicted; you will strengthen their heart; you will incline your ear

18 to do justice to the fatherless and the oppressed, so that man who is of the earth may strike terror no more.

PSALM 11

To the choirmaster. Of David.

1 In the LORD I take refuge; how can you say to my soul, "Flee like a bird to your mountain,

2 "for behold, the wicked bend the bow; they have fitted their arrow to the string to shoot in the dark at the upright in heart;

3 "if the foundations are destroyed, what can the righteous do?"

4 The LORD is in his holy temple; the LORD's throne is in heaven; his eyes see,

his eyelids test the children of man.

5 The LORD tests the righteous, but his soul hates the wicked and the one who loves violence.

6 Let him rain coals on the wicked; fire and sulfur and a scorching wind shall be the portion of their cup.

7 For the LORD is righteous; he loves righteous deeds; the upright shall behold his face.

PSALM 12

To the choirmaster: according to The Sheminith. A Psalm of David.

1 Save, O LORD, for the godly one is gone; for the faithful have vanished from among the children of man.

2 Everyone utters lies to his neighbor; with flattering lips and a double heart they speak.

3 May the LORD cut off all flattering lips, the tongue that makes great boasts,

4 those who say, "With our tongue we will prevail, our lips are with us; who is master over us?"

5 "Because the poor are plundered, because the needy groan, I will now arise," says the LORD; "I will place him in the safety for which he longs."

6 The words of the LORD are pure words, like silver

refined in a furnace on the ground, purified seven times.

⁷ You, O LORD, will keep them; you will guard us from this generation forever.

⁸ On every side the wicked prowl, as vileness is exalted among the children of man.

PSALM 13

To the choirmaster.
A Psalm of David.

¹ How long, O LORD? Will you forget me forever? How long will you hide your face from me?

² How long must I take counsel in my soul and have sorrow in my heart all the day? How long shall my enemy be exalted over me?

³ Consider and answer me, O LORD my God; light up my eyes, lest I sleep the sleep of death,

⁴ lest my enemy say, "I have prevailed over him," lest my foes rejoice because I am shaken.

⁵ But I have trusted in your steadfast love; my heart shall rejoice in your salvation.

⁶ I will sing to the LORD, because he has dealt bountifully with me.

PSALM 14

To the choirmaster. Of David.

¹ The fool says in his heart, "There is no God." They are corrupt, they do abominable deeds, there is none who does good.

² The LORD looks down from heaven on the children of man, to see if there are any who understand, who seek after God.

³ They have all turned aside; together they have become corrupt; there is none who does good, not even one.

⁴ Have they no knowledge, all the evildoers who eat up my people as they eat bread and do not call upon the LORD?

⁵ There they are in great terror, for God is with the generation of the righteous.

⁶ You would shame the plans of the poor, but the LORD is his refuge.

⁷ Oh, that salvation for Israel would come out of Zion! When the LORD restores the fortunes of his people, let Jacob rejoice, let Israel be glad.

PSALM 15

A Psalm of David.

¹ O LORD, who shall sojourn in your tent? Who shall dwell on your holy hill?

² He who walks blamelessly and does what is right and speaks truth in his heart;

³ who does not slander with his tongue and does

no evil to his neighbor, nor takes up a reproach against his friend;

4 in whose eyes a vile person is despised, but who honors those who fear the LORD; who swears to his own hurt and does not change;

5 who does not put out his money at interest and does not take a bribe against the innocent. He who does these things shall never be moved.

PSALM 16

A Miktam of David.

1 Preserve me, O God, for in you I take refuge.

2 I say to the LORD, "You are my Lord; I have no good apart from you."

3 As for the saints in the land, they are the excellent ones, in whom is all my delight.

4 The sorrows of those who run after another god shall multiply; their drink offerings of blood I will not pour out or take their names on my lips.

5 The LORD is my chosen portion and my cup; you hold my lot.

6 The lines have fallen for me in pleasant places; indeed, I have a beautiful inheritance.

7 I bless the LORD who gives me counsel; in the night also my heart instructs me.

8 I have set the LORD always before me; because he is at my right hand, I shall not be shaken.

9 Therefore my heart is glad, and my whole being rejoices; my flesh also dwells secure.

10 For you will not abandon my soul to Sheol, or let your holy one see corruption.

11 You make known to me the path of life; in your presence there is fullness of joy; at your right hand are pleasures forevermore.

PSALM 17

A Prayer of David.

1 Hear a just cause, O LORD; attend to my cry! Give ear to my prayer from lips free of deceit!

2 From your presence let my vindication come! Let your eyes behold the right!

3 You have tried my heart, you have visited me by night, you have tested me, and you will find nothing; I have purposed that my mouth will not transgress.

4 With regard to the works of man, by the word of your lips I have avoided the ways of the violent.

5 My steps have held fast to your paths; my feet have not slipped.

⁶ I call upon you, for you will answer me, O God; incline your ear to me; hear my words.

⁷ Wondrously show your steadfast love, O Savior of those who seek refuge from their adversaries at your right hand.

⁸ Keep me as the apple of your eye; hide me in the shadow of your wings,

⁹ from the wicked who do me violence, my deadly enemies who surround me.

¹⁰ They close their hearts to pity; with their mouths they speak arrogantly.

¹¹ They have now surrounded our steps; they set their eyes to cast us to the ground.

¹² He is like a lion eager to tear, as a young lion lurking in ambush.

¹³ Arise, O Lord! Confront him, subdue him! Deliver my soul from the wicked by your sword,

¹⁴ from men by your hand, O Lord, from men of the world whose portion is in this life. You fill their womb with treasure; they are satisfied with children, and they leave their abundance to their infants.

¹⁵ As for me, I shall behold your face in righteousness; when I awake, I shall be satisfied with your likeness.

PSALM 18

To the choirmaster. A Psalm of David, the servant of the Lord, who addressed the words of this song to the Lord on the day when the Lord rescued him from the hand of all his enemies, and from the hand of Saul. He said:

¹ I love you, O Lord, my strength.

² The Lord is my rock and my fortress and my deliverer, my God, my rock, in whom I take refuge, my shield, and the horn of my salvation, my stronghold.

³ I call upon the Lord, who is worthy to be praised, and I am saved from my enemies.

⁴ The cords of death encompassed me; the torrents of destruction assailed me;

⁵ the cords of Sheol entangled me; the snares of death confronted me.

⁶ In my distress I called upon the Lord; to my God I cried for help. From his temple he heard my voice, and my cry to him reached his ears.

⁷ Then the earth reeled and rocked; the foundations also of the mountains trembled and quaked, because he was angry.

⁸ Smoke went up from his nostrils, and devouring fire from his mouth;

glowing coals flamed forth from him.

9 He bowed the heavens and came down; thick darkness was under his feet.

10 He rode on a cherub and flew; he came swiftly on the wings of the wind.

11 He made darkness his covering, his canopy around him, thick clouds dark with water.

12 Out of the brightness before him hailstones and coals of fire broke through his clouds.

13 The LORD also thundered in the heavens, and the Most High uttered his voice, hailstones and coals of fire.

14 And he sent out his arrows and scattered them; he flashed forth lightnings and routed them.

15 Then the channels of the sea were seen, and the foundations of the world were laid bare at your rebuke, O LORD, at the blast of the breath of your nostrils.

16 He sent from on high, he took me; he drew me out of many waters.

17 He rescued me from my strong enemy and from those who hated me, for they were too mighty for me.

18 They confronted me in the day of my calamity, but the LORD was my support.

19 He brought me out into a broad place; he rescued me, because he delighted in me.

20 The LORD dealt with me according to my righteousness; according to the cleanness of my hands he rewarded me.

21 For I have kept the ways of the LORD, and have not wickedly departed from my God.

22 For all his rules were before me, and his statutes I did not put away from me.

23 I was blameless before him, and I kept myself from my guilt.

24 So the LORD has rewarded me according to my righteousness, according to the cleanness of my hands in his sight.

25 With the merciful you show yourself merciful; with the blameless man you show yourself blameless;

26 with the purified you show yourself pure; and with the crooked you make yourself seem tortuous.

27 For you save a humble people, but the haughty eyes you bring down.

28 For it is you who light my lamp; the LORD my God lightens my darkness.

29 For by you I can run against a troop, and by my God I can leap over a wall.

30 This God—his way is perfect; the word of the LORD proves true; he is a shield for all those who take refuge in him.

31 For who is God, but the LORD? And who is a rock, except our God?—

32 the God who equipped me with strength and made my way blameless.

33 He made my feet like the feet of a deer and set me secure on the heights.

34 He trains my hands for war, so that my arms can bend a bow of bronze.

35 You have given me the shield of your salvation, and your right hand supported me, and your gentleness made me great.

36 You gave a wide place for my steps under me, and my feet did not slip.

37 I pursued my enemies and overtook them, and did not turn back till they were consumed.

38 I thrust them through, so that they were not able to rise; they fell under my feet.

39 For you equipped me with strength for the battle; you made those who rise against me sink under me.

40 You made my enemies turn their backs to me, and those who hated me I destroyed.

41 They cried for help, but there was none to save; they cried to the LORD, but he did not answer them.

42 I beat them fine as dust before the wind; I cast them out like the mire of the streets.

43 You delivered me from strife with the people; you made me the head of the nations; people whom I had not known served me.

44 As soon as they heard of me they obeyed me; foreigners came cringing to me.

45 Foreigners lost heart and came trembling out of their fortresses.

46 The LORD lives, and blessed be my rock, and exalted be the God of my salvation—

47 the God who gave me vengeance and subdued peoples under me,

48 who delivered me from my enemies; yes, you exalted me above those who rose against me; you rescued me from the man of violence.

49 For this I will praise you, O LORD, among the nations, and sing to your name.

50 Great salvation he brings to his king, and shows steadfast love to his anointed, to David and his offspring forever.

PSALM 19

To the choirmaster.
A Psalm of David.

¹ The heavens declare the glory of God, and the sky above proclaims his handiwork.

² Day to day pours out speech, and night to night reveals knowledge.

³ There is no speech, nor are there words, whose voice is not heard.

⁴ Their voice goes out through all the earth, and their words to the end of the world. In them he has set a tent for the sun,

⁵ which comes out like a bridegroom leaving his chamber, and, like a strong man, runs its course with joy.

⁶ Its rising is from the end of the heavens, and its circuit to the end of them, and there is nothing hidden from its heat.

⁷ The law of the LORD is perfect, reviving the soul; the testimony of the LORD is sure, making wise the simple;

⁸ the precepts of the LORD are right, rejoicing the heart; the commandment of the LORD is pure, enlightening the eyes;

⁹ the fear of the LORD is clean, enduring forever; the rules of the LORD are true, and righteous altogether.

¹⁰ More to be desired are they than gold, even much fine gold; sweeter also than honey and drippings of the honeycomb.

¹¹ Moreover, by them is your servant warned; in keeping them there is great reward.

¹² Who can discern his errors? Declare me innocent from hidden faults.

¹³ Keep back your servant also from presumptuous sins; let them not have dominion over me! Then I shall be blameless, and innocent of great transgression.

¹⁴ Let the words of my mouth and the meditation of my heart be acceptable in your sight, O LORD, my rock and my redeemer.

PSALM 20

To the choirmaster.
A Psalm of David.

¹ May the LORD answer you in the day of trouble! May the name of the God of Jacob protect you!

² May he send you help from the sanctuary and give you support from Zion!

³ May he remember all your offerings and regard with favor your burnt sacrifices! Selah.

⁴ May he grant you your heart's desire and fulfill all your plans!

⁵ May we shout for joy over your salvation, and in the name of our God set up our banners! May the LORD fulfill all your petitions!

⁶ Now I know that the LORD saves his anointed; he will answer him from his holy heaven with the saving might of his right hand.

⁷ Some trust in chariots and some in horses, but we trust in the name of the LORD our God.

⁸ They collapse and fall, but we rise and stand upright.

⁹ O LORD, save the king! May he answer us when we call.

PSALM 21

To the choirmaster.
A Psalm of David.

¹ O LORD, in your strength the king rejoices, and in your salvation how greatly he exults!

² You have given him his heart's desire and have not withheld the request of his lips. Selah.

³ For you meet him with rich blessings; you set a crown of fine gold upon his head.

⁴ He asked life of you; you gave it to him, length of days forever and ever.

⁵ His glory is great through your salvation; splendor and majesty you bestow on him.

⁶ For you make him most blessed forever; you make him glad with the joy of your presence.

⁷ For the king trusts in the LORD, and through the steadfast love of the Most High he shall not be moved.

⁸ Your hand will find out all your enemies; your right hand will find out those who hate you.

⁹ You will make them as a blazing oven when you appear. The LORD will swallow them up in his wrath, and fire will consume them.

¹⁰ You will destroy their descendants from the earth, and their offspring from among the children of man.

¹¹ Though they plan evil against you, though they devise mischief, they will not succeed.

¹² For you will put them to flight; you will aim at their faces with your bows.

¹³ Be exalted, O LORD, in your strength! We will sing and praise your power.

PSALM 22

To the choirmaster: according to The Doe of the Dawn.
A Psalm of David.

¹ My God, my God, why have you forsaken me? Why are you so far from saving me, from the words of my groaning?

2 O my God, I cry by day, but you do not answer, and by night, but I find no rest.

3 Yet you are holy, enthroned on the praises of Israel.

4 In you our fathers trusted; they trusted, and you delivered them.

5 To you they cried and were rescued; in you they trusted and were not put to shame.

6 But I am a worm and not a man, scorned by mankind and despised by the people.

7 All who see me mock me; they make mouths at me; they wag their heads;

8 "He trusts in the LORD; let him deliver him; let him rescue him, for he delights in him!"

9 Yet you are he who took me from the womb; you made me trust you at my mother's breasts.

10 On you was I cast from my birth, and from my mother's womb you have been my God.

11 Be not far from me, for trouble is near, and there is none to help.

12 Many bulls encompass me; strong bulls of Bashan surround me;

13 they open wide their mouths at me, like a ravening and roaring lion.

14 I am poured out like water, and all my bones are out of joint; my heart is like wax; it is melted within my breast;

15 my strength is dried up like a potsherd, and my tongue sticks to my jaws; you lay me in the dust of death.

16 For dogs encompass me; a company of evildoers encircles me; they have pierced my hands and feet—

17 I can count all my bones— they stare and gloat over me;

18 they divide my garments among them, and for my clothing they cast lots.

19 But you, O LORD, do not be far off! O you my help, come quickly to my aid!

20 Deliver my soul from the sword, my precious life from the power of the dog!

21 Save me from the mouth of the lion! You have rescued me from the horns of the wild oxen!

22 I will tell of your name to my brothers; in the midst of the congregation I will praise you:

23 You who fear the LORD, praise him! All you offspring of Jacob, glorify him, and stand in awe of him, all you offspring of Israel!

24 For he has not despised or abhorred the affliction of the afflicted, and he has not hidden his face from him, but has heard, when he cried to him.

²⁵ From you comes my praise in the great congregation; my vows I will perform before those who fear him.

²⁶ The afflicted shall eat and be satisfied; those who seek him shall praise the LORD! May your hearts live forever!

²⁷ All the ends of the earth shall remember and turn to the LORD, and all the families of the nations shall worship before you.

²⁸ For kingship belongs to the LORD, and he rules over the nations.

²⁹ All the prosperous of the earth eat and worship; before him shall bow all who go down to the dust, even the one who could not keep himself alive.

³⁰ Posterity shall serve him; it shall be told of the Lord to the coming generation;

³¹ they shall come and proclaim his righteousness to a people yet unborn, that he has done it.

PSALM 23
A Psalm of David.

¹ The LORD is my shepherd; I shall not want.

² He makes me lie down in green pastures. He leads me beside still waters.

³ He restores my soul. He leads me in paths of righteousness for his name's sake.

⁴ Even though I walk through the valley of the shadow of death, I will fear no evil, for you are with me; your rod and your staff, they comfort me.

⁵ You prepare a table before me in the presence of my enemies; you anoint my head with oil; my cup overflows.

⁶ Surely goodness and mercy shall follow me all the days of my life, and I shall dwell in the house of the LORD forever.

PSALM 24
A Psalm of David.

¹ The earth is the LORD's and the fullness thereof, the world and those who dwell therein,

² for he has founded it upon the seas and established it upon the rivers.

³ Who shall ascend the hill of the LORD? And who shall stand in his holy place?

⁴ He who has clean hands and a pure heart, who does not lift up his soul to what is false and does not swear deceitfully.

⁵ He will receive blessing from the LORD and righteousness from the God of his salvation.

⁶ Such is the generation of those who seek him, who seek the face of the God of Jacob. Selah.

⁷ Lift up your heads, O gates! And be lifted up, O ancient doors, that the King of glory may come in.

⁸ Who is this King of glory? The LORD, strong and mighty, the LORD, mighty in battle!

⁹ Lift up your heads, O gates! And lift them up, O ancient doors, that the King of glory may come in.

¹⁰ Who is this King of glory? The LORD of hosts, he is the King of glory! Selah.

PSALM 25
Of David.

¹ To you, O LORD, I lift up my soul.

² O my God, in you I trust; let me not be put to shame; let not my enemies exult over me.

³ Indeed, none who wait for you shall be put to shame; they shall be ashamed who are wantonly treacherous.

⁴ Make me to know your ways, O LORD; teach me your paths.

⁵ Lead me in your truth and teach me, for you are the God of my salvation; for you I wait all the day long.

⁶ Remember your mercy, O LORD, and your steadfast love, for they have been from of old.

⁷ Remember not the sins of my youth or my transgressions; according to your steadfast love remember me, for the sake of your goodness, O LORD!

⁸ Good and upright is the LORD; therefore he instructs sinners in the way.

⁹ He leads the humble in what is right, and teaches the humble his way.

¹⁰ All the paths of the LORD are steadfast love and faithfulness, for those who keep his covenant and his testimonies.

¹¹ For your name's sake, O LORD, pardon my guilt, for it is great.

¹² Who is the man who fears the LORD? Him will he instruct in the way that he should choose.

¹³ His soul shall abide in well-being, and his offspring shall inherit the land.

¹⁴ The friendship of the LORD is for those who fear him, and he makes known to them his covenant.

¹⁵ My eyes are ever toward the LORD, for he will pluck my feet out of the net.

¹⁶ Turn to me and be gracious to me, for I am lonely and afflicted.

¹⁷ The troubles of my heart are enlarged; bring me out of my distresses.

¹⁸ Consider my affliction

and my trouble, and forgive all my sins.

¹⁹ Consider how many are my foes, and with what violent hatred they hate me.

²⁰ Oh, guard my soul, and deliver me! Let me not be put to shame, for I take refuge in you.

²¹ May integrity and uprightness preserve me, for I wait for you.

²² Redeem Israel, O God, out of all his troubles.

PSALM 26

Of David.

¹ Vindicate me, O LORD, for I have walked in my integrity, and I have trusted in the LORD without wavering.

² Prove me, O LORD, and try me; test my heart and my mind.

³ For your steadfast love is before my eyes, and I walk in your faithfulness.

⁴ I do not sit with men of falsehood, nor do I consort with hypocrites.

⁵ I hate the assembly of evildoers, and I will not sit with the wicked.

⁶ I wash my hands in innocence and go around your altar, O LORD,

⁷ proclaiming thanksgiving aloud, and telling all your wondrous deeds.

⁸ O LORD, I love the habitation of your house and the place where your glory dwells.

⁹ Do not sweep my soul away with sinners, nor my life with bloodthirsty men,

¹⁰ in whose hands are evil devices, and whose right hands are full of bribes.

¹¹ But as for me, I shall walk in my integrity; redeem me, and be gracious to me.

¹² My foot stands on level ground; in the great assembly I will bless the LORD.

PSALM 27

Of David.

¹ The LORD is my light and my salvation; whom shall I fear? The LORD is the stronghold of my life; of whom shall I be afraid?

² When evildoers assail me to eat up my flesh, my adversaries and foes, it is they who stumble and fall,

³ Though an army encamp against me, my heart shall not fear; though war arise against me, yet I will be confident.

⁴ One thing have I asked of the LORD, that will I seek after: that I may dwell in the house of the LORD all the days of my life, to gaze upon the beauty of the LORD and to inquire in his temple.

⁵ For he will hide me in his

shelter in the day of trouble; he will conceal me under the cover of his tent; he will lift me high upon a rock.

⁶ And now my head shall be lifted up above my enemies all around me, and I will offer in his tent sacrifices with shouts of joy; I will sing and make melody to the LORD.

⁷ Hear, O LORD, when I cry aloud; be gracious to me and answer me!

⁸ You have said, "Seek my face." My heart says to you, "Your face, LORD, do I seek."

⁹ Hide not your face from me. Turn not your servant away in anger, O you who have been my help. Cast me not off; forsake me not, O God of my salvation!

¹⁰ For my father and my mother have forsaken me, but the LORD will take me in.

¹¹ Teach me your way, O LORD, and lead me on a level path because of my enemies.

¹² Give me not up to the will of my adversaries; for false witnesses have risen against me, and they breathe out violence.

¹³ I believe that I shall look upon the goodness of the LORD in the land of the living!

¹⁴ Wait for the LORD; be strong, and let your heart take courage; wait for the LORD!

PSALM 28
Of David.

¹ To you, O LORD, I call; my rock, be not deaf to me, lest, if you be silent to me, I become like those who go down to the pit.

² Hear the voice of my pleas for mercy, when I cry to you for help, when I lift up my hands toward your most holy sanctuary.

³ Do not drag me off with the wicked, with the workers of evil, who speak peace with their neighbors while evil is in their hearts.

⁴ Give to them according to their work and according to the evil of their deeds; give to them according to the work of their hands; render them their due reward.

⁵ Because they do not regard the works of the LORD or the work of his hands, he will tear them down and build them up no more.

⁶ Blessed be the LORD! For he has heard the voice of my pleas for mercy.

⁷ The LORD is my strength and my shield; in him my heart trusts, and I am helped; my heart exults, and with my song I give thanks to him.

⁸ The LORD is the strength of his people; he is the saving refuge of his anointed.

⁹ Oh, save your people and

bless your heritage! Be their shepherd and carry them forever.

PSALM 29

A Psalm of David.

¹ Ascribe to the LORD, O heavenly beings, ascribe to the LORD glory and strength.
² Ascribe to the LORD the glory due his name; worship the LORD in the splendor of holiness.
³ The voice of the LORD is over the waters; the God of glory thunders, the LORD, over many waters.
⁴ The voice of the LORD is powerful; the voice of the LORD is full of majesty.
⁵ The voice of the LORD breaks the cedars; the LORD breaks the cedars of Lebanon.
⁶ He makes Lebanon to skip like a calf, and Sirion like a young wild ox.
⁷ The voice of the LORD flashes forth flames of fire.
⁸ The voice of the LORD shakes the wilderness; the LORD shakes the wilderness of Kadesh.
⁹ The voice of the LORD makes the deer give birth and strips the forests bare, and in his temple all cry, "Glory!"
¹⁰ The LORD sits enthroned over the flood; the LORD sits enthroned as king forever.
¹¹ May the LORD give strength to his people! May the LORD bless his people with peace!

PSALM 30

A Psalm of David. A song at the dedication of the temple.

¹ I will extol you, O LORD, for you have drawn me up and have not let my foes rejoice over me.
² O LORD my God, I cried to you for help, and you have healed me.
³ O LORD, you have brought up my soul from Sheol; you restored me to life from among those who go down to the pit.
⁴ Sing praises to the LORD, O you his saints, and give thanks to his holy name.
⁵ For his anger is but for a moment, and his favor is for a lifetime. Weeping may tarry for the night, but joy comes with the morning.
⁶ As for me, I said in my prosperity, "I shall never be moved."
⁷ By your favor, O LORD, you made my mountain stand strong; you hid your face; I was dismayed.
⁸ To you, O LORD, I cry, and to the Lord I plead for mercy:
⁹ "What profit is there in my death, if I go down to the pit? Will the dust praise

you? Will it tell of your faithfulness?

¹⁰ "Hear, O LORD, and be merciful to me! O LORD, be my helper!"

¹¹ You have turned for me my mourning into dancing; you have loosed my sackcloth and clothed me with gladness,

¹² that my glory may sing your praise and not be silent. O LORD my God, I will give thanks to you forever!

PSALM 31

To the choirmaster.
A Psalm of David.

¹ In you, O LORD, do I take refuge; let me never be put to shame; in your righteousness deliver me!

² Incline your ear to me; rescue me speedily! Be a rock of refuge for me, a strong fortress to save me!

³ For you are my rock and my fortress; and for your name's sake you lead me and guide me;

⁴ you take me out of the net they have hidden for me, for you are my refuge.

⁵ Into your hand I commit my spirit; you have redeemed me, O LORD, faithful God.

⁶ I hate those who pay regard to worthless idols, but I trust in the LORD.

⁷ I will rejoice and be glad in your steadfast love, because you have seen my affliction; you have known the distress of my soul,

⁸ and you have not delivered me into the hand of the enemy; you have set my feet in a broad place.

⁹ Be gracious to me, O LORD, for I am in distress; my eye is wasted from grief; my soul and my body also.

¹⁰ For my life is spent with sorrow, and my years with sighing; my strength fails because of my iniquity, and my bones waste away.

¹¹ Because of all my adversaries I have become a reproach, especially to my neighbors, and an object of dread to my acquaintances; those who see me in the street flee from me.

¹² I have been forgotten like one who is dead; I have become like a broken vessel.

¹³ For I hear the whispering of many— terror on every side!— as they scheme together against me, as they plot to take my life.

¹⁴ But I trust in you, O LORD; I say, "You are my God."

¹⁵ My times are in your hand; rescue me from the hand of my enemies and from my persecutors!

¹⁶ Make your face shine on

your servant; save me in your steadfast love!

¹⁷ O LORD, let me not be put to shame, for I call upon you; let the wicked be put to shame; let them go silently to Sheol.

¹⁸ Let the lying lips be mute, which speak insolently against the righteous in pride and contempt.

¹⁹ Oh, how abundant is your goodness, which you have stored up for those who fear you and worked for those who take refuge in you, in the sight of the children of mankind!

²⁰ In the cover of your presence you hide them from the plots of men; you store them in your shelter from the strife of tongues.

²¹ Blessed be the LORD, for he has wondrously shown his steadfast love to me when I was in a besieged city.

²² I had said in my alarm, "I am cut off from your sight." But you heard the voice of my pleas for mercy when I cried to you for help.

²³ Love the LORD, all you his saints! The LORD preserves the faithful but abundantly repays the one who acts in pride.

²⁴ Be strong, and let your heart take courage, all you who wait for the LORD!

PSALM 32
A Maskil of David.

¹ Blessed is the one whose transgression is forgiven, whose sin is covered.

² Blessed is the man against whom the LORD counts no iniquity, and in whose spirit there is no deceit.

³ For when I kept silent, my bones wasted away through my groaning all day long.

⁴ For day and night your hand was heavy upon me; my strength was dried up as by the heat of summer. Selah.

⁵ I acknowledged my sin to you, and I did not cover my iniquity; I said, "I will confess my transgressions to the LORD," and you forgave the iniquity of my sin. Selah.

⁶ Therefore let everyone who is godly offer prayer to you at a time when you may be found; surely in the rush of great waters, they shall not reach him.

⁷ You are a hiding place for me; you preserve me from trouble; you surround me with shouts of deliverance. Selah.

⁸ I will instruct you and teach you in the way you should go; I will counsel you with my eye upon you.

⁹ Be not like a horse or a mule, without understanding, which must be curbed

with bit and bridle, or it will not stay near you.

¹⁰ Many are the sorrows of the wicked, but steadfast love surrounds the one who trusts in the LORD.

¹¹ Be glad in the LORD, and rejoice, O righteous, and shout for joy, all you upright in heart!

PSALM 33

¹ Shout for joy in the LORD, O you righteous! Praise befits the upright.

² Give thanks to the LORD with the lyre; make melody to him with the harp of ten strings!

³ Sing to him a new song; play skillfully on the strings, with loud shouts.

⁴ For the word of the LORD is upright, and all his work is done in faithfulness.

⁵ He loves righteousness and justice; the earth is full of the steadfast love of the LORD.

⁶ By the word of the LORD the heavens were made, and by the breath of his mouth all their host.

⁷ He gathers the waters of the sea as a heap; he puts the deeps in storehouses.

⁸ Let all the earth fear the LORD; let all the inhabitants of the world stand in awe of him!

⁹ For he spoke, and it came to be; he commanded, and it stood firm.

¹⁰ The LORD brings the counsel of the nations to nothing; he frustrates the plans of the peoples.

¹¹ The counsel of the LORD stands forever, the plans of his heart to all generations.

¹² Blessed is the nation whose God is the LORD, the people whom he has chosen as his heritage!

¹³ The LORD looks down from heaven; he sees all the children of man;

¹⁴ from where he sits enthroned he looks out on all the inhabitants of the earth,

¹⁵ he who fashions the hearts of them all and observes all their deeds.

¹⁶ The king is not saved by his great army; a warrior is not delivered by his great strength.

¹⁷ The war horse is a false hope for salvation, and by its great might it cannot rescue.

¹⁸ Behold, the eye of the LORD is on those who fear him, on those who hope in his steadfast love,

¹⁹ that he may deliver their soul from death and keep them alive in famine.

²⁰ Our soul waits for the LORD; he is our help and our shield.

²¹ For our heart is glad in

him, because we trust in his holy name.

²² Let your steadfast love, O LORD, be upon us, even as we hope in you.

PSALM 34

*Of David, when he changed
his behavior before Abimelech,
so that he drove him out,
and he went away.*

¹ I will bless the LORD at all times; his praise shall continually be in my mouth.

² My soul makes its boast in the LORD; let the humble hear and be glad.

³ Oh, magnify the LORD with me, and let us exalt his name together!

⁴ I sought the LORD, and he answered me and delivered me from all my fears.

⁵ Those who look to him are radiant, and their faces shall never be ashamed.

⁶ This poor man cried, and the LORD heard him and saved him out of all his troubles.

⁷ The angel of the LORD encamps around those who fear him, and delivers them.

⁸ Oh, taste and see that the LORD is good! Blessed is the man who takes refuge in him!

⁹ Oh, fear the LORD, you his saints, for those who fear him have no lack!

¹⁰ The young lions suffer want and hunger; but those who seek the LORD lack no good thing.

¹¹ Come, O children, listen to me; I will teach you the fear of the LORD.

¹² What man is there who desires life and loves many days, that he may see good?

¹³ Keep your tongue from evil and your lips from speaking deceit.

¹⁴ Turn away from evil and do good; seek peace and pursue it.

¹⁵ The eyes of the LORD are toward the righteous and his ears toward their cry.

¹⁶ The face of the LORD is against those who do evil, to cut off the memory of them from the earth.

¹⁷ When the righteous cry for help, the LORD hears and delivers them out of all their troubles.

¹⁸ The LORD is near to the brokenhearted and saves the crushed in spirit.

¹⁹ Many are the afflictions of the righteous, but the LORD delivers him out of them all.

²⁰ He keeps all his bones; not one of them is broken.

²¹ Affliction will slay the wicked, and those who hate the righteous will be condemned.

²² The LORD redeems the life of his servants; none of

those who take refuge in him will be condemned.

PSALM 35
Of David.

¹ Contend, O LORD, with those who contend with me; fight against those who fight against me!

² Take hold of shield and buckler and rise for my help!

³ Draw the spear and javelin against my pursuers! Say to my soul, "I am your salvation!"

⁴ Let them be put to shame and dishonor who seek after my life! Let them be turned back and disappointed who devise evil against me!

⁵ Let them be like chaff before the wind, with the angel of the LORD driving them away!

⁶ Let their way be dark and slippery, with the angel of the LORD pursuing them!

⁷ For without cause they hid their net for me; without cause they dug a pit for my life.

⁸ Let destruction come upon him when he does not know it! And let the net that he hid ensnare him; let him fall into it—to his destruction!

⁹ Then my soul will rejoice in the LORD, exulting in his salvation.

¹⁰ All my bones shall say, "O LORD, who is like you, delivering the poor from him who is too strong for him, the poor and needy from him who robs him?"

¹¹ Malicious witnesses rise up; they ask me of things that I do not know.

¹² They repay me evil for good; my soul is bereft.

¹³ But I, when they were sick— I wore sackcloth; I afflicted myself with fasting; I prayed with head bowed on my chest.

¹⁴ I went about as though I grieved for my friend or my brother; as one who laments his mother, I bowed down in mourning.

¹⁵ But at my stumbling they rejoiced and gathered; they gathered together against me; wretches whom I did not know tore at me without ceasing;

¹⁶ like profane mockers at a feast, they gnash at me with their teeth.

¹⁷ How long, O Lord, will you look on? Rescue me from their destruction, my precious life from the lions!

¹⁸ I will thank you in the great congregation; in the mighty throng I will praise you.

¹⁹ Let not those rejoice over me who are wrongfully my

foes, and let not those wink the eye who hate me without cause.

²⁰ For they do not speak peace, but against those who are quiet in the land they devise words of deceit.

²¹ They open wide their mouths against me; they say, "Aha, Aha! Our eyes have seen it!"

²² You have seen, O LORD; be not silent! O Lord, be not far from me!

²³ Awake and rouse yourself for my vindication, for my cause, my God and my Lord!

²⁴ Vindicate me, O LORD, my God, according to your righteousness, and let them not rejoice over me!

²⁵ Let them not say in their hearts, "Aha, our heart's desire!" Let them not say, "We have swallowed him up."

²⁶ Let them be put to shame and disappointed altogether who rejoice at my calamity! Let them be clothed with shame and dishonor who magnify themselves against me!

²⁷ Let those who delight in my righteousness shout for joy and be glad and say evermore, "Great is the LORD, who delights in the welfare of his servant!"

²⁸ Then my tongue shall tell of your righteousness and of your praise all the day long.

PSALM 36

To the choirmaster. Of David,
the servant of the LORD.

¹ Transgression speaks to the wicked deep in his heart; there is no fear of God before his eyes.

² For he flatters himself in his own eyes that his iniquity cannot be found out and hated.

³ The words of his mouth are trouble and deceit; he has ceased to act wisely and do good.

⁴ He plots trouble while on his bed; he sets himself in a way that is not good; he does not reject evil.

⁵ Your steadfast love, O LORD, extends to the heavens, your faithfulness to the clouds.

⁶ Your righteousness is like the mountains of God; your judgments are like the great deep; man and beast you save, O LORD.

⁷ How precious is your steadfast love, O God! The children of mankind take refuge in the shadow of your wings.

⁸ They feast on the abundance of your house, and you give them drink from the river of your delights.

⁹ For with you is the fountain of life; in your light do we see light.

¹⁰ Oh, continue your steadfast love to those who know you, and your righteousness to the upright of heart!

¹¹ Let not the foot of arrogance come upon me, nor the hand of the wicked drive me away.

¹² There the evildoers lie fallen; they are thrust down, unable to rise.

PSALM 37
Of David.

¹ Fret not yourself because of evildoers; be not envious of wrongdoers!

² For they will soon fade like the grass and wither like the green herb.

³ Trust in the LORD, and do good; dwell in the land and befriend faithfulness.

⁴ Delight yourself in the LORD, and he will give you the desires of your heart.

⁵ Commit your way to the LORD; trust in him, and he will act.

⁶ He will bring forth your righteousness as the light, and your justice as the noonday.

⁷ Be still before the LORD and wait patiently for him; fret not yourself over the one who prospers in his way, over the man who carries out evil devices!

⁸ Refrain from anger, and forsake wrath! Fret not yourself; it tends only to evil.

⁹ For the evildoers shall be cut off, but those who wait for the LORD shall inherit the land.

¹⁰ In just a little while, the wicked will be no more; though you look carefully at his place, he will not be there.

¹¹ But the meek shall inherit the land and delight themselves in abundant peace.

¹² The wicked plots against the righteous and gnashes his teeth at him,

¹³ but the Lord laughs at the wicked, for he sees that his day is coming.

¹⁴ The wicked draw the sword and bend their bows to bring down the poor and needy, to slay those whose way is upright;

¹⁵ their sword shall enter their own heart, and their bows shall be broken.

¹⁶ Better is the little that the righteous has than the abundance of many wicked.

¹⁷ For the arms of the wicked shall be broken, but the LORD upholds the righteous.

¹⁸ The LORD knows the days of the blameless, and their heritage will remain forever;

¹⁹ they are not put to shame

in evil times; in the days of famine they have abundance.

²⁰ But the wicked will perish; the enemies of the LORD are like the glory of the pastures; they vanish—like smoke they vanish away.

²¹ The wicked borrows but does not pay back, but the righteous is generous and gives;

²² for those blessed by the LORD shall inherit the land, but those cursed by him shall be cut off.

²³ The steps of a man are established by the LORD, when he delights in his way;

²⁴ though he fall, he shall not be cast headlong, for the LORD upholds his hand.

²⁵ I have been young, and now am old, yet I have not seen the righteous forsaken or his children begging for bread.

²⁶ He is ever lending generously, and his children become a blessing.

²⁷ Turn away from evil and do good; so shall you dwell forever.

²⁸ For the LORD loves justice; he will not forsake his saints. They are preserved forever, but the children of the wicked shall be cut off.

²⁹ The righteous shall inherit the land and dwell upon it forever.

³⁰ The mouth of the righteous utters wisdom, and his tongue speaks justice.

³¹ The law of his God is in his heart; his steps do not slip.

³² The wicked watches for the righteous and seeks to put him to death.

³³ The LORD will not abandon him to his power or let him be condemned when he is brought to trial.

³⁴ Wait for the LORD and keep his way, and he will exalt you to inherit the land; you will look on when the wicked are cut off.

³⁵ I have seen a wicked, ruthless man, spreading himself like a green laurel tree.

³⁶ But he passed away, and behold, he was no more; though I sought him, he could not be found.

³⁷ Mark the blameless and behold the upright, for there is a future for the man of peace.

³⁸ But transgressors shall be altogether destroyed; the future of the wicked shall be cut off.

³⁹ The salvation of the righteous is from the LORD; he is their stronghold in the time of trouble.

⁴⁰ The LORD helps them and delivers them; he delivers them from the wicked and

saves them, because they take refuge in him.

PSALM 38

A Psalm of David, for the memorial offering.

¹ O LORD, rebuke me not in your anger, nor discipline me in your wrath!

² For your arrows have sunk into me, and your hand has come down on me.

³ There is no soundness in my flesh because of your indignation; there is no health in my bones because of my sin.

⁴ For my iniquities have gone over my head; like a heavy burden, they are too heavy for me.

⁵ My wounds stink and fester because of my foolishness,

⁶ I am utterly bowed down and prostrate; all the day I go about mourning.

⁷ For my sides are filled with burning, and there is no soundness in my flesh.

⁸ I am feeble and crushed; I groan because of the tumult of my heart.

⁹ O Lord, all my longing is before you; my sighing is not hidden from you.

¹⁰ My heart throbs; my strength fails me, and the light of my eyes—it also has gone from me.

¹¹ My friends and companions stand aloof from my plague, and my nearest kin stand far off.

¹² Those who seek my life lay their snares; those who seek my hurt speak of ruin and meditate treachery all day long.

¹³ But I am like a deaf man; I do not hear, like a mute man who does not open his mouth.

¹⁴ I have become like a man who does not hear, and in whose mouth are no rebukes.

¹⁵ But for you, O LORD, do I wait; it is you, O Lord my God, who will answer.

¹⁶ For I said, "Only let them not rejoice over me, who boast against me when my foot slips!"

¹⁷ For I am ready to fall, and my pain is ever before me.

¹⁸ I confess my iniquity; I am sorry for my sin.

¹⁹ But my foes are vigorous, they are mighty, and many are those who hate me wrongfully.

²⁰ Those who render me evil for good accuse me because I follow after good.

²¹ Do not forsake me, O LORD! O my God, be not far from me!

²² Make haste to help me, O Lord, my salvation!

PSALM 39

*To the choirmaster: to
Jeduthun. A Psalm of David.*

¹ I said, "I will guard my ways,
that I may not sin with my
tongue; I will guard my
mouth with a muzzle, so
long as the wicked are in my
presence."

² I was mute and silent; I
held my peace to no avail,
and my distress grew worse.

³ My heart became hot within me. As I mused, the fire
burned; then I spoke with
my tongue:

⁴ "O LORD, make me know
my end and what is the measure of my days; let me know
how fleeting I am!

⁵ "Behold, you have made
my days a few handbreadths,
and my lifetime is as nothing before you. Surely all
mankind stands as a mere
breath! Selah.

⁶ "Surely a man goes about
as a shadow! Surely for nothing they are in turmoil; man
heaps up wealth and does
not know who will gather!

⁷ "And now, O Lord, for
what do I wait? My hope is
in you.

⁸ "Deliver me from all my
transgressions. Do not make
me the scorn of the fool!

⁹ "I am mute; I do not open
my mouth, for it is you who
have done it.

¹⁰ "Remove your stroke
from me; I am spent by the
hostility of your hand.

¹¹ "When you discipline a
man with rebukes for sin,
you consume like a moth
what is dear to him; surely
all mankind is a mere breath!
Selah.

¹² "Hear my prayer, O LORD,
and give ear to my cry; hold
not your peace at my tears!
For I am a sojourner with
you, a guest, like all my fathers.

¹³ "Look away from me, that
I may smile again, before I depart and am no more!"

PSALM 40

*To the choirmaster.
A Psalm of David.*

¹ I waited patiently for the
LORD; he inclined to me and
heard my cry.

² He drew me up from the
pit of destruction, out of the
miry bog, and set my feet
upon a rock, making my
steps secure.

³ He put a new song in my
mouth, a song of praise to
our God. Many will see and
fear, and put their trust in
the LORD.

⁴ Blessed is the man who
makes the LORD his trust,
who does not turn to the
proud, to those who go astray
after a lie!

⁵ You have multiplied, O LORD my God, your wondrous deeds and your thoughts toward us; none can compare with you! I will proclaim and tell of them, yet they are more than can be told.

⁶ In sacrifice and offering you have not delighted, but you have given me an open ear. Burnt offering and sin offering you have not required.

⁷ Then I said, "Behold, I have come; in the scroll of the book it is written of me:

⁸ "I delight to do your will, O my God; your law is within my heart."

⁹ I have told the glad news of deliverance in the great congregation; behold, I have not restrained my lips, as you know, O LORD.

¹⁰ I have not hidden your deliverance within my heart; I have spoken of your faithfulness and your salvation; I have not concealed your steadfast love and your faithfulness from the great congregation.

¹¹ As for you, O LORD, you will not restrain your mercy from me; your steadfast love and your faithfulness will ever preserve me!

¹² For evils have encompassed me beyond number; my iniquities have overtaken me, and I cannot see; they are more than the hairs of my head; my heart fails me.

¹³ Be pleased, O LORD, to deliver me! O LORD, make haste to help me!

¹⁴ Let those be put to shame and disappointed altogether who seek to snatch away my life; let those be turned back and brought to dishonor who delight in my hurt!

¹⁵ Let those be appalled because of their shame who say to me, "Aha, Aha!"

¹⁶ But may all who seek you rejoice and be glad in you; may those who love your salvation say continually, "Great is the LORD!"

¹⁷ As for me, I am poor and needy, but the Lord takes thought for me. You are my help and my deliverer; do not delay, O my God!

PSALM 41

To the choirmaster.
A Psalm of David.

¹ Blessed is the one who considers the poor! In the day of trouble the LORD delivers him;

² the LORD protects him and keeps him alive; he is called blessed in the land; you do not give him up to the will of his enemies.

³ The LORD sustains him on his sickbed; in his

illness you restore him to full health.

⁴ As for me, I said, "O LORD, be gracious to me; heal me, for I have sinned against you!"

⁵ My enemies say of me in malice, "When will he die, and his name perish?"

⁶ And when one comes to see me, he utters empty words, while his heart gathers iniquity; when he goes out, he tells it abroad.

⁷ All who hate me whisper together about me; they imagine the worst for me.

⁸ They say, "A deadly thing is poured out on him; he will not rise again from where he lies."

⁹ Even my close friend in whom I trusted, who ate my bread, has lifted his heel against me.

¹⁰ But you, O LORD, be gracious to me, and raise me up, that I may repay them!

¹¹ By this I know that you delight in me: my enemy will not shout in triumph over me.

¹² But you have upheld me because of my integrity, and set me in your presence forever.

¹³ Blessed be the LORD, the God of Israel, from everlasting to everlasting! Amen and Amen.

PSALM 42

To the choirmaster. A Maskil of the Sons of Korah.

¹ As a deer pants for flowing streams, so pants my soul for you, O God.

² My soul thirsts for God, for the living God. When shall I come and appear before God?

³ My tears have been my food day and night, while they say to me all the day long, "Where is your God?"

⁴ These things I remember, as I pour out my soul: how I would go with the throng and lead them in procession to the house of God with glad shouts and songs of praise, a multitude keeping festival.

⁵ Why are you cast down, O my soul, and why are you in turmoil within me? Hope in God; for I shall again praise him, my salvation

⁶ and my God. My soul is cast down within me; therefore I remember you from the land of Jordan and of Hermon, from Mount Mizar.

⁷ Deep calls to deep at the roar of your waterfalls; all your breakers and your waves have gone over me.

⁸ By day the LORD commands his steadfast love, and at night his song is with me, a prayer to the God of my life.

⁹ I say to God, my rock: "Why have you forgotten

me? Why do I go mourning because of the oppression of the enemy?"

¹⁰ As with a deadly wound in my bones, my adversaries taunt me, while they say to me all the day long, "Where is your God?"

¹¹ Why are you cast down, O my soul, and why are you in turmoil within me? Hope in God; for I shall again praise him, my salvation and my God.

PSALM 43

¹ Vindicate me, O God, and defend my cause against an ungodly people, from the deceitful and unjust man deliver me!

² For you are the God in whom I take refuge; why have you rejected me? Why do I go about mourning because of the oppression of the enemy?

³ Send out your light and your truth; let them lead me; let them bring me to your holy hill and to your dwelling!

⁴ Then I will go to the altar of God, to God my exceeding joy, and I will praise you with the lyre, O God, my God.

⁵ Why are you cast down, O my soul, and why are you in turmoil within me? Hope in God; for I shall again praise him, my salvation and my God.

PSALM 44

To the choirmaster. A Maskil of the Sons of Korah.

¹ O God, we have heard with our ears, our fathers have told us, what deeds you performed in their days, in the days of old:

² you with your own hand drove out the nations, but them you planted; you afflicted the peoples, but them you set free;

³ for not by their own sword did they win the land, nor did their own arm save them, but your right hand and your arm, and the light of your face, for you delighted in them.

⁴ You are my King, O God; ordain salvation for Jacob!

⁵ Through you we push down our foes; through your name we tread down those who rise up against us.

⁶ For not in my bow do I trust, nor can my sword save me.

⁷ But you have saved us from our foes and have put to shame those who hate us.

⁸ In God we have boasted continually, and we will give thanks to your name forever. Selah.

⁹ But you have rejected us and disgraced us and have not gone out with our armies.

¹⁰ You have made us turn

back from the foe, and those who hate us have gotten spoil.

¹¹ You have made us like sheep for slaughter and have scattered us among the nations.

¹² You have sold your people for a trifle, demanding no high price for them.

¹³ You have made us the taunt of our neighbors, the derision and scorn of those around us.

¹⁴ You have made us a byword among the nations, a laughingstock among the peoples.

¹⁵ All day long my disgrace is before me, and shame has covered my face

¹⁶ at the sound of the taunter and reviler, at the sight of the enemy and the avenger.

¹⁷ All this has come upon us, though we have not forgotten you, and we have not been false to your covenant.

¹⁸ Our heart has not turned back, nor have our steps departed from your way;

¹⁹ yet you have broken us in the place of jackals and covered us with the shadow of death.

²⁰ If we had forgotten the name of our God or spread out our hands to a foreign god,

²¹ would not God discover this? For he knows the secrets of the heart.

²² Yet for your sake we are killed all the day long; we are regarded as sheep to be slaughtered.

²³ Awake! Why are you sleeping, O Lord? Rouse yourself! Do not reject us forever!

²⁴ Why do you hide your face? Why do you forget our affliction and oppression?

²⁵ For our soul is bowed down to the dust; our belly clings to the ground.

²⁶ Rise up; come to our help! Redeem us for the sake of your steadfast love!

PSALM 45

To the choirmaster: according to Lilies. A Maskil of the Sons of Korah; a love song.

¹ My heart overflows with a pleasing theme; I address my verses to the king; my tongue is like the pen of a ready scribe.

² You are the most handsome of the sons of men; grace is poured upon your lips; therefore God has blessed you forever.

³ Gird your sword on your thigh, O mighty one, in your splendor and majesty!

⁴ In your majesty ride out victoriously for the cause of truth and meekness and righteousness; let your right

hand teach you awesome deeds!

⁵ Your arrows are sharp in the heart of the king's enemies; the peoples fall under you.

⁶ Your throne, O God, is forever and ever. The scepter of your kingdom is a scepter of uprightness;

⁷ you have loved righteousness and hated wickedness. Therefore God, your God, has anointed you with the oil of gladness beyond your companions;

⁸ your robes are all fragrant with myrrh and aloes and cassia. From ivory palaces stringed instruments make you glad;

⁹ daughters of kings are among your ladies of honor; at your right hand stands the queen in gold of Ophir.

¹⁰ Hear, O daughter, and consider, and incline your ear: forget your people and your father's house,

¹¹ and the king will desire your beauty. Since he is your lord, bow to him.

¹² The people of Tyre will seek your favor with gifts, the richest of the people.

¹³ All glorious is the princess in her chamber, with robes interwoven with gold.

¹⁴ In many-colored robes she is led to the king, with her virgin companions following behind her.

¹⁵ With joy and gladness they are led along as they enter the palace of the king.

¹⁶ In place of your fathers shall be your sons; you will make them princes in all the earth.

¹⁷ I will cause your name to be remembered in all generations; therefore nations will praise you forever and ever.

PSALM 46

To the choirmaster. Of the Sons of Korah. According to Alamoth. A Song.

¹ God is our refuge and strength, a very present help in trouble.

² Therefore we will not fear though the earth gives way, though the mountains be moved into the heart of the sea,

³ though its waters roar and foam, though the mountains tremble at its swelling. Selah.

⁴ There is a river whose streams make glad the city of God, the holy habitation of the Most High.

⁵ God is in the midst of her; she shall not be moved; God will help her when morning dawns.

⁶ The nations rage, the kingdoms totter; he utters his voice, the earth melts.

⁷ The LORD of hosts is with us; the God of Jacob is our fortress. Selah.

⁸ Come, behold the works of the LORD, how he has brought desolations on the earth.

⁹ He makes wars cease to the end of the earth; he breaks the bow and shatters the spear; he burns the chariots with fire.

¹⁰ "Be still, and know that I am God. I will be exalted among the nations, I will be exalted in the earth!"

¹¹ The LORD of hosts is with us; the God of Jacob is our fortress. Selah.

PSALM 47

To the choirmaster. A Psalm of the Sons of Korah.

¹ Clap your hands, all peoples! Shout to God with loud songs of joy!

² For the LORD, the Most High, is to be feared, a great king over all the earth.

³ He subdued peoples under us, and nations under our feet.

⁴ He chose our heritage for us, the pride of Jacob whom he loves. Selah.

⁵ God has gone up with a shout, the LORD with the sound of a trumpet.

⁶ Sing praises to God, sing praises! Sing praises to our King, sing praises!

⁷ For God is the King of all the earth; sing praises with a psalm!

⁸ God reigns over the nations; God sits on his holy throne.

⁹ The princes of the peoples gather as the people of the God of Abraham. For the shields of the earth belong to God; he is highly exalted!

PSALM 48

A Song. A Psalm of the Sons of Korah.

¹ Great is the LORD and greatly to be praised in the city of our God! His holy mountain,

² beautiful in elevation, is the joy of all the earth, Mount Zion, in the far north, the city of the great King.

³ Within her citadels God has made himself known as a fortress.

⁴ For behold, the kings assembled; they came on together.

⁵ As soon as they saw it, they were astounded; they were in panic; they took to flight.

⁶ Trembling took hold of them there, anguish as of a woman in labor.

⁷ By the east wind you shattered the ships of Tarshish.

⁸ As we have heard, so have we seen in the city of the LORD of hosts, in the city of

our God, which God will establish forever. Selah.

⁹ We have thought on your steadfast love, O God, in the midst of your temple.

¹⁰ As your name, O God, so your praise reaches to the ends of the earth. Your right hand is filled with righteousness.

¹¹ Let Mount Zion be glad! Let the daughters of Judah rejoice because of your judgments!

¹² Walk about Zion, go around her, number her towers,

¹³ consider well her ramparts, go through her citadels, that you may tell the next generation

¹⁴ that this is God, our God forever and ever. He will guide us forever.

PSALM 49

To the choirmaster. A Psalm of the Sons of Korah.

¹ Hear this, all peoples! Give ear, all inhabitants of the world,

² both low and high, rich and poor together!

³ My mouth shall speak wisdom; the meditation of my heart shall be understanding.

⁴ I will incline my ear to a proverb; I will solve my riddle to the music of the lyre.

⁵ Why should I fear in times of trouble, when the iniquity of those who cheat me surrounds me,

⁶ those who trust in their wealth and boast of the abundance of their riches?

⁷ Truly no man can ransom another, or give to God the price of his life,

⁸ for the ransom of their life is costly and can never suffice,

⁹ that he should live on forever and never see the pit.

¹⁰ For he sees that even the wise die; the fool and the stupid alike must perish and leave their wealth to others.

¹¹ Their graves are their homes forever, their dwelling places to all generations, though they called lands by their own names.

¹² Man in his pomp will not remain; he is like the beasts that perish.

¹³ This is the path of those who have foolish confidence; yet after them people approve of their boasts. Selah.

¹⁴ Like sheep they are appointed for Sheol; death shall be their shepherd; and the upright shall rule over them in the morning. Their form shall be consumed in Sheol, with no place to dwell.

¹⁵ But God will ransom my soul from the power of Sheol, for he will receive me. Selah.

¹⁶ Be not afraid when a man becomes rich, when the glory of his house increases.

¹⁷ For when he dies he will carry nothing away; his glory will not go down after him.

¹⁸ For though, while he lives, he counts himself blessed —and though you get praise when you do well for yourself—

¹⁹ his soul will go to the generation of his fathers, who will never again see light.

²⁰ Man in his pomp yet without understanding is like the beasts that perish.

PSALM 50

A Psalm of Asaph.

¹ The Mighty One, God the LORD, speaks and summons the earth from the rising of the sun to its setting.

² Out of Zion, the perfection of beauty, God shines forth.

³ Our God comes; he does not keep silence; before him is a devouring fire, around him a mighty tempest.

⁴ He calls to the heavens above and to the earth, that he may judge his people:

⁵ "Gather to me my faithful ones, who made a covenant with me by sacrifice!"

⁶ The heavens declare his righteousness, for God himself is judge! Selah.

⁷ "Hear, O my people, and I will speak; O Israel, I will testify against you. I am God, your God.

⁸ "Not for your sacrifices do I rebuke you; your burnt offerings are continually before me.

⁹ "I will not accept a bull from your house or goats from your folds.

¹⁰ "For every beast of the forest is mine, the cattle on a thousand hills.

¹¹ "I know all the birds of the hills, and all that moves in the field is mine.

¹² "If I were hungry, I would not tell you, for the world and its fullness are mine.

¹³ "Do I eat the flesh of bulls or drink the blood of goats?

¹⁴ "Offer to God a sacrifice of thanksgiving, and perform your vows to the Most High,

¹⁵ "and call upon me in the day of trouble; I will deliver you, and you shall glorify me."

¹⁶ But to the wicked God says: "What right have you to recite my statutes or take my covenant on your lips?

¹⁷ "For you hate discipline, and you cast my words behind you.

¹⁸ "If you see a thief, you are pleased with him, and you keep company with adulterers.

¹⁹ "You give your mouth free

rein for evil, and your tongue frames deceit.

²⁰ "You sit and speak against your brother; you slander your own mother's son.

²¹ "These things you have done, and I have been silent; you thought that I was one like yourself. But now I rebuke you and lay the charge before you.

²² "Mark this, then, you who forget God, lest I tear you apart, and there be none to deliver!

²³ "The one who offers thanksgiving as his sacrifice glorifies me; to one who orders his way rightly I will show the salvation of God!"

PSALM 51

To the choirmaster. A Psalm of David, when Nathan the prophet went to him, after he had gone in to Bathsheba.

¹ Have mercy on me, O God, according to your steadfast love; according to your abundant mercy blot out my transgressions.

² Wash me thoroughly from my iniquity, and cleanse me from my sin!

³ For I know my transgressions, and my sin is ever before me.

⁴ Against you, you only, have I sinned and done what is evil in your sight, so that you may be justified in your words and blameless in your judgment.

⁵ Behold, I was brought forth in iniquity, and in sin did my mother conceive me.

⁶ Behold, you delight in truth in the inward being, and you teach me wisdom in the secret heart.

⁷ Purge me with hyssop, and I shall be clean; wash me, and I shall be whiter than snow.

⁸ Let me hear joy and gladness; let the bones that you have broken rejoice.

⁹ Hide your face from my sins, and blot out all my iniquities.

¹⁰ Create in me a clean heart, O God, and renew a right spirit within me.

¹¹ Cast me not away from your presence, and take not your Holy Spirit from me.

¹² Restore to me the joy of your salvation, and uphold me with a willing spirit.

¹³ Then I will teach transgressors your ways, and sinners will return to you.

¹⁴ Deliver me from bloodguiltiness, O God, O God of my salvation, and my tongue will sing aloud of your righteousness.

¹⁵ O Lord, open my lips, and my mouth will declare your praise.

16 For you will not delight in sacrifice, or I would give it; you will not be pleased with a burnt offering.

17 The sacrifices of God are a broken spirit; a broken and contrite heart, O God, you will not despise.

18 Do good to Zion in your good pleasure; build up the walls of Jerusalem;

19 then will you delight in right sacrifices, in burnt offerings and whole burnt offerings; then bulls will be offered on your altar.

PSALM 52

To the choirmaster. A Maskil of David, when Doeg, the Edomite, came and told Saul, "David has come to the house of Ahimelech."

1 Why do you boast of evil, O mighty man? The steadfast love of God endures all the day.

2 Your tongue plots destruction, like a sharp razor, you worker of deceit.

3 You love evil more than good, and lying more than speaking what is right. Selah.

4 You love all words that devour, O deceitful tongue.

5 But God will break you down forever; he will snatch and tear you from your tent; he will uproot you from the land of the living. Selah.

6 The righteous shall see and fear, and shall laugh at him, saying,

7 "See the man who would not make God his refuge, but trusted in the abundance of his riches and sought refuge in his own destruction!"

8 But I am like a green olive tree in the house of God. I trust in the steadfast love of God forever and ever.

9 I will thank you forever, because you have done it. I will wait for your name, for it is good, in the presence of the godly.

PSALM 53

To the choirmaster: according to Mahalath. A Maskil of David.

1 The fool says in his heart, "There is no God." They are corrupt, doing abominable iniquity; there is none who does good.

2 God looks down from heaven on the children of man to see if there are any who understand, who seek after God.

3 They have all fallen away; together they have become corrupt; there is none who does good, not even one.

4 Have those who work evil no knowledge, who eat up my people as they eat bread, and do not call upon God?

5 There they are, in great terror, where there is no

terror! For God scatters the bones of him who encamps against you; you put them to shame, for God has rejected them.

⁶ Oh, that salvation for Israel would come out of Zion! When God restores the fortunes of his people, let Jacob rejoice, let Israel be glad.

PSALM 54

To the choirmaster: with stringed instruments. A Maskil of David, when the Ziphites went and told Saul, "Is not David hiding among us?"

¹ O God, save me by your name, and vindicate me by your might.

² O God, hear my prayer; give ear to the words of my mouth.

³ For strangers have risen against me; ruthless men seek my life; they do not set God before themselves. Selah.

⁴ Behold, God is my helper; the Lord is the upholder of my life.

⁵ He will return the evil to my enemies; in your faithfulness put an end to them.

⁶ With a freewill offering I will sacrifice to you; I will give thanks to your name, O Lord, for it is good.

⁷ For he has delivered me from every trouble, and my eye has looked in triumph on my enemies.

PSALM 55

To the choirmaster: with stringed instruments. A Maskil of David.

¹ Give ear to my prayer, O God, and hide not yourself from my plea for mercy!

² Attend to me, and answer me; I am restless in my complaint and I moan,

³ because of the noise of the enemy, because of the oppression of the wicked. For they drop trouble upon me, and in anger they bear a grudge against me.

⁴ My heart is in anguish within me; the terrors of death have fallen upon me.

⁵ Fear and trembling come upon me, and horror overwhelms me.

⁶ And I say, "Oh, that I had wings like a dove! I would fly away and be at rest;

⁷ "yes, I would wander far away; I would lodge in the wilderness; Selah,

⁸ "I would hurry to find a shelter from the raging wind and tempest."

⁹ Destroy, O Lord, divide their tongues; for I see violence and strife in the city.

¹⁰ Day and night they go around it on its walls, and iniquity and trouble are within it;

11 ruin is in its midst; oppression and fraud do not depart from its marketplace.

12 For it is not an enemy who taunts me— then I could bear it; it is not an adversary who deals insolently with me— then I could hide from him.

13 But it is you, a man, my equal, my companion, my familiar friend.

14 We used to take sweet counsel together; within God's house we walked in the throng.

15 Let death steal over them; let them go down to Sheol alive; for evil is in their dwelling place and in their heart.

16 But I call to God, and the LORD will save me.

17 Evening and morning and at noon I utter my complaint and moan, and he hears my voice.

18 He redeems my soul in safety from the battle that I wage, for many are arrayed against me.

19 God will give ear and humble them, he who is enthroned from of old, Selah, because they do not change and do not fear God.

20 My companion stretched out his hand against his friends; he violated his covenant.

21 His speech was smooth as butter, yet war was in his heart; his words were softer than oil, yet they were drawn swords.

22 Cast your burden on the LORD, and he will sustain you; he will never permit the righteous to be moved.

23 But you, O God, will cast them down into the pit of destruction; men of blood and treachery shall not live out half their days. But I will trust in you.

PSALM 56

To the choirmaster: according to The Dove on Far-off Terebinths. A Miktam of David, when the Philistines seized him in Gath.

1 Be gracious to me, O God, for man tramples on me; all day long an attacker oppresses me;

2 my enemies trample on me all day long, for many attack me proudly.

3 When I am afraid, I put my trust in you.

4 In God, whose word I praise, in God I trust; I shall not be afraid. What can flesh do to me?

5 All day long they injure my cause; all their thoughts are against me for evil.

6 They stir up strife, they lurk; they watch my steps, as they have waited for my life.

7 For their crime will they escape? In wrath cast down the peoples, O God!

⁸ You have kept count of my tossings; put my tears in your bottle. Are they not in your book?

⁹ Then my enemies will turn back in the day when I call. This I know, that God is for me.

¹⁰ In God, whose word I praise, in the LORD, whose word I praise,

¹¹ in God I trust; I shall not be afraid. What can man do to me?

¹² I must perform my vows to you, O God; I will render thank offerings to you.

¹³ For you have delivered my soul from death, yes, my feet from falling, that I may walk before God in the light of life.

PSALM 57

To the choirmaster: according to Do Not Destroy. A Miktam of David, when he fled from Saul, in the cave.

¹ Be merciful to me, O God, be merciful to me, for in you my soul takes refuge; in the shadow of your wings I will take refuge, till the storms of destruction pass by.

² I cry out to God Most High, to God who fulfills his purpose for me.

³ He will send from heaven and save me; he will put to shame him who tramples on me. Selah. God will send out his steadfast love and his faithfulness!

⁴ My soul is in the midst of lions; I lie down amid fiery beasts— the children of man, whose teeth are spears and arrows, whose tongues are sharp swords.

⁵ Be exalted, O God, above the heavens! Let your glory be over all the earth!

⁶ They set a net for my steps; my soul was bowed down. They dug a pit in my way, but they have fallen into it themselves. Selah.

⁷ My heart is steadfast, O God, my heart is steadfast! I will sing and make melody!

⁸ Awake, my glory! Awake, O harp and lyre! I will awake the dawn!

⁹ I will give thanks to you, O Lord, among the peoples; I will sing praises to you among the nations.

¹⁰ For your steadfast love is great to the heavens, your faithfulness to the clouds.

¹¹ Be exalted, O God, above the heavens! Let your glory be over all the earth!

PSALM 58

To the choirmaster: according to Do Not Destroy. A Miktam of David.

¹ Do you indeed decree what is right, you gods? Do you

judge the children of man uprightly?

² No, in your hearts you devise wrongs; your hands deal out violence on earth.

³ The wicked are estranged from the womb; they go astray from birth, speaking lies.

⁴ They have venom like the venom of a serpent, like the deaf adder that stops its ear,

⁵ so that it does not hear the voice of charmers or of the cunning enchanter.

⁶ O God, break the teeth in their mouths; tear out the fangs of the young lions, O LORD!

⁷ Let them vanish like water that runs away; when he aims his arrows, let them be blunted.

⁸ Let them be like the snail that dissolves into slime, like the stillborn child who never sees the sun.

⁹ Sooner than your pots can feel the heat of thorns, whether green or ablaze, may he sweep them away!

¹⁰ The righteous will rejoice when he sees the vengeance; he will bathe his feet in the blood of the wicked.

¹¹ Mankind will say, "Surely there is a reward for the righteous; surely there is a God who judges on earth."

PSALM 59

To the choirmaster: according to Do Not Destroy. A Miktam of David, when Saul sent men to watch his house in order to kill him.

¹ Deliver me from my enemies, O my God; protect me from those who rise up against me;

² deliver me from those who work evil, and save me from bloodthirsty men.

³ For behold, they lie in wait for my life; fierce men stir up strife against me. For no transgression or sin of mine, O LORD,

⁴ for no fault of mine, they run and make ready. Awake, come to meet me, and see!

⁵ You, LORD God of hosts, are God of Israel. Rouse yourself to punish all the nations; spare none of those who treacherously plot evil. Selah.

⁶ Each evening they come back, howling like dogs and prowling about the city.

⁷ There they are, bellowing with their mouths with swords in their lips— for "Who," they think, "will hear us?"

⁸ But you, O LORD, laugh at them; you hold all the nations in derision.

⁹ O my Strength, I will

watch for you, for you, O God, are my fortress.

¹⁰ My God in his steadfast love will meet me; God will let me look in triumph on my enemies.

¹¹ Kill them not, lest my people forget; make them totter by your power and bring them down, O Lord, our shield!

¹² For the sin of their mouths, the words of their lips, let them be trapped in their pride. For the cursing and lies that they utter,

¹³ consume them in wrath; consume them till they are no more, that they may know that God rules over Jacob to the ends of the earth. Selah.

¹⁴ Each evening they come back, howling like dogs and prowling about the city.

¹⁵ They wander about for food and growl if they do not get their fill.

¹⁶ But I will sing of your strength; I will sing aloud of your steadfast love in the morning. For you have been to me a fortress and a refuge in the day of my distress.

¹⁷ O my Strength, I will sing praises to you, for you, O God, are my fortress, the God who shows me steadfast love.

PSALM 60

To the choirmaster: according to Shushan Eduth. A Miktam of David; for instruction; when he strove with Aram-naharaim and with Aram-zobah, and when Joab on his return struck down twelve thousand of Edom in the Valley of Salt.

¹ O God, you have rejected us, broken our defenses; you have been angry; oh, restore us.

² You have made the land to quake; you have torn it open; repair its breaches, for it totters.

³ You have made your people see hard things; you have given us wine to drink that made us stagger.

⁴ You have set up a banner for those who fear you, that they may flee to it from the bow. Selah.

⁵ That your beloved ones may be delivered, give salvation by your right hand and answer us!

⁶ God has spoken in his holiness: "With exultation I will divide up Shechem and portion out the Vale of Succoth.

⁷ "Gilead is mine; Manasseh is mine; Ephraim is my helmet; Judah is my scepter.

⁸ "Moab is my washbasin; upon Edom I cast my shoe; over Philistia I shout in triumph."

⁹ Who will bring me to the fortified city? Who will lead me to Edom?

¹⁰ Have you not rejected us, O God? You do not go forth, O God, with our armies.

¹¹ Oh, grant us help against the foe, for vain is the salvation of man!

¹² With God we shall do valiantly; it is he who will tread down our foes.

PSALM 61

To the choirmaster: with stringed instruments. Of David.

¹ Hear my cry, O God, listen to my prayer;

² from the end of the earth I call to you when my heart is faint. Lead me to the rock that is higher than I,

³ for you have been my refuge, a strong tower against the enemy.

⁴ Let me dwell in your tent forever! Let me take refuge under the shelter of your wings! Selah.

⁵ For you, O God, have heard my vows; you have given me the heritage of those who fear your name.

⁶ Prolong the life of the king; may his years endure to all generations!

⁷ May he be enthroned forever before God; appoint steadfast love and faithfulness to watch over him!

⁸ So will I ever sing praises to your name, as I perform my vows day after day.

PSALM 62

To the choirmaster: according to Jeduthun. A Psalm of David.

¹ For God alone my soul waits in silence; from him comes my salvation.

² He alone is my rock and my salvation, my fortress; I shall not be greatly shaken.

³ How long will all of you attack a man to batter him, like a leaning wall, a tottering fence?

⁴ They only plan to thrust him down from his high position. They take pleasure in falsehood. They bless with their mouths, but inwardly they curse. Selah.

⁵ For God alone, O my soul, wait in silence, for my hope is from him.

⁶ He only is my rock and my salvation, my fortress; I shall not be shaken.

⁷ On God rests my salvation and my glory; my mighty rock, my refuge is God.

⁸ Trust in him at all times, O people; pour out your heart before him; God is a refuge for us. Selah.

⁹ Those of low estate are but a breath; those of high estate are a delusion; in the balances they go up; they

are together lighter than a breath.

¹⁰ Put no trust in extortion; set no vain hopes on robbery; if riches increase, set not your heart on them.

¹¹ Once God has spoken; twice have I heard this: that power belongs to God,

¹² and that to you, O Lord, belongs steadfast love. For you will render to a man according to his work.

PSALM 63

A Psalm of David, when he was in the wilderness of Judah.

¹ O God, you are my God; earnestly I seek you; my soul thirsts for you; my flesh faints for you, as in a dry and weary land where there is no water.

² So I have looked upon you in the sanctuary, beholding your power and glory.

³ Because your steadfast love is better than life, my lips will praise you.

⁴ So I will bless you as long as I live; in your name I will lift up my hands.

⁵ My soul will be satisfied as with fat and rich food, and my mouth will praise you with joyful lips,

⁶ when I remember you upon my bed, and meditate on you in the watches of the night;

⁷ for you have been my help, and in the shadow of your wings I will sing for joy.

⁸ My soul clings to you; your right hand upholds me.

⁹ But those who seek to destroy my life shall go down into the depths of the earth;

¹⁰ they shall be given over to the power of the sword; they shall be a portion for jackals.

¹¹ But the king shall rejoice in God; all who swear by him shall exult, for the mouths of liars will be stopped.

PSALM 64

To the choirmaster. A Psalm of David.

¹ Hear my voice, O God, in my complaint; preserve my life from dread of the enemy.

² Hide me from the secret plots of the wicked, from the throng of evildoers,

³ who whet their tongues like swords, who aim bitter words like arrows,

⁴ shooting from ambush at the blameless, shooting at him suddenly and without fear.

⁵ They hold fast to their evil purpose; they talk of laying snares secretly, thinking, "Who can see them?"

⁶ They search out injustice,

saying, "We have accomplished a diligent search." For the inward mind and heart of a man are deep.

⁷ But God shoots his arrow at them; they are wounded suddenly.

⁸ They are brought to ruin, with their own tongues turned against them; all who see them will wag their heads.

⁹ Then all mankind fears; they tell what God has brought about and ponder what he has done.

¹⁰ Let the righteous one rejoice in the Lᴏʀᴅ and take refuge in him! Let all the upright in heart exult!

PSALM 65

To the choirmaster.
A Psalm of David. A Song.

¹ Praise is due to you, O God, in Zion, and to you shall vows be performed.

² O you who hear prayer, to you shall all flesh come.

³ When iniquities prevail against me, you atone for our transgressions.

⁴ Blessed is the one you choose and bring near, to dwell in your courts! We shall be satisfied with the goodness of your house, the holiness of your temple!

⁵ By awesome deeds you answer us with righteousness, O God of our salvation, the hope of all the ends of the earth and of the farthest seas;

⁶ the one who by his strength established the mountains, being girded with might;

⁷ who stills the roaring of the seas, the roaring of their waves, the tumult of the peoples,

⁸ so that those who dwell at the ends of the earth are in awe at your signs. You make the going out of the morning and the evening to shout for joy.

⁹ You visit the earth and water it; you greatly enrich it; the river of God is full of water; you provide their grain, for so you have prepared it.

¹⁰ You water its furrows abundantly, settling its ridges, softening it with showers, and blessing its growth.

¹¹ You crown the year with your bounty; your wagon tracks overflow with abundance.

¹² The pastures of the wilderness overflow, the hills gird themselves with joy,

¹³ the meadows clothe themselves with flocks, the valleys deck themselves with grain, they shout and sing together for joy.

PSALM 66

To the choirmaster.
A Song. A Psalm.

¹ Shout for joy to God, all the earth;

² sing the glory of his name; give to him glorious praise!

³ Say to God, "How awesome are your deeds! So great is your power that your enemies come cringing to you.

⁴ "All the earth worships you and sings praises to you; they sing praises to your name." Selah.

⁵ Come and see what God has done: he is awesome in his deeds toward the children of man.

⁶ He turned the sea into dry land; they passed through the river on foot. There did we rejoice in him,

⁷ who rules by his might forever, whose eyes keep watch on the nations— let not the rebellious exalt themselves. Selah.

⁸ Bless our God, O peoples; let the sound of his praise be heard,

⁹ who has kept our soul among the living and has not let our feet slip.

¹⁰ For you, O God, have tested us; you have tried us as silver is tried.

¹¹ You brought us into the net; you laid a crushing burden on our backs;

¹² you let men ride over our heads; we went through fire and through water; yet you have brought us out to a place of abundance.

¹³ I will come into your house with burnt offerings; I will perform my vows to you,

¹⁴ that which my lips uttered and my mouth promised when I was in trouble.

¹⁵ I will offer to you burnt offerings of fattened animals, with the smoke of the sacrifice of rams; I will make an offering of bulls and goats. Selah.

¹⁶ Come and hear, all you who fear God, and I will tell what he has done for my soul.

¹⁷ I cried to him with my mouth, and high praise was on my tongue.

¹⁸ If I had cherished iniquity in my heart, the Lord would not have listened.

¹⁹ But truly God has listened; he has attended to the voice of my prayer.

²⁰ Blessed be God, because he has not rejected my prayer or removed his steadfast love from me!

PSALM 67

To the choirmaster: with stringed instruments. A Psalm. A Song.

¹ May God be gracious to us and bless us and make his face to shine upon us, Selah,

2 that your way may be known on earth, your saving power among all nations.

3 Let the peoples praise you, O God; let all the peoples praise you!

4 Let the nations be glad and sing for joy, for you judge the peoples with equity and guide the nations upon earth. Selah.

5 Let the peoples praise you, O God; let all the peoples praise you!

6 The earth has yielded its increase; God, our God, shall bless us.

7 God shall bless us; let all the ends of the earth fear him!

PSALM 68

To the choirmaster.
A Psalm of David. A Song.

1 God shall arise, his enemies shall be scattered; and those who hate him shall flee before him!

2 As smoke is driven away, so you shall drive them away; as wax melts before fire, so the wicked shall perish before God!

3 But the righteous shall be glad; they shall exult before God; they shall be jubilant with joy!

4 Sing to God, sing praises to his name; lift up a song to him who rides through the deserts; his name is the LORD; exult before him!

5 Father of the fatherless and protector of widows is God in his holy habitation.

6 God settles the solitary in a home; he leads out the prisoners to prosperity, but the rebellious dwell in a parched land.

7 O God, when you went out before your people, when you marched through the wilderness, Selah,

8 the earth quaked, the heavens poured down rain, before God, the One of Sinai, before God, the God of Israel.

9 Rain in abundance, O God, you shed abroad; you restored your inheritance as it languished;

10 your flock found a dwelling in it; in your goodness, O God, you provided for the needy.

11 The Lord gives the word; the women who announce the news are a great host:

12 "The kings of the armies—they flee, they flee!" The women at home divide the spoil—

13 though you men lie among the sheepfolds— the wings of a dove covered with silver, its pinions with shimmering gold.

14 When the Almighty scat-

ters kings there, let snow fall on Zalmon.

¹⁵ O mountain of God, mountain of Bashan; O many-peaked mountain, mountain of Bashan!

¹⁶ Why do you look with hatred, O many-peaked mountain, at the mount that God desired for his abode, yes, where the Lord will dwell forever?

¹⁷ The chariots of God are twice ten thousand, thousands upon thousands; the Lord is among them; Sinai is now in the sanctuary.

¹⁸ You ascended on high, leading a host of captives in your train and receiving gifts among men, even among the rebellious, that the Lord God may dwell there.

¹⁹ Blessed be the Lord, who daily bears us up; God is our salvation. Selah.

²⁰ Our God is a God of salvation, and to God, the Lord, belong deliverances from death.

²¹ But God will strike the heads of his enemies, the hairy crown of him who walks in his guilty ways.

²² The Lord said, "I will bring them back from Bashan, I will bring them back from the depths of the sea,

²³ "that you may strike your feet in their blood, that the tongues of your dogs may have their portion from the foe."

²⁴ Your procession is seen, O God, the procession of my God, my King, into the sanctuary—

²⁵ the singers in front, the musicians last, between them virgins playing tambourines:

²⁶ "Bless God in the great congregation, the Lord; O you who are of Israel's fountain!"

²⁷ There is Benjamin, the least of them, in the lead, the princes of Judah in their throng, the princes of Zebulun, the princes of Naphtali.

²⁸ Summon your power, O God, the power, O God, by which you have worked for us.

²⁹ Because of your temple at Jerusalem kings shall bear gifts to you.

³⁰ Rebuke the beasts that dwell among the reeds, the herd of bulls with the calves of the peoples. Trample underfoot those who lust after tribute; scatter the peoples who delight in war.

³¹ Nobles shall come from Egypt; Cush shall hasten to stretch out her hands to God.

³² O kingdoms of the earth, sing to God; sing praises to the Lord, Selah,

³³ to him who rides in the heavens, the ancient heavens; behold, he sends out his voice, his mighty voice.

³⁴ Ascribe power to God, whose majesty is over Israel, and whose power is in the skies.

³⁵ Awesome is God from his sanctuary; the God of Israel—he is the one who gives power and strength to his people. Blessed be God!

PSALM 69

To the choirmaster: according to Lilies. Of David.

¹ Save me, O God! For the waters have come up to my neck.

² I sink in deep mire, where there is no foothold; I have come into deep waters, and the flood sweeps over me.

³ I am weary with my crying out; my throat is parched. My eyes grow dim with waiting for my God.

⁴ More in number than the hairs of my head are those who hate me without cause; mighty are those who would destroy me, those who attack me with lies. What I did not steal must I now restore?

⁵ O God, you know my folly; the wrongs I have done are not hidden from you.

⁶ Let not those who hope in you be put to shame through me, O Lord GOD of hosts; let not those who seek you be brought to dishonor through me, O God of Israel.

⁷ For it is for your sake that I have borne reproach, that dishonor has covered my face.

⁸ I have become a stranger to my brothers, an alien to my mother's sons.

⁹ For zeal for your house has consumed me, and the reproaches of those who reproach you have fallen on me.

¹⁰ When I wept and humbled my soul with fasting, it became my reproach.

¹¹ When I made sackcloth my clothing, I became a byword to them.

¹² I am the talk of those who sit in the gate, and the drunkards make songs about me.

¹³ But as for me, my prayer is to you, O LORD. At an acceptable time, O God, in the abundance of your steadfast love answer me in your saving faithfulness.

¹⁴ Deliver me from sinking in the mire; let me be delivered from my enemies and from the deep waters.

¹⁵ Let not the flood sweep over me, or the deep swallow me up, or the pit close its mouth over me.

¹⁶ Answer me, O LORD, for your steadfast love is good; according to your abundant mercy, turn to me.

¹⁷ Hide not your face from your servant; for I am in distress; make haste to answer me.

¹⁸ Draw near to my soul, redeem me; ransom me because of my enemies!

¹⁹ You know my reproach, and my shame and my dishonor; my foes are all known to you.

²⁰ Reproaches have broken my heart, so that I am in despair. I looked for pity, but there was none, and for comforters, but I found none.

²¹ They gave me poison for food, and for my thirst they gave me sour wine to drink.

²² Let their own table before them become a snare; and when they are at peace, let it become a trap.

²³ Let their eyes be darkened, so that they cannot see, and make their loins tremble continually.

²⁴ Pour out your indignation upon them, and let your burning anger overtake them.

²⁵ May their camp be a desolation; let no one dwell in their tents.

²⁶ For they persecute him whom you have struck down, and they recount the pain of those you have wounded.

²⁷ Add to them punishment upon punishment; may they have no acquittal from you.

²⁸ Let them be blotted out of the book of the living; let them not be enrolled among the righteous.

²⁹ But I am afflicted and in pain; let your salvation, O God, set me on high!

³⁰ I will praise the name of God with a song; I will magnify him with thanksgiving.

³¹ This will please the LORD more than an ox or a bull with horns and hoofs.

³² When the humble see it they will be glad; you who seek God, let your hearts revive.

³³ For the LORD hears the needy and does not despise his own people who are prisoners.

³⁴ Let heaven and earth praise him, the seas and everything that moves in them.

³⁵ For God will save Zion and build up the cities of Judah, and people shall dwell there and possess it;

³⁶ the offspring of his servants shall inherit it, and those who love his name shall dwell in it.

PSALM 70

To the choirmaster. Of David,
for the memorial offering.

¹ Make haste, O God, to deliver me! O LORD, make haste to help me!

² Let them be put to shame and confusion who seek my life! Let them be turned back and brought to dishonor who delight in my hurt!

³ Let them turn back because of their shame who say, "Aha, Aha!"

⁴ May all who seek you rejoice and be glad in you! May those who love your salvation say evermore, "God is great!"

⁵ But I am poor and needy; hasten to me, O God! You are my help and my deliverer; O LORD, do not delay!

PSALM 71

¹ In you, O LORD, do I take refuge; let me never be put to shame!

² In your righteousness deliver me and rescue me; incline your ear to me, and save me!

³ Be to me a rock of refuge, to which I may continually come; you have given the command to save me, for you are my rock and my fortress.

⁴ Rescue me, O my God, from the hand of the wicked, from the grasp of the unjust and cruel man.

⁵ For you, O Lord, are my hope, my trust, O LORD, from my youth.

⁶ Upon you I have leaned from before my birth; you are he who took me from my mother's womb. My praise is continually of you.

⁷ I have been as a portent to many, but you are my strong refuge.

⁸ My mouth is filled with your praise, and with your glory all the day.

⁹ Do not cast me off in the time of old age; forsake me not when my strength is spent.

¹⁰ For my enemies speak concerning me; those who watch for my life consult together

¹¹ and say, "God has forsaken him; pursue and seize him, for there is none to deliver him."

¹² O God, be not far from me; O my God, make haste to help me!

¹³ May my accusers be put to shame and consumed; with scorn and disgrace may they be covered who seek my hurt.

¹⁴ But I will hope continually and will praise you yet more and more.

¹⁵ My mouth will tell of your righteous acts, of your deeds of salvation all the day, for their number is past my knowledge.

¹⁶ With the mighty deeds of the Lord GOD I will come; I will remind them of your righteousness, yours alone.

¹⁷ O God, from my youth you

have taught me, and I still proclaim your wondrous deeds.

18 So even to old age and gray hairs, O God, do not forsake me, until I proclaim your might to another generation, your power to all those to come.

19 Your righteousness, O God, reaches the high heavens. You who have done great things, O God, who is like you?

20 You who have made me see many troubles and calamities will revive me again; from the depths of the earth you will bring me up again.

21 You will increase my greatness and comfort me again.

22 I will also praise you with the harp for your faithfulness, O my God; I will sing praises to you with the lyre, O Holy One of Israel.

23 My lips will shout for joy, when I sing praises to you; my soul also, which you have redeemed.

24 And my tongue will talk of your righteous help all the day long, for they have been put to shame and disappointed who sought to do me hurt.

PSALM 72
Of Solomon.

1 Give the king your justice, O God, and your righteousness to the royal son!

2 May he judge your people with righteousness, and your poor with justice!

3 Let the mountains bear prosperity for the people, and the hills, in righteousness!

4 May he defend the cause of the poor of the people, give deliverance to the children of the needy, and crush the oppressor!

5 May they fear you while the sun endures, and as long as the moon, throughout all generations!

6 May he be like rain that falls on the mown grass, like showers that water the earth!

7 In his days may the righteous flourish, and peace abound, till the moon be no more!

8 May he have dominion from sea to sea, and from the River to the ends of the earth!

9 May desert tribes bow down before him, and his enemies lick the dust!

10 May the kings of Tarshish and of the coastlands render him tribute; may the kings of Sheba and Seba bring gifts!

11 May all kings fall down before him, all nations serve him!

12 For he delivers the needy when he calls, the poor and him who has no helper.

¹³ He has pity on the weak and the needy, and saves the lives of the needy.

¹⁴ From oppression and violence he redeems their life, and precious is their blood in his sight.

¹⁵ Long may he live; may gold of Sheba be given to him! May prayer be made for him continually, and blessings invoked for him all the day!

¹⁶ May there be abundance of grain in the land; on the tops of the mountains may it wave; may its fruit be like Lebanon; and may people blossom in the cities like the grass of the field!

¹⁷ May his name endure forever, his fame continue as long as the sun! May people be blessed in him, all nations call him blessed!

¹⁸ Blessed be the LORD, the God of Israel, who alone does wondrous things!

¹⁹ Blessed be his glorious name forever; may the whole earth be filled with his glory! Amen and Amen!

²⁰ The prayers of David, the son of Jesse, are ended.

PSALM 73

A Psalm of Asaph.

¹ Truly God is good to Israel, to those who are pure in heart.

² But as for me, my feet had almost stumbled, my steps had nearly slipped.

³ For I was envious of the arrogant when I saw the prosperity of the wicked.

⁴ For they have no pangs until death; their bodies are fat and sleek.

⁵ They are not in trouble as others are; they are not stricken like the rest of mankind.

⁶ Therefore pride is their necklace; violence covers them as a garment.

⁷ Their eyes swell out through fatness; their hearts overflow with follies.

⁸ They scoff and speak with malice; loftily they threaten oppression.

⁹ They set their mouths against the heavens, and their tongue struts through the earth.

¹⁰ Therefore his people turn back to them, and find no fault in them.

¹¹ And they say, "How can God know? Is there knowledge in the Most High?"

¹² Behold, these are the wicked; always at ease, they increase in riches.

¹³ All in vain have I kept my heart clean and washed my hands in innocence.

¹⁴ For all the day long I have been stricken and rebuked every morning.

¹⁵ If I had said, "I will speak thus," I would have betrayed the generation of your children.

¹⁶ But when I thought how to understand this, it seemed to me a wearisome task,

¹⁷ until I went into the sanctuary of God; then I discerned their end.

¹⁸ Truly you set them in slippery places; you make them fall to ruin.

¹⁹ How they are destroyed in a moment, swept away utterly by terrors!

²⁰ Like a dream when one awakes, O Lord, when you rouse yourself, you despise them as phantoms.

²¹ When my soul was embittered, when I was pricked in heart,

²² I was brutish and ignorant; I was like a beast toward you.

²³ Nevertheless, I am continually with you; you hold my right hand.

²⁴ You guide me with your counsel, and afterward you will receive me to glory.

²⁵ Whom have I in heaven but you? And there is nothing on earth that I desire besides you.

²⁶ My flesh and my heart may fail, but God is the strength of my heart and my portion forever.

²⁷ For behold, those who are far from you shall perish; you put an end to everyone who is unfaithful to you.

²⁸ But for me it is good to be near God; I have made the Lord God my refuge, that I may tell of all your works.

PSALM 74

A Maskil of Asaph.

¹ O God, why do you cast us off forever? Why does your anger smoke against the sheep of your pasture?

² Remember your congregation, which you have purchased of old, which you have redeemed to be the tribe of your heritage! Remember Mount Zion, where you have dwelt.

³ Direct your steps to the perpetual ruins; the enemy has destroyed everything in the sanctuary!

⁴ Your foes have roared in the midst of your meeting place; they set up their own signs for signs.

⁵ They were like those who swing axes in a forest of trees.

⁶ And all its carved wood they broke down with hatchets and hammers.

⁷ They set your sanctuary on fire; they profaned the dwelling place of your name, bringing it down to the ground.

8 They said to themselves, "We will utterly subdue them"; they burned all the meeting places of God in the land.

9 We do not see our signs; there is no longer any prophet, and there is none among us who knows how long.

10 How long, O God, is the foe to scoff? Is the enemy to revile your name forever?

11 Why do you hold back your hand, your right hand? Take it from the fold of your garment and destroy them!

12 Yet God my King is from of old, working salvation in the midst of the earth.

13 You divided the sea by your might; you broke the heads of the sea monsters on the waters.

14 You crushed the heads of Leviathan; you gave him as food for the creatures of the wilderness.

15 You split open springs and brooks; you dried up ever-flowing streams.

16 Yours is the day, yours also the night; you have established the heavenly lights and the sun.

17 You have fixed all the boundaries of the earth; you have made summer and winter.

18 Remember this, O LORD, how the enemy scoffs, and a foolish people reviles your name.

19 Do not deliver the soul of your dove to the wild beasts; do not forget the life of your poor forever.

20 Have regard for the covenant, for the dark places of the land are full of the habitations of violence.

21 Let not the downtrodden turn back in shame; let the poor and needy praise your name.

22 Arise, O God, defend your cause; remember how the foolish scoff at you all the day!

23 Do not forget the clamor of your foes, the uproar of those who rise against you, which goes up continually!

PSALM 75

To the choirmaster: according to Do Not Destroy. A Psalm of Asaph. A Song.

1 We give thanks to you, O God; we give thanks, for your name is near. We recount your wondrous deeds.

2 "At the set time that I appoint I will judge with equity.

3 "When the earth totters, and all its inhabitants, it is I who keep steady its pillars. Selah.

4 "I say to the boastful, 'Do not boast,' and to the wicked, 'Do not lift up your horn;

⁵ "'do not lift up your horn on high, or speak with haughty neck.'"

⁶ For not from the east or from the west and not from the wilderness comes lifting up,

⁷ but it is God who executes judgment, putting down one and lifting up another.

⁸ For in the hand of the LORD there is a cup with foaming wine, well mixed, and he pours out from it, and all the wicked of the earth shall drain it down to the dregs.

⁹ But I will declare it forever; I will sing praises to the God of Jacob.

¹⁰ All the horns of the wicked I will cut off, but the horns of the righteous shall be lifted up.

PSALM 76

To the choirmaster: with stringed instruments. A Psalm of Asaph. A Song.

¹ In Judah God is known; his name is great in Israel.

² His abode has been established in Salem, his dwelling place in Zion.

³ There he broke the flashing arrows, the shield, the sword, and the weapons of war. Selah.

⁴ Glorious are you, more majestic than the mountains full of prey.

⁵ The stouthearted were stripped of their spoil; they sank into sleep; all the men of war were unable to use their hands.

⁶ At your rebuke, O God of Jacob, both rider and horse lay stunned.

⁷ But you, you are to be feared! Who can stand before you when once your anger is roused?

⁸ From the heavens you uttered judgment; the earth feared and was still,

⁹ when God arose to establish judgment, to save all the humble of the earth. Selah.

¹⁰ Surely the wrath of man shall praise you; the remnant of wrath you will put on like a belt.

¹¹ Make your vows to the LORD your God and perform them; let all around him bring gifts to him who is to be feared,

¹² who cuts off the spirit of princes, who is to be feared by the kings of the earth.

PSALM 77

To the choirmaster: according to Jeduthun. A Psalm of Asaph.

¹ I cry aloud to God, aloud to God, and he will hear me.

² In the day of my trouble I seek the Lord; in the night my hand is stretched out without

wearying; my soul refuses to be comforted.

³ When I remember God, I moan; when I meditate, my spirit faints. Selah.

⁴ You hold my eyelids open; I am so troubled that I cannot speak.

⁵ I consider the days of old, the years long ago.

⁶ I said, "Let me remember my song in the night; let me meditate in my heart." Then my spirit made a diligent search:

⁷ "Will the Lord spurn forever, and never again be favorable?

⁸ "Has his steadfast love forever ceased? Are his promises at an end for all time?

⁹ "Has God forgotten to be gracious? Has he in anger shut up his compassion?" Selah.

¹⁰ Then I said, "I will appeal to this, to the years of the right hand of the Most High."

¹¹ I will remember the deeds of the Lᴏʀᴅ; yes, I will remember your wonders of old.

¹² I will ponder all your work, and meditate on your mighty deeds.

¹³ Your way, O God, is holy. What god is great like our God?

¹⁴ You are the God who works wonders; you have made known your might among the peoples.

¹⁵ You with your arm redeemed your people, the children of Jacob and Joseph. Selah.

¹⁶ When the waters saw you, O God, when the waters saw you, they were afraid; indeed, the deep trembled.

¹⁷ The clouds poured out water; the skies gave forth thunder; your arrows flashed on every side.

¹⁸ The crash of your thunder was in the whirlwind; your lightnings lighted up the world; the earth trembled and shook.

¹⁹ Your way was through the sea, your path through the great waters; yet your footprints are unseen.

²⁰ You led your people like a flock by the hand of Moses and Aaron.

PSALM 78
A Maskil of Asaph.

¹ Give ear, O my people, to my teaching; incline your ears to the words of my mouth!

² I will open my mouth in a parable; I will utter dark sayings from of old,

³ things that we have heard and known, that our fathers have told us.

⁴ We will not hide them from their children, but tell

to the coming generation the glorious deeds of the LORD, and his might, and the wonders that he has done.

5 He established a testimony in Jacob and appointed a law in Israel, which he commanded our fathers to teach to their children,

6 that the next generation might know them, the children yet unborn, and arise and tell them to their children,

7 so that they should set their hope in God and not forget the works of God, but keep his commandments;

8 and that they should not be like their fathers, a stubborn and rebellious generation, a generation whose heart was not steadfast, whose spirit was not faithful to God.

9 The Ephraimites, armed with the bow, turned back on the day of battle.

10 They did not keep God's covenant, but refused to walk according to his law.

11 They forgot his works and the wonders that he had shown them.

12 In the sight of their fathers he performed wonders in the land of Egypt, in the fields of Zoan.

13 He divided the sea and let them pass through it, and made the waters stand like a heap.

14 In the daytime he led them with a cloud, and all the night with a fiery light.

15 He split rocks in the wilderness and gave them drink abundantly as from the deep.

16 He made streams come out of the rock and caused waters to flow down like rivers.

17 Yet they sinned still more against him, rebelling against the Most High in the desert.

18 They tested God in their heart by demanding the food they craved.

19 They spoke against God, saying, "Can God spread a table in the wilderness?

20 "He struck the rock so that water gushed out and streams overflowed. Can he also give bread or provide meat for his people?"

21 Therefore, when the LORD heard, he was full of wrath; a fire was kindled against Jacob; his anger rose against Israel,

22 because they did not believe in God and did not trust his saving power.

23 Yet he commanded the skies above and opened the doors of heaven,

24 and he rained down on

them manna to eat and gave them the grain of heaven.

25 Man ate of the bread of the angels; he sent them food in abundance.

26 He caused the east wind to blow in the heavens, and by his power he led out the south wind;

27 he rained meat on them like dust, winged birds like the sand of the seas;

28 he let them fall in the midst of their camp, all around their dwellings.

29 And they ate and were well filled, for he gave them what they craved.

30 But before they had satisfied their craving, while the food was still in their mouths,

31 the anger of God rose against them, and he killed the strongest of them and laid low the young men of Israel.

32 In spite of all this, they still sinned; despite his wonders, they did not believe.

33 So he made their days vanish like a breath, and their years in terror.

34 When he killed them, they sought him; they repented and sought God earnestly.

35 They remembered that God was their rock, the Most High God their redeemer.

36 But they flattered him with their mouths; they lied to him with their tongues.

37 Their heart was not steadfast toward him; they were not faithful to his covenant.

38 Yet he, being compassionate, atoned for their iniquity and did not destroy them; he restrained his anger often and did not stir up all his wrath.

39 He remembered that they were but flesh, a wind that passes and comes not again.

40 How often they rebelled against him in the wilderness and grieved him in the desert!

41 They tested God again and again and provoked the Holy One of Israel.

42 They did not remember his power or the day when he redeemed them from the foe,

43 when he performed his signs in Egypt and his marvels in the fields of Zoan.

44 He turned their rivers to blood, so that they could not drink of their streams.

45 He sent among them swarms of flies, which devoured them, and frogs, which destroyed them.

46 He gave their crops to the destroying locust and the fruit of their labor to the locust.

47 He destroyed their vines

with hail and their sycamores with frost.

⁴⁸ He gave over their cattle to the hail and their flocks to thunderbolts.

⁴⁹ He let loose on them his burning anger, wrath, indignation, and distress, a company of destroying angels.

⁵⁰ He made a path for his anger; he did not spare them from death, but gave their lives over to the plague.

⁵¹ He struck down every firstborn in Egypt, the first-fruits of their strength in the tents of Ham.

⁵² Then he led out his people like sheep and guided them in the wilderness like a flock.

⁵³ He led them in safety, so that they were not afraid, but the sea overwhelmed their enemies.

⁵⁴ And he brought them to his holy land, to the mountain which his right hand had won.

⁵⁵ He drove out nations before them; he apportioned them for a possession and settled the tribes of Israel in their tents.

⁵⁶ Yet they tested and rebelled against the Most High God and did not keep his testimonies,

⁵⁷ but turned away and acted treacherously like their fathers; they twisted like a deceitful bow.

⁵⁸ For they provoked him to anger with their high places; they moved him to jealousy with their idols.

⁵⁹ When God heard, he was full of wrath, and he utterly rejected Israel.

⁶⁰ He forsook his dwelling at Shiloh, the tent where he dwelt among mankind,

⁶¹ and delivered his power to captivity, his glory to the hand of the foe.

⁶² He gave his people over to the sword and vented his wrath on his heritage.

⁶³ Fire devoured their young men, and their young women had no marriage song.

⁶⁴ Their priests fell by the sword, and their widows made no lamentation.

⁶⁵ Then the Lord awoke as from sleep, like a strong man shouting because of wine.

⁶⁶ And he put his adversaries to rout; he put them to everlasting shame.

⁶⁷ He rejected the tent of Joseph; he did not choose the tribe of Ephraim,

⁶⁸ but he chose the tribe of Judah, Mount Zion, which he loves.

⁶⁹ He built his sanctuary like the high heavens, like the earth, which he has founded forever.

70 He chose David his servant and took him from the sheepfolds;

71 from following the nursing ewes he brought him to shepherd Jacob his people, Israel his inheritance.

72 With upright heart he shepherded them and guided them with his skillful hand.

PSALM 79

A Psalm of Asaph.

1 O God, the nations have come into your inheritance; they have defiled your holy temple; they have laid Jerusalem in ruins.

2 They have given the bodies of your servants to the birds of the heavens for food, the flesh of your faithful to the beasts of the earth.

3 They have poured out their blood like water all around Jerusalem, and there was no one to bury them.

4 We have become a taunt to our neighbors, mocked and derided by those around us.

5 How long, O LORD? Will you be angry forever? Will your jealousy burn like fire?

6 Pour out your anger on the nations that do not know you, and on the kingdoms that do not call upon your name!

7 For they have devoured Jacob and laid waste his habitation.

8 Do not remember against us our former iniquities; let your compassion come speedily to meet us, for we are brought very low.

9 Help us, O God of our salvation, for the glory of your name; deliver us, and atone for our sins, for your name's sake!

10 Why should the nations say, "Where is their God?" Let the avenging of the outpoured blood of your servants be known among the nations before our eyes!

11 Let the groans of the prisoners come before you; according to your great power, preserve those doomed to die!

12 Return sevenfold into the lap of our neighbors the taunts with which they have taunted you, O Lord!

13 But we your people, the sheep of your pasture, will give thanks to you forever; from generation to generation we will recount your praise.

PSALM 80

To the choirmaster: according to Lilies. A Testimony. Of Asaph, a Psalm.

1 Give ear, O Shepherd of Israel, you who lead Joseph

like a flock. You who are enthroned upon the cherubim, shine forth.

2 Before Ephraim and Benjamin and Manasseh, stir up your might and come to save us!

3 Restore us, O God; let your face shine, that we may be saved!

4 O LORD God of hosts, how long will you be angry with your people's prayers?

5 You have fed them with the bread of tears and given them tears to drink in full measure.

6 You make us an object of contention for our neighbors, and our enemies laugh among themselves.

7 Restore us, O God of hosts; let your face shine, that we may be saved!

8 You brought a vine out of Egypt; you drove out the nations and planted it.

9 You cleared the ground for it; it took deep root and filled the land.

10 The mountains were covered with its shade, the mighty cedars with its branches.

11 It sent out its branches to the sea and its shoots to the River.

12 Why have you broken down its walls, so that all who pass along the way pluck its fruit?

13 The boar from the forest ravages it, and all that move in the field feed on it.

14 Turn again, O God of hosts! Look down from heaven, and see; have regard for this vine,

15 the stock that your right hand planted, and for the son whom you made strong for yourself.

16 They have burned it with fire; they have cut it down; may they perish at the rebuke of your face!

17 But let your hand be on the man of your right hand, the son of man whom you have made strong for yourself!

18 Then we shall not turn back from you; give us life, and we will call upon your name!

19 Restore us, O LORD God of hosts! Let your face shine, that we may be saved!

PSALM 81

To the choirmaster: according to The Gittith. Of Asaph.

1 Sing aloud to God our strength; shout for joy to the God of Jacob!

2 Raise a song; sound the tambourine, the sweet lyre with the harp.

3 Blow the trumpet at the new moon, at the full moon, on our feast day.

⁴ For it is a statute for Israel, a rule of the God of Jacob.

⁵ He made it a decree in Joseph when he went out over the land of Egypt. I hear a language I had not known:

⁶ "I relieved your shoulder of the burden; your hands were freed from the basket.

⁷ "In distress you called, and I delivered you; I answered you in the secret place of thunder; I tested you at the waters of Meribah. Selah.

⁸ "Hear, O my people, while I admonish you! O Israel, if you would but listen to me!

⁹ "There shall be no strange god among you; you shall not bow down to a foreign god.

¹⁰ "I am the Lᴏʀᴅ your God, who brought you up out of the land of Egypt. Open your mouth wide, and I will fill it.

¹¹ "But my people did not listen to my voice; Israel would not submit to me.

¹² "So I gave them over to their stubborn hearts, to follow their own counsels.

¹³ "Oh, that my people would listen to me, that Israel would walk in my ways!

¹⁴ "I would soon subdue their enemies and turn my hand against their foes.

¹⁵ "Those who hate the Lᴏʀᴅ would cringe toward him, and their fate would last forever.

¹⁶ "But he would feed you with the finest of the wheat, and with honey from the rock I would satisfy you."

PSALM 82
A Psalm of Asaph.

¹ God has taken his place in the divine council; in the midst of the gods he holds judgment:

² "How long will you judge unjustly and show partiality to the wicked? Selah.

³ "Give justice to the weak and the fatherless; maintain the right of the afflicted and the destitute.

⁴ "Rescue the weak and the needy; deliver them from the hand of the wicked."

⁵ They have neither knowledge nor understanding, they walk about in darkness; all the foundations of the earth are shaken.

⁶ I said, "You are gods, sons of the Most High, all of you;

⁷ "nevertheless, like men you shall die, and fall like any prince."

⁸ Arise, O God, judge the earth; for you shall inherit all the nations!

PSALM 83
A Song. A Psalm of Asaph.

¹ O God, do not keep silence; do not hold your peace or be still, O God!

2 For behold, your enemies make an uproar; those who hate you have raised their heads.

3 They lay crafty plans against your people; they consult together against your treasured ones.

4 They say, "Come, let us wipe them out as a nation; let the name of Israel be remembered no more!"

5 For they conspire with one accord; against you they make a covenant—

6 the tents of Edom and the Ishmaelites, Moab and the Hagrites,

7 Gebal and Ammon and Amalek, Philistia with the inhabitants of Tyre;

8 Asshur also has joined them; they are the strong arm of the children of Lot. Selah.

9 Do to them as you did to Midian, as to Sisera and Jabin at the river Kishon,

10 who were destroyed at En-dor, who became dung for the ground.

11 Make their nobles like Oreb and Zeeb, all their princes like Zebah and Zalmunna,

12 who said, "Let us take possession for ourselves of the pastures of God."

13 O my God, make them like whirling dust, like chaff before the wind.

14 As fire consumes the forest, as the flame sets the mountains ablaze,

15 so may you pursue them with your tempest and terrify them with your hurricane!

16 Fill their faces with shame, that they may seek your name, O LORD.

17 Let them be put to shame and dismayed forever; let them perish in disgrace,

18 that they may know that you alone, whose name is the LORD, are the Most High over all the earth.

PSALM 84

To the choirmaster: according to The Gittith. A Psalm of the Sons of Korah.

1 How lovely is your dwelling place, O LORD of hosts!

2 My soul longs, yes, faints for the courts of the LORD; my heart and flesh sing for joy to the living God.

3 Even the sparrow finds a home, and the swallow a nest for herself, where she may lay her young, at your altars, O LORD of hosts, my King and my God.

4 Blessed are those who dwell in your house, ever singing your praise! Selah.

5 Blessed are those whose strength is in you, in whose heart are the highways to Zion.

⁶ As they go through the Valley of Baca they make it a place of springs; the early rain also covers it with pools.

⁷ They go from strength to strength; each one appears before God in Zion.

⁸ O LORD God of hosts, hear my prayer; give ear, O God of Jacob! Selah.

⁹ Behold our shield, O God; look on the face of your anointed!

¹⁰ For a day in your courts is better than a thousand elsewhere. I would rather be a doorkeeper in the house of my God than dwell in the tents of wickedness.

¹¹ For the LORD God is a sun and shield; the LORD bestows favor and honor. No good thing does he withhold from those who walk uprightly.

¹² O LORD of hosts, blessed is the one who trusts in you!

PSALM 85

To the choirmaster. A Psalm of the Sons of Korah.

¹ LORD, you were favorable to your land; you restored the fortunes of Jacob.

² You forgave the iniquity of your people; you covered all their sin. Selah.

³ You withdrew all your wrath; you turned from your hot anger.

⁴ Restore us again, O God of our salvation, and put away your indignation toward us!

⁵ Will you be angry with us forever? Will you prolong your anger to all generations?

⁶ Will you not revive us again, that your people may rejoice in you?

⁷ Show us your steadfast love, O LORD, and grant us your salvation.

⁸ Let me hear what God the LORD will speak, for he will speak peace to his people, to his saints; but let them not turn back to folly.

⁹ Surely his salvation is near to those who fear him, that glory may dwell in our land.

¹⁰ Steadfast love and faithfulness meet; righteousness and peace kiss each other.

¹¹ Faithfulness springs up from the ground, and righteousness looks down from the sky.

¹² Yes, the LORD will give what is good, and our land will yield its increase.

¹³ Righteousness will go before him and make his footsteps a way.

PSALM 86

A Prayer of David.

¹ Incline your ear, O LORD, and answer me, for I am poor and needy.

² Preserve my life, for I am godly; save your servant,

who trusts in you—you are my God.

³ Be gracious to me, O Lord, for to you do I cry all the day.

⁴ Gladden the soul of your servant, for to you, O Lord, do I lift up my soul.

⁵ For you, O Lord, are good and forgiving, abounding in steadfast love to all who call upon you.

⁶ Give ear, O LORD, to my prayer; listen to my plea for grace.

⁷ In the day of my trouble I call upon you, for you answer me.

⁸ There is none like you among the gods, O Lord, nor are there any works like yours.

⁹ All the nations you have made shall come and worship before you, O Lord, and shall glorify your name.

¹⁰ For you are great and do wondrous things; you alone are God.

¹¹ Teach me your way, O LORD, that I may walk in your truth; unite my heart to fear your name.

¹² I give thanks to you, O Lord my God, with my whole heart, and I will glorify your name forever.

¹³ For great is your steadfast love toward me; you have delivered my soul from the depths of Sheol.

¹⁴ O God, insolent men have risen up against me; a band of ruthless men seeks my life, and they do not set you before them.

¹⁵ But you, O Lord, are a God merciful and gracious, slow to anger and abounding in steadfast love and faithfulness.

¹⁶ Turn to me and be gracious to me; give your strength to your servant, and save the son of your maidservant.

¹⁷ Show me a sign of your favor, that those who hate me may see and be put to shame because you, LORD, have helped me and comforted me.

PSALM 87

A Psalm of the Sons of Korah. A Song.

¹ On the holy mount stands the city he founded;

² the LORD loves the gates of Zion more than all the dwelling places of Jacob.

³ Glorious things of you are spoken, O city of God. Selah.

⁴ Among those who know me I mention Rahab and Babylon; behold, Philistia and Tyre, with Cush— "This one was born there," they say.

⁵ And of Zion it shall be said, "This one and that one were born in her"; for the

Most High himself will establish her.

⁶ The LORD records as he registers the peoples, "This one was born there." Selah.

⁷ Singers and dancers alike say, "All my springs are in you."

PSALM 88

A Song. A Psalm of the Sons of Korah. To the choirmaster: according to Mahalath Leannoth. A Maskil of Heman the Ezrahite.

¹ O LORD, God of my salvation; I cry out day and night before you.

² Let my prayer come before you; incline your ear to my cry!

³ For my soul is full of troubles, and my life draws near to Sheol.

⁴ I am counted among those who go down to the pit; I am a man who has no strength,

⁵ like one set loose among the dead, like the slain that lie in the grave, like those whom you remember no more, for they are cut off from your hand.

⁶ You have put me in the depths of the pit, in the regions dark and deep.

⁷ Your wrath lies heavy upon me, and you overwhelm me with all your waves. Selah.

⁸ You have caused my companions to shun me; you have made me a horror to them. I am shut in so that I cannot escape;

⁹ my eye grows dim through sorrow. Every day I call upon you, O LORD; I spread out my hands to you.

¹⁰ Do you work wonders for the dead? Do the departed rise up to praise you? Selah.

¹¹ Is your steadfast love declared in the grave, or your faithfulness in Abaddon?

¹² Are your wonders known in the darkness, or your righteousness in the land of forgetfulness?

¹³ But I, O LORD, cry to you; in the morning my prayer comes before you.

¹⁴ O LORD, why do you cast my soul away? Why do you hide your face from me?

¹⁵ Afflicted and close to death from my youth up, I suffer your terrors; I am helpless.

¹⁶ Your wrath has swept over me; your dreadful assaults destroy me.

¹⁷ They surround me like a flood all day long; they close in on me together.

¹⁸ You have caused my beloved and my friend to shun me; my companions have become darkness.

PSALM 89

A Maskil of Ethan the Ezrahite.

¹ I will sing of the steadfast love of the LORD, forever; with my mouth I will make known your faithfulness to all generations.

² For I said, "Steadfast love will be built up forever; in the heavens you will establish your faithfulness."

³ You have said, "I have made a covenant with my chosen one; I have sworn to David my servant:

⁴ "'I will establish your offspring forever, and build your throne for all generations.'" Selah.

⁵ Let the heavens praise your wonders, O LORD, your faithfulness in the assembly of the holy ones!

⁶ For who in the skies can be compared to the LORD? Who among the heavenly beings is like the LORD,

⁷ a God greatly to be feared in the council of the holy ones, and awesome above all who are around him?

⁸ O LORD God of hosts, who is mighty as you are, O LORD, with your faithfulness all around you?

⁹ You rule the raging of the sea; when its waves rise, you still them.

¹⁰ You crushed Rahab like a carcass; you scattered your enemies with your mighty arm.

¹¹ The heavens are yours; the earth also is yours; the world and all that is in it, you have founded them.

¹² The north and the south, you have created them; Tabor and Hermon joyously praise your name.

¹³ You have a mighty arm; strong is your hand, high your right hand.

¹⁴ Righteousness and justice are the foundation of your throne; steadfast love and faithfulness go before you.

¹⁵ Blessed are the people who know the festal shout, who walk, O LORD, in the light of your face,

¹⁶ who exult in your name all the day and in your righteousness are exalted.

¹⁷ For you are the glory of their strength; by your favor our horn is exalted.

¹⁸ For our shield belongs to the LORD, our king to the Holy One of Israel.

¹⁹ Of old you spoke in a vision to your godly one, and said: "I have granted help to one who is mighty; I have exalted one chosen from the people.

²⁰ "I have found David, my servant; with my holy oil I have anointed him,

21 "so that my hand shall be established with him; my arm also shall strengthen him.

22 "The enemy shall not outwit him; the wicked shall not humble him.

23 "I will crush his foes before him and strike down those who hate him.

24 "My faithfulness and my steadfast love shall be with him, and in my name shall his horn be exalted.

25 "I will set his hand on the sea and his right hand on the rivers.

26 "He shall cry to me, 'You are my Father, my God, and the Rock of my salvation.'

27 "And I will make him the firstborn, the highest of the kings of the earth.

28 "My steadfast love I will keep for him forever, and my covenant will stand firm for him.

29 "I will establish his offspring forever and his throne as the days of the heavens.

30 "If his children forsake my law and do not walk according to my rules,

31 "if they violate my statutes and do not keep my commandments,

32 "then I will punish their transgression with the rod and their iniquity with stripes,

33 "but I will not remove from him my steadfast love or be false to my faithfulness.

34 "I will not violate my covenant or alter the word that went forth from my lips.

35 "Once for all I have sworn by my holiness; I will not lie to David.

36 "His offspring shall endure forever, his throne as long as the sun before me.

37 "Like the moon it shall be established forever, a faithful witness in the skies." Selah.

38 But now you have cast off and rejected; you are full of wrath against your anointed.

39 You have renounced the covenant with your servant; you have defiled his crown in the dust.

40 You have breached all his walls; you have laid his strongholds in ruins.

41 All who pass by plunder him; he has become the scorn of his neighbors.

42 You have exalted the right hand of his foes; you have made all his enemies rejoice.

43 You have also turned back the edge of his sword, and you have not made him stand in battle.

44 You have made his splen-

dor to cease and cast his throne to the ground.

⁴⁵ You have cut short the days of his youth; you have covered him with shame. Selah.

⁴⁶ How long, O LORD? Will you hide yourself forever? How long will your wrath burn like fire?

⁴⁷ Remember how short my time is! For what vanity have you created all the children of man!

⁴⁸ What man can live and never see death? Who can deliver his soul from the power of Sheol? Selah.

⁴⁹ Lord, where is your steadfast love of old, which by your faithfulness you swore to David?

⁵⁰ Remember, O Lord, how your servants are mocked, and how I bear in my heart the insults of all the many nations,

⁵¹ with which your enemies mock, O LORD, with which they mock the footsteps of your anointed.

⁵² Blessed be the LORD forever! Amen and Amen.

PSALM 90

A Prayer of Moses,
the man of God.

¹ Lord, you have been our dwelling place in all generations.

² Before the mountains were brought forth, or ever you had formed the earth and the world, from everlasting to everlasting you are God.

³ You return man to dust and say, "Return, O children of man!"

⁴ For a thousand years in your sight are but as yesterday when it is past, or as a watch in the night.

⁵ You sweep them away as with a flood; they are like a dream, like grass that is renewed in the morning:

⁶ in the morning it flourishes and is renewed; in the evening it fades and withers.

⁷ For we are brought to an end by your anger; by your wrath we are dismayed.

⁸ You have set our iniquities before you, our secret sins in the light of your presence.

⁹ For all our days pass away under your wrath; we bring our years to an end like a sigh.

¹⁰ The years of our life are seventy, or even by reason of strength eighty; yet their span is but toil and trouble; they are soon gone, and we fly away.

¹¹ Who considers the power of your anger, and your wrath according to the fear of you?

12 So teach us to number our days that we may get a heart of wisdom.

13 Return, O LORD! How long? Have pity on your servants!

14 Satisfy us in the morning with your steadfast love, that we may rejoice and be glad all our days.

15 Make us glad for as many days as you have afflicted us, and for as many years as we have seen evil.

16 Let your work be shown to your servants, and your glorious power to their children.

17 Let the favor of the Lord our God be upon us, and establish the work of our hands upon us; yes, establish the work of our hands!

PSALM 91

1 He who dwells in the shelter of the Most High will abide in the shadow of the Almighty.

2 I will say to the LORD, "My refuge and my fortress, my God, in whom I trust."

3 For he will deliver you from the snare of the fowler and from the deadly pestilence.

4 He will cover you with his pinions, and under his wings you will find refuge; his faithfulness is a shield and buckler.

5 You will not fear the terror of the night, nor the arrow that flies by day,

6 nor the pestilence that stalks in darkness, nor the destruction that wastes at noonday.

7 A thousand may fall at your side, ten thousand at your right hand, but it will not come near you.

8 You will only look with your eyes and see the recompense of the wicked.

9 Because you have made the LORD your dwelling place— the Most High, who is my refuge—

10 no evil shall be allowed to befall you, no plague come near your tent.

11 For he will command his angels concerning you to guard you in all your ways.

12 On their hands they will bear you up, lest you strike your foot against a stone.

13 You will tread on the lion and the adder; the young lion and the serpent you will trample underfoot.

14 "Because he holds fast to me in love, I will deliver him; I will protect him, because he knows my name.

15 "When he calls to me, I will answer him; I will be with him in trouble; I will rescue him and honor him.

16 "With long life I will sat-

isfy him and show him my salvation."

PSALM 92

A Psalm. A Song for the Sabbath.

[1] It is good to give thanks to the LORD, to sing praises to your name, O Most High;

[2] to declare your steadfast love in the morning, and your faithfulness by night,

[3] to the music of the lute and the harp, to the melody of the lyre.

[4] For you, O LORD, have made me glad by your work; at the works of your hands I sing for joy.

[5] How great are your works, O LORD! Your thoughts are very deep!

[6] The stupid man cannot know; the fool cannot understand this:

[7] that though the wicked sprout like grass and all evildoers flourish, they are doomed to destruction forever;

[8] but you, O LORD, are on high forever.

[9] For behold, your enemies, O LORD, for behold, your enemies shall perish; all evildoers shall be scattered.

[10] But you have exalted my horn like that of the wild ox; you have poured over me fresh oil.

[11] My eyes have seen the downfall of my enemies; my ears have heard the doom of my evil assailants.

[12] The righteous flourish like the palm tree and grow like a cedar in Lebanon.

[13] They are planted in the house of the LORD; they flourish in the courts of our God.

[14] They still bear fruit in old age; they are ever full of sap and green,

[15] to declare that the LORD is upright; he is my rock, and there is no unrighteousness in him.

PSALM 93

[1] The LORD reigns; he is robed in majesty; the LORD is robed; he has put on strength as his belt. Yes, the world is established; it shall never be moved.

[2] Your throne is established from of old; you are from everlasting.

[3] The floods have lifted up, O LORD, the floods have lifted up their voice; the floods lift up their roaring.

[4] Mightier than the thunders of many waters, mightier than the waves of the sea, the LORD on high is mighty!

[5] Your decrees are very trustworthy; holiness befits your house, O LORD, forevermore.

¹ O LORD, God of vengeance, O God of vengeance, shine forth!

² Rise up, O judge of the earth; repay to the proud what they deserve!

³ O LORD, how long shall the wicked, how long shall the wicked exult?

⁴ They pour out their arrogant words; all the evildoers boast.

⁵ They crush your people, O LORD, and afflict your heritage.

⁶ They kill the widow and the sojourner, and murder the fatherless;

⁷ and they say, "The LORD does not see; the God of Jacob does not perceive."

⁸ Understand, O dullest of the people! Fools, when will you be wise?

⁹ He who planted the ear, does he not hear? He who formed the eye, does he not see?

¹⁰ He who disciplines the nations, does he not rebuke? He who teaches man knowledge—

¹¹ the LORD—knows the thoughts of man, that they are but a breath.

¹² Blessed is the man whom you discipline, O LORD, and whom you teach out of your law,

¹³ to give him rest from days of trouble, until a pit is dug for the wicked.

¹⁴ For the LORD will not forsake his people; he will not abandon his heritage;

¹⁵ for justice will return to the righteous, and all the upright in heart will follow it.

¹⁶ Who rises up for me against the wicked? Who stands up for me against evildoers?

¹⁷ If the LORD had not been my help, my soul would soon have lived in the land of silence.

¹⁸ When I thought, "My foot slips," your steadfast love, O LORD, held me up.

¹⁹ When the cares of my heart are many, your consolations cheer my soul.

²⁰ Can wicked rulers be allied with you, those who frame injustice by statute?

²¹ They band together against the life of the righteous and condemn the innocent to death.

²² But the LORD has become my stronghold, and my God the rock of my refuge.

²³ He will bring back on them their iniquity and wipe them out for their wickedness; the LORD our God will wipe them out.

PSALM 95

¹ Oh come, let us sing to the LORD; let us make a joyful noise to the rock of our salvation!

² Let us come into his presence with thanksgiving; let us make a joyful noise to him with songs of praise!

³ For the LORD is a great God, and a great King above all gods.

⁴ In his hand are the depths of the earth; the heights of the mountains are his also.

⁵ The sea is his, for he made it, and his hands formed the dry land.

⁶ Oh come, let us worship and bow down; let us kneel before the LORD, our Maker!

⁷ For he is our God, and we are the people of his pasture, and the sheep of his hand. Today, if you hear his voice,

⁸ do not harden your hearts, as at Meribah, as on the day at Massah in the wilderness,

⁹ when your fathers put me to the test and put me to the proof, though they had seen my work.

¹⁰ For forty years I loathed that generation and said, "They are a people who go astray in their heart, and they have not known my ways."

¹¹ Therefore I swore in my wrath, "They shall not enter my rest."

PSALM 96

¹ Oh sing to the LORD a new song; sing to the LORD, all the earth!

² Sing to the LORD, bless his name; tell of his salvation from day to day.

³ Declare his glory among the nations, his marvelous works among all the peoples!

⁴ For great is the LORD, and greatly to be praised; he is to be feared above all gods.

⁵ For all the gods of the peoples are worthless idols, but the LORD made the heavens.

⁶ Splendor and majesty are before him; strength and beauty are in his sanctuary.

⁷ Ascribe to the LORD, O families of the peoples, ascribe to the LORD glory and strength!

⁸ Ascribe to the LORD the glory due his name; bring an offering, and come into his courts!

⁹ Worship the LORD in the splendor of holiness; tremble before him, all the earth!

¹⁰ Say among the nations, "The LORD reigns! Yes, the world is established; it shall never be moved; he will judge the peoples with equity."

¹¹ Let the heavens be glad, and let the earth rejoice; let the sea roar, and all that fills it;

¹² let the field exult, and

everything in it! Then shall all the trees of the forest sing for joy

13 before the LORD, for he comes, for he comes to judge the earth. He will judge the world in righteousness, and the peoples in his faithfulness.

PSALM 97

1 The LORD reigns, let the earth rejoice; let the many coastlands be glad!

2 Clouds and thick darkness are all around him; righteousness and justice are the foundation of his throne.

3 Fire goes before him and burns up his adversaries all around.

4 His lightnings light up the world; the earth sees and trembles.

5 The mountains melt like wax before the LORD, before the Lord of all the earth.

6 The heavens proclaim his righteousness, and all the peoples see his glory.

7 All worshipers of images are put to shame, who make their boast in worthless idols; worship him, all you gods!

8 Zion hears and is glad, and the daughters of Judah rejoice, because of your judgments, O LORD.

9 For you, O LORD, are most high over all the earth; you are exalted far above all gods.

10 O you who love the LORD, hate evil! He preserves the lives of his saints; he delivers them from the hand of the wicked.

11 Light is sown for the righteous, and joy for the upright in heart.

12 Rejoice in the LORD, O you righteous, and give thanks to his holy name!

PSALM 98

A Psalm.

1 Oh sing to the LORD a new song, for he has done marvelous things! His right hand and his holy arm have worked salvation for him.

2 The LORD has made known his salvation; he has revealed his righteousness in the sight of the nations.

3 He has remembered his steadfast love and faithfulness to the house of Israel. All the ends of the earth have seen the salvation of our God.

4 Make a joyful noise to the LORD, all the earth; break forth into joyous song and sing praises!

5 Sing praises to the LORD with the lyre, with the lyre and the sound of melody!

6 With trumpets and the sound of the horn make a

joyful noise before the King, the LORD!

⁷ Let the sea roar, and all that fills it; the world and those who dwell in it!

⁸ Let the rivers clap their hands; let the hills sing for joy together

⁹ before the LORD, for he comes to judge the earth. He will judge the world with righteousness, and the peoples with equity.

PSALM 99

¹ The LORD reigns; let the peoples tremble! He sits enthroned upon the cherubim; let the earth quake!

² The LORD is great in Zion; he is exalted over all the peoples.

³ Let them praise your great and awesome name! Holy is he!

⁴ The King in his might loves justice. You have established equity; you have executed justice and righteousness in Jacob.

⁵ Exalt the LORD our God; worship at his footstool! Holy is he!

⁶ Moses and Aaron were among his priests, Samuel also was among those who called upon his name. They called to the LORD, and he answered them.

⁷ In the pillar of the cloud he spoke to them; they kept his testimonies and the statute that he gave them.

⁸ O LORD our God, you answered them; you were a forgiving God to them, but an avenger of their wrongdoings.

⁹ Exalt the LORD our God, and worship at his holy mountain; for the LORD our God is holy!

PSALM 100

A Psalm for giving thanks.

¹ Make a joyful noise to the LORD, all the earth!

² Serve the LORD with gladness! Come into his presence with singing!

³ Know that the LORD, he is God! It is he who made us, and we are his; we are his people, and the sheep of his pasture.

⁴ Enter his gates with thanksgiving, and his courts with praise! Give thanks to him; bless his name!

⁵ For the LORD is good; his steadfast love endures forever, and his faithfulness to all generations.

PSALM 101

A Psalm of David.

¹ I will sing of steadfast love and justice; to you, O LORD, I will make music.

² I will ponder the way that

is blameless. Oh when will you come to me? I will walk with integrity of heart within my house;

³ I will not set before my eyes anything that is worthless. I hate the work of those who fall away; it shall not cling to me.

⁴ A perverse heart shall be far from me; I will know nothing of evil.

⁵ Whoever slanders his neighbor secretly I will destroy. Whoever has a haughty look and an arrogant heart I will not endure.

⁶ I will look with favor on the faithful in the land, that they may dwell with me; he who walks in the way that is blameless shall minister to me.

⁷ No one who practices deceit shall dwell in my house; no one who utters lies shall continue before my eyes.

⁸ Morning by morning I will destroy all the wicked in the land, cutting off all the evildoers from the city of the Lord.

PSALM 102

A Prayer of one afflicted, when he is faint and pours out his complaint before the Lord.

¹ Hear my prayer, O Lord; let my cry come to you!

² Do not hide your face from me in the day of my distress! Incline your ear to me; answer me speedily in the day when I call!

³ For my days pass away like smoke, and my bones burn like a furnace.

⁴ My heart is struck down like grass and has withered; I forget to eat my bread.

⁵ Because of my loud groaning my bones cling to my flesh.

⁶ I am like a desert owl of the wilderness, like an owl of the waste places;

⁷ I lie awake; I am like a lonely sparrow on the housetop.

⁸ All the day my enemies taunt me; those who deride me use my name for a curse.

⁹ For I eat ashes like bread and mingle tears with my drink,

¹⁰ because of your indignation and anger; for you have taken me up and thrown me down.

¹¹ My days are like an evening shadow; I wither away like grass.

¹² But you, O Lord, are enthroned forever; you are remembered throughout all generations.

¹³ You will arise and have pity on Zion; it is the time to favor her; the appointed time has come.

14 For your servants hold her stones dear and have pity on her dust.

15 Nations will fear the name of the LORD, and all the kings of the earth will fear your glory.

16 For the LORD builds up Zion; he appears in his glory;

17 he regards the prayer of the destitute and does not despise their prayer.

18 Let this be recorded for a generation to come, so that a people yet to be created may praise the LORD:

19 that he looked down from his holy height; from heaven the LORD looked at the earth,

20 to hear the groans of the prisoners, to set free those who were doomed to die,

21 that they may declare in Zion the name of the LORD, and in Jerusalem his praise,

22 when peoples gather together, and kingdoms, to worship the LORD.

23 He has broken my strength in midcourse; he has shortened my days.

24 "O my God," I say, "take me not away in the midst of my days— you whose years endure throughout all generations!"

25 Of old you laid the foundation of the earth, and the heavens are the work of your hands.

26 They will perish, but you will remain; they will all wear out like a garment. You will change them like a robe, and they will pass away,

27 but you are the same, and your years have no end.

28 The children of your servants shall dwell secure; their offspring shall be established before you.

PSALM 103

Of David.

1 Bless the LORD, O my soul, and all that is within me, bless his holy name!

2 Bless the LORD, O my soul, and forget not all his benefits,

3 who forgives all your iniquity, who heals all your diseases,

4 who redeems your life from the pit, who crowns you with steadfast love and mercy,

5 who satisfies you with good so that your youth is renewed like the eagle's.

6 The LORD works righteousness and justice for all who are oppressed.

7 He made known his ways to Moses, his acts to the people of Israel.

8 The LORD is merciful and gracious, slow to anger and abounding in steadfast love.

9 He will not always chide,

nor will he keep his anger forever.

¹⁰ He does not deal with us according to our sins, nor repay us according to our iniquities.

¹¹ For as high as the heavens are above the earth, so great is his steadfast love toward those who fear him;

¹² as far as the east is from the west, so far does he remove our transgressions from us.

¹³ As a father shows compassion to his children, so the LORD shows compassion to those who fear him.

¹⁴ For he knows our frame; he remembers that we are dust.

¹⁵ As for man, his days are like grass; he flourishes like a flower of the field;

¹⁶ for the wind passes over it, and it is gone, and its place knows it no more.

¹⁷ But the steadfast love of the LORD is from everlasting to everlasting on those who fear him, and his righteousness to children's children,

¹⁸ to those who keep his covenant and remember to do his commandments.

¹⁹ The LORD has established his throne in the heavens, and his kingdom rules over all.

²⁰ Bless the LORD, O you his angels, you mighty ones who do his word, obeying the voice of his word!

²¹ Bless the LORD, all his hosts, his ministers, who do his will!

²² Bless the LORD, all his works, in all places of his dominion. Bless the LORD, O my soul!

PSALM 104

¹ Bless the LORD, O my soul! O LORD my God, you are very great! You are clothed with splendor and majesty,

² covering yourself with light as with a garment, stretching out the heavens like a tent.

³ He lays the beams of his chambers on the waters; he makes the clouds his chariot; he rides on the wings of the wind;

⁴ he makes his messengers winds, his ministers a flaming fire.

⁵ He set the earth on its foundations, so that it should never be moved.

⁶ You covered it with the deep as with a garment; the waters stood above the mountains.

⁷ At your rebuke they fled; at the sound of your thunder they took to flight.

⁸ The mountains rose, the valleys sank down to the

place that you appointed for them.

⁹ You set a boundary that they may not pass, so that they might not again cover the earth.

¹⁰ You make springs gush forth in the valleys; they flow between the hills;

¹¹ they give drink to every beast of the field; the wild donkeys quench their thirst.

¹² Beside them the birds of the heavens dwell; they sing among the branches.

¹³ From your lofty abode you water the mountains; the earth is satisfied with the fruit of your work.

¹⁴ You cause the grass to grow for the livestock and plants for man to cultivate, that he may bring forth food from the earth

¹⁵ and wine to gladden the heart of man, oil to make his face shine and bread to strengthen man's heart.

¹⁶ The trees of the LORD are watered abundantly, the cedars of Lebanon that he planted.

¹⁷ In them the birds build their nests; the stork has her home in the fir trees.

¹⁸ The high mountains are for the wild goats; the rocks are a refuge for the rock badgers.

¹⁹ He made the moon to mark the seasons; the sun knows its time for setting.

²⁰ You make darkness, and it is night, when all the beasts of the forest creep about.

²¹ The young lions roar for their prey, seeking their food from God.

²² When the sun rises, they steal away and lie down in their dens.

²³ Man goes out to his work and to his labor until the evening.

²⁴ O LORD, how manifold are your works! In wisdom have you made them all; the earth is full of your creatures.

²⁵ Here is the sea, great and wide, which teems with creatures innumerable, living things both small and great.

²⁶ There go the ships, and Leviathan, which you formed to play in it.

²⁷ These all look to you, to give them their food in due season.

²⁸ When you give it to them, they gather it up; when you open your hand, they are filled with good things.

²⁹ When you hide your face, they are dismayed; when you take away their breath, they die and return to their dust.

³⁰ When you send forth your Spirit, they are created, and you renew the face of the ground.

³¹ May the glory of the LORD endure forever; may the LORD rejoice in his works,

³² who looks on the earth and it trembles, who touches the mountains and they smoke!

³³ I will sing to the LORD as long as I live; I will sing praise to my God while I have being.

³⁴ May my meditation be pleasing to him, for I rejoice in the LORD.

³⁵ Let sinners be consumed from the earth, and let the wicked be no more! Bless the LORD, O my soul! Praise the LORD!

PSALM 105

¹ Oh give thanks to the LORD; call upon his name; make known his deeds among the peoples!

² Sing to him, sing praises to him; tell of all his wondrous works!

³ Glory in his holy name; let the hearts of those who seek the LORD rejoice!

⁴ Seek the LORD and his strength; seek his presence continually!

⁵ Remember the wondrous works that he has done, his miracles, and the judgments he uttered,

⁶ O offspring of Abraham, his servant, children of Jacob, his chosen ones!

⁷ He is the LORD our God; his judgments are in all the earth.

⁸ He remembers his covenant forever, the word that he commanded, for a thousand generations,

⁹ the covenant that he made with Abraham, his sworn promise to Isaac,

¹⁰ which he confirmed to Jacob as a statute, to Israel as an everlasting covenant,

¹¹ saying, "To you I will give the land of Canaan as your portion for an inheritance."

¹² When they were few in number, of little account, and sojourners in it,

¹³ wandering from nation to nation, from one kingdom to another people,

¹⁴ he allowed no one to oppress them; he rebuked kings on their account,

¹⁵ saying, "Touch not my anointed ones, do my prophets no harm!"

¹⁶ When he summoned a famine on the land and broke all supply of bread,

¹⁷ he had sent a man ahead of them, Joseph, who was sold as a slave.

¹⁸ His feet were hurt with fetters; his neck was put in a collar of iron;

¹⁹ until what he had said came to pass, the word of the LORD tested him.

²⁰ The king sent and released him; the ruler of the peoples set him free;

²¹ he made him lord of his house and ruler of all his possessions,

²² to bind his princes at his pleasure and to teach his elders wisdom.

²³ Then Israel came to Egypt; Jacob sojourned in the land of Ham.

²⁴ And the LORD made his people very fruitful and made them stronger than their foes.

²⁵ He turned their hearts to hate his people, to deal craftily with his servants.

²⁶ He sent Moses, his servant, and Aaron, whom he had chosen.

²⁷ They performed his signs among them and miracles in the land of Ham.

²⁸ He sent darkness, and made the land dark; they did not rebel against his words.

²⁹ He turned their waters into blood and caused their fish to die.

³⁰ Their land swarmed with frogs, even in the chambers of their kings.

³¹ He spoke, and there came swarms of flies, and gnats throughout their country.

³² He gave them hail for rain, and fiery lightning bolts through their land.

³³ He struck down their vines and fig trees, and shattered the trees of their country.

³⁴ He spoke, and the locusts came, young locusts without number,

³⁵ which devoured all the vegetation in their land and ate up the fruit of their ground.

³⁶ He struck down all the firstborn in their land, the firstfruits of all their strength.

³⁷ Then he brought out Israel with silver and gold, and there was none among his tribes who stumbled.

³⁸ Egypt was glad when they departed, for dread of them had fallen upon it.

³⁹ He spread a cloud for a covering, and fire to give light by night.

⁴⁰ They asked, and he brought quail, and gave them bread from heaven in abundance.

⁴¹ He opened the rock, and water gushed out; it flowed through the desert like a river.

⁴² For he remembered his holy promise, and Abraham, his servant.

⁴³ So he brought his people out with joy, his chosen ones with singing.

⁴⁴ And he gave them the

lands of the nations, and they took possession of the fruit of the peoples' toil,

⁴⁵ that they might keep his statutes and observe his laws. Praise the LORD!

PSALM 106

¹ Praise the LORD! Oh give thanks to the LORD, for he is good, for his steadfast love endures forever!

² Who can utter the mighty deeds of the LORD, or declare all his praise?

³ Blessed are they who observe justice, who do righteousness at all times!

⁴ Remember me, O LORD, when you show favor to your people; help me when you save them,

⁵ that I may look upon the prosperity of your chosen ones, that I may rejoice in the gladness of your nation, that I may glory with your inheritance.

⁶ Both we and our fathers have sinned; we have committed iniquity; we have done wickedness.

⁷ Our fathers, when they were in Egypt, did not consider your wondrous works; they did not remember the abundance of your steadfast love, but rebelled by the sea, at the Red Sea.

⁸ Yet he saved them for his name's sake, that he might make known his mighty power.

⁹ He rebuked the Red Sea, and it became dry, and he led them through the deep as through a desert.

¹⁰ So he saved them from the hand of the foe and redeemed them from the power of the enemy.

¹¹ And the waters covered their adversaries; not one of them was left.

¹² Then they believed his words; they sang his praise.

¹³ But they soon forgot his works; they did not wait for his counsel.

¹⁴ But they had a wanton craving in the wilderness, and put God to the test in the desert;

¹⁵ he gave them what they asked, but sent a wasting disease among them.

¹⁶ When men in the camp were jealous of Moses and Aaron, the holy one of the LORD,

¹⁷ the earth opened and swallowed up Dathan, and covered the company of Abiram.

¹⁸ Fire also broke out in their company; the flame burned up the wicked.

¹⁹ They made a calf in Horeb and worshiped a metal image.

²⁰ They exchanged the glory of God for the image of an ox that eats grass.

²¹ They forgot God, their Savior, who had done great things in Egypt,

²² wondrous works in the land of Ham, and awesome deeds by the Red Sea.

²³ Therefore he said he would destroy them— had not Moses, his chosen one, stood in the breach before him, to turn away his wrath from destroying them.

²⁴ Then they despised the pleasant land, having no faith in his promise.

²⁵ They murmured in their tents, and did not obey the voice of the LORD.

²⁶ Therefore he raised his hand and swore to them that he would make them fall in the wilderness,

²⁷ and would make their offspring fall among the nations, scattering them among the lands.

²⁸ Then they yoked themselves to the Baal of Peor, and ate sacrifices offered to the dead;

²⁹ they provoked the LORD to anger with their deeds, and a plague broke out among them.

³⁰ Then Phinehas stood up and intervened, and the plague was stayed.

³¹ And that was counted to him as righteousness from generation to generation forever.

³² They angered him at the waters of Meribah, and it went ill with Moses on their account,

³³ for they made his spirit bitter, and he spoke rashly with his lips.

³⁴ They did not destroy the peoples, as the LORD commanded them,

³⁵ but they mixed with the nations and learned to do as they did.

³⁶ They served their idols, which became a snare to them.

³⁷ They sacrificed their sons and their daughters to the demons;

³⁸ they poured out innocent blood, the blood of their sons and daughters, whom they sacrificed to the idols of Canaan, and the land was polluted with blood.

³⁹ Thus they became unclean by their acts, and played the whore in their deeds.

⁴⁰ Then the anger of the LORD was kindled against his people, and he abhorred his heritage;

⁴¹ he gave them into the hand of the nations, so that

those who hated them ruled over them.

⁴² Their enemies oppressed them, and they were brought into subjection under their power.

⁴³ Many times he delivered them, but they were rebellious in their purposes and were brought low through their iniquity.

⁴⁴ Nevertheless, he looked upon their distress, when he heard their cry.

⁴⁵ For their sake he remembered his covenant, and relented according to the abundance of his steadfast love.

⁴⁶ He caused them to be pitied by all those who held them captive.

⁴⁷ Save us, O Lord our God, and gather us from among the nations, that we may give thanks to your holy name and glory in your praise.

⁴⁸ Blessed be the Lord, the God of Israel, from everlasting to everlasting! And let all the people say, "Amen!" Praise the Lord!

PSALM 107

¹ Oh give thanks to the Lord, for he is good, for his steadfast love endures forever!

² Let the redeemed of the Lord say so, whom he has redeemed from trouble

³ and gathered in from the lands, from the east and from the west, from the north and from the south.

⁴ Some wandered in desert wastes, finding no way to a city to dwell in;

⁵ hungry and thirsty, their soul fainted within them.

⁶ Then they cried to the Lord in their trouble, and he delivered them from their distress.

⁷ He led them by a straight way till they reached a city to dwell in.

⁸ Let them thank the Lord for his steadfast love, for his wondrous works to the children of man!

⁹ For he satisfies the longing soul, and the hungry soul he fills with good things.

¹⁰ Some sat in darkness and in the shadow of death, prisoners in affliction and in irons,

¹¹ for they had rebelled against the words of God, and spurned the counsel of the Most High.

¹² So he bowed their hearts down with hard labor; they fell down, with none to help.

¹³ Then they cried to the Lord in their trouble, and he delivered them from their distress.

¹⁴ He brought them out of darkness and the shadow of

death, and burst their bonds apart.

¹⁵ Let them thank the LORD for his steadfast love, for his wondrous works to the children of man!

¹⁶ For he shatters the doors of bronze and cuts in two the bars of iron.

¹⁷ Some were fools through their sinful ways, and because of their iniquities suffered affliction;

¹⁸ they loathed any kind of food, and they drew near to the gates of death.

¹⁹ Then they cried to the LORD in their trouble, and he delivered them from their distress.

²⁰ He sent out his word and healed them, and delivered them from their destruction.

²¹ Let them thank the LORD for his steadfast love, for his wondrous works to the children of man!

²² And let them offer sacrifices of thanksgiving, and tell of his deeds in songs of joy!

²³ Some went down to the sea in ships, doing business on the great waters;

²⁴ they saw the deeds of the LORD, his wondrous works in the deep.

²⁵ For he commanded and raised the stormy wind, which lifted up the waves of the sea.

²⁶ They mounted up to heaven; they went down to the depths; their courage melted away in their evil plight;

²⁷ they reeled and staggered like drunken men and were at their wits' end.

²⁸ Then they cried to the LORD in their trouble, and he delivered them from their distress.

²⁹ He made the storm be still, and the waves of the sea were hushed.

³⁰ Then they were glad that the waters were quiet, and he brought them to their desired haven.

³¹ Let them thank the LORD for his steadfast love, for his wondrous works to the children of man!

³² Let them extol him in the congregation of the people, and praise him in the assembly of the elders.

³³ He turns rivers into a desert, springs of water into thirsty ground,

³⁴ a fruitful land into a salty waste, because of the evil of its inhabitants.

³⁵ He turns a desert into pools of water, a parched land into springs of water.

³⁶ And there he lets the hungry dwell, and they establish a city to live in;

³⁷ they sow fields and plant

vineyards and get a fruitful yield.

³⁸ By his blessing they multiply greatly, and he does not let their livestock diminish.

³⁹ When they are diminished and brought low through oppression, evil, and sorrow,

⁴⁰ he pours contempt on princes and makes them wander in trackless wastes;

⁴¹ but he raises up the needy out of affliction and makes their families like flocks.

⁴² The upright see it and are glad, and all wickedness shuts its mouth.

⁴³ Whoever is wise, let him attend to these things; let them consider the steadfast love of the LORD.

PSALM 108

A Song. A Psalm of David.

¹ My heart is steadfast, O God! I will sing and make melody with all my being!

² Awake, O harp and lyre! I will awake the dawn!

³ I will give thanks to you, O LORD, among the peoples; I will sing praises to you among the nations.

⁴ For your steadfast love is great above the heavens; your faithfulness reaches to the clouds.

⁵ Be exalted, O God, above the heavens! Let your glory be over all the earth!

⁶ That your beloved ones may be delivered, give salvation by your right hand and answer me!

⁷ God has promised in his holiness: "With exultation I will divide up Shechem and portion out the Valley of Succoth.

⁸ "Gilead is mine; Manasseh is mine; Ephraim is my helmet, Judah my scepter.

⁹ "Moab is my washbasin; upon Edom I cast my shoe; over Philistia I shout in triumph."

¹⁰ Who will bring me to the fortified city? Who will lead me to Edom?

¹¹ Have you not rejected us, O God? You do not go out, O God, with our armies.

¹² Oh grant us help against the foe, for vain is the salvation of man!

¹³ With God we shall do valiantly; it is he who will tread down our foes.

PSALM 109

To the choirmaster.
A Psalm of David.

¹ Be not silent, O God of my praise!

² For wicked and deceitful mouths are opened against me, speaking against me with lying tongues.

³ They encircle me with words of hate, and attack me without cause.

⁴ In return for my love they accuse me, but I give myself to prayer.

⁵ So they reward me evil for good, and hatred for my love.

⁶ Appoint a wicked man against him; let an accuser stand at his right hand.

⁷ When he is tried, let him come forth guilty; let his prayer be counted as sin!

⁸ May his days be few; may another take his office!

⁹ May his children be fatherless and his wife a widow!

¹⁰ May his children wander about and beg, seeking food far from the ruins they inhabit!

¹¹ May the creditor seize all that he has; may strangers plunder the fruits of his toil!

¹² Let there be none to extend kindness to him, nor any to pity his fatherless children!

¹³ May his posterity be cut off; may his name be blotted out in the second generation!

¹⁴ May the iniquity of his fathers be remembered before the Lord, and let not the sin of his mother be blotted out!

¹⁵ Let them be before the Lord continually, that he may cut off the memory of them from the earth!

¹⁶ For he did not remember to show kindness, but pursued the poor and needy and the brokenhearted, to put them to death.

¹⁷ He loved to curse; let curses come upon him! He did not delight in blessing; may it be far from him!

¹⁸ He clothed himself with cursing as his coat; may it soak into his body like water, like oil into his bones!

¹⁹ May it be like a garment that he wraps around him, like a belt that he puts on every day!

²⁰ May this be the reward of my accusers from the Lord, of those who speak evil against my life!

²¹ But you, O God my Lord, deal on my behalf for your name's sake; because your steadfast love is good, deliver me!

²² For I am poor and needy, and my heart is stricken within me.

²³ I am gone like a shadow at evening; I am shaken off like a locust.

²⁴ My knees are weak through fasting; my body has become gaunt, with no fat.

²⁵ I am an object of scorn to my accusers; when they see me, they wag their heads.

²⁶ Help me, O LORD my God! Save me according to your steadfast love!

²⁷ Let them know that this is your hand; you, O LORD, have done it!

²⁸ Let them curse, but you will bless! They arise and are put to shame, but your servant will be glad!

²⁹ May my accusers be clothed with dishonor; may they be wrapped in their own shame as in a cloak!

³⁰ With my mouth I will give great thanks to the LORD; I will praise him in the midst of the throng.

³¹ For he stands at the right hand of the needy one, to save him from those who condemn his soul to death.

PSALM 110
A Psalm of David.

¹ The LORD says to my Lord: "Sit at my right hand, until I make your enemies your footstool."

² The LORD sends forth from Zion your mighty scepter. Rule in the midst of your enemies!

³ Your people will offer themselves freely on the day of your power, in holy garments; from the womb of the morning, the dew of your youth will be yours.

⁴ The LORD has sworn and will not change his mind, "You are a priest forever after the order of Melchizedek."

⁵ The Lord is at your right hand; he will shatter kings on the day of his wrath.

⁶ He will execute judgment among the nations, filling them with corpses; he will shatter chiefs over the wide earth.

⁷ He will drink from the brook by the way; therefore he will lift up his head.

PSALM 111

¹ Praise the LORD! I will give thanks to the LORD with my whole heart, in the company of the upright, in the congregation.

² Great are the works of the LORD, studied by all who delight in them.

³ Full of splendor and majesty is his work, and his righteousness endures forever.

⁴ He has caused his wondrous works to be remembered; the LORD is gracious and merciful.

⁵ He provides food for those who fear him; he remembers his covenant forever.

⁶ He has shown his people the power of his works, in giving them the inheritance of the nations.

7 The works of his hands are faithful and just; all his precepts are trustworthy;

8 they are established forever and ever, to be performed with faithfulness and uprightness.

9 He sent redemption to his people; he has commanded his covenant forever. Holy and awesome is his name!

10 The fear of the LORD is the beginning of wisdom; all those who practice it have a good understanding. His praise endures forever!

PSALM 112

1 Praise the LORD! Blessed is the man who fears the LORD, who greatly delights in his commandments!

2 His offspring will be mighty in the land; the generation of the upright will be blessed.

3 Wealth and riches are in his house, and his righteousness endures forever.

4 Light dawns in the darkness for the upright; he is gracious, merciful, and righteous.

5 It is well with the man who deals generously and lends; who conducts his affairs with justice.

6 For the righteous will never be moved; he will be remembered forever.

7 He is not afraid of bad news; his heart is firm, trusting in the LORD.

8 His heart is steady; he will not be afraid, until he looks in triumph on his adversaries.

9 He has distributed freely; he has given to the poor; his righteousness endures forever; his horn is exalted in honor.

10 The wicked man sees it and is angry; he gnashes his teeth and melts away; the desire of the wicked will perish!

PSALM 113

1 Praise the LORD! Praise, O servants of the LORD, praise the name of the LORD!

2 Blessed be the name of the LORD from this time forth and forevermore!

3 From the rising of the sun to its setting, the name of the LORD is to be praised!

4 The LORD is high above all nations, and his glory above the heavens!

5 Who is like the LORD our God, who is seated on high,

6 who looks far down on the heavens and the earth?

7 He raises the poor from the dust and lifts the needy from the ash heap,

8 to make them sit with princes, with the princes of his people.

⁹ He gives the barren woman a home, making her the joyous mother of children. Praise the LORD!

PSALM 114

¹ When Israel went out from Egypt, the house of Jacob from a people of strange language,

² Judah became his sanctuary, Israel his dominion.

³ The sea looked and fled; Jordan turned back.

⁴ The mountains skipped like rams, the hills like lambs.

⁵ What ails you, O sea, that you flee? O Jordan, that you turn back?

⁶ O mountains, that you skip like rams? O hills, like lambs?

⁷ Tremble, O earth, at the presence of the Lord, at the presence of the God of Jacob,

⁸ who turns the rock into a pool of water, the flint into a spring of water.

PSALM 115

¹ Not to us, O LORD, not to us, but to your name give glory, for the sake of your steadfast love and your faithfulness!

² Why should the nations say, "Where is their God?"

³ Our God is in the heavens; he does all that he pleases.

⁴ Their idols are silver and gold, the work of human hands.

⁵ They have mouths, but do not speak; eyes, but do not see.

⁶ They have ears, but do not hear; noses, but do not smell.

⁷ They have hands, but do not feel; feet, but do not walk; and they do not make a sound in their throat.

⁸ Those who make them become like them; so do all who trust in them.

⁹ O Israel, trust in the LORD! He is their help and their shield.

¹⁰ O house of Aaron, trust in the LORD! He is their help and their shield.

¹¹ You who fear the LORD, trust in the LORD! He is their help and their shield.

¹² The LORD has remembered us; he will bless us; he will bless the house of Israel; he will bless the house of Aaron;

¹³ he will bless those who fear the LORD, both the small and the great.

¹⁴ May the LORD give you increase, you and your children!

¹⁵ May you be blessed by the LORD, who made heaven and earth!

¹⁶ The heavens are the LORD's heavens, but the earth

he has given to the children of man.

¹⁷ The dead do not praise the LORD, nor do any who go down into silence.

¹⁸ But we will bless the LORD from this time forth and forevermore. Praise the LORD!

PSALM 116

¹ I love the LORD, because he has heard my voice and my pleas for mercy.

² Because he inclined his ear to me, therefore I will call on him as long as I live.

³ The snares of death encompassed me; the pangs of Sheol laid hold on me; I suffered distress and anguish.

⁴ Then I called on the name of the LORD: "O LORD, I pray, deliver my soul!"

⁵ Gracious is the LORD, and righteous; our God is merciful.

⁶ The LORD preserves the simple; when I was brought low, he saved me.

⁷ Return, O my soul, to your rest; for the LORD has dealt bountifully with you.

⁸ For you have delivered my soul from death, my eyes from tears, my feet from stumbling;

⁹ I will walk before the LORD in the land of the living.

¹⁰ I believed, even when I spoke: "I am greatly afflicted";

¹¹ I said in my alarm, "All mankind are liars."

¹² What shall I render to the LORD for all his benefits to me?

¹³ I will lift up the cup of salvation and call on the name of the LORD,

¹⁴ I will pay my vows to the LORD in the presence of all his people.

¹⁵ Precious in the sight of the LORD is the death of his saints.

¹⁶ O LORD, I am your servant; I am your servant, the son of your maidservant. You have loosed my bonds.

¹⁷ I will offer to you the sacrifice of thanksgiving and call on the name of the LORD.

¹⁸ I will pay my vows to the LORD in the presence of all his people,

¹⁹ in the courts of the house of the LORD, in your midst, O Jerusalem. Praise the LORD!

PSALM 117

¹ Praise the LORD, all nations! Extol him, all peoples!

² For great is his steadfast love toward us, and the faithfulness of the LORD endures forever. Praise the LORD!

PSALM 118

¹ Oh give thanks to the LORD, for he is good; for his steadfast love endures forever!

2 Let Israel say, "His steadfast love endures forever."

3 Let the house of Aaron say, "His steadfast love endures forever."

4 Let those who fear the LORD say, "His steadfast love endures forever."

5 Out of my distress I called on the LORD; the LORD answered me and set me free.

6 The LORD is on my side; I will not fear. What can man do to me?

7 The LORD is on my side as my helper; I shall look in triumph on those who hate me.

8 It is better to take refuge in the LORD than to trust in man.

9 It is better to take refuge in the LORD than to trust in princes.

10 All nations surrounded me; in the name of the LORD I cut them off!

11 They surrounded me, surrounded me on every side; in the name of the LORD I cut them off!

12 They surrounded me like bees; they went out like a fire among thorns; in the name of the LORD I cut them off!

13 I was pushed hard, so that I was falling, but the LORD helped me.

14 The LORD is my strength and my song; he has become my salvation.

15 Glad songs of salvation are in the tents of the righteous: "The right hand of the LORD does valiantly,

16 "the right hand of the LORD exalts, the right hand of the LORD does valiantly!"

17 I shall not die, but I shall live, and recount the deeds of the LORD.

18 The LORD has disciplined me severely, but he has not given me over to death.

19 Open to me the gates of righteousness, that I may enter through them and give thanks to the LORD.

20 This is the gate of the LORD; the righteous shall enter through it.

21 I thank you that you have answered me and have become my salvation.

22 The stone that the builders rejected has become the cornerstone.

23 This is the LORD's doing; it is marvelous in our eyes.

24 This is the day that the LORD has made; let us rejoice and be glad in it.

25 Save us, we pray, O LORD! O LORD, we pray, give us success!

26 Blessed is he who comes in the name of the LORD! We

bless you from the house of the LORD.

27 The LORD is God, and he has made his light to shine upon us. Bind the festal sacrifice with cords, up to the horns of the altar!

28 You are my God, and I will give thanks to you; you are my God; I will extol you.

29 Oh give thanks to the LORD, for he is good; for his steadfast love endures forever!

PSALM 119

ALEPH

1 Blessed are those whose way is blameless, who walk in the law of the LORD!

2 Blessed are those who keep his testimonies, who seek him with their whole heart,

3 who also do no wrong, but walk in his ways!

4 You have commanded your precepts to be kept diligently.

5 Oh that my ways may be steadfast in keeping your statutes!

6 Then I shall not be put to shame, having my eyes fixed on all your commandments.

7 I will praise you with an upright heart, when I learn your righteous rules.

8 I will keep your statutes; do not utterly forsake me!

BETH

9 How can a young man keep his way pure? By guarding it according to your word.

10 With my whole heart I seek you; let me not wander from your commandments!

11 I have stored up your word in my heart, that I might not sin against you.

12 Blessed are you, O LORD; teach me your statutes!

13 With my lips I declare all the rules of your mouth.

14 In the way of your testimonies I delight as much as in all riches.

15 I will meditate on your precepts and fix my eyes on your ways.

16 I will delight in your statutes; I will not forget your word.

GIMEL

17 Deal bountifully with your servant, that I may live and keep your word.

18 Open my eyes, that I may behold wondrous things out of your law.

19 I am a sojourner on the earth; hide not your commandments from me!

20 My soul is consumed with longing for your rules at all times.

21 You rebuke the insolent,

accursed ones, who wander from your commandments.

²² Take away from me scorn and contempt, for I have kept your testimonies.

²³ Even though princes sit plotting against me, your servant will meditate on your statutes.

²⁴ Your testimonies are my delight; they are my counselors.

DALETH

²⁵ My soul clings to the dust; give me life according to your word!

²⁶ When I told of my ways, you answered me; teach me your statutes!

²⁷ Make me understand the way of your precepts, and I will meditate on your wondrous works.

²⁸ My soul melts away for sorrow; strengthen me according to your word!

²⁹ Put false ways far from me and graciously teach me your law!

³⁰ I have chosen the way of faithfulness; I set your rules before me.

³¹ I cling to your testimonies, O LORD; let me not be put to shame!

³² I will run in the way of your commandments when you enlarge my heart!

HE

³³ Teach me, O LORD, the way of your statutes; and I will keep it to the end.

³⁴ Give me understanding, that I may keep your law and observe it with my whole heart.

³⁵ Lead me in the path of your commandments, for I delight in it.

³⁶ Incline my heart to your testimonies, and not to selfish gain!

³⁷ Turn my eyes from looking at worthless things; and give me life in your ways.

³⁸ Confirm to your servant your promise, that you may be feared.

³⁹ Turn away the reproach that I dread, for your rules are good.

⁴⁰ Behold, I long for your precepts; in your righteousness give me life!

WAW

⁴¹ Let your steadfast love come to me, O LORD, your salvation according to your promise;

⁴² then shall I have an answer for him who taunts me, for I trust in your word.

⁴³ And take not the word of truth utterly out of my mouth, for my hope is in your rules.

⁴⁴ I will keep your law continually, forever and ever,

⁴⁵ and I shall walk in a wide place, for I have sought your precepts.

⁴⁶ I will also speak of your testimonies before kings and shall not be put to shame,

⁴⁷ for I find my delight in your commandments, which I love.

⁴⁸ I will lift up my hands toward your commandments, which I love, and I will meditate on your statutes.

ZAYIN

⁴⁹ Remember your word to your servant, in which you have made me hope.

⁵⁰ This is my comfort in my affliction, that your promise gives me life.

⁵¹ The insolent utterly deride me, but I do not turn away from your law.

⁵² When I think of your rules from of old, I take comfort, O LORD.

⁵³ Hot indignation seizes me because of the wicked, who forsake your law.

⁵⁴ Your statutes have been my songs in the house of my sojourning.

⁵⁵ I remember your name in the night, O LORD, and keep your law.

⁵⁶ This blessing has fallen to me, that I have kept your precepts.

HETH

⁵⁷ The LORD is my portion; I promise to keep your words.

⁵⁸ I entreat your favor with all my heart; be gracious to me according to your promise.

⁵⁹ When I think on my ways, I turn my feet to your testimonies;

⁶⁰ I hasten and do not delay to keep your commandments.

⁶¹ Though the cords of the wicked ensnare me, I do not forget your law.

⁶² At midnight I rise to praise you, because of your righteous rules.

⁶³ I am a companion of all who fear you, of those who keep your precepts.

⁶⁴ The earth, O LORD, is full of your steadfast love; teach me your statutes!

TETH

⁶⁵ You have dealt well with your servant, O LORD, according to your word.

⁶⁶ Teach me good judgment and knowledge, for I believe in your commandments.

⁶⁷ Before I was afflicted I went astray, but now I keep your word.

68 You are good and do good; teach me your statutes.

69 The insolent smear me with lies, but with my whole heart I keep your precepts;

70 their heart is unfeeling like fat, but I delight in your law.

71 It is good for me that I was afflicted, that I might learn your statutes.

72 The law of your mouth is better to me than thousands of gold and silver pieces.

YODH

73 Your hands have made and fashioned me; give me understanding that I may learn your commandments.

74 Those who fear you shall see me and rejoice, because I have hoped in your word.

75 I know, O LORD, that your rules are righteous, and that in faithfulness you have afflicted me.

76 Let your steadfast love comfort me according to your promise to your servant.

77 Let your mercy come to me, that I may live; for your law is my delight.

78 Let the insolent be put to shame, because they have wronged me with falsehood; as for me, I will meditate on your precepts.

79 Let those who fear you turn to me, that they may know your testimonies.

80 May my heart be blameless in your statutes, that I may not be put to shame!

KAPH

81 My soul longs for your salvation; I hope in your word.

82 My eyes long for your promise; I ask, "When will you comfort me?"

83 For I have become like a wineskin in the smoke, yet I have not forgotten your statutes.

84 How long must your servant endure? When will you judge those who persecute me?

85 The insolent have dug pitfalls for me; they do not live according to your law.

86 All your commandments are sure; they persecute me with falsehood; help me!

87 They have almost made an end of me on earth, but I have not forsaken your precepts.

88 In your steadfast love give me life, that I may keep the testimonies of your mouth.

LAMEDH

89 Forever, O LORD, your word is firmly fixed in the heavens.

⁹⁰ Your faithfulness endures to all generations; you have established the earth, and it stands fast.

⁹¹ By your appointment they stand this day, for all things are your servants.

⁹² If your law had not been my delight, I would have perished in my affliction.

⁹³ I will never forget your precepts, for by them you have given me life.

⁹⁴ I am yours; save me, for I have sought your precepts.

⁹⁵ The wicked lie in wait to destroy me, but I consider your testimonies.

⁹⁶ I have seen a limit to all perfection, but your commandment is exceedingly broad.

MEM

⁹⁷ Oh how I love your law! It is my meditation all the day.

⁹⁸ Your commandment makes me wiser than my enemies, for it is ever with me.

⁹⁹ I have more understanding than all my teachers, for your testimonies are my meditation.

¹⁰⁰ I understand more than the aged, for I keep your precepts.

¹⁰¹ I hold back my feet from every evil way, in order to keep your word.

¹⁰² I do not turn aside from your rules, for you have taught me.

¹⁰³ How sweet are your words to my taste, sweeter than honey to my mouth!

¹⁰⁴ Through your precepts I get understanding; therefore I hate every false way.

NUN

¹⁰⁵ Your word is a lamp to my feet and a light to my path.

¹⁰⁶ I have sworn an oath and confirmed it, to keep your righteous rules.

¹⁰⁷ I am severely afflicted; give me life, O LORD, according to your word!

¹⁰⁸ Accept my freewill offerings of praise, O LORD, and teach me your rules.

¹⁰⁹ I hold my life in my hand continually, but I do not forget your law.

¹¹⁰ The wicked have laid a snare for me, but I do not stray from your precepts.

¹¹¹ Your testimonies are my heritage forever, for they are the joy of my heart.

¹¹² I incline my heart to perform your statutes forever, to the end.

SAMEKH

¹¹³ I hate the double-minded, but I love your law.

¹¹⁴ You are my hiding place

and my shield; I hope in your word.

115 Depart from me, you evildoers, that I may keep the commandments of my God.

116 Uphold me according to your promise, that I may live, and let me not be put to shame in my hope!

117 Hold me up, that I may be safe and have regard for your statutes continually!

118 You spurn all who go astray from your statutes, for their cunning is in vain.

119 All the wicked of the earth you discard like dross, therefore I love your testimonies.

120 My flesh trembles for fear of you, and I am afraid of your judgments.

AYIN

121 I have done what is just and right; do not leave me to my oppressors.

122 Give your servant a pledge of good; let not the insolent oppress me.

123 My eyes long for your salvation and for the fulfillment of your righteous promise.

124 Deal with your servant according to your steadfast love, and teach me your statutes.

125 I am your servant; give me understanding, that I may know your testimonies!

126 It is time for the LORD to act, for your law has been broken.

127 Therefore I love your commandments above gold, above fine gold.

128 Therefore I consider all your precepts to be right; I hate every false way.

PE

129 Your testimonies are wonderful; therefore my soul keeps them.

130 The unfolding of your words gives light; it imparts understanding to the simple.

131 I open my mouth and pant, because I long for your commandments.

132 Turn to me and be gracious to me, as is your way with those who love your name.

133 Keep steady my steps according to your promise, and let no iniquity get dominion over me.

134 Redeem me from man's oppression, that I may keep your precepts.

135 Make your face shine upon your servant, and teach me your statutes.

136 My eyes shed streams of tears, because people do not keep your law.

TSADHE

¹³⁷ Righteous are you, O LORD, and right are your rules.

¹³⁸ You have appointed your testimonies in righteousness and in all faithfulness.

¹³⁹ My zeal consumes me, because my foes forget your words.

¹⁴⁰ Your promise is well tried, and your servant loves it.

¹⁴¹ I am small and despised, yet I do not forget your precepts.

¹⁴² Your righteousness is righteous forever, and your law is true.

¹⁴³ Trouble and anguish have found me out, but your commandments are my delight.

¹⁴⁴ Your testimonies are righteous forever; give me understanding that I may live.

QOPH

¹⁴⁵ With my whole heart I cry; answer me, O LORD! I will keep your statutes.

¹⁴⁶ I call to you; save me, that I may observe your testimonies.

¹⁴⁷ I rise before dawn and cry for help; I hope in your words.

¹⁴⁸ My eyes are awake before the watches of the night, that I may meditate on your promise.

¹⁴⁹ Hear my voice according to your steadfast love; O LORD, according to your justice give me life.

¹⁵⁰ They draw near who persecute me with evil purpose; they are far from your law.

¹⁵¹ But you are near, O LORD, and all your commandments are true.

¹⁵² Long have I known from your testimonies that you have founded them forever.

RESH

¹⁵³ Look on my affliction and deliver me, for I do not forget your law.

¹⁵⁴ Plead my cause and redeem me; give me life according to your promise!

¹⁵⁵ Salvation is far from the wicked, for they do not seek your statutes.

¹⁵⁶ Great is your mercy, O LORD; give me life according to your rules.

¹⁵⁷ Many are my persecutors and my adversaries, but I do not swerve from your testimonies.

¹⁵⁸ I look at the faithless with disgust, because they do not keep your commands.

¹⁵⁹ Consider how I love your precepts! Give me life according to your steadfast love.

¹⁶⁰ The sum of your word is

truth, and every one of your righteous rules endures forever.

SIN AND SHIN

161 Princes persecute me without cause, but my heart stands in awe of your words.

162 I rejoice at your word like one who finds great spoil.

163 I hate and abhor falsehood, but I love your law.

164 Seven times a day I praise you for your righteous rules.

165 Great peace have those who love your law; nothing can make them stumble.

166 I hope for your salvation, O LORD, and I do your commandments.

167 My soul keeps your testimonies; I love them exceedingly.

168 I keep your precepts and testimonies, for all my ways are before you.

TAW

169 Let my cry come before you, O LORD; give me understanding according to your word!

170 Let my plea come before you; deliver me according to your word.

171 My lips will pour forth praise, for you teach me your statutes.

172 My tongue will sing of your word, for all your commandments are right.

173 Let your hand be ready to help me, for I have chosen your precepts.

174 I long for your salvation, O LORD, and your law is my delight.

175 Let my soul live and praise you, and let your rules help me.

176 I have gone astray like a lost sheep; seek your servant, for I do not forget your commandments.

PSALM 120

A Song of Ascents.

1 In my distress I called to the LORD, and he answered me.

2 Deliver me, O LORD, from lying lips, from a deceitful tongue.

3 What shall be given to you, and what more shall be done to you, you deceitful tongue?

4 A warrior's sharp arrows, with glowing coals of the broom tree!

5 Woe to me, that I sojourn in Meshech, that I dwell among the tents of Kedar!

6 Too long have I had my dwelling among those who hate peace.

7 I am for peace, but when I speak, they are for war!

PSALM 121

A Song of Ascents.

1 I lift up my eyes to the hills. From where does my help come?

2 My help comes from the LORD, who made heaven and earth.

3 He will not let your foot be moved; he who keeps you will not slumber.

4 Behold, he who keeps Israel will neither slumber nor sleep.

5 The LORD is your keeper; the LORD is your shade on your right hand.

6 The sun shall not strike you by day, nor the moon by night.

7 The LORD will keep you from all evil; he will keep your life.

8 The LORD will keep your going out and your coming in from this time forth and forevermore.

PSALM 122

A Song of Ascents. Of David.

1 I was glad when they said to me, "Let us go to the house of the LORD!"

2 Our feet have been standing within your gates, O Jerusalem!

3 Jerusalem—built as a city that is bound firmly together,

4 to which the tribes go up, the tribes of the LORD, as was decreed for Israel, to give thanks to the name of the LORD.

5 There thrones for judgment were set, the thrones of the house of David.

6 Pray for the peace of Jerusalem! "May they be secure who love you!

7 "Peace be within your walls and security within your towers!"

8 For my brothers and companions' sake I will say, "Peace be within you!"

9 For the sake of the house of the LORD our God, I will seek your good.

PSALM 123

A Song of Ascents.

1 To you I lift up my eyes, O you who are enthroned in the heavens!

2 Behold, as the eyes of servants look to the hand of their master, as the eyes of a maidservant to the hand of her mistress, so our eyes look to the LORD our God, till he has mercy upon us.

3 Have mercy upon us, O LORD, have mercy upon us, for we have had more than enough of contempt.

4 Our soul has had more than enough of the scorn of those who are at ease, the contempt of the proud.

PSALM 124

A Song of Ascents. Of David.

¹ If it had not been the LORD who was on our side— let Israel now say—

² if it had not been the LORD who was on our side when people rose up against us,

³ then they would have swallowed us up alive, when their anger was kindled against us;

⁴ then the flood would have swept us away, the torrent would have gone over us;

⁵ then over us would have gone the raging waters.

⁶ Blessed be the LORD, who has not given us as prey to their teeth!

⁷ We have escaped like a bird from the snare of the fowlers; the snare is broken, and we have escaped!

⁸ Our help is in the name of the LORD, who made heaven and earth.

PSALM 125

A Song of Ascents.

¹ Those who trust in the LORD are like Mount Zion, which cannot be moved, but abides forever.

² As the mountains surround Jerusalem, so the LORD surrounds his people, from this time forth and forevermore.

³ For the scepter of wickedness shall not rest on the land allotted to the righteous, lest the righteous stretch out their hands to do wrong.

⁴ Do good, O LORD, to those who are good, and to those who are upright in their hearts!

⁵ But those who turn aside to their crooked ways the LORD will lead away with evildoers! Peace be upon Israel!

PSALM 126

A Song of Ascents.

¹ When the LORD restored the fortunes of Zion, we were like those who dream.

² Then our mouth was filled with laughter, and our tongue with shouts of joy; then they said among the nations, "The LORD has done great things for them."

³ The LORD has done great things for us; we are glad.

⁴ Restore our fortunes, O LORD, like streams in the Negeb!

⁵ Those who sow in tears shall reap with shouts of joy!

⁶ He who goes out weeping, bearing the seed for sowing, shall come home with shouts of joy, bringing his sheaves with him.

PSALM 127

A Song of Ascents. Of Solomon.

¹ Unless the LORD builds the house, those who build

it labor in vain. Unless the LORD watches over the city, the watchman stays awake in vain.

² It is in vain that you rise up early and go late to rest, eating the bread of anxious toil; for he gives to his beloved sleep.

³ Behold, children are a heritage from the LORD, the fruit of the womb a reward.

⁴ Like arrows in the hand of a warrior are the children of one's youth.

⁵ Blessed is the man who fills his quiver with them! He shall not be put to shame when he speaks with his enemies in the gate.

PSALM 128
A Song of Ascents.

¹ Blessed is everyone who fears the LORD, who walks in his ways!

² You shall eat the fruit of the labor of your hands; you shall be blessed, and it shall be well with you.

³ Your wife will be like a fruitful vine within your house; your children will be like olive shoots around your table.

⁴ Behold, thus shall the man be blessed who fears the LORD.

⁵ The LORD bless you from Zion! May you see the prosperity of Jerusalem all the days of your life!

⁶ May you see your children's children! Peace be upon Israel!

PSALM 129
A Song of Ascents.

¹ "Greatly have they afflicted me from my youth"— let Israel now say—

² "Greatly have they afflicted me from my youth, yet they have not prevailed against me.

³ "The plowers plowed upon my back; they made long their furrows."

⁴ The LORD is righteous; he has cut the cords of the wicked.

⁵ May all who hate Zion be put to shame and turned backward!

⁶ Let them be like the grass on the housetops, which withers before it grows up,

⁷ with which the reaper does not fill his hand nor the binder of sheaves his arms,

⁸ nor do those who pass by say, "The blessing of the LORD be upon you! We bless you in the name of the LORD!"

PSALM 130
A Song of Ascents.

¹ Out of the depths I cry to you, O LORD!

2 O Lord, hear my voice! Let your ears be attentive to the voice of my pleas for mercy!

3 If you, O Lord, should mark iniquities, O Lord, who could stand?

4 But with you there is forgiveness, that you may be feared.

5 I wait for the Lord, my soul waits, and in his word I hope;

6 my soul waits for the Lord more than watchmen for the morning, more than watchmen for the morning.

7 O Israel, hope in the Lord! For with the Lord there is steadfast love, and with him is plentiful redemption.

8 And he will redeem Israel from all his iniquities.

PSALM 131
A Song of Ascents. Of David.

1 O Lord, my heart is not lifted up; my eyes are not raised too high; I do not occupy myself with things too great and too marvelous for me.

2 But I have calmed and quieted my soul, like a weaned child with its mother; like a weaned child is my soul within me.

3 O Israel, hope in the Lord from this time forth and forevermore.

PSALM 132
A Song of Ascents.

1 Remember, O Lord, in David's favor, all the hardships he endured,

2 how he swore to the Lord and vowed to the Mighty One of Jacob,

3 "I will not enter my house or get into my bed,

4 "I will not give sleep to my eyes or slumber to my eyelids,

5 "until I find a place for the Lord, a dwelling place for the Mighty One of Jacob."

6 Behold, we heard of it in Ephrathah; we found it in the fields of Jaar.

7 "Let us go to his dwelling place; let us worship at his footstool!"

8 Arise, O Lord, and go to your resting place, you and the ark of your might.

9 Let your priests be clothed with righteousness, and let your saints shout for joy.

10 For the sake of your servant David, do not turn away the face of your anointed one.

11 The Lord swore to David a sure oath from which he will not turn back: "One of the sons of your body I will set on your throne.

12 "If your sons keep my covenant and my testimonies that I shall teach them, their sons also forever shall sit on your throne."

¹³ For the LORD has chosen Zion; he has desired it for his dwelling place:

¹⁴ "This is my resting place forever; here I will dwell, for I have desired it.

¹⁵ "I will abundantly bless her provisions; I will satisfy her poor with bread.

¹⁶ "Her priests I will clothe with salvation, and her saints will shout for joy.

¹⁷ "There I will make a horn to sprout for David; I have prepared a lamp for my anointed.

¹⁸ "His enemies I will clothe with shame, but on him his crown will shine."

PSALM 133

A Song of Ascents. Of David.

¹ Behold, how good and pleasant it is when brothers dwell in unity!

² It is like the precious oil on the head, running down on the beard, on the beard of Aaron, running down on the collar of his robes!

³ It is like the dew of Hermon, which falls on the mountains of Zion! For there the LORD has commanded the blessing, life forevermore.

PSALM 134

A Song of Ascents.

¹ Come, bless the LORD, all you servants of the LORD, who stand by night in the house of the LORD!

² Lift up your hands to the holy place and bless the LORD!

³ May the LORD bless you from Zion, he who made heaven and earth!

PSALM 135

¹ Praise the LORD! Praise the name of the LORD, give praise, O servants of the LORD,

² who stand in the house of the LORD, in the courts of the house of our God!

³ Praise the LORD, for the LORD is good; sing to his name, for it is pleasant!

⁴ For the LORD has chosen Jacob for himself, Israel as his own possession.

⁵ For I know that the LORD is great, and that our Lord is above all gods.

⁶ Whatever the LORD pleases, he does, in heaven and on earth, in the seas and all deeps.

⁷ He it is who makes the clouds rise at the end of the earth, who makes lightnings for the rain and brings forth the wind from his storehouses.

⁸ He it was who struck down the firstborn of Egypt, both of man and of beast;

⁹ who in your midst, O

Egypt, sent signs and wonders against Pharaoh and all his servants;

¹⁰ who struck down many nations and killed mighty kings,

¹¹ Sihon, king of the Amorites, and Og, king of Bashan, and all the kingdoms of Canaan,

¹² and gave their land as a heritage, a heritage to his people Israel.

¹³ Your name, O LORD, endures forever, your renown, O LORD, throughout all ages.

¹⁴ For the LORD will vindicate his people and have compassion on his servants.

¹⁵ The idols of the nations are silver and gold, the work of human hands.

¹⁶ They have mouths, but do not speak; they have eyes, but do not see;

¹⁷ they have ears, but do not hear, nor is there any breath in their mouths.

¹⁸ Those who make them become like them, so do all who trust in them.

¹⁹ O house of Israel, bless the LORD! O house of Aaron, bless the LORD!

²⁰ O house of Levi, bless the LORD! You who fear the LORD, bless the LORD!

²¹ Blessed be the LORD from Zion, he who dwells in Jerusalem! Praise the LORD!

PSALM 136

¹ Give thanks to the LORD, for he is good, for his steadfast love endures forever.

² Give thanks to the God of gods, for his steadfast love endures forever.

³ Give thanks to the Lord of lords, for his steadfast love endures forever;

⁴ to him who alone does great wonders, for his steadfast love endures forever;

⁵ to him who by understanding made the heavens, for his steadfast love endures forever;

⁶ to him who spread out the earth above the waters, for his steadfast love endures forever;

⁷ to him who made the great lights, for his steadfast love endures forever;

⁸ the sun to rule over the day, for his steadfast love endures forever;

⁹ the moon and stars to rule over the night, for his steadfast love endures forever;

¹⁰ to him who struck down the firstborn of Egypt, for his steadfast love endures forever;

¹¹ and brought Israel out from among them, for his steadfast love endures forever;

¹² with a strong hand and an outstretched arm, for

his steadfast love endures forever;

¹³ to him who divided the Red Sea in two, for his steadfast love endures forever;

¹⁴ and made Israel pass through the midst of it, for his steadfast love endures forever;

¹⁵ but overthrew Pharaoh and his host in the Red Sea, for his steadfast love endures forever;

¹⁶ to him who led his people through the wilderness, for his steadfast love endures forever;

¹⁷ to him who struck down great kings, for his steadfast love endures forever;

¹⁸ and killed mighty kings, for his steadfast love endures forever;

¹⁹ Sihon, king of the Amorites, for his steadfast love endures forever;

²⁰ and Og, king of Bashan, for his steadfast love endures forever;

²¹ and gave their land as a heritage, for his steadfast love endures forever;

²² a heritage to Israel his servant, for his steadfast love endures forever.

²³ It is he who remembered us in our low estate, for his steadfast love endures forever;

²⁴ and rescued us from our foes, for his steadfast love endures forever;

²⁵ he who gives food to all flesh, for his steadfast love endures forever.

²⁶ Give thanks to the God of heaven, for his steadfast love endures forever.

PSALM 137

¹ By the waters of Babylon, there we sat down and wept, when we remembered Zion.

² On the willows there we hung up our lyres.

³ For there our captors required of us songs, and our tormentors, mirth, saying, "Sing us one of the songs of Zion!"

⁴ How shall we sing the LORD's song in a foreign land?

⁵ If I forget you, O Jerusalem, let my right hand forget its skill!

⁶ Let my tongue stick to the roof of my mouth, if I do not remember you, if I do not set Jerusalem above my highest joy!

⁷ Remember, O LORD, against the Edomites the day of Jerusalem, how they said, "Lay it bare, lay it bare, down to its foundations!"

⁸ O daughter of Babylon, doomed to be destroyed, blessed shall he be who repays you with what you have done to us!

9 Blessed shall he be who takes your little ones and dashes them against the rock!

PSALM 138
Of David.

1 I give you thanks, O LORD, with my whole heart; before the gods I sing your praise;

2 I bow down toward your holy temple and give thanks to your name for your steadfast love and your faithfulness, for you have exalted above all things your name and your word.

3 On the day I called, you answered me; my strength of soul you increased.

4 All the kings of the earth shall give you thanks, O LORD, for they have heard the words of your mouth,

5 and they shall sing of the ways of the LORD, for great is the glory of the LORD.

6 For though the LORD is high, he regards the lowly, but the haughty he knows from afar.

7 Though I walk in the midst of trouble, you preserve my life; you stretch out your hand against the wrath of my enemies, and your right hand delivers me.

8 The LORD will fulfill his purpose for me; your steadfast love, O LORD, endures forever. Do not forsake the work of your hands.

PSALM 139
To the choirmaster.
A Psalm of David.

1 O LORD, you have searched me and known me!

2 You know when I sit down and when I rise up; you discern my thoughts from afar.

3 You search out my path and my lying down and are acquainted with all my ways.

4 Even before a word is on my tongue, behold, O LORD, you know it altogether.

5 You hem me in, behind and before, and lay your hand upon me.

6 Such knowledge is too wonderful for me; it is high; I cannot attain it.

7 Where shall I go from your Spirit? Or where shall I flee from your presence?

8 If I ascend to heaven, you are there! If I make my bed in Sheol, you are there!

9 If I take the wings of the morning and dwell in the uttermost parts of the sea,

10 even there your hand shall lead me, and your right hand shall hold me.

11 If I say, "Surely the darkness shall cover me, and the light about me be night,"

12 even the darkness is not dark to you; the night is

bright as the day, for darkness is as light with you.

13 For you formed my inward parts; you knitted me together in my mother's womb.

14 I praise you, for I am fearfully and wonderfully made. Wonderful are your works; my soul knows it very well.

15 My frame was not hidden from you, when I was being made in secret, intricately woven in the depths of the earth.

16 Your eyes saw my unformed substance; in your book were written, every one of them, the days that were formed for me, when as yet there was none of them.

17 How precious to me are your thoughts, O God! How vast is the sum of them!

18 If I would count them, they are more than the sand. I awake, and I am still with you.

19 Oh that you would slay the wicked, O God! O men of blood, depart from me!

20 They speak against you with malicious intent; your enemies take your name in vain.

21 Do I not hate those who hate you, O LORD? And do I not loathe those who rise up against you?

22 I hate them with complete hatred; I count them my enemies.

23 Search me, O God, and know my heart! Try me and know my thoughts!

24 And see if there be any grievous way in me, and lead me in the way everlasting!

PSALM 140

To the choirmaster.
A Psalm of David.

1 Deliver me, O LORD, from evil men; preserve me from violent men,

2 who plan evil things in their heart and stir up wars continually.

3 They make their tongue sharp as a serpent's, and under their lips is the venom of asps. Selah.

4 Guard me, O LORD, from the hands of the wicked; preserve me from violent men, who have planned to trip up my feet.

5 The arrogant have hidden a trap for me, and with cords they have spread a net; beside the way they have set snares for me. Selah.

6 I say to the LORD, You are my God; give ear to the voice of my pleas for mercy, O LORD!

7 O LORD, my Lord, the strength of my salvation, you have covered my head in the day of battle.

⁸ Grant not, O Lord, the desires of the wicked; do not further their evil plot, or they will be exalted! Selah.

⁹ As for the head of those who surround me, let the mischief of their lips overwhelm them!

¹⁰ Let burning coals fall upon them! Let them be cast into fire, into miry pits, no more to rise!

¹¹ Let not the slanderer be established in the land; let evil hunt down the violent man speedily!

¹² I know that the Lord will maintain the cause of the afflicted, and will execute justice for the needy.

¹³ Surely the righteous shall give thanks to your name; the upright shall dwell in your presence.

PSALM 141
A Psalm of David.

¹ O Lord, I call upon you; hasten to me! Give ear to my voice when I call to you!

² Let my prayer be counted as incense before you, and the lifting up of my hands as the evening sacrifice!

³ Set a guard, O Lord, over my mouth; keep watch over the door of my lips!

⁴ Do not let my heart incline to any evil, to busy myself with wicked deeds in company with men who work iniquity, and let me not eat of their delicacies!

⁵ Let a righteous man strike me—it is a kindness; let him rebuke me—it is oil for my head; let my head not refuse it. Yet my prayer is continually against their evil deeds.

⁶ When their judges are thrown over the cliff, then they shall hear my words, for they are pleasant.

⁷ As when one plows and breaks up the earth, so shall our bones be scattered at the mouth of Sheol.

⁸ But my eyes are toward you, O God, my Lord; in you I seek refuge; leave me not defenseless!

⁹ Keep me from the trap that they have laid for me and from the snares of evildoers!

¹⁰ Let the wicked fall into their own nets, while I pass by safely.

PSALM 142
A Maskil of David, when he was in the cave. A Prayer.

¹ With my voice I cry out to the Lord; with my voice I plead for mercy to the Lord.

² I pour out my complaint before him; I tell my trouble before him.

³ When my spirit faints within me, you know my way! In the path where I

walk they have hidden a trap for me.

⁴ Look to the right and see: there is none who takes notice of me; no refuge remains to me; no one cares for my soul.

⁵ I cry to you, O LORD; I say, "You are my refuge, my portion in the land of the living,"

⁶ Attend to my cry, for I am brought very low! Deliver me from my persecutors, for they are too strong for me!

⁷ Bring me out of prison, that I may give thanks to your name! The righteous will surround me, for you will deal bountifully with me.

PSALM 143
A Psalm of David.

¹ Hear my prayer, O LORD; give ear to my pleas for mercy! In your faithfulness answer me, in your righteousness!

² Enter not into judgment with your servant, for no one living is righteous before you.

³ For the enemy has pursued my soul; he has crushed my life to the ground; he has made me sit in darkness like those long dead.

⁴ Therefore my spirit faints within me; my heart within me is appalled.

⁵ I remember the days of old; I meditate on all that

you have done; I ponder the work of your hands.

⁶ I stretch out my hands to you; my soul thirsts for you like a parched land. Selah.

⁷ Answer me quickly, O LORD! My spirit fails! Hide not your face from me, lest I be like those who go down to the pit.

⁸ Let me hear in the morning of your steadfast love, for in you I trust. Make me know the way I should go, for to you I lift up my soul.

⁹ Deliver me from my enemies, O LORD! I have fled to you for refuge.

¹⁰ Teach me to do your will, for you are my God! Let your good Spirit lead me on level ground!

¹¹ For your name's sake, O LORD, preserve my life! In your righteousness bring my soul out of trouble!

¹² And in your steadfast love you will cut off my enemies, and you will destroy all the adversaries of my soul, for I am your servant.

PSALM 144
Of David.

¹ Blessed be the LORD, my rock, who trains my hands for war, and my fingers for battle;

² he is my steadfast love and my fortress, my stronghold

and my deliverer, my shield and he in whom I take refuge, who subdues peoples under me.

3 O LORD, what is man that you regard him, or the son of man that you think of him?

4 Man is like a breath; his days are like a passing shadow.

5 Bow your heavens, O LORD, and come down! Touch the mountains so that they smoke!

6 Flash forth the lightning and scatter them; send out your arrows and rout them!

7 Stretch out your hand from on high; rescue me and deliver me from the many waters, from the hand of foreigners,

8 whose mouths speak lies and whose right hand is a right hand of falsehood.

9 I will sing a new song to you, O God; upon a ten-stringed harp I will play to you,

10 who gives victory to kings, who rescues David his servant from the cruel sword.

11 Rescue me and deliver me from the hand of foreigners, whose mouths speak lies and whose right hand is a right hand of falsehood.

12 May our sons in their youth be like plants full grown, our daughters like corner pillars cut for the structure of a palace;

13 may our granaries be full, providing all kinds of produce; may our sheep bring forth thousands and ten thousands in our fields;

14 may our cattle be heavy with young, suffering no mishap or failure in bearing; may there be no cry of distress in our streets!

15 Blessed are the people to whom such blessings fall! Blessed are the people whose God is the LORD!

PSALM 145

A Song of Praise. Of David.

1 I will extol you, my God and King, and bless your name forever and ever.

2 Every day I will bless you and praise your name forever and ever.

3 Great is the LORD, and greatly to be praised, and his greatness is unsearchable.

4 One generation shall commend your works to another, and shall declare your mighty acts.

5 On the glorious splendor of your majesty, and on your wondrous works, I will meditate.

6 They shall speak of the might of your awesome deeds, and I will declare your greatness.

⁷ They shall pour forth the fame of your abundant goodness and shall sing aloud of your righteousness.

⁸ The LORD is gracious and merciful, slow to anger and abounding in steadfast love.

⁹ The LORD is good to all, and his mercy is over all that he has made.

¹⁰ All your works shall give thanks to you, O LORD, and all your saints shall bless you!

¹¹ They shall speak of the glory of your kingdom and tell of your power,

¹² to make known to the children of man your mighty deeds, and the glorious splendor of your kingdom.

¹³ Your kingdom is an everlasting kingdom, and your dominion endures throughout all generations. [The LORD is faithful in all his words and kind in all his works.]

¹⁴ The LORD upholds all who are falling and raises up all who are bowed down.

¹⁵ The eyes of all look to you, and you give them their food in due season.

¹⁶ You open your hand; you satisfy the desire of every living thing.

¹⁷ The LORD is righteous in all his ways and kind in all his works.

¹⁸ The LORD is near to all who call on him, to all who call on him in truth.

¹⁹ He fulfills the desire of those who fear him; he also hears their cry and saves them.

²⁰ The LORD preserves all who love him, but all the wicked he will destroy.

²¹ My mouth will speak the praise of the LORD, and let all flesh bless his holy name forever and ever.

PSALM 146

¹ Praise the LORD! Praise the LORD, O my soul!

² I will praise the LORD as long as I live; I will sing praises to my God while I have my being.

³ Put not your trust in princes, in a son of man, in whom there is no salvation.

⁴ When his breath departs, he returns to the earth; on that very day his plans perish.

⁵ Blessed is he whose help is the God of Jacob, whose hope is in the LORD his God,

⁶ who made heaven and earth, the sea, and all that is in them, who keeps faith forever;

⁷ who executes justice for the oppressed, who gives food to the hungry. The LORD sets the prisoners free;

⁸ the LORD opens the eyes of the blind. The LORD lifts up those who are bowed down; the LORD loves the righteous.

⁹ The LORD watches over the sojourners; he upholds the widow and the fatherless, but the way of the wicked he brings to ruin.

¹⁰ The LORD will reign forever, your God, O Zion, to all generations. Praise the LORD!

PSALM 147

¹ Praise the LORD! For it is good to sing praises to our God; for it is pleasant, and a song of praise is fitting.

² The LORD builds up Jerusalem; he gathers the outcasts of Israel.

³ He heals the brokenhearted and binds up their wounds.

⁴ He determines the number of the stars; he gives to all of them their names.

⁵ Great is our Lord, and abundant in power; his understanding is beyond measure.

⁶ The LORD lifts up the humble; he casts the wicked to the ground.

⁷ Sing to the LORD with thanksgiving; make melody to our God on the lyre!

⁸ He covers the heavens with clouds; he prepares rain for the earth; he makes grass grow on the hills.

⁹ He gives to the beasts their food, and to the young ravens that cry.

¹⁰ His delight is not in the strength of the horse, nor his pleasure in the legs of a man,

¹¹ but the LORD takes pleasure in those who fear him, in those who hope in his steadfast love.

¹² Praise the LORD, O Jerusalem! Praise your God, O Zion!

¹³ For he strengthens the bars of your gates; he blesses your children within you.

¹⁴ He makes peace in your borders; he fills you with the finest of the wheat.

¹⁵ He sends out his command to the earth; his word runs swiftly.

¹⁶ He gives snow like wool; he scatters frost like ashes.

¹⁷ He hurls down his crystals of ice like crumbs; who can stand before his cold?

¹⁸ He sends out his word, and melts them; he makes his wind blow and the waters flow.

¹⁹ He declares his word to Jacob, his statutes and rules to Israel.

²⁰ He has not dealt thus with any other nation; they do not know his rules. Praise the LORD!

PSALM 148

¹ Praise the LORD! Praise the LORD from the heavens; praise him in the heights!

² Praise him, all his angels; praise him, all his hosts!

³ Praise him, sun and moon, praise him, all you shining stars!

⁴ Praise him, you highest heavens, and you waters above the heavens!

⁵ Let them praise the name of the LORD! For he commanded and they were created.

⁶ And he established them forever and ever; he gave a decree, and it shall not pass away.

⁷ Praise the LORD from the earth, you great sea creatures and all deeps,

⁸ fire and hail, snow and mist, stormy wind fulfilling his word!

⁹ Mountains and all hills, fruit trees and all cedars!

¹⁰ Beasts and all livestock, creeping things and flying birds!

¹¹ Kings of the earth and all peoples, princes and all rulers of the earth!

¹² Young men and maidens together, old men and children!

¹³ Let them praise the name of the LORD, for his name alone is exalted; his majesty is above earth and heaven.

¹⁴ He has raised up a horn for his people, praise for all his saints, for the people of Israel who are near to him. Praise the LORD!

PSALM 149

¹ Praise the LORD! Sing to the LORD a new song, his praise in the assembly of the godly!

² Let Israel be glad in his Maker; let the children of Zion rejoice in their King!

³ Let them praise his name with dancing, making melody to him with tambourine and lyre!

⁴ For the LORD takes pleasure in his people; he adorns the humble with salvation.

⁵ Let the godly exult in glory; let them sing for joy on their beds.

⁶ Let the high praises of God be in their throats and two-edged swords in their hands,

⁷ to execute vengeance on the nations and punishments on the peoples,

⁸ to bind their kings with chains and their nobles with fetters of iron,

⁹ to execute on them the judgment written! This is honor for all his godly ones. Praise the LORD!

PSALM 150

[1] Praise the LORD! Praise God in his sanctuary; praise him in his mighty heavens!

[2] Praise him for his mighty deeds; praise him according to his excellent greatness!

[3] Praise him with trumpet sound; praise him with lute and harp!

[4] Praise him with tambourine and dance; praise him with strings and pipe!

[5] Praise him with sounding cymbals; praise him with loud clashing cymbals!

[6] Let everything that has breath praise the LORD! Praise the LORD!

PROVERBS

PROVERBS

¹ The proverbs of Solomon, son of David, king of Israel:

² To know wisdom and instruction, to understand words of insight,

³ to receive instruction in wise dealing, in righteousness, justice, and equity;

⁴ to give prudence to the simple, knowledge and discretion to the youth—

⁵ Let the wise hear and increase in learning, and the one who understands obtain guidance,

⁶ to understand a proverb and a saying, the words of the wise and their riddles.

⁷ The fear of the LORD is the beginning of knowledge; fools despise wisdom and instruction.

⁸ Hear, my son, your father's instruction, and forsake not your mother's teaching,

⁹ for they are a graceful garland for your head and pendants for your neck.

¹⁰ My son, if sinners entice you, do not consent.

¹¹ If they say, "Come with us, let us lie in wait for blood; let us ambush the innocent without reason;

¹² "like Sheol let us swallow them alive, and whole, like those who go down to the pit;

¹³ "we shall find all precious goods, we shall fill our houses with plunder;

¹⁴ "throw in your lot among us; we will all have one purse"—

¹⁵ my son, do not walk in the way with them; hold back your foot from their paths,

¹⁶ for their feet run to evil, and they make haste to shed blood.

¹⁷ For in vain is a net spread in the sight of any bird,

¹⁸ but these men lie in wait for their own blood; they set an ambush for their own lives.

¹⁹ Such are the ways of everyone who is greedy for unjust gain; it takes away the life of its possessors.

²⁰ Wisdom cries aloud in the street, in the markets she raises her voice;

²¹ at the head of the noisy streets she cries out; at the entrance of the city gates she speaks:

²² "How long, O simple ones, will you love being simple? How long will scoffers delight in their scoffing and fools hate knowledge?

²³ "If you turn at my reproof, behold, I will pour out my spirit to you; I will make my words known to you.

²⁴ "Because I have called and you refused to listen, have stretched out my hand and no one has heeded,

²⁵ "because you have ignored all my counsel and would have none of my reproof,

²⁶ "I also will laugh at your calamity; I will mock when terror strikes you,

²⁷ "when terror strikes you like a storm and your calamity comes like a whirlwind, when distress and anguish come upon you.

²⁸ "Then they will call upon me, but I will not answer; they will seek me diligently but will not find me.

²⁹ "Because they hated knowledge and did not choose the fear of the LORD,

³⁰ "would have none of my counsel and despised all my reproof,

³¹ "therefore they shall eat the fruit of their way, and have their fill of their own devices.

³² "For the simple are killed by their turning away, and the complacency of fools destroys them;

³³ "but whoever listens to me will dwell secure and will be at ease, without dread of disaster."

CHAPTER 2

¹ My son, if you receive my words and treasure up my commandments with you,

² making your ear attentive to wisdom and inclining your heart to understanding;

³ yes, if you call out for insight and raise your voice for understanding,

⁴ if you seek it like silver and search for it as for hidden treasures,

⁵ then you will understand the fear of the LORD and find the knowledge of God.

⁶ For the LORD gives wisdom; from his mouth come knowledge and understanding;

⁷ he stores up sound wisdom for the upright; he is a shield to those who walk in integrity,

⁸ guarding the paths of justice and watching over the way of his saints.

⁹ Then you will understand righteousness and justice and equity, every good path;

¹⁰ for wisdom will come into your heart, and knowl-

edge will be pleasant to your soul;

¹¹ discretion will watch over you, understanding will guard you,

¹² delivering you from the way of evil, from men of perverted speech,

¹³ who forsake the paths of uprightness to walk in the ways of darkness,

¹⁴ who rejoice in doing evil and delight in the perverseness of evil,

¹⁵ men whose paths are crooked, and who are devious in their ways.

¹⁶ So you will be delivered from the forbidden woman, from the adulteress with her smooth words,

¹⁷ who forsakes the companion of her youth and forgets the covenant of her God;

¹⁸ for her house sinks down to death, and her paths to the departed;

¹⁹ none who go to her come back, nor do they regain the paths of life.

²⁰ So you will walk in the way of the good and keep to the paths of the righteous.

²¹ For the upright will inhabit the land, and those with integrity will remain in it,

²² but the wicked will be cut off from the land, and the treacherous will be rooted out of it.

CHAPTER 3

¹ My son, do not forget my teaching, but let your heart keep my commandments,

² for length of days and years of life and peace they will add to you.

³ Let not steadfast love and faithfulness forsake you; bind them around your neck; write them on the tablet of your heart.

⁴ So you will find favor and good success in the sight of God and man.

⁵ Trust in the LORD with all your heart, and do not lean on your own understanding.

⁶ In all your ways acknowledge him, and he will make straight your paths.

⁷ Be not wise in your own eyes; fear the LORD, and turn away from evil.

⁸ It will be healing to your flesh and refreshment to your bones.

⁹ Honor the LORD with your wealth and with the firstfruits of all your produce;

¹⁰ then your barns will be filled with plenty, and your vats will be bursting with wine.

¹¹ My son, do not despise the LORD's discipline or be weary of his reproof,

¹² for the LORD reproves him whom he loves, as a father the son in whom he delights.

¹³ Blessed is the one who finds wisdom, and the one who gets understanding,

¹⁴ for the gain from her is better than gain from silver and her profit better than gold.

¹⁵ She is more precious than jewels, and nothing you desire can compare with her.

¹⁶ Long life is in her right hand; in her left hand are riches and honor.

¹⁷ Her ways are ways of pleasantness, and all her paths are peace.

¹⁸ She is a tree of life to those who lay hold of her; those who hold her fast are called blessed.

¹⁹ The LORD by wisdom founded the earth; by understanding he established the heavens;

²⁰ by his knowledge the deeps broke open, and the clouds drop down the dew.

²¹ My son, do not lose sight of these— keep sound wisdom and discretion,

²² and they will be life for your soul and adornment for your neck.

²³ Then you will walk on your way securely, and your foot will not stumble.

²⁴ If you lie down, you will not be afraid; when you lie down, your sleep will be sweet.

²⁵ Do not be afraid of sudden terror or of the ruin of the wicked, when it comes,

²⁶ for the LORD will be your confidence and will keep your foot from being caught.

²⁷ Do not withhold good from those to whom it is due, when it is in your power to do it.

²⁸ Do not say to your neighbor, "Go, and come again, tomorrow I will give it"—when you have it with you.

²⁹ Do not plan evil against your neighbor, who dwells trustingly beside you.

³⁰ Do not contend with a man for no reason, when he has done you no harm.

³¹ Do not envy a man of violence and do not choose any of his ways,

³² for the devious person is an abomination to the LORD, but the upright are in his confidence.

³³ The LORD's curse is on the house of the wicked, but he blesses the dwelling of the righteous.

³⁴ Toward the scorners he is scornful, but to the humble he gives favor.

³⁵ The wise will inherit honor, but fools get disgrace.

CHAPTER 4

¹ Hear, O sons, a father's instruction, and be attentive, that you may gain insight,

2 for I give you good precepts; do not forsake my teaching.

3 When I was a son with my father, tender, the only one in the sight of my mother,

4 he taught me and said to me, "Let your heart hold fast my words; keep my commandments, and live.

5 "Get wisdom; get insight; do not forget, and do not turn away from the words of my mouth.

6 "Do not forsake her, and she will keep you; love her, and she will guard you.

7 "The beginning of wisdom is this: Get wisdom, and whatever you get, get insight.

8 "Prize her highly, and she will exalt you; she will honor you if you embrace her.

9 "She will place on your head a graceful garland; she will bestow on you a beautiful crown."

10 Hear, my son, and accept my words, that the years of your life may be many.

11 I have taught you the way of wisdom; I have led you in the paths of uprightness.

12 When you walk, your step will not be hampered, and if you run, you will not stumble.

13 Keep hold of instruction; do not let go; guard her, for she is your life.

14 Do not enter the path of the wicked, and do not walk in the way of the evil.

15 Avoid it; do not go on it; turn away from it and pass on.

16 For they cannot sleep unless they have done wrong; they are robbed of sleep unless they have made someone stumble.

17 For they eat the bread of wickedness and drink the wine of violence.

18 But the path of the righteous is like the light of dawn, which shines brighter and brighter until full day.

19 The way of the wicked is like deep darkness; they do not know over what they stumble.

20 My son, be attentive to my words; incline your ear to my sayings.

21 Let them not escape from your sight; keep them within your heart.

22 For they are life to those who find them, and healing to all their flesh.

23 Keep your heart with all vigilance, for from it flow the springs of life.

24 Put away from you crooked speech, and put devious talk far from you.

25 Let your eyes look directly forward, and your gaze be straight before you.

26 Ponder the path of your feet; then all your ways will be sure.

27 Do not swerve to the right or to the left; turn your foot away from evil.

CHAPTER 5

1 My son, be attentive to my wisdom; incline your ear to my understanding,

2 that you may keep discretion, and your lips may guard knowledge.

3 For the lips of a forbidden woman drip honey, and her speech is smoother than oil,

4 but in the end she is bitter as wormwood, sharp as a two-edged sword.

5 Her feet go down to death; her steps follow the path to Sheol;

6 she does not ponder the path of life; her ways wander, and she does not know it.

7 And now, O sons, listen to me, and do not depart from the words of my mouth.

8 Keep your way far from her, and do not go near the door of her house,

9 lest you give your honor to others and your years to the merciless;

10 lest strangers take their fill of your strength, and your labors go to the house of a foreigner,

11 and at the end of your life you groan, when your flesh and body are consumed,

12 and you say, "How I hated discipline, and my heart despised reproof!

13 "I did not listen to the voice of my teachers or incline my ear to my instructors.

14 "I am at the brink of utter ruin in the assembled congregation."

15 Drink water from your own cistern, flowing water from your own well.

16 Should your springs be scattered abroad, streams of water in the streets?

17 Let them be for yourself alone, and not for strangers with you.

18 Let your fountain be blessed, and rejoice in the wife of your youth,

19 a lovely deer, a graceful doe. Let her breasts fill you at all times with delight; be intoxicated always in her love.

20 Why should you be intoxicated, my son, with a forbidden woman and embrace the bosom of an adulteress?

21 For a man's ways are before the eyes of the LORD, and he ponders all his paths.

22 The iniquities of the wicked ensnare him, and he is held fast in the cords of his sin.

23 He dies for lack of dis-

cipline, and because of his great folly he is led astray.

CHAPTER 6

¹ My son, if you have put up security for your neighbor, have given your pledge for a stranger,

² if you are snared in the words of your mouth, caught in the words of your mouth,

³ then do this, my son, and save yourself, for you have come into the hand of your neighbor: go, hasten, and plead urgently with your neighbor.

⁴ Give your eyes no sleep and your eyelids no slumber;

⁵ save yourself like a gazelle from the hand of the hunter, like a bird from the hand of the fowler.

⁶ Go to the ant, O sluggard; consider her ways, and be wise.

⁷ Without having any chief, officer, or ruler,

⁸ she prepares her bread in summer and gathers her food in harvest.

⁹ How long will you lie there, O sluggard? When will you arise from your sleep?

¹⁰ A little sleep, a little slumber, a little folding of the hands to rest,

¹¹ and poverty will come upon you like a robber, and want like an armed man.

¹² A worthless person, a wicked man, goes about with crooked speech,

¹³ winks with his eyes, signals with his feet, points with his finger,

¹⁴ with perverted heart devises evil, continually sowing discord;

¹⁵ therefore calamity will come upon him suddenly; in a moment he will be broken beyond healing.

¹⁶ There are six things that the LORD hates, seven that are an abomination to him:

¹⁷ haughty eyes, a lying tongue, and hands that shed innocent blood,

¹⁸ a heart that devises wicked plans, feet that make haste to run to evil,

¹⁹ a false witness who breathes out lies, and one who sows discord among brothers.

²⁰ My son, keep your father's commandment, and forsake not your mother's teaching.

²¹ Bind them on your heart always; tie them around your neck.

²² When you walk, they will lead you; when you lie down, they will watch over you; and when you awake, they will talk with you.

²³ For the commandment is a lamp and the teaching

a light, and the reproofs of discipline are the way of life,

²⁴ to preserve you from the evil woman, from the smooth tongue of the adulteress.

²⁵ Do not desire her beauty in your heart, and do not let her capture you with her eyelashes;

²⁶ for the price of a prostitute is only a loaf of bread, but a married woman hunts down a precious life.

²⁷ Can a man carry fire next to his chest and his clothes not be burned?

²⁸ Or can one walk on hot coals and his feet not be scorched?

²⁹ So is he who goes in to his neighbor's wife; none who touches her will go unpunished.

³⁰ People do not despise a thief if he steals to satisfy his appetite when he is hungry,

³¹ but if he is caught, he will pay sevenfold; he will give all the goods of his house.

³² He who commits adultery lacks sense; he who does it destroys himself.

³³ He will get wounds and dishonor, and his disgrace will not be wiped away.

³⁴ For jealousy makes a man furious, and he will not spare when he takes revenge.

³⁵ He will accept no compensation; he will refuse though you multiply gifts.

CHAPTER 7

¹ My son, keep my words and treasure up my commandments with you;

² keep my commandments and live; keep my teaching as the apple of your eye;

³ bind them on your fingers; write them on the tablet of your heart.

⁴ Say to wisdom, "You are my sister," and call insight your intimate friend,

⁵ to keep you from the forbidden woman, from the adulteress with her smooth lips.

⁶ For at the window of my house I have looked out through my lattice,

⁷ and I have seen among the simple, I have perceived among the youths, a young man lacking sense,

⁸ passing along the street near her corner, taking the road to her house

⁹ in the twilight, in the evening, at the time of night and darkness.

¹⁰ And behold, the woman meets him, dressed as a prostitute, wily of heart.

¹¹ She is loud and wayward; her feet do not stay at home;

¹² now in the street, now in the market, and at every corner she lies in wait.

¹³ She seizes him and kisses him, and with bold face she says to him,

¹⁴ "I had to offer sacrifices, and today I have paid my vows;

¹⁵ "so now I have come out to meet you, to seek you eagerly, and I have found you.

¹⁶ "I have spread my couch with coverings, colored linens from Egyptian linen;

¹⁷ "I have perfumed my bed with myrrh, aloes, and cinnamon.

¹⁸ "Come, let us take our fill of love till morning; let us delight ourselves with love.

¹⁹ "For my husband is not at home; he has gone on a long journey;

²⁰ "he took a bag of money with him; at full moon he will come home."

²¹ With much seductive speech she persuades him; with her smooth talk she compels him.

²² All at once he follows her, as an ox goes to the slaughter, or as a stag is caught fast

²³ till an arrow pierces its liver; as a bird rushes into a snare; he does not know that it will cost him his life.

²⁴ And now, O sons, listen to me, and be attentive to the words of my mouth.

²⁵ Let not your heart turn aside to her ways; do not stray into her paths,

²⁶ for many a victim has she laid low, and all her slain are a mighty throng.

²⁷ Her house is the way to Sheol, going down to the chambers of death.

CHAPTER 8

¹ Does not wisdom call? Does not understanding raise her voice?

² On the heights beside the way, at the crossroads she takes her stand;

³ beside the gates in front of the town, at the entrance of the portals she cries aloud:

⁴ "To you, O men, I call, and my cry is to the children of man.

⁵ "O simple ones, learn prudence; O fools, learn sense.

⁶ "Hear, for I will speak noble things, and from my lips will come what is right,

⁷ "for my mouth will utter truth; wickedness is an abomination to my lips.

⁸ "All the words of my mouth are righteous; there is nothing twisted or crooked in them.

⁹ "They are all straight to him who understands, and right to those who find knowledge.

¹⁰ "Take my instruction instead of silver, and knowledge rather than choice gold,

11 "for wisdom is better than jewels, and all that you may desire cannot compare with her.

12 "I, wisdom, dwell with prudence, and I find knowledge and discretion.

13 "The fear of the LORD is hatred of evil. Pride and arrogance and the way of evil and perverted speech I hate.

14 "I have counsel and sound wisdom; I have insight; I have strength.

15 "By me kings reign, and rulers decree what is just;

16 "by me princes rule, and nobles, all who govern justly.

17 "I love those who love me, and those who seek me diligently find me.

18 "Riches and honor are with me, enduring wealth and righteousness.

19 "My fruit is better than gold, even fine gold, and my yield than choice silver.

20 "I walk in the way of righteousness, in the paths of justice,

21 "granting an inheritance to those who love me, and filling their treasuries.

22 "The LORD possessed me at the beginning of his work, the first of his acts of old.

23 "Ages ago I was set up, at the first, before the beginning of the earth.

24 "When there were no depths I was brought forth, when there were no springs abounding with water.

25 "Before the mountains had been shaped, before the hills, I was brought forth,

26 "before he had made the earth with its fields, or the first of the dust of the world.

27 "When he established the heavens, I was there; when he drew a circle on the face of the deep,

28 "when he made firm the skies above, when he established the fountains of the deep,

29 "when he assigned to the sea its limit, so that the waters might not transgress his command, when he marked out the foundations of the earth,

30 "then I was beside him, like a master workman, and I was daily his delight, rejoicing before him always,

31 "rejoicing in his inhabited world and delighting in the children of man.

32 "And now, O sons, listen to me: blessed are those who keep my ways.

33 "Hear instruction and be wise, and do not neglect it.

34 "Blessed is the one who listens to me, watching daily at my gates, waiting beside my doors.

35 "For whoever finds me

...ds life and obtains favor
...rom the LORD,

³⁶ "but he who fails to find
me injures himself; all who
hate me love death."

CHAPTER 9

¹ Wisdom has built her house;
she has hewn her seven pillars.

² She has slaughtered her
beasts; she has mixed her wine;
she has also set her table.

³ She has sent out her young
women to call from the highest places in the town,

⁴ "Whoever is simple, let
him turn in here!" To him
who lacks sense she says,

⁵ "Come, eat of my bread
and drink of the wine I have
mixed.

⁶ "Leave your simple ways,
and live, and walk in the way
of insight."

⁷ Whoever corrects a scoffer gets himself abuse, and he
who reproves a wicked man
incurs injury.

⁸ Do not reprove a scoffer,
or he will hate you; reprove
a wise man, and he will love
you.

⁹ Give instruction to a
wise man, and he will be
still wiser; teach a righteous
man, and he will increase in
learning.

¹⁰ The fear of the LORD is
the beginning of wisdom,
and the knowledge of the
Holy One is insight.

¹¹ For by me your days will
be multiplied, and years will
be added to your life.

¹² If you are wise, you are
wise for yourself; if you scoff,
you alone will bear it.

¹³ The woman Folly is loud;
she is seductive and knows
nothing.

¹⁴ She sits at the door of her
house; she takes a seat on the
highest places of the town,

¹⁵ calling to those who pass
by, who are going straight on
their way,

¹⁶ "Whoever is simple, let
him turn in here!" And to
him who lacks sense she
says,

¹⁷ "Stolen water is sweet,
and bread eaten in secret is
pleasant."

¹⁸ But he does not know
that the dead are there, that
her guests are in the depths
of Sheol.

CHAPTER 10

¹ The proverbs of Solomon. A
wise son makes a glad father,
but a foolish son is a sorrow
to his mother.

² Treasures gained by wickedness do not profit, but
righteousness delivers from
death.

³ The LORD does not let the
righteous go hungry, but he

thwarts the craving of the wicked.

⁴ A slack hand causes poverty, but the hand of the diligent makes rich.

⁵ He who gathers in summer is a prudent son, but he who sleeps in harvest is a son who brings shame.

⁶ Blessings are on the head of the righteous, but the mouth of the wicked conceals violence.

⁷ The memory of the righteous is a blessing, but the name of the wicked will rot.

⁸ The wise of heart will receive commandments, but a babbling fool will come to ruin.

⁹ Whoever walks in integrity walks securely, but he who makes his ways crooked will be found out.

¹⁰ Whoever winks the eye causes trouble, and a babbling fool will come to ruin.

¹¹ The mouth of the righteous is a fountain of life, but the mouth of the wicked conceals violence.

¹² Hatred stirs up strife, but love covers all offenses.

¹³ On the lips of him who has understanding, wisdom is found, but a rod is for the back of him who lacks sense.

¹⁴ The wise lay up knowledge, but the mouth of a fool brings ruin near.

¹⁵ A rich man's wealth is ₁ strong city; the poverty of the poor is their ruin.

¹⁶ The wage of the righteous leads to life, the gain of the wicked to sin.

¹⁷ Whoever heeds instruction is on the path to life, but he who rejects reproof leads others astray.

¹⁸ The one who conceals hatred has lying lips, and whoever utters slander is a fool.

¹⁹ When words are many, transgression is not lacking, but whoever restrains his lips is prudent.

²⁰ The tongue of the righteous is choice silver; the heart of the wicked is of little worth.

²¹ The lips of the righteous feed many, but fools die for lack of sense.

²² The blessing of the LORD makes rich, and he adds no sorrow with it.

²³ Doing wrong is like a joke to a fool, but wisdom is pleasure to a man of understanding.

²⁴ What the wicked dreads will come upon him, but the desire of the righteous will be granted.

²⁵ When the tempest passes, the wicked is no more, but the righteous is established forever.

²⁶ Like vinegar to the teeth

and smoke to the eyes, so is the sluggard to those who send him.

27 The fear of the LORD prolongs life, but the years of the wicked will be short.

28 The hope of the righteous brings joy, but the expectation of the wicked will perish.

29 The way of the LORD is a stronghold to the blameless, but destruction to evildoers.

30 The righteous will never be removed, but the wicked will not dwell in the land.

31 The mouth of the righteous brings forth wisdom, but the perverse tongue will be cut off.

32 The lips of the righteous know what is acceptable, but the mouth of the wicked, what is perverse.

CHAPTER 11

1 A false balance is an abomination to the LORD, but a just weight is his delight.

2 When pride comes, then comes disgrace, but with the humble is wisdom.

3 The integrity of the upright guides them, but the crookedness of the treacherous destroys them.

4 Riches do not profit in the day of wrath, but righteousness delivers them from death.

5 The righteousness of the blameless keeps his way straight, but the wicked falls by his own wickedness.

6 The righteousness of the upright delivers them, but the treacherous are taken captive by their lust.

7 When the wicked dies, his hope will perish, and the expectation of wealth perishes too.

8 The righteous is delivered from trouble, and the wicked walks into it instead.

9 With his mouth the godless man would destroy his neighbor, but by knowledge the righteous are delivered.

10 When it goes well with the righteous, the city rejoices, and when the wicked perish there are shouts of gladness.

11 By the blessing of the upright a city is exalted, but by the mouth of the wicked it is overthrown.

12 Whoever belittles his neighbor lacks sense, but a man of understanding remains silent.

13 Whoever goes about slandering reveals secrets, but he who is trustworthy in spirit keeps a thing covered.

14 Where there is no guidance, a people falls, but in an abundance of counselors there is safety.

15 Whoever puts up security for a stranger will surely

suffer harm, but he who hates striking hands in pledge is secure.

¹⁶ A gracious woman gets honor, and violent men get riches.

¹⁷ A man who is kind benefits himself, but a cruel man hurts himself.

¹⁸ The wicked earns deceptive wages, but one who sows righteousness gets a sure reward.

¹⁹ Whoever is steadfast in righteousness will live, but he who pursues evil will die.

²⁰ Those of crooked heart are an abomination to the LORD, but those of blameless ways are his delight.

²¹ Be assured, an evil person will not go unpunished, but the offspring of the righteous will be delivered.

²² Like a gold ring in a pig's snout is a beautiful woman without discretion.

²³ The desire of the righteous ends only in good; the expectation of the wicked is in wrath.

²⁴ One gives freely, yet grows all the richer; another withholds what he should give, and only suffers want.

²⁵ Whoever brings blessing will be enriched, and one who waters will himself be watered.

²⁶ The people curse him who holds back grain, but a blessing is on the head of him who sells it.

²⁷ Whoever diligently seeks good seeks favor, but evil comes to him who searches for it.

²⁸ Whoever trusts in his riches will fall, but the righteous will flourish like a green leaf.

²⁹ Whoever troubles his own household will inherit the wind, and the fool will be servant to the wise of heart.

³⁰ The fruit of the righteous is a tree of life, and whoever captures souls is wise.

³¹ If the righteous is repaid on earth, how much more the wicked and the sinner!

CHAPTER 12

¹ Whoever loves discipline loves knowledge, but he who hates reproof is stupid.

² A good man obtains favor from the LORD, but a man of evil devices he condemns.

³ No one is established by wickedness, but the root of the righteous will never be moved.

⁴ An excellent wife is the crown of her husband, but she who brings shame is like rottenness in his bones.

⁵ The thoughts of the righteous are just; the counsels of the wicked are deceitful.

⁶ The words of the wicked lie in wait for blood, but the mouth of the upright delivers them.

⁷ The wicked are overthrown and are no more, but the house of the righteous will stand.

⁸ A man is commended according to his good sense, but one of twisted mind is despised.

⁹ Better to be lowly and have a servant than to play the great man and lack bread.

¹⁰ Whoever is righteous has regard for the life of his beast, but the mercy of the wicked is cruel.

¹¹ Whoever works his land will have plenty of bread, but he who follows worthless pursuits lacks sense.

¹² Whoever is wicked covets the spoil of evildoers, but the root of the righteous bears fruit.

¹³ An evil man is ensnared by the transgression of his lips, but the righteous escapes from trouble.

¹⁴ From the fruit of his mouth a man is satisfied with good, and the work of a man's hand comes back to him.

¹⁵ The way of a fool is right in his own eyes, but a wise man listens to advice.

¹⁶ The vexation of a fool is known at once, but the prudent ignores an insult.

¹⁷ Whoever speaks the truth gives honest evidence, but a false witness utters deceit.

¹⁸ There is one whose rash words are like sword thrusts, but the tongue of the wise brings healing.

¹⁹ Truthful lips endure forever, but a lying tongue is but for a moment.

²⁰ Deceit is in the heart of those who devise evil, but those who plan peace have joy.

²¹ No ill befalls the righteous, but the wicked are filled with trouble.

²² Lying lips are an abomination to the LORD, but those who act faithfully are his delight.

²³ A prudent man conceals knowledge, but the heart of fools proclaims folly.

²⁴ The hand of the diligent will rule, while the slothful will be put to forced labor.

²⁵ Anxiety in a man's heart weighs him down, but a good word makes him glad.

²⁶ One who is righteous is a guide to his neighbor, but the way of the wicked leads them astray.

²⁷ Whoever is slothful will not roast his game, but the diligent man will get precious wealth.

²⁸ In the path of righteousness is life, and in its pathway there is no death.

¹ A wise son hears his father's instruction, but a scoffer does not listen to rebuke.

² From the fruit of his mouth a man eats what is good, but the desire of the treacherous is for violence.

³ Whoever guards his mouth preserves his life; he who opens wide his lips comes to ruin.

⁴ The soul of the sluggard craves and gets nothing, while the soul of the diligent is richly supplied.

⁵ The righteous hates falsehood, but the wicked brings shame and disgrace.

⁶ Righteousness guards him whose way is blameless, but sin overthrows the wicked.

⁷ One pretends to be rich, yet has nothing; another pretends to be poor, yet has great wealth.

⁸ The ransom of a man's life is his wealth, but a poor man hears no threat.

⁹ The light of the righteous rejoices, but the lamp of the wicked will be put out.

¹⁰ By insolence comes nothing but strife, but with those who take advice is wisdom.

¹¹ Wealth gained hastily will dwindle, but whoever gathers little by little will increase it.

¹² Hope deferred makes the heart sick, but a desire fulfilled is a tree of life.

¹³ Whoever despises the word brings destruction on himself, but he who reveres the commandment will be rewarded.

¹⁴ The teaching of the wise is a fountain of life, that one may turn away from the snares of death.

¹⁵ Good sense wins favor, but the way of the treacherous is their ruin.

¹⁶ In everything the prudent acts with knowledge, but a fool flaunts his folly.

¹⁷ A wicked messenger falls into trouble, but a faithful envoy brings healing.

¹⁸ Poverty and disgrace come to him who ignores instruction, but whoever heeds reproof is honored.

¹⁹ A desire fulfilled is sweet to the soul, but to turn away from evil is an abomination to fools.

²⁰ Whoever walks with the wise becomes wise, but the companion of fools will suffer harm.

²¹ Disaster pursues sinners, but the righteous are rewarded with good.

²² A good man leaves an

inheritance to his children's children, but the sinner's wealth is laid up for the righteous.

23 The fallow ground of the poor would yield much food, but it is swept away through injustice.

24 Whoever spares the rod hates his son, but he who loves him is diligent to discipline him.

25 The righteous has enough to satisfy his appetite, but the belly of the wicked suffers want.

CHAPTER 14

1 The wisest of women builds her house, but folly with her own hands tears it down.

2 Whoever walks in uprightness fears the LORD, but he who is devious in his ways despises him.

3 By the mouth of a fool comes a rod for his back, but the lips of the wise will preserve them.

4 Where there are no oxen, the manger is clean, but abundant crops come by the strength of the ox.

5 A faithful witness does not lie, but a false witness breathes out lies.

6 A scoffer seeks wisdom in vain, but knowledge is easy for a man of understanding.

7 Leave the presence of a fool, for there you do not meet words of knowledge.

8 The wisdom of the prudent is to discern his way, but the folly of fools is deceiving.

9 Fools mock at the guilt offering, but the upright enjoy acceptance.

10 The heart knows its own bitterness, and no stranger shares its joy.

11 The house of the wicked will be destroyed, but the tent of the upright will flourish.

12 There is a way that seems right to a man, but its end is the way to death.

13 Even in laughter the heart may ache, and the end of joy may be grief.

14 The backslider in heart will be filled with the fruit of his ways, and a good man will be filled with the fruit of his ways.

15 The simple believes everything, but the prudent gives thought to his steps.

16 One who is wise is cautious and turns away from evil, but a fool is reckless and careless.

17 A man of quick temper acts foolishly, and a man of evil devices is hated.

18 The simple inherit folly, but the prudent are crowned with knowledge.

19 The evil bow down before

the good, the wicked at the gates of the righteous.

²⁰ The poor is disliked even by his neighbor, but the rich has many friends.

²¹ Whoever despises his neighbor is a sinner, but blessed is he who is generous to the poor.

²² Do they not go astray who devise evil? Those who devise good meet steadfast love and faithfulness.

²³ In all toil there is profit, but mere talk tends only to poverty.

²⁴ The crown of the wise is their wealth, but the folly of fools brings folly.

²⁵ A truthful witness saves lives, but one who breathes out lies is deceitful.

²⁶ In the fear of the LORD one has strong confidence, and his children will have a refuge.

²⁷ The fear of the LORD is a fountain of life, that one may turn away from the snares of death.

²⁸ In a multitude of people is the glory of a king, but without people a prince is ruined.

²⁹ Whoever is slow to anger has great understanding, but he who has a hasty temper exalts folly.

³⁰ A tranquil heart gives life to the flesh, but envy makes the bones rot.

³¹ Whoever oppresses a poor man insults his Maker, but he who is generous to the needy honors him.

³² The wicked is overthrown through his evildoing, but the righteous finds refuge in his death.

³³ Wisdom rests in the heart of a man of understanding, but it makes itself known even in the midst of fools.

³⁴ Righteousness exalts a nation, but sin is a reproach to any people.

³⁵ A servant who deals wisely has the king's favor, but his wrath falls on one who acts shamefully.

CHAPTER 15

¹ A soft answer turns away wrath, but a harsh word stirs up anger.

² The tongue of the wise commends knowledge, but the mouths of fools pour out folly.

³ The eyes of the LORD are in every place, keeping watch on the evil and the good.

⁴ A gentle tongue is a tree of life, but perverseness in it breaks the spirit.

⁵ A fool despises his father's instruction, but whoever heeds reproof is prudent.

⁶ In the house of the righteous there is much trea-

sure, but trouble befalls the income of the wicked.

⁷ The lips of the wise spread knowledge; not so the hearts of fools.

⁸ The sacrifice of the wicked is an abomination to the LORD, but the prayer of the upright is acceptable to him.

⁹ The way of the wicked is an abomination to the LORD, but he loves him who pursues righteousness.

¹⁰ There is severe discipline for him who forsakes the way; whoever hates reproof will die.

¹¹ Sheol and Abaddon lie open before the LORD; how much more the hearts of the children of man!

¹² A scoffer does not like to be reproved; he will not go to the wise.

¹³ A glad heart makes a cheerful face, but by sorrow of heart the spirit is crushed.

¹⁴ The heart of him who has understanding seeks knowledge, but the mouths of fools feed on folly.

¹⁵ All the days of the afflicted are evil, but the cheerful of heart has a continual feast.

¹⁶ Better is a little with the fear of the LORD than great treasure and trouble with it.

¹⁷ Better is a dinner of herbs where love is than a fattened ox and hatred with it.

¹⁸ A hot-tempered man stirs up strife, but he who is slow to anger quiets contention.

¹⁹ The way of a sluggard is like a hedge of thorns, but the path of the upright is a level highway.

²⁰ A wise son makes a glad father, but a foolish man despises his mother.

²¹ Folly is a joy to him who lacks sense, but a man of understanding walks straight ahead.

²² Without counsel plans fail, but with many advisers they succeed.

²³ To make an apt answer is a joy to a man, and a word in season, how good it is!

²⁴ The path of life leads upward for the prudent, that he may turn away from Sheol beneath.

²⁵ The LORD tears down the house of the proud but maintains the widow's boundaries.

²⁶ The thoughts of the wicked are an abomination to the LORD, but gracious words are pure.

²⁷ Whoever is greedy for unjust gain troubles his own household, but he who hates bribes will live.

²⁸ The heart of the righteous ponders how to answer, but the mouth of the wicked pours out evil things.

29 The LORD is far from the wicked, but he hears the prayer of the righteous.

30 The light of the eyes rejoices the heart, and good news refreshes the bones.

31 The ear that listens to life-giving reproof will dwell among the wise.

32 Whoever ignores instruction despises himself, but he who listens to reproof gains intelligence.

33 The fear of the LORD is instruction in wisdom, and humility comes before honor.

CHAPTER 16

1 The plans of the heart belong to man, but the answer of the tongue is from the LORD.

2 All the ways of a man are pure in his own eyes, but the LORD weighs the spirit.

3 Commit your work to the LORD, and your plans will be established.

4 The LORD has made everything for its purpose, even the wicked for the day of trouble.

5 Everyone who is arrogant in heart is an abomination to the LORD; be assured, he will not go unpunished.

6 By steadfast love and faithfulness iniquity is atoned for, and by the fear of the LORD one turns away from evil.

7 When a man's ways please the LORD, he makes even his enemies to be at peace with him.

8 Better is a little with righteousness than great revenues with injustice.

9 The heart of man plans his way, but the LORD establishes his steps.

10 An oracle is on the lips of a king; his mouth does not sin in judgment.

11 A just balance and scales are the LORD's; all the weights in the bag are his work.

12 It is an abomination to kings to do evil, for the throne is established by righteousness.

13 Righteous lips are the delight of a king, and he loves him who speaks what is right.

14 A king's wrath is a messenger of death, and a wise man will appease it.

15 In the light of a king's face there is life, and his favor is like the clouds that bring the spring rain.

16 How much better to get wisdom than gold! To get understanding is to be chosen rather than silver.

17 The highway of the upright turns aside from evil; whoever guards his way preserves his life.

18 Pride goes before destruc-

tion, and a haughty spirit before a fall.

¹⁹ It is better to be of a lowly spirit with the poor than to divide the spoil with the proud.

²⁰ Whoever gives thought to the word will discover good, and blessed is he who trusts in the LORD.

²¹ The wise of heart is called discerning, and sweetness of speech increases persuasiveness.

²² Good sense is a fountain of life to him who has it, but the instruction of fools is folly.

²³ The heart of the wise makes his speech judicious and adds persuasiveness to his lips.

²⁴ Gracious words are like a honeycomb, sweetness to the soul and health to the body.

²⁵ There is a way that seems right to a man, but its end is the way to death.

²⁶ A worker's appetite works for him; his mouth urges him on.

²⁷ A worthless man plots evil, and his speech is like a scorching fire.

²⁸ A dishonest man spreads strife, and a whisperer separates close friends.

²⁹ A man of violence entices his neighbor and leads him in a way that is not good.

³⁰ Whoever winks his eyes plans dishonest things; he who purses his lips brings evil to pass.

³¹ Gray hair is a crown of glory; it is gained in a righteous life.

³² Whoever is slow to anger is better than the mighty, and he who rules his spirit than he who takes a city.

³³ The lot is cast into the lap, but its every decision is from the LORD.

CHAPTER 17

¹ Better is a dry morsel with quiet than a house full of feasting with strife.

² A servant who deals wisely will rule over a son who acts shamefully and will share the inheritance as one of the brothers.

³ The crucible is for silver, and the furnace is for gold, and the LORD tests hearts.

⁴ An evildoer listens to wicked lips, and a liar gives ear to a mischievous tongue.

⁵ Whoever mocks the poor insults his Maker; he who is glad at calamity will not go unpunished.

⁶ Grandchildren are the crown of the aged, and the glory of children is their fathers.

⁷ Fine speech is not becoming to a fool; still less is false speech to a prince.

⁸ A bribe is like a magic stone in the eyes of the one who gives it; wherever he turns he prospers.

⁹ Whoever covers an offense seeks love, but he who repeats a matter separates close friends.

¹⁰ A rebuke goes deeper into a man of understanding than a hundred blows into a fool.

¹¹ An evil man seeks only rebellion, and a cruel messenger will be sent against him.

¹² Let a man meet a she-bear robbed of her cubs rather than a fool in his folly.

¹³ If anyone returns evil for good, evil will not depart from his house.

¹⁴ The beginning of strife is like letting out water, so quit before the quarrel breaks out.

¹⁵ He who justifies the wicked and he who condemns the righteous are both alike an abomination to the LORD.

¹⁶ Why should a fool have money in his hand to buy wisdom when he has no sense?

¹⁷ A friend loves at all times, and a brother is born for adversity.

¹⁸ One who lacks sense gives a pledge and puts up security in the presence of his neighbor.

¹⁹ Whoever loves transgression loves strife; he who makes his door high seeks destruction.

²⁰ A man of crooked heart does not discover good, and one with a dishonest tongue falls into calamity.

²¹ He who sires a fool gets himself sorrow, and the father of a fool has no joy.

²² A joyful heart is good medicine, but a crushed spirit dries up the bones.

²³ The wicked accepts a bribe in secret to pervert the ways of justice.

²⁴ The discerning sets his face toward wisdom, but the eyes of a fool are on the ends of the earth.

²⁵ A foolish son is a grief to his father and bitterness to her who bore him.

²⁶ To impose a fine on a righteous man is not good, nor to strike the noble for their uprightness.

²⁷ Whoever restrains his words has knowledge, and he who has a cool spirit is a man of understanding.

²⁸ Even a fool who keeps silent is considered wise; when he closes his lips, he is deemed intelligent.

CHAPTER 18

¹ Whoever isolates himself seeks his own desire; he

breaks out against all sound judgment.

2 A fool takes no pleasure in understanding, but only in expressing his opinion.

3 When wickedness comes, contempt comes also, and with dishonor comes disgrace.

4 The words of a man's mouth are deep waters; the fountain of wisdom is a bubbling brook.

5 It is not good to be partial to the wicked or to deprive the righteous of justice.

6 A fool's lips walk into a fight, and his mouth invites a beating.

7 A fool's mouth is his ruin, and his lips are a snare to his soul.

8 The words of a whisperer are like delicious morsels; they go down into the inner parts of the body.

9 Whoever is slack in his work is a brother to him who destroys.

10 The name of the LORD is a strong tower; the righteous man runs into it and is safe.

11 A rich man's wealth is his strong city, and like a high wall in his imagination.

12 Before destruction a man's heart is haughty, but humility comes before honor.

13 If one gives an answer before he hears, it is his folly and shame.

14 A man's spirit will endure sickness, but a crushed spirit who can bear?

15 An intelligent heart acquires knowledge, and the ear of the wise seeks knowledge.

16 A man's gift makes room for him and brings him before the great.

17 The one who states his case first seems right, until the other comes and examines him.

18 The lot puts an end to quarrels and decides between powerful contenders.

19 A brother offended is more unyielding than a strong city, and quarreling is like the bars of a castle.

20 From the fruit of a man's mouth his stomach is satisfied; he is satisfied by the yield of his lips.

21 Death and life are in the power of the tongue, and those who love it will eat its fruits.

22 He who finds a wife finds a good thing and obtains favor from the LORD.

23 The poor use entreaties, but the rich answer roughly.

24 A man of many companions may come to ruin, but there is a friend who sticks closer than a brother.

¹ Better is a poor person who walks in his integrity than one who is crooked in speech and is a fool.

² Desire without knowledge is not good, and whoever makes haste with his feet misses his way.

³ When a man's folly brings his way to ruin, his heart rages against the LORD.

⁴ Wealth brings many new friends, but a poor man is deserted by his friend.

⁵ A false witness will not go unpunished, and he who breathes out lies will not escape.

⁶ Many seek the favor of a generous man, and everyone is a friend to a man who gives gifts.

⁷ All a poor man's brothers hate him; how much more do his friends go far from him! He pursues them with words, but does not have them.

⁸ Whoever gets sense loves his own soul; he who keeps understanding will discover good.

⁹ A false witness will not go unpunished, and he who breathes out lies will perish.

¹⁰ It is not fitting for a fool to live in luxury, much less for a slave to rule over princes.

¹¹ Good sense makes one slow to anger, and it is his glory to overlook an offense.

¹² A king's wrath is like the growling of a lion, but his favor is like dew on the grass.

¹³ A foolish son is ruin to his father, and a wife's quarreling is a continual dripping of rain.

¹⁴ House and wealth are inherited from fathers, but a prudent wife is from the LORD.

¹⁵ Slothfulness casts into a deep sleep, and an idle person will suffer hunger.

¹⁶ Whoever keeps the commandment keeps his life; he who despises his ways will die.

¹⁷ Whoever is generous to the poor lends to the LORD, and he will repay him for his deed.

¹⁸ Discipline your son, for there is hope; do not set your heart on putting him to death.

¹⁹ A man of great wrath will pay the penalty, for if you deliver him, you will only have to do it again.

²⁰ Listen to advice and accept instruction, that you may gain wisdom in the future.

²¹ Many are the plans in the mind of a man, but it is the purpose of the LORD that will stand.

22 What is desired in a man is steadfast love, and a poor man is better than a liar.

23 The fear of the LORD leads to life, and whoever has it rests satisfied; he will not be visited by harm.

24 The sluggard buries his hand in the dish and will not even bring it back to his mouth.

25 Strike a scoffer, and the simple will learn prudence; reprove a man of understanding, and he will gain knowledge.

26 He who does violence to his father and chases away his mother is a son who brings shame and reproach.

27 Cease to hear instruction, my son, and you will stray from the words of knowledge.

28 A worthless witness mocks at justice, and the mouth of the wicked devours iniquity.

29 Condemnation is ready for scoffers, and beating for the backs of fools.

CHAPTER 20

1 Wine is a mocker, strong drink a brawler, and whoever is led astray by it is not wise.

2 The terror of a king is like the growling of a lion; whoever provokes him to anger forfeits his life.

3 It is an honor for a man to keep aloof from strife, but every fool will be quarreling.

4 The sluggard does not plow in the autumn; he will seek at harvest and have nothing.

5 The purpose in a man's heart is like deep water, but a man of understanding will draw it out.

6 Many a man proclaims his own steadfast love, but a faithful man who can find?

7 The righteous who walks in his integrity— blessed are his children after him!

8 A king who sits on the throne of judgment winnows all evil with his eyes.

9 Who can say, "I have made my heart pure; I am clean from my sin"?

10 Unequal weights and unequal measures are both alike an abomination to the LORD.

11 Even a child makes himself known by his acts, by whether his conduct is pure and upright.

12 The hearing ear and the seeing eye, the LORD has made them both.

13 Love not sleep, lest you come to poverty; open your eyes, and you will have plenty of bread.

14 "Bad, bad," says the buyer, but when he goes away, then he boasts.

¹⁵ There is gold and abundance of costly stones, but the lips of knowledge are a precious jewel.

¹⁶ Take a man's garment when he has put up security for a stranger, and hold it in pledge when he puts up security for foreigners.

¹⁷ Bread gained by deceit is sweet to a man, but afterward his mouth will be full of gravel.

¹⁸ Plans are established by counsel; by wise guidance wage war.

¹⁹ Whoever goes about slandering reveals secrets; therefore do not associate with a simple babbler.

²⁰ If one curses his father or his mother, his lamp will be put out in utter darkness.

²¹ An inheritance gained hastily in the beginning will not be blessed in the end.

²² Do not say, "I will repay evil"; wait for the LORD, and he will deliver you.

²³ Unequal weights are an abomination to the LORD, and false scales are not good.

²⁴ A man's steps are from the LORD; how then can man understand his way?

²⁵ It is a snare to say rashly, "It is holy," and to reflect only after making vows.

²⁶ A wise king winnows the wicked and drives the wheel over them.

²⁷ The spirit of man is the lamp of the LORD, searching all his innermost parts.

²⁸ Steadfast love and faithfulness preserve the king, and by steadfast love his throne is upheld.

²⁹ The glory of young men is their strength, but the splendor of old men is their gray hair.

³⁰ Blows that wound cleanse away evil; strokes make clean the innermost parts.

CHAPTER 21

¹ The king's heart is a stream of water in the hand of the LORD; he turns it wherever he will.

² Every way of a man is right in his own eyes, but the LORD weighs the heart.

³ To do righteousness and justice is more acceptable to the LORD than sacrifice.

⁴ Haughty eyes and a proud heart, the lamp of the wicked, are sin.

⁵ The plans of the diligent lead surely to abundance, but everyone who is hasty comes only to poverty.

⁶ The getting of treasures by a lying tongue is a fleeting vapor and a snare of death.

⁷ The violence of the wicked will sweep them away,

because they refuse to do what is just.

⁸ The way of the guilty is crooked, but the conduct of the pure is upright.

⁹ It is better to live in a corner of the housetop than in a house shared with a quarrelsome wife.

¹⁰ The soul of the wicked desires evil; his neighbor finds no mercy in his eyes.

¹¹ When a scoffer is punished, the simple becomes wise; when a wise man is instructed, he gains knowledge.

¹² The Righteous One observes the house of the wicked; he throws the wicked down to ruin.

¹³ Whoever closes his ear to the cry of the poor will himself call out and not be answered.

¹⁴ A gift in secret averts anger, and a concealed bribe, strong wrath.

¹⁵ When justice is done, it is a joy to the righteous but terror to evildoers.

¹⁶ One who wanders from the way of good sense will rest in the assembly of the dead.

¹⁷ Whoever loves pleasure will be a poor man; he who loves wine and oil will not be rich.

¹⁸ The wicked is a ransom for the righteous, and the traitor for the upright.

¹⁹ It is better to live in a desert land than with a quarrelsome and fretful woman.

²⁰ Precious treasure and oil are in a wise man's dwelling, but a foolish man devours it.

²¹ Whoever pursues righteousness and kindness will find life, righteousness, and honor.

²² A wise man scales the city of the mighty and brings down the stronghold in which they trust.

²³ Whoever keeps his mouth and his tongue keeps himself out of trouble.

²⁴ "Scoffer" is the name of the arrogant, haughty man who acts with arrogant pride.

²⁵ The desire of the sluggard kills him, for his hands refuse to labor.

²⁶ All day long he craves and craves, but the righteous gives and does not hold back.

²⁷ The sacrifice of the wicked is an abomination; how much more when he brings it with evil intent.

²⁸ A false witness will perish, but the word of a man who hears will endure.

²⁹ A wicked man puts on a bold face, but the upright gives thought to his ways.

30 No wisdom, no understanding, no counsel can avail against the LORD.

31 The horse is made ready for the day of battle, but the victory belongs to the LORD.

CHAPTER 22

1 A good name is to be chosen rather than great riches, and favor is better than silver or gold.

2 The rich and the poor meet together; the LORD is the maker of them all.

3 The prudent sees danger and hides himself, but the simple go on and suffer for it.

4 The reward for humility and fear of the LORD is riches and honor and life.

5 Thorns and snares are in the way of the crooked; whoever guards his soul will keep far from them.

6 Train up a child in the way he should go; even when he is old he will not depart from it.

7 The rich rules over the poor, and the borrower is the slave of the lender.

8 Whoever sows injustice will reap calamity, and the rod of his fury will fail.

9 Whoever has a bountiful eye will be blessed, for he shares his bread with the poor.

10 Drive out a scoffer, and strife will go out, and quarreling and abuse will cease.

11 He who loves purity of heart, and whose speech is gracious, will have the king as his friend.

12 The eyes of the LORD keep watch over knowledge, but he overthrows the words of the traitor.

13 The sluggard says, "There is a lion outside! I shall be killed in the streets!"

14 The mouth of forbidden women is a deep pit; he with whom the LORD is angry will fall into it.

15 Folly is bound up in the heart of a child, but the rod of discipline drives it far from him.

16 Whoever oppresses the poor to increase his own wealth, or gives to the rich, will only come to poverty.

17 Incline your ear, and hear the words of the wise, and apply your heart to my knowledge,

18 for it will be pleasant if you keep them within you, if all of them are ready on your lips.

19 That your trust may be in the LORD, I have made them known to you today, even to you.

20 Have I not written for you thirty sayings of counsel and knowledge,

²¹ to make you know what is right and true, that you may give a true answer to those who sent you?

²² Do not rob the poor, because he is poor, or crush the afflicted at the gate,

²³ for the LORD will plead their cause and rob of life those who rob them.

²⁴ Make no friendship with a man given to anger, nor go with a wrathful man,

²⁵ lest you learn his ways and entangle yourself in a snare.

²⁶ Be not one of those who give pledges, who put up security for debts.

²⁷ If you have nothing with which to pay, why should your bed be taken from under you?

²⁸ Do not move the ancient landmark that your fathers have set.

²⁹ Do you see a man skillful in his work? He will stand before kings; he will not stand before obscure men.

CHAPTER 23

¹ When you sit down to eat with a ruler, observe carefully what is before you,

² and put a knife to your throat if you are given to appetite.

³ Do not desire his delicacies, for they are deceptive food.

⁴ Do not toil to acquire wealth; be discerning enough to desist.

⁵ When your eyes light on it, it is gone, for suddenly it sprouts wings, flying like an eagle toward heaven.

⁶ Do not eat the bread of a man who is stingy; do not desire his delicacies,

⁷ for he is like one who is inwardly calculating. "Eat and drink!" he says to you, but his heart is not with you.

⁸ You will vomit up the morsels that you have eaten, and waste your pleasant words.

⁹ Do not speak in the hearing of a fool, for he will despise the good sense of your words.

¹⁰ Do not move an ancient landmark or enter the fields of the fatherless,

¹¹ for their Redeemer is strong; he will plead their cause against you.

¹² Apply your heart to instruction and your ear to words of knowledge.

¹³ Do not withhold discipline from a child; if you strike him with a rod, he will not die.

¹⁴ If you strike him with the rod, you will save his soul from Sheol.

¹⁵ My son, if your heart is wise, my heart too will be glad.

16 My inmost being will exult when your lips speak what is right.

17 Let not your heart envy sinners, but continue in the fear of the LORD all the day.

18 Surely there is a future, and your hope will not be cut off.

19 Hear, my son, and be wise, and direct your heart in the way.

20 Be not among drunkards or among gluttonous eaters of meat,

21 for the drunkard and the glutton will come to poverty, and slumber will clothe them with rags.

22 Listen to your father who gave you life, and do not despise your mother when she is old.

23 Buy truth, and do not sell it; buy wisdom, instruction, and understanding.

24 The father of the righteous will greatly rejoice; he who fathers a wise son will be glad in him.

25 Let your father and mother be glad; let her who bore you rejoice.

26 My son, give me your heart, and let your eyes observe my ways.

27 For a prostitute is a deep pit; an adulteress is a narrow well.

28 She lies in wait like a robber and increases the traitors among mankind.

29 Who has woe? Who has sorrow? Who has strife? Who has complaining? Who has wounds without cause? Who has redness of eyes?

30 Those who tarry long over wine; those who go to try mixed wine.

31 Do not look at wine when it is red, when it sparkles in the cup and goes down smoothly.

32 In the end it bites like a serpent and stings like an adder.

33 Your eyes will see strange things, and your heart utter perverse things.

34 You will be like one who lies down in the midst of the sea, like one who lies on the top of a mast.

35 "They struck me," you will say, "but I was not hurt; they beat me, but I did not feel it. When shall I awake? I must have another drink."

CHAPTER 24

1 Be not envious of evil men, nor desire to be with them,

2 for their hearts devise violence, and their lips talk of trouble.

3 By wisdom a house is built, and by understanding it is established;

4 by knowledge the rooms

are filled with all precious and pleasant riches.

5 A wise man is full of strength, and a man of knowledge enhances his might,

6 for by wise guidance you can wage your war, and in abundance of counselors there is victory.

7 Wisdom is too high for a fool; in the gate he does not open his mouth.

8 Whoever plans to do evil will be called a schemer.

9 The devising of folly is sin, and the scoffer is an abomination to mankind.

10 If you faint in the day of adversity, your strength is small.

11 Rescue those who are being taken away to death; hold back those who are stumbling to the slaughter.

12 If you say, "Behold, we did not know this," does not he who weighs the heart perceive it? Does not he who keeps watch over your soul know it, and will he not repay man according to his work?

13 My son, eat honey, for it is good, and the drippings of the honeycomb are sweet to your taste.

14 Know that wisdom is such to your soul; if you find it, there will be a future, and your hope will not be cut off.

15 Lie not in wait as a wicked man against the dwelling of the righteous; do no violence to his home;

16 for the righteous falls seven times and rises again, but the wicked stumble in times of calamity.

17 Do not rejoice when your enemy falls, and let not your heart be glad when he stumbles,

18 lest the LORD see it and be displeased, and turn away his anger from him.

19 Fret not yourself because of evildoers, and be not envious of the wicked,

20 for the evil man has no future; the lamp of the wicked will be put out.

21 My son, fear the LORD and the king, and do not join with those who do otherwise,

22 for disaster will arise suddenly from them, and who knows the ruin that will come from them both?

23 These also are sayings of the wise. Partiality in judging is not good.

24 Whoever says to the wicked, "You are in the right," will be cursed by peoples, abhorred by nations,

25 but those who rebuke the wicked will have delight, and a good blessing will come upon them.

26 Whoever gives an honest answer kisses the lips.

27 Prepare your work outside; get everything ready for yourself in the field, and after that build your house.

28 Be not a witness against your neighbor without cause, and do not deceive with your lips.

29 Do not say, "I will do to him as he has done to me; I will pay the man back for what he has done."

30 I passed by the field of a sluggard, by the vineyard of a man lacking sense,

31 and behold, it was all overgrown with thorns; the ground was covered with nettles, and its stone wall was broken down.

32 Then I saw and considered it; I looked and received instruction.

33 A little sleep, a little slumber, a little folding of the hands to rest,

34 and poverty will come upon you like a robber, and want like an armed man.

CHAPTER 25

1 These also are proverbs of Solomon which the men of Hezekiah king of Judah copied.

2 It is the glory of God to conceal things, but the glory of kings is to search things out.

3 As the heavens for height, and the earth for depth, so the heart of kings is unsearchable.

4 Take away the dross from the silver, and the smith has material for a vessel;

5 take away the wicked from the presence of the king, and his throne will be established in righteousness.

6 Do not put yourself forward in the king's presence or stand in the place of the great,

7 for it is better to be told, "Come up here," than to be put lower in the presence of a noble. What your eyes have seen

8 do not hastily bring into court, for what will you do in the end, when your neighbor puts you to shame?

9 Argue your case with your neighbor himself, and do not reveal another's secret,

10 lest he who hears you bring shame upon you, and your ill repute have no end.

11 A word fitly spoken is like apples of gold in a setting of silver.

12 Like a gold ring or an ornament of gold is a wise reprover to a listening ear.

13 Like the cold of snow in the time of harvest is a faithful messenger to those who send him; he refreshes the soul of his masters.

14 Like clouds and wind without rain is a man who boasts of a gift he does not give.

15 With patience a ruler may be persuaded, and a soft tongue will break a bone.

16 If you have found honey, eat only enough for you, lest you have your fill of it and vomit it.

17 Let your foot be seldom in your neighbor's house, lest he have his fill of you and hate you.

18 A man who bears false witness against his neighbor is like a war club, or a sword, or a sharp arrow.

19 Trusting in a treacherous man in time of trouble is like a bad tooth or a foot that slips.

20 Whoever sings songs to a heavy heart is like one who takes off a garment on a cold day, and like vinegar on soda.

21 If your enemy is hungry, give him bread to eat, and if he is thirsty, give him water to drink,

22 for you will heap burning coals on his head, and the LORD will reward you.

23 The north wind brings forth rain, and a backbiting tongue, angry looks.

24 It is better to live in a corner of the housetop than in a house shared with a quarrelsome wife.

25 Like cold water to a thirsty soul, so is good news from a far country.

26 Like a muddied spring or a polluted fountain is a righteous man who gives way before the wicked.

27 It is not good to eat much honey, nor is it glorious to seek one's own glory.

28 A man without self-control is like a city broken into and left without walls.

CHAPTER 26

1 Like snow in summer or rain in harvest, so honor is not fitting for a fool.

2 Like a sparrow in its flitting, like a swallow in its flying, a curse that is causeless does not alight.

3 A whip for the horse, a bridle for the donkey, and a rod for the back of fools.

4 Answer not a fool according to his folly, lest you be like him yourself.

5 Answer a fool according to his folly, lest he be wise in his own eyes.

6 Whoever sends a message by the hand of a fool cuts off his own feet and drinks violence.

7 Like a lame man's legs, which hang useless, is a proverb in the mouth of fools.

⁸ Like one who binds the stone in the sling is one who gives honor to a fool.

⁹ Like a thorn that goes up into the hand of a drunkard is a proverb in the mouth of fools.

¹⁰ Like an archer who wounds everyone is one who hires a passing fool or drunkard.

¹¹ Like a dog that returns to his vomit is a fool who repeats his folly.

¹² Do you see a man who is wise in his own eyes? There is more hope for a fool than for him.

¹³ The sluggard says, "There is a lion in the road! There is a lion in the streets!"

¹⁴ As a door turns on its hinges, so does a sluggard on his bed.

¹⁵ The sluggard buries his hand in the dish; it wears him out to bring it back to his mouth.

¹⁶ The sluggard is wiser in his own eyes than seven men who can answer sensibly.

¹⁷ Whoever meddles in a quarrel not his own is like one who takes a passing dog by the ears.

¹⁸ Like a madman who throws firebrands, arrows, and death

¹⁹ is the man who deceives his neighbor and says, "I am only joking!"

²⁰ For lack of wood the fire goes out, and where there is no whisperer, quarreling ceases.

²¹ As charcoal to hot embers and wood to fire, so is a quarrelsome man for kindling strife.

²² The words of a whisperer are like delicious morsels; they go down into the inner parts of the body.

²³ Like the glaze covering an earthen vessel are fervent lips with an evil heart.

²⁴ Whoever hates disguises himself with his lips and harbors deceit in his heart;

²⁵ when he speaks graciously, believe him not, for there are seven abominations in his heart;

²⁶ though his hatred be covered with deception, his wickedness will be exposed in the assembly.

²⁷ Whoever digs a pit will fall into it, and a stone will come back on him who starts it rolling.

²⁸ A lying tongue hates its victims, and a flattering mouth works ruin.

CHAPTER 27

¹ Do not boast about tomorrow, for you do not know what a day may bring.

² Let another praise you, and not your own mouth; a stranger, and not your own lips.

³ A stone is heavy, and sand is weighty, but a fool's provocation is heavier than both.

⁴ Wrath is cruel, anger is overwhelming, but who can stand before jealousy?

⁵ Better is open rebuke than hidden love.

⁶ Faithful are the wounds of a friend; profuse are the kisses of an enemy.

⁷ One who is full loathes honey, but to one who is hungry everything bitter is sweet.

⁸ Like a bird that strays from its nest is a man who strays from his home.

⁹ Oil and perfume make the heart glad, and the sweetness of a friend comes from his earnest counsel.

¹⁰ Do not forsake your friend and your father's friend, and do not go to your brother's house in the day of your calamity. Better is a neighbor who is near than a brother who is far away.

¹¹ Be wise, my son, and make my heart glad, that I may answer him who reproaches me.

¹² The prudent sees danger and hides himself, but the simple go on and suffer for it.

¹³ Take a man's garment when he has put up security for a stranger, and hold it in pledge when he puts up security for an adulteress.

¹⁴ Whoever blesses his neighbor with a loud voice, rising early in the morning, will be counted as cursing.

¹⁵ A continual dripping on a rainy day and a quarrelsome wife are alike;

¹⁶ to restrain her is to restrain the wind or to grasp oil in one's right hand.

¹⁷ Iron sharpens iron, and one man sharpens another.

¹⁸ Whoever tends a fig tree will eat its fruit, and he who guards his master will be honored.

¹⁹ As in water face reflects face, so the heart of man reflects the man.

²⁰ Sheol and Abaddon are never satisfied, and never satisfied are the eyes of man.

²¹ The crucible is for silver, and the furnace is for gold, and a man is tested by his praise.

²² Crush a fool in a mortar with a pestle along with crushed grain, yet his folly will not depart from him.

²³ Know well the condition of your flocks, and give attention to your herds,

²⁴ for riches do not last forever; and does a crown endure to all generations?

25 When the grass is gone and the new growth appears and the vegetation of the mountains is gathered,

26 the lambs will provide your clothing, and the goats the price of a field.

27 There will be enough goats' milk for your food, for the food of your household and maintenance for your girls.

CHAPTER 28

1 The wicked flee when no one pursues, but the righteous are bold as a lion.

2 When a land transgresses, it has many rulers, but with a man of understanding and knowledge, its stability will long continue.

3 A poor man who oppresses the poor is a beating rain that leaves no food.

4 Those who forsake the law praise the wicked, but those who keep the law strive against them.

5 Evil men do not understand justice, but those who seek the LORD understand it completely.

6 Better is a poor man who walks in his integrity than a rich man who is crooked in his ways.

7 The one who keeps the law is a son with understanding, but a compan-ion of gluttons shames his father.

8 Whoever multiplies his wealth by interest and profit gathers it for him who is generous to the poor.

9 If one turns away his ear from hearing the law, even his prayer is an abomination.

10 Whoever misleads the upright into an evil way will fall into his own pit, but the blameless will have a goodly inheritance.

11 A rich man is wise in his own eyes, but a poor man who has understanding will find him out.

12 When the righteous triumph, there is great glory, but when the wicked rise, people hide themselves.

13 Whoever conceals his transgressions will not prosper, but he who confesses and forsakes them will obtain mercy.

14 Blessed is the one who fears the LORD always, but whoever hardens his heart will fall into calamity.

15 Like a roaring lion or a charging bear is a wicked ruler over a poor people.

16 A ruler who lacks understanding is a cruel oppressor, but he who hates unjust gain will prolong his days.

17 If one is burdened with the blood of another, he will

wrapped up the waters in a garment? Who has established all the ends of the earth? What is his name, and what is his son's name? Surely you know!

⁵ Every word of God proves true; he is a shield to those who take refuge in him.

⁶ Do not add to his words, lest he rebuke you and you be found a liar.

⁷ Two things I ask of you; deny them not to me before I die:

⁸ Remove far from me falsehood and lying; give me neither poverty nor riches; feed me with the food that is needful for me,

⁹ lest I be full and deny you and say, "Who is the LORD?" or lest I be poor and steal and profane the name of my God.

¹⁰ Do not slander a servant to his master, lest he curse you, and you be held guilty.

¹¹ There are those who curse their fathers and do not bless their mothers.

¹² There are those who are clean in their own eyes but are not washed of their filth.

¹³ There are those—how lofty are their eyes, how high their eyelids lift!

¹⁴ There are those whose teeth are swords, whose fangs are knives, to devour the poor from off the earth, the needy from among mankind.

¹⁵ The leech has two daughters: Give and Give. Three things are never satisfied; four never say, "Enough":

¹⁶ Sheol, the barren womb, the land never satisfied with water, and the fire that never says, "Enough."

¹⁷ The eye that mocks a father and scorns to obey a mother will be picked out by the ravens of the valley and eaten by the vultures.

¹⁸ Three things are too wonderful for me; four I do not understand:

¹⁹ the way of an eagle in the sky, the way of a serpent on a rock, the way of a ship on the high seas, and the way of a man with a virgin.

²⁰ This is the way of an adulteress: she eats and wipes her mouth and says, "I have done no wrong."

²¹ Under three things the earth trembles; under four it cannot bear up:

²² a slave when he becomes king, and a fool when he is filled with food;

²³ an unloved woman when she gets a husband, and a maidservant when she displaces her mistress.

²⁴ Four things on earth are small, but they are exceedingly wise:

25 the ants are a people not strong, yet they provide their food in the summer;

26 the rock badgers are a people not mighty, yet they make their homes in the cliffs;

27 the locusts have no king, yet all of them march in rank;

28 the lizard you can take in your hands, yet it is in kings' palaces.

29 Three things are stately in their tread; four are stately in their stride:

30 the lion, which is mightiest among beasts and does not turn back before any;

31 the strutting rooster, the he-goat, and a king whose army is with him.

32 If you have been foolish, exalting yourself, or if you have been devising evil, put your hand on your mouth.

33 For pressing milk produces curds, pressing the nose produces blood, and pressing anger produces strife.

CHAPTER 31

1 The words of King Lemuel. An oracle that his mother taught him:

2 What are you doing, my son? What are you doing, son of my womb? What are you doing, son of my vows?

3 Do not give your strength to women, your ways to those who destroy kings.

4 It is not for kings, O Lemuel, it is not for kings to drink wine, or for rulers to take strong drink,

5 lest they drink and forget what has been decreed and pervert the rights of all the afflicted.

6 Give strong drink to the one who is perishing, and wine to those in bitter distress;

7 let them drink and forget their poverty and remember their misery no more.

8 Open your mouth for the mute, for the rights of all who are destitute.

9 Open your mouth, judge righteously, defend the rights of the poor and needy.

10 An excellent wife who can find? She is far more precious than jewels.

11 The heart of her husband trusts in her, and he will have no lack of gain.

12 She does him good, and not harm, all the days of her life.

13 She seeks wool and flax, and works with willing hands.

14 She is like the ships of the merchant; she brings her food from afar.

15 She rises while it is yet night and provides food for

her household and portions for her maidens.

¹⁶ She considers a field and buys it; with the fruit of her hands she plants a vineyard.

¹⁷ She dresses herself with strength and makes her arms strong.

¹⁸ She perceives that her merchandise is profitable. Her lamp does not go out at night.

¹⁹ She puts her hands to the distaff, and her hands hold the spindle.

²⁰ She opens her hand to the poor and reaches out her hands to the needy.

²¹ She is not afraid of snow for her household, for all her household are clothed in scarlet.

²² She makes bed coverings for herself; her clothing is fine linen and purple.

²³ Her husband is known in the gates when he sits among the elders of the land.

²⁴ She makes linen garments and sells them; she delivers sashes to the merchant.

²⁵ Strength and dignity are her clothing, and she laughs at the time to come.

²⁶ She opens her mouth with wisdom, and the teaching of kindness is on her tongue.

²⁷ She looks well to the ways of her household and does not eat the bread of idleness.

²⁸ Her children rise up and call her blessed; her husband also, and he praises her:

²⁹ "Many women have done excellently, but you surpass them all."

³⁰ Charm is deceitful, and beauty is vain, but a woman who fears the LORD is to be praised.

³¹ Give her of the fruit of her hands, and let her works praise her in the gates.

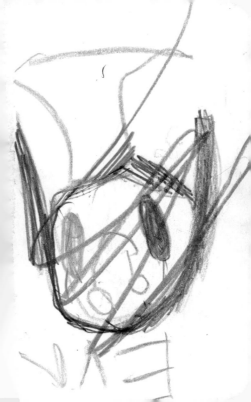

GOD LOVES YOU

For God so loved the world, that he gave his only Son, that whoever believes in him should not perish but have eternal life.

John 3:16   Page 167

But God shows his love for us in that while we were still sinners, Christ died for us.

Romans 5:8   Page 281

ALL ARE SINNERS

For all have sinned and fall short of the glory of God.

Romans 3:23   Page 279

As it is written: "None is righteous, no, not one."

Romans 3:10   Page 278

GOD'S REMEDY FOR SIN

For the wages of sin is death, but the free gift of God is eternal life in Christ Jesus our Lord.

Romans 6:23   Page 283

But to all who did receive him, who believed in his name, he gave the right to become children of God.

John 1:12   Page 163

For I delivered to you as of first importance what I also received: that Christ died for our sins in accordance with the Scriptures, that he was buried, that he was raised on the third day in accordance with the Scriptures.   1 Corinthians 15:3, 4   Page 320

ALL MAY BE SAVED NOW

Behold, I stand at the door and knock. If anyone hears my voice and opens the door, I will come in to him.   Revelation 3:20   Page 443

For everyone who calls on the name of the Lord will be saved.   Romans 10:13   Page 290